Advancing Sustainable Development Goals With Educational Technology

Froilan Delute Mobo
Philippine Merchant Marine Academy, Philippines

Vice President of Editorial: Melissa Wagner
Managing Editor of Acquisitions: Mikaela Felty
Managing Editor of Book Development: Jocelynn Hessler
Production Manager: Mike Brehm
Cover Design: Phillip Shickler

Published in the United States of America by
IGI Global Scientific Publishing
701 East Chocolate Avenue
Hershey, PA, 17033, USA
Tel: 717-533-8845
Fax: 717-533-8661
E-mail: cust@igi-global.com
Website: https://www.igi-global.com

Copyright © 2025 by IGI Global Scientific Publishing. All rights reserved. No part of this publication may be reproduced, stored or distributed in any form or by any means, electronic or mechanical, including photocopying, without written permission from the publisher.
Product or company names used in this set are for identification purposes only. Inclusion of the names of the products or companies does not indicate a claim of ownership by IGI Global Scientific Publishing of the trademark or registered trademark.

Library of Congress Cataloging-in-Publication Data

CIP Data Pending
ISBN:979-8-3693-8242-4
eISBN:979-8-3693-8244-8

British Cataloguing in Publication Data
A Cataloguing in Publication record for this book is available from the British Library.

All work contributed to this book is new, previously-unpublished material.
The views expressed in this book are those of the authors, but not necessarily of the publisher.
This book contains information sourced from authentic and highly regarded references, with reasonable efforts made to ensure the reliability of the data and information presented. The authors, editors, and publisher believe the information in this book to be accurate and true as of the date of publication. Every effort has been made to trace and credit the copyright holders of all materials included. However, the authors, editors, and publisher cannot assume responsibility for the validity of all materials or the consequences of their use. Should any copyright material be found unacknowledged, please inform the publisher so that corrections may be made in future reprints.

Table of Contents

Preface xiv

Chapter 1
Digital Mandarin Learning Enhances SDG 8 for Tourism and Hospitality Management Students 1
> Wes Harven Guillemer Maravilla, Suan Sunandha Rajabhat University, Thailand

Chapter 2
Addressing SDG 1 (No Poverty) Through Philippine Higher Education Institutions: Challenges, Gaps, and Opportunities 35
> Elreen Aguilar Delavin, Dr. Emilio B. Espinosa Sr. Memorial State College of Agriculture and Technology, Philippines

Chapter 3
Advancing Sustainable Development Goals With Educational Technology: Supporting STEM Education and Fostering Innovation Through Educational Technology 65
> Rodulfo Tumacay Aunzo, Jr., Visayas State University Isabel, Isabel, Philippines

Chapter 4
Analysis of Student Affairs and Services Programs and SDG Sustainability Knowledge and Behavior in One State University: Alignment of Services to Sustainable Development Goals 99
> Jherwin Pagkaliwagan Hermosa, Laguna State Polytechnic University, Philippines
> Alberto B. Castillo, Laguna State Polytechnic University, Philippines

Chapter 5
Circular Economy in Tourism Industry: A Sustainable Approach 117
> Vandana Sharma, DCRUST Murthal, India
> Chinu Bumra, DCRUST Murthal, India
> Vidhu Vats, DCRUST Murthal, India

Chapter 6
Digital Mental Health Education: Alleviating Stigma and Enhancing Well-Being in Schools 143
    Anjali Daisy, Loyola Institute of Business Administration, India

Chapter 7
Digital Platforms as Catalysts for Public-Private Partnerships in Achieving Sustainable Development Goals 181
    Kongkon Bordoloi, Majuli College, India
    Bijoy Timung, Majuli College, India
    Acharjya Mohan Das, Majuli College, India
    Gargi Doloi, Mahapurusha Srimanta Sankaradeva Viswavidyalaya, India

Chapter 8
E-Learning as a Global Vessel Towards Inclusive and Quality Education 209
    John Marvin D. Renacido, Aklan State University, Philippines
    Ersyl T. Biray, Aklan State University, Philippines

Chapter 9
Enhancing Peer Engagement and Student Motivation Through AI-Gamified Interactive Learning Tools 277
    John Marvin D. Renacido, Aklan State University, Philippines
    Ersyl T. Biray, Aklan State University, Philippines

Chapter 10
Exploring Faculty Research Engagement: A Cultural Perspective at Maritime Institutions for Achieving Sustainable Development Goals 343
    Froilan Delute Mobo, Philippine Merchant Marine Academy, Philippines
    Roldan C. Cabiles, Bicol University Open University, Philippines

Chapter 11
Facilitating Global Partnerships for Knowledge Sharing by Mediating Role of Digital Platforms in Achieving SDG 17 in Ethiopia 359
    Shashi Kant, Bule Hora University, Ethiopia
    Metasebia Adula, Bule Hora University, Ethiopia
    Tamire Ashuro, Bule Hora University, Ethiopia

Chapter 12
Innovative Teaching Methods Using Technology in Accounting and Business Management 387
    Michael B. Bongalonta, Sorsogon State University, Philippines

Chapter 13
Quality Education in Artificial Intelligence: Promising Technologically Sustainable Transformation for Future Education 401
    Miftachul Huda, Universiti Pendidikan Sultan Idris Malaysia, Malaysia

Chapter 14
Shaping the Future of Education and the Futures of Learning Spaces in the Philippines Beyond 2050 425
    Jimmy Maming, Nuevo School of Technology and Humanities Inc., Philippines
    Eugene Escalona Toring, Indiana Aerospace University, Philippines
    Kimberly Cui Nuevo-Toring, Indian Aerospace University, Philippines & University of the Visayas, Philippines

Chapter 15
The Effect of Experiment Videos Supported by Case Studies on High School Students' Environmental Awareness 439
    Gamze Tunçay, Gazi University, Turkey
    Zeynep Melike Güçlü, Gazi University, Turkey
    Özge Özyalçin Oskay, Hacettepe University, Turkey

Compilation of References 481

About the Contributors 555

Index 559

Detailed Table of Contents

Preface xiv

Chapter 1
Digital Mandarin Learning Enhances SDG 8 for Tourism and Hospitality
Management Students 1
    *Wes Harven Guillemer Maravilla, Suan Sunandha Rajabhat University,
    Thailand*

This chapter examines digital Mandarin learning's impact on Tourism and Hospitality Management (THM) students in Malay, Aklan, Philippines, preparing them for the rising number of Chinese tourists on Boracay Island. Digital Mandarin education strengthens students' 21st-century skills and career prospects, supporting Sustainable Development Goal 8 (SDG 8) by promoting decent work and economic growth. A review of the literature assesses digital tools' role in language proficiency and career growth. Findings reveal digital Mandarin learning enhances critical thinking, teamwork, and communication, increasing employability and job satisfaction. Effective strategies are also identified to address implementation challenges, maximizing its benefits. This approach bridges cultural divides, elevates service quality, and supports sustainable tourism, offering valuable guidance for educators, policymakers, and industry leaders in the Philippines.

Chapter 2
Addressing SDG 1 (No Poverty) Through Philippine Higher Education
Institutions: Challenges, Gaps, and Opportunities... 35
    Elreen Aguilar Delavin, Dr. Emilio B. Espinosa Sr. Memorial State
      College of Agriculture and Technology, Philippines

This chapter explores the role of Philippine higher education institutions (HEIs) in addressing Sustainable Development Goal 1 through education, research, and community engagement. With poverty remaining a critical challenge in the Philippines, HEIs are uniquely positioned to contribute to poverty alleviation by equipping students with relevant skills, conducting research, and fostering sustainable community development programs. However, challenges such as fragmented initiatives, limited interdisciplinary collaboration, and inadequate funding often constrain HEIs' capacity to make a substantial impact. Through analysis of local and international case studies, this chapter identifies best practices for effective poverty reduction in HEIs. Recommendations include fostering long-term community partnerships, developing sustainable funding models, and translating research into actionable policies.

Chapter 3
Advancing Sustainable Development Goals With Educational Technology:
Supporting STEM Education and Fostering Innovation Through Educational
Technology.. 65
    Rodulfo Tumacay Aunzo, Jr., Visayas State University Isabel, Isabel,
      Philippines

STEM education, covering Science, Technology, Engineering, and Mathematics, equips students with critical problem-solving skills and prepares them for advanced studies and careers in these fields. Originating from the National Science Foundation's initiative to drive innovation, STEM integrates hands-on, problem-based learning to tackle real-world challenges. Its growing importance aligns with global competitiveness goals, enhancing student readiness for high-tech careers and fueling economic growth. Educational technology plays a key role in this transformation through interactive tools and multimedia resources. However, challenges like resource limitations and teacher training gaps hinder effective integration. Continuous research and professional development are needed to fully harness technology's potential, ensuring it supports educational goals and enhances learning outcomes.

Chapter 4
Analysis of Student Affairs and Services Programs and SDG Sustainability Knowledge and Behavior in One State University: Alignment of Services to Sustainable Development Goals 99
    Jherwin Pagkaliwagan Hermosa, Laguna State Polytechnic University,
        Philippines
    Alberto B. Castillo, Laguna State Polytechnic University, Philippines

This study conducted an analysis of the current student affairs and services programs at The Laguna State Polytechnic University, with a particular focus on aligning these services with the Sustainable Development Goals (SDGs) set by the United Nations. It utilized a descriptive design and surveyed 200 students. It is revealed that the Office of Student Affairs offers accessible and well-utilized Services and programs. The students know the Sustainable Development Goals (SDGs) and can make valuable contributions to sustainability initiatives. Thus, it is essential to align initiatives in student affairs and services with institutional strategies and objectives related to the SDGs. Higher education institutions serve as crucial platforms for advancing the SDGs. By engaging faculty members as SDG experts and incorporating the goals into their teaching, institutions can effectively integrate these principles into their curriculum. Additionally, supporting student organizations in participating in SDG-related events and collaborations further enhances the promotion of these global objectives.

Chapter 5
Circular Economy in Tourism Industry: A Sustainable Approach 117
    Vandana Sharma, DCRUST Murthal, India
    Chinu Bumra, DCRUST Murthal, India
    Vidhu Vats, DCRUST Murthal, India

The linear economy of today does not maximize resources or encourage their recycling, reuse, or healing. Therefore, enhancement of interest can be seen in the idea of the Circular Economy (CE) and between the relationship of global stakeholders and policymakers. Accepting a circular economy approach offerings an opportunity for tourism businesses to enhance their innovation and achieve resource efficiency through a system extensive approach. The existing article deals with the transition to a new economic model i.e., the circular economy, a more suited model for the current tendencies that confirm to the sustainable economic process. Given the planet's finite, but particularly non-regenerative, resources, there is currently rising worry about the detrimental effects of human activity on the ecosystem. Consequently, sustainable development turns into a style of rational and doing for the populace and the commercial environment, and in this regard, clearly defined guidelines and measures intended to guarantee environmental preservation are required.

Chapter 6
Digital Mental Health Education: Alleviating Stigma and Enhancing Well-Being in Schools 143
Anjali Daisy, Loyola Institute of Business Administration, India

In today's fast-paced world, mental health education is more crucial than ever, particularly for students. This paper examines how digital mental health education can transform school environments by making mental health discussions more accessible and supportive. Utilizing engaging, interactive tools such as virtual counseling, mindfulness applications, and digital activities, students can effectively learn to manage stress and emotions in a way that aligns with their tech-savvy lifestyles. These digital resources help break the stigma surrounding mental health, fostering an open and supportive environment where students feel comfortable discussing their feelings. The objective is clear: to make mental health education approachable, impactful, and seamlessly integrated into school life, thereby promoting students' emotional and mental well-being.

Chapter 7
Digital Platforms as Catalysts for Public-Private Partnerships in Achieving Sustainable Development Goals 181
Kongkon Bordoloi, Majuli College, India
Bijoy Timung, Majuli College, India
Acharjya Mohan Das, Majuli College, India
Gargi Doloi, Mahapurusha Srimanta Sankaradeva Viswavidyalaya, India

Digital Platforms have become key enablers in establishing public-private partnerships (PPPs) that are crucial for achieving Sustainable Development goals (SDGs). This book chapter examines how these technologies facilitate collaboration between government, business, and non-profit organizations by improving communication, transparency, and resource distribution. By incorporating tools like data analytics, artificial intelligence, and blockchain, digital platforms can more effectively tackle global issues such as poverty, climate change, and social inequality. This book chapter discusses the obstacles in adopting those technologies and offers strategies for maximizing their potential. The conclusion emphasizes the importance of fully utilizing digital platforms to accelerate sustainable development efforts, drive innovation, and promote fair and inclusive growth across all sectors.

Chapter 8
E-Learning as a Global Vessel Towards Inclusive and Quality Education 209
    John Marvin D. Renacido, Aklan State University, Philippines
    Ersyl T. Biray, Aklan State University, Philippines

E-learning is easily accessible on the Internet, which opens up countless opportunities for the learning population and academic institutions. As the technological world skyrockets, so does the educational system that serves us at the forefront of other advancements. This chapter will discuss how the new learning model has proven that growth does not only lean toward one area but knows no bounds—a digital classroom where flexibility and creativity are at its center.

Chapter 9
Enhancing Peer Engagement and Student Motivation Through AI-Gamified Interactive Learning Tools 277
    John Marvin D. Renacido, Aklan State University, Philippines
    Ersyl T. Biray, Aklan State University, Philippines

Artificial Intelligence (AI) has become widely accepted in diverse fields and applications in the fast-paced development of technology. It has even penetrated the threshold of education. This chapter will tackle the potential benefits of utilizing AI-powered gamification and interactive learning tools and lay down approaches to attaining a responsible approach to AI Integration. It will also explore interactive learning tools teachers can employ in the classroom and determine the impact of AI-powered gamification on peer engagement. By this, some drawbacks of using AI in education will be revealed to avoid frustration in coping with its mechanisms. Further, it will also provide virtual and augmented reality applications for a clearer view of how these devices work. This chapter will uncover the psychology of gamification to realize the underlying mental implications of this pedagogy for students.

Chapter 10
Exploring Faculty Research Engagement: A Cultural Perspective at Maritime Institutions for Achieving Sustainable Development Goals 343
Froilan Delute Mobo, Philippine Merchant Marine Academy, Philippines
Roldan C. Cabiles, Bicol University Open University, Philippines

The mission of the Commission for Higher Education (CHED) is to assist in the development of a quality community that can address the social, political, economic, cultural, and ethical problems that impede the nation's human growth and ability to compete internationally. Additionally, it adopts a vertical typology within each horizontal type as well as a horizontal typology based on the functional differentiation of HEIs about service to the nation. The study was conducted at the Central Luzon College of Science and Technology, Philippines during the 1st Semester of Academic Year, 2023-2024. The respondents of the study were 80 fulltime and part-time faculty. The researcher recommends that the faculty maintain high standards in terms of conducting research to comply with international standards.

Chapter 11
Facilitating Global Partnerships for Knowledge Sharing by Mediating Role of Digital Platforms in Achieving SDG 17 in Ethiopia 359
Shashi Kant, Bule Hora University, Ethiopia
Metasebia Adula, Bule Hora University, Ethiopia
Tamire Ashuro, Bule Hora University, Ethiopia

In the context of SDG 17, this study looks at how digital platforms might support international collaborations for knowledge exchange. Surveying a sample of 400 participants—this included international organization officials, development practitioners, and policymaker. The study employed both exploratory factor analysis (EFA) and confirmatory factor analysis (CFA) techniques to determine the principal aspects that underlie the utilization of digital platforms for international knowledge exchange. The data's appropriateness for factor analysis was evaluated using Bartlett's test of sphericity and the Kaiser-Meyer-Olkin (KMO) measure of sampling adequacy. After that, SEM, was used to investigate the mediating function of digital platforms. The study's conclusions give development organizations, governments, and digital platform providers with insightful information on how to use digital technologies to promote international cooperation and knowledge sharing, which will eventually assist the larger objectives of sustainable development.

Chapter 12
Innovative Teaching Methods Using Technology in Accounting and Business Management 387
Michael B. Bongalonta, Sorsogon State University, Philippines

This chapter thus examines how technology can be embraced in teaching accounting and business management. The fast development of digital technologies impacted the traditional approaches and methodologies of teaching and learning and it provided educators the opportunity to incorporate innovative instructional techniques to engage and accommodate students and improve their understanding and memorizing capabilities. This chapter explores how accounting and business management curriculum integrates online simulations, VR, AR, AI, and big data analytics. By these technologies, learning activities are designed to be more engaging and challenging thus enabling students to be equipped with knowledge and skills for actual business settings. Furthermore, the challenges and future developments of using technology in teaching accounting and business management are presented highlighting the opportunity for educators in today's constantly developing educational environment

Chapter 13
Quality Education in Artificial Intelligence: Promising Technologically Sustainable Transformation for Future Education 401
Miftachul Huda, Universiti Pendidikan Sultan Idris Malaysia, Malaysia

This chapter aims to examine the quality education in the age of Artificial Intelligence (AI) as an attempt to shape the future education through technologically sustainable transformation. The critical review from recently related literature will be employed in providing the perceptions concerning from both significant benefits and potential limitations of AI in the context of quality education. Utilizing the qualitative research design in focusing on the main objective, the findings revealed that the way to enhance quality education actualised into both teaching and learning practices amidst AI should do with enhancing the active involvement on questioning norms, analysing context, and evaluating evidence. The strategic potentials of AI adoption and development refers to enrich the utility of various facets of quality education including academic research and theory scrutiny. The study concludes that AI can be an asset in the development of quality education with caveats that require careful management.for quality education with AI applications effectively.

Chapter 14
Shaping the Future of Education and the Futures of Learning Spaces in the
Philippines Beyond 2050 425
    Jimmy Maming, Nuevo School of Technology and Humanities Inc.,
       Philippines
    Eugene Escalona Toring, Indiana Aerospace University, Philippines
    Kimberly Cui Nuevo-Toring, Indian Aerospace University, Philippines
       & University of the Visayas, Philippines

The foreseeable future educational environment in the Philippines is influenced by a complex interaction of elements such as technical improvements, shifts in population, economic expansion, and social changes. As we move beyond 2050, it is vital to conceive and investigate creative learning environments that promote innovation, analytical thinking, and lifelong education. This article investigates the Philippines' problems and prospects for building innovative learning spaces. It emphasizes the importance of fair opportunity for technological advances, training for educators, and suitable infrastructure. The report also looks at upcoming themes including individualized instruction, blended education, learning through experience, and lifelong learning.

Chapter 15
The Effect of Experiment Videos Supported by Case Studies on High School
Students' Environmental Awareness 439
    Gamze Tunçay, Gazi University, Turkey
    Zeynep Melike Güçlü, Gazi University, Turkey
    Özge Özyalçin Oskay, Hacettepe University, Turkey

In 2015, the United Nations set the 2030 Sustainable Development Goals (SDGs) to address global challenges like poverty, inequality, health, education, and climate change. One key goal is quality education, aiming to provide free, equitable, and high-quality education for all. This study focused on improving environmental awareness and educational equality by using technology in schools without laboratories. A booklet with YouTube links and QR codes for experiments was developed, enabling 475 students across four cities to access experiment videos. Results showed a significant increase in students' environmental awareness and contributed to equal learning opportunities.

Compilation of References 481

About the Contributors 555

Index 559

Preface

The world today is caught at the crossroads of the sustainable development agenda with more challenges now than ever before. From the challenges of climate change to those of equity, poverty, and justice, the world is part of an ambitious international mission to achieve the United Nations Sustainable Development Goals. However, the fast development of educational technology contributes to the disorder and provides a lot of chances to resolve the above-stated challenges, especially in the educational domain. In this book titled Advancing Sustainable Development Goals with Educational Technology, we explores how the role of educational technology as a transformative tool for education is capable of advancing the achievement of the SDGs. In this work, we focus on the potential of educational technology as a means to support SD, for which we discuss how digital resources, effective teaching practices, and the use of big data are initiators of change for individuals, organizations, and communities. Hence, the present chapter utilizes the findings of various studies, case perspectives, and authentic examples to substantiate how the use of technologies to deliver teaching and learning enhances participation, access, and equality because these are values in the SDGs. Furthermore, possible problems of using technology for development are highlighted alongside our dedication to accountable innovation and sustainable and ethical approaches towards harnessing technology for development for diverse groups of people. Educationally integrated technology is not solely a question of the application of innovative instruments; it is a question of remodeling the process of learning, teaching, and addressing the challenges of global society. In recommending the practical use of technology in learning institutions, this chapter presents the possible path to influence the education sector, leaders, and the world at large to advance in attaining sustainable solutions and development for the future generation. From this research endeavor, we aim to expand knowledge on how educational technology can enhance the achievement of the SDGs and offer practical guidelines to turn knowledge into practice. So here is what I propose: a road map to a world where technology, education, and sustainability are concomitance for the benefit of society.

CHAPTER OVERVIEW

Chapter 1: Digital Mandarin Learning Enhances SDG 8 for Tourism and Hospitality Management Students

This chapter examines digital Mandarin learning's impact on Tourism and Hospitality Management (THM) students in Malay, Aklan, Philippines, preparing them for the rising number of Chinese tourists on Boracay Island. Digital Mandarin education strengthens students' 21st-century skills and career prospects, supporting Sustainable Development Goal 8 (SDG 8) by promoting decent work and economic growth. A review of the literature assesses digital tools' role in language proficiency and career growth. Findings reveal digital Mandarin learning enhances critical thinking, teamwork, and communication, increasing employability and job satisfaction. Effective strategies are also identified to address implementation challenges, maximizing its benefits. This approach bridges cultural divides, elevates service quality, and supports sustainable tourism, offering valuable guidance for educators, policymakers, and industry leaders in the Philippines.

Chapter 2: Addressing SDG 1 (No Poverty) through Philippine Higher Education Institutions Challenges, Gaps, and Opportunities

This chapter explores the role of Philippine higher education institutions (HEIs) in addressing Sustainable Development Goal 1 through education, research, and community engagement. With poverty remaining a critical challenge in the Philippines, HEIs are uniquely positioned to contribute to poverty alleviation by equipping students with relevant skills, conducting research, and fostering sustainable community development programs. However, challenges such as fragmented initiatives, limited interdisciplinary collaboration, and inadequate funding often constrain HEIs' capacity to make a substantial impact. Through analysis of local and international case studies, this chapter identifies best practices for effective poverty reduction in HEIs. Recommendations include fostering long-term community partnerships, developing sustainable funding models, and translating research into actionable policies.

Chapter 3: Advancing Sustainable Development Goals With Educational Technology: Supporting STEM Education and Fostering Innovation Through Educational Technology

STEM education, covering Science, Technology, Engineering, and Mathematics, equips students with critical problem-solving skills and prepares them for advanced studies and careers in these fields. Originating from the National Science Foundation's initiative to drive innovation, STEM integrates hands-on, problem-based learning to tackle real-world challenges. Its growing importance aligns with global competitiveness goals, enhancing student readiness for high-tech careers and fueling economic growth. Educational technology plays a key role in this transformation through interactive tools and multimedia resources. However, challenges like resource limitations and teacher training gaps hinder effective integration. Continuous research and professional development are needed to fully harness technology's potential, ensuring it supports educational goals and enhances learning outcomes.

Chapter 4: Analysis of Student Affairs and Services Programs and SDG Sustainability Knowledge and Behavior in One State University: Alignment of Services to Sustainable Development Goals

This study conducted an analysis of the current student affairs and services programs at The Laguna State Polytechnic University, with a particular focus on aligning these services with the Sustainable Development Goals (SDGs) set by the United Nations. It utilized a descriptive design and surveyed 200 students. It is revealed that the Office of Student Affairs offers accessible and well-utilized Services and programs. They are well-versed in the SDGs and contribute positively to sustainability efforts. Thus, it is essential to align initiatives in student affairs and services with institutional strategies and objectives related to the SDGs. Higher education institutions serve as crucial platforms for advancing the SDGs. By engaging faculty members as SDG experts and incorporating the goals into their teaching, institutions can effectively integrate these principles into their curriculum. Additionally, supporting student organizations in participating in SDG-related events and collaborations further enhances the promotion of these global objectives.

Chapter 5: Circular Economy in Tourism Industry A Sustainable Approach: Integrating Resource Efficiency and Waste Reduction to Enhance Sustainable Tourism Practices

The linear economy of today does not maximize resources or encourage their recycling, reuse, or healing. Therefore, enhancement of interest can be seen in the idea of the Circular Economy (CE) and between the relationship of global stakeholders and policymakers. Accepting a circular economy approach offerings an opportunity for tourism businesses to enhance their innovation and achieve resource efficiency through a system extensive approach. The existing article deals with the transition to a new economic model i.e., the circular economy, a more suited model for the current tendencies that confirm to the sustainable economic process. Given the planet's finite, but particularly non-regenerative, resources, there is currently rising worry about the detrimental effects of human activity on the ecosystem. Consequently, sustainable development turns into a style of rational and doing for the populace and the commercial environment, and in this regard, clearly defined guidelines and measures intended to guarantee environmental preservation are required.

Chapter 6: Digital Mental Health Education: Alleviating Stigma and Enhancing Well-being in Schools

In today's fast-paced world, mental health education is more crucial than ever, particularly for students. This paper examines how digital mental health education can transform school environments by making mental health discussions more accessible and supportive. Utilizing engaging, interactive tools such as virtual counseling, mindfulness applications, and digital activities, students can effectively learn to manage stress and emotions in a way that aligns with their tech-savvy lifestyles. These digital resources help break the stigma surrounding mental health, fostering an open and supportive environment where students feel comfortable discussing their feelings. The objective is clear: to make mental health education approachable, impactful, and seamlessly integrated into school life, thereby promoting students' emotional and mental well-being.

Chapter 7: Digital Platforms as Catalysts for Public-Private Partnerships in Achieving Sustainable Development Goals

Digital Platforms have become key enablers in establishing public-private partnerships (PPPs) that are crucial for achieving Sustainable Development goals (SDGs). This book chapter examines how these technologies facilitate collaboration between government, business, and non-profit organizations by improving communication, transparency, and resource distribution. By incorporating tools like data analytics, artificial intelligence, and blockchain, digital platforms can more effectively tackle global issues such as poverty, climate change, and social inequality. This book chapter discusses the obstacles in adopting those technologies and offers strategies for maximizing their potential. The conclusion emphasizes the importance of fully utilizing digital platforms to accelerate sustainable development efforts, drive innovation, and promote fair and inclusive growth across all sectors.

Chapter 8: E-Learning as a Global Vessel Towards Inclusive and Quality Education

E-learning is currently available on the Internet, allowing students and practitioners access to information and development with a swipe of their hands. This adaptive approach enables countless opportunities in a wide range of industries. As the technological world skyrockets, so does the educational system that serves us at the forefront of other advancements. This chapter will discuss how the new learning model has proven that growth does not only lean toward one area but knows no bounds—a digital classroom where flexibility and creativity are at its center.

Chapter 9: Enhancing Peer Engagement and Student Motivation through AI-Gamified Interactive Learning Tools

Artificial Intelligence (AI) has become widely accepted in diverse fields and applications in the fast-paced development of technology. It has even penetrated the threshold of education. This chapter will tackle the potential benefits of utilizing AI-powered gamification and interactive learning tools and lay down approaches to attaining a responsible approach to AI Integration. It will also explore interactive learning tools teachers can employ in the classroom and determine the impact of AI-powered gamification on peer engagement. By this, some drawbacks of using AI in education will be revealed to avoid frustration in coping with its mechanisms. Further, it will also provide virtual and augmented reality applications for a clearer view of how these devices work. This chapter will uncover the psychology of gamification to realize the underlying mental implications of this pedagogy for students.

Chapter 10: Exploring Faculty Research Engagement: A Cultural Perspective at Maritime Institutions for Achieving Sustainable Development Goals through

The mission of the Commission for Higher Education (CHED) is to assist in the development of a quality community that can address the social, political, economic, cultural, and ethical problems that impede the nation's human growth and ability to compete internationally. Additionally, it adopts a vertical typology within each horizontal type as well as a horizontal typology based on the functional differentiation of HEIs about service to the nation. The study was conducted at the Central Luzon College of Science and Technology, Philippines during the 1st Semester of Academic Year, 2023-2024. The respondents of the study were 80 fulltime and part-time faculty. The researcher recommends that the faculty maintain high standards in terms of conducting research to comply with international standards.

Chapter 11: Facilitating Global Partnerships for Knowledge Sharing by Mediating Role of Digital Platforms in Achieving SDG 17 in Ethiopia

In the context of SDG 17, this study looks at how digital platforms might support international collaborations for knowledge exchange. Surveying a sample of 400 participants—this included international organization officials, development practitioners, and policymaker. The study employed both exploratory factor analysis (EFA) and confirmatory factor analysis (CFA) techniques to determine the principal aspects that underlie the utilization of digital platforms for international knowledge exchange. The data's appropriateness for factor analysis was evaluated using Bartlett's test of sphericity and the Kaiser-Meyer-Olkin (KMO) measure of sampling adequacy. After that, SEM, was used to investigate the mediating function of digital platforms. The study's conclusions give development organizations, governments, and digital platform providers with insightful information on how to use digital technologies to promote international cooperation and knowledge sharing, which will eventually assist the larger objectives of sustainable development.

Chapter 12: Innovative Teaching Methods Using Technology in Accounting and Business Management

This chapter thus examines how technology can be embraced in teaching accounting and business management. The fast development of digital technologies impacted the traditional approaches and methodologies of teaching and learning and it provided educators the opportunity to incorporate innovative instructional techniques to engage and accommodate students and improve their understanding and memorizing capabilities. This chapter explores how accounting and business management curriculum integrates online simulations, VR, AR, AI, and big data analytics. By these technologies, learning activities are designed to be more engaging and challenging thus enabling students to be equipped with knowledge and skills for actual business settings. Furthermore, the challenges and future developments of using technology in teaching accounting and business management are presented highlighting the opportunity for educators in today's constantly developing educational environment

Chapter 13: Quality Education in Artificial Intelligence: Promising technologically sustainable transformation for future education

This chapter aims to examine the quality education in the age of Artificial Intelligence (AI) as an attempt to shape the future education through technologically sustainable transformation. The critical review from recently related literature will be employed in providing the perceptions concerning from both significant benefits and potential limitations of AI in the context of quality education. Utilizing the qualitative research design in focusing on the main objective, the findings revealed that the way to enhance quality education actualised into both teaching and learning practices amidst AI should do with enhancing the active involvement on questioning norms, analysing context, and evaluating evidence. The strategic potentials of AI adoption and development refers to enrich the utility of various facets of quality education including academic research and theory scrutiny. The study concludes that AI can be an asset in the development of quality education with caveats that require careful management.for quality education with AI applications effectively.

Chapter 14: Shaping the Future of Education and the Futures of Learning Spaces in the Philippines Beyond 2050

The foreseeable future educational environment in the Philippines is influenced by a complex interaction of elements such as technical improvements, shifts in population, economic expansion, and social changes. As we move beyond 2050, it is vital to conceive and investigate creative learning environments that promote innovation, analytical thinking, and lifelong education. This article investigates the Philippines' problems and prospects for building innovative learning spaces. It emphasizes the importance of fair opportunity for technological advances, training for educators, and suitable infrastructure. The report also looks at upcoming themes including individualized instruction, blended education, learning through experience, and lifelong learning.

Chapter 15: The Effect of Experiment Videos Supported by Case Studies on High School Students' Environmental Awareness

In 2015, the United Nations set the 2030 Sustainable Development Goals (SDGs) to address global challenges like poverty, inequality, health, education, and climate change. One key goal is quality education, aiming to provide free, equitable, and high-quality education for all. This study focused on improving environmental awareness and educational equality by using technology in schools without laboratories. A booklet with YouTube links and QR codes for experiments was developed, enabling 475 students across four cities to access experiment videos. Results showed a significant increase in students' environmental awareness and contributed to equal learning opportunities.

Advancing the United Nations Sustainable Development Goals (SDGs) through the strategic use of educational technology has proven to be an effective approach in addressing the multifaceted challenges of our time. Throughout this book, we have explored a diverse range of applications where technology enhances education, supports sustainable practices, and drives social change. From improving language skills in hospitality management to fostering critical thinking in STEM, educational technology offers tangible solutions to promote economic growth, reduce poverty, and empower future generations.

The chapters demonstrate how digital tools, from e-learning platforms to AI-powered gamification, are revolutionizing teaching methodologies, enhancing student engagement, and fostering inclusive learning environments. These innovations not only bridge gaps in access but also create opportunities for individuals to thrive in an increasingly interconnected world. Additionally, the integration of technology in addressing SDGs like mental health, environmental sustainability, and global partnerships highlights the importance of a collaborative approach between educators, policymakers, and industry leaders.

However, the journey toward achieving the SDGs is not without its challenges. Issues such as resource limitations, ethical concerns, and disparities in access to technology require careful consideration and solutions that are both sustainable and inclusive. As we continue to harness the power of educational technology, it is crucial to remain mindful of its impact on diverse communities and ensure that innovation is used responsibly to create equitable opportunities for all.

The insights gathered in this book underscore the potential of educational technology to not only transform the education sector but also to play a pivotal role in shaping a more sustainable and just future. By embracing the strategic integration of technology, we can create a world where education and sustainability go hand in hand, empowering individuals and communities to contribute to the global goals of development and well-being. The road ahead is one of collaboration, innovation, and commitment to ensuring that educational technology remains a catalyst for positive, lasting change in the pursuit of the SDGs.

Chapter 1
Digital Mandarin Learning Enhances SDG 8 for Tourism and Hospitality Management Students

Wes Harven Guillemer Maravilla
https://orcid.org/0000-0001-5592-3425
Suan Sunandha Rajabhat University, Thailand

ABSTRACT

This chapter examines digital Mandarin learning's impact on Tourism and Hospitality Management (THM) students in Malay, Aklan, Philippines, preparing them for the rising number of Chinese tourists on Boracay Island. Digital Mandarin education strengthens students' 21st-century skills and career prospects, supporting Sustainable Development Goal 8 (SDG 8) by promoting decent work and economic growth. A review of the literature assesses digital tools' role in language proficiency and career growth. Findings reveal digital Mandarin learning enhances critical thinking, teamwork, and communication, increasing employability and job satisfaction. Effective strategies are also identified to address implementation challenges, maximizing its benefits. This approach bridges cultural divides, elevates service quality, and supports sustainable tourism, offering valuable guidance for educators, policymakers, and industry leaders in the Philippines.

DOI: 10.4018/979-8-3693-8242-4.ch001

INTRODUCTION

The Rise of Chinese Tourism and the Demand for Mandarin Proficiency

The recent surge in Chinese tourist arrivals to Boracay Island presents a significant opportunity for economic growth. It aligns with the United Nations' Sustainable Development Goal 8, which promotes sustained, inclusive, and sustainable economic growth, full and productive employment, and decent work for all (United Nations, 2015). This demographic shift necessitates a corresponding adaptation within the local workforce, particularly among Tourism and Hospitality Management (THM) graduates. To effectively cater to the needs and expectations of this growing market segment, these graduates must possess strong Mandarin language skills and intercultural competence. This highlights the need for a shift in language education, moving beyond traditional rote learning towards a more dynamic and communicative approach that fosters genuine intercultural understanding and interaction.

The challenge lies in equipping THM graduates with the necessary linguistic and cultural competencies to excel in this evolving tourism landscape. Traditional language education often needs more practical communication skills and cultural sensitivity to interact effectively with Chinese tourists (Hu, 2018). To bridge this gap, adopting innovative teaching methodologies that prioritize active learning, authentic communication, and cultural immersion is essential. By incorporating interactive activities, real-life scenarios, and opportunities for cultural exchange, language education can better prepare THM graduates to confidently engage with Chinese tourists, fostering positive experiences and contributing to the sustainable growth of Boracay's tourism industry.

Integrating digital learning tools emerges as a beacon of hope in bridging this proficiency gap in Boracay. By harnessing the power of technology, THM programs can revolutionize Mandarin language acquisition, making it more accessible, engaging, and tailored to the specific needs of the island's tourism industry. Digital platforms offer immersive experiences, personalized feedback, and real-time interactions with native speakers, fostering linguistic fluency and the 21st-century skills essential for success in today's globalized workforce. This paradigm shift in language education promises to empower THM graduates, enhance service quality, and unlock the full potential of Boracay's burgeoning Chinese tourist market, ultimately driving sustainable economic growth and decent work opportunities on the island and beyond.

The Mandarin Proficiency Gap and Its Impact on Sustainable Development

The Philippine tourism industry finds itself at a crossroads, with the burgeoning influx of Chinese tourists presenting a stark paradox. While this surge promises significant economic growth and aligns with the United Nations' Sustainable Development Goal 8 (SDG 8) of decent Work and economic growth, a critical linguistic barrier threatens to undermine this potential. The demand for Mandarin proficiency has skyrocketed, yet a significant gap persists between the language skills of Tourism and Hospitality Management (THM) graduates and the linguistic needs of this lucrative market. This mismatch impedes effective communication and cultural exchange and risks compromising the quality of service provided, potentially deterring future visitors and hindering the industry's overall growth.

Compounding this challenge is the need for more traditional language instruction, which often prioritizes rote memorization and grammar drills at the expense of cultivating essential 21st-century skills such as critical thinking, collaboration, and communication (Voogt & Rublin, 2010). This deficiency not only curtails the career prospects of THM graduates but also hampers the industry's capacity to provide high-quality employment opportunities, a cornerstone of SDG 8. This dual challenge necessitates a paradigm shift in language education that transcends mere linguistic competence and embraces a holistic approach that equips THM graduates with the multifaceted skills required to thrive in a dynamic and culturally diverse global landscape. This shift is crucial for unlocking the full potential of the Chinese tourist market, fostering sustainable tourism development, and driving economic growth in the Philippines.

Digital Mandarin Learning: A Catalyst for SDG 8

The convergence of surging Chinese tourism and the demand for Mandarin proficiency in the Philippine tourism sector presents a unique opportunity to leverage digital innovation for sustainable development. Digital Mandarin learning is a potent catalyst for achieving Sustainable Development Goal 8 (SDG 8) by equipping Tourism and Hospitality Management (THM) graduates with the linguistic and cultural competencies essential for thriving in this evolving landscape. This approach transcends traditional language instruction, fostering language acquisition and critical 21st-century skills that underpin decent Work and economic growth.

By harnessing the power of technology, digital Mandarin learning platforms offer immersive, interactive, and personalized experiences that accelerate language acquisition and cultural understanding. This transformative approach empowers THM graduates to effectively communicate with Chinese tourists, enhancing service quality and fostering cross-cultural exchange. Furthermore, digital learning cultivates essential critical thinking, collaboration, and problem-solving skills, positioning graduates for success in the dynamic and competitive tourism industry. This study seeks to unravel the multifaceted impact of digital Mandarin learning in the Philippine context through the following research objectives and questions:

This innovative approach to digital Mandarin learning in support of SDG 8 invites further investigation. To advance this goal, this study embarks with three primary objectives:

- To investigate the impact of digital Mandarin learning on the development of 21st-century skills among THM students.
- To examine the relationship between Mandarin language proficiency and employability outcomes for THM graduates.
- To identify the challenges and opportunities associated with integrating digital Mandarin learning into THM curricula.

To guide this exploration of how digital Mandarin learning can support SDG 8 for Tourism and Hospitality Management students, the following research questions are posed:

- How does digital Mandarin learning contribute to developing critical thinking, collaboration, and communication skills among THM students?
- What is the correlation between Mandarin language proficiency and employment rates, job satisfaction, and career advancement among THM graduates?
- What factors influence the successful integration of digital Mandarin learning into THM programs?

LITERATURE REVIEW

Global Perspectives on Digital Language Learning in Tourism

Digital language learning is transforming the landscape of language education, offering innovative tools and platforms to enhance language acquisition and cultural understanding. (Lee & Li, 2021) This approach is particularly relevant in the tourism and hospitality sector, where effective communication and cross-cultural competence are essential for providing quality service to international tourists. Studies from various countries have highlighted the positive impact of digital language learning on language proficiency, cultural awareness, and employability outcomes in the tourism industry.

For example, research in China has shown that incorporating virtual reality (VR) and augmented reality (AR) technologies into Mandarin language learning can create immersive simulations of real-life tourism scenarios, allowing students to practice their communication skills in a safe and interactive environment. (Liu & Tang, 2022) In Europe, studies have explored using language learning apps and online platforms to personalize the learning experience and cater to individual needs and learning styles. These approaches have increased student engagement and motivation, improving language proficiency and cultural understanding.

Furthermore, research in North America has examined the role of digital language learning in fostering intercultural competence among tourism professionals. By providing opportunities for virtual exchanges and online interactions with native speakers, digital platforms can facilitate authentic communication and cultural immersion. This can help tourism professionals develop a deeper understanding of different cultures, values, and communication styles, leading to more positive and respectful interactions with international tourists.

The Impact of Digital Language Learning on 21st Century Skills Development

Table 1. The Impact of Digital Language Learning on 21st-Century Skills

Aspect	Description
Sustainable Development Goal	Supports SDG 8: Promotes fair Work and economic growth through skill development.
Key Skills Developed	- **Communication**: Enhances language proficiency and cultural understanding.
	- **Critical Thinking**: Encourages analytical skills through interactive content.
	- **Collaboration**: Fosters teamwork via group activities and discussions.
Learning Environment	- **Active Learning**: Engages students in the learning process.
	- **Personalized Feedback**: Provides tailored guidance to improve individual skills.
Tools and Methods	- **Interactive Exercises**: Engages learners through gamified content.
	- **Multimedia Resources**: Utilizes videos, audio, and visuals for immersive learning.
	- **Real-time Communication**: Connects learners with native speakers for practical experience.
Industry Relevance	- Particularly beneficial in **Tourism and Hospitality**, where communication is crucial.

The table illustrates the multifaceted benefits of digital language learning in enhancing essential skills for the 21st century. It emphasizes how integrating technology into language education fosters active participation, collaboration, and personalized feedback, which are critical for preparing students for the modern workforce. By aligning educational practices with industry standards, this approach improves language proficiency. It equips learners with the cultural awareness necessary to thrive in diverse environments, particularly in sectors like tourism and hospitality (Voogt & Rublin, 2010).

Digital language learning is vital in sectors like tourism and hospitality, where cultural competence and effective communication are crucial. Interactive exercises and real-time interactions with native speakers enrich learners' understanding of different cultures, equipping them to thrive in globalized industries. As demand for skilled workers in multicultural environments increases, integrating digital language learning becomes essential for economic growth and sustainable development.

Utilizing digital tools in language learning fosters critical thinking, collaboration, and effective communication, aligning with Sustainable Development Goal 8 for decent Work and economic growth. Digital platforms offer immersive learning experiences with interactive exercises, multimedia content, and real-time interactions, empowering students with the necessary skills and cultural understanding for successful careers in the evolving tourism industry.

The Correlation Between Language Proficiency and Employability Outcomes in the Tourism and Hospitality Sector

The Tourism and Hospitality Industry is a primary global economic driver, significantly contributing to employment and GDP worldwide (World Travel and Tourism Council, 2023). Within this dynamic industry, language proficiency is increasingly vital for employability and career progression, particularly in languages spoken by key tourist demographics. Research consistently demonstrates a positive correlation between language skills and positive employment outcomes, including higher earning potential, increased job satisfaction, and enhanced career mobility (Akar, 2015). This highlights the importance of equipping future tourism professionals with the necessary language skills to cater to diverse international tourists effectively.

Mandarin proficiency is becoming particularly valuable in tourism hotspots experiencing a surge in Chinese tourist arrivals, such as the Philippines. However, a study by Gonzales and Soriano (2022) revealed a concerning gap in Mandarin proficiency among Filipino THM graduates, hindering their ability to communicate with Chinese tourists effectively. This language barrier negatively impacts service quality and tourist satisfaction and limits employment opportunities and career advancement for these graduates. This deficiency directly impedes their ability to contribute to the SDG 8 goals of decent Work and economic growth, emphasizing the urgent need for targeted interventions in language education.

To address this challenge, innovative educational approaches are crucial to equip THM graduates with the necessary Mandarin language skills to thrive in this evolving landscape. This includes incorporating communicative language teaching methodologies, authentic materials, and immersive experiences that foster linguistic proficiency and intercultural competence (Hu, 2018). By bridging this language gap, the tourism industry can unlock the full potential of THM graduates, enhance the tourist experience, and contribute to sustainable economic growth in the Philippines.

Challenges and Opportunities in Integrating Digital Language Learning into THM Curricula

Integrating digital language learning into Tourism and Hospitality Management (THM) curricula presents challenges and opportunities. A significant obstacle is the need for essential technological infrastructure and resources, particularly in developing regions. Many institutions need help with unreliable internet access, outdated equipment, and limited software licenses, which hinder effective digital tool integration (Garcia & Li, 2021). Faculty often require extra training to use these platforms efficiently, potentially delaying successful implementation (Chen et al., 2022).

Conversely, digital language learning offers substantial opportunities for innovation in THM education. Its interactive nature allows educators to design engaging, student-centered learning experiences that foster motivation and active participation. Furthermore, digital platforms promote collaboration among students and instructors from various backgrounds, enhancing cross-cultural understanding and global citizenship—crucial skills in tourism and hospitality (Wang & Zhang, 2020).

More in-depth studies are essential to examine THM institutions' specific challenges in adopting digital language learning and identify effective strategies for overcoming them. Further research should investigate the long-term impacts of digital language learning on employability and career advancement within tourism and hospitality, helping to clarify its full potential in advancing SDG 8 (Tan, 2023).

Addressing the Gaps: The Role of This Study in Promoting SDG 8

This study aims to bridge the identified gaps in the literature by conducting a comprehensive investigation into the impact of digital Mandarin learning on Tourism and Hospitality Management (THM) students in the Philippines. It will go beyond existing research by examining the development of 21st-century skills and analyzing the correlation between Mandarin language proficiency and employability outcomes in the context of SDG 8 – Decent Work and Economic Growth.

Specifically, this study will delve into several key areas. First, it will employ rigorous quantitative and qualitative methods to measure the impact of digital Mandarin learning on 21st-century skills, assessing how it enhances critical thinking, collaboration, and communication among THM students. This will provide empirical evidence supporting the effectiveness of digital tools in fostering these essential skills. Additionally, the study will investigate the correlation between Mandarin proficiency and employability outcomes, examining how language skills influence job placement rates, salary levels, and career advancement opportunities for THM graduates. This analysis will highlight the economic value of Mandarin proficiency in the Philippine tourism and hospitality sector, contributing to understanding how language skills drive decent Work and economic growth. Finally, the research will explore the challenges faced by Philippine THM institutions in integrating digital Mandarin learning into their curricula and identify opportunities that digital tools offer for enhancing language education and promoting SDG 8. This will provide valuable insights and recommendations for educators, policymakers, and industry stakeholders aiming to leverage digital language learning for sustainable development.

Methodology

This study adopts a narrative review methodology to consolidate research and current practices in digital Mandarin learning within Tourism and Hospitality Management (THM) education in the Philippines, particularly in Malay, Aklan. This approach allows for a thorough and detailed exploration of the field's current status, focusing on how digital tools impact language learning, 21st-century skill enhancement, and employability outcomes, aligning with the goals of SDG 8.

To gather relevant data, the study systematically searches for sources in peer-reviewed journals, conference proceedings, government publications, and credible websites, covering topics such as digital language learning, Mandarin education, and the tourism and hospitality sector. Keywords like "digital Mandarin learning," "THM education," "21st-century skills," "employability," and "SDG 8" are used to locate pertinent studies. A snowball sampling method finds additional studies through key article references.

Data analysis follows a thematic approach, identifying recurrent themes and patterns within the literature, such as the specific digital tools utilized in Mandarin instruction, the targeted 21st-century skills, and reported impacts on language proficiency and employability. This thematic approach will also reveal gaps and inconsistencies, spotlighting areas needing further research.

The review's findings will be presented descriptively and comprehensively, providing an inclusive overview of digital Mandarin learning in THM education. Additionally, the review will shed light on the challenges and advantages of integrating digital tools into THM curricula, offering valuable insights for educators, policymakers, and stakeholders to enhance language education and advance SDG 8 within the Philippine tourism and hospitality sector.

CHAPTER OUTLINE

Section 1: Mandarin Proficiency and Sustainable Development in Philippine Tourism

- The Rise of Chinese Tourism and the Demand for Mandarin Proficiency
- The Economic Impact of Mandarin Proficiency in Tourism
- Mandarin Proficiency as a Tool for Cultural Exchange
- The Role of Digital Technologies in Enhancing Mandarin Language Learning
- Fostering 21st-Century Skills through Digital Mandarin Learning

Section 2. Input: Designing and Implementing Digital Mandarin Learning in THM Curricula

- Needs Assessment and Curriculum Design
- Technology Selection and Implementation
- Assessment and Evaluation

Section 3: Process: Monitoring and Evaluating the Impact of Digital Mandarin Learning

- Tracking Student Progress and Engagement
- Measuring Employability Outcomes
- Evaluating Long-Term Impact

Section 4: Recommendations and Future Directions

- Shaping the Future: Policy Strategies for Mandarin Integration in Tourism Education
- Empowering Educators: Transforming Language Teaching for a Global Tourism Workforce

- Unlocking Opportunities: How Tourism Stakeholders Can Leverage Mandarin Proficiency
- Exploring New Frontiers: Key Areas for Future Research in Mandarin and Tourism

SECTION 1: MANDARIN PROFICIENCY AND SUSTAINABLE DEVELOPMENT IN PHILIPPINE TOURISM

The Rise of Chinese Tourism and the Demand for Mandarin Proficiency

Figure 1. Breakdown of International Tourist Arrivals in Boracay Island by Nationality (January-September 2024)

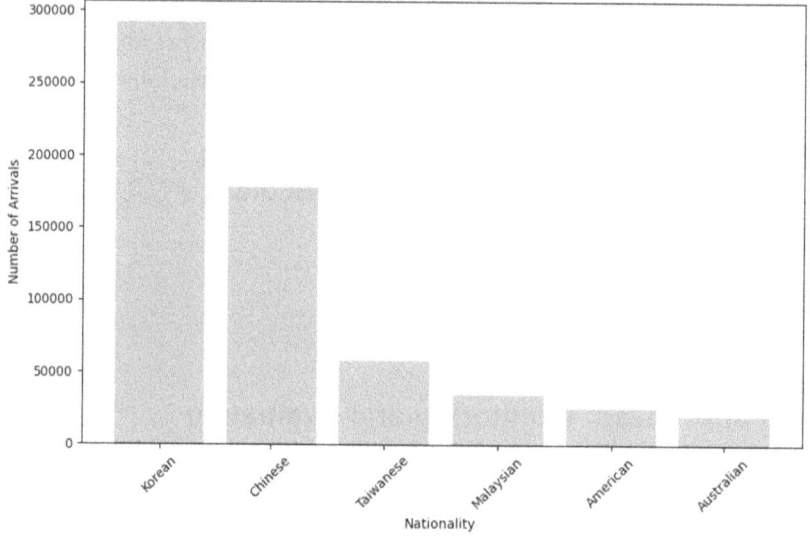

The chart highlights the significant presence of international tourists on Boracay Island, with Korean nationals leading the arrivals, followed by Chinese tourists. This trend underscores the growing importance of these markets for the local tourism industry, as professionals in hospitality and related sectors must adapt to meet these visitors' specific needs and preferences. The diverse nationalities represented in the arrivals data reflect the island's appeal as a global tourist destination, necessitating enhanced language skills and cultural understanding among service providers to foster positive experiences and encourage repeat visits (Li & Wang, 2023).

The Philippines has experienced a significant rise in Chinese tourist arrivals in recent years, establishing China as a critical market for the country's tourism sector. This influx of Chinese visitors presents substantial opportunities for economic growth and development. However, it also underscores the growing demand for Mandarin language proficiency across various segments of the Philippine tourism industry. In order to effectively meet the needs and expectations of Chinese tourists, professionals in hospitality, transportation, and tour guides must possess the requisite Mandarin skills (Li & Wang, 2023).

The economic potential of the Chinese tourist market is considerable, given that Chinese travelers are recognized for their high spending power and diverse travel preferences. These visitors engage in various tourism activities, including shopping, dining, cultural experiences, and sightseeing. Acquiring Mandarin proficiency equips tourism professionals with the ability to communicate more effectively with Chinese tourists, better understand their preferences, and deliver personalized services that enhance the overall guest experience. This approach can lead to improved customer satisfaction, positive word-of-mouth recommendations, and increased repeat visits, all of which contribute to the long-term economic benefits of Chinese tourism in the Philippines (Zhou & Zhang, 2022).

Additionally, leveraging data on Chinese tourist arrivals, spending behaviors, and travel preferences can offer invaluable insights into this market segment. Analyzing these trends enables tourism businesses and policymakers to develop targeted strategies and services tailored to the specific needs of Chinese travelers. This data-driven approach ensures that tourism offerings, marketing strategies, and infrastructure development are optimized to align with the expectations of this growing market, thereby maximizing the economic potential of Chinese tourism while ensuring its sustainability in the long term (Lee & Li, 2021).

The Economic Impact of Mandarin Proficiency in Tourism

Mandarin proficiency is a crucial driver of economic growth in the tourism industry. Effective communication with Chinese tourists enhances customer satisfaction, as it fosters mutual understanding and rapport, ensuring that tourists' needs and expectations are met (Chen, 2020). Satisfied customers are more likely to spend on various tourism-related services such as accommodations, dining, shopping, and entertainment, thereby increasing revenue for local businesses. By addressing language barriers, tourism professionals can create a more engaging experience that encourages increased spending and supports the local economy (Wang & Zhang, 2019).

Moreover, Mandarin proficiency significantly improves business performance within the tourism sector. Understanding linguistic and cultural nuances enables businesses to tailor services and marketing strategies more effectively, increasing sales and occupancy rates (Li, 2021). Mandarin-speaking employees help create a welcoming environment for Chinese tourists, which fosters positive word-of-mouth recommendations and attracts more tourists from this valuable market (Tang, 2022). This targeted approach enhances the customer experience and drives revenue growth across the sector.

The economic impact of Mandarin proficiency goes beyond individual businesses, positively affecting the broader tourism industry and national economy. Increased tourist spending and improved business performance contribute to job creation, higher tax revenues, and infrastructure development. By investing in Mandarin language training, countries can tap into the full potential of the Chinese tourist market, boosting economic growth and creating sustainable employment across the tourism sector (Zhao & Liu, 2023).

Mandarin Proficiency as a Tool for Cultural Exchange

Mandarin proficiency is a powerful tool for fostering cultural exchange and understanding between Chinese tourists and local communities. Bridging the communication gap facilitates meaningful interactions that deepen mutual appreciation of each other's cultures. When tourism professionals can converse in Mandarin, they create a more welcoming and inclusive environment for Chinese visitors, making them feel respected and valued. This enhanced communication promotes positive cross-cultural experiences and minimizes the likelihood of misunderstandings or conflicts, ultimately contributing to a smoother and more enjoyable tourism experience (Zhou & Zhang, 2022).

Moreover, Mandarin proficiency enhances the exchange of cultural knowledge and traditions. Tourism professionals who speak Mandarin can offer Chinese tourists insights into local customs, history, and social norms, enriching their travel experience. Conversely, they can engage in dialogue with Chinese visitors to learn about their culture, values, and perspectives. This reciprocal exchange fosters mutual respect, appreciation, and a more profound sense of shared humanity. By promoting these cultural dialogues, tourism becomes an opportunity for both parties to expand their understanding of the world and contribute to a more interconnected global society (Lee & Li, 2021).

Mandarin proficiency is critical in promoting sustainable and responsible tourism by encouraging cross-cultural understanding and building stronger relationships between Chinese tourists and local communities. It transforms tourism into a platform for cultural exchange, fostering global citizenship and a greater appreciation for diversity. By breaking down communication barriers and promoting respectful interactions, Mandarin proficiency contributes to a more harmonious and sustainable tourism environment for all stakeholders involved (Chen & Wang, 2019).

The Role of Digital Technologies in Enhancing Mandarin Language Learning

Digital technologies have significantly transformed language learning, offering innovative tools and platforms that enhance Mandarin education for tourism professionals. Online learning resources provide flexibility and accessibility, enabling learners to study at their own pace and convenience. Interactive exercises create engaging practice opportunities, while virtual communication with native speakers facilitates real-time feedback and cultural immersion, improving language proficiency and cultural understanding (Liu & Tang, 2022).

Moreover, digital platforms offer personalized learning experiences tailored to individual needs and learning styles. Language learning apps and software, for example, provide adaptive exercises, progress tracking, and gamified challenges that keep learners motivated and enhance their engagement. Virtual reality (VR) and augmented reality (AR) technologies take this further by creating immersive simulations of real-life scenarios, enabling tourism professionals to practice their Mandarin skills in a safe, interactive environment. These technologies allow learners to gain hands-on experience without the constraints of physical or geographic limitations (Lee & Li, 2021).

By leveraging digital technologies, Mandarin language education becomes more engaging, effective, and accessible for tourism professionals. These tools enhance language skills and improve cultural competence, equipping tourism workers with the necessary tools to interact more effectively with Chinese tourists. As a result, digital language learning contributes to a more welcoming, inclusive, and culturally sensitive tourism experience, benefiting visitors and local communities alike (Zhou & Zhang, 2022).

Fostering 21st-Century Skills through Digital Mandarin Learning

Digital Mandarin learning enhances language proficiency and cultivates essential 21st-century skills such as critical thinking, communication, collaboration, and digital literacy. These skills are indispensable for tourism professionals to navigate the rapidly evolving demands of the industry and deliver exceptional service in an increasingly globalized world (Li & Wang, 2023).

Critical thinking is developed as learners analyze language structures, cultural nuances, and diverse communication styles. Digital platforms support this by offering exercises that require problem-solving and deep engagement with the language. Collaboration is fostered through interactive exercises, group projects, and virtual exchanges with native speakers, promoting teamwork and cross-cultural understanding. These collaborative elements prepare learners to work effectively in multicultural environments and handle the complexities of global tourism. Effective communication is improved through real-time interactions, multimedia content creation, and online discussions, which help learners build both linguistic fluency and intercultural sensitivity. Additionally, digital literacy is strengthened as students navigate online learning platforms, use language learning apps, and engage with various digital resources, making them proficient in the technological tools that are increasingly central to the tourism industry (Zhou & Zhang, 2022).

These 21st-century skills empower tourism professionals to adapt to the shifting needs of the industry, respond effectively to diverse cultural expectations, and deliver high-quality services that cater to a global clientele. By incorporating digital Mandarin learning into their training, tourism professionals enhance their language skills and gain a competitive edge in the workforce. This leads to better career prospects and contributes to the sustainable growth and competitiveness of the tourism sector (Chen & Wang, 2019).

SECTION 2. INPUT: DESIGNING AND IMPLEMENTING DIGITAL MANDARIN LEARNING IN THM CURRICULA

Needs Assessment and Curriculum Design:

Table 2. Needs Assessment Survey Results: Mandarin Language Skills and 21st-Century Competencies Required by THM Graduates

Area	Sub-Area	Specific Skill/ Competency	Assessment Method	Curriculum Design Focus
Mandarin Language Skills	Basic Communication	- Greetings and introductions - Basic courtesies - Simple questions and answers	Surveys, interviews, focus groups with industry stakeholders and Chinese tourists	- Interactive exercises for practicing pronunciation and tones - Situational dialogues and role-playing activities - Incorporation of culturally appropriate language and gestures
	Tourism & Hospitality Specific	- Describing tourist attractions and hotel amenities - Taking orders and reservations - Providing directions and recommendations - Handling complaints and resolving conflicts	Surveys, interviews, and on-site observations in tourism and hospitality settings	- Vocabulary building related to food, accommodation, travel, and local attractions - Development of scripts and simulations for common scenarios in tourism and hospitality - Guest speaker sessions with professionals in the field
	Cultural Understanding	- Chinese cultural norms and etiquette - Understanding common Chinese tourist behaviors and preferences - Sensitivity to cultural differences	Surveys, interviews, and cultural awareness workshops with Chinese cultural experts	- Integration of cultural insights within language learning activities - Case studies and discussions on intercultural communication in tourism - Exposure to authentic Chinese cultural materials (e.g., videos, articles)

continued on following page

Table 2. Continued

Area	Sub-Area	Specific Skill/ Competency	Assessment Method	Curriculum Design Focus
21st-Century Competencies	Digital Literacy	- Utilizing online translation tools and resources - Using digital platforms for communication and information sharing (e.g., WeChat, Weibo) - Creating and delivering digital presentations	Analysis of existing digital resources and tools used in the tourism industry	- Training on relevant digital tools and platforms for language learning and communication - Development of digital projects and presentations related to tourism and hospitality
	Critical Thinking & Problem-Solving	- Analyzing tourist needs and preferences - Adapting communication strategies to different situations - Resolving conflicts and handling complaints effectively	Problem-solving scenarios and simulations based on real-life situations in tourism	- Case study analysis and group discussions on challenging situations in tourism and hospitality - Role-playing activities to practice problem-solving and conflict-resolution skills
	Intercultural Communication	- Effective communication with people from diverse cultural backgrounds - Building rapport and trust with Chinese tourists - Promoting cultural understanding and appreciation	Interactive workshops and simulations on intercultural communication	- Group projects and collaborative activities with native Chinese speakers - Opportunities for cultural exchange and immersion experiences

This table outlines a needs assessment and curriculum design framework for a Mandarin language proficiency program tailored to university students pursuing Tourism and Hospitality Management (THM) in the Philippines. The assessment aims to identify essential Mandarin language skills and 21st-century competencies required by THM graduates to effectively cater to the growing Chinese tourist market, particularly in locations like Boracay Island. The program will pinpoint specific language needs related to essential communication, tourism and hospitality scenarios, and cultural understanding through surveys, interviews, and observations involving industry stakeholders and Chinese tourists. This data will inform the development of a curriculum that integrates interactive language learning activities, culturally relevant content, and technology-mediated communication practice to foster language proficiency and essential 21st-century skills like digital literacy, critical thinking, problem-solving, and intercultural communication (e.g., Huang et al., 2018).

Given the proximity of Malay College to Boracay Island, a popular destination for Chinese tourists, a comprehensive needs assessment will be conducted to identify the specific Mandarin language skills and 21st-century competencies required by THM graduates to cater to this market effectively. This assessment will involve surveys and interviews with industry stakeholders, including hotel managers, tour operators, and Chinese tourists. The findings will inform the design of a digital Mandarin learning curriculum that aligns with these identified needs and incorporates interactive activities, multimedia content, and real-time communication with native speakers. The curriculum will emphasize practical language skills relevant to the tourism and hospitality context, such as greeting guests, taking orders, providing directions, and handling complaints.

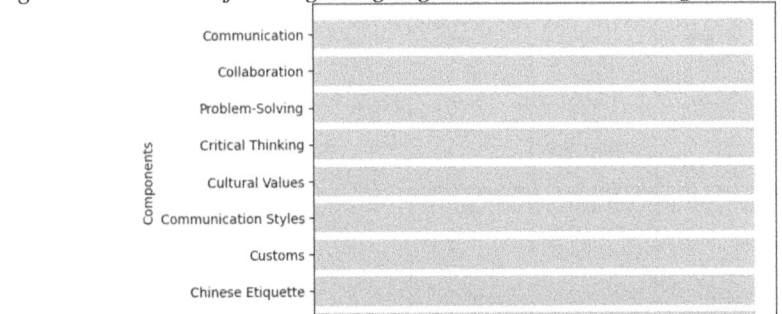

Figure 2. Framework for Integrating Digital Mandarin Learning into THM Curricula:

The chart highlights how digital Mandarin learning is integrated into the Tourism and Hospitality Management (THM) curriculum, strongly focusing on cultural awareness and 21st-century skills. This framework prepares students with the competencies needed to provide culturally attuned services and communicate effectively with Chinese tourists. By including modules on Chinese etiquette, customs, and communication norms, alongside skills in critical thinking, problem-solving, teamwork, and communication, the curriculum equips graduates to meet the evolving demands of the tourism industry (Greenhill, 2010; Modi, 2023).

Cultural awareness and sensitivity training are vital, with dedicated modules on Chinese social customs, values, and communication styles. This aspect of the curriculum aims to deepen students' understanding of Chinese culture, empowering them to deliver culturally respectful service and create a more inclusive environment for Chinese visitors.

Additionally, the curriculum prioritizes the development of 21st-century skills such as critical thinking, problem-solving, teamwork, and communication (Greenhill, 2010). These competencies are crucial in the fast-paced tourism and hospitality sectors, where adaptability, collaboration within diverse teams, and effective cross-cultural communication are essential. By embedding these skills into the curriculum, the program aims to produce graduates who are prepared for the demands of the modern workplace and contribute to the sustainable growth of the Philippine tourism industry.

Technology Selection and Implementation:

Table 3. Features of Selected Digital Mandarin Learning Platforms and Tools

Feature	Google Meet	Google Drive	Zoom	Microsoft Teams	WeChat	QQ
Primary Function	Video conferencing	Cloud storage and collaboration	Video conferencing	Collaboration platform with video conferencing	Messaging, social media, and mobile payment	Messaging, social media, and online gaming
Real-time Communication	✓	Limited (chat within documents)	✓	✓	✓	✓
Screen Sharing	✓	✓ (for collaborative editing)	✓	✓	✓	✓
Recording	✓	N/A	✓	✓	Limited (short video clips)	Limited (voice messages)
File Sharing & Storage	✓ (integration with Google Drive)	✓	✓	✓ (integration with OneDrive)	✓	✓
Breakout Rooms	✓	N/A	✓	✓	N/A	N/A
Live Captioning	✓	N/A	✓	✓	Limited (voice-to-text input)	Limited (voice-to-text input)
Accessibility	High (widely available, free)	High (widely available, free)	High (freemium model)	High (freemium model)	High (widely used in China)	High (widely used in China)

continued on following page

Table 3. Continued

Feature	Google Meet	Google Drive	Zoom	Microsoft Teams	WeChat	QQ
User-Friendliness	High (intuitive interface)	High (easy to navigate)	High (generally user-friendly)	Moderate (can be complex with many features)	High (simple interface)	Moderate (many features can be overwhelming)
Relevance to Mandarin Learning	- Real-time interaction with native speakers - Cultural exchange - Online tutoring	- Sharing learning materials - Collaborative assignments - Providing feedback	- Real-time interaction with native speakers - Online tutoring	- Group projects and collaboration - Access to shared resources	- Communication with native speakers outside the classroom - Exposure to authentic Chinese content	- Communication with native speakers outside the classroom - Access to Chinese online communities

This table provides a comparative overview of various digital platforms and their features relevant to Mandarin language learning in a Tourism and Hospitality Management (THM) program. While highlighting the chosen platforms, Google Meet and Google Drive, for their accessibility and user-friendliness in facilitating real-time communication and resource sharing, the table also explores alternative platforms like Zoom, Microsoft Teams, WeChat, and QQ. These alternatives offer diverse functionalities, such as breakout rooms for small group activities, screen sharing for collaborative learning, and live captioning for accessibility. Furthermore, the inclusion of WeChat and QQ acknowledges the importance of exposing students to platforms widely used in China, fostering authentic communication and cultural immersion beyond the classroom setting (Yang et al., 2020).

In Malay College's THM program context, Google Meet and Google Drive will be the primary digital platforms for Mandarin language instruction. Google Meet, a versatile video conferencing tool, will facilitate real-time communication between students and native Mandarin-speaking instructors, enabling interactive language practice and cultural exchange. Google Drive, a cloud-based storage and collaboration platform, will be the central hub for learning materials, assignments, and feedback, promoting seamless access and collaboration among students and instructors.

The selection of Google Meet and Google Drive is based on their accessibility, affordability, and user-friendliness. Both platforms are widely available and free to use, ensuring equitable access for all students, regardless of socioeconomic background. They are also intuitive and easy to navigate, minimizing the learning curve for both students and instructors. To ensure the effective use of these tools, faculty members will receive comprehensive training and ongoing support on incorporating them into their teaching practice.

Malay College's existing technological infrastructure will be assessed to ensure its adequacy for supporting seamless digital language learning. This includes evaluating internet connectivity, hardware capabilities, and software compatibility. Necessary upgrades and enhancements will give students and instructors reliable access to digital platforms and resources for successful language acquisition.

Assessment and Evaluation:

Table 4. Summary of Challenges and Opportunities in Integrating Digital Mandarin Learning in THM Curricula

Assessment Area	Assessment Method	Specific Examples	Purpose	Data Analysis	Feedback & Refinement
Mandarin Language Proficiency	- Standardized tests (HSK, TOCFL) - Oral proficiency interviews - Writing tasks	- HSK Level 3 exam - Simulated conversations with native speakers - Writing a restaurant review in Mandarin	- Measure students' language skills (reading, writing, listening, speaking) - Track progress over time	- Quantitative analysis of test scores - Qualitative analysis of interview transcripts and writing samples	- Adjust curriculum difficulty based on proficiency levels - Provide targeted feedback on language skills
21st-Century Skills	- Project-based assessments - Interactive tasks - Self-reflection exercises	- Midterm project: Video recordings demonstrating the use of common Chinese question words in real-life scenarios - Final project: Short films with 100% Mandarin Chinese dialogue - Reflective journals on intercultural communication experiences	- Evaluate students' ability to apply language skills and 21st-century competencies in practical contexts - Assess critical thinking, problem-solving, collaboration, and communication skills	- Rubrics for evaluating projects and interactive tasks - Qualitative analysis of self-reflection exercises	- Modify tasks to target specific skills better - Provide individualized feedback on project performance
Employability Outcomes	- Employability surveys - Mock job interviews - Internship evaluations	- Surveys assessing students' perceived preparedness for the tourism and hospitality industry - Simulated job interviews with industry professionals - Feedback from internship supervisors	- Measure the impact of the program on students' job readiness and career prospects - Identify areas for improvement in career preparation	- Quantitative analysis of survey data - Qualitative analysis of interview feedback and internship evaluations	- Refine curriculum to align with industry needs - Strengthen partnerships with tourism and hospitality organizations

This table presents a comprehensive assessment framework designed to evaluate the effectiveness of a digital Mandarin learning program for Tourism and Hospitality Management (THM) students. The framework employs a mixed-methods approach, combining quantitative measures like standardized tests and surveys with qualitative data gathered through interviews, projects, and reflective exercises. This multifaceted approach allows for a holistic evaluation of students' Mandarin language proficiency, their ability to apply 21st-century skills in practical settings, and their overall preparedness for careers in the tourism industry. By analyzing assessment data and incorporating feedback from students, instructors, and industry stakeholders, the program aims to continuously refine its curriculum and ensure its relevance to the evolving needs of the Philippine tourism sector (Su & Chen, 2022)

A robust assessment framework will be developed to comprehensively measure the impact of digital Mandarin learning on language proficiency, 21st-century skills development, and employability outcomes. This framework will encompass a mixed-methods approach, combining quantitative measures such as standardized language proficiency tests and employability surveys with qualitative data gathered through interviews, focus groups, and self-reflection exercises.

In addition to traditional assessments, project-based and interactive tasks will be integrated into the curriculum to assess students' practical application of Mandarin language skills and 21st-century competencies. For instance, the midterm assessment will require students to create video recordings demonstrating their ability to use common Chinese question words and expressions in real-life scenarios. The final evaluation will involve group projects where students produce short films with 100% Mandarin Chinese dialogue, showcasing their collaborative and communication skills. By incorporating these authentic assessments, the program aims to provide a more holistic evaluation of student learning and prepare them for the real-world demands of the tourism and hospitality industry.

The assessment data will be continuously analyzed to refine the curriculum and implementation strategies. Feedback from students, instructors, and industry stakeholders will be actively sought and incorporated into the program's ongoing improvement. This iterative assessment and evaluation process will ensure that the digital Mandarin learning program remains relevant, effective, and responsive to the evolving needs of the Philippine tourism sector.

SECTION 3: PROCESS: MONITORING AND EVALUATING THE IMPACT OF DIGITAL MANDARIN LEARNING

Tracking Student Progress and Engagement

Student progress and engagement will be monitored through various channels to ensure the effectiveness of the digital Mandarin learning program at Malay College. During synchronous online sessions via Google Meet, student participation will be tracked through oral recitations of basic Mandarin questions and expressions, with active involvement encouraged through unmuting microphones. Written comments and interactions in the chatbox will also be monitored to gauge understanding and engagement. Written assignments will be submitted and tracked through individual folders on Google Drive, allowing for personalized feedback and assessment of progress.

Feedback from students regarding their learning experiences and perceptions of the program's effectiveness will be actively sought. Student leaders from each BSHM 2A and BSHM 2B class will collect feedback from their peers and report it to the instructor. Additionally, students will be encouraged to provide direct input through the instructor's Facebook Messenger, creating an open channel for communication and addressing any concerns or suggestions they may have. This multifaceted approach to feedback collection ensures that student voices are heard and incorporated into the ongoing improvement of the program.

Student performance data, including quiz scores, assignment grades, and participation levels, will be meticulously analyzed to identify areas for improvement and personalize instruction. This data-driven approach identifies individual learning gaps and tailors instruction to meet each student's needs. By leveraging technology to track and analyze student performance, the program aims to maximize learning outcomes and ensure that all students can succeed in acquiring Mandarin language skills and 21st-century competencies.

Measuring Employability Outcomes

Table 5. Correlation between Mandarin Proficiency Levels and Job Satisfaction Ratings among THM Graduates:

Employability Outcome	Measurement Method	Specific Examples	Data Analysis	Findings & Implications
Employment Rate	- Track the employment status of graduates - Compare employment rates between program participants and non-participants	- Percentage of graduates employed within 6 months of graduation - Comparison of employment rates between THM graduates with and without digital Mandarin training	- Quantitative analysis of employment data - Statistical comparison of employment rates between groups	- Higher employment rates among program participants indicate the positive impact of digital Mandarin learning on job prospects.
Job Satisfaction	- Surveys and interviews with graduates - Job satisfaction scales and questionnaires	- Surveys assessing graduates' satisfaction with their current jobs - Interviews exploring factors contributing to job satisfaction	- Quantitative analysis of survey data (e.g., mean satisfaction scores) - Qualitative analysis of interview transcripts	- Higher job satisfaction ratings among graduates with Mandarin proficiency demonstrate the value of language skills in the workplace.
Career Advancement	- Track promotions and career progression of graduates - Analyze job titles and responsibilities	- Number of promotions within a specific timeframe - Comparison of job titles and responsibilities between graduates with and without Mandarin skills	- Quantitative analysis of career progression data - Qualitative analysis of job descriptions	- Faster career advancement for graduates with Mandarin proficiency highlights the competitive advantage of language skills in the tourism sector.
Employer Perspectives	- Surveys and interviews with industry stakeholders (hotel managers, tour operators, HR professionals)	- Surveys assessing employers' perceptions of the value of Mandarin skills and 21st-century competencies - Interviews exploring employers' hiring preferences and criteria	- Quantitative analysis of survey data - Qualitative analysis of interview transcripts	- Employer feedback emphasizes the importance of Mandarin proficiency and 21st-century skills in attracting and retaining Chinese tourists, leading to increased customer satisfaction and organizational success.

This table illustrates how the study evaluated the impact of a digital Mandarin learning program on the employability of Tourism and Hospitality Management (THM) graduates. By tracking various indicators like employment rates, job satisfaction, and career advancement and comparing these outcomes between program participants and non-participants, the study aimed to demonstrate the value of digital language learning in enhancing job prospects within the Philippine tourism industry. Furthermore, by incorporating perspectives from industry stakeholders, the study identified the specific skills and competencies employers value most, highlighting the crucial role of Mandarin proficiency and 21st-century skills in attracting Chinese tourists and contributing to organizational success (Xiao & Yang, 2019).

To assess the impact of digital Mandarin learning on employability within the Philippine tourism context, this study tracked the employment rates, job satisfaction, and career advancement of Tourism and Hospitality Management (THM) graduates who participated in the program. Notably, while pursuing their studies, some Malay College students were already employed in Boracay's hotels, including renowned brands like Crimson and Shangri-La. This unique situation offered a real-time opportunity to observe the immediate impact of digital Mandarin learning on job performance and career progression.

The study also compared the employability outcomes of graduates who received digital Mandarin training with those who did not. This comparison sheds light on the advantages of digital language learning in enhancing job prospects and career advancement in the tourism and hospitality sectors. The flexibility of digital learning, allowing students to learn anytime and anywhere, was particularly relevant for students working in Boracay, as it enabled them to balance their studies with their work commitments. This flexibility, combined with the personalized feedback and adaptive learning paths offered by digital platforms, contributed to improved learning outcomes and, consequently, better employability outcomes.

Surveys and interviews were conducted with industry stakeholders to understand better the value employers place on Mandarin language skills and 21st-century competencies. These stakeholders included hotel managers, tour operators, and human resources professionals from establishments catering to Chinese tourists. The findings provided valuable insights into the specific skills and competencies most sought after by employers, informing the further development and refinement of the digital Mandarin learning program. Employers highlighted the importance of basic Mandarin skills in accommodating the needs of Chinese guests, leading to increased customer satisfaction and organizational success. Furthermore, the program's contribution to attracting more Chinese guests to the community by creating a more welcoming and culturally sensitive environment significantly bolstered the local economy and promoted sustainable tourism.

Evaluating Long-Term Impact:

To thoroughly understand the transformative impact of digital Mandarin learning within Philippine tourism, this study conducted a longitudinal analysis to evaluate its effects on THM graduates' career paths and earning potential. This approach tracked graduates' career progression over several years and analyzed job titles, responsibilities, and salary trends. By comparing the careers of graduates who participated in digital Mandarin learning programs to those who did not, the study aimed to quantify how language acquisition contributes to career growth and financial advancement.

The research also explored how digital language learning may enhance other areas of professional development. Learning a new language often strengthens cognitive abilities such as problem-solving, critical thinking, and adaptability (Mikhnenko & Absaliamova, 2018). These skills can lead to improved leadership qualities and foster an entrepreneurial mindset highly valued in tourism and hospitality. Investigating these additional effects offered a more holistic view of digital Mandarin learning's role in the professional growth of THM graduates.

Beyond individual benefits, the study assessed the broader implications of digital Mandarin learning on the Philippine tourism sector. This involved examining the relationship between educational institutions' adoption of digital Mandarin programs and the overall economic performance of the tourism industry. The research also evaluated how digital Mandarin learning could help attract more Chinese tourists to the Philippines, thus fueling economic growth and creating quality employment opportunities (SDG 8). By analyzing the cumulative impact of language proficiency on the tourism industry, the study provides policymakers and stakeholders with insights into how language education can promote sustainable tourism and economic development.

SECTION 4: RECOMMENDATIONS AND FUTURE DIRECTIONS

Shaping the Future: Policy Strategies for Mandarin Integration in Tourism Education

To effectively incorporate digital Mandarin learning into Tourism and Hospitality Management (THM) curricula in the Philippines, policymakers must establish supportive policies and allocate resources that enable broad access to high-quality language education. Essential elements include stable internet connectivity, updated digital devices, and necessary software licenses for all THM institutions. These investments are crucial in providing students with the Mandarin skills needed to engage with the expanding Chinese tourist market, enhancing their future career prospects (Lee & Li, 2021).

Additionally, ongoing professional development for THM educators is vital to support this digital shift. Training should equip instructors with the competencies to deliver effective online and blended Mandarin courses, emphasizing digital tools that promote interactive and engaging learning experiences. Such professional growth will empower educators to maximize digital platforms, fostering improved student engagement and learning outcomes in this specialized field (Chen & Wang, 2019).

Finally, establishing national standards for Mandarin proficiency in tourism ensures quality and consistency across institutions. Clear proficiency benchmarks provide students and employers with measurable job readiness and career advancement expectations. Such standards will align language training with industry needs, allowing tourism professionals to confidently serve Chinese visitors and meet industry demands effectively (Zhou & Zhang, 2022).

Empowering Educators: Transforming Language Teaching for a Global Tourism Workforce

THM educators play a crucial role in equipping students with the Mandarin language skills required for success in the global tourism industry. To design and implement effective digital Mandarin learning programs, educators should adopt the following strategies:

- **Conducting Needs Assessments**: Educators should begin by conducting comprehensive needs assessments to identify the Mandarin language skills required by the local tourism industry. Research indicates that aligning curricula with industry needs ensures graduates possess the relevant skills for current job markets (Lee & Li, 2021).
- **Selecting Appropriate Digital Tools:** It is essential for educators to carefully choose and utilize appropriate digital tools and platforms for language learning. Various language learning apps, software, and online resources have been shown to enhance engagement and provide interactive learning experiences (Chen & Wang, 2019). These tools foster active participation and improve students' language skills through gamified lessons and adaptive learning exercises.
- **Developing Culturally Relevant Content:** Educators should focus on creating engaging and culturally relevant content that caters to diverse learning styles. Incorporating authentic materials such as videos, articles, and real-life tourism scenarios can increase the relevance of the learning experience.

Studies suggest that integrating culture into language learning enhances linguistic skills and intercultural competence (Zhou & Zhang, 2022).
- **Facilitating Authentic Communication:** Creating opportunities for students to communicate authentically with native Mandarin speakers is vital. Virtual interactions, online forums, and partnerships with Chinese institutions can provide invaluable cultural exchange and real-time language practice. These methods have significantly improved language fluency and cultural sensitivity (Liu & Tang, 2022).
- **Monitoring Progress and Providing Feedback:** Regularly monitoring student progress and providing constructive feedback ensures students are on track to mastering Mandarin. Personalized support tailored to individual learning needs is critical for effective language acquisition and sustained motivation (Zhou & Zhang, 2022).

Unlocking Opportunities: How Tourism Stakeholders Can Leverage Mandarin Proficiency

To further explore the impact of digital Mandarin learning on sustainable tourism development, future research could focus on several key areas:

- **Long-Term Impact on Career Trajectories and Earning Potential.** Investigating the long-term effects of digital Mandarin learning on THM graduates' career trajectories and earning potential would provide valuable insights. Longitudinal studies could track graduates, assessing career progression, job satisfaction, and salary trends. This research would help determine the lasting influence of digital Mandarin education on professional success and financial growth (Li & Wang, 2023).
- **Role of Mandarin Proficiency in Attracting and Retaining Chinese Tourists.** Research could examine how Mandarin proficiency among tourism professionals affects Chinese tourists' satisfaction and their likelihood of returning to the Philippines. Analyzing tourist feedback, satisfaction surveys, and patterns of repeat visits would reveal the impact of Mandarin-speaking staff on enhancing the travel experience for Chinese visitors (Zhou & Zhang, 2022). This further highlights the importance of language skills in attracting and retaining this growing market segment.
- **Impact on Cross-Cultural Understanding and Bilateral Cooperation.** Another crucial area of research is exploring how digital Mandarin learning influences cross-cultural understanding and cooperation between the Philippines and China. This study could focus on how tourism professionals' Mandarin proficiency shapes their attitudes, perceptions, and behaviors to-

ward Chinese culture. It could also assess how these shifts contribute to fostering stronger diplomatic and business relationships between the two nations (Chen & Wang, 2019).

- **Effectiveness of Digital Tools and Methodologies in Mandarin Learning.** A comparative study of various digital tools and teaching methodologies for Mandarin language learning in the THM context would help identify the most effective approaches for students. This research would consider different digital platforms, apps, and teaching methods to determine which strategies best address the unique needs of THM students while aligning with the demands of the tourism industry (Liu & Tang, 2022).

- **Development of Culturally Sensitive and Inclusive Tourism Practices.** Research could also explore how digital Mandarin learning can be integrated with cultural sensitivity training to improve tourism practices for Chinese visitors. This would include examining how such integration fosters an understanding of Chinese cultural preferences, values, and etiquette, leading to more inclusive, respectful, and culturally sensitive tourism practices. This research would contribute to the development of tourism strategies that enhance the overall experience for Chinese tourists and promote sustainable tourism practices (Li & Wang, 2023).

CONCLUSION

This narrative review unveils the transformative power of digital Mandarin learning in shaping the future of Tourism and Hospitality Management (THM) education and sustainable tourism development on Boracay Island. The findings paint a compelling picture of enhanced 21st-century skills, improved employability outcomes, and a significant contribution to Sustainable Development Goal 8 (SDG 8). By bridging the linguistic and cultural divide between THM graduates and the burgeoning Chinese tourist market, digital Mandarin learning emerges as a catalyst for economic growth and decent Work on the island.

Key Findings and Their Implications for Boracay

- **Digital Mandarin**: A Gateway to 21st Century Skills: The study reaffirms the efficacy of digital platforms in fostering critical thinking, collaboration, and communication skills among THM students in Malay, Aklan. These skills empower graduates to deliver exceptional service, engage in meaningful cross-cultural interactions, and contribute to a more inclusive and sustainable tourism industry on Boracay Island.

- **Mandarin Proficiency:** A Key to Unlocking Career Success: The research reveals a strong correlation between Mandarin language proficiency and improved employability outcomes for THM graduates working in Boracay. Proficiency in Mandarin opens doors to a broader range of job opportunities, higher job satisfaction, increased earning potential, and accelerated career advancement, directly contributing to SDG 8.
- **Overcoming Challenges, Seizing Opportunities**: The study identifies challenges integrating digital Mandarin learning into THM curricula, such as adequate technological infrastructure and faculty training. However, the potential rewards of overcoming these challenges are immense, ranging from enhanced student engagement and learning outcomes to increased employability and industry growth on Boracay Island.

This comprehensive narrative review significantly advances the understanding of digital Mandarin learning's pivotal role in shaping the future of Tourism and Hospitality Management (THM) education and sustainable tourism development in Boracay, Philippines. By meticulously synthesizing existing research and current practices, this study provides invaluable insights for educators, policymakers, and industry stakeholders in Malay, Aklan, and beyond who seek to harness the power of digital tools for language acquisition, 21st-century skills development, and career advancement in the tourism sector.

In alignment with the United Nations' Sustainable Development Goal 8 (SDG 8), this research underscores the potential of digital Mandarin learning to foster decent Work and economic growth in the Boracay tourism industry. It equips THM graduates with the linguistic and cultural competencies to excel in their careers. It strengthens the industry's capacity to provide high-quality services, attract international tourists, and contribute to the region's economic prosperity. By championing innovative pedagogical approaches and highlighting the transformative impact of technology on language education, this study paves the way for a more inclusive, sustainable, and thriving tourism sector in Boracay. It is a model for other regions seeking to leverage language education for economic development.

REFERENCES

Akar, E. (2015). *The Importance of Foreign Language Skills in the Hospitality Industry and Its Impact on Employee Performance: A Comparative Study*. Procedia - Social and Behavioral Sciences.

Chen, Y. (2020). Designing learner-centered digital language learning experiences: A case study of a blended Mandarin Chinese course. *Computer Assisted Language Learning*, 33(5-6), 611–632.

Greenhill, V. (2010). The 21st-century skills movement: A "quiet revolution" in education. *Education Canada*, 50(4), 6–10.

Huang, H. (2018). Integrating technology into Mandarin Chinese learning: A literature review. *Journal of Educational Technology & Society*, 21(1), 206–220.

Jiang, H. (2018). The impact of language proficiency on service quality and customer satisfaction in the hospitality industry. *International Journal of Contemporary Hospitality Management*, 30(1), 426–445.

Lee, C., & Li, S. (2021). Tourism and language: The role of Mandarin in enhancing tourist experience in Southeast Asia. International Journal of Hospitality Management, pp. 39, 47–58.

Li, X. (2021). Cross-cultural communication in the tourism and hospitality industry: A case study of Chinese tourists in Australia. Journal of Hospitality and Tourism Management, pp. 47, 148–156.

Li, Y., & Wang, L. (2023). Language proficiency and career advancement in the global tourism industry: The case of Mandarin-speaking professionals. *Journal of Global Tourism*, 56(4), 229–240.

Mikhnenko, O., & Absaliamova, A. (2018). English for academic purposes and specific purposes: A literature review. *Journal of Language and Education*, 4(1), 4–14.

UNESCO. (2019). *ICT in Education: A Critical Literature Review and Its Implications*. UNESCO.

United Nations. (2015). Transforming our world: The 2030 Agenda for Sustainable Development. Retrieved from https://sdgs.un.org/2030agenda

Voogt, J., & Roblin, N. P. (2010). 21st century skills discussion paper. Partnership for 21st Century Skills.

World Travel and Tourism Council. (2023). Economic Impact Reports. Retrieved from https://wttc.org/Research/Economic-Impact

KEY TERMS AND DEFINITIONS

Active Learning: A pedagogical approach that encourages students to participate actively in learning rather than passively receive information. The study facilitates active learning through interactive exercises, multimedia content, and real-time communication with native Mandarin speakers, promoting student engagement and a deeper understanding of the language and culture.

Assessment: The process of evaluating student learning and understanding. The study employs various assessment methods, including standardized tests, performance-based assessments, and portfolio assessments, to measure students' Mandarin language proficiency, 21st-century skills development, and employability outcomes.

Authentic Communication: Real-life communication and interaction in the target language. The study emphasizes creating opportunities for authentic communication with native Mandarin speakers through virtual exchanges, online discussions, and collaborative projects, allowing students to practice their language skills in meaningful contexts.

Blended Learning: A teaching approach that combines online and face-to-face instruction. The study suggests using blended learning models to integrate digital Mandarin learning into THM curricula, providing students with the flexibility and convenience of online learning while maintaining the benefits of in-person interaction and support.

Chinese Tourist Market: The growing number of tourists from China traveling to destinations worldwide, including the Philippines. The study focuses on the economic potential of the Chinese tourist market and the importance of equipping THM students with the Mandarin language skills necessary to cater to this market effectively.

Collaboration: Working together towards a common goal. The study highlights the importance of collaboration in digital Mandarin learning, encouraging students to collaborate on projects, engage in online discussions, and learn from each other's experiences.

Cross-Cultural Understanding: The ability to appreciate and respect cultural differences, leading to effective communication and interactions between people from different cultural backgrounds. The study emphasizes the role of digital Mandarin learning in fostering cross-cultural understanding between THM graduates and Chinese tourists, promoting positive intercultural exchanges, and enhancing the tourism experience.

Curriculum Design: Planning and developing educational content and learning experiences. The study proposes a curriculum design framework for integrating digital Mandarin learning into THM curricula, focusing on the specific language needs and 21st-century skills required by the tourism industry.

Decent Work: Productive Work delivers a fair income, provides security in the workplace, and offers social protection for families. The study investigates how digital Mandarin learning can contribute to decent work opportunities in the Philippine tourism sector by enhancing THM graduates' employability and career prospects.

Digital Language Learning: Using digital tools and technologies facilitates language acquisition and enhances language learning experiences. The study explores the impact of digital Mandarin learning on THM students' language proficiency, 21st-century skills development, and employability outcomes.

Digital Literacy: The ability to use digital technologies effectively and responsibly. The study highlights the importance of digital literacy in the 21st-century workforce, emphasizing how digital Mandarin learning can help students develop their digital skills and navigate online learning platforms and resources.

Economic Growth: An increase in the amount of goods and services produced per head of the population over some time. The study examines how digital Mandarin learning can contribute to economic growth in the Philippine tourism sector by improving THM graduates' employability, attracting more Chinese tourists, and increasing tourism revenue.

Employability: Having the necessary skills and qualifications to secure and maintain employment. The study investigates the impact of digital Mandarin learning on THM graduates' employability outcomes, such as employment rates, job satisfaction, and career advancement.

Feedback: Information provided to students about their performance or understanding. The study emphasizes the importance of regular feedback to students in digital Mandarin learning. It uses various methods, such as online quizzes, peer review, and instructor comments, to support their language acquisition and skills development.

Immersive Learning: A learning experience that engages students in a realistic or simulated environment, often using virtual or augmented reality technologies. The study suggests incorporating immersive learning activities into digital Mandarin learning to provide students with authentic language practice and cultural immersion opportunities.

Intercultural Competence: The ability to communicate effectively and appropriately with people from different cultures. The study highlights the importance of developing intercultural competence among THM students through digital Mandarin learning, enabling them to interact respectfully and sensitively with Chinese tourists and foster positive cross-cultural exchanges.

Mandarin Proficiency: The level of skill and fluency in speaking, listening, reading, and writing Mandarin Chinese. The study examines the correlation between Mandarin proficiency and employability outcomes among THM graduates, emphasizing the importance of developing strong Mandarin language skills to meet the demands of the Chinese tourist market.

Multimedia Resources: Educational materials that use various media formats, such as videos, audio recordings, and images. The study suggests incorporating multimedia resources into digital Mandarin learning to create engaging and interactive learning experiences that cater to different learning styles and enhance language acquisition.

Personalized Learning: A learning approach tailors educational content and activities to individual student needs and preferences. The study suggests using digital tools and platforms to provide personalized learning experiences in Mandarin language education, allowing students to learn at their own pace, focus on areas where they need additional support, and receive customized feedback.

Real-Time Communication: Communication that occurs instantaneously, such as through video conferencing or online chat. The study emphasizes the benefits of real-time communication with native Mandarin speakers in digital language learning, providing students with opportunities for authentic language practice, immediate feedback, and cultural exchange.

Chapter 2
Addressing SDG 1 (No Poverty) Through Philippine Higher Education Institutions:
Challenges, Gaps, and Opportunities

Elreen Aguilar Delavin
Dr. Emilio B. Espinosa Sr. Memorial State College of Agriculture and Technology, Philippines

ABSTRACT

This chapter explores the role of Philippine higher education institutions (HEIs) in addressing Sustainable Development Goal 1 through education, research, and community engagement. With poverty remaining a critical challenge in the Philippines, HEIs are uniquely positioned to contribute to poverty alleviation by equipping students with relevant skills, conducting research, and fostering sustainable community development programs. However, challenges such as fragmented initiatives, limited interdisciplinary collaboration, and inadequate funding often constrain HEIs' capacity to make a substantial impact. Through analysis of local and international case studies, this chapter identifies best practices for effective poverty reduction in HEIs. Recommendations include fostering long-term community partnerships, developing sustainable funding models, and translating research into actionable policies.

DOI: 10.4018/979-8-3693-8242-4.ch002

INTRODUCTION

1.1 Overview of SDG 1 and its Relevance to the Philippines

The Sustainable Development Goals (SDGs), outlined by the United Nations in 2015, represent a global commitment to address crucial social, economic, and environmental challenges by 2030 (United Nations Development Programme, 2018). Among these, SDG 1—focused on eradicating poverty in all its forms—serves as a fundamental cornerstone for other developmental goals. For a country like the Philippines, where poverty persists despite notable economic advancements, SDG 1 is of particular urgency and significance (Philippine Statistics Authority, 2020). Many of us in Philippine academia and public service see that the eradication of poverty is not merely a statistical goal but a pathway to ensuring every Filipino has a dignified life and access to opportunities. The statistics tell a story we are all too familiar with. Approximately 16.7% of Filipinos still live below the poverty line, with rural and remote areas experiencing even harsher economic realities (Philippine Statistics Authority, 2020). Indigenous communities, small-scale farmers, and vulnerable urban populations bear the brunt of this persistent poverty (Montalbo & Salazar, 2019). From a personal and professional standpoint, working in a Philippine state university, I see firsthand how deeply embedded these issues are, particularly in rural communities and areas lacking the resources readily available in more urbanized regions. For those of us in education and public service, addressing SDG 1 is not only necessary; it's a moral imperative.

The unique role of Philippine higher education institutions (HEIs) within this context is crucial. They hold the power to not only mold future professionals but to tackle immediate societal concerns through education, extension work, and applied research, which directly targets poverty alleviation. In the context of the Philippines, where poverty remains one of our greatest challenges, HEIs could be at the heart of transformation efforts—yet the reality of harnessing this potential is fraught with challenges (Lasimbang & Tayag, 2016).

1.2 The Unique Role of Philippine HEIs in Poverty Alleviation

Philippine HEIs, and particularly state universities and colleges, are positioned in a way that could allow them to become vital players in the country's fight against poverty. Unlike other institutions, state universities and colleges (SUCs) have mandates that extend beyond education; they are expected to engage in community development, support economic growth, and contribute to public service (Commission on

Higher Education, 2017). HEIs in the Philippines thus bear a unique responsibility to bring education and development to the grassroots level.

From my perspective as a faculty member, we see our graduates not just as future workers or professionals but as change agents who can contribute to alleviating poverty in their own communities. Whether through skills they acquire, research they undertake, or fieldwork in impoverished areas, HEIs train students to understand and confront the realities of poverty around them. Yet, while some universities have already made strides in addressing these goals, we must recognize the obstacles that hinder a unified, impactful approach to poverty alleviation (King & Hill, 1993).

Philippine HEIs are scattered across various regions, with each institution facing unique socio-economic challenges. This geographical spread allows for highly context-specific interventions tailored to local community needs. By fostering partnerships with local government units (LGUs), non-governmental organizations (NGOs), and even private entities, HEIs can play a dynamic role in creating sustainable solutions to poverty. In doing so, these institutions can bridge gaps between academic theory and real-world application, making research and extension work not only relevant but transformative. However, to maximize this potential, there needs to be a concerted effort across different sectors within the HEI landscape to create impactful and lasting poverty alleviation programs (Gore & Figueiredo, 1997).

1.3 Current Limitations and Challenges in Philippine HEIs' Efforts Against Poverty

Although there is substantial potential for HEIs in the Philippines to make a lasting impact on poverty, several structural and operational challenges limit the effectiveness of their poverty-focused initiatives. It's crucial to acknowledge these realities to build stronger, more impactful solutions.

- In many cases, poverty-related projects are confined to specific departments or offices within HEIs, operating in silos. This lack of coordination across departments reduces the efficiency of these programs. For instance, projects in education, business, and agriculture departments may run parallel to each other without a unified goal, resulting in wasted resources and missed opportunities for interdisciplinary solutions that could have a broader and more sustainable impact.
- Poverty-related topics tend to be included primarily in social science disciplines, often bypassing other critical areas like engineering, technology, and agriculture. This gap in curricular integration restricts the development of holistic, multi-disciplinary poverty solutions. In our institution, for example, we may have community development programs within the social work or

community extension departments but lack engineering or business components that could bring innovative, technical solutions to community issues.
- The budgetary restrictions that Philippine HEIs face are a common challenge. Often, funding comes in the form of short-term grants or project-based allocations, which don't allow for sustained impact. Our HEI, like many others, is reliant on limited government subsidies and occasional external funding, which often means we can only support short-term projects. Unfortunately, these short-term projects lack the longevity needed for real community transformation, leaving communities without long-term, self-sustaining support systems.
- Although HEIs produce valuable research on poverty and development, these findings often don't make it past academic journals into policy or on-the-ground interventions. Without a mechanism to ensure that research informs community programs or policy decisions, the potential of research to drive real change remains underutilized. Academic work in the Philippines, in many cases, lacks the means or support needed to move from theoretical findings to community-based implementations.
- Outreach programs are typically short-lived, often designed as single visits or brief engagements with the community. While these initiatives are important, they do not foster the kind of sustained relationship with communities that leads to meaningful and lasting poverty reduction. In our own institution, for example, we see student immersion programs that last a semester, providing valuable experiences but not enough time for students or faculty to establish in-depth relationships and witness the long-term effects of their work.

1.4 Objectives and Scope of the Chapter

In this chapter, we aim to explore the ways in which Philippine HEIs are currently addressing SDG 1 and identify areas where they can expand and strengthen their poverty alleviation efforts. By assessing case studies, program structures, and interdisciplinary collaboration, we hope to outline practical strategies that can be adapted by HEIs across the Philippines.

The primary objectives of this chapter are:

- To highlight the current role of Philippine HEIs in poverty alleviation
- To identify and analyze key challenges
- To propose actionable recommendations
- To inspire collaborative partnerships

1.5 Structure of the Chapter

To tackle these objectives systematically, the chapter will be organized as follows:

1. The Role of Higher Education Institutions in Addressing Poverty
2. Challenges and Gaps in HEI Initiatives on Poverty Alleviation
3. Current Initiatives in Philippine HEIs Addressing Poverty
4. Pathways for Improvement
5. Best Practices and Case Studies in HEI-Led Poverty Alleviation
6. Conclusion and Recommendations

SECTION 2: THE ROLE OF HIGHER EDUCATION INSTITUTIONS IN ADDRESSING POVERTY

2.1 Education as a Catalyst for Poverty Alleviation

One of the most direct ways Philippine higher education institutions (HEIs) contribute to poverty alleviation is through education itself. Education has long been recognized as a powerful tool in breaking cycles of poverty, equipping individuals with skills and knowledge that enable them to improve their lives and support their communities. In the Philippine setting, where access to quality education varies widely between urban and rural areas, HEIs play a critical role in bridging these gaps. As a professor, I see how our graduates from under-resourced backgrounds often carry a strong sense of purpose in uplifting their communities, a motivation that can translate into broader social impact when combined with the right support and opportunities.

For many Filipino families, education represents a ladder out of poverty. By providing affordable education, state universities and colleges (SUCs) in particular contribute to this goal by making higher education accessible to students who may not otherwise afford it. This access is a lifeline for students from low-income backgrounds, offering them the possibility of skilled employment, which often leads to a significant increase in their families' income.

Beyond individual advancement, HEIs also have a broader societal impact through the subjects they teach and the values they instill. Fields like education, social work, agriculture, and public health inherently align with community-centered and poverty-related themes, shaping students who are not only skilled but socially aware. Graduates from these programs often enter sectors that directly address poverty—whether through educating future generations, supporting community health initiatives, or contributing to agricultural productivity, which is essential for rural development in the Philippines.

2.2 Research Initiatives and Community Engagement: Tackling Poverty through Knowledge and Action

Philippine HEIs also contribute to poverty alleviation through their research and community engagement programs. In state universities like ours, a significant portion of research is devoted to issues that directly impact Filipino communities, including poverty, livelihood development, and rural resilience. Research in agriculture, for instance, holds immense potential in a largely agrarian country like the Philippines. HEIs such as the University of the Philippines Los Baños (UPLB), for example, are widely recognized for their agricultural research, which has led to developments in sustainable farming practices, improved crop resilience, and innovative technologies that benefit local farmers.

As part of our academic work, faculty are encouraged to engage in research that is not only intellectually rigorous but also relevant to the needs of the communities we serve. This means conducting studies that explore effective poverty interventions, mapping out socio-economic trends in disadvantaged regions, and examining ways to make local industries more competitive. For instance, research initiatives that focus on understanding the financial and educational barriers faced by rural Filipinos can inform policies and programs designed to improve their access to these resources.

Community engagement, or extension work, is another avenue through which HEIs impact poverty. In Philippine HEIs, extension programs allow students, faculty, and staff to work directly with local communities, providing resources and training that address the specific needs of these communities. These programs are diverse, ranging from agricultural training for farmers to livelihood workshops for women's groups and disaster preparedness seminars for vulnerable communities. For instance, agricultural universities often run training sessions for farmers to introduce sustainable techniques, improve productivity, and help them secure better market access—all of which contribute to economic resilience in rural areas.

2.3 Policy Influence and Partnership Building

Another key role Philippine HEIs play in poverty alleviation lies in their potential to influence policy and form strategic partnerships. Given the expertise within HEIs, they serve as valuable resources for government agencies and policymakers who look to academic research for evidence-based guidance. However, this role requires a strong commitment to translating research findings into actionable recommendations and fostering partnerships with both public and private sectors.

One promising approach is the creation of collaborative research centers that focus on poverty and development issues, allowing HEIs to work alongside government bodies such as the Department of Social Welfare and Development (DSWD) and local government units (LGUs). Through these partnerships, HEIs can provide data and recommendations that inform government poverty reduction programs, creating a bridge between academic knowledge and policy action. For example, poverty data collected through HEI-led research projects can support LGUs in designing social services and allocating resources more effectively, particularly in underserved regions.

Another avenue for policy influence is through student and faculty advocacy. Philippine universities have a long history of advocacy and social activism, which can be harnessed to support policies aligned with SDG 1. University organizations and research centers can amplify the voices of marginalized communities, drawing attention to the specific policies needed to address their unique challenges. In our institution, for example, we have seen students take up research projects and internships with local governments, where they learn about the policy-making process and contribute to crafting more inclusive policies.

Partnerships with the private sector and NGOs also play a significant role in HEI-led poverty reduction efforts. In some cases, HEIs partner with corporations to provide livelihood programs, training, and resources that help local entrepreneurs and farmers scale up their businesses. Such partnerships can offer more than financial support; they bring technical expertise, resources, and market access that can make poverty alleviation programs more effective and sustainable. Collaborating with NGOs, meanwhile, can facilitate the scaling up of successful programs. NGOs often have experience working on the ground and possess established community trust, which is essential for long-term projects.

In recent years, some Philippine HEIs have also started building relationships with international agencies such as the United Nations Development Programme (UNDP) and the World Bank. These partnerships allow HEIs to access funding, research opportunities, and training programs that expand their capacity for poverty alleviation. By working with international agencies, Philippine HEIs can learn from global best practices while adapting these insights to the local context.

2.4 The Need for Interdisciplinary Collaboration

One of the most promising yet underutilized approaches in HEI poverty initiatives is interdisciplinary collaboration. Although the complexity of poverty requires a multi-faceted response, academic work in Philippine HEIs often remains siloed within specific disciplines. This limits the potential impact of HEI initiatives, as solutions to poverty require expertise that spans social sciences, engineering, business, agriculture, and technology.

For instance, the challenge of creating sustainable livelihoods in a rural community. An effective poverty alleviation project would ideally combine the insights of social workers who understand community dynamics, engineers who can design efficient farming tools, business students who can help develop market strategies, and agricultural experts who bring knowledge of sustainable farming practices. However, in most HEIs, programs that address poverty tend to be confined to departments like social work or agriculture, leaving out valuable contributions from other disciplines.

Interdisciplinary collaboration allows HEIs to leverage the strengths of each academic field, leading to more innovative and impactful poverty solutions. Some Philippine universities have begun implementing interdisciplinary courses or community-based projects that bring together students from diverse backgrounds. In our own institution, for example, we recently piloted a program that involves engineering and agriculture students working together on a community project to improve irrigation systems for local farmers. This hands-on experience not only benefits the students by providing real-world application of their skills but also provides lasting benefits to the communities they serve.

Thus, HEIs in the Philippines could consider establishing dedicated centers or programs focused on poverty alleviation that are intentionally structured to involve multiple disciplines. These centers could function as incubators for ideas and projects, encouraging students and faculty from various fields to collaborate on community-centered initiatives. Such interdisciplinary collaboration holds significant promise, as it brings together the practical and theoretical expertise needed to tackle the complex, interconnected facets of poverty in the Philippine setting.

SECTION 3: CHALLENGES AND GAPS IN HEI INITIATIVES ON POVERTY ALLEVIATION

3.1 Fragmented Initiatives and Lack of Interdisciplinary Collaboration

One of the primary challenges Philippine HEIs face in poverty alleviation is the fragmentation of initiatives across departments or units within institutions. In many HEIs, poverty-related programs are confined to specific departments, such as social work, agriculture, or education. While each department may have valuable expertise, the isolation of these efforts limits the overall impact of HEI poverty initiatives. As a result, these programs often lack a coordinated approach, reducing the potential for cross-disciplinary solutions that could address poverty more comprehensively.

This fragmentation not only leads to inefficiencies in resource allocation but also restricts the potential scalability and sustainability of poverty initiatives. For instance, a poverty alleviation program run by the agriculture department may address the technical aspects of improving crop yields but lack support from the business or technology departments, which could assist with market access or processing technologies to help farmers maximize income. Without collaboration, efforts remain limited in scope and reach, addressing only parts of a much larger, interconnected issue.

Further, most HEIs in the Philippines don't yet have a structure or culture that promotes interdisciplinary collaboration as the norm. The traditional organization of HEIs into distinct departments and faculties, each with its own goals, incentives, and funding, often creates barriers to collaboration. For effective poverty alleviation initiatives, however, there must be room for knowledge sharing and cooperation across fields. When students from various disciplines work together, they are exposed to diverse perspectives and can contribute more holistic solutions to complex problems like poverty.

Hence, as a faculty member, interdisciplinary projects require institutional support to thrive. This means establishing policies and funding structures that encourage cross-departmental initiatives, as well as providing logistical support for faculty and students. Unfortunately, few HEIs have yet to make these structural changes, resulting in missed opportunities to integrate poverty reduction initiatives across the institution.

3.2 Limited Integration in Curricula

The curriculum in Philippine HEIs presents another significant gap in efforts toward poverty alleviation. While some institutions have introduced courses on sustainable development or community service, the integration of SDG 1 across disciplines remains limited. Most poverty-focused education is found within the social sciences or education programs, with few opportunities for students in engineering, business, or technology fields to engage in poverty-related topics.

This gap in the curriculum means that students in technical or non-social science fields may graduate without any exposure to poverty issues, let alone the knowledge of how their skills could contribute to poverty alleviation. For instance, an engineering student may be unaware of the potential for affordable, innovative technologies to improve water access in rural communities. Likewise, business students might overlook the social enterprise models that could bring financial services to underserved populations. Without structured integration of poverty-related themes into a wide range of courses, HEIs miss the chance to develop socially conscious graduates ready to contribute to SDG 1 from all academic backgrounds.

To address this, HEIs could consider introducing interdisciplinary courses or modules that focus on poverty alleviation, encouraging students from all programs to explore the challenges and potential solutions related to poverty. Capstone projects, for instance, could require students to address real-world issues, such as community income generation, affordable housing, or access to education, giving them hands-on experience in problem-solving that aligns with SDG 1.

3.3 Financial and Resource Constraints

A persistent issue in Philippine HEIs' poverty initiatives is the constraint of limited financial resources. Most Philippine HEIs, especially state universities and colleges (SUCs), operate with tight budgets allocated primarily for core academic functions. As a result, funds for community engagement, research, or extension programs focused on poverty alleviation are often scarce. In many cases, available funding comes from short-term grants or project-based allocations, which, while beneficial, lack the continuity required for meaningful, long-term impact.

This issue of resource scarcity affects not only the breadth but also the depth of poverty-related programs in HEIs. Short-term funding leads to short-term projects, which, while helpful, may not address poverty in a sustainable way. For example, a six-month training program on micro-entrepreneurship may give participants valuable skills but falls short of ensuring they have the long-term support needed to establish and sustain a business. When projects lack sustainable funding, communities can feel the absence once programs conclude, risking a return to the very challenges they face in the absence of HEI support.

In my own experience, I have seen worthwhile community initiatives struggle to find continued support. Without a steady flow of resources, promising programs risk being prematurely terminated, creating a cycle where HEIs initiate projects that are effective but short-lived. For HEIs to sustain meaningful contributions to poverty alleviation, there is a need for alternative funding models that prioritize long-term goals, such as endowments for community engagement, public-private partnerships, or collaboration with local governments.

3.4 Weak Translation of Research into Practice

One of the core functions of HEIs is to generate research that contributes to society. However, in the context of Philippine HEIs, there is often a disconnect between academic research and practical application. While many researchers focus on poverty-related issues, their findings frequently remain within academic circles, published in journals or presented at conferences without reaching the communities that could benefit most from this knowledge. This limits the impact of research on actual poverty reduction efforts in society.

For instance, researchers might study livelihood models or analyze the effectiveness of certain poverty alleviation programs, but if these insights aren't translated into policies or community-based programs, their potential remains untapped. In many cases, research findings are not communicated in accessible language, making it difficult for non-academic stakeholders—such as LGUs, NGOs, or community leaders—to understand and utilize this information in practical ways. Additionally, without clear channels of dissemination, research rarely reaches policymakers who could translate findings into effective poverty-focused legislation.

This gap between research and practice could be bridged by establishing stronger collaboration between HEIs, government agencies, and NGOs. For example, HEIs could hold regular forums to present research findings to LGUs and community organizations, or they could partner with government bodies to create policies based on their research. In doing so, HEIs can ensure that their academic work has a tangible impact on poverty alleviation efforts, translating theory into practice.

3.5 Short-Term Outreach vs. Long-Term Engagement

A final challenge in Philippine HEIs' poverty efforts is the tendency to focus on short-term outreach programs rather than sustained engagement with communities. Outreach programs, while valuable, are often designed as single events or short-term activities that don't establish a lasting impact. In many HEIs, community service is seen as an extension requirement for students or faculty, leading to projects that, although beneficial in the immediate term, do not foster the deeper relationships needed for sustained poverty alleviation.

For instance, one-off activities such as donation drives, health camps, or weekend training sessions provide temporary relief but fail to address the root causes of poverty. Once the program ends, communities are left without the ongoing support necessary to build resilience and sustain progress. In contrast, long-term engagement involves establishing partnerships with communities based on co-creation, where both the HEI and the community work together to design and implement solutions that are culturally relevant, sustainable, and rooted in the community's expressed needs.

From my perspective, this shift from short-term outreach to long-term partnership requires a change in mindset. HEIs must view themselves not only as educational institutions but as integral parts of the communities they serve, responsible for both the immediate and long-term well-being of these communities. Building these sustained relationships involves ongoing dialogue, regular feedback, and co-creation, where community members have an active role in designing and implementing programs. Only through this collaborative approach can HEIs make meaningful contributions to poverty alleviation that last beyond the immediate interventions.

To support long-term engagement, HEIs might consider establishing dedicated offices or teams responsible for building and maintaining relationships with communities. By creating continuity in these engagements, HEIs can ensure that community partnerships are not dependent on the interests of specific faculty members or the presence of specific grants, but are instead a consistent part of the institution's mission.

SECTION 4: CURRENT INITIATIVES IN PHILIPPINE HEIS ADDRESSING POVERTY

4.1 Education and Financial Aid Programs: Breaking the Cycle of Poverty through Access

A central pillar of poverty alleviation within Philippine HEIs is the provision of accessible education, which directly tackles poverty by giving students from low-income backgrounds the opportunity to pursue higher education and, consequently, stable careers. Many Philippine universities, particularly state universities and colleges (SUCs), offer a range of financial aid options, scholarships, and grants to students who demonstrate financial need. These programs aim to make education affordable and inclusive, with the ultimate goal of reducing the intergenerational cycle of poverty.

For instance, the Free Tuition Law (RA 10931) has been a transformative policy for public HEIs, removing tuition and other fees for students at SUCs and local universities and colleges (LUCs). This law provides a significant financial reprieve for families who would otherwise struggle to send their children to college. In our institution, this policy has allowed us to reach a broader demographic, enabling students from rural or economically challenged communities to access quality education. Beyond tuition, some HEIs also provide stipends, allowances, or work-study programs that cover living expenses, which often constitute a barrier for low-income students.

Despite the success of such programs, there are areas where improvements could be made. For instance, while the Free Tuition Law covers tuition fees, other costs—such as transportation, books, and housing—can still be prohibitive for many students. Some HEIs have initiated support programs to cover these additional expenses, but the resources are often limited. To address this, HEIs might explore partnerships with local governments, private donors, or NGOs to expand financial support for students who face substantial non-tuition costs. This would create a more inclusive environment, ensuring that financial limitations do not impede students from completing their education.

Another consideration is the impact of scholarships on students' academic performance and well-being. While scholarship requirements often set high academic standards, these can be stressful for students already balancing economic challenges. As educators, we witness how the pressure to maintain high grades affects our students' mental health and academic experience. Some HEIs have begun offering counseling and academic support services to help scholarship recipients manage these demands. This comprehensive support, which includes financial aid, academic guidance, and mental health resources, is essential for creating an environment where low-income students can truly thrive.

4.2 Community Development Projects: Building Capacity and Self-Reliance

Community development is another area where Philippine HEIs contribute significantly to poverty alleviation. Many universities operate extension programs and community development initiatives that aim to improve local livelihoods, provide skills training, and promote economic self-reliance in surrounding communities. These projects, typically led by faculty and students, involve close collaboration with communities to identify local needs and co-create solutions that are relevant, sustainable, and empowering.

For example, universities with strong agriculture programs, such as the University of the Philippines Los Baños (UPLB), have developed community-based projects that provide training for farmers on sustainable agriculture techniques, climate-resilient farming, and crop diversification. These projects not only improve agricultural productivity but also increase farmers' income, contributing directly to poverty reduction in rural areas. In our institution, we run a similar program where agriculture and business students work with local farmers to enhance their farming practices, assist with market access, and increase the economic value of their crops. Such projects foster self-sufficiency and economic stability, which are vital for poverty alleviation.

Beyond agriculture, other HEIs engage in community development initiatives tailored to specific local needs. For example, universities in coastal regions may focus on sustainable fishing practices or marine conservation, while institutions in urban centers might emphasize livelihood training, micro-entrepreneurship, or community health. Community-based programs that address local concerns allow HEIs to make a meaningful impact, as they leverage regional knowledge and expertise.

However, one challenge of community development projects is sustainability. Many HEI-led projects are grant-funded or limited to a specific academic term, making it difficult to establish long-term programs that can create enduring impact. While short-term projects provide immediate benefits, their impact may fade if the community does not have the capacity to sustain the programs independently. To address this, HEIs can focus on capacity-building approaches, such as training community leaders who can continue the work after the project ends. Additionally, establishing partnerships with local governments or NGOs can ensure continuity, as these partners can provide ongoing support and resources to maintain the programs.

4.3 Research on Poverty Solutions: Knowledge-Driven Approaches to Community Development

Research on poverty-related issues is another critical avenue through which Philippine HEIs contribute to SDG 1. Many HEIs conduct studies that explore factors contributing to poverty, evaluate the effectiveness of existing poverty alleviation programs, and develop innovative solutions tailored to the Philippine context. These research efforts provide valuable insights that can inform local government policies, influence program design, and support evidence-based approaches to poverty alleviation.

For instance, faculty at our university are involved in researching livelihood opportunities for smallholder farmers in our region. This research not only examines economic barriers but also considers cultural and environmental factors that impact rural poverty. By understanding these underlying causes, researchers can recommend more holistic solutions that address the specific needs of local communities. Moreover, these studies often involve participatory methods where researchers engage directly with community members, ensuring that the research reflects the community's realities and aspirations.

HEIs with research centers dedicated to poverty alleviation also play a crucial role in policy influence. Universities like the University of the Philippines and Ateneo de Manila University regularly publish research on poverty, social inequality, and development issues, contributing to public discourse and providing a knowledge base that government agencies can use to shape poverty reduction programs. This research not only informs policy but also provides a training ground for students, who gain experience in conducting socially relevant research and analyzing real-world issues.

However, one gap in HEI research on poverty is the limited application of findings into practical solutions. While universities produce high-quality studies, their insights often remain within academic journals or conferences without being translated into programs or policies. To address this, HEIs could create platforms for knowledge exchange with local government units, NGOs, and community organizations. By holding forums or workshops where researchers present their findings in accessible language, HEIs can bridge the gap between academia and practice, ensuring that research insights directly inform poverty alleviation efforts on the ground.

4.4 Skills Training and Livelihood Programs: Empowering Communities through Economic Opportunities

Philippine HEIs contribute to poverty alleviation by offering skills training and livelihood programs that empower communities to generate stable incomes. These initiatives often focus on providing practical skills that enable individuals to start their own businesses, improve productivity, or access better employment opportunities. In our institution, for example, we have a livelihood training program designed for low-income mothers, teaching skills in food processing, handicraft, and small-scale entrepreneurship. Such programs are crucial for communities where formal employment opportunities are limited, as they offer an alternative pathway to economic self-reliance.

Skills training initiatives are typically hands-on, allowing participants to apply what they learn immediately. For instance, students in technical courses may work with local carpenters, masons, or electricians, providing training on newer techniques or technologies that improve their efficiency and expand their client base. These skills-based initiatives not only benefit community members but also provide valuable learning experiences for students, allowing them to apply their academic knowledge in real-world contexts.

One innovative approach seen in some HEIs is the establishment of on-campus incubation centers for micro-entrepreneurs. The Technological Institute of the Philippines (TIP), for instance, has an innovation hub that supports aspiring entrepreneurs from disadvantaged backgrounds. This hub provides mentorship, technical training, and access to resources, enabling individuals to start and grow their businesses. Programs like this highlight how HEIs can support not only academic success but also entrepreneurship, creating multiple avenues for poverty alleviation.

While skills training and livelihood programs offer significant benefits, they also face challenges, particularly in terms of funding and sustainability. Many livelihood programs rely on project-based funding, which may not always be sufficient to meet the long-term needs of participants. To enhance sustainability, HEIs can consider partnering with local businesses or cooperatives, creating a network of support that extends beyond the initial training phase. By linking livelihood programs with local industry, HEIs can also ensure that the skills taught are relevant to market demands, increasing the likelihood of successful entrepreneurship.

4.5 Collaborative Extension Services: Leveraging Partnerships for Greater Impact

HEIs often collaborate with government agencies, NGOs, and private organizations to implement poverty alleviation programs, recognizing that partnerships amplify the impact of their initiatives. For example, the Ateneo de Manila University has partnered with Gawad Kalinga, a renowned poverty alleviation movement, to provide community development services. This partnership engages both students and faculty in building sustainable housing, providing education, and offering livelihood programs in disadvantaged communities.

Collaborative extension services allow HEIs to combine their resources with the expertise of partner organizations, creating a synergistic effect. Partnerships with local government units (LGUs), for instance, can streamline resources and extend the reach of HEI programs to areas that are most in need. For example, our institution has collaborated with LGUs in conducting health and nutrition campaigns in rural areas, where medical services are often scarce. By pooling resources, HEIs and LGUs can deliver comprehensive services that neither could achieve alone.

However, collaborative extension services require effective coordination and mutual understanding between HEIs and their partners. For these partnerships to succeed, it's essential to establish clear roles and shared goals, ensuring that each party understands their responsibilities and contributions. HEIs also need to be mindful of the power dynamics that may arise in these collaborations, ensuring that community voices are prioritized and respected in decision-making processes. In our experience, projects that involve community members in leadership roles tend to be more sustainable and have a greater impact, as they are shaped by local knowledge and values.

SECTION 5: PATHWAYS FOR IMPROVEMENT

5.1 Strengthening Interdisciplinary Integration and Collaboration

One of the most promising ways to enhance the impact of Philippine HEIs on poverty alleviation is to foster greater interdisciplinary integration. Poverty is a complex issue influenced by multiple factors, including economic, social, environmental, and technological considerations. Addressing it requires input from diverse academic fields, yet HEI programs aimed at poverty alleviation often remain siloed within single departments. By creating mechanisms that encourage interdisciplinary collaboration, HEIs can bring together expertise from various fields to develop more comprehensive and effective poverty reduction strategies.

One approach could be to establish centers within HEIs dedicated to interdisciplinary poverty research and initiatives. These centers could bring together faculty, students, and external partners from various fields, such as business, engineering, social work, agriculture, and public health, to work on collaborative projects. In these centers, students from different programs could participate in joint community-based projects, where their varied skills contribute to holistic solutions that address both the economic and social aspects of poverty. For instance, a project to develop sustainable livelihoods in a rural community could involve engineering students creating appropriate technology for agriculture, business students devising marketing strategies, and social work students providing community support.

Moreover, HEIs could encourage interdisciplinary capstone projects or community immersion programs that require students from diverse fields to collaborate. By integrating interdisciplinary collaboration into course requirements or extracurricular projects, HEIs would cultivate a generation of graduates who are equipped to approach poverty alleviation with a multi-dimensional perspective. These cross-disciplinary experiences also provide students with real-world skills in teamwork, problem-solving, and cultural sensitivity, which are essential in poverty-related work.

5.2 Developing Sustainable Funding Models

As noted earlier, one of the primary challenges Philippine HEIs face in their poverty alleviation initiatives is the lack of sustainable funding. To overcome this, HEIs must explore alternative funding models that support long-term poverty alleviation programs, rather than relying solely on short-term grants. Sustainable funding would allow HEIs to plan and execute more comprehensive, impactful projects that can address the root causes of poverty over time.

One effective model could be the establishment of dedicated endowment funds for poverty alleviation. These endowment funds could be built through partnerships with alumni, local businesses, and philanthropic organizations. By building a stable source of funding, HEIs can ensure that key programs and initiatives continue to receive support regardless of fluctuations in external funding.

Additionally, HEIs could explore public-private partnerships to fund poverty-related initiatives. For example, partnering with companies that have corporate social responsibility (CSR) programs could provide additional resources for HEI-led projects in low-income communities. Companies in agriculture, technology, and healthcare sectors, in particular, may find value in supporting HEI initiatives that align with their industry expertise. By collaborating with businesses, HEIs can access resources and technical support that may be outside the institution's traditional funding channels.

Some HEIs in the Philippines have also started pursuing international grants or partnerships with development organizations, such as the United Nations Development Programme (UNDP) and the World Bank. These partnerships provide access to international best practices and resources, allowing HEIs to scale up successful poverty reduction models and adapt them to local conditions. By diversifying their funding sources and cultivating partnerships with both local and international organizations, HEIs can create a stable financial base for poverty alleviation efforts.

5.3 Building Robust Monitoring and Evaluation Frameworks

For poverty alleviation initiatives to be effective, it is essential to establish monitoring and evaluation (M&E) frameworks that assess the outcomes and impacts of these programs. In Philippine HEIs, many poverty-related programs lack structured M&E processes, which makes it difficult to determine their effectiveness or identify areas for improvement. Without a robust M&E system, HEIs cannot accurately measure the progress of their initiatives or make data-informed decisions to improve their approaches.

Implementing an M&E framework involves setting clear objectives, defining performance indicators, and regularly collecting data on program outcomes. HEIs could benefit from dedicating specific personnel or offices to oversee M&E processes, ensuring that all poverty-related projects undergo systematic evaluation. This team could work with faculty and students involved in these initiatives to track progress and gather both quantitative and qualitative data, which could then be analyzed to refine the programs.

An effective M&E framework also requires a feedback loop, where community members are given the opportunity to provide input on the programs. By involving community stakeholders in the evaluation process, HEIs can gain valuable insights into the lived experiences of those they aim to help, ensuring that programs are not only effective but also culturally relevant and aligned with community needs. Moreover, sharing the results of evaluations with both internal and external stakeholders can increase transparency and attract more partners or funders who are interested in supporting successful poverty reduction programs.

5.4 Fostering Long-Term Community Partnerships and Engagement

To make a meaningful impact on poverty, HEIs in the Philippines must shift from short-term outreach programs to long-term community engagement. Long-term partnerships with communities create opportunities for sustained impact, allowing HEIs to address poverty in ways that are not only relevant but sustainable. By building enduring relationships with communities, HEIs can move beyond one-off projects to create programs that have lasting effects.

Building long-term partnerships begins with establishing trust and mutual respect between HEIs and communities. This involves listening to the community's needs and goals, co-creating programs with local leaders, and maintaining open lines of communication. Rather than approaching communities with pre-set objectives, HEIs should work collaboratively with community members to design programs that are locally relevant and community-driven. By involving community members in leadership roles, HEIs empower them to take ownership of the initiatives, which is essential for long-term sustainability.

One effective model for long-term engagement is the "anchor institution" approach, where an HEI commits to supporting the development of a specific community or region over a multi-year period. This model, seen in universities such as Arizona State University in the United States, involves the HEI dedicating resources, faculty, and students to work with a community over the long term, addressing poverty, education, health, and other social issues holistically. Philippine HEIs could adopt a similar approach, focusing on underserved communities within their geographic area, where they can have the most impact.

Another strategy is the establishment of community advisory boards composed of local leaders, HEI representatives, and students, which would oversee poverty-related initiatives and ensure that they align with the community's evolving needs. These advisory boards create a formal structure for community feedback, enabling HEIs to adapt their programs to the shifting dynamics of poverty in the local context.

5.5 Translating Research into Actionable Policies and Programs

As discussed, Philippine HEIs produce valuable research on poverty-related issues, yet these insights are often underutilized in policy and practice. For HEIs to maximize their impact on SDG 1, there must be a stronger emphasis on translating research findings into practical applications. This involves creating pathways for research to inform community programs, influence policy decisions, and provide guidance to organizations working in poverty alleviation.

One way to achieve this is through the establishment of research extension units within HEIs. These units could serve as bridges between researchers and policymakers, translating academic findings into accessible reports and policy briefs targeted at government agencies and NGOs. For example, an HEI researching poverty among indigenous communities could produce a policy brief that recommends specific interventions, which could then be shared with local government units (LGUs) and national agencies. By distilling research into actionable insights, HEIs can ensure that their findings reach the right stakeholders and lead to real-world impact.

Moreover, HEIs could create platforms for regular dialogue between researchers, policymakers, and community leaders. Hosting public forums, policy workshops, or roundtable discussions provides opportunities for HEIs to share their research and advocate for evidence-based solutions to poverty. These events also give policymakers direct access to experts and allow community members to voice their concerns, creating a collaborative environment where research directly informs local poverty reduction efforts.

Another strategy is to embed research projects within poverty alleviation programs, so that findings are immediately applied and tested in real-time. For instance, a research project on micro-entrepreneurship could be integrated into a community program that supports local businesses, allowing researchers to work alongside practitioners and make data-driven adjustments to program design. This approach ensures that research doesn't remain theoretical but directly impacts community development, resulting in programs that are both informed by evidence and practically applicable.

5.6 Cultivating a Culture of Social Responsibility and Innovation

Finally, Philippine HEIs can enhance their contributions to SDG 1 by fostering a culture of social responsibility and innovation among students, faculty, and staff. Instilling values of community service and social entrepreneurship encourages all members of the HEI community to think creatively about poverty solutions and actively participate in poverty alleviation efforts. Cultivating this culture starts with integrating social responsibility into the institution's mission, values, and educational practices.

One effective approach is to include community service or social entrepreneurship courses as part of the general curriculum, allowing students from all disciplines to engage with poverty-related issues. For example, courses on social innovation or sustainable development could be made available to students from various fields, exposing them to the social and economic realities of poverty and challenging them to think of innovative ways to address these issues. Student organizations focused on community development or social advocacy can also be supported to provide additional opportunities for students to get involved in poverty alleviation.

HEIs can further encourage social responsibility by establishing entrepreneurship hubs or innovation labs focused on poverty-related solutions. These hubs could provide resources, mentorship, and funding to students and faculty interested in creating products, services, or business models that address poverty. For example, a business student might develop a social enterprise that provides affordable healthcare in rural areas, while an engineering student could design a low-cost water filtration system for communities without clean water. By providing a supportive environment, HEIs can empower their students to become change agents who contribute actively to poverty reduction.

Moreover, HEIs can recognize and celebrate contributions to poverty alleviation, whether through awards, research grants, or public recognition. By valuing community impact alongside academic achievement, HEIs reinforce the importance of social responsibility and inspire others to contribute to SDG 1.

SECTION 6: BEST PRACTICES AND CASE STUDIES IN HEI-LED POVERTY ALLEVIATION

6.1 Local Case Studies: Philippine HEIs in Action

In recent years, several Philippine HEIs have developed noteworthy poverty alleviation programs that demonstrate the potential of HEIs to make a meaningful impact. By examining these local examples, we can gain insights into successful models and identify strategies that other institutions might adopt or adapt.

The Ateneo de Manila University's Gawad Kalinga Partnership

Ateneo de Manila University has a long-standing partnership with Gawad Kalinga, a prominent poverty alleviation movement in the Philippines. This collaboration exemplifies the power of partnerships between academia and civil society in addressing poverty. Through this initiative, Ateneo faculty and students engage in community development projects, including building sustainable housing, providing education, and offering livelihood programs. These projects aim to empower communities by addressing their immediate needs and helping them achieve long-term self-sufficiency.

Impact: The Gawad Kalinga partnership has improved housing conditions for hundreds of families and created new livelihood opportunities. The program has also fostered a culture of social responsibility among Ateneo students, exposing them to the realities of poverty and equipping them with the skills necessary for community leadership. This model of collaborative, immersive learning could serve as a template for other HEIs seeking to engage students meaningfully in poverty-related projects.

University of the Philippines Los Baños (UPLB) Rural Development Initiatives

UPLB is well-known for its expertise in agricultural education and research, which it applies to support rural communities. One of its flagship programs focuses on providing technical assistance to smallholder farmers, particularly those in marginalized areas. This program includes training on sustainable farming techniques, access to financial resources, and market linkages, all designed to improve agricultural productivity and economic resilience.

Impact: By supporting smallholder farmers, UPLB's initiative helps to address rural poverty directly. The program has contributed to increased income for participating farmers and promoted more sustainable agricultural practices. This approach illustrates how HEIs with specific areas of expertise, such as agriculture, can leverage their strengths to create scalable, community-centered models of poverty alleviation.

Technological Institute of the Philippines (TIP) Innovation Hub for Micro-entrepreneurs

The Technological Institute of the Philippines (TIP) has developed an innovation hub that supports micro-entrepreneurs in disadvantaged communities. This program offers technical training, business mentorship, and access to resources for local entrepreneurs. By providing support services tailored to the needs of small-scale business owners, TIP's initiative promotes entrepreneurship as a pathway out of poverty.

Impact: TIP's innovation hub has enabled many individuals to start and grow businesses, creating stable income streams for families previously living in poverty. The program highlights how HEIs can contribute to poverty alleviation by fostering economic self-reliance and empowering individuals to build their own livelihoods.

These local examples demonstrate the impact of HEIs in addressing poverty through targeted programs. Each initiative leverages the institution's strengths—be it agriculture, entrepreneurship, or community engagement—to create positive social change. They also emphasize the importance of partnerships, hands-on training, and community involvement, all of which are essential elements of successful poverty alleviation models.

6.2 International Case Studies: Adaptable Models for the Philippine Context

Examining international best practices provides valuable insights into innovative approaches to poverty alleviation that Philippine HEIs could adapt. These examples highlight programs from Ghana, South Africa, and the United States, which illustrate various strategies HEIs can use to address poverty.

Ashesi University's Poverty Action Lab (Ghana)

Ashesi University in Ghana has developed a unique model that combines research, education, and community engagement to tackle poverty. The university's Poverty Action Lab conducts randomized controlled trials (RCTs) to test the effectiveness of poverty reduction interventions. By rigorously evaluating community-based programs, Ashesi ensures that its initiatives are data-driven and tailored to the needs of specific communities.

Adaptation Potential: Philippine HEIs could benefit from adopting a similar approach by conducting localized evaluations of poverty interventions in collaboration with government agencies and NGOs. Through partnerships with LGUs and development organizations, HEIs in the Philippines could implement evidence-based strategies that maximize impact. This data-driven approach not only improves program effectiveness but also provides a reliable foundation for scaling up successful initiatives.

University of Cape Town's Bertha Centre for Social Innovation and Entrepreneurship (South Africa)

The University of Cape Town (UCT) established the Bertha Centre to support social enterprises addressing poverty and inequality. This center offers training, mentorship, and funding for students and community members who wish to create businesses with a social mission. By fostering social entrepreneurship, the Bertha Centre empowers individuals to develop innovative solutions to local challenges, such as job creation, access to education, and healthcare.

Adaptation Potential: Philippine HEIs could replicate this model by creating centers for social innovation and entrepreneurship that focus on poverty alleviation. These centers could support students and community members interested in launching social enterprises that address specific issues related to poverty. For example, an entrepreneurship center might help students develop low-cost housing solutions or provide affordable healthcare services. By integrating entrepreneurship with social responsibility, HEIs can equip future leaders with the tools needed to address poverty through business and innovation.

Arizona State University's Social Embeddedness Initiative (United States)

Arizona State University (ASU) has developed a comprehensive "social embeddedness" strategy that integrates teaching, research, and community outreach to address local and global challenges. This approach involves deep community engagement, where ASU faculty, students, and staff work closely with local communities to co-create solutions that are contextually appropriate and sustainable. ASU's model emphasizes long-term partnerships with communities, ensuring that programs are both responsive to local needs and sustainable.

Adaptation Potential: Philippine HEIs can learn from ASU's model of social embeddedness by fostering deeper and longer-lasting partnerships with communities. By committing to sustained, multi-year engagement with specific communities, HEIs can address complex issues like poverty more effectively. This approach encourages HEIs to move beyond temporary outreach programs and build lasting relationships with communities, allowing for the co-creation of programs that are rooted in local contexts and supported over the long term.

6.3 Lessons Learned and Best Practices for Philippine HEIs

The local and international examples discussed above offer several best practices that Philippine HEIs could adopt to strengthen their poverty alleviation efforts. Key lessons from these case studies include:

1. **Emphasize Community Partnership and Co-Creation**. Both local and international examples highlight the importance of working closely with communities to identify needs and design solutions collaboratively. This approach ensures that programs are culturally relevant, locally driven, and more likely to be sustained by the community over time.
2. **Leverage HEI Expertise to Address Specific Community Needs**. Each HEI has unique strengths and resources that can be directed toward poverty alleviation. Agricultural universities, for example, can support rural communities through training and research in sustainable farming, while institutions with strong business programs can focus on entrepreneurship and livelihood development.

By aligning HEI initiatives with institutional expertise, programs can be more impactful and resource-efficient.
3. **Incorporate Social Innovation and Entrepreneurship**. The case studies from South Africa and the Philippines underscore the potential of social entrepreneurship as a tool for poverty alleviation. HEIs can create hubs or incubators that support students and community members in launching enterprises with a social mission. This approach promotes economic self-reliance and empowers individuals to address poverty within their communities.
4. **Commit to Long-Term Engagement**. Temporary outreach programs provide immediate benefits but often lack sustained impact. Philippine HEIs could adopt models of long-term engagement, where institutions work with communities over several years. This commitment to continuity fosters trust, encourages deeper relationships, and allows for the co-creation of solutions that evolve with the community's needs.
5. **Implement Data-Driven and Evidence-Based Approaches**. Initiatives like the Poverty Action Lab demonstrate the value of using data to inform poverty alleviation programs. Philippine HEIs can implement monitoring and evaluation frameworks to assess the effectiveness of their programs, making adjustments based on empirical evidence. This not only improves program quality but also provides a basis for advocating policy changes at the local and national levels.
6. **Foster a Culture of Social Responsibility and Innovation**. Integrating social responsibility into the curriculum, student organizations, and institutional values encourages students to approach their careers with a sense of purpose. By promoting a culture of community service, HEIs can inspire students to actively engage in poverty alleviation and become advocates for social change.

6.4 Adapting Best Practices to the Philippine Context

While the international examples provide valuable insights, adapting these models to the Philippine context requires careful consideration of the local socio-economic environment. For instance, poverty in the Philippines is closely tied to geographic factors, as remote rural areas face unique challenges in terms of access to education, healthcare, and economic opportunities. Philippine HEIs could adopt a regional approach, focusing on poverty alleviation models that are tailored to the specific needs of rural, urban, and indigenous communities.

Another consideration is the cultural diversity within the Philippines, as poverty alleviation programs that succeed in one region may require modifications in others. For example, livelihood programs in indigenous communities should incorporate traditional knowledge and respect cultural practices, ensuring that poverty alleviation efforts are not only economically beneficial but culturally empowering. By customizing international best practices to suit local needs, Philippine HEIs can create poverty reduction programs that are both effective and sensitive to the diverse communities they serve.

SECTION 7: CONCLUSION AND RECOMMENDATIONS

7.1 Summary of Key Insights

Addressing SDG 1 (No Poverty) in the Philippines through higher education institutions (HEIs) presents both significant opportunities and challenges. Throughout this chapter, we've examined the unique role that Philippine HEIs can play in poverty alleviation through education, research, and community engagement. By leveraging their intellectual, social, and practical resources, HEIs hold the potential to impact not only the lives of individual students but also the communities they serve.

However, the analysis has also highlighted critical gaps in the current efforts of Philippine HEIs. From fragmented initiatives and limited interdisciplinary collaboration to financial constraints and short-term outreach programs, there are significant barriers that reduce the overall impact of HEI poverty alleviation efforts. While successful programs exist, many HEI initiatives would benefit from greater coordination, sustained engagement, and strategic partnerships that enable long-term, sustainable poverty reduction.

The case studies explored in this chapter—both local and international—illustrate a variety of effective models and practices that HEIs can adapt to strengthen their contributions to SDG 1. Programs like the Ateneo de Manila University's partnership with Gawad Kalinga, the University of the Philippines Los Baños's agricultural initiatives, and the Technological Institute of the Philippines' innovation hub for micro-entrepreneurs demonstrate that HEIs can make meaningful, lasting changes when they align their programs with community needs and institutional strengths. International examples, such as Ashesi University's Poverty Action Lab, the University of Cape Town's Bertha Centre for Social Innovation, and Arizona State University's social embeddedness strategy, also provide valuable insights for Philippine HEIs seeking to enhance their poverty alleviation efforts.

7.2 Strategic Recommendations for Philippine HEIs

To bridge the gap between potential and actual impact, Philippine HEIs can consider the following strategic recommendations for expanding and refining their poverty alleviation efforts:

1. **Foster Interdisciplinary Collaboration.** HEIs can establish dedicated centers or initiatives that bring together multiple disciplines to address poverty. By involving faculty and students from fields such as agriculture, business, engineering, social work, and public health, HEIs can develop holistic, cross-disciplinary solutions that are better suited to address the complexity of poverty.
2. **Develop Sustainable Funding Models.** To avoid reliance on short-term grants, HEIs should consider creating endowment funds specifically for poverty-related programs. Partnerships with private companies, alumni, and philanthropic organizations can provide stable funding sources, enabling HEIs to invest in long-term poverty reduction projects. Public-private partnerships with companies interested in corporate social responsibility (CSR) can also provide valuable resources and expertise.
3. **Implement Robust Monitoring and Evaluation Frameworks.** A structured M&E framework allows HEIs to measure the impact of their poverty-related initiatives, make data-driven improvements, and communicate their results to stakeholders. By creating dedicated teams or offices for M&E, HEIs can ensure that programs are continuously improved based on evidence and feedback, maximizing their long-term impact on poverty.
4. **Prioritize Long-Term Community Engagement.** Philippine HEIs should shift from short-term outreach to long-term, community-based partnerships. This involves co-creating programs with community members and establishing community advisory boards to oversee initiatives, ensuring that they are locally relevant and sustainable. Long-term engagement not only fosters trust but also enables HEIs to address poverty in a manner that evolves with community needs.
5. **Translate Research into Actionable Policies and Programs.** HEIs should create mechanisms for translating research findings into practical applications that directly benefit communities. Establishing research extension units and organizing regular forums where researchers, policymakers, and community leaders can engage with each other would bridge the gap between academic research and real-world poverty alleviation efforts. This translation of knowledge is essential to ensure that academic work has a tangible impact on society.
6. **Cultivate a Culture of Social Responsibility and Innovation.** Philippine HEIs can instill a sense of social responsibility in students, faculty, and staff by integrating community service and social entrepreneurship into curricula, student organizations, and institutional values. By fostering a culture that values community impact alongside academic success, HEIs empower their members to contribute actively to poverty reduction efforts.

7.3 Future Directions

Looking ahead, Philippine HEIs have an opportunity to redefine their role in society by committing to SDG 1 and positioning themselves as key players in the national effort to eradicate poverty. Future research could explore the specific needs of different types of communities—urban, rural, indigenous—and identify poverty reduction models that are customized to these contexts. Furthermore, HEIs could expand partnerships with international agencies, such as the United Nations and the World Bank, to access global resources, best practices, and opportunities for collaboration.

Philippine HEIs may also consider creating networks among themselves to share resources, collaborate on large-scale poverty reduction projects, and develop a united front in addressing SDG 1. By pooling resources, knowledge, and expertise, HEIs across the country could support one another in overcoming financial and operational challenges, creating a stronger, more cohesive impact on poverty.

Finally, advancing digital and technological solutions for poverty alleviation represents a promising area for future exploration. Philippine HEIs can tap into innovations in information technology, mobile banking, e-learning, and telemedicine to provide greater access to resources for underserved communities. This technology-driven approach aligns well with the Philippines' growing digital economy and offers a scalable way for HEIs to address poverty on a broader level.

7.4 CONCLUSION

The fight against poverty in the Philippines requires the collective efforts of all sectors, and higher education institutions have a unique and pivotal role to play. Philippine HEIs possess the knowledge, resources, and reach needed to create lasting social change, impacting both students and communities in significant ways. By adopting more strategic, sustainable, and interdisciplinary approaches, HEIs can bridge the gaps in their current efforts and become even more effective agents of poverty reduction.

The journey toward SDG 1 is complex, but Philippine HEIs are well-positioned to lead the way by harnessing the power of education, research, and community partnership. With a strong commitment to social responsibility and an emphasis on long-term impact, HEIs can make a meaningful difference in the lives of millions of Filipinos, creating a future where poverty is no longer a barrier to opportunity and well-being.

REFERENCES:

Arizona State University. (2019). Social embeddedness initiative at ASU: Addressing community needs through deep engagement. https://www.asu.edu

Ashesi University. (2019). Poverty Action Lab: Testing effective interventions in Ghana. https://www.ashesi.edu.gh

Ateneo de Manila University. (2018). *Partnerships for sustainable development: Ateneo de Manila and Gawad Kalinga*. Ateneo Press.

Commission on Higher Education. (2017). *Higher education reform agenda for poverty reduction in the Philippines*. CHED Publications.

Gawad Kalinga Foundation. (2020). Building sustainable communities: The Gawad Kalinga experience. https://gk1world.com

Gore, C., & Figueiredo, J. B. (1997). *Social exclusion and anti-poverty policy: A debate*. International Institute for Labour Studies.

International Labor Organization. (2018). *Decent work and poverty reduction in Southeast Asia*. International Labour Organization Publications.

King, E. M., & Hill, M. A. (1993). *Women's education in developing countries: Barriers, benefits, and policies*. Johns Hopkins University Press. DOI: 10.1596/0-8018-4534-3

Lasimbang, B., & Tayag, J. (2016). The role of state universities and colleges in poverty alleviation: An ASEAN perspective. *ASEAN Journal of Higher Education*, 10(3), 245–265.

Montalbo, M. T., & Salazar, J. P. (2019). Poverty in the Philippines: An analysis of urban and rural disparities. *Philippine Social Science Journal*, 14(2), 112–130.

Philippine Statistics Authority. (2020). Poverty incidence among families: Annual report. https://psa.gov.ph

Ravallion, M. (2016). *The economics of poverty: History, measurement, and policy*. Oxford University Press. DOI: 10.1093/acprof:oso/9780190212766.001.0001

Technological Institute of the Philippines. (2020). *Innovating for change: The TIP innovation hub for micro-entrepreneurs*. TIP Manila.

United Nations Development Programme. (2018). Sustainable development goals in the Philippines: A progress report. https://www.ph.undp.org

University of Cape Town's Bertha Centre for Social Innovation and Entrepreneurship. (2021). *Social innovation as a catalyst for poverty alleviation*. Bertha Centre Publications.

University of the Philippines Los Baños. (2021). *Empowering rural communities through sustainable agriculture: UPLB initiatives*. UPLB Extension Office Publications.

World Bank. (2018). *Higher education and poverty reduction: Evidence from low-income countries*. World Bank.

World Health Organization. (2021). *The social determinants of health and poverty reduction in Asia: An overview*. World Health Organization Publications.

Yap, J., & Ravago, M.-L. V. (2021). *Economics and poverty in the Philippines: Policy, research, and practice*. University of the Philippines Press.

Chapter 3
Advancing Sustainable Development Goals With Educational Technology:
Supporting STEM Education and Fostering Innovation Through Educational Technology

Rodulfo Tumacay Aunzo, Jr.
 https://orcid.org/0009-0000-3368-1605
Visayas State University Isabel, Isabel, Philippines

ABSTRACT

STEM education, covering Science, Technology, Engineering, and Mathematics, equips students with critical problem-solving skills and prepares them for advanced studies and careers in these fields. Originating from the National Science Foundation's initiative to drive innovation, STEM integrates hands-on, problem-based learning to tackle real-world challenges. Its growing importance aligns with global competitiveness goals, enhancing student readiness for high-tech careers and fueling economic growth. Educational technology plays a key role in this transformation through interactive tools and multimedia resources. However, challenges like resource limitations and teacher training gaps hinder effective integration. Continuous research and professional development are needed to fully harness technology's potential, ensuring it supports educational goals and enhances learning outcomes.

DOI: 10.4018/979-8-3693-8242-4.ch003

INTRODUCTION

STEM education, which stands for Science, Technology, Engineering, and Mathematics, is a comprehensive interdisciplinary program aimed at preparing students from primary to secondary levels for higher education and careers in these fields. It emphasizes hands-on, problem-based learning that develops critical skills such as logical reasoning, inquiry, and collaboration (Hasanah, 2020). Initially termed Science, Mathematics, Engineering, and Technology (SMET), the program was introduced by the National Science Foundation (NSF) to foster innovation and problem-solving abilities (Sanders, 2009). STEM education plays a crucial role in preparing students to tackle real-world challenges using cross-disciplinary approaches.

The significance of STEM education has grown in recent years, particularly due to its role in addressing workforce demands and fostering innovation. The U.S. has emphasized STEM as a key driver of global competitiveness, aiming to increase the number of qualified workers in high-tech industries (Butz et al., 2004). Reeve (2013) points out that STEM is often used as a broad label for programs and policies involving one or more STEM disciplines, reflecting its importance in various sectors. This focus on STEM has contributed to economic growth, helping students develop the skills needed to address complex societal problems.

STEM education equips students with essential skills for success in an increasingly knowledge-based economy. Students well-versed in STEM subjects are better prepared to transition into higher education and are more likely to secure high-paying jobs in fields such as engineering, technology, and data science (Reeve, 2013). Additionally, Bybee (2010) highlights that STEM education integrates multiple disciplines, encouraging students to apply their learning to solve real-world problems, ultimately improving their communities and enhancing their career prospects.

Moreover, STEM education fosters technological advancement and innovation by promoting participation in research and collaborative projects. Universities and industries benefit from STEM programs, as evidenced by initiatives like the University of Minnesota's antiviral drug development project (Bybee, 2010). The U.S. government also supports programs that attract STEM talent, recognizing its critical role in maintaining global competitiveness and driving long-term economic success (Hasanah, 2020).

Educational technology is a multifaceted field designed to enhance the teaching and learning process through the use of hardware like computers and digital devices, as well as software including educational programs and applications (Opara, 2023). This dual approach supports individualized instruction, multimedia learning, and effective classroom management. The scope of educational technology encompasses teaching technology, instructional technology, and instructional design technology, each contributing to improved educational practices and outcomes (Arockiasamy,

2018). This integration helps create interactive and engaging learning environments, catering to diverse learner needs and enhancing overall educational experiences.

Historically, the role of technology in STEM education has evolved significantly. Initially, technology in education focused on the introduction of various tools without a specific focus on STEM contexts (Flick & Bell, 2000). Over time, there has been a shift towards utilizing technology that mirrors real-world practices in STEM disciplines. Perspective 4, which emphasizes technology as tools and practices used by professionals in science, mathematics, and engineering, is particularly impactful. This approach allows students to engage with technologies similar to those used by practitioners, thereby gaining a deeper understanding of STEM content and methodologies (Ellis et al., 2020).

Despite advancements in educational technology, challenges remain in its integration into STEM education. According to Hıdıroğlu et al. (2022), while technology can enhance students' focus from operational tasks to conceptual understanding, integrating these tools effectively remains complex. The lack of consensus on technology's role in education highlights the need for ongoing research to explore various integration strategies and their impacts on teaching and learning (Hıdıroğlu & Karakaş, 2022). Effective integration necessitates not only selecting appropriate technologies but also aligning them with educational goals and learning outcomes.

Gamification and other technology-enhanced methods have been shown to boost student performance, motivation, and participation (Ortiz Rojas et al., 2017). However, the effectiveness of these methods depends on their application. Teachers must be discerning, focusing on how technology supports educational objectives rather than merely incorporating popular tools. For instance, technologies such as 3D printers must be utilized in ways that align with educational goals to avoid superficial implementation (Ellis et al., 2020).

The evolving nature of educational technology underscores the need for continuous adaptation and thoughtful application. Opara (2023) highlights that while technology has the potential to enhance educational outcomes, its integration must be strategic and purpose-driven. Professional development for in-service teachers and training for preservice teachers should encompass various perspectives on technology use to ensure comprehensive understanding and effective application in STEM education (El Morabit, 2021). This approach helps educators harness technology's potential to foster meaningful learning experiences.

Ahmadigol (2016) defines educational technology as a dynamic system that integrates study and ethical action to create interactive learning environments supporting effective education. This definition underscores the importance of both theoretical and practical components in educational technology. The field's dynamic nature requires educators to continuously adapt their practices and incorporate new technological advancements to meet evolving educational needs. Ethical considerations are crucial to ensure that technology use upholds human rights and moral principles.

Educational technology has significantly transformed teaching and learning, particularly in STEM fields. The integration of authentic tools and techniques, as advocated by Perspective 4, offers considerable potential for enhancing student understanding and engagement (Ellis et al., 2020). Nevertheless, the field must address ongoing challenges related to technology's application and effectiveness. Continued research and professional development are essential to ensure technology is used strategically to support educational goals and improve learning outcomes (Hıdıroğlu & Karakaş, 2022; Ortiz Rojas et al., 2017). Educators must stay informed and adaptable to leverage technology's benefits fully and meet the needs of diverse learners.

Nguyen et al. (2024) conducted a systematic review based on the PRISMA model to examine the role of information technology (IT) in STEM education, revealing a positive relationship between IT and STEM outcomes while highlighting challenges such as resource limitations and inadequate teacher training. This underscores the need for addressing these issues to enhance IT's effectiveness in STEM education and encourages teachers to implement effective measures. Complementarily, McDonald (2016) reviewed global initiatives aimed at increasing student participation in STEM and preparing them for STEM careers, identifying key factors such as maintaining student interest through junior secondary schooling, implementing effective pedagogical practices, and developing high-quality teachers to positively impact student attitudes and achievement in STEM fields.

PEDAGOGICAL THEORIES IN STEM EDUCATION

Constructivist Learning Theory

Constructivist learning theory emphasizes that individuals actively construct their understanding of the world through the interaction of prior knowledge and new experiences (Resnick, 1989). Learning is seen as an active, reflective process where knowledge is built through engagement rather than passive reception. Piaget (1967) argues that learners construct knowledge by questioning, investigating, interacting, and reflecting. Dewey (1916) supports this, emphasizing that meaningful, authentic experiences are essential for effective education.

In constructivist teaching, the instructor shifts from being a primary knowledge source to a facilitator (Brau, n.d.). Teachers guide learners by promoting active engagement, encouraging inquiry-based learning, and fostering dialogue. This approach contrasts with traditional methods where knowledge is transferred through lectures and rigid curricula. Constructivist teaching encourages students to take responsibility for their learning and achieve deeper understanding, focusing on inquiry and critical thinking (D'Silva, 2010).

The theory is rooted in developmental approaches from Piaget, Vygotsky, Dewey, and Bruner. Piaget's cognitive constructivism stresses that learning results from individuals interacting with new experiences. In contrast, Vygotsky's social constructivism highlights the importance of social and cultural interactions in learning (Prince & Felder, 2006). Dewey (1997) argues for integrating real-world activities into learning, asserting that inquiry-based approaches enrich education through authentic experiences.

Constructivist classrooms reflect these principles by fostering active student participation. Teachers create motivating environments, present real-world problems, and facilitate prior knowledge retrieval, emphasizing the learning process over mere outcomes (Olsen, 1999). This environment nurtures higher-order thinking and problem-solving skills, helping students to construct knowledge more effectively. However, implementing constructivist approaches requires well-trained teachers who understand its principles and practices (Prince & Felder, 2006).

Dewey's (1916) advocacy for learning through doing set the foundation for project-based learning, where students engage in authentic activities to construct knowledge meaningfully. His focus on inquiry shapes how educators integrate practical experiences with theoretical concepts, particularly in STEM education.

Piaget (1972) and Vygotsky (1978) have significantly influenced constructivist pedagogy. Piaget highlights that learners build knowledge through interactions with their environment, while Vygotsky emphasizes peer learning and the cultural context in knowledge acquisition. Together, these theories demonstrate how students integrate new information with existing knowledge, facilitating deeper understanding (Brau, n.d.).

Despite its promise, implementing constructivism in the classroom presents challenges. Teachers need a strong grasp of constructivist theory and the ability to create environments that support student-driven learning. Olsen (1999) notes that this process requires significant shifts in teaching approaches, with teachers fostering problem-solving, motivation, and active participation.

Overall, constructivism offers a transformative approach to education, especially in STEM. It moves away from teacher-centered models, emphasizing student responsibility and learning through inquiry, action, reflection, and collaboration, leading to deeper understanding of complex concepts.

Inquiry-based Learning

Inquiry-based learning (IBL) is a student-centered pedagogical approach that promotes active learning through questioning, investigation, and problem-solving (Kuhlthau & Maniotes, 2015). This method fosters critical thinking, collaboration, and reflection, encouraging students to actively engage with material rather than passively absorb information (Barron & Hammond, 2008). IBL's structured phases, as outlined by Pedaste et al. (2015), include Orientation to stimulate curiosity, Conceptualization where students form hypotheses, Investigation to explore answers, Conclusion to validate hypotheses, and finally, Discussion/Communication to share findings and reflect.

IBL has roots in scientific inquiry and is particularly effective in STEM education, where it promotes student motivation, problem-solving abilities, and critical thinking (Blumenfeld et al., 1991; Bruder & Prescott, 2013). The approach differs from problem-based learning by emphasizing smaller-scale, student-led projects, making it ideal for STEM subjects. Banchi and Bell (2008) describe four levels of inquiry: Confirmation, Structured, Guided, and Open Inquiry, with Open Inquiry providing the highest level of student autonomy. They recommend starting at lower inquiry levels and gradually advancing to more open formats to ensure skill development.

A well-known framework in IBL is the 5E Inquiry-Based Instructional Model (Bybee & Landes, 1990), which includes five phases: Engage, Explore, Explain, Elaborate, and Evaluate. This model helps teachers guide students through the inquiry process and has shown positive outcomes in fostering scientific inquiry skills (Bybee, 2009). Grounded in cognitive psychology and constructivist theory, IBL encourages students to build knowledge through experience and active participation, improving both scientific inquiry and socio-emotional development (Darling-Hammond et al., 2020).

Despite its benefits, some critics argue that IBL may be less effective than direct instruction for students lacking prior knowledge or skills (Hattie, 2009). However, research by Alfieri et al. (2011) and Darling-Hammond et al. (2020) suggests that well-designed inquiry activities, which balance direct instruction with student autonomy, lead to improved learning outcomes. Effective implementation of IBL requires careful scaffolding, with teachers gradually releasing control as students develop their inquiry skills (Banchi & Bell, 2008).

Finally, Fichtman-Dana et al. (2011) highlight the varying levels of teacher control in different IBL models, ranging from structured inquiry, where teachers direct much of the process, to free inquiry, where students take full ownership. To ensure success, teachers must support students in their transition from guided inquiry to independent learning, creating a balance that enhances both engagement and learning outcomes.

Benefits of Inquiry-based Learning in STEM

Research supports the effectiveness of IBL in enhancing student engagement in STEM fields. Attard et al. (2021) found that integrating IBL with industry-based partnerships significantly increased student engagement in STEM disciplines. Wang et al. (2010) further emphasize that inquiry-based approaches allow students to uncover first-hand understandings about their environment, themselves, and academic subjects through collaborative investigation and evidence-based reasoning.

In addition to engagement, IBL promotes critical thinking and problem-solving skills. Bell et al. (2010) note that students in IBL settings develop their own questions, gather and analyze evidence, and construct arguments based on their findings. These processes are essential for developing higher-order thinking skills, which are critical for success in STEM careers. Moreover, Dostál (2015) highlights how IBL helps students practice critical thinking and problem-solving in authentic contexts, preparing them for real-world challenges.

However, the successful implementation of IBL requires thoughtful guidance. Meta-analyses indicate that inquiry-based learning is most effective when teachers provide scaffolding tailored to students' individual learning needs, prior knowledge, and experience (Alfieri et al., 2011). Teachers need to strike a balance between offering guidance and allowing students the autonomy to explore and construct their understanding.

Challenges of Inquiry-based Learning

Despite its effectiveness, some educators are reluctant to adopt IBL due to the perceived complexity of classroom management and the alignment of IBL activities with standardized curricula (Blumenfeld & Krajcik, 2006). Additionally, there are concerns about whether students can remain motivated and on task during open-ended inquiry activities (Hattie, 2009). However, peer assessment strategies and thoughtful classroom management practices can help mitigate issues like social loafing (Perry, n.d.).

Inquiry-based learning remains a powerful pedagogical tool, particularly in STEM education, where it helps students build critical thinking and problem-solving skills. The structured phases of inquiry, combined with the flexibility to adapt IBL to various levels and learning contexts, make it a valuable approach for modern classrooms. With ongoing research supporting its benefits, IBL continues to evolve as an essential component of effective STEM instruction.

Project-based Learning

Project-based learning (PBL) is a student-centered instructional approach that engages learners in real-world problem-solving and investigation, promoting deeper understanding through active participation. According to Blumenfeld et al. (1991), PBL encourages students to explore meaningful, multidisciplinary questions, refine their inquiries, collect data, and present findings through artifacts such as reports or presentations. It fosters critical thinking and autonomy, especially in STEM education, where students apply inquiry and decision-making skills to solve real-world problems (Jumaat et al., 2017).

PBL differs from traditional learning methods by demanding higher-order thinking and student autonomy. As Perry (n.d.) notes, PBL is rooted in inquiry-based learning, emphasizing exploration and active engagement over passive instruction. It involves students in design, problem-solving, and investigation over extended periods, shifting the teacher's role from an authority figure to a facilitator (Thomas, 2000). Dewey and Small (1897) stress that in PBL, teachers guide rather than impose ideas, cultivating a learning environment that fosters both hands-on and minds-on activities.

Hannafin and Hannafin (2010) highlight that PBL encourages collaboration and critical thinking, with students managing their time and learning goals while teachers act as coaches. Assessment occurs throughout the project, rather than relying solely on traditional exams. Research suggests that PBL leads to better factual knowledge retention compared to traditional methods, although empirical evidence on its overall effectiveness remains mixed (Barron & Hammond, 2008). Despite this, PBL is considered a high-engagement instructional method, particularly in STEM fields, where students working on multiple PBL units demonstrate improved performance on standardized tests (Krajcik & Blumenfeld, 2006).

The versatility of PBL extends beyond STEM, with its capacity to address real-world problems in various contexts (Perry, n.d.). However, educators may face challenges in aligning PBL with strict curricular standards and standardized testing (Blumenfeld & Krajcik, 2006). Successful implementation requires careful planning, collaboration, and ongoing formative assessments (Barron & Darling-Hammond, 2008). Technology integration can enhance PBL's potential, as demonstrated by Eskrootchi and Oskrochi (2010), who found that combining PBL with computer simulations fosters deeper learning. Peer assessment also helps mitigate challenges such as social loafing in group projects.

PBL positively impacts students' attitudes toward learning. Tseng et al. (2013) found that students in Taiwan who engaged in PBL developed more positive attitudes toward learning, especially in STEM fields, perceiving the experience as meaningful and relevant to future career aspirations. While PBL presents logistical and pedagogical challenges, its ability to foster critical thinking, engagement, and deeper learning across disciplines remains evident, though further research is needed to establish best practices and consistent outcomes (Barron & Darling-Hammond, 2008).

Technological Pedagogical Content Knowledge

Technological Pedagogical Content Knowledge (TPACK), introduced by Mishra and Koehler (2006), is a framework designed to improve the integration of technology in education. It encompasses seven components: Technology Knowledge, Content Knowledge, Pedagogical Knowledge, Pedagogical Content Knowledge, Technological Content Knowledge, Technological Pedagogical Knowledge, and Technological Pedagogical Content Knowledge. TPACK helps educators blend technology, pedagogy, and content to enhance teaching and learning outcomes, particularly in STEM education (Bell et al., 2009).

The application of TPACK in classrooms significantly improves students' engagement with complex scientific concepts, fostering problem-solving skills and critical thinking (Bell et al., 2009). Despite these benefits, challenges such as limited resources and the need for continuous technological advancement hinder its full implementation (Harris & Hofer, 2011).

Research by Atmojo et al. (2022) found that while TPACK is integrated with STEAM (Science, Technology, Engineering, Arts, Mathematics) activities, mathematics is often underrepresented. Similarly, Putri et al. (2020) identified that biology teachers were still in the pre-TPACK stage, facing difficulties in integrating content, pedagogy, and technology.

The global demand for skilled STEM teachers has highlighted TPACK's crucial role in teacher education. Srisawasdi (2012) demonstrated that TPACK competency is essential for preparing high-quality STEM educators, with case-based learning approaches proving effective in developing these skills. Graham et al. (2012) also found that TPACK-based interventions enhance student engagement, motivation, and achievement.

In science and mathematics education, integrating technology through simulations and multimedia improves student engagement (Harris & Hofer, 2011). However, Mansour (2024) noted that teachers often struggle to master both subject expertise and pedagogical skills, particularly in project-based learning, underscoring the need for tailored professional development.

Fei (2024) revealed that pre-service teachers are enthusiastic about educational technologies but lack sufficient experience, while in-service teachers are less inclined to adopt new technologies. Continuous professional development is necessary to address these gaps and enhance educators' TPACK competencies.

Anud (2022) demonstrated that science and mathematics teachers with high TPACK self-efficacy effectively use technology in project-based learning, employing tools like digital simulations and multimedia. This underscores the importance of TPACK in facilitating exploration and data analysis in STEM education, ultimately improving teaching practices and preparing effective STEM educators.

Current Trends in Educational Technology for STEM.

Interactive simulations and virtual labs

Interactive simulations and virtual labs have become pivotal in modern STEM education, offering dynamic learning environments that enhance student engagement and understanding. According to Sellberg et al. (2024), synthetic learning environments like virtual laboratories are increasingly used in higher education across various study programs. These virtual labs simulate experiments and hands-on activities, allowing students to explore scientific principles in a flexible and convenient manner. This approach can supplement or even replace traditional lab experiences, providing students with a more adaptable learning tool.

Virtual labs can be categorized into two-dimensional (2D) desktop-based simulations and three-dimensional (3D) virtual reality (VR) environments, as described by Reeves and Crippen (2021). While 2D simulations offer basic interactive experiences, 3D VR environments provide a more immersive experience using head-mounted displays. This differentiation caters to various learning preferences and enhances the educational experience by offering different levels of interaction and immersion.

Chudaeva emphasizes that virtual science labs are advanced online simulators that allow students to test ideas and observe results in a safe digital space. These labs not only improve engagement and curiosity but also facilitate the visualization of complex scientific concepts. By interacting with these simulations, students can develop practical skills such as experimentation and report-writing, which are valuable for their future careers. The flexibility and broad access of virtual labs further support a wider reach in science education.

Brinson (2015) highlights that synthetic learning environments, including virtual labs, enable educators and students to simulate experiments that might be challenging to perform in a physical lab. This interactive approach allows learners to test hypotheses, collect data, and analyze results using virtual equipment. Stanney and Cohn (2012) support this view by describing VR environments as immersive technologies that emulate physical laboratories, providing intuitive and hands-on interactions that enrich the learning experience.

Reimagine Education (n.d.) and the Open Education Community (n.d.) both note that interactive simulations and virtual labs are transforming STEM education by offering cost-effective, accessible, and immersive learning experiences. These digital tools replicate real-world lab environments, enabling students to conduct experiments and visualize complex concepts that might be impractical in physical labs. The tools also support diverse learning styles and help bridge the gap between theoretical knowledge and practical application, democratizing education and increasing the accessibility of high-quality STEM resources.

Nelson (2022) identifies several key resources that illustrate the impact of interactive simulations and virtual labs. NOVA Labs, an extension of the PBS science documentary series, engages high school and older students with immersive games and interactive elements. The PhET Interactive Simulations project from the University of Colorado Boulder features over 150 simulations across various scientific subjects, offering accessibility features and adaptability for diverse learning needs. NASA's space exploration simulations and NOAA's weather laboratories further enhance STEM education by providing interactive and engaging experiences in space science and meteorology, respectively.

Coding and Robotics Platforms

Coding and robotics are increasingly becoming integral parts of STEM (Science, Technology, Engineering, and Mathematics) education. These fields foster hands-on learning, encourage creativity, and develop problem-solving skills, making them essential for preparing students for future technological challenges. By integrating coding and robotics into the curriculum, educators can provide interactive and engaging experiences that enhance students' understanding of STEM concepts. Various platforms cater to different educational levels, helping both beginners and advanced learners excel in these fields.

Key Platforms for Coding and Robotics in STEM

CoderZ. CoderZ is an innovative online platform that combines coding and robotics with virtual 3D robots, making it accessible and cost-effective for all educational settings. By eliminating the need for physical hardware, CoderZ provides a cloud-based solution that fosters critical thinking, creativity, and collaboration among students of all levels. It supports multiple programming languages, including

Blockly and Python, and offers a tiered mission structure that accommodates both younger and older students (CoderZ, n.d.).

Scratch. Developed by MIT Media Lab, Scratch is a versatile block-based programming platform. It allows students to create animations, games, and interactive projects, making it an excellent resource for teaching foundational coding concepts. Scratch's integration with various robotics kits such as Finch Robot, Strawbees, and Edison Robot enhances its educational value by providing students with hands-on experience in robotics (Scatch, n.d.).

STEMLAB by RobotLAB. STEMLAB offers an online platform that supports 11 different robotics platforms, including NAO and Sphero. This centralized hub provides educators with curriculum-aligned resources, software updates, and tutorials that facilitate the integration of robotics into the classroom. It helps streamline access to STEM tools, making it a valuable asset for teachers and students alike (Common Sense Education, n.d.).

STEMpedia. STEMpedia provides diverse tools for enhancing STEM education through hands-on learning. With resources like the tinker kit and GoPiGo robot, STEMpedia encourages students to engage in coding and robotics activities that promote problem-solving and creativity. Its curriculum-aligned lessons make it a practical tool for classroom integration, offering students a comprehensive suite of coding, robotics, and electronics resources (STEMpedia, n.d.).

Daran Robot. The Daran Robot is a versatile and affordable platform designed to enhance STEM education by offering reconfigurable features. This modularity allows educators to adapt the robot to various educational activities, making it a valuable resource for teaching both basic and advanced STEM concepts. Its affordability and ease of use make it accessible to schools with limited budgets, while fostering critical thinking and problem-solving skills through hands-on robotics projects (Wang et al., 2021).

Hopscotch. Hopscotch is an engaging iPad app aimed at students aged 8-11, offering a drag-and-drop interface that introduces basic coding concepts through game and animation creation. With video tutorials and lesson plans, it provides educators with the tools they need to effectively incorporate coding into their STEM curriculum (Erickson, 2019).

Kodable. Kodable offers a comprehensive coding curriculum for students aged five and older, featuring 49 levels of challenges that promote creativity and collaboration. This platform is available on both iPad and web-based platforms, making it an accessible tool for fostering essential coding skills in young learners (Erickson, 2019).

Code.org. Code.org is a widely-used platform that provides a variety of curriculum options, including lesson plans, offline activities, and online tutorials. Its Computer Science Fundamentals courses and Hour of Code events help students of all ages learn essential coding skills. With features like a teacher dashboard, Code.org is an excellent resource for educators integrating coding into their classroom activities (Erickson, 2019).

Google CS First. Google CS First offers a range of coding activities that use Scratch, catering to students aged 9-14. The platform provides themed activities such as animation and game design, with video tutorials and practice sessions. Recognized for aligning with ISTE standards, Google CS First offers structured content that enhances coding education (Erickson, 2019).

Tynker. Tynker provides a comprehensive coding curriculum for students in grades K-8, including STEM courses and classroom management tools. It supports teachers with free training, helping them deliver effective coding instruction to students of all levels. Tynker's engaging activities and structured approach make it a key resource for integrating coding into STEM education (Common Sense Education, n.d.).

Augmented Reality (AR) and Virtual Reality (VR) applications.

Augmented Reality (AR) and Virtual Reality (VR) have become instrumental in transforming STEM education by offering immersive and interactive learning experiences. These technologies enable students to engage with complex concepts in novel ways, enhancing their understanding and retention. For instance, the AR Geometry Hololens 2 allows for collaborative manipulation of geometric objects in both 2D and 3D, facilitating interactive learning regardless of physical location (DC7, n.d.). Similarly, the VR STEM Lab Oculus Quest provides a platform for remote manipulation of scientific and mathematical models, overcoming geographical barriers to create a more connected educational environment (DC7, n.d.). Additionally, the AR Chemistry Mobile App allows students to visualize and interact with molecular structures, offering a hands-on approach to understanding abstract chemical concepts (DC7, n.d.). Such applications highlight how AR and VR can bridge the gap between theoretical knowledge and practical application, enhancing STEM education (Augmentastic PVT. LTD, 2023).

The integration of AR and VR technologies also addresses challenges in practical STEM education by providing virtual labs and simulations. For example, Labster offers a VR platform for virtual science labs, enabling students to conduct experiments without physical equipment, thus making science education more accessible (Marr, 2021). Google Expeditions uses AR and VR to provide immersive virtual field trips, allowing students to explore historical landmarks and outer space, which enhances learning through experiential engagement (Marr, 2021). zSpace creates AR and VR experiences for interactive learning in subjects such as biology and engineering, enabling students to engage with 3D models and simulations (Marr, 2021). ClassVR offers a range of educational content, including virtual field trips and interactive lessons, which complement traditional teaching methods and enhance conceptual understanding (Marr, 2021). These examples demonstrate how AR and VR can provide hands-on practice and improve student engagement (HundrED, 2024).

AR and VR technologies also support the development of crucial soft skills in STEM education. For instance, VR simulations allow students to navigate social and emotional challenges, building resilience and problem-solving abilities (Parlier, 2024). These technologies can help manage anxiety and build confidence by providing virtual environments for practicing social interactions and handling real-world scenarios, such as job interviews (Parlier, 2024). Additionally, AR and VR foster cultural exposure and empathy by enabling virtual exploration of different countries and historical periods, broadening students' understanding of global issues and human experiences (Parlier, 2024). This immersive approach not only enhances academic learning but also supports the development of well-rounded, confident individuals (Parlier, 2024).

In higher education, AR and VR are making a significant impact through innovative projects that illustrate their potential. The Stanford Ocean Acidification Experience, developed by Stanford University's Virtual Human Interaction Lab, uses VR to educate students about the effects of carbon dioxide on marine ecosystems, offering a virtual exploration of ocean environments (Craig & Georgieva, 2017). The University of Michigan–Ann Arbor's MIDEN system employs immersive technologies to project 3D models on room surfaces, aiding in the understanding of complex structures like architectural designs and archaeological reconstructions (Craig & Georgieva, 2017). Texas A&M University's Immersive Mechanics Visualization Lab utilizes AR and VR for refining 3D CAD models, enhancing industrial design and student projects through virtual experimentation (Craig & Georgieva, 2017). These projects demonstrate how AR and VR are revolutionizing STEM education by integrating virtual and physical elements for deeper learning experiences (Craig & Georgieva, 2017).

Looking ahead, AR and VR technologies promise to further reshape STEM education by expanding their applications and capabilities. Innovations such as Labster's virtual lab simulations and NASA's use of HoloLens for Martian Rover simulations illustrate the future potential of these technologies for global collaboration and advanced scientific research (Craig & Georgieva, 2017). Microsoft HoloLens provides mixed reality experiences to visualize complex data in educational contexts, enhancing students' understanding of intricate concepts (Marr, 2021). Pico Interactive's VR headsets are used in educational settings to facilitate immersive learning (Marr, 2021). These advancements indicate that AR and VR will continue to enrich STEM education by making learning more interactive, accessible, and effective (Augmentastic PVT. LTD, 2023; Marr, 2021).

Enhancing STEM Curriculum with Technology.

Integrating Technology in STEM Education

Integrating technology into STEM education has proven to enhance student engagement and motivation significantly. Chacko et.al., (2015) demonstrate this through a bioengineering summer program that employed a technology-rich lesson plan. This program, featuring interactive labs and lessons as well as exposure to scientists, fostered independent research and learning among students. The use of a paperless classroom model not only improved students' understanding but also heightened their interest in science-related fields. Notably, the percentage of students who initially thought science was not for them decreased from 13% to 0% by the program's end, highlighting the effectiveness of technology in enriching education (Chacko et al., 2015).

The Engineering byDesign™ (EbD) framework exemplifies how technology can enhance STEM education by emphasizing design and inquiry-based learning. According to Burke et.al., (n.d.), the EbD framework integrates technology to facilitate hands-on learning and critical thinking. This approach bridges the gap between theoretical concepts and practical applications through design challenges and simulations, which are crucial for understanding complex STEM topics (Burke et.al., n.d.). By incorporating technology as a central component, the framework enables students to engage in real-world problem-solving and project-based learning, effectively supporting their STEM education.

Further, the EbD framework provides a model for integrating technology into STEM lesson plans, demonstrating that such integration can significantly improve student learning outcomes. Burke et.al., (n.d.) outline strategies for incorporating technology into the curriculum, making lessons more interactive and engaging. This approach not only enhances students' grasp of STEM concepts but also prepares them for future challenges by developing essential technological skills. The framework's alignment with current educational trends highlights the importance of digital literacy and technological proficiency in preparing students for STEM careers (Burke et.al., n.d.).

Manosuttirit (2019) addresses the challenges of integrating technology in STEM education within Thailand, contrasting it with more established systems in countries like the U.S. In Thailand, STEM education is still somewhat abstract, facing issues related to contextual factors, teacher development, and the capability of educators (Manosuttirit, 2019). In contrast, the U.S. has a more established STEM education system, with a significant portion of its workforce educated in STEM fields, demonstrating a strong commitment to STEM integration. To overcome these challenges,

Thai STEM teachers need to acquire skills such as technological awareness, mathematical integration, and the ability to create reasoning charts (Manosuttirit, 2019).

Yang and Baldwin (2020) emphasize the importance of effectively utilizing technology-use strategies within integrated STEM learning environments. They argue that while both integrated STEM learning and technology offer substantial potential, their combined capabilities have not been fully realized (Chiu et al., 2013). Yang and Baldwin (2020) highlight the need to connect technology-use strategies with integrated STEM learning to enhance student outcomes. By providing authentic contexts and real-world experiences, technology can facilitate a deeper understanding of STEM subjects, demonstrating how mathematics, science, and engineering are interlinked and applied in practical scenarios (Wu, 2010).

Collaborative and interdisciplinary Projects

In collaborative and interdisciplinary STEM projects, several key factors influence the success of the model, including team size, teaching goals, and the structure of collaboration (Wang et al., 2020). Effective interdisciplinary teams typically consist of three to five teachers from diverse subject areas, aligning with both practical recommendations and existing literature (Wang et al., 2020). Larger teams, however, can face challenges such as coordination issues, which can be mitigated by incorporating dedicated collaborative planning time (Wang et al., 2020). Teaching goals in interdisciplinary settings often involve addressing real-world problems, allowing students to apply STEM concepts in practical contexts. Differences in pedagogical approaches between subject areas, such as science and agriculture, highlight the need for alignment in teaching methods to enhance collaborative effectiveness and achieve shared educational goals (Wang et al., 2020; Sahin, 2019).

The structure of interdisciplinary collaboration can vary significantly and impact its effectiveness (Wang et al., 2020). For example, a multi-classroom model allows teachers to specialize in different content areas while working together on complex systems, offering students diverse perspectives. Conversely, an extracurricular activity model emphasizes interdisciplinary work within a single classroom setting (Wang et al., 2020). This variation, influenced by factors such as state standards and school culture, demonstrates how contextual elements affect collaboration practices (21st Century Education, 2024). Afterschool programs are also critical for applying STEM knowledge, though challenges may arise if teachers perceive their contributions as misaligned with project goals, highlighting the importance of teacher beliefs and external factors in the effectiveness of interdisciplinary STEM integration (Wang et al., 2020; 21st Century Education, 2024).

Interdisciplinary approaches to STEM education dismantle traditional subject silos by integrating STEM skills—such as critical thinking, problem-solving, creativity, and collaboration—with insights from the humanities (21st Century Education, 2024.). This holistic approach fosters a learning environment that mirrors real-world complexities and better prepares students for a modern workforce that values adaptability and broad knowledge. By connecting various disciplines, students gain an understanding of how different fields interact and develop essential 21st-century skills, while educators benefit from opportunities for collaborative teaching and innovative methods (21st Century Education, 2024; Sahin, 2019).

Collaborative projects further enhance the interdisciplinary approach by encouraging students to tackle real-world problems through a blend of STEM and humanities skills (21st Century Education, 2024). For instance, projects that integrate art, science, and environmental issues enable students to apply their knowledge in practical contexts and work together to devise creative solutions. Such activities enrich the learning experience and foster intellectual curiosity and practical problem-solving skills. These projects ultimately prepare students to address the complexities of the contemporary world effectively (21st Century Education, 2024; Sahin, 2019).

Sahin (2019) underscores the critical role of Project-Based Learning (PBL) in enhancing K-12 STEM education through collaborative and interdisciplinary methods. PBL is identified as an engaging approach that allows students to investigate real-life problems or curriculum-related issues with guidance from their teachers (Sahin, 2019). The chapter emphasizes the need for ongoing professional development for teachers, including visits to schools with successful PBL implementations and access to rigorous PBL curricula to improve teaching practices. Such professional development is essential for the effective implementation of PBL, which can significantly enhance the quality of STEM education and provide meaningful learning experiences (Sahin, 2019).

The integration of PBL into STEM education requires a focus on continuous professional development for teachers, as highlighted by Sahin (2019). This includes exposure to successful PBL models and high-quality curricula, which are crucial for refining and improving teaching strategies. These initiatives have the potential to drive significant improvements in STEM education, benefiting all students by providing them with meaningful learning experiences and preparing them for future challenges (Sahin, 2019; Wang et al., 2020).

Combining insights from Wang et al. (2020), 21st Century Education (2024), and Sahin (2019), it is clear that interdisciplinary and collaborative approaches are vital for advancing STEM education. These methods not only enhance students' understanding of complex systems but also foster the development of critical 21st-century skills. Educators are encouraged to embrace these approaches and invest in professional development to effectively integrate PBL and other interdisciplinary practices into their teaching (Wang et al., 2020; 21st Century Education, 2024; Sahin, 2019).

Overall, the success of interdisciplinary and collaborative STEM projects relies on factors such as effective team composition, alignment of teaching goals, and the adoption of innovative teaching methods (Wang et al., 2020; Sahin, 2019). Addressing these factors and focusing on continuous professional development can enhance the effectiveness of STEM education, ultimately preparing students to navigate and address the complexities of the modern world (21st Century Education, 2024; Sahin, 2019).

Hands-on and Experiential Learning

Hands-on and experiential learning in STEM education foster active student engagement and real-world applications, making abstract concepts more relatable and improving motivation and understanding (21st Century Education, 2024). By encouraging students to participate in practical activities, these methods extend beyond traditional rote learning. Students can solve problems and think critically, which enhances their ability to grasp STEM concepts and apply them in everyday situations, such as designing experiments or managing budgets (21st Century Education, 2024). The focus is on creating learning experiences where knowledge retention is deepened and long-lasting.

The integration of experiential learning equips students with essential skills, including communication, collaboration, and creative problem-solving, which are highly valuable in STEM careers (Aldridge, 2023). Educators are tasked with embedding real-world tasks in the curriculum, such as coding projects, engineering challenges, or mathematical modeling activities. These tasks allow students to actively apply theoretical knowledge, preparing them for careers in STEM fields by developing both technical and soft skills (21st Century Education, 2024). The hands-on approach also provides insights into various STEM professions, linking classroom learning to the real world (Aldridge, 2023).

A crucial aspect of experiential learning is the shift from traditional, passive instruction to active learning, which involves students in STEM subjects in more meaningful ways (Aldridge, 2023). Many students today are disengaged from traditional lecture-based methods, particularly in STEM, which can feel disconnected from real life. However, hands-on approaches, such as conducting science experiments or coding projects, enable students to understand how STEM principles work practically. This active involvement cultivates critical skills like teamwork and problem-solving, which are essential for success in future STEM careers (Aldridge, 2023; 21st Century Education, 2024).

Through experiential learning, students not only grasp STEM concepts more effectively but also become more engaged and motivated. The practical nature of hands-on learning keeps students invested in their education, turning STEM subjects from challenging and abstract to exciting and accessible (STEAM Powered Kids, 2023). For instance, building simple circuits to learn about electricity gives students a tangible understanding of the concept, reinforcing how STEM works in real-world contexts. This deeper engagement through practical tasks makes STEM learning both interactive and meaningful (STEAM Powered Kids, 2023).

Programs like *Engineering is Elementary* and the *FIRST Robotics Competition* showcase the success of hands-on learning by engaging students in real-world STEM challenges. These initiatives help students to apply theoretical knowledge in practical scenarios, leading to a deeper understanding and improved skill development (STEAM Powered Kids, 2023). By allowing students to engage directly with STEM projects, such programs significantly boost student interest and motivation, creating a more engaging learning environment that aligns with 21st-century career demands (STEAM Powered Kids, 2023).

Experiential learning, grounded in constructivist theory, emphasizes the active participation of students, allowing them to bridge the gap between theory and practice. This approach not only strengthens knowledge retention but also fosters the development of metacognitive skills, enabling students to reflect on their learning processes and problem-solving strategies (Conchas et al., 2023). Educators play a key role in creating dynamic and interactive learning environments by utilizing laboratories and applying diverse instructional techniques tailored to meet student needs (Conchas et al., 2023). Such methods ensure that learning is both collaborative and personalized.

In higher education, the development of scientific process skills is critical for fostering students' research capabilities. However, the lack of adequate focus on these skills poses challenges for student engagement in research-based activities (Conchas et al., 2023). To address this, educators must incorporate hands-on tasks that allow students to engage deeply with scientific methods, promoting the integration of theory with practical inquiry (Conchas et al., 2023). This integration is key to equipping students with the skills needed for advanced STEM careers.

Academic success in science education is intricately linked to factors such as motivation, engagement, and a supportive learning environment. Experiential learning can significantly enhance these aspects by creating opportunities for peer collaboration, creativity, and inquiry-based learning (21st Century Education, 2024). When students are motivated and supported, they are more likely to engage in the learning process, leading to better outcomes in STEM subjects. Collaborative activities and peer interactions also promote teamwork, a crucial skill in STEM professions (Aldridge, 2023; Conchas et al., 2023).

Innovative teaching strategies such as inquiry-based instruction and technology integration have great potential to optimize learning outcomes in STEM education. These strategies encourage students to explore problems from multiple perspectives and devise creative solutions (STEAM Powered Kids, 2023). While implementing these methods can present challenges, particularly in resource-limited settings, they offer substantial benefits by making learning more interactive and reflective of real-world STEM tasks (STEAM Powered Kids, 2023).

Overcoming the barriers to integrating hands-on and experiential learning into STEM education is essential for aligning instruction with future career demands. Educators, institutions, and policymakers must collaborate to provide the necessary resources, training, and support to ensure the seamless incorporation of these transformative learning approaches (Aldridge, 2023). When effectively implemented, experiential learning offers a powerful way to engage students, foster essential skills, and prepare them for the evolving STEM landscape.

Best Practices.

In high-quality STEM education, several best practices emerge as essential for effective teaching and learning. **Integration of Disciplines** is a cornerstone of these practices. Combining elements of science, technology, engineering, and mathematics into a unified curriculum supports STEM literacy and engagement by presenting these subjects as interconnected rather than isolated. This interdisciplinary approach helps students see the relevance of STEM concepts in a cohesive context, facilitating a deeper understanding of how these fields interact and apply to real-world problems (Vernier, n.d.; Wilkinson, 2020).

Active Learning is another critical best practice, where students engage directly with material through hands-on experiments and problem-solving tasks. Active learning strategies such as collaborative projects and inquiry-based activities enable students to apply concepts in practical scenarios, promoting deeper understanding and retention. This method aligns with the principle of making learning more interactive and experiential, thus enhancing students' critical thinking and problem-solving skills (Wilkinson, 2020; K-Rockets, 2024).

Real-World Connections in STEM education are vital for demonstrating the relevance of STEM skills. By linking content to real-world applications and case studies, educators make learning more engaging and motivating for students. This practice not only highlights the importance of STEM skills but also illustrates how these skills are applicable across various fields, making the educational experience more meaningful (Vernier, n.d.; August, 2023).

Technology Utilization enhances STEM education by integrating modern digital tools and resources. Tools such as simulation software, educational apps, and online resources provide interactive learning experiences and prepare students for the technological demands of the future. Effective technology integration should complement traditional teaching methods, ensuring that digital tools enhance rather than distract from learning objectives (August, 2023; Wilkinson, 2020).

Collaborative Learning is essential for developing teamwork and communication skills among students. Group projects, peer reviews, and collaborative problem-solving activities foster a learning environment where students work together, share ideas, and leverage each other's strengths. This practice not only enhances problem-solving abilities but also prepares students for collaborative work environments in their future careers (Wilkinson, 2020; Huang et al., 2022).

Professional Development for Educators is crucial for maintaining effective STEM education practices. Continuous training and development help teachers stay current with the latest STEM teaching methods and technologies. Providing educators with ongoing support ensures they are equipped to implement best practices and adapt to new challenges in their teaching environments (National Academies of Sciences, Engineering, and Medicine, 2011; Huang et al., 2022).

Assessment and Feedback are important for monitoring student progress and guiding instruction. Regular formative assessments and timely feedback help identify areas for improvement and tailor teaching strategies to meet individual student needs. This practice supports continuous improvement in student learning and helps educators refine their teaching methods based on student performance (Wilkinson, 2020; K-Rockets, 2024).

Culturally Relevant and Collaborative Activities play a significant role in making STEM education more inclusive and engaging. By honoring and incorporating students' cultural backgrounds and fostering teamwork, educators create a more meaningful learning experience for diverse student populations. This approach helps address various learning styles and backgrounds, promoting better engagement and understanding (Vernier, n.d.; August, 2023).

Inquiry-Based Learning involves moving beyond traditional methods to include project-based and experiential learning. This approach encourages students to engage in real-world tasks, facilitating a deeper connection to the material and preparing them for future career paths. Inquiry-based learning fosters curiosity and critical thinking, essential components of effective STEM education (Vernier, n.d.; K-Rockets, 2024).

Holistic Development addresses the intellectual, social, and emotional growth of students. High-quality STEM education should support overall development, including social and emotional learning. This approach helps students become well-rounded individuals who are academically proficient and prepared for future challenges. Integrating social and emotional aspects into STEM education ensures that students are equipped with a balanced skill set for their future endeavors (Vernier, n.d.; August, 2023).

Collectively, these best practices in STEM education—integrating disciplines, employing active learning, making real-world connections, utilizing technology, fostering collaboration, supporting professional development, and addressing diverse needs—create a dynamic and effective learning environment. By implementing these strategies, educators can enhance student engagement, deepen understanding, and prepare students for success in an increasingly technology-driven world (Wilkinson, 2020; Huang et al., 2022; National Academies of Sciences, Engineering, and Medicine, 2011; K-Rockets, 2024; August, 2023).

Challenges and Barriers.

The integration of educational technology in STEM education has been a focal point in recent research, highlighting both its potential benefits and inherent challenges. Triplett (2023) emphasizes the dual nature of technology integration in STEM: it can significantly enhance educational outcomes but also presents obstacles, such as limited access to resources and the need for comprehensive teacher training. This aligns with the findings of Nadelson and Seifert (2017), who stress the importance of bridging the digital divide and providing continuous professional development for educators. Effective integration of technology requires not only access to the necessary tools but also the pedagogical skills to use them effectively, a notion supported by Estapa and Tank (2017) who argue that both STEM content knowledge and pedagogical strategies are crucial for successful technology-enhanced education.

Johnson et al. (2016) add to this discussion by identifying the barriers that impede technology integration in STEM classrooms, distinguishing between first-order barriers, like resource limitations, and second-order barriers, such as teachers' attitudes and beliefs. Their research suggests that overcoming these barriers involves securing additional funding and developing robust professional development programs. This is complemented by their advocacy for training that focuses on constructivism and student-centered learning approaches, rather than just administrative tasks. The emphasis on teachers' active involvement in technology adoption and the use of frameworks like Technological Pedagogical Content Knowledge (TPACK) underscores the importance of aligning technology with instructional needs.

Dong et al. (2020) further investigate the intrinsic challenges faced by teachers, particularly in the Chinese context. They find that teachers with a solid understanding of STEM pedagogy encounter fewer obstacles than those who rely heavily on their primary discipline. This highlights the need for targeted professional development that enhances teachers' STEM knowledge and pedagogical skills. Dong et al. (2020)

argue that bridging the gap between teachers' beliefs and the practical challenges they face requires innovative practices in teacher preparation, suggesting that continued support and training are essential for effective STEM integration.

Portz (2015) critiques the traditional siloed approach to STEM education, advocating for a more integrated and applied method of teaching. He suggests that hands-on engineering and technology labs, along with Project-Based Learning (PBL), can effectively bridge the gap between theoretical knowledge and real-world applications. This approach aligns with the call for more interdisciplinary learning and the need for curricula that prepare students for practical STEM careers. Chiangpradit (2024) echoes this sentiment, pointing out the challenges of integrating STEM from early education through to higher levels. Key issues include resource limitations, curriculum integration difficulties, and the need to counter stereotypes and engage students through relevant and inclusive methods.

In summary, the integration of technology into STEM education is multifaceted, involving both external and internal challenges. Research highlights the importance of equitable access to resources, effective teacher training, and curriculum integration to address these challenges. The need for professional development is a recurring theme, with various authors emphasizing that teachers must be equipped with both the technological tools and pedagogical strategies necessary for successful integration. As technology continues to evolve, ongoing support and adaptation are crucial for maintaining effective STEM education practices.

Triplett's (2023) research, along with contributions from Nadelson and Seifert (2017) and Estapa and Tank (2017), underscores the need for a comprehensive approach to technology integration, balancing access, training, and curriculum alignment. Johnson et al. (2016) add depth to this discussion by identifying specific barriers and solutions, while Dong et al. (2020) provide insights into the intrinsic challenges faced by educators. Portz (2015) and Chiangpradit (2024) offer practical solutions and highlight the importance of integrating STEM education from early schooling through to higher education.

By addressing these barriers and leveraging the potential of technology, educators can enhance STEM learning experiences, foster student engagement, and better prepare students for future careers. The collective insights from these studies illustrate the complex interplay between technology, pedagogy, and curriculum, and the necessity for a coordinated effort among educators, administrators, and policymakers to overcome the challenges and harness the benefits of technology in STEM education.

CONCLUSION

Integrating educational technology into STEM education presents a transformative opportunity for enhancing learning experiences and preparing students for future challenges. Pedagogical theories such as constructivism, inquiry-based learning, and project-based learning underscore the value of active, hands-on engagement in knowledge construction. Constructivist theory emphasizes learners' active role in building their understanding through experience, which aligns seamlessly with the hands-on approach of inquiry-based and project-based learning. These methods encourage students to explore, experiment, and apply their knowledge to real-world problems, fostering deeper engagement and practical application. Technological Pedagogical Content Knowledge (TPACK) plays a crucial role in this process, ensuring that educators effectively integrate technology with their pedagogical strategies to enhance content delivery and student comprehension.

Current trends in educational technology, including interactive simulations, virtual labs, coding and robotics platforms, and Augmented Reality (AR) and Virtual Reality (VR) applications, further enrich STEM education. Interactive simulations and virtual labs provide dynamic and immersive experiences, allowing students to experiment with STEM concepts in a virtual setting. Coding and robotics platforms introduce foundational programming and engineering principles, promoting problem-solving and creativity. AR and VR applications offer innovative ways to visualize and interact with complex STEM concepts, making abstract ideas more tangible and accessible to students.

To enhance the STEM curriculum, technology should be integrated in ways that align with educational goals and standards. Collaborative and interdisciplinary projects are particularly effective, as they encourage teamwork and reflect the interconnected nature of real-world STEM fields. Hands-on and experiential learning approaches, supported by technology, provide practical experiences that reinforce theoretical knowledge and improve problem-solving skills.

Implementing educational technology successfully requires adherence to best practices, including aligning technology with curriculum standards, providing ongoing professional development for educators, and creating a supportive learning environment. Technology should enhance teaching practices rather than overshadow them, ensuring that it complements and supports core content and pedagogical objectives.

Despite these advantages, challenges such as limited resources, resistance to change, and disparities in access to technology persist. Addressing these challenges involves securing adequate funding, providing comprehensive training for educators, and developing inclusive policies to ensure equitable access to technology. By overcoming these barriers, schools can better utilize educational technology to support STEM education and foster innovation.

In conclusion, the thoughtful integration of educational technology into STEM education holds significant promise for enhancing learning outcomes and preparing students for future careers. By leveraging pedagogical theories, embracing current technological trends, and adhering to best practices, educators can create engaging and effective STEM learning environments that inspire and equip students for success.

REFERENCES

21st Century Education. (2024). Interdisciplinary approaches to STEM education: Bridging STEM with humanities. 21st Century Education. Retrieved September 15, 2024, from https://21stcented.com/interdisciplinary-approaches-to-stem-education-bridging-stem-with-humanities/

Ahmadigol, J. (2016). New definition of educational technology. In 30th Annual Proceedings: Selected Research and Development Papers (Vol. 1). Presented at the Annual Convention of the Association for Educational Communications and Technology.

Aldridge, D. (2023). Making learning engaging: Hands-on STEM education. LinkedIn. Retrieved September 15, 2024, from https://www.linkedin.com/pulse/making-learning-engaging-hands-on-stem-education-damien-aldridge-51bnc

Alfieri, L., Brooks, P. J., Aldrich, N. J., & Tenenbaum, H. R. (2011). Does discovery-based instruction enhance learning? *Journal of Educational Psychology*, 103(1), 1–18. https://doi.org/10.1037/a0021017

Anud, E. (2022). Teaching performance of science teachers in the new normal and their technological pedagogical and content knowledge (TPACK) self-efficacy. International Journal of Applied Science and Research.https://doi.org/10.56293/ijasr.2022.5410

Arockiasamy, S. (2018). Concept of educational technology. Viswa Bharathi College of Education for Women. Retrieved from https://drarockiasamy.wordpress.com/unit-i-concept-of-educational-technology/

Atmojo, I. R. W., Saputri, D. Y., & Fajri, A. K. (2022). Analysis of STEAM-based TPACK integrated activities in elementary school thematic books. *Mimbar Sekolah Dasar*, 9(2), 317–335. https://doi.org/10.53400/mimbar-sd.v9i2.49131

Attard, C., Berger, N., & Mackenzie, E. (2021). The positive influence of inquiry-based learning, teacher professional learning, and industry partnerships on student engagement with STEM. *Frontiers in Education*, 6. Advance online publication. https://doi.org/10.3389/feduc.2021.693221

Augmentastic, P. V. T. LTD. (2023, April 12). How AR/VR is transforming STEM education: Unlocking new learning opportunities. Augmentastic PVT. LTD. Retrieved from https://www.augmentastic.com/how-arvr-is-transforming-stem-education

August, S. E. (2023, April 26). Integrating technology with best practices paves the way. American Association for the Advancement of Science. Retrieved September 15, 2024, from https://aaas-iuse.org/integrating-technology-with-best-practices-paves-the-way/

Banchi, H., & Bell, R. (2008, October). The many levels of inquiry. *Science and Children*, 26–29.

Barron, B., & Darling-Hammond, L. (2008). Teaching for meaningful learning: A review of research on inquiry-based and cooperative learning. In Darling-Hammond, L., Barron, B., Pearson, P. D., Schoenfeld, A., Stage, E., Zimmerman, T., Cervetti, G., & Tilson, J. (Eds.), *Powerful learning: What we know about teaching for understanding* (pp. 11–70). Jossey-Bass.

Bell, P., Lewenstein, B., Shouse, A. W., & Feder, M. A. (2009). *Learning science in informal environments: People, places, and pursuits*. National Academies Press.

Bell, T., Urhahne, D., Schanze, S., & Ploetzner, R. (2010). Collaborative inquiry learning: Models, tools, and challenges. *International Journal of Science Education*, 32(1), 349–377. https://doi.org/10.1080/09500690802582241

Blumenfeld, P. C., & Krajcik, J. S. (2006). Project-based learning. In Sawyer, R. K. (Ed.), *The Cambridge handbook of learning sciences* (pp. 317–334). Cambridge University Press.

Brau, B. (n.d.). Constructivism. In Student guide to learning with technology. EdTech Books. Retrieved September 14, 2024, from https://edtechbooks.org/studentguide/constructivism

Brinson, J. R. (2015). Learning outcome achievement in non-traditional (virtual and remote) versus traditional (hands-on) laboratories: A review of the empirical research. *Computers & Education*, 87, 218–237. https://doi.org/10.1016/j.compedu.2015.07.003

Bruder, R., & Prescott, A. (2013). Research evidence on the benefits of IBL. *ZDM Mathematics Education*, 45(6), 811–822. https://doi.org/10.1007/s11858-013-0542-2

Burke, B. N., Reed, P. A., & Wells, J. G. (n.d.). Engineering byDesign™ – Maximizing design and inquiry through integrative STEM education: The setting. International Technology and Engineering Educators Association. Retrieved from https://assets-002.noviams.com/novi-file-uploads/iteea/resource_hub/ESP_EbD_v12.pdf

Butz, W. P., Kelly, T. K., Adamson, D. M., Bloom, G. A., Fossum, D., & Gross, M. E. (2004). *Will the scientific and technology workforce meet the requirements of the federal government?* RAND Corporation.

Bybee, R. (2010). Advancing STEM education: A 2020 vision. *Technology and Engineering Teacher*, 70(1), 30–35.

Bybee, R. W. (2009). *The BSCS 5E instructional model and 21st century skills*. BSCS.

Bybee, R. W., & Landes, N. M. (1990). Science for life & living: An elementary school science program from Biological Sciences Curriculum Study. *The American Biology Teacher*, 52(2), 92–98.

Chacko, P., Appelbaum, S., Kim, H., Zhao, J., & Kim Montclare, J. (2013). Integrating technology in STEM education. *Journal of Technology and Science Education*, 5(1). Advance online publication. https://doi.org/10.3926/jotse.124

Chiangpradit, L. (2024, July 10). 9 challenges of teaching STEM & how to overcome them. STEM Sports. Reviewed by S. Barton & H. MacLean. Retrieved from https://stemsports.com/8-challenges-of-teaching-stem/

Chiu, J. L., Malcolm, P. T., Hecht, D., DeJaegher, C. J., Pan, E. A., Bradley, M., & Burghardt, M. D. (2013). WISEngineering: Supporting precollege engineering design and mathematical understanding. *Computers & Education*, 67, 142–155.

Coder, Z. (n.d.). CoderZ: Engage students in STEM with coding and robotics. Retrieved September 14, 2024, from https://gocoderz.com/learn/

Common Sense Education. (n.d.). Best robotics apps and websites for STEM classrooms. Common Sense Education. Retrieved September 14, 2024, from https://www.commonsense.org/education/lists/best-robotics-apps-and-websites-for-stem-classrooms

Conchas, D. M., Montilla, A. R. Y., Romblon, K. D. C., Torion, M. P., Reyes, J. J. R., & Tinapay, A. O. (2023). Assessing the experiential learning and scientific process skills of senior high school STEM students: A literature review. *International Journal of Multidisciplinary Research and Publications*, 6(2), 81–90.

Craig, E., & Georgieva, M. (2017, August 4). AR and VR in STEM: The new frontiers in science. Retrieved from https://www.emorycraig.com/ar-and-vr-in-stem-the-new-frontiers-in-science

D'Silva, I. (2010). Active learning. *Journal of Education Administration and Policy Studies*, 2(6), 77–82.

DC7. (n.d.). AR and VR STEM learning prototypes. Retrieved from https://www.dc7.co/research

Darling-Hammond, L., Flook, L., Cook-Harvey, C., Barron, B., & Osher, D. (2020). Implications for educational practice of the science of learning and development. *Applied Developmental Science*, 24(2), 97–140. https://doi.org/10.1080/10888691.2018.1537791

Dewey, J. (1916). *Democracy and education: An introduction to the philosophy of education* (1966 ed.). Free Press.

Dewey, J. (1997). *How we think*.

Dong, Y., Wang, J., & Yang, Y.. (2020). Understanding intrinsic challenges to STEM instructional practices for Chinese teachers based on their beliefs and knowledge base. *International Journal of STEM Education*, 7(1), 47. https://doi.org/10.1186/s40594-020-00245-0

Dostál, J. (2015). *Inquiry-based instruction: Concept, essence, importance and contribution*. Palacký University., https://doi.org/10.5507/pdf.15.24445076

El Morabit, N. (2021). Educational technology: From a historical perspective to an empirical exploration of Moroccan learners' EFL speaking fluency. Global Journal of Human-Social Science: G Linguistics & Education, 21(11). https://doi.org/10.34257/GJHSSGV21N11

Ellis, J., Wieselmann, J., Sivaraj, R., Roehrig, G., Dare, E., & Ring-Whalen, E. (2020). Toward a productive definition of technology in science and STEM education. CITE Journal, 20(3). Retrieved from https://citejournal.org/volume-20/issue-3-20/science/toward-a-productive-definition-of-technology-in-science-and-stem-education/

Erickson, L. (2019, November 14). [STEM resources for robotics and coding. Mimio Educator. Retrieved from https://www.mimio.com/educator-blog/top-10-stem-resources-for-robotics-and-coding]. *Top (Madrid)*, 10, •••.

Eskrootchi, R., & Oskrochi, G. R. (2010). A study of the efficacy of project-based learning integrated with computer-based simulation – Stella. *Journal of Educational Technology & Society*, 13(1), 236–245.

Estapa, A. T., & Tank, K. M. (2017). Supporting integrated STEM in the elementary classroom: A professional development approach centered on an engineering design challenge. *International Journal of STEM Education*, 4(1), 1–16.

Fei, C., & Tse, A. W. C. (2024). Examining the Technological Pedagogical Content Knowledge (TPACK) of biology educators: A case study on pre-service and in-service teachers in preparation for applying STEM education. In Kubincová, Z. (Eds.), Lecture Notes in Computer Science: Vol. 14606. *Emerging technologies for education. SETE 2023* (pp. 108–119). Springer., https://doi.org/10.1007/978-981-97-4243-1_8

Fichtman-Dana, N., Thomas, C., & Boynton, S. (2011). *Inquiry: A districtwide approach to staff and student learning*. Corwin Press.

Flick, L., & Bell, R. (2000). Preparing tomorrow's science teachers to use technology: Guidelines for science educators. *Contemporary Issues in Technology & Teacher Education*, 1(1), 39–60.

Graham, C. R., Borup, J., & Smith, N. B. (2012). Using TPACK as a framework to understand teacher candidates' technology integration decisions. *Journal of Computer Assisted Learning*, 28(6), 530–546. https://doi.org/10.1111/j.1365-2729.2011.00472.x

Hannafin, M. J., & Hannafin, K. M. (2010). Cognition and student-centered, web-based learning: Issues and implications for research and theory. In M. Spector, D. Ifenthaler, & Kinshuk (Eds.), Learning and instruction in the digital age (pp. 11–23). Springer.

Harris, J., & Hofer, M. (2011). Technological pedagogical content knowledge (TPACK) in action: A descriptive study of secondary teachers' curriculum-based, technology-related instructional planning. *Journal of Research on Technology in Education*, 43(3), 211–229. https://doi.org/10.1080/15391523.2011.10782570

Hasanah, U. (2020). Key definitions of STEM education: Literature review. *Interdisciplinary Journal of Environmental and Science Education*, 16(3), e2217. https://doi.org/10.29333/ijese/8336

Hattie, J. (2009). *Visible learning: A synthesis of over 800 meta-analyses relating to achievement*. Routledge.

Hıdıroğlu, Ç. N., & Karakaş, A. (2022). Transdisciplinary role of technology in STEM education. *Malaysian Online Journal of Educational Technology*, 10(4), 276–293. https://doi.org/10.52380/mojet.2022.10.4.411

Huang, B., Jong, M. S.-Y., Tu, Y.-F., Hwang, G.-J., Chai, C. S., & Jiang, M. Y.-C. (2022). Trends and exemplary practices of STEM teacher professional development programs in K-12 contexts: A systematic review of empirical studies. *Computers & Education*, 189, 104577. https://doi.org/10.1016/j.compedu.2022.104577

HundrED. (2024). The impact of AR and VR on STEM education: A case study of Qatar Science and Technology Secondary School.

Johnson, A. M., Jacovina, M. E., Russell, D. E., & Soto, C. M. (2016). Challenges and solutions when using technologies in the classroom. In Crossley, S. A., & McNamara, D. S. (Eds.), *Adaptive educational technologies for literacy instruction* (pp. 13–29). Taylor & Francis.

Jumaat, N. F., Tasir, Z., Abd Halim, N. D., & Mohamad Ashari, Z. (2017). Project-based learning from constructivism point of view. *Advanced Science Letters*, 23(8), 7904–7906.

K-Rockets. (2024, July 14). STEM education: Top ten best practices for teaching and learning. K-Rockets. https://k-rockets.com/stem-education-top-ten-best-practices-for-teaching-and-learning/

Koehler, M. J., Mishra, P., & Yahya, K. (2007). Tracing the development of teacher knowledge in a design seminar: Integrating content, pedagogy, & technology. *Computers & Education*, 49(3), 740–762.

Kuhlthau, C., & Maniotes, L. K. (2015). *Guided inquiry: Learning in the 21st century* (2nd ed.). Libraries Unlimited.

Manosuttirit, A. (2019). How to apply technology in STEM education lesson by project-based learning. *Journal of Physics: Conference Series*, 1340(1), 012044. https://doi.org/10.1088/1742-6596/1340/1/012044

Mansour, N., Said, Z., & Abu-Tineh, A. (2024). Factors impacting science and mathematics teachers' competencies and self-efficacy in TPACK for PBL and STEM. *Eurasia Journal of Mathematics, Science and Technology Education*, 20(5), em2442. Advance online publication. https://doi.org/10.29333/ejmste/14467

Marr, B. (2021, July 23). 10 best examples of VR and AR in education. Forbes. https://www.forbes.com/sites/bernardmarr/2021/07/23/10-best-examples-of-vr-and-ar-in-education/

McDonald, C. V. (2016). STEM education: A review of the contribution of the disciplines of science, technology, engineering and mathematics. *Science Education International*, 27(4), 530–569.

Nadelson, L. S., & Seifert, A. L. (2017). Integrated STEM defined: Contexts, challenges, and the future. *The Journal of Educational Research*, 110(3), 221–223.

National Academies of Sciences, Engineering, and Medicine. (2011). Chapter 3: Practices that support effective STEM education. In Successful STEM education: A workshop summary (pp. 25–42). The National Academies Press. https://doi.org/10.17226/13230

Nelson, C. E. (2022, January 30). STEM educational activities with virtual labs: Curriculum & skills. Connections Academy. https://www.connectionsacademy.com/support/resources/article/stem-educational-activities-with-virtual-labs/

Nguyen, T. C., Nguyen, T. C., & Nguyen, H. B. (2024). The role of information technology in STEM education. *Asian Journal of Education and Training*, 10(1), 18–26. https://doi.org/10.20448/edu.v10i1.532

Olsen, D. (1999). Constructivist principles of learning and teaching methods. *Education*, •••, 120.

Opara, E. C. (2023). *Educational technology for beginners: Basics of educational technology*. Printed in the United States of America.

Ortiz Rojas, M. E., Chiluiza, K., & Valcke, M. (2017). Gamification in computer programming: Effects on learning, engagement, self-efficacy, and intrinsic motivation. Retrieved from https://biblio.ugent.be/publication/8542410/file/8549234

Parlier, M. (2024). The role of AR and VR in developing soft skills in STEM education.

Pedaste, M., Mäeotos, M., Siiman, L., de Jong, T., van Riesen, S., Kamp, E., Manoli, C., Zacharia, Z., & Tsourlidaki, E. (2015). Phases of inquiry-based learning: Definitions and the inquiry cycle. *Educational Research Review*, 14, 47–61.

Perry, S. B. (n.d.). Project-based learning. The student's guide to learning design and research. EdTech Books. https://edtechbooks.org/studentguide/project-based_learning

Piaget, J. (1972). *The psychology of the child*. Basic Books.

Portz, S. (2015). The challenges of STEM education. The Space Congress® Proceedings, 3. https://commons.erau.edu/space-congress-proceedings/proceedings-2015-43rd/proceedings-2015-43rd/3

Powered Kids, S. T. E. A. M. (2023). The importance of incorporating hands-on learning in STEM education. Retrieved September 15, 2024, from https://www.steampoweredkids.com.au/post/the-importance-of-incorporating-hands-on-learning-in-stem-education

Prince, M. J., & Felder, R. M. (2006). Inductive teaching and learning methods: Definitions, comparisons, and research bases.

Putri, A. R. A., Hidayat, T., & Purwianingsih, W. (2020). Analysis of technological pedagogical content knowledge (TPACK) of biology teachers in classification of living things learning. *Journal of Physics: Conference Series*, 1521, 042033. https://doi.org/10.1088/1742-6596/1521/4/042033

Reeve, E. M. (2013). Implementing science, technology, mathematics, and engineering (STEM) education in Thailand and in ASEAN. *International Journal of Technology and Design Education*, 23(3).

Reeves, S. M., & Crippen, K. J. (2021). Virtual laboratories in undergraduate science and engineering courses: A systematic review, 2009–2019. *Journal of Science Education and Technology*, 30(1), 16–30. https://doi.org/10.1007/s10956-020-09866-0

Reimagine Education. (n.d.). How virtual labs are revolutionizing science education. Retrieved September 14, 2024, from https://www.reimagineeducation.com/virtual-labs-science-education

Resnick, L. B. (1989). Introduction. In Resnick, L. B. (Ed.), *Knowing, learning, and instruction: Essays in honor of Robert Glaser* (pp. 1–4). Erlbaum.

Sahin, A. (2019). The role of interdisciplinary project-based learning in integrated STEM education. In STEM education 2.0 (pp. [page numbers]). https://doi.org/10.1163/9789004405400_006

Sanders, M. (2009). STEM, STEM education, STEMmania. *Technology Teacher*, 68(4), 20–26.

Scratch. (n.d.). Coding and robotics platforms for STEM. Retrieved September 14, 2024, from https://scratch.mit.edu

Sellberg, C., Nazari, Z., & Solberg, M. (2024). Virtual laboratories in STEM higher education: A scoping review. *Nordic Journal of Systematic Reviews in Education*, 2, 58–75.

Srisawasdi, N. (2012). Fostering pre-service STEM teachers' technological pedagogical content knowledge: A lesson learned from case-based learning approach. *Journal of The Korean Association for Science Education*, 32(8), 1356–1370. https://doi.org/10.14697/jkase.2012.32.8.1356

Stanney, K. M., & Cohn, J. V. (2009). Virtual environments. In Human-computer interaction (pp. 311–328).

STEMpedia. (n.d.). STEMpedia: Innovating STEM education through coding and robotics. Retrieved September 14, 2024, from https://thestempedia.com

Thomas, J. W. (2000). *A review of research on project-based learning*. Autodesk Foundation.

Triplett, W. J. (2023). Impact of technology integration in STEM education. *Cybersecurity and Innovation Technology Journal*, 1(1), 16–22. https://doi.org/10.52889/citj.v1i1.295

Tseng, K., Chang, C., Lou, S., & Chen, W. (2013). Attitudes towards science, technology, engineering and mathematics (STEM) in a project-based learning (PjBL) environment. *International Journal of Technology and Design Education*, 23(1), 87–102.

Vernier Science Education. (n.d.). Five research-based best practices for STEM education. Retrieved September 15, 2024, from https://www.vernier.com/blog/five-research-based-best-practices-for-stem-education/

Vygotsky, L. S. (1978). *Mind in society*. Harvard University Press.

Wang, F., Kinzie, M. B., McGuire, P., & Pan, E. (2010). Applying technology to inquiry-based learning in early childhood education. *Early Childhood Education Journal*, 37(5), 381–389. https://doi.org/10.1007/s10643-009-0364-6

Wang, H. H., Charoenmuang, M., & Knobloch, N. A.. (2020). Defining interdisciplinary collaboration based on high school teachers' beliefs and practices of STEM integration using a complex designed system. *International Journal of STEM Education*, 7(1), 3. https://doi.org/10.1186/s40594-019-0201-4

Wang, M., Liu, R., Zhang, C., & Tang, Z. (2021). Daran robot: A reconfigurable, powerful, and affordable robotic platform for STEM education. *STEM Education*, 1(4), 299–308. https://doi.org/10.3934/steme.2021019

Wilkinson, M. (2020). Best practices in STEM education. Retrieved from https://www.utc.edu/sites/default/files/2020-12/wilkinsonm2powerpoint.pdf

Wu, H.-K. (2010). Modeling a complex system: Using novice-expert analysis for developing an effective technology-enhanced learning environment. *International Journal of Science Education*, 32(2), 195–219.

Yang, D., & Baldwin, S. J. (2020). Using technology to support student learning in an integrated STEM learning environment. [IJTES]. *International Journal of Technology in Education and Science*, 4(1), 1–11.

Chapter 4
Analysis of Student Affairs and Services Programs and SDG Sustainability Knowledge and Behavior in One State University:
Alignment of Services to Sustainable Development Goals

Jherwin Pagkaliwagan Hermosa
https://orcid.org/0000-0001-8562-3028
Laguna State Polytechnic University, Philippines

Alberto B. Castillo
https://orcid.org/0000-0001-5427-0194
Laguna State Polytechnic University, Philippines

ABSTRACT

This study conducted an analysis of the current student affairs and services programs at The Laguna State Polytechnic University, with a particular focus on aligning these services with the Sustainable Development Goals (SDGs) set by the United Nations. It utilized a descriptive design and surveyed 200 students. It is revealed that the Office of Student Affairs offers accessible and well-utilized Services and programs. The students know the Sustainable Development Goals (SDGs) and can make valuable contributions to sustainability initiatives. Thus, it is essential to align initiatives in

DOI: 10.4018/979-8-3693-8242-4.ch004

student affairs and services with institutional strategies and objectives related to the SDGs. Higher education institutions serve as crucial platforms for advancing the SDGs. By engaging faculty members as SDG experts and incorporating the goals into their teaching, institutions can effectively integrate these principles into their curriculum. Additionally, supporting student organizations in participating in SDG-related events and collaborations further enhances the promotion of these global objectives.

INTRODUCTION

The educational landscape in the Philippines has seen significant changes with the implementation of the K-to-12 program and RA 10931, also referred to as the Universal Access to Quality Tertiary Education Act. These developments have introduced new challenges and heightened demands for universities to provide effective student service programs. Educators recognize the crucial role of these services in improving academic performance, fostering social growth, and nurturing positive student attitudes. In 2013, the Commission on Higher Education (CHED) introduced CMO No. 09, s. 2013, which outlines the Guidelines on Student Affairs and Services Program. This policy requires all Higher Education Institutions (HEIs) to comply with the set standards for their Student Affairs and Services Program.

The memorandum sets forth guidelines, objectives, and minimum standards for student services to improve access to high-quality and relevant student affairs and services, foster student development and welfare, and ensure that Higher Education Institutions (HEIs) provide a comprehensive approach to Student Affairs and Services while meeting minimum requirements. As a result, the quality of university programs' output and outcomes can be evaluated based on the established minimum standards. By the guidelines specified in CHED CMO no. 9, s. 2013, the Institution must furnish all students with access to informational materials detailing the institutional mission, vision, and goals, academic regulations, student conduct policies, student programs, services, facilities, and any other pertinent information essential for student growth and development. (Ibarrientos, 2015)

Currently, universities are increasingly aligning themselves with the Sustainable Development Goals (SDGs). The appeal of the SDGs lies in their ability to drive societal and institutional transformations. This study seeks to explore the impact of the SDGs on universities. Parr (2022) highlights the importance of universities embracing the Agenda 2030 for it to be successfully implemented. The SDGs not only serve as a common platform for collaboration between universities and other stakeholders to tackle global issues (Purcell et al., 2019) but also act as a framework for driving internal changes within universities. The growing focus on Higher

Education Institutions (HEIs) and the SDGs has led to an increase in universities worldwide showing interest in engaging with the Goals (Mallow et al., 2020; Chankseliani & McCowan, 2021).

While several studies have examined the significance of SDGs in enhancing the quality of education and student services, one area that has received little attention is the alignment of Student Affairs and Services Programs with SDG Sustainability Knowledge and Behavior in a particular state university. Therefore, this research seeks to illuminate the factors that contribute to consistent academic performance. In the Philippines, there is a growing enthusiasm among universities towards the SDGs, with various instances of university involvement in the Goals coming to light. However, uncertainties persist regarding the impact of the SDGs on university evolution. Despite this, there is a lack of concerted efforts to align University Student Affairs and Services Programs with the Sustainable Development Goals.

LITERATURE REVIEW

Sustainable Development Goals

The concept of Sustainable Development (SD) on a global scale can be characterized as the promotion of development that fulfills current needs without jeopardizing the ability of future generations to meet their own needs. This involves considering sustainability in economic, environmental, and social aspects with the active engagement of multiple stakeholders (Olawumi & Chan, 2018). The forefront of SD is marked by the United Nations Sustainable Development Goals (SDGs), which were introduced in 2015 with a target to be achieved by 2030. These goals aim to spur collective global efforts in achieving sustainable development through a harmonious and integrated approach across its three pillars (United Nations, 2015). They play a crucial role in rallying institutions worldwide (both public and private) to step up their contributions (Blasco et al., 2020) and collaborate towards the realization of genuine sustainable development for all. The concept of Higher Education Institutions (HEIs) playing a crucial role in promoting sustainable development (SD) is relatively recent, as highlighted by Montenegro de Lima et al. (2020). The Sustainable Development Goals (SDGs) have been identified as a tool for HEIs to address their sustainability challenges, While HEIs have long recognized the importance of sustainable development, the full integration of these principles into their operations and systems is still a work in progress, as noted by Aleixo et al. (2018).

In 2014, UNESCO convened a World Conference in Japan, urging HEIs to enhance their Education for Sustainable Development (ESD) efforts. This call emphasized the significance of integrating sustainable development principles into education at all levels and in all disciplines, enabling citizens to make informed decisions that promote sustainable living and working practices. Achieving this goal could involve implementing Education for Sustainable Development (ESD), which not only involves influencing policies but also raising awareness about sustainability goals and implementing best practices in various learning and education contexts. Numerous studies have urged Higher Education Institutions (HEIs) to integrate ESD into their practices (Leicht et al., 2018). Educators are called upon to adopt competency-based and participatory approaches within their institutions. Consequently, many HEIs have undergone structural changes to enhance their sustainability initiatives by modernizing their operations and expanding research, education, and community engagement activities.

Importance of Aligning the Student Services to SGDs

Patton et al. (2016) contend that it is essential for higher education institutions in the Philippines to align student affairs and services with the Sustainable Development Goals (SDGs). This alignment allows universities to significantly contribute to promoting sustainable development and play a transformative role in society. By integrating the SDGs into the framework of student services, higher education institutions can actively support the global sustainability agenda and help address both local and national challenges. The significance of this alignment is in its capacity to cultivate students into socially conscious and environmentally conscious global citizens. By engaging in customized programs and activities aligned with the Sustainable Development Goals (SDGs), such as community service initiatives, environmental advocacy campaigns, and leadership development, students acquire practical experience in addressing real-world challenges. This not only enriches their academic education but also equips them with the necessary skills, values, and ethical awareness to effectively tackle intricate societal issues (Saputra & Prabowo, 2021). Meanwhile, Sultana et al. (2021) affirmed that by aligning student affairs with Sustainable Development Goals (SDGs), universities can enhance their social impact and promote a culture of engagement and accountability. In the Philippines, urgent issues like poverty, inequality, disaster risk, and environmental degradation are prevalent. This presents an invaluable opportunity for higher education institutions to cultivate a dedication to sustainability among their student body. Initiatives centered on health and well-being, quality education, and climate action have the potential to empower students to make a meaningful difference in their communities, ultimately fostering positive, lasting change. Moreover, the integration of student affairs with the Sustainable Development Goals (SDGs) not only ensures the institution's relevance and global connectivity, but also has the potential to elevate the university's reputation, secure partnerships and funding for sustainable initiatives, and equip students for success in a job market that is increasingly focusing on sustainability. Ultimately, incorporating the SDGs into student affairs is a strategic investment in cultivating empowered and forward-thinking leaders who are poised to drive positive change at both local and international levels (Ouellette& Wanger, 2022).

HEIs and the Importance of SDGs Awareness and Engagement

HEIs have a substantial role to play in raising awareness and promoting engagement with the Sustainable Development Goals (SDGs) among the general public, as emphasized by Kräusche & Pilz (2018). As leaders in innovation, education, and research, HEIs are essential in driving societal change and fostering the development of economies and societies, according to Lozano et al. (2015). Whether in theory or in practice, HEIs are pivotal in articulating the necessary societal transformations. It has been recognized that HEIs have a moral obligation and responsibility to ensure that their graduates depart with a deep understanding of their role in advancing the quality of life for future generations. The rise in challenges surrounding survival, politics, societies, and peace has made sustainability a pressing global issue. Higher Education Institutions (HEIs) worldwide are increasingly incorporating sustainability into their core mission to address the existing knowledge gap (Soini et al., 2018). In alignment with the global push for a sustainable future, HEIs are integrating sustainable initiatives into their curriculum, communities, operations, activities. Furthermore, they are enhancing their collaboration and contribution efforts to instill sustainable values, attributes, and behaviors in the future generation.

In order to achieve the Sustainable Development Goals (SDGs), Hajer et al. (2015) emphasized the importance of introducing new and diverse agents of change, such as Higher Education Institutions (HEIs). According to Leal Filho (2018), HEIs possess a unique capability to promote impartial and resilient societies by serving as "knowledge disseminators, behavior consolidators, and idea innovators" within their distinctive learning environments and campus experiences. This underscores the significance of integrating sustainability principles universally. HEIs can play a crucial role in educating individuals about the necessary processes for accomplishing the SDGs (Frandoloso et al., 2019). It is widely believed that HEIs need to implement sustainability policies to effectively address sustainability-related challenges. This not only demonstrates the institution's dedication to reaching its objectives but also acts as a vital measurement of its commitment to sustainability (Leal Filho, 2018).

Higher Education Institutions (HEIs) have played a crucial role in furthering the Sustainable Development Goals (SDGs) by assisting in local and national implementation, embodying Education for Sustainable Development (ESD), aligning governance and operations with the SDGs, integrating the SDGs into university reporting, and promoting transdisciplinary and interdisciplinary research (Montenegro de Lima et al., 2020). HEIs are recognized as key contributors to the achievement of the SDGs particularly in relation to Goal 4 - Quality Education, which emphasizes the importance of HEIs in teaching and learning about the goals (Blasco et al., 2020). The emphasis on education as a means to promote sustainable development and achieve the SDGs underscores the significant role of HEIs in driving progress towards all the goals (Kestin et al., 2017) as highlighted by the United Nations (2015).

This has led to increased participation in Higher Education for Sustainable Development. Given their extensive reach, Higher Education Institutions (HEIs) can actively promote the Sustainable Development Goals thereby raising awareness and engagement levels towards these goals. As highlighted by Paletta & Bonoli (2019), HEIs play a crucial role not only in supporting the implementation of policies to achieve the SDGs but also in enhancing awareness among their stakeholders, especially their students. HEIS needs to educate students on their role in the 2030 SDGs agenda and equip them with the necessary skills and mindsets through knowledge transfer. The pursuit of embodying education for sustainable development (SD) and engaging with the goals at higher education institutions (HEIs) is met with obstacles, particularly in terms of staff involvement and inadequate funding (Fiselieret al., 2018). Various studies have focused on evaluating how HEIs are implementing sustainability and the SDGs, as well as how these goals are being integrated into the educational programs offered by the institution (Shiel et al., 2020). There is a growing demand for HEIs to explore and implement new and innovative methods, content, and approaches to learning within their institutions to enhance awareness and engagement with these goals.

MATERIALS AND METHODS

The research employed a descriptive survey methodology to investigate the perception of students towards Student Affairs and Services Programs and SDG Sustainability Knowledge and Behavior in a particular State University. This approach aims to provide a detailed description of a phenomenon and ascertain its cause, value, and importance. The study involved 200 students as its primary participants, who completed a researcher-developed questionnaire. This questionnaire was designed based on indicators from previous studies by Sison (2019) and Ciobanu (2013). It consisted of two parts: the first part focused on the respondents' perception of the student affairs services provided by the university, while the second part aimed to gauge their perception of Sustainable Development Goals and their impact on the quality of education. To ensure adherence to ethical standards, a consent letter was provided to the respondents. The letter outlined the extent of their participation and guaranteed confidentiality and privacy regarding their personal information.

Meanwhile, the instrument was validated through an evaluation by university tool validators. Given that the tool used is a self-report survey, it was crucial to consider various factors (such as halo effect or reference group bias) that could affect participant responses (Robertson-Kraft & Duckworth, 2020). Once validation was complete, the questionnaire was converted into an electronic format using Google Forms. Assistance was also sought from university deans to encourage student participation in the online survey. Despite efforts to maximize participation, 200 completed online survey questionnaires were obtained. The percentage of collected data may impact the analysis results. Subsequently, participant responses were compiled, tallied, and tabulated.

RESULTS AND DISCUSSION

Table 1. Services Provided by the Office of Students Affairs

Services Provided by OSAS	Mean	SD	VI
1. Student council/government	3.47	.701	A
2. Economic Enterprise, Handbook Development, Student Organization and activities	3.46	.693	A
3. Leadership training	3.46	.721	A
4. Information and orientation services, Guidance and counseling services, and Career and job placement services	3.42	.738	A
5. Student discipline	3.47	.712	A
6. Student publication	3.49	.707	A
7. Admission services	3.49	.710	A
8. Scholarship and financial assistance and Food services	3.52	.702	HA
9. Health services	3.51	.707	HA
10. Safety and security services	3.50	.710	HA
Overall	3.48	.655	A

Legend: 3.50 – 4.00 - Highly Available (HA); 2.50 – 3.49 - Available (A); 1.50 – 2.49 - Moderately Available (MA); 1.00 – 1.49 - Not Available (NA)

The data presented in Table 1 illustrates the perceptions of students regarding the services offered by the Office of Student Affairs at Laguna State Polytechnic University. The findings indicate that the majority of respondents agree on the availability of scholarships and financial assistance, as well as the university food services center, which received the highest mean score of 3.51. These services were deemed to effectively meet the needs of students during their time at the university. Conversely, information and orientation services, guidance and counseling services, and career and job placement services, although considered available, received the lowest mean score of 3.42. The overall mean availability of services offered by the Office of Student Affairs is 3.48, indicating that these services are generally accessible to students.

The respondents acknowledged that the various services and programs offered by the support offices were helpful in enhancing student performance. This suggests that the support offices effectively provided services and programs that benefited LSPU students as they progressed through their educational journey. According to Dagdag et al. (2019), support services and programs that are tailored to meet student needs play a significant role in students' academic success. Similarly, the research findings by Twum-Ampofo & Osei-Owusu (2015) demonstrated that well-rounded institutional student services, which cater to students' needs, positively impact student outcomes.

The services and programs offered by support offices were instrumental in enhancing student performance. These resources encompassed a variety of supportive measures such as academic advising, tutoring, mental health support, and career counseling, providing customized and easily accessible aid to cater to individual student needs. By tackling academic and personal hurdles, these support systems cultivated a conducive learning environment that empowered students to achieve their maximum potential.

Table 2. Perceived Level of Knowledge on Sustainable Development Goals

Knowledge on Sustainable Development Goals	Mean	SD	VI
1. I am familiar with the concept of Sustainable Development Goals (SDGs) and understand their purpose.	3.33	.848	K
2. I am knowledgeable about the specific countries targeted by the SDGs.	3.32	.843	K
3. I am aware of the timeframe set for achieving the SDGs.	3.32	.836	K
4. I recognize the significance of aligning programs and activities with the SDG goals.	3.37	.833	K
5. I can identify at least one of the SDGs and understand their overall objectives.	3.33	.845	K
Overall	3.33	.8012	K

Legend: 3.50 – 4.00 - Highly Knowledgeable (HK); 2.50 – 3.49 – Knowledgeable (K); 1.50 – 2.49 - Moderately Knowledgeable (MK); 1.00 – 1.49 - Not Knowledgeable (NK)

In Table 2, the data showcases the perception of students regarding their understanding of sustainable development goals. The majority of respondents express agreement with the importance of aligning programs and activities with SDG goals, with a mean score of 3.37, indicating a level of knowledge deemed as "knowledgeable". Although respondents' familiarity with the specific countries targeted by the

SDGs and the awareness of the set timeframe for achieving the goals both have a lower mean of 3.32, they still fall under the category of "knowledgeable". The overall mean for Perceived Knowledge of Sustainable Development Goals is 3.33, also categorized as "knowledgeable".

Edwards et al. (2020), posited that the level of awareness and understanding of the Sustainable Development Goals (SDGs) by students has a notable impact on the incorporation of these goals into various subjects, activities, and programs at the university. Anderson (2017) suggested that students' knowledge of the SDGs, as well as their access to information sources, play a crucial role in enhancing their understanding of sustainability and motivating them to participate in global sustainable development efforts.

In a study by Zamora-Polo et al. (2019), it was stated that the Sustainable Development Goals (SDGs) serve as a plan for creating a more sustainable future for upcoming generations. Igbinovia and Osuchukwu (2018) also emphasized the importance of universities in disseminating knowledge and information related to the SDGs, as many students are unaware of these goals. Consequently, higher education institutions are tasked with the challenge of equipping students with the necessary skills and knowledge to contribute to the achievement of the SDGs (Zamora-Polo et al., 2019).

The inclusion of these objectives greatly influenced a wide range of subjects, activities, and programs at the university. By incorporating these goals, educational aims were effectively integrated into both the curriculum and extracurricular activities, creating a comprehensive learning experience. This approach allowed students to interact with these objectives in various settings, improving their comprehension and practical implementation, as well as cultivating a cohesive educational atmosphere.

Table 3. Perceived Behavior Towards Sustainable Development Goals

Display Sustainability Behavior	Mean	SD	VI
1. Whenever feasible, I opt for cycling or walking over using a motor vehicle for transportation.	3.31	.841	P
2. I have modified my lifestyle to minimize waste, such as reducing food waste and conserving materials.	3.32	.843	P
3. I demonstrate equal respect towards all individuals regardless of their gender or age.	3.38	.837	P
4. I prioritize the importance of receiving a quality education in my personal life.	3.37	.833	P
5. I treat everyone with equal respect, regardless of any cultural differences that may exist.	3.34	.845	P
Overall	3.34	.8012	P

Legend: 3.50 – 4.00 - Highly Practiced (HP); 2.50 – 3.49 – Practiced (P); 1.50 – 2.49 - Moderately Practiced (MP); 1.00 – 1.49 - Not Practiced (NP)

In Table 3, the students' perceptions of display behavior related to sustainable development goals are presented. It is evident that the majority of respondents agree on the importance of showing equal respect to individuals regardless of their gender or age, with a mean score of 3.38, indicating a "Practiced" behavior. In contrast, the option to choose cycling or walking over using a motor vehicle for transportation received the lowest mean score of 3.31, still categorized as "Practiced." The overall mean score for Perceived Behavior on Sustainable Development Goals is 3.34, which is also interpreted as "Practiced."

In their study, Yuan et al. (2020) proposed that adopting a proactive attitude toward sustainability could facilitate the development of students' awareness, knowledge, and competencies in this area, leading to increased engagement in global sustainable development efforts. Mohd et al., (2019) support this view, defining sustainability as a holistic approach that takes into account ecological, social, and economic factors, emphasizing the importance of integrating these elements for sustained success.

According to Eizaguirre et al. (2019), there is a belief among some commentators that universities play a crucial role in addressing sustainable development issues through education. These institutions serve as a vital platform for exploring, testing, developing, and communicating the necessary conditions for long-term growth. At university, students are exposed to social changes and have the opportunity to engage in sustainable development efforts through various channels, including organizational, educational, curricular, and research avenues (Caeiro & Azeiteiro, 2020). Ultimately, education indirectly influences changes in students' behavior.

Thus, taking a proactive stance on sustainability can have a substantial impact on raising students' awareness, understanding, and skills in this vital field. By integrating sustainability into educational methods, schools can motivate students to become more involved and dedicated to global sustainability initiatives. This proactive approach fosters a sense of accountability and readies students to implement sustainable practices across different sectors, empowering them to tackle urgent global issues proficiently.

Table 4. Correlation analysis (Pearson r) examining the relationship between OSAS services, knowledge of SDGs, and behavior towards sustainable development goals.

Services and Program by OSAS	Knowledge of SDG Goals			Display Sustainable Behavior		
	r value	p-value	VI	r value	p-value	VI
	.597	.000	Significant	.590	.000	Significant

* p> 0 .05 not significant, p< 0 .05 significant

In Table 4, the correlations test between the services and programs provided by OSAS, knowledge of SDG Goals, and the sustainable behavior of the respondents is presented. The data shows a significant relationship between the services and programs offered by the Office of the Students' Affairs and the knowledge of the SDG goals, with an r-value of .597 and a p-value of .000. Additionally, a significant relationship is observed between the services and programs provided by OSAS and the respondents' display of sustainable behavior at the Laguna State Polytechnic University, San Pablo City Campus. The research hypothesis posited that a greater knowledge and awareness of the SDGs among students would lead to more sustainable behavior, and vice versa. Higher education institutions play a vital role in promoting the Sustainable Development Goals (SDG). Utilizing faculty members as experts in SDG and incorporating the goals into their teaching allows institutions to seamlessly integrate SDG principles into their curriculum. Supporting student clubs and organizations in participating in SDG-related events and collaborations further bolsters the advancement of these global objectives.

These findings align with previous research conducted by Barloa et al. (2016) on solid waste management, which found that respondents with higher knowledge scores were more likely to demonstrate good practices and behavior. Education for sustainability aims to reconsider and enhance educational programs aligned with the Sustainable Development Goals (SDGs) that are crucial for present and future communities (Joshi et al., 2017). Research has shown various gaps in understanding the impact of SDGs on learning concepts and educational practices, including discrepancies, methodological inconsistencies, and curriculum deficiencies (Kioupi & Voulvoulis, 2019). As a result, the implementation of SDGs is not progressing as rapidly as anticipated, indicating a general lack of knowledge about these goals (Zamora-Polo et al., 2019). Ang (2021) proposed that educational strategies can be applied across all levels of education, from preschool to university, to educate students on knowledge, sustainability principles, skills, perspectives, and values.

The findings indicated that the relationship between the services provided by the Office of Student Affairs and Services (OSAS), students' understanding of the Sustainable Development Goals (SDGs), and their actions towards these goals are complex and interconnected. OSAS offers essential support through a range of programs, such as educational workshops, leadership training, community involvement opportunities, and well-being initiatives. These resources are designed not only to improve students' academic and personal growth but also to act as a way to share information about the SDGs and their importance on a global scale. Through the utilization of these services, students enhance their comprehension of the Sustainable Development Goals (SDGs) and develop a heightened awareness of the complex global issues at play, such as climate change, inequality, and responsible consumption. This newfound knowledge shapes their attitudes and values, prompting them to embrace a more deliberate and proactive stance on sustainability. Additionally, the incorporation of SDG-related material into OSAS programs equips students with tangible illustrations and practical applications, underscoring the significance of sustainable development in both their academic endeavors and everyday experiences.

As students gain more knowledge and awareness, they are inclined to adopt more sustainable practices like engaging in environmental initiatives, promoting equity and inclusivity, and making mindful lifestyle decisions. This shift in behavior not only benefits the individual students but also has a significant impact on the institution as a whole. OSAS services are pivotal in integrating sustainability into the student experience, demonstrating the power of student affairs programming in cultivating meaningful involvement in sustainable development. Ultimately, this dynamic relationship highlights the potential for student affairs to shape a cohort of graduates who are equipped to contribute effectively to global sustainability efforts.

CONCLUSION

Universities worldwide are adapting their instructional mission and methods to integrate sustainability into the educational system. Zamora-Polo et al. (2019) emphasized the importance of considering various aspects of a university's activities, including governance, the university environment, and societal responsibility, when evaluating its overall impact. At Laguna State Polytechnic University, San Pablo City Campus, the Office of Student Affairs offers services and programs focused on sustainability, ensuring that students are well-informed about the Sustainable Development Goals and consistently demonstrate positive sustainability practices. These efforts across different university aspects have the potential to foster a more equitable society and instill sustainable knowledge and behavior in students within higher education institutions. However, further education and promotion are necessary to fully achieve these objectives.

Higher education institutions serve as crucial platforms for advancing the Sustainable Development Goals (SDG). By engaging faculty members as SDG experts and incorporating the goals into their teaching, institutions can effectively integrate SDG principles into their curriculum. Additionally, supporting student clubs and organizations in participating in SDG-related events and collaborations further enhances the promotion of these global objectives. This research can inform and guide the alignment of student affairs initiatives with institutional strategies and goals related to the SDGs, highlighting the importance of these goals in shaping the overall mission of higher education institutions. Future research could investigate the use of a larger and more diverse sample of participants, as well as the implementation of a mixed methods approach to determine if the qualitative feedback aligns with the quantitative data. In this, efforts may explore the effectiveness of different implementation strategies and analyze comparisons among institutions and regions to provide valuable insights into the incorporation of SDGs within higher education. Since this case study was conducted at a single campus, it is not representative of all students nationwide and cannot be generalized to the entire population. However, as it was conducted in a real-life setting, it is reasonable to draw pedagogical implications from these findings, as they offer insights into the characteristics of Student Affairs and Services Programs and SDG Sustainability Knowledge and Behavior in One State University.

DECLARATION OF CONFLICT

The authors declare that they have no known competing financial interests or personal relationships that could have appeared to influence the work reported in this paper.

ACKNOWLEDGMENT

The researchers would like to acknowledge the Laguna State Polytechnic University Academic Community for always inspiring us to be the agents of innovation, progress, and quality education.

REFERENCES

Aleixo, A., Azeiteiro, U., & Leal, S. (2016). *Toward sustainability through higher education: Sustainable Development Incorporation in Portuguese Higher Education Institutions.* In Challenges in Higher Education for Sustainability (pp. 159-187). Springer. DOI: 10.1007/978-3-319-23705-3_7

Anderson, K., Ryan, B., Sonntag, W., Kavvada, A., & Friedl, L. (2017). Earth observation in service of the 2030 Agenda for Sustainable Development. *Geo-Spatial Information Science*, 20(2), 77–96. DOI: 10.1080/10095020.2017.1333230

Ang, S. M. (2021). Awareness on sustainable development goals among university students in Malaysia. *Asian Journal of Research in Education and Social Sciences*, 3(1), 105–116.

Blasco, N., Brusca, I., & Labrador, M. (2020). Drivers for universities' contribution to the sustainable development goals: An analysis of Spanish public universities. *Sustainability (Basel)*, 13(1), 1–19. DOI: 10.3390/su13010089

Caeiro, S., & Azeiteiro, U. M. (2020). Sustainability Assessment in Higher Education Institutions. *Sustainability (Basel)*, 12(8), 10–13. DOI: 10.3390/su12083433

Chankseliani, M., & McCowan, T. (2021). Higher education and the sustainable development goals. *Higher Education*, 81(1), 1–8. DOI: 10.1007/s10734-020-00652-w PMID: 33173242

Ciobanu, A. (2013). *The role of student services in the improving of student experience in higher education.* Lumen Research Center in Social and Humanistic Sciences, Asociatia Lumen. DOI: 10.1016/j.sbspro.2013.08.654

Dagdag, J., Cuizon, H., & Bete, A. (2019). College students' problems and their link to academic performance: Basis for needs-driven student programs. *Journal of Research, Policy & Practice of Teachers &. Teaching Education*. Advance online publication. DOI: 10.37134/jrpptte.vol9.no2.5.201

Edwards, D. B., Sustarsic, M., Chiba, M., McCormick, M., Goo, M., & Perriton, S. (2014). Achieving and Monitoring Education for Sustainable Development and Global Citizenship: A Systematic Review of the Literature. *Sustainability 2020, 12, 1383. S. Awareness of School Students about Sustainable Development in Education. PolySciTech*, 2014(1), 112–116.

Eizaguirre, A., García-Feijoo, M., & Laka, J. P. (2019). Defining Sustainability Core Competencies in Business and Management Studies Based on Multinational Stakeholders' Perceptions. *Sustainability (Switzerland), 11(8)*.

Fiselier, E. S., Longhurst, J. W. S., & Gough, G. K. (2018). Exploring the current position of ESD in UK higher education institutions. *International Journal of Sustainability in Higher Education*, 19(2), 393–412. DOI: 10.1108/IJSHE-06-2017-0084

Frandoloso, M. A., & Gasparetto Rebelatto, B. (2019). The participatory process of planning social and environmental responsibility at a Brazilian university. *International Journal of Sustainability in Higher Education*, 20(5), 917–931. DOI: 10.1108/IJSHE-01-2019-0017

Hajer, M., Nilsson, M., Raworth, K., Bakker, P., Berkhout, F., de Boer, Y., Rockström, J., Ludwig, K., & Kok, M. (2015). Beyond Cockpit-ism: Four Insights to Enhance the Transformative Potential of the Sustainable Development Goals. *Sustainability (Basel)*, 7(2), 1651–1660. DOI: 10.3390/su7021651

Han, Q. (2015). Education for sustainable development and climate change education in China: A status report. [The SPSSAU Project. SPSSA.]. *Journal of Education for Sustainable Development*, 2015(9), 62–77. DOI: 10.1177/0973408215569114

Ibarrientos, J. R. (2015). Implementation and Effectiveness of Student Affairs Services Program in One Polytechnic College. *Asia Pacific Journal of Multidisciplinary Research*, 3(5), 144–156.

Joshi, Y., & Rahman, Z. (2017). Investigating the Determinants of Consumers' Sustainable Purchase Behaviour. *Sustainable Production and Consumption*, 10, 110–120. DOI: 10.1016/j.spc.2017.02.002

Kestin, T., den Belt, M., Denby, L., Ross, K., Thwaitea, J., & Hawkes, M. (2017). *Getting started with the SDGs in universities: A Guide for universities, higher education institutions, and the academic sector.* Sustainable Development Solutions Network.

Kioupi, V., & Voulvoulis, N. (2019). *Education for Sustainable Development: A Systemic Framework for Connecting the SDGs to Educational Outcomes.* Sustainable Education and Approaches., DOI: 10.3390/su11216104

Kräusche, K., & Pilz, S. (2018). Integrated sustainability reporting at HNE Eberswalde–a practice report. *International Journal of Sustainability in Higher Education*, 19(2), 291–312. DOI: 10.1108/IJSHE-07-2016-0145

Leicht, A., Heiss, J., & Byun, W. (Eds.). (2018). Issues and trends in education for sustainable development. *UNESCO Publishing*.https://unesdoc.unesco.org/ark:/48223/pf0000261445

Lozano, R., Ceulemans, K., Alonso-Almeida, M., Huisingh, D., Lozano, F. J., Waas, T., Lambrechts, W., Lukman, R., & Hugé, J. (2015). A review of commitment and implementation of sustainable development in higher education: Results from a worldwide survey. *Journal of Cleaner Production*, 108, 1–18. DOI: 10.1016/j.jclepro.2014.09.048

Mallow, S., Toman, I., & Van't Land, H. (2020). Higher Education and the 2030 Agenda: Moving into the 'Decade of Action and Delivery for the SDGs'. *IAU 2nd Global Survey Report on Higher Education and Research for Sustainable Development*.

Manolas, F. Alves, U. Azeiteiro, J. Rogers, C. Shiel, & A. Do Paco (Eds.), Universities as Living Labs for Sustainable Development: Supporting the Implementation of the Sustainable Development Goals (pp. 11–27). Springer International Publishing.

Memorandum Order No, CHED. 09, s. 2013.

Mohd Nizar, N., Ab Mutalib, N. H., & Taha, H. (2019). The Status of Knowledge, Attitude, And Behaviour of Postgraduate Students towards Education for Sustainable Development (ESD). *Jurnal Pendidikan Sains dan Matematik Malaysia, 9(2)*, 35–41. *https://doi.org/*DOI: 10.37134/jpsmm.vol9.2.5.2019

Montenegro de Lima, C. R., Coelho Soares, T., Andrade de Lima, M., Oliveira Veras, M., & Andrade Guerra, J. B. S. O. D. A. (2020). Sustainability funding in higher education: A literature-based review. *International Journal of Sustainability in Higher Education*, 21(3), 441–464. DOI: 10.1108/IJSHE-07-2019-0229

Olawumi, T. O., & Chan, D. W. (2018). A scientometric review of global research on sustainability and sustainable development. *Journal of Cleaner Production*, 183, 231–250. DOI: 10.1016/j.jclepro.2018.02.162

Ouellette, A. M., & Wanger, S. P. (2022). Emerging International Issues in Student Affairs Research and Practice. *International Perspectives on Educational Policy, Research and Practice. Library of Congress Cataloging-in-Publication*.http://loc.gov

Paletta, A., & Bonoli, A. (2019). Governing the university in the perspective of the United Nations 2030 Agenda: The case of the University of Bologna. *International Journal of Sustainability in Higher Education*, 20(3), 500–514. DOI: 10.1108/IJSHE-02-2019-0083

Parr, A. (2022). *Knowledge-driven actions: transforming higher education for global sustainability*. UNESCO.

Patton, L. D., Renn, K. A., Guido, F. M., & Quaye, S. J. (2016). *Student development in college: Theory, research, and practice* (3rd ed.). John Wiley & Sons., https://books.google.com.ph/books

Purcell, W. M., Henriksen, H., & Spengler, J. D. (2019). Universities as the engine of transformational sustainability toward delivering the sustainable development goals: "Living labs" for sustainability. *International Journal of Sustainability in Higher Education*, 20(8), 1343–1357. DOI: 10.1108/IJSHE-02-2019-0103

Robertson-Kraft, C., & Duckworth, A. (2020). *Positive psychology: character, grit and research methods*. University of Pennsylvania.

Saputra, J., & Prabowo, A. (2021). The Role of the School in Developing Student Development Tasks. *International Journal of Ethno Sciences and Education Research*, 1(4), 84–87. Advance online publication. DOI: 10.46336/ijeer.v1i4.244

Shiel, C., Smith, N., & Cantarello, E. (2020). *Aligning campus strategy with the SDGs: An institutional case study*. In W. Leal Filho, A. L. Salvia, R. W. Pretorius, L. L. Brandli, E. DOI: 10.1007/978-3-030-15604-6_2

Sison, M. (2019). Evaluation of Student Affairs and Services Programs: A Tool for Quality Improvement. *International Journal of Education and Research*.

Soini, K., Jurgilevich, A., Pietikäinen, J., & Korhonen-Kurki, K. (2018). Universities responding to the call for sustainability: A typology of sustainability centres. *Journal of Cleaner Production*, 170, 1423–1432. DOI: 10.1016/j.jclepro.2017.08.228

Sultana, S. A., Rahman, M. T. M., Indhumathi, M., Keerthana, J., Kannadasan, & Nair, D. P. 2021. Student Welfare Services in Higher Educational Institution Hei in Puducherry:Study, A. (●●●).. . *Global Journal for Research Analysis*, 10(05). Advance online publication. DOI: 10.36106/gjra/0609142

Twum-Ampofo, E. &O sei-Owusu, B. Students' academic performance as mediated by students' academic ambition and effort in the public senior high schools in Ashanti Mampong Municipality of Ghana. *Selected Topics in Humanities and Social Sciences*. DOI: 10.9734/bpi/sthss/v7/13406D

United Nations. (2015). *Transforming our world: The 2030 agenda for sustainable development (Report)*. United Nations. https://undocs.org/A/RES/70/1

Yuan, X., Yu, L., Wu, H., (2021). Awareness of Sustainable Development Goals among Students from a Chinese Senior High School. Educ. Sci. 11, 458. *Special Issue Including Sustainable Development Goals (SDGs) Transversally in Education* DOI: 10.3390/educsci11090458

Zamora-Polo, F., Sanchez-martin, J., Corrales-Serrano, M., & Espejo-Antunez, L. (2019). What Do University Students Now About Sustainable Development Goals? A Realistic Approach to the Reception of this UN Program amongst the Youth Population. *Sustainability (Basel)*, 11(13), 3533–3552. DOI: 10.3390/su11133533

Chapter 5
Circular Economy in Tourism Industry:
A Sustainable Approach

Vandana Sharma
https://orcid.org/0009-0000-8686-806X
DCRUST Murthal, India

Chinu Bumra
DCRUST Murthal, India

Vidhu Vats
DCRUST Murthal, India

ABSTRACT

The linear economy of today does not maximize resources or encourage their recycling, reuse, or healing. Therefore, enhancement of interest can be seen in the idea of the Circular Economy (CE) and between the relationship of global stakeholders and policymakers. Accepting a circular economy approach offerings an opportunity for tourism businesses to enhance their innovation and achieve resource efficiency through a system extensive approach. The existing article deals with the transition to a new economic model i.e., the circular economy, a more suited model for the current tendencies that confirm to the sustainable economic process. Given the planet's finite, but particularly non-regenerative, resources, there is currently rising worry about the detrimental effects of human activity on the ecosystem. Consequently, sustainable development turns into a style of rational and doing for the populace and the commercial environment, and in this regard, clearly defined guidelines and measures intended to guarantee environmental preservation are required.

DOI: 10.4018/979-8-3693-8242-4.ch005

1. INTRODUCTION

Tourism has both good and bad consequences. It has a substantial impact on service and GDP in numbers of nations and areas. Tourism contributes 10% of global GDP, one in every ten jobs, and 7% of global exports (UNWTO, 2018). But it has a variety of severe environmental consequences and places a strain on local resources as a result of resource use and trash generation. In fact, global tourist consumption has grown to the point of unsustainable and contributing to global climate change (Manniche et al., 2021). Tourism is expected to account for 8% of world CO2 emissions and will continue to rise (Lenzen et al., 2018). There has been widespread criticism of the immense CO2 emissions and that's the reason of rising population. According to the United Nations World Tourism Organization and United Nations Environmental Programme (2012), tourism results in over 35 million tons of solid waste annually, increases the use of water and land, emits greenhouse gases, diverts animals, and reduces biodiversity (Gossling, 2002; Hall, 2010). According to the most current data, the hotels generate 289,000 tons of solid waste per year, of which 79.000 tons is related to food waste and accounting for 9% of the total waste produced. Waste of food in the hospitality industry accounts for half a billion tons (or $376 billion) of the waste produced in the United States of America by hotels, restaurants, and supermarkets. More than $35 billion year on catering and banquets that is actually spend by hotel industry which results in solid waste like rinds and trimmings, among other leftovers (Mettler et al., 2023). According to the 2021, Food Waste Index Report, India creates around 68.7 million tons of food waste per year, with the food service industry accounting for 11.9 million tons. Since tourism is one of the main drivers of economic growth, it is anticipated that all these negative environmental effects will get worse in the future (United Nations World Tourism Organization, 2020). According to United Nations Tourism Organization (2023) it is also anticipated that tourism will return to pre-pandemic level 2024. One important measure of environmental health in the sustainability of tourism is waste production and responsible management. The involved management and the produced waste are main indicator of environmental well-being in tourism's sustainability (Global Sustainable Tourism Council, 2012).

According to the United Nations World Tourism Organization and United Nations Environmental the litter generated by hospitality and tourism globally contains of this table:

Table 1. Waste Generation Patterns for Hotels and Hospitality Sectors

Waste materials	Percentages
organic waste	37-72%
Paper and cardboard	6-40%
Plastic	5-15%
Glass	3-14%

Sources: Pirani & Arafat, 2014

According to Gaffar et al., (2021) the requirement of the people to balance nature and sustainability of the environment force companies to change their business model towards a friendlier and comfortable environment. This is in harmony with one of the Sustainable Development Goals (SDGs) goals, which is to make a more sustainable better and advance future for all (Gaffar et al., 2021). The circular economy is a novel idea that may be able to solve the issue. It is a restorative industrial system by intention and design (MacArthur, 2012). Circular Economy is an economic system that reflects a paradigm shift in how humans interact with nature and all (Sandoval et al., 2018). According to Sorin and Sirajavah (2021), CE is a system-level economic model that aims to regenerate both natural and social capital while functioning within global boundaries. In other words, CE strives to modify the way resources are used by reusing them and keeping them in a cycle of production and consumption. The circular economy holds significant importance in the global tourism industry, promoting both environmental and economic sustainability. In tourism, the circular economy framework seeks to reduce waste, boost resource efficiency, and maximize the lifecycle of products and services (García & Tugores, 2021). Traditional tourism models often lead to high levels of waste, pollution, and resource depletion. However, by adopting circular practices such as recycling, reusing materials, and implementing renewable energy, the industry can lower its ecological footprint, helping preserve natural resources essential to tourism, like clean beaches, forests, and water bodies (World Tourism Organization, 2018). Moreover, economic benefits arise as businesses cut costs by reducing raw material consumption and waste disposal needs. This model can also create job opportunities through recycling and upcycling efforts, which helps diversify local economies (Daly & Farley, 2019). The shift toward a circular economy aligns with the broader goals of sustainable development by fostering more resilient tourism destinations that prioritize long-term viability over short-term gains, thereby addressing the climate crisis while meeting consumer demand for eco-friendly travel options (Lew et al., 2020). The concept of the circular economy (CE) originates from ecological economics and systems thinking, which emphasize sustainable resource use and the need to shift away from linear economic models (Geissdoerfer et al., 2017).

Empirical studies showcase various applications of CE in tourism, including waste reduction initiatives, renewable energy usage, and resource efficiency improvements in areas like hospitality and transport (García & Tugores, 2021). These efforts highlight the potential for CE principles to drive sustainable innovation within tourism. Nonetheless, implementing circular practices in the sector faces several challenges, including the complexity of engaging multiple stakeholders with different interests, limited regulatory support, and the difficulty of integrating CE models into traditional, linear business structures (Ellen MacArthur Foundation, 2019). Addressing these gaps requires a comprehensive understanding of the barriers to CE adoption in tourism, offering insights valuable for researchers and policymakers. These insights can support strategies that foster collaboration across the public and private sectors and encourage regulatory reforms that facilitate circular practices, ultimately advancing sustainability in global tourism (Lew et al., 2020). Hence the study aims to answer the following research questions:

RQ1. How can the principles of the circular economy be effectively integrated into the tourism industry to promote sustainability and resilience?

RQ2. This study seeks to fill the existing gaps in knowledge, highlight best practices, and propose actionable strategies for implementation.

2. THEORETICAL BACKGROUND AND HYPOTHESES DEVELOPMENT

The CE idea advocates for a closed-loop economy that prioritizes sustainability and eliminates waste, as opposed to the linear economy (MacArthur, 2012). CE is founded on the balancing principle, which requires accounting for all material flows. However, economic values rather than physical flows are used to direct management (Andersen, 2007). CE aims to balance environmental protection and economic growth by analyzing different levels and lifecycle stages. CE refers to the whole environmental effect of an economic sector or process, including manufacturing, transportation, design, distribution, recycling, and consumption. According to Ellen Macarthur foundation, in a "circular economy, resources never go to waste and the environment is replenished. Products and resources are kept in circulation in a circular economy through recycling, composting, refurbishing, reusing, and maintaining. By severing the link between economic activity and the use of limited resources, the circular economy addresses issues such as pollution, waste, and biodiversity loss in addition to climate change". According to Rheeder, (2012) the circular economy refers to a restorative system, substituting restoration for the phrase "end of life cycle." The path involves employing sustainable energy, getting rid of harmful substances, cutting down on waste, and improving the design of goods, systems, materials, and, indirectly, business models. Circular economy is a substitute to the conventional linear economy of "make, use, dispose," where sources are used providing possible, maximum value is take out during use, and products and materials are improved and regenerate at the end of their useful lives. The concept of a circular economy has its roots in various schools of thought rather than a single date or source. Many academics believed that the environmental economists Pearce and Turner, based their theoretical framework on past research by the ecological economist Kenneth Boulding, were majorly responsible for the introduction of the CE system (Anderson, 2007; Murray et al., 2017; Su et al., 2013). This model is the antithesis of the linear economy in that nothing is wasted (Aestimum, 2017). An economy that maximizes value from its resources through efficient use is known as a circular economy. By slowing, and narrowing materials, CE could lower down resource input and scrap, emissions, and energy leakage (Geissdoerfer et al., 2018). The hotel sector is one of industry where CE principles can be applied.

Amsterdam faces significant over-tourism challenges, with a steadily growing annual visitor population, pushing the city to explore sustainable solutions. Since 2015, Amsterdam has pioneered initiatives to examine the benefits of a circular economy, especially given the environmental pressures from its tourism sector, which operates largely on a linear economic model (Boronnia, 2021). Globally, urban areas grapple with resource depletion, climate change, and increased waste production, using 60-80% of all natural resources and generating over 75% of greenhouse gas emissions (Atanasova et al., 2021; Williams, 2019). Projections suggest that by 2050, 68% of the global population will reside in cities, emphasizing the urgent need for sustainable urban solutions (UN, 2018). While circular economy principles are acknowledged, practical applications in tourism are limited, primarily addressing waste and pollution reduction and despite greater knowledge of sustainability concerns through laws, scientific publications, and public conversations, many consumers remain unaware of the CE principles. Many CE concepts neglect the social dimension, including customers, which may contribute to this lack of understanding (Geissdoerfer et al., 2017).

Recent research suggests more efforts are required to foster visitor awareness, contributing to a more sustainable tourism model (Kaszás et al., 2022; Bosone & Nocca, 2022). Museums in Amsterdam are innovating to reduce environmental impacts by collaborating with energy and sustainability experts, thus preserving artifacts and promoting sustainability through educational outreach (Paehlke, 1999; Worts, 2006). Implementing circularity in museums within Amsterdam encounters financial, policy, technical, and awareness barriers. For example, the high costs and lack of market demand for secondary materials hinder circular initiatives, while policy challenges such as inadequate legislation and fragmented administration further complicate implementation (Kampasakali et al., 2021). Key enablers include financial support for innovation, public procurement with circular criteria, and promoting stakeholder education. Networking with other cities and continuous assessment of circular initiatives are also vital in overcoming these barriers (Campbell-Johnston et al., 2019; Montenegro Navarro & Jonker, 2018).

3. THE PRESENT RESEARCH

The tourism and other like hospitality sectors, of which the hotel industry is a part, are known to contribute significantly to the economy. It directly affects the environment and the usage of natural resources. The hotel industry is compelled by this phenomenon to manage its operations sustainably, which includes minimizing the negative impact and reducing the energy use and managing waste (Gaffar et al., 2021). The tourism industry is largely characterized by linear consumption patterns, which contribute significantly to environmental degradation and resource depletion. Although there is an increasing interest in adopting circular economy (CE) principles to address these issues, evidence of CE's effectiveness in tourism remains inconsistent (Garcia & Tugores, 2021). Gaps in theoretical foundations, inconclusive empirical findings, and limited understanding of the localized context challenge the widespread implementation of CE practices in tourism (Geissdoerfer et al., 2017). This study aims to address these barriers by providing a nuanced examination of CE's role in tourism and outlining a roadmap for future research and application. To inform the study, several theories related to sustainability and resource management are critical, including systems theory, ecological modernization, and the triple bottom line. Systems theory serves as the primary theoretical framework, offering a holistic perspective on how interconnected elements within the tourism ecosystem-including businesses, communities, and natural resources-can be aligned to promote CE practices (Meadows, 2008). By viewing the tourism sector as an interdependent network, systems theory emphasizes the relationships among stakeholders and highlights how collaborative efforts can foster sustainable resource use (Sterman, 2000). The ecological modernization theory, which posits that economic growth and environmental sustainability can coexist through technological and regulatory advancements, supports the alignment of CE strategies with modern tourism (Mol & Spaargaren, 2000). Additionally, the triple bottom line approach, focusing on economic, environmental, and social pillars of sustainability, underpins the conceptual framework by demonstrating how CE can benefit each of these aspects (Elkington, 1998).

In this context, "circular economy" refers to an economic model that prioritizes sustainable resource management, emphasizing the reduction, recycling and reuse, of materials to create closed-loop systems that minimize waste and pollution (Ellen

MacArthur Foundation, 2019). The origins of CE are rooted in ecological economics and systems thinking, dating back to the 1960s and 1970s, which focused on sustainable resource use and minimized environmental impacts (Boulding, 1966).

A comprehensive review of empirical literature reveals diverse applications of CE principles across the tourism industry. Some studies highlight successful CE strategies, such as implementing waste reduction programs, utilizing renewable energy sources, and promoting eco-friendly products and services, all of which can enhance resource efficiency and improve visitor experiences (Lew et al., 2020). Evidence suggests that such strategies can reduce resource consumption, improve economic performance, and promote sustainable tourism development (García & Tugores, 2021). Implementing circular economy principles in the tourism industry can significantly reduce environmental impacts while promoting sustainable practices. One primary approach is to minimize waste by transitioning from single-use products to reusable or compostable alternatives in accommodations, restaurants, and tourist facilities. For instance, hotels can replace plastic toiletries with refillable dispensers and encourage guests to reduce water and energy usage (Gossling & Peeters, 2015). Another critical area is resource efficiency; eco-friendly tourism operators can invest in renewable energy sources and water-saving technologies to minimize their environmental footprint (Garcia-Navarro et al., 2020). Additionally, destinations can foster a "closed-loop" approach by recycling waste within the community, composting organic materials, and reusing treated water for irrigation purposes (Ellen MacArthur Foundation, 2013). This closed-loop system not only reduces waste but also inspires local economies by creating jobs in recycling and waste management sectors (Scheyvens, 2020). Finally, circular economy principles encourage collaboration among stakeholders, such as local governments, businesses, and tourists, to develop guidelines that support sustainable practices across the tourism sector (UNWTO, 2018). By embedding these principles, the tourism industry can achieve sustainable growth that benefits both the environment and local communities.

However, much of the literature remains focused on theoretical frameworks rather than practical applications, revealing a gap in actionable insights for industry stakeholders. Moreover, many studies lack a focus on the unique challenges faced by different regions and types of tourism businesses, such as small-scale versus large-scale tourism operators and differences in regulatory support across countries (Manniche et al., 2017) and many existing studies focus on theoretical frameworks rather than practical applications, revealing a significant gap in actionable insights for industry stakeholders. Furthermore, the literature often lacks a focus on the unique challenges faced by different regions and types of tourism businesses. Focusing on all the limitations this study develops a conceptual framework based on system theory. The conceptual framework integrates multiple dimensions of the circular economy within the tourism context, focusing on economic, environmental, and social factors. By illustrating how these components intersect, the framework provides a foundation for analyzing case studies and making recommendations for practitioners and policymakers. This approach is informed by systems theory, which emphasizes the interconnectedness of various tourism ecosystem elements, demonstrating how they can collectively contribute to a sustainable tourism model (Sterman, 2000). The framework underscores the importance of stakeholder collaboration and the need for flexible regulatory frameworks that accommodate regional differences, ultimately advancing CE implementation in the tourism sector.

By developing new business models, CE implementation seeks to improve economic growth and lessen its negative effects on the environment (Kalmykovaet al., 2018). Additionally, it aims to address environmental problems (Sauve et al., 2016). System theory in the context of circular economy helps in conceptualizing tourism as an interconnected system where resources, processes, and outcomes influence each other. It provides a structured approach to understanding how different factors within the circular economy model interact to affect visitor satisfaction and, ultimately, influence the likelihood of tourists revisiting a destination. System theory emphasizes the feedback loops, interdependence, and adaptability within the circular economy, facilitating a dynamic model where sustainability practices directly contribute to satisfaction levels by enhancing the quality and authenticity of the tourist experience (Murray et al., 2017).

In this framework, the circular economy emotions operate as an independent variable, encompassing practices like waste reduction, resource efficiency, and sustainable resource management. These practices create value for tourists by aligning with their environmental values and expectations, thus enhancing their satisfaction (Geissdoerfer et al., 2017). Satisfaction then acts as a mediating variable, translating the positive impact of sustainable practices into favorable tourist experiences, which strengthens their intention to revisit. Studies show that tourists are more likely to return to destinations where they perceive a commitment to sustainable practices, as it enriches their experience and aligns with their environmental consciousness (Tse & Tse, 2019).

Thus, system theory helps by framing the circular economy model as an integrated approach where sustainable practices (independent variable) drive visitor satisfaction (mediating variable) and encourage tourists' likelihood of revisiting (dependent variable), contributing to a sustainable tourism industry (Esposito et al., 2020). On the basis of above literature two hypothesis was proposed

H1: Circular economy emotions lead to satisfaction and revisit of tourists.

H2: Satisfaction of the tourists is positively related to revisit, thus mediates between circular economy emotions and revisit of employees

4. RESEARCH DESIGN

4.1. Samples, Research Tools and Methodology

Systematic sampling and stratified sampling are used to ensure the samples are representative. 130 tourists from Delhi-NCR were taken and questionnaire were sent to them, 100 were recovered. In this study, three variables are used for circular economy emotions which contains 15 items from Hosany and Gilbert's (2010) was adopted, tourist's satisfaction was measured by Cong (2016) 2 item scale and tourist revisit was measured by Sato et al., (2018) 6 items scale.

Figure 1. Research Model

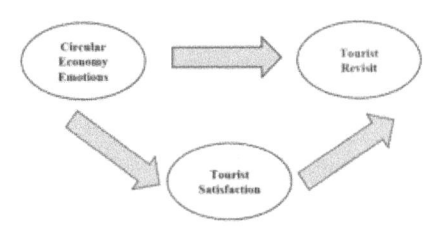

Figure 1. Research Model

4.2. Statistical and Data Analysis

In this study, SPSS 22.0 are used to analysis of the data. The methods of statistical analysis mainly include descriptive statistics, correlation analysis and regression analysis.

4.3. Descriptive Statistics

We use SPASS 22.0 to do the descriptive statistics analysis. From Table 2 we can see that the mean value and the standard deviation of all three variables.

Table 2. Descriptive Statistics Analysis

Variables	Mean	Std. Deviation
Circular Economy Emotions	59.11	11.27
Tourist Satisfaction	6.26	1.44
Tourist Revisit	20.95	4.08

4.4. Correlation Analysis

For correlation analysis, we use SPASS 22.0. coefficient of each variable is shown in Table 3. From Table 3 we can see that the correlation coefficient between circular economy emotions and tourist satisfaction reached a significant level of $P < 0.01$, in addition, each of circular economy emotions and tourist satisfaction reached a significant level of $P < 0.01$ with tourist revisit respectively. Furthermore, the correlation coefficients are between 0.692 and 0.721, all are significantly positive correlation.

Table 3. Correlation Analysis

Variables	Circular Economy Emotions	Tourist Satisfaction	Tourist Revisit
Circular Economy Emotions		0.721**	0.709
Tourist Satisfaction	0.721**		0.692**
Tourist Revisit	0.709**	0.692**	

**Correlation is significant at the 0.01 level (2-tailed)

4.5. Regression Analysis

From Table 4 we can see that in M1, circular economy emotions have a significant impact on tourist satisfaction in the significant level of 0.001, so as to verify the hypothesis 1. In M2, we explored the role of tourist satisfaction on tourist revisit, and the regression equation was significant. In M3, the circular economy emotions have a positive effect on tourist revisit at the significance level of 0.001 and the regression equation was significant, So the tourist satisfaction played a mediating role in the relationship between circular economy emotions and tourist revisit

Table 4. Regression Analysis

Dependent Variables	Tourist Satisfaction	Tourist Revisit	
Independent Variables	M1	M2	M3
Circular Economy Emotions	0.092***		5.76***
Tourist Satisfaction		1.96***	
Change in R^2	0.519	0.479	0.502
Adjusted R^2	0.514	0.473	0.497

***Regression is significant at the 0.001 level (2-tailed)

4.6. Mediation Analysis

Table 5. Mediation Analysis

Path	Effect	SE	95% CI (LL)	95% CI (UL)
X → Y (total)	0.257	0.027	0.204	0.310
X → Y (direct)	0.158	0.036	0.086	0.230
Indirect Effect (X → M → Y)	0.099	0.038	0.034	0.185
Standardized Indirect Effect (X → M → Y)	0.272	0.101	0.095	0.487

The mediation study was performed to look into the linkages between the independent variable (X: circular economy emotions), the mediator (M: tourist satisfaction), and the dependent variable (Y: tourist revisit). The results show that X substantially predicts M (β=0.092, p<0.001), which predicts Y (β=1.072, p<0.001). X has a considerable influence on Y (β=0.257, p<0.001), with a direct effect of β=0.158 and an indirect effect via M of β=0.099. The confidence intervals for these effects exclude 0, demonstrating mediation. The standardized indirect effect is β=0.272, suggesting a significant mediation effect. The interaction term (X by M) was not significant (p=0.783), indicating that this model lacks moderation. Overall, the study provides significant evidence for the mediator impact of visitor satisfaction in the link between circular economy emotions and tourist revisit.

5. CONCLUSIONS AND DISCUSSIONS

The study highlights the importance of circular economy emotions in influencing tourist satisfaction, which, in turn, impacts tourists' intentions to revisit. Circular economy emotions, reflecting tourists' emotional responses to sustainable practices, create a foundation for satisfaction with environmentally responsible destinations. When tourists perceive that a destination upholds circular economy principles, they are more likely to experience positive emotions, such as pride or fulfillment, that enhance their satisfaction. This satisfaction acts as a mediating factor, directly linking circular economy emotions to revisit intentions. Thus, when tourism businesses prioritize circular economy strategies, they not only foster sustainable practices but also cultivate emotional satisfaction that encourages tourists to return, creating a sustainable tourism model (Gossling & Higham, 2020; Kozak & Rimmington, 2000). Future research should continue exploring the nuanced emotional responses within circular economy frameworks to better understand how these elements affect tourist behaviour and sustainability in the tourism industry. Over the last ten years, academics, businesses, and government have conducted extensive study on the concepts of the CE. Circular economy is gaining popularity as a way to minimize emissions and raw material consumption, develop new market possibilities, and, most significantly, make consumption more sustainable and resource efficient (Tunn et al., 2019, Shpak et al., 2020).

All things considered, the tourism sector is essential to job creation and economic expansion. But perhaps more significantly, it plays a critical role in sustainable resource management, which reduces, if not completely eliminates, waste generation and enhances environmental sustainability and protection. primarily characterized using a consumption and production model at the micro level. If when circular approaches are implemented, sustainability outcomes improve.

Jones and Wynn (2019) state that developing a CE strategy in the tourist industry is challenging and requires proper laws. Regulations and policies shape customers and supplier's environmental habits, impacting CE implementation (Sandoval et al., 2018). Furthermore, national tourist regulations should include directives for promoting CE in the tourism business. As a result, it would be beneficial to do research analyzing the government's position as a driver and implementor of CE in tourism from many viewpoints, as this function has been mostly disregarded. The findings align with Rodriguez et al., (2020) observations on the research of CE in tourism focuses on environmental and business management expertise. Further studies might discover the social impact of CE in tourism at various levels. Circular cultural tourism is becoming more popular at the destination level, but socio-cultural aspects are often overlooked (Iodice et al., 2020; Rudan et al., 2021). According to Einarsson and Sorin (2020), the shift to CE can lead to more prosperous and equitable societies. This is especially pertinent in the tourist industry, which focuses on people, communities, and their connections.

Therefore, it is crucial for all of us that the industry evolves toward a CE path in order to reduce its environmental footprint.

6. PRACTICAL IMPLICATIONS

Companies have an important part in CE as they create services and products. While the linear economic model prioritizes throughout improvement and cost efficiency, some organizations are adopting sustainability measures (Mac Arthur, 2012). Identifying reasons and arguments for firms to implement CE and circular technologies, including cleaner production and eco-design, is the problem, mostly influenced by public awareness and restrictions (Dangelico et al., 2010), product design can help facilitate this integration. CE standards emphasize the need of designing durable products and services for reuse, allowing for easy disassembly and recirculation. MacArthur's reasoning might encourage corporations to adopt circular goods (Mac Arthur, 2012). Several researches have proven that integrating environmentally sustainable solutions leads to a competitive advantage (Wong, 2012). Companies may see lowering environmental impact as a cost-effective chance to improve goods, processes, and operations (Porter and Linde, 1995). Consumers have a significant role in implementing CE principles by purchasing products and services and influencing governments (Juliao et al., 2019). Companies have the difficulty of adopting business strategies that leverage current resources instead of relying on new ones. (Juliao et al., 2019). Customers wants to purchase items created on the supposed value for money in comparison to its price value and quality ratio (Mandese, 1991). Criteria of quality can include non-economic factors such as the environment (Witjes and Lozano, 2016.

Now a days, green practices are becoming more popular in restaurants, just as they are in companies. Restaurants consume significant amounts of disposable items, water, and electricity. Improving environmental performance may benefit the business (Ravell and Blackburn, 2007). Restaurants rely heavily on their image and brand, making green practices vital for commercial success (Schubert et al., 2010). Research shows that these activities improve brand image, leading to economic sustainability and financial advantages for the local community (Schubert et al., 2010). As a result, green restaurant concept was developed, much like hotels. Focus on reducing and recycling, as well as energy and efficiency (Gilg et al., 2005). Restaurants use green measures such as energy and water-saving equipment, waste reduction and recycling, bans on disposable containers, use of locally-grown and organic materials, and employee training (Schubert et al., 2010). Green restaurant practices are applied strategically, addressing health, environmental, and social problems (Chao and Parsa, 2007). According to a 2011 National Restaurant Association survey, customers are more likely to patronize environmentally friendly restaurants. Green food and practices strongly affect patronage selections (Hu et al., 2010). Health-conscious consumers prioritize food-focused practices like organic or locally farmed foods (Hu et al., 2010). Administration-focused related practices, like green certifications and CSR, positively impact consumer decisions by reducing perceived uncertainty and dangers associated with food items (Juliao et al., 2019).

The tourist industry's expansion directly impacts usage of natural resource and the environment (Shan & Man, 2011). Hotel buildings are amongst the most energy-intensive building because of their multi-purpose uses and 24/7 operations (Huang et al., 2012). The hotel business is increasingly focusing on green practices (Han et al., 2010). Hotels are implementing environmental steps to reduce energy and water usage, as well as garbage generation (Rehman and Reynolds, 2016), this has run to the development of "green hotels". This market segment is gaining popularity among both major hotel brands and small and medium-sized companies (Rehman et al., 2015). Green management has been shown to enhance cost savings, staff loyalty, customer retention, and short- term operational objectives (Chen, 2008). As customers become more mindful of pollution and waste, they seek out hotels that prioritize green operations (Manaktola and Jauhari, 2007). Hotels are offering ecologically friendly products and services to attract more sophisticated customers (Dief and Font, 2010). Guests are increasingly prepared to pay more for ecologically friendly items and services (Kang et al., 2010), Green hotel clients are ready to sacrifice convenience and comfort, and some luxury standards for the process (Rehman and Reynolds, 2016). Consumer behaviour is favorably affecting the hotel industry's adoption of green initiatives. According to surveys, most hotels have moderate to extensive expertise with green practices and recognize the need of implementing them (Aomer and Hussain, 2017). The hotel business is increasingly adopting sustainable practices, as seen by the points presented above. However, existing research doesn't show if the hotel business is aware of CE procedures or applies its principles (Juliao et al., 2019).

6.1. A Sustainable Economic Model - Circular Economy

According to (United Nations, 2015) successful endeavor to lower the amount of fossil fuel and resources that each economic agent uses would not change the fact that these resources are finite; rather, it will merely postpone the inevitable, necessitating additional significant reforms. The term "circular economy" has gained increasing traction in this context in recent years.

It is based on three concepts (World Economic Forum, 2016):

Principle 1:

Preservation and to enhance the natural capital via management of inadequate resources and equilibrium of the flow of renewable resources (e.g., substituting renewable energy for fossil fuels or employing the extreme sustainable yield technique to preserve fish stocks).

Principle 2:

Maximizing resource efficiency by creating resources, components, and products that are always as useful as possible for both biological and technological cycles like sharing goods and also prolonging their use cycles).

Principle 3:

Involves enhancing the system's efficacy by the identification and design of negative externalities, like pollution of the water, soil, and noise, climate change, or health-related injury resulting from resource usage.

Now a days, the term "circular economy" has gained increasing traction in this context. It is better defined as a recreating economy, which distinguishes between technical and biological cycles and tries to retain resources components, and products at their highest level of usefulness. It is a continuous cycle of positive development that manages finished goods and renewable streams to demonstrate efficiency at all levels while protecting and also enhancing the natural capital, to optimize the resource efficiency, and also reduce system risks.

6.2. The Adoption of Circular Economy Principles in the Hotel Industry

There are six principles of circular economy which is very important for hotel industry and also explained in below:

Table 6. Hotel industry principles

1.	Cascade orientation
2.	Elimination of waste
3.	Optimization of Economy
4.	Retained value maximization
5.	Consciousness of environment
6.	Minimization of leakage

Source: Gaffer et al., 2021

Cascade orientation- Cascade orientation, which involves storing a product longer in circulation and transforming it into multiple different types of products, is the first CE principle. While some hotels are still in the initial stages, most hotels have already recycled some of their products, such as amenities (Gaffer et al.,2021).

Elimination of waste- The elimination of waste is the second principle. This principle highlights the need to cut waste at every stage of the product design process, from the beginning to the end. Except for the trash can, one hotel uses no plastic at all. They employ biodegradable plastic, despite the fact that it costs 25% more than regular plastic (Gaffer et al.,2021).

Optimization of Economy- The third principle concerns economic optimization, the realization of which will build a robust economy. Hotels are not confronted with challenges related with rising costs in this pandemic scenario. Certain hotels modified their pricing tactics by enhancing their menu offerings, while maintaining a focus on health precautions (Gaffer et al.,2021).

Retained value maximization- Hotels have implemented a regular treatment system that has grown to be the industry standard. This is required to keep the machinery in good working order and prevent breakage. To address this issue, certain hotels have a dedicated team and program (Gaffer et al.,2021).

Consciousness of environment- The awareness of the environment is the next principle. Some hotels are using sensors to reduce their electricity use. Many hotels have offered their guests tips on how to cut back on waste and conserve energy. But ultimately, it's up to the visitors. While some people are conscious of the harm done to the environment, others are still unaware of it. Some hotels are beginning to minimize the use of plastics, particularly those found in guest room like amenities plastic like amenities plastic toothbrush rods (Gaffer., 2021).

Minimization of leakage- The sixth and final principle is the minimization of leakage. This idea raises the concern of maximizing the amount of time that products can be used before they are lost. For example, how to guarantee pollutant-free rooms and that waste does not leak into clean streams (Gaffer et al.,20

Manniche et al. (2017) suggest a circular economy (CE) approach in tourism by dividing the value chain into pre-travel and destination supply phases, which applies well to hotel management. Each segment's unique challenges and resources should be addressed for effective CE integration. They also highlight the importance of distinguishing between "near future" and "not-so-near future" goals. According to Sorensen and Baerenholdt (2020), tourists, not just providers, play a key role in minimizing environmental impact, advocating for reduced reliance on recycling alone in favor of reducing and reusing resources (Stahel, 2013; Manniche et al., 2017)

6.3. How Hierarchy is Helpful in Circular Economy?

Figure 2. Waste hierarchy Source: Waste in Line (2006)

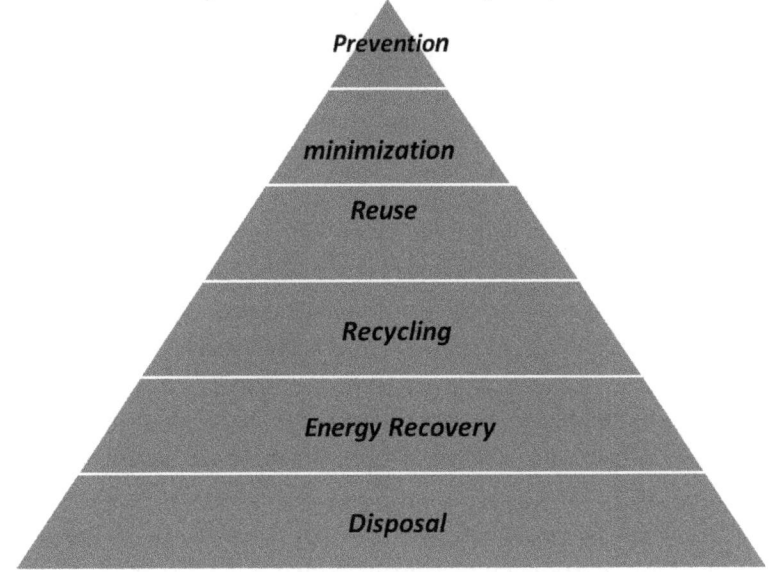

```
        Prevention
       minimization
          Reuse
        Recycling
      Energy Recovery
         Disposal
```

A variety of options are available to adjust various waste streams that is describe in below. This waste hierarchy introduced by this author Waste on Line (2006).

Waste prevention is the main process of getting rid of waste earlier it is produced.

- Minimization is the process of lessening waste generated all over a product's life cycle.
- The practice of reusing waste materials prevents them from entering the waste stream.
- Recovery is the process of improving some of the material's value via energy and recycling.
- At the last stage of the pyramid, disposal typically entails landfill and waste burning (Baker & Vandepeer, 2004).
- Composting, a crucial SWM choice for managing organic waste in a sustainable manner, was not covered by the waste hierarchy, though (Webster, 2000).

Acampora et al. (2020) outline 11 Rs as best practices for circular economy (CE) in tourism to promote sustainability. First,

- Refuse involves opting not to use or purchase certain products, particularly hazardous materials, and to limit overconsumption at the start of the life cycle (Potting et al., 2017).
- Re-sterilization emphasizes the shift towards digital and shared economies, integrating virtual tools and reducing emissions to support CE (Acampora et al., 2020).
- Reduce focuses on minimizing raw material use, waste, and resource consumption by enhancing efficiency through innovative packaging and resource-light products, positively impacting hotel economies (Manniche et al., 2017).
- Regenerate applies mostly to food waste, with natural and systematized composting methods to restore resources to the biosphere (Reike et al., 2017).
- Re-use is crucial economically, as it avoids resource-intensive production by reusing products multiple times, such as second-hand goods (Potting et al., 2017).
- Repair extends the lifecycle of products by making fixes either within hotels or through professional services, often with minimal energy costs (Reike et al., 2017).
- Refurbish is similar, involving partial repairs or aesthetic changes to extend usage at a lower cost than replacement (Reike et al., 2017).
- Remanufacture entails disassembly and reassembly to create a product that meets the original function, though some structure may change (Potting et al., 2017).
- Repurpose involves using products or their parts for entirely new purposes (Potting et al., 2017).
- Recycle, one of the most common CE practices, repurposes waste into new goods or resources without involving energy recovery (Manniche et al., 2017).
- Recover is a final option where energy or biomass is extracted from waste, the closest process to linear economics (Reike et al., 2017).

Travelers must be mindful of their environmental, sociocultural, and economic effects at all stages—from planning to sharing experiences (Nocca et al., 2023; Flognfeldt, 2005).

Bosone and Nocca (2022) identify three CE dimensions in tourism: environmental, economic, and socio-cultural. The environmental dimension urges tourists to reduce waste, emissions, and non-renewable resource use, focusing on pre-departure decisions such as selecting eco-friendly accommodations that actively convey sustainable practices (Pencarelli et al., 2011).

The economic dimension recommends tourists support local economies, such as purchasing locally made goods and crafts, which in turn preserves local culture and encourages sustainable economic practices. The socio-cultural dimension involves the cultural exchange and knowledge-sharing between tourists and locals, promoting the preservation of local heritage and fostering respect for natural and cultural assets (Bosone & Nocca, 2022).

Together, these practices emphasize the need for hoteliers and tourists to align with CE principles, which support sustainability across environmental, economic, and socio-cultural levels in tourism (Acampora et al., 2020).

7. LIMITATIONS AND FUTURE SUGGESTIONS OF THE STUDY

While this study demonstrates how emotion influences satisfaction and behavioural intentions, certain limitations must be acknowledged. Firstly, the use of stratified sampling and a relatively small sample size restricts the generalizability of the findings to broader contexts (Vatensever et al., 2021). To enhance the robustness of the model analyzed, it is essential to test it in various destinations and include a more diverse sample of tourists from different nationalities. Secondly, the chapter lacks a comprehensive examination of several relevant topics that could add to its depth. For instance, incorporating a section on how specific circular economy practices, like waste management or resource optimization, apply to sub-sectors (hotels, restaurants, tour operators) would enhance the scope. It would also be beneficial to include a segment on the challenges and barriers that tourism stakeholders face in implementing circular economy practices, as this could provide readers with a more realistic view of the industry's landscape.

Future research should prioritize longitudinal studies to evaluate the long-term impacts of circular economy initiatives in tourism. Looking ahead, integrating circular economy principles into tourism offers significant potential for fostering innovation and sustainability. Given that the circular economy (CE) is a relatively novel concept in the Turkish tourism sector, identifying industry experts with adequate knowledge of CE proved challenging. Consequently, our study was conducted with only four industry experts. As awareness and understanding of CE continue to grow within the tourism industry, future studies will benefit from collaboration with a larger pool of experts, thereby increasing the accuracy and reliability of findings (Vatensever et al., 2021).

REFERENCES

Acampora, A., Preziosi, M., & Merli, R. (2020). Framing the tourism industry into circular economy practices. In *Proceedings of the 26th Annual Conference of the International Sustainable Development Research Society* (pp. 15-17).

Al-Aomar, R., & Hussain, M. (2017). An assessment of green practices in a hotel supply chain: A study of UAE hotels. *Journal of Hospitality and Tourism Management*, 32, 71–81. DOI: 10.1016/j.jhtm.2017.04.002

Andersen, M. S. (2007). An introductory note on the environmental economics of the circular economy. *Sustainability Science*, 2(1), 133–140. DOI: 10.1007/s11625-006-0013-6

Atanasova, N., Castellar, J. A., Pineda-Martos, R., Nika, C. E., Katsou, E., Istenic, D., Pucher, B., Andreucci, M. B., & Langergraber, G. (2021). Nature-based solutions and circularity in cities. *Circular Economy and Sustainability*, 1(1), 319–332. DOI: 10.1007/s43615-021-00024-1

Bacova, M., Bohme, K., Guitton, M., Herwijnen, M. V., Kállay, T., Koutsomarkou, J., & Rok, A. (2016). *Pathways to a circular economy in cities and regions*. Interreg Europe Joint Secretariat.

Baker, S., & Vandepeer, B. (2004). *Deployed force waste management report* (1st ed.). DSTO Systems Sciences Laboratory.

Bosone, M., & Nocca, F. (2022). Human Circular Tourism as the tourism of tomorrow: The role of travelers in achieving a more sustainable and circular tourism. *Sustainability (Basel)*, 14(19), 12218. DOI: 10.3390/su141912218

Boulding, K. E. (1966). The economics of the coming spaceship Earth. In Jarrett, H. (Ed.), *Environmental quality in a growing economy* (pp. 3–14). Johns Hopkins University Press.

Campbell-Johnston, K., ten Cate, J., Elfering-Petrovic, M., & Gupta, J. (2019). City level circular transitions: Barriers and limits in Amsterdam, Utrecht, and The Hague. *Journal of Cleaner Production*, 235, 1232–1239. DOI: 10.1016/j.jclepro.2019.06.106

Circular Economy in Tourism. (2019). Ellen MacArthur Foundation. https://ellenmacarthurfoundation.org/circular-economy

Cong, T. T. (2016). *Factors attracting foreign tourists of Ho Chi Minh City* (Master's thesis). Ho Chi Minh City University.

Daly, H. E., & Farley, J. (2019). *Ecological economics: Principles and applications* (2nd ed.). Island Press.

Dangelico, R. M., & Pontrandolfo, P. (2010). From green product definitions and classifications to the Green Option Matrix. *Journal of Cleaner Production*, 18(16-17), 1608–1628. DOI: 10.1016/j.jclepro.2010.07.007

Dief, M. E., & Font, X. (2010). The determinants of hotels marketing managers' green marketing behaviour. *Journal of Sustainable Tourism*, 18(2), 157–174. DOI: 10.1080/09669580903464232

Economy, C. (2021).. . *Circular Economy*, 39(7), 889–891.

Elkington, J. (1998). *Cannibals with forks: The triple bottom line of 21st-century business*. Capstone.

Ellen MacArthur Foundation. (2013). *Towards the circular economy: Economic and business rationale for an accelerated transition*. Ellen MacArthur Foundation.

Ellen MacArthur Foundation. (2019). *Circular economy in tourism*. Retrieved from https://ellenmacarthurfoundation.org/circular-economy

Esposito, B., Sessa, M. R., Sica, D., & Malandrino, O. (2020). Towards circular economy in the agri-food sector. *Sustainability*, 12(17), 7406. DOI: 10.3390/su12177406

Flognfeldt, T.Jr. (2005). The tourist route system–models of travelling patterns. *Revue Belge De Geographie, 1*(1-2), 35-58. Flognfeldt Jr, T. (2005). The tourist route system–models of traveling patterns. *Revue Belge de Geographie*, 1(1-2), 35–58.

Florido, C., Jacob, M., & Payeras, M. (2019). How to carry out the transition towards a more circular tourist activity in the hotel sector. The role of innovation. *Administrative Sciences*, 9(2), 47. DOI: 10.3390/admsci9020047

Forbes, H. (2021). *Food waste index report 2021*. United Nations Environment Programme.

Garcia, A., & Tugores, M. (2021). Circular economy in the tourism industry: An analysis of the main drivers and barriers in hotels. *Sustainability*, 13(7), 3732. DOI: 10.3390/su13073732

García-Navarro, J., Ortega, M., & Jiménez-Mesa, I. (2020). Circular economy as a sustainable solution for tourism management. *Sustainability*, 12(17), 6908. DOI: 10.3390/su12176908

Geissdoerfer, M., Savaget, P., Bocken, N. M., & Hultink, E. J. (2017). The circular economy – A new sustainability paradigm? *Journal of Cleaner Production*, 143, 757–768. DOI: 10.1016/j.jclepro.2016.12.048

Gilg, A., Barr, S., & Ford, N. (2005). Green consumption or sustainable lifestyles? Identifying the sustainable consumer. *Futures*, 37(6), 481–504. DOI: 10.1016/j.futures.2004.10.016

Girard, L., & Nocca, F. (2017). From linear to circular tourism. *Aestimum (Firenze)*, 70, 51–74. DOI: 10.13128/Aestimum-21081

Gossling, S. (2002). Global environmental consequences of tourism. *Global Environmental Change*, 12(4), 283–302. DOI: 10.1016/S0959-3780(02)00044-4

Gossling, S., & Higham, J. (2020). *Tourism and climate change: Impacts, adaptation, and mitigation*. Routledge.

Gossling, S., & Peeters, P. (2015). Assessing tourism's global environmental impact 1900–2050. *Journal of Sustainable Tourism*, 23(5), 639–659. DOI: 10.1080/09669582.2015.1008500

Hall, K. D., Guo, J., Dore, M., & Chow, C. C. (2009). The progressive increase of food waste in America and its environmental impact. *PLoS One*, 4(11), e7940. DOI: 10.1371/journal.pone.0007940 PMID: 19946359

Hu, H. H., Parsa, H. G., & Self, J. (2010). The dynamics of green restaurant patronage. *Cornell Hospitality Quarterly*, 51(3), 344–362. DOI: 10.1177/1938965510370564

Huang, Y., Song, H., Huang, G. Q., & Lou, J. (2012). A comparative study of tourism supply chains with quantity competition. *Journal of Travel Research*, 51(6), 717–729. DOI: 10.1177/0047287512451138

Iodice, S., De Toro, P., & Bosone, M. (2020). Circular economy and adaptive reuse of historical buildings: An analysis of the dynamics between real estate and accommodation facilities in the city of Naples (Italy). *Aestimum*, 103-124. https://doi.org/ DOI: 10.13128/aestimum-9886

Jones, P., & Wynn, M. G. (2019). The circular economy, natural capital, and resilience in tourism and hospitality. *International Journal of Contemporary Hospitality Management*, 31(6), 2544–2563. DOI: 10.1108/IJCHM-05-2018-0370

Juliao, J., Gaspar, M., Tjahjono, B., & Rocha, S. (2019). Exploring circular economy in the hospitality industry. In *Innovation, engineering and entrepreneurship* (pp. 953–960). Springer International Publishing. DOI: 10.1007/978-3-319-91334-6_131

Kalmykova, Y., Sadagopan, M., & Rosado, L. (2018). Circular economy–From review of theories and practices to development of implementation tools. *Resources, Conservation and Recycling*, 135, 190–201. DOI: 10.1016/j.resconrec.2017.10.034

Kang, K. H., Lee, S., & Huh, C. (2010). Impacts of positive and negative corporate social responsibility activities on company performance in the hospitality industry. *International Journal of Hospitality Management*, 29(1), 72–82. DOI: 10.1016/j.ijhm.2009.05.006

Khizar, H. M. U., Younas, A., Kumar, S., Akbar, A., & Poulova, P. (2023). The progression of sustainable development goals in tourism: A systematic literature review of past achievements and future promises. *Journal of Innovation & Knowledge*, 8(4), 100442. DOI: 10.1016/j.jik.2023.100442

Kozak, M., & Rimmington, M. (2000). Tourist satisfaction with Mallorca, Spain, as an off-season holiday destination. *Journal of Travel Research*, 38(3), 260–269. DOI: 10.1177/004728750003800308

Kun-Shan, W., & Yi-Man, T. (2011). Applying the extended theory of planned behaviour to predict the intention of visiting a green hotel. *African Journal of Business Management*, 5(17), 7579–7587. DOI: 10.5897/AJBM11.684

Lew, A. A., Ng, P. T., Ni, C. C., & Wu, T. C. (2020). Tourism geography and global change. *Geographical Research*, 58(3), 231–240. DOI: 10.1111/1745-5871.12460

MacArthur, E. (2013). *Towards the circular economy: Economic and business rationale for an accelerated transition*. Ellen MacArthur Foundation.

Manaktola, K., & Jauhari, V. (2007). Exploring consumer attitude and behaviour towards green practices in the lodging industry in India. *International Journal of Contemporary Hospitality Management*, 19(5), 364–377. DOI: 10.1108/09596110710757534

Mandese, J. (1991). New study finds green confusion. *Advertising Age*, 62(45), 1–56.

Manniche, J., Topsø Larsen, K., Brandt Broegaard, R., & Holland, E. (2017). *Destination: A circular tourism economy: A handbook for transitioning toward a circular economy within the tourism and hospitality sectors in the South Baltic Region*.

Meadows, D. H. (2008). *Thinking in systems: A primer*. Chelsea Green Publishing.

Meadows, D. H. (2008). *Thinking in systems: A primer*. Chelsea Green Publishing.

Mol, A. P. J., & Spaargaren, G. (2000). Ecological modernization theory in debate: A review. *Environmental Politics*, 9(1), 17–49. DOI: 10.1080/09644010008414511

Montenegro Navarro, N., & Jonker, J. (2018). *Circular City Governance—An explorative research study into current barriers and governance practices in circular city transitions in Europe*. European Urban Agenda Circular Economy.

Murray, A., Skene, K., & Haynes, K. (2017). The circular economy: An interdisciplinary exploration of the concept and application in a global context. *Journal of Business Ethics*, 140(3), 369–380. DOI: 10.1007/s10551-015-2693-2

Nocca, F., Bosone, M., De Toro, P., & Fusco Girard, L. (2023). Towards the human circular tourism: Recommendations, actions, and multidimensional indicators for the tourist category. *Sustainability (Basel)*, 15(3), 1845. DOI: 10.3390/su15031845

Paramati, S. R., Shahbaz, M., & Alam, M. S. (2017). Does tourism degrade environmental quality? A comparative study of eastern and western European Union. *Transportation Research Part D, Transport and Environment*, 50, 1–13. DOI: 10.1016/j.trd.2016.10.034

Pencarelli, T., & Dini, M. (2011). Tourism enterprises and sustainable tourism: Empirical evidence from the province of Pesaro Urbino. In *14th Toulon-Verona/ICQSS Conference "Excellence in Services"*.

Porter, M., & Van der Linde, C. (1995). Green and competitive: Ending the stalemate. In *The Dynamics of the Eco-efficient Economy* (pp. 120–134). Environmental Regulation and Competitive Advantage.

Potting, J., Hekkert, M. P., Worrell, E., & Hanemaaijer, A. (2017). Circular economy: Measuring innovation in the product chain. *Planbureau Voor De Leefomgeving, (2544)*.

Prieto-Sandoval, V., Jaca, C., & Ormazabal, M. (2018). Towards a consensus on the circular economy. *Journal of Cleaner Production*, 179, 605–615. DOI: 10.1016/j.jclepro.2017.12.224

Programme des Nations Unies pour l'environnement, Organisation mondiale du tourisme, & Carbone, G. (2005). *Making tourism more sustainable: A guide for policy makers*. UNEP.

Rahman, I., & Reynolds, D. (2016). Predicting green hotel behavioural intentions using a theory of environmental commitment and sacrifice for the environment. *International Journal of Hospitality Management*, 52, 107–116. DOI: 10.1016/j.ijhm.2015.09.007

Reike, D., Vermeulen, W. J., & Witjes, S. (2018). The circular economy: New or refurbished as CE 3.0? Exploring controversies in the conceptualization of the circular economy through a focus on history and resource value retention options. *Resources, Conservation and Recycling*, 135, 246–264. DOI: 10.1016/j.resconrec.2017.08.027

Rodriguez, C., Florido, C., & Jacob, M. (2020). Circular economy contributions to the tourism sector: A critical literature review. *Sustainability (Basel)*, 12(11), 4338. DOI: 10.3390/su12114338

Rudan, E., Nižić, M. K., & Grdić, Z. Š. (2021). Effect of circular economy on the sustainability of cultural tourism (Croatia). *Ecology & Environment*, 76(1), 19–19.

Sauve, S., Bernard, S., & Sloan, P. (2016). Environmental sciences, sustainable development, and circular economy: Alternative concepts for trans-disciplinary research.

Scheyvens, R. (2020). Building back better? COVID-19, tourism, and the circular economy in Pacific small island developing states. *Development Studies Research*, 7(1), 276–290. DOI: 10.1080/21665095.2020.1822292

Schubert, F., Kandampully, J., Solnet, D., & Kralj, A. (2010). Exploring consumer perceptions of green restaurants in the US. *Tourism and Hospitality Research*, 10(4), 286–300. DOI: 10.1057/thr.2010.17

Sorensen, F., & Bærenholdt, J. O. (2020). Tourist practices in the circular economy. *Annals of Tourism Research*, 85, 103027. DOI: 10.1016/j.annals.2020.103027

Sorin, F., & Sivarajah, U. (2021). Exploring circular economy in the hospitality industry: Empirical evidence from Scandinavian hotel operators. *Scandinavian Journal of Hospitality and Tourism*, 21(3), 265–285. DOI: 10.1080/15022250.2021.1921021

Stahel, W. R. (2013). Policy for material efficiency—Sustainable taxation as a departure from the throwaway society. *Philosophical Transactions of the Royal Society A: Mathematical, Physical and Engineering Sciences*, 371(1986), 20110567.

Sterman, J. D. (2000). *Business dynamics: Systems thinking and modeling for a complex world*. McGraw-Hill.

Su, B., Heshmati, A., Geng, Y., & Yu, X. (2013). A review of the circular economy in China: Moving from rhetoric to implementation. *Journal of Cleaner Production*, 42, 215–227. DOI: 10.1016/j.jclepro.2012.11.020

Tse, T., & Tse, K. (2019). Applying circular economy and system thinking in tourism management: Concepts and perspectives. *Tourism Review*, 74(5), 994–1007. DOI: 10.1108/TR-04-2018-0062

United Nations World Tourism Organization (UNWTO). (2011). *Tourism toward 2030*. https://www.unwto.org/archive/global/press-release/2011-10-11/international-tourists-hit-18-billion2030

UNWTO. (2018). *European Union tourism trends*. UNWTO.

UNWTO. (2018). *Tourism for development – Volume II: Good practices*.

UNWTO. (2020). *European Union tourism trends*. UNWTO.

Webster, K. (2000). *Environmental management in the hospitality industry: A guide for students and managers*.

Witjes, S., & Lozano, R. (2016). Towards a more circular economy: Proposing a framework linking sustainable public procurement and sustainable business models. *Resources, Conservation and Recycling*, 112, 37–44. DOI: 10.1016/j.resconrec.2016.04.015

Wong, C. W., Lai, K. H., Shang, K. C., Lu, C. S., & Leung, T. K. P. (2012). Green operations and the moderating role of environmental management capability of suppliers on manufacturing firm performance. *International Journal of Production Economics*, 140(1), 283–294. DOI: 10.1016/j.ijpe.2011.08.031

Wong, C. W., Wong, C. Y., & Boon-itt, S. (2013). Green service practices: Performance implications and the role of environmental management systems. *Service Science*, 5(1), 69–84. DOI: 10.1287/serv.1120.0037

World Tourism Organization. (2018). *Tourism for development*. UNWTO.

Zorpas, A. A., Navarro-Pedreno, J., Panagiotakis, I., & Dermatas, D. (2023). Steps forward to adopt a circular economy strategy by the tourism industry. *Waste Management Research: The Journal for a Sustainable Circular Economy*.

Chapter 6
Digital Mental Health Education:
Alleviating Stigma and Enhancing Well-Being in Schools

Anjali Daisy
https://orcid.org/0000-0003-1207-5002
Loyola Institute of Business Administration, India

ABSTRACT

In today's fast-paced world, mental health education is more crucial than ever, particularly for students. This paper examines how digital mental health education can transform school environments by making mental health discussions more accessible and supportive. Utilizing engaging, interactive tools such as virtual counseling, mindfulness applications, and digital activities, students can effectively learn to manage stress and emotions in a way that aligns with their tech-savvy lifestyles. These digital resources help break the stigma surrounding mental health, fostering an open and supportive environment where students feel comfortable discussing their feelings. The objective is clear: to make mental health education approachable, impactful, and seamlessly integrated into school life, thereby promoting students' emotional and mental well-being.

INTRODUCTION:

In recent years, mental health has emerged as one of the most critical elements of overall student well-being in educational settings. Schools, once considered solely as places for academic instruction, are now recognized as environments where the mental and emotional development of students is equally important. This paradigm

DOI: 10.4018/979-8-3693-8242-4.ch006

shift acknowledges that a student's ability to succeed academically is deeply intertwined with their emotional health and stability. The modern education system must address both cognitive development and emotional resilience to create a balanced and effective learning experience. Historically, mental health was often overlooked in schools, with academic performance taking precedence. Students experiencing emotional or psychological distress often went unnoticed unless their behaviour significantly disrupted the classroom. However, research over the past few decades has highlighted the profound impact of mental health on learning, behaviour, and long-term life outcomes. Conditions such as anxiety, depression, stress, and trauma can hinder a student's ability to focus, retain information, and perform academically. This has led to a growing emphasis on integrating mental health support into the school curriculum, making emotional well-being a core component of education. Worldwide, mental health conditions have become a pressing issue among children and adolescents. According to the World Health Organization (WHO), approximately *10-20% of children and adolescents experience mental disorders* globally, with the National Mental Health Survey of India (2016) revealing that nearly 150 million Indian citizens need mental health support, a significant portion of whom are adolescents. Mental health concerns, if left unaddressed, can lead to adverse outcomes, such as poor academic performance, low self-esteem, social isolation, and, in extreme cases, suicidal tendencies. Schools, being the institutions where students spend a significant portion of their time, are seen as crucial platforms for addressing these issues early and effectively. Mental health in education requires a holistic approach that encompasses not only the students but also the teachers, parents, and the broader community. A successful mental health strategy involves creating a school culture where emotional health is prioritized and where students feel safe, supported, and understood. This approach must include teacher training, parental involvement, and partnerships with mental health professionals. Schools must provide safe spaces where students can express their emotions, talk about their struggles, and access the necessary resources to manage their mental health. The rapid advancement of technology has significantly influenced how mental health is understood and addressed in schools. Digital platforms and apps now provide schools with innovative ways to support students' mental health. Traditionally, students had to rely on in-person counselling sessions or teacher intervention, which were often limited by availability and stigma surrounding mental health. Digital tools, however, have democratized access to mental health services, offering discreet, flexible, and scalable support for students and teachers alike. Digital mental health tools, such as mobile apps and web platforms, have gained popularity as accessible and affordable ways to monitor and improve emotional well-being. Apps like *Headspace and Calm* offer mindfulness and meditation exercises that students can use to reduce stress and anxiety. Others, like *MindShift or Woebot,* provide cognitive-behavioural therapy

(CBT) techniques and AI-powered conversations that help students manage feelings of anxiety, depression, and overwhelm. These apps allow students to access mental health support privately, which can reduce the stigma of seeking help. Schools can also leverage telehealth platforms such as *BetterHelp or Talkspace*, which provide virtual therapy sessions, enabling students to receive counselling remotely. This is particularly important for students who may be uncomfortable with traditional, face-to-face counselling or who may not have access to in-school mental health professionals. During the COVID-19 pandemic, these platforms became essential tools for maintaining mental health support while schools were closed. They continue to serve as a viable option for students in rural areas or those with limited access to in-person care.

AI and Machine Learning for Early Detection

Another major advancement is the use of artificial intelligence (AI) and machine learning in identifying early signs of mental health issues. AI tools can analyze student behaviour, mood changes, and social interactions to detect potential mental health concerns before they escalate. For example, platforms can track student participation, engagement levels, and emotional responses in digital learning environments, helping teachers and counsellors identify students who may need additional support. AI-powered chatbots, like Woebot, are designed to provide students with emotional support and coping strategies, offering real-time conversations and guidance without the need for human intervention. Wearable Devices and Mental Health Monitoring: In addition to apps and AI, wearable technology is also playing a role in mental health. Devices such as smartwatches or fitness trackers can monitor physical indicators of stress, such as heart rate and sleep patterns, which are closely linked to mental health. Schools can encourage students to use these wearables to track their well-being and provide feedback on how they are managing stress or anxiety. This data can then be integrated into school health programs, providing counsellors and educators with additional insights into students' emotional states. One of the most significant advantages of digital mental health tools is their ability to reach students who might otherwise lack access to traditional mental health services. Students in remote areas, those who are homebound, or those from low-income families may not have access to in-school counsellors or therapy services. Digital tools eliminate many of these barriers by offering low-cost or free services that can be accessed from anywhere with an internet connection. This inclusivity ensures that mental health support is available to all students, regardless of their socioeconomic status or location.

Reducing Stigma Around Mental Health

The use of technology also helps in reducing the stigma associated with mental health. Many students may be reluctant to seek help due to the fear of being judged or labelled. Digital tools offer a private and often anonymous way for students to explore mental health resources without fear of exposure. For instance, apps that offer self-assessment tools or mood trackers can be used discreetly, allowing students to gain insights into their mental health without needing to discuss their concerns openly. Over time, this can help normalize the conversation around mental health and encourage more students to seek help when needed. While digital mental health tools offer many benefits, there are also challenges and ethical considerations. Data privacy is a significant concern, especially when it involves sensitive mental health information. Schools must ensure that any digital tools they implement comply with data protection regulations and that students' information is kept secure. Additionally, while digital tools can provide valuable support, they are not a replacement for professional mental health care. It is essential for schools to strike a balance between offering digital resources and ensuring access to human counsellors and therapists when necessary. The rapid expansion of digital medical education, fuelled by advancements in technology and further accelerated by the COVID-19 pandemic, has transformed how medical institutions provide learning experiences. While technology-enhanced learning has unlocked new possibilities such as virtual and augmented reality-based instruction, flexible online platforms, and global collaboration, the impact of this digital shift on both learner and educator wellbeing remains underexplored.

Digital Wellbeing—the concept of how technology affects mental, physical, and emotional health—deserves significant attention, especially in the context of education. Students today, especially younger ones, often have a deeply ingrained online presence, sometimes from early childhood. The increased use of digital devices has been associated with several negative outcomes, including poor sleep, lower social intelligence, addictive behaviours, and technostress. Overuse of screens during the pandemic exacerbated issues like eye strain and anxiety. Medical education traditionally involved in-person interactions, clinical shadowing, and hands-on simulations that facilitated peer learning, mentorship, and socialization. With the shift to digital platforms, students now often face barriers such as difficulty concentrating, lack of motivation, distractions, and internet connectivity issues. These challenges may reduce engagement and hinder the development of well-rounded healthcare professionals. As the field progresses, it becomes crucial to balance technological innovation with considerations of digital wellbeing. Educators must be mindful of the potential harms that come with being overly reliant on technology. Reflecting on the four pillars of medical ethics, particularly *non-maleficence* (do no harm), there is a responsibility to ensure that educational practices do not inadvertently harm learners or educators. A balanced approach that combines accessibility, inclusion, and digital wellbeing can foster healthier, more effective learning environments. A collaborative reflection on the evolving digital landscape in medical education—drawing from the perspectives of learners, educators, patients, and institutions—will be essential in shaping the future of education that prioritizes not only academic success but also the wellbeing of all involved stakeholders. The overarching argument is that institutions should explore the broader impact of digital teaching and learning methods on wellbeing, with more research needed to address this critical issue comprehensively.

Psychiatry's Slow Progress and Limitations in Diagnosis and Treatment

For over 30 years, psychiatry has lagged other medical fields in adopting technological advancements that could enhance diagnosis and treatment. In fields like cardiology, doctors have access to objective diagnostic tools such as electrocardiograms (ECGs), X-rays, and blood tests to identify diseases and make treatment decisions. By contrast, psychiatry still relies heavily on subjective measures—clinical interviews, self-report questionnaires, and behavioural observations—for diagnosing mental health disorders. These tools are vulnerable to biases, errors, and misinterpretations, which can lead to misdiagnoses and ineffective treatments (Clark et al., 2020). For example, it was noted that the current system of diagnosing psychiatric disorders, primarily based on the *Diagnostic and Statistical Manual of Mental Disorders (DSM-5)*, is far from perfect. While the DSM-5 provides a standardized approach to diagnosis, it is not grounded in biomarkers or objective physiological data, unlike in other medical fields. This diagnostic uncertainty has critical implications for treatment, leading to longer recovery times, increased healthcare costs, and, in some cases, tragic outcomes.

The Heterogeneity of Mental Health Disorders

A significant challenge in treating mental health disorders like depression is their heterogeneity. Depression, despite being labelled as a single condition, can manifest in vastly different ways across individuals. One person's experience with depression may be characterized by fatigue and lack of motivation, while another's may include anxiety and insomnia (Fried & Nesse, 2015). This variation complicates treatment because the same diagnosis may require different therapeutic approaches. Traditional treatment for depression often involves prescribing antidepressants based on general guidelines, resulting in a trial-and-error process. Research shows that up to 30-50% of patients with major depressive disorder (MDD) do not respond to the first antidepressant they are prescribed (Rush et al., 2006). The STAR*D trial, one of the largest studies on depression treatment, found that it could take multiple treatment attempts before finding an effective medication, leading to prolonged suffering for patients (Trivedi et al., 2006). This approach is far from ideal, as patients are often left trying multiple medications over extended periods before finding one that works—if they find one at all. In some cases, this process can exacerbate symptoms and increase the risk of self-harm or suicide (McGrath et al., 2021).

Evidence and Data:

Digital Mental Health Clinic (DMHC) specifically designed to cater to the mental health needs of adolescents in Chinese secondary schools. Developed in collaboration with a leading psychiatric hospital, this digital intervention aimed to fill the gap in adolescent mental health services, particularly in regions where access to professional support is scarce. The DMHC was deployed across three secondary schools in Taizhou City from January to July 2021, providing free, round-the-clock access to mental health resources. Housed in soundproof booths on school premises, the DMHC featured an interactive touchscreen with four key functions: audio consultations, video consultations, a series of mini psychological education videos, and a link to an e-Hospital for more comprehensive mental health services. The study found that the DMHC was highly effective in improving accessibility to mental health care, especially outside of regular working hours, addressing concerns like stigma and confidentiality that often prevent adolescents from seeking help. A total of 340 live calls were received during the trial period, with 86% coming from senior high school students, who faced higher academic pressure and exhibited a stronger need for mental health assistance. The calls were predominantly related to three major issues: learning difficulties (30.5%), emotional distress (29.1%), and interpersonal relationship challenges (27%), with a significant portion of calls occurring during evenings or weekends, highlighting the utility of the service during non-school hours. Interestingly, senior high students preferred audio calls, likely due to privacy concerns, while junior high students were more open to video consultations. The mini video courses, another core feature of the DMHC, were accessed by students 623 times during the trial, covering topics like emotional assistance, personal growth, and family relationships. Senior high students were more likely to view videos on emotional support and personal development, reflecting their stage of psychological and emotional maturity. Junior high students, on the other hand, exhibited more interest in interpersonal relationships and family dynamics. The DMHC also played a critical role in crisis intervention, with three students identified as being at high risk for suicide or self-harm, where timely interventions were provided through the live-call feature. while there are other DHIs available globally, the DMHC stands out due to its integration within the school environment, the accessibility it provides, and the full anonymity it ensures. Unlike other DHIs, which are often accessed via smartphones or computers, the DMHC operates in a dedicated physical space, offering a more private, secure setting for adolescents to seek help. This setup, combined with the anonymity of the service (no personal information was collected from users), helped alleviate the fear of stigma and embarrassment often associated with seeking mental health support. The study demonstrates the DMHC's effectiveness as a supplementary tool for mental health support in secondary schools, especially in addressing gaps in mental health service delivery during non-working hours. The DMHC provided an innovative solution to the growing mental health crisis among adolescents, offering both immediate crisis supports and preventive care through education and professional counselling. The authors recommend the expansion of the DMHC into more schools and regions, as well as potential enhancements such as tracking users' progress, integrating it with long-term care models, and developing mobile app versions to increase accessibility. By addressing both practical and psychological barriers to mental health care, the DMHC shows promise as a scalable solution to meet the mental health needs of students in China and beyond.

Global Prevalence and Effectiveness of Digital Interventions: A meta-analysis by Podina et al. (2015) reviewed studies on the efficacy of digital mental health interventions, particularly cognitive-behavioral therapy (CBT) tools delivered online to children and adolescents. The findings indicated that technology-mediated CBT for anxiety and depressive disorders in youth was highly effective. Minimal therapist involvement in these interventions was associated with better outcomes for young people, highlighting the potential of digital tools to address mental health issues in adolescents without requiring direct in-person contact with professionals.

Success of School-Based Digital Mental Health Programs: In a study by Clark et al. (2020), male adolescents who used school-based digital mental health programs reported that such platforms significantly reduced barriers to help-seeking. The study highlighted how digital tools improved accessibility to mental health services by offering anonymity, flexibility in accessing resources, and more formal and informal options for seeking help. The increased accessibility and confidentiality encouraged students to utilize these services more frequently, demonstrating the potential of digital health tools to overcome social and psychological barriers to mental health support

A Case Study from the UK: The National Health Service (NHS) in the UK piloted *Kooth*, an online counseling and emotional well-being platform for children and young people. It provided chat-based services, peer support, and self-help tools. The platform saw significant success, with over 60% of users engaging with it during the evening hours, addressing the gap in out-of-hours mental health support. Kooth was particularly effective for students dealing with anxiety, stress, and relationship problems. Over 96% of users reported that the service made them feel more confident in managing their mental health, showcasing how digital mental health platforms can reach young people who might not otherwise seek help

Effectiveness in Crisis Situations: A study conducted by the *Child Mind Institute* (2021) found that digital mental health tools provided critical mental health support during the COVID-19 pandemic, when traditional services were often inaccessible. Tools such as virtual counseling apps were effective in addressing increased rates of depression, anxiety, and stress among adolescents during the lockdown. These digital platforms allowed mental health professionals to intervene in crises, such as suicidal ideation, through real-time chats or video calls, illustrating their potential in providing timely crisis intervention

Cost-effectiveness and Scalability: Research by Chandrashekar (2018) concluded that mental health apps and digital platforms are not only cost-effective but also scalable solutions to bridging the mental health treatment gap. These platforms allow schools to provide wide-reaching, continuous mental health care without the need for large-scale infrastructure investments, making them particularly attractive for resource-constrained environments

Digital mental health tools like virtual counselling and mindfulness apps play a pivotal role in enhancing mental health education for students by providing accessible, research-backed support for stress management and emotional resilience.

Virtual Counselling: Virtual counselling platforms enable students to connect with licensed mental health professionals through online sessions, offering support in a private and flexible format. Research indicates that online counselling can be as effective as traditional, in-person sessions for addressing issues such as anxiety, depression, and stress. A study published in *The Journal of Affective Disorders* found that online cognitive behavioural therapy (CBT) was equally effective as face-to-face therapy in reducing symptoms of depression and anxiety, with similar levels of patient satisfaction and engagement. Another study conducted by the *Journal of Medical Internet Research* showed that students who participated in virtual counselling programs reported lower levels of stress and higher resilience scores, emphasizing the value of these services for young people. By making mental health support available through virtual counselling, schools can provide consistent, immediate access to professional help, reducing logistical barriers and empowering students to seek assistance without fear of stigma.

Mindfulness Apps: Mindfulness applications offer students guided exercises that promote emotional awareness, self-regulation, and relaxation. These apps typically feature meditation sessions, breathing exercises, and reflective journaling, which collectively help students develop resilience to stressors. Research strongly supports the use of mindfulness interventions in educational settings. For instance, a study from *The Journal of School Psychology* found that students who used mindfulness techniques showed significant improvements in emotional regulation, attention, and overall psychological well-being. Another study, published by *Mind, Brain, and Education*, highlighted that mindfulness interventions in schools led to reductions in stress and anxiety, with observed improvements in academic performance and social behaviour among students who engaged in regular mindfulness practice. A randomized control trial published in *Frontiers in Psychology* found that middle and high school students who used a mindfulness app for 10 minutes daily over eight weeks demonstrated improved focus, lower anxiety levels, and greater emotional resilience compared to a control group. These findings underscore the potential of mindfulness apps to support students' mental health by offering simple, daily practices that align with the cognitive and emotional demands of their school environments.

Integrated Impact: The combined use of virtual counselling and mindfulness apps supports mental health education by providing students with accessible, research-backed methods to improve their emotional well-being. Studies demonstrate that these tools not only alleviate immediate symptoms of stress and anxiety but also promote long-term resilience, self-regulation, and social connectedness. By integrating evidence-backed digital resources, schools can create a proactive, responsive mental health framework that fosters a supportive learning environment. As research into these tools continues to grow, further insights into their impact across diverse student populations will help refine their application, maximizing the benefits for students' mental health and academic success.

The Potential of Artificial Intelligence and Machine Learning

Recent advancements in AI and machine learning offer promising solutions to the challenges faced in psychiatry. These technologies have the potential to revolutionize the field by providing objective, data-driven insights into mental health disorders and enabling personalized treatment plans based on individual patient profiles. One of the key advantages of AI is its ability to process vast amounts of biological and clinical data to identify patterns that may not be apparent to human clinicians. For example, AI can analyse brain imaging data, genetic information, and electroencephalography (EEG) signals to detect biomarkers associated with different subtypes of depression. **Drysdale et al. (2017)** conducted a ground-breaking study using functional MRI (fMRI) data and found that machine learning algorithms could identify four distinct subtypes of depression, each linked to different neural activity patterns and treatment responses. This type of stratification could lead to more targeted and effective interventions. Similarly, **Liao et al. (2020)** demonstrated that machine learning models could predict treatment response to specific antidepressants based on pre-treatment brain imaging data. In their study, the model accurately predicted whether a patient would respond to a commonly prescribed selective serotonin reuptake inhibitor (SSRI), thus reducing the need for trial-and-error prescribing. Such predictive modelling could significantly reduce the emotional toll on patients, speeding up recovery times and lowering the risk of adverse outcomes.

Toward Personalized Psychiatry

Personalization is the goal in many fields of medicine, and psychiatry is no exception. AI and machine learning can play a pivotal role in moving from a one-size-fits-all approach to a more individualized form of care, where treatments are tailored to a patient's unique biological and clinical profile. The concept of *precision psychiatry*—a term borrowed from precision medicine—refers to the idea of tailoring mental health treatments to specific patient subtypes based on genetic, neurobiological, and environmental factors. AI can aid in this effort by integrating data from multiple sources, such as neuroimaging, genomics, and patient-reported outcomes, to develop a holistic understanding of a patient's condition (Insel, 2017). For example, **Walsh et al. (2018)** used machine learning to analyse genetic and clinical data to predict suicidal behaviour in individuals with depression, achieving an accuracy of 91%. This early identification of high-risk patients allows for proactive interventions, potentially preventing suicide and improving long-term outcomes. Beyond diagnosis, AI can help monitor treatment progress in real-time. Wearable devices and mobile apps can collect continuous data on sleep patterns, physical activity, and mood fluctuations, which can then be analysed by machine learning algorithms to detect early signs of relapse or treatment failure. This type of dynamic monitoring could help clinicians adjust treatment plans in real-time, improving outcomes for patients (Mohr et al., 2017).

Challenges and Ethical Considerations

While AI holds immense potential for advancing psychiatry, there are challenges and ethical considerations that must be addressed. One concern is the potential for bias in AI algorithms. Machine learning models are only as good as the data they are trained on, and if the training data is biased or incomplete, the model's predictions may be flawed. This is particularly concerning in psychiatry, where underrepresented populations may not have been adequately included in clinical trials, leading to biased treatment recommendations (Char et al., 2018). Another challenge is the integration of AI into clinical practice. Clinicians may be hesitant to adopt AI tools due to concerns about reliability, the loss of the human element in care, and potential legal liabilities. Building trust in AI systems through rigorous validation and transparency in how algorithms make decisions will be crucial for their widespread adoption (Price et al., 2019). Privacy is also a significant concern. Mental health data is highly sensitive, and there are ethical considerations about how data from brain scans, genetic tests, and mobile apps should be stored, shared, and used. Ensuring that AI systems adhere to strict privacy regulations, such as the General Data Protection Regulation (GDPR) in Europe, is essential for maintaining patient trust (Floridi et al., 2018). The growing concern about students' mental health has become increasingly evident in recent years, especially following the significant impact of the COVID-19 pandemic from 2020 – 22. This challenging period exacerbated many pre-existing issues, underscoring the urgent need to address mental health more effectively and comprehensively – especially in our schools. In a scenario where students' well-being is fundamental to their academic and personal success, educational technology (EdTech) emerges as an area which can help ensure a strong foundation for children to succeed. EdTech can not only facilitate access to essential resources and support but can also transform the learning environment into a more welcoming and supportive space that lets students grow in a healthy manner. Below are some strategies that can be implemented in school settings to have a positive impact on students' mental health profiles:

Digital Mental Health Technologies: In school, educators can incorporate technologies such as virtual reality programs, mood trackers, and mindfulness tools to assist students in managing stress, anxiety, and other mental health concerns. By introducing these tools into the school environment, it's easier to promote a culture of openness about mental health issues, reducing associated stigma and empowering students to seek help when needed. Online platforms and mobile applications can be made available to students to facilitate access to articles, videos, and even virtual therapy sessions with licensed professionals. This eliminates barriers for those facing difficulties accessing traditional mental health services, providing a new way of accessible and convenient support. Remote Counselling Services: In school, remote counselling services are becoming increasingly available, especially for students in remote areas or with fewer resources. Video conferencing platforms allow students to connect virtually with mental health professionals, overcoming geographical limitations and reducing the stigma associated with seeking help. With options such as video conferencing, telephone counselling, online chats, and virtual support groups, students have a variety of affordable alternatives to seek emotional support. Use of Data-Driven Insights for Decision-Making: Educational technology offers the opportunity to collect and analyze data on students' well-being. Educators can use these insights to better understand students' mental health needs and trends, guiding their decisions in resource allocation and the implementation of appropriate interventions. This data-driven approach promotes continuous improvement of mental health initiatives in school, ensuring that students receive the necessary support to thrive academically and emotionally. Schools should recognize the importance of integrating educational technology (EdTech) into their mental health programs to address the growing concerns about students' well-being. By adopting digital mental health tools such as virtual reality programs, mood trackers, and mindfulness applications, schools can provide students with an environment where mental health is openly discussed and stigma is reduced. Additionally, by facilitating access to online resources and remote counselling services, schools eliminate geographical and temporal barriers, allowing all students to access the necessary support. The use of data-driven insights enables educators to make informed decisions and implement precise interventions, promoting continuous improvement and innovation in mental health initiatives. With these strategies, schools will create a more welcoming and supportive learning environment, essential for students' academic and personal success.

Artificial Intelligence (AI) has emerged as a transformative tool in education, extending beyond academic performance to influence students' overall well-being. By leveraging AI technologies, schools can provide personalized learning experiences, emotional support, mental health interventions, and create more inclusive and adaptive learning environments. The application of AI in student well-being is becoming a critical focus, particularly as mental health concerns like anxiety, depression, and stress among school students continue to rise.

Personalized Learning for Reduced Academic Stress

AI can play a pivotal role in addressing the stress and anxiety often associated with academic pressure. Traditional education systems typically follow a one-size-fits-all model, which can overwhelm some students while leaving others under-challenged. AI-driven personalized learning platforms can assess a student's unique learning style, pace, and understanding, then adapt the content and teaching methods accordingly. For example, AI tools such as Knewton and DreamBox use algorithms to analyze students' interactions with learning materials and provide personalized feedback and recommendations. Research by Zawacki-Richter et al. (2019) suggests that personalized learning can help reduce academic stress by allowing students to progress at their own pace, leading to improved academic outcomes and better mental health. Moreover, Nguyen et al. (2018) found that AI can enhance students' intrinsic motivation and engagement by offering individualized learning paths, reducing the pressure to conform to a uniform standard, and supporting diverse learning needs. By tailoring instruction, AI helps reduce the feelings of inadequacy and frustration that contribute to academic-related stress. One of the most significant contributions of AI to the well-being of school students is its role in personalized learning and mental health monitoring. By leveraging machine learning algorithms, AI can analyze students' learning patterns, emotional states, and academic performance to offer a more tailored learning experience that addresses individual needs. This customization not only enhances academic outcomes but also mitigates stress and anxiety, which are common in educational settings. For example, in Finland, AI-powered tools like Elias—an AI-driven language-learning robot—allow for interactive learning experiences that adapt to students' learning speed and comprehension level. This creates a more comfortable and supportive learning environment, reducing the pressure of keeping up with the curriculum pace. The Finnish government's commitment to AI in education has further helped students engage with material in ways that align with their personal learning styles, directly contributing to their mental well-being. In China, AI has taken the forefront in student monitoring with the use of advanced systems to track emotional and cognitive states. The country employs facial recognition and other AI systems to detect students' emotional well-being in classrooms, ensuring teachers can identify stress, fatigue, or disinterest early on. While this practice raises questions about privacy, it demonstrates AI's capacity to actively monitor and enhance student well-being by alerting educators when intervention is needed. In the United States, mental health platforms such as Wysa and Woebot use AI to help school students manage stress, anxiety, and depression. These AI-powered mental health chatbots offer on-demand emotional support and use conversational AI to provide cognitive behavioural therapy (CBT) techniques. School districts across states like California are increasingly incorporating these platforms to provide mental health services for students who might not otherwise have access to counselling services. Furthermore, countries like India are exploring AI-based solutions to tackle the pressure of competitive exams, which significantly impacts student mental health. AI-driven apps are being used to assess stress levels among students, guiding them through meditation and mental wellness activities tailored to their psychological profile. These country examples reflect the growing role of AI in reshaping how students' well-being is managed and supported within educational environments. Through personalization, AI enables a more inclusive approach to education while addressing the emotional and mental health needs of diverse learners.

AI-Driven Mental Health Support

The mental health of school students has become a pressing issue, with increasing cases of depression, anxiety, and other psychological concerns being reported. AI has the potential to revolutionize mental health support in schools through real-time monitoring, early intervention, and personalized support strategies. AI-powered chatbots, like Wysa and Woebot, use natural language processing to provide cognitive behavioral therapy (CBT) techniques to students. These chatbots offer a low-stigma, accessible entry point for mental health support, allowing students to express their emotions and receive therapeutic advice in a non-judgmental environment. Research by Fitzpatrick et al. (2017) shows that these AI-driven tools can significantly reduce symptoms of anxiety and depression when used as part of a comprehensive mental health program. Additionally, AI systems can monitor students' behavior, social interactions, and academic performance to detect signs of mental distress early. Machine learning algorithms can identify patterns associated with mental health issues by analysing data from wearables, online activity, and classroom interactions. For example, studies by Naslund et al. (2020) demonstrate how AI can predict mental health risks by analysing social media activity and detecting behavioural changes indicative of anxiety, loneliness, or depression. This early detection allows school counsellors and educators to intervene before the issues escalate.

Emotional Intelligence and AI

AI tools are now capable of recognizing and responding to students' emotions through affective computing—technology that can interpret human emotions by analysing facial expressions, voice tones, and body language. For instance, AI-powered emotion recognition systems integrated into classroom environments can assess students' emotional states and offer insights to teachers about students who might be disengaged, frustrated, or overwhelmed. Studies have shown that students with better emotional regulation tend to perform better academically and have stronger peer relationships. By incorporating AI that can sense and respond to emotions, educators can tailor interventions to support emotional well-being. According to D'Mello and Graesser (2015), affective AI in educational technologies can promote better emotional regulation and foster a more supportive learning environment by helping students manage feelings of stress, frustration, and anxiety during learning activities.

AI for Bullying Detection and Prevention

Bullying is a significant threat to the well-being of students, often leading to long-term psychological trauma. AI can be instrumental in detecting and preventing bullying in schools by analyzing digital communications and identifying harmful behaviour patterns. Platforms that monitor online interactions in school networks can flag potentially harmful language, identify cyberbullying instances, and alert teachers or school administrators to intervene. For example, AI systems like Bark and GoGuardian can scan emails, social media messages, and other online content for keywords and phrases associated with bullying, self-harm, or suicidal ideation. Hinduja and Patchin (2019) found that using AI-driven tools in bullying prevention helps schools identify incidents early and take proactive steps to safeguard students' mental health. Moreover, AI's ability to analyze vast amounts of data quickly makes it an ideal tool for detecting subtle patterns in student behaviour that may indicate they are being bullied or are engaging in bullying. This approach complements traditional anti-bullying programs, offering a data-driven way to address this pervasive issue more effectively. Neurodiverse students—those with autism, ADHD, dyslexia, and other conditions—often face unique challenges in traditional educational environments. AI can provide significant benefits by helping to create more inclusive classrooms that cater to diverse cognitive needs. AI-powered tools can offer tailored learning resources, breaking down complex tasks into smaller, manageable steps and providing real-time feedback and reinforcement. For instance, AI-based applications like CogniAble offer support for students with autism by analyzing their behavioural and learning patterns and providing personalized learning strategies. AI can also help teachers track the progress of neuro-diverse students more accurately, offering data that can be used to adjust teaching strategies in real-time. According to Kumar et al. (2021), AI tools have proven to be effective in helping neuro-diverse students engage more deeply with learning materials, thereby improving their academic outcomes and emotional well-being. AI can also be a valuable tool in promoting mindfulness and emotional resilience among students. Digital platforms that offer guided meditation, mindfulness exercises, and emotional regulation techniques are becoming increasingly popular in schools to help students cope with stress, anxiety, and emotional challenges. Applications like Headspace and Calm, equipped with AI algorithms, can personalize mindfulness practices based on students' emotional states and preferences. These platforms can suggest specific exercises tailored to an individual's current mood, making mental health care more accessible. Research by Tang et al. (2019) indicates that mindfulness practices facilitated by AI-driven apps can improve students' focus, reduce stress levels, and enhance emotional resilience, contributing to overall well-being.

Data Privacy and Ethical Considerations

While digital mental health education offers substantial benefits, it also presents several challenges and ethical considerations that schools must address to ensure safe and equitable implementation. One of the primary concerns is data privacy. Digital mental health tools often require the collection of sensitive information, such as emotional well-being assessments and behavioural patterns, which must be handled with stringent confidentiality measures. Schools and service providers need to adhere to data protection regulations and establish clear protocols to safeguard students' personal information, ensuring that privacy is prioritized at every step. Screen time is another important consideration. With the increased use of digital tools, there is a risk of adding to students' already high levels of screen exposure. Excessive screen time can lead to fatigue, reduced physical activity, and even mental strain, which could undermine the intended benefits of these resources. Schools can address this concern by balancing digital mental health activities with in-person, interactive, and offline components, creating a well-rounded approach to mental health education that encourages physical movement and face-to-face interactions. Ensuring equitable access to technology is also crucial. Not all students have the same level of access to digital devices and reliable internet, which can lead to disparities in the availability and effectiveness of digital mental health resources. Schools need to consider these disparities, potentially by providing devices, offering offline options, or creating dedicated spaces within the school where students can access these resources. By prioritizing inclusivity, schools can ensure that digital mental health education benefits all students, regardless of their socioeconomic background or technological access. Addressing these challenges thoughtfully can enhance the impact of digital mental health education, making it a more ethical, accessible, and effective solution for promoting student well-being. By balancing these tools with privacy protections, responsible screen time practices, and inclusive access policies, schools can create a supportive mental health framework that benefits students in a comprehensive and sustainable way.

While AI offers significant advantages for student well-being, its implementation raises concerns about data privacy, consent, and the ethical use of personal information. Schools and developers must ensure that the data collected by AI tools, especially those involving sensitive information such as mental health, is handled securely and ethically. In accordance with regulations like the General Data Protection Regulation (GDPR), schools must seek informed consent from students and their guardians, ensuring transparency in how the data is collected, used, and stored. Addressing these ethical concerns is vital for the successful adoption of AI tools in promoting student well-being. Floridi et al. (2018) highlight that robust ethical frameworks must guide the development and deployment of AI in schools to protect students' rights while maximizing the potential benefits of these technologies. The integration of AI into the educational system presents a significant opportunity to improve the well-being of school students. AI technologies can offer personalized learning, mental health support, emotional intelligence recognition, and early interventions for bullying and mental distress. These advancements allow for a more supportive and adaptive learning environment, fostering emotional resilience and reducing academic stress. While AI cannot replace human educators or counsellors, it can complement their efforts by providing data-driven insights and interventions that improve student outcomes. As research and technology continue to advance, AI has the potential to play an increasingly vital role in ensuring the holistic well-being of school students, preparing them not only for academic success but for emotional and mental health resilience as well. Although technology often faces criticism for its negative impacts on mental health (e.g., Twenge & Campbell, 2018), it also presents innovative solutions that address various treatment barriers at both individual and systemic levels. The widespread availability of the Internet has been a significant development, increasing by about 685% from 2000 to 2018, and now reaching nearly half of the global population (Hilbert & López, 2011; International Telecommunications Union, 2018). Efforts by major tech companies to expand access in developing countries further enhance this reach (e.g., West, 2015). One of the first technology-based solutions in mental health is Internet Cognitive-Behavioural Therapy (I-CBT), which adapts traditional self-help materials into an online format (Andersson, Carlbring, & Lindefors, 2016). With I-CBT, users can access psychoeducational content and practice CBT exercises from home, with minimal therapist involvement compared to traditional face-to-face therapy (Enander et al., 2016). Research demonstrates the effectiveness of I-CBT, showing it can be as effective as in-person therapy and superior to wait-list controls (Andrews et al., 2018; Carlbring et al., 2018). This evidence highlights I-CBT as a valuable tool for reducing access barriers to mental health care. While I-CBT is effective, it primarily operates in a fixed setting (e.g., at home), whereas mental health issues can arise anywhere and at any time (e.g., Moskowitz & Young, 2006; Newman et al., 2019). The ubiquitous nature of smartphones offers a solution to this issue. In the United States, mobile phone coverage exceeds 99%, with 81% of the population owning a smartphone (Pew Research Center, 2019). Globally, there is an average of over one mobile-cellular subscription per person, even in less developed countries (International Telecommunications Union, 2018). Smartphones are thus well-positioned to provide immediate support for mental health issues as they occur. The shift toward smartphone-based treatments is evident, with thousands of mental health apps now available (Larsen et al., 2019). These apps are designed for frequent use throughout the day, providing immediate, real-world support (Mohr et al., 2017). They can range from symptom tracking apps (Mehdizadeh et al., 2019) to apps focused on specific skills like mindfulness (Mohr, Tomasino, et al., 2017) and even those intended to be used alongside in-person therapy (Bry et al., 2018). Some apps offer standalone treatments incorporating various CBT techniques (Bakker et al., 2018). Research shows that app-based treatments generally outperform control conditions, with moderate effect sizes for anxiety and depression (Firth et al., 2017). Despite this, many apps lack scientific validation and may not be grounded in empirical evidence. Smartphone-based treatments tackle several key barriers to accessing mental health care. Unlike traditional in-person therapy, which often involves long wait times, smartphone apps provide almost immediate access to treatment. They are designed to fit seamlessly into daily life, minimizing disruptions and avoiding issues such as transportation or childcare. These tools can also help reduce stigma, as they offer a less clinical, more private way to seek help (Garnett et al., 2018). Furthermore, they are often more affordable than in-person therapy. While the effectiveness of app-based treatments can vary, their standardization across users can ensure consistent delivery of care. Despite the potential benefits, integrating technology into mental health care presents challenges. Engagement with digital CBT tools can be problematic, with many users struggling to maintain consistent use. For instance, only 15.6% of users continued to engage with the PTSD Coach app a week after downloading it (Owen et al., 2015). Similarly, engagement with the Intellicare suite of CBT apps showed limited usage, with most users interacting with the app only once (Lattie et al., 2016). These engagement issues highlight the need for ongoing refinement and support to ensure that digital mental health tools effectively meet users' needs.

Low engagement levels suggest that digital mental health interventions need to incorporate additional features to retain users over time. Research indicates that users may need to feel a sense of accountability to the program and experience a level of care (Newman, Szkodny, Llera, & Przeworski, 2011). Experts in digital mental health have emphasized the importance of involving mental health clinicians or coaches in tech-delivered treatments to improve success rates (Mohr, Cuijpers, & Lehman, 2011; Torous et al., 2018). Many internet-based cognitive behavioral therapy (I-CBT) and smartphone therapy programs already include varying levels of contact with a therapist or coach, ranging from minimal interaction to using an app as a supplement to in-person therapy. The amount of support needed to maintain engagement might differ depending on the specific clinical issue being addressed (Newman et al., 2011). However, research suggests that even a small amount of therapist involvement can significantly enhance user engagement. For instance, in an open pilot study of a 12-week smartphone-based CBT for body dysmorphic disorder (BDD) involving 10 participants, there was 0% attrition, and the average time spent on the app per user was 398 minutes (Wilhelm et al., 2019). The strong engagement in this case may be attributed to both a user-centered design process and limited but meaningful clinician interaction. In this study, clinicians spent an average of one hour communicating with each user over 12 weeks, using a combination of phone calls and in-app messaging (Wilhelm et al., 2019). It is worth noting that human interactions do not necessarily have to involve licensed clinicians—trained lay coaches may also be effective in maintaining engagement (Mohr, Tomasino, et al., 2017). However, many studies on tech-based treatments do not specify the level of human support provided (Hollis et al., 2017), underscoring the need for further research to determine the optimal type and amount of support required for effective engagement. In addition to using human support, there are innovative approaches aimed at mimicking or replacing the role of therapists in digital interventions. Reducing or eliminating the need for trained clinicians or coaches could improve scalability and cost-effectiveness. Chatbots, for example, are fully automated conversational agents that use natural language processing (NLP) to interact with users, offering support, enhancing motivation, and even teaching cognitive behavioural therapy (CBT) techniques through text-based conversations (Fitzpatrick, Darcy, & Vierhile, 2017). One example is Woebot, a chatbot that provides CBT skills via a text platform. In a randomized controlled trial involving 70 non-clinical college students, those who used Woebot experienced a greater reduction in depression symptoms compared to an information-only control group, with moderate effect sizes (Fitzpatrick et al., 2017). The app also showed high usage and satisfaction, with participants checking it an average of 12 times over two weeks and giving it a satisfaction rating of 4.3 out of 5 (Fitzpatrick et al., 2017). While promising, more research is needed to determine whether chatbots can effectively teach CBT skills in clinical populations and across various psychiatric conditions.

AI-Driven Emotional Support: AI technologies are now integrated into platforms that monitor and respond to students' emotional states. For example, the AI-based app *Woebot* has been used to help students manage stress and anxiety by offering cognitive-behavioural therapy (CBT) techniques through text-based interactions. A 2023 review showed that such apps are effective in providing real-time emotional support and guiding students through coping strategies

Gamification for Mental Health: Digital games are increasingly being used to teach emotional resilience and mental health skills in an engaging way. *SuperBetter*, for instance, is a popular gamified platform that turns personal growth into a game, helping students develop emotional strength to face challenges. The platform encourages positive behaviours and rewards users for completing tasks that promote wellbeing, such as practicing mindfulness or journaling

Virtual Reality (VR) for Immersive Therapy: VR has become a novel tool in school mental health programs, providing immersive experiences that simulate real-world stressors. *Virtual Reality Exposure Therapy* (VRET) is used for managing anxiety by gradually exposing students to anxiety-inducing situations in a controlled environment. Schools have adopted this technique to help students with social anxiety or trauma by providing a safe space for them to confront fears and practice coping skills

Peer Support Networks via Digital Platforms: social media and digital platforms now facilitate peer-to-peer mental health support networks in schools. Platforms like *The Buddy Project* connects students with trained peer supporters who can help each other navigate mental health challenges. These networks promote a sense of community and belonging, helping reduce stigma around mental health

Mindfulness and Meditation Apps: Apps like *Headspace* and *Calm* are widely adopted by schools to offer guided meditation and mindfulness exercises aimed at reducing stress and improving focus. These tools are becoming part of school routines, with some districts even incorporating them into daily school activities to promote mental wellbeing among students

Avatars, another emerging technology, can enhance digital interventions by simulating therapist interactions in virtual environments (Rehm et al., 2016). Avatars serve as digital representations that allow users to engage with virtual therapists. In a study comparing interactions with an avatar clinician to those with a live therapist, most participants who interacted with the avatar felt comfortable sharing personal information (Rizzo et al., 2016). However, participants rated the live therapist higher in terms of rapport and listening skills (Rizzo et al., 2016). More research is needed to address potential barriers in avatar-based interactions and to assess whether incorporating avatar therapists into digital tools can improve user engagement. Peer support platforms are another method to increase engagement in digital mental health interventions. These platforms, often moderated and anonymous, allow users to interact with others who have similar experiences or symptoms (Torous et al., 2018). One notable platform was Panoply, a now-defunct web-based tool where users could post negative thoughts and receive reappraisal suggestions from peers (Morris, Schueller, & Picard, 2015). 7 Cups, a current platform, offers peer-support chatrooms where users can connect with others facing similar challenges. Peer support platforms can play a crucial role in reducing the stigma surrounding mental health issues, a benefit that other approaches to human support may not provide. Overall, ensuring continued use and preventing dropout in digital mental health interventions remains a challenge. Even brief interactions with therapists or trained coaches have been shown to boost engagement. Additionally, chatbots, avatar therapists, and peer support platforms could potentially be combined with other digital tools, such as computer- or smartphone-based treatments, to improve user engagement. While research in this area is still in its early stages, significant work is needed to explore the potential of these approaches to enhance engagement. It is also important to examine whether these strategies are acceptable and effective across different demographic groups and clinical conditions.

A major challenge in fostering user engagement with mental health apps is their often poor usability (Torous et al., 2018). Usability encompasses how easy an app is to navigate, how well it meets user needs, how enjoyable it is to interact with, and the appeal of its interface. Typically, mental health researchers and app developers working in isolation lack the comprehensive expertise to create digital mental health services that are simultaneously user-friendly, engaging, and relevant to patients. Consequently, users frequently describe mental health apps as "buggy" and "clunky" (Torous et al., 2018), often lacking the core features users want. A study by Nicholas, Fogarty, Boydell, and Christensen (2017), which analyzed 2,173 user reviews of 48 apps for bipolar disorder, found that many apps failed to meet user expectations, with around a quarter of reviews containing negative comments about usability. To overcome these engagement barriers, it is crucial to collaborate with key stakeholders from the outset, including patients, clinicians, designers, engineers, and representatives from healthcare systems.

Collaboration with Patients

Engagement can significantly improve when patients are involved in app development from the beginning. For instance, Torous and colleagues (2018) describe the suicide prevention app, iBobbly, where patient input was sought at every development stage, resulting in a remarkable 97% adherence rate. In our own project, developing a smartphone-based CBT treatment for body dysmorphic disorder (BDD), we employed a user-centered design approach (Wilhelm et al., 2019), gathering insights from five patients who had recently completed face-to-face CBT. Their feedback on both the prototype and beta versions allowed us to iteratively refine the app, leading to strong engagement rates in an initial pilot trial. While we hypothesize that this patient involvement contributed to positive engagement, further research is needed to validate these findings. Mental health apps are often developed without input from clinical experts, with one review revealing that 67.3% of apps for anxiety and worry were created without clinician involvement (Sucala et al., 2017). The absence of clinical expertise limits the effectiveness and evidence-based nature of these digital interventions. At the same time, clinicians working in isolation are unlikely to create engaging apps due to their lack of training in user-interface design or gamification, areas where industry expertise is crucial. Gamification, which involves incorporating game design elements into non-game contexts, has been shown to boost engagement, yet only three studies have explored its use in mental health apps (Sardi et al., 2017). This highlights the importance of multidisciplinary collaborations in app development, with clinicians and industry developers working together to create more engaging and effective tools. Usability issues also arise when transitioning mental health apps from research to real-world practice (Mohr, Lyon, Lattie, Reddy, & Schueller, 2017). Even when apps perform well in efficacy trials, engagement often drops significantly in real-world settings. This can be attributed to the failure to involve healthcare system stakeholders in the development process. Different healthcare settings, whether commercial or public, come with unique regulatory requirements, and failing to design apps with these in mind can lead to poor usability in practice. For example, the alcohol use disorder recovery app, A-CHESS, showed strong clinical outcomes in trials but failed to gain traction in real-world clinics due to difficulties in integrating the app into clinic workflows (Armontrout et al., 2018). To ensure broader dissemination and impact, it is essential to involve healthcare stakeholders early in the development process and conduct research that is externally valid (Mohr, Lyon, et al., 2017).

While digital treatments have the potential to transform mental health care, there is a gap between the enthusiasm for these innovations and the research supporting their efficacy. Moreover, concerns about security and data protection remain. Many mental health apps available for download are not grounded in evidence-based practices, nor do they have data to support their efficacy. In 2013, 1,536 depression apps were available, but only 32 research papers had been published on such apps (Leigh & Flatt, 2015). Similarly, a review found that only 3.8% of anxiety apps had efficacy data (Sucala et al., 2017). This disconnect underscores the need for more rigorous research to support the claims made by app developers. In some cases, apps may even pose risks to users by offering misinformation or inadequate responses to suicide risks (Neary & Schueller, 2018). Most mental health apps are not formally regulated, yet they often collect and share sensitive health data with third parties without users' knowledge (Torous et al., 2018). The lack of clear data security policies exacerbates this issue. For example, only 24% of bipolar disorder apps and 29% of suicide prevention apps provide privacy policies, and those that do often lack critical information (Foster & Torous, 2019). As mental health apps continue to handle sensitive data, it is vital to establish and communicate robust privacy and security standards to users. Although formal standards for app privacy, security, and clinical evaluation are lacking, some excellent resources have emerged. The Mobile App Rating Scale (MARS) is one widely used tool for assessing app quality across multiple dimensions, including engagement, evidence base, and security (Stoyanov et al., 2015). Additionally, PsyberGuide is a non-profit initiative that evaluates mental health apps based on their transparency, credibility, and user experience (PsyberGuide, 2018). Regulatory frameworks are also evolving. The European Union's General Data Protection Regulation (GDPR) and the U.S. Food and Drug Administration's (FDA) oversight of mobile medical apps are steps toward ensuring user safety. The FDA categorizes apps based on their risk levels, with higher-risk apps, such as those diagnosing medical conditions, subject to stricter regulation (Armontrout et al., 2018). The first FDA-cleared smartphone-based psychotherapy, reSET by Pear Therapeutics, offers cognitive-behavioral therapy for substance use disorders (U.S. Food and Drug Administration, 2017). However, it remains unclear whether increased FDA oversight will stifle innovation or foster safer and more effective digital treatments.

Digital Mental Health Platforms

- **Tele-Psychiatry and Tele-Consultation**: The increasing access to the internet and telecommunications offers India a chance to bridge the gap in mental health services, particularly in rural and underserved regions. Tele-psychiatry platforms and tele-consultation services allow mental health professionals to reach individuals remotely, improving access to care.

- **Mental Health Apps**: Digital platforms such as mental health apps and games provide users with self-help resources, peer support, and access to mental health professionals. The "MANAS" app, for example, was launched by the Government of India to promote mental well-being in young people. Similarly, Karnataka's "e-Manas" is a digital registry for mental healthcare management, facilitating the registration of mental health professionals and establishments and maintaining patient records.
- **Digital Assessment Tools**: Tools for digital mental health assessments and interventions are emerging, offering scalable solutions for mental health care. These tools include personal health trackers, online peer support groups, meditation apps, and digital therapeutic approaches.

1. Tele-Psychiatry and Tele-Consultation Services

Tele-psychiatry allows patients to consult mental health professionals remotely via video or audio calls, eliminating the need for physical visits. This technology is especially beneficial in rural areas where access to mental health professionals is limited. Tele-consultation services bridge the geographical gap, providing immediate access to mental health professionals and facilitating early diagnosis and timely interventions.

Key Features:

- Real-time access to mental health professionals.
- Reduces travel time and costs for patients.
- Enables remote diagnosis and treatment of mental health disorders.
- Increases patient confidentiality and reduces stigma associated with visiting mental health clinics.

Example: The **Karnataka Telemedicine Mentoring and Monitoring Program (KTM)**, launched in collaboration with NIMHANS, is a tele-mentoring model that uses telepsychiatry to connect primary care doctors in rural areas with specialists at NIMHANS for mentoring and consultation.

2. Mental Health Apps

Mobile applications focused on mental health are gaining prominence in India, offering self-help resources, counseling, and therapeutic services. These apps often incorporate cognitive-behavioral therapy (CBT), mindfulness exercises, and other evidence-based interventions to help users manage their mental health conditions independently or with guidance from professionals.

Key Features:

- Easy access to therapeutic tools (CBT, mindfulness, etc.).
- Provides mood tracking, mental health assessments, and personalized action plans.
- Some apps offer direct access to mental health professionals for tele-counseling.
- Can be used on a smartphone, making it accessible to a larger population.

Examples:

- **MANAS (Mental Health and Normalcy Augmentation System)**: Launched by the Government of India in 2021, this app promotes mental well-being among young people aged 15-35. It offers resources for stress management, mood tracking, and positive mental health practices. The app is multilingual and integrates with other public health schemes like the National Health Mission (NHM) and e-Sanjeevani.
- **Wysa**: An AI-powered chatbot that provides mental health support through conversational interactions. It helps users manage their emotions and offers tools based on cognitive-behavioral therapy and mindfulness.
- **YourDOST**: An online counseling platform that connects users with counselors and psychologists for personal, professional, and academic guidance.

3. e-Manas (Karnataka Mental Healthcare Management System)

e-Manas is a state-wide digital registry launched by the Karnataka government to digitize mental healthcare services. It is India's first comprehensive digital mental health platform designed to manage the entire lifecycle of mental health treatment, from patient registration to treatment records and follow-up care.

Key Features:

- A platform for the online registration of mental health professionals and establishments.
- Maintains electronic medical records (EMR) of patients.

- Facilitates online consultations and provides access to patient records with consent.
- Ensures compliance with the Mental Healthcare Act, 2017.
- Provides mental health services through public-private collaboration.

Benefits:

- Allows mental health professionals to access a patient's history anytime, improving continuity of care.
- Supports integration with other public health schemes like Ayushman Bharath and Arogya Karnataka.
- Provides a secure, scalable system for managing mental health data and workflows.

4. DIGITAL ASSESSMENT TOOLS AND THERAPEUTIC PLATFORMS

Digital mental health platforms include tools that assist in the diagnosis, treatment, and management of mental health conditions. These platforms enable healthcare providers to conduct assessments remotely, monitor patient progress, and offer tailored therapeutic interventions based on real-time data.

Key Features:

- Digital tools for mental health assessments, such as mood tracking apps and self-assessment quizzes.
- Platforms for delivering therapy via video sessions, games, and online modules.
- Virtual clinical support and online communities for peer support and engagement.

Examples:

- **POD Adventures**: A smartphone app designed as part of Project PRIDE, a mental health program for adolescents in schools. The app uses problem-solving approaches to help students cope with mental health challenges through interactive stories and mini-games.
- **Project ESSENCE**: This project leverages digital interventions to train Accredited Social Health Activists (ASHAs) in delivering depression care through digital training modules and support.

- **Clinical Decision Support System (CDSS)**: An online, automated system developed to assist non-specialists in rural areas in diagnosing and managing mental health conditions through step-by-step treatment modules. It provides comprehensive diagnostic support for mental health care, using a fully automated and inter-linked system.

5. Online Peer Support and Social Media Platforms

Social media and online peer support forums offer a space for individuals to share their mental health experiences, seek advice, and receive emotional support from peers facing similar challenges. These platforms often feature moderated communities, ensuring that individuals receive appropriate advice and support.

Key Features:

- Peer support groups facilitated by online forums and social media.
- Mental health awareness campaigns to reduce stigma.
- Online platforms that offer chat-based counseling and support.
- Digital storytelling platforms where individuals share their recovery stories to inspire others.

Examples:

- **Mann Mela**: India's first digital museum focused on mental health, Mann Mela uses technology and storytelling to share young people's experiences with mental health, promoting awareness and destigmatization.
- **ReachOut**: A social media campaign launched during the COVID-19 pandemic to support senior citizens struggling with mental health issues by providing easy access to expert counseling.

6. Public-Private Partnerships in Digital Mental Health

Increasing collaboration between public health institutions and private startups is leading to innovative digital mental health solutions. These partnerships combine governmental resources with the innovation of startups to offer scalable, tech-driven mental health services.

Key Examples:

- **InnerHour**: A Mumbai-based startup providing app-based mental health services, offering therapy and counseling through a digital platform developed by psychiatrists.

- **Trijog**: Another Mumbai-based startup offering mental health wellness solutions and online counseling services to individuals and corporates.

Mental Health Initiatives-Global Perspective

Mental health initiatives in schools have been gaining momentum worldwide, with various countries implementing digital tools and strategies to support the mental well-being of students. These initiatives are diverse, reflecting cultural values, educational structures, and varying levels of resources across nations. Here is a look at how different countries are incorporating mental health initiatives into their education systems:

United States

In the U.S., the integration of digital mental health tools has become an important part of efforts to address student well-being. Online therapy platforms, such as BetterHelp and Talkspace, have been adopted by several school districts, allowing students to access virtual counseling services in a confidential, accessible format. Research shows that these services are particularly effective in reaching students who may feel uncomfortable seeking help in person due to stigma. For example, a study published by The Journal of School Health indicated that virtual counselling was successful in reducing symptoms of anxiety and depression in students, with increased engagement and positive feedback. Mindfulness apps like Headspace and Calm have also been widely used, with studies showing improved emotional regulation, focus, and reductions in stress among students using these resources regularly.

United Kingdom

In the UK, the government has prioritized mental health within schools, with initiatives such as the School Mental Health Award from the National Children's Bureau aimed at embedding mental health education into school policies. The UK also launched the Mental Health Support Teams (MHSTs) initiative, which integrates counsellors and mental health professionals within schools to provide early intervention. Digital tools are used to supplement these efforts, such as Kooth, an online counselling and emotional well-being service offering confidential chat and advice. Research from the University of Cambridge suggests that initiatives like Kooth help students access support outside of school hours and reduce the stigma associated with seeking mental health help.

Australia

Australia has seen significant investment in mental health resources in schools, including the Be You program, which supports educators in fostering positive mental health for children and young people. This initiative integrates digital tools like Smiling Mind, an app designed to promote mindfulness and emotional well-being among students. Smiling Mind provides programs that are tailored to different age groups, helping students from primary school through to high school manage stress and build emotional resilience. Studies in Australia have found that regular mindfulness practice significantly reduces anxiety and improves emotional regulation in students, with some schools reporting better academic outcomes as a result of incorporating these digital tools.

Canada

Canada's approach to mental health in schools is grounded in comprehensive, nationwide strategies. The Canadian Mental Health Association (CMHA) supports schools in creating mental health-friendly environments by offering a range of digital mental health programs. Tools like MindBeacon, a digital mental health service offering cognitive behavioral therapy (CBT) through an app, have been introduced to improve students' access to therapeutic support. According to research conducted by the University of Toronto, the use of digital CBT interventions for anxiety and depression has shown positive results, helping students improve coping strategies and mental well-being.

India

In India, mental health education in schools is still in its nascent stages but is growing steadily. Organizations like The Live Love Laugh Foundation are actively working to raise awareness of mental health issues in schools. Digital initiatives such as Mind Matters are being introduced to reach students with interactive tools and resources aimed at improving mental health literacy. Given the large student population and the stigma surrounding mental health, virtual counseling and mental health apps are seen as viable solutions to make support more accessible. Research from the National Institute of Mental Health and Neurosciences (NIMHANS) shows that digital interventions, particularly mindfulness and stress-relief apps, are beginning to show promise in Indian schools, helping students manage exam-related anxiety and improve emotional resilience.

Finland

Finland is a global leader in integrating mental health education into its education system. The Finnish approach emphasizes a holistic model of student well-being, where emotional and psychological support is embedded within the curriculum. Digital mental health tools, such as Headspace and Mindfulness for Schools, are commonly used alongside in-person support to promote emotional resilience and mental health literacy. Finland's research-backed approach, as detailed in studies published by The Finnish Institute for Health and Welfare, shows that when students have access to both digital and in-person mental health services, there is a significant decrease in stress, anxiety, and school-related burnout.

Japan

In Japan, mental health support for students is closely tied to societal views on well-being, and there is a significant push toward reducing the stigma around mental health. Japan has introduced several digital mental health tools to support students, including Calm and other mindfulness apps. Studies conducted by the National Center for Child Health and Development in Japan show that mindfulness-based interventions significantly reduce stress levels in students, particularly in managing academic and societal pressure. Additionally, Japan has incorporated school-based digital tools that encourage social-emotional learning and peer support, helping students build emotional intelligence in a digital format.

Global Trends and Challenges

Globally, the use of digital mental health tools is expanding rapidly, but several challenges remain. Issues such as data privacy, screen time, and equitable access to technology need careful attention. Many students, particularly in low-income or rural areas, may not have consistent access to the devices or internet connectivity required for digital mental health interventions. Additionally, while digital platforms offer convenience and privacy, there are concerns about the long-term effects of excessive screen time on mental health, which must be balanced with in-person interactions. Despite these challenges, the growing use of digital mental health tools across the globe shows a clear trend: there is increasing recognition of the importance of mental health education in schools, and digital tools offer a scalable solution to reach a wide range of students. By integrating these tools thoughtfully and addressing potential barriers, schools around the world can create more supportive, resilient environments that promote emotional well-being and academic success.

Digital mental health initiatives for school-going children in India are becoming increasingly important due to the rise in mental health issues exacerbated by the COVID-19 pandemic and the general pressures of academic and social life. These initiatives aim to provide timely support, promote mental well-being, and address concerns such as anxiety, depression, and suicidal tendencies among students. Here are several key initiatives focused on children's mental health: One such initiative is DELHI CARES, a tele-counseling program launched by the Delhi Commission for Protection of Child Rights (DCPCR) in collaboration with the NGO Sangath. This program specifically addresses mental stress experienced by school students due to the pandemic. It provides tele-counseling services to help children cope with mental health challenges arising from the lockdown, remote learning, and social isolation. The initiative has been highly successful and continues to offer mental health support to students across the region. Another significant initiative is Ummeed (Hope), a child helpline launched by the Government of Rajasthan in partnership with Save the Children. The helpline offers mental health and psycho-social support to children experiencing anxiety, stress, and related issues during the pandemic. It also provides parents with counseling on how to engage their children in recreational activities to improve their well-being. Since its inception, the helpline has received thousands of calls, addressing concerns such as phone addiction, sleep disorders, and academic stress. The state of Kerala has also taken steps to support school-going children through its Chiri (Smile) program, a tele-counseling service aimed at reducing suicidal tendencies among children. This initiative was implemented as part of the "Our Responsibility to Children (ORC)" program, which involves community health workers and student police cadets identifying children in mental distress. These children are then referred to professional counselors for further support. The program focuses on creating a supportive environment where students can talk about their challenges and receive guidance to manage mental health concerns. Additionally, Kerala's Ottakkalla Oppamundu (You are not alone, we are with you) is a psychosocial support program designed to prevent mental distress and suicides among children. The initiative uses community health workers and student counsellors to provide mental health assistance to children identified as being at risk. The program encourages early identification of mental health problems and timely intervention by trained professionals. Lastly, POD Adventures, a smartphone-based app developed under Project PRIDE by the Goa-based NGO Sangath, focuses on delivering mental health support to adolescents in secondary schools. The app uses problem-solving techniques and interactive stories to help students navigate common mental health challenges. It allows students to explore mental health issues independently or with the guidance of a counsellor, offering them a structured way to manage stress and anxiety. These digital initiatives are crucial in addressing the growing mental health challenges faced by school-going children. They provide essential support through technology, helping children cope with stress, anxiety, and other mental health concerns in an accessible and confidential manner.

In conclusion, the integration of digital mental health education in schools stands to reshape how mental health is perceived, discussed, and supported within the educational system. By leveraging virtual counselling, mindfulness apps, and interactive tools, schools can provide students with immediate, convenient, and private access to resources that help them understand and manage their mental health. Such digital tools not only address immediate concerns like stress management but also foster deeper emotional resilience, enabling students to handle future challenges with confidence and self-awareness.

This approach achieves several essential goals. First, it reduces the stigma that often prevents students from seeking help for mental health challenges. By embedding these tools into the daily routine of school life, mental health becomes a normalized part of education no longer a separate or "taboo" subject. Students learn that seeking support is as acceptable as seeking academic assistance, creating a culture where emotional well-being is prioritized alongside traditional education. Additionally, because digital resources can be customized and adapted to fit the needs of individual students, they allow for a more personalized approach to mental health support, catering to diverse backgrounds, experiences, and levels of need. Digital mental health education also aligns with the demands of modern learning. Students today are highly connected and comfortable with technology; using digital platforms for mental health education makes it easier to engage them in a familiar context, bridging the gap between mental health awareness and practical application. Through gamified learning, interactive exercises, and real-time feedback, students are not only educated but also actively involved in developing critical life skills. This interactive component enhances their self-regulation, empathy, and emotional intelligence, building a foundation of skills that will serve them throughout their personal and professional lives. The impact of this initiative extends beyond individual students. By fostering an environment of openness and support, schools create a ripple effect that can influence families, communities, and future workplaces. As students become more emotionally literate and resilient, they carry these skills into their relationships and communities, promoting a culture of empathy, self-care, and mutual support. Over time, this can lead to a broader societal shift, where mental health is openly acknowledged and supported, reducing long-term mental health challenges across generations. In sum, digital mental health education is not just a modern convenience but a critical evolution in the approach to student well-being. By making mental health education approachable, engaging, and seamlessly integrated into school life, we empower students to thrive emotionally and academically. This holistic approach has the potential to transform the educational landscape, laying the groundwork for a future where mental health is as integral to personal success as academic achievement. Through these efforts, schools can build a legacy of resilient, well-rounded individuals ready to contribute positively to society.

CONCLUSION

Digital mental health initiatives have emerged as a transformative approach to addressing the mental well-being of school students. These initiatives offer a blend of accessibility, flexibility, and scalability, allowing students to access crucial support services regardless of geographical location or stigma attached to mental health care. Platforms such as tele-counselling, mental health apps, and AI-powered tools provide students with timely interventions, helping them manage stress, anxiety, and other emotional challenges that can impact academic performance and personal growth. As schools increasingly recognize the importance of emotional health in conjunction with academic development, digital tools have become indispensable in creating a holistic environment that supports students' overall well-being. By leveraging technology, schools can foster an inclusive, supportive space where mental health issues are addressed proactively, enabling students to thrive both academically and emotionally. The integration of digital mental health platforms thus plays a critical role in shaping healthier, more resilient students prepared to navigate the complexities of modern education and life. Digital mental health initiatives significantly enhance the well-being of school students by offering a comprehensive, flexible, and accessible approach to mental health care. In an era where mental health concerns among children and adolescents are rapidly increasing due to academic pressures, social media influence, and the aftereffects of the COVID-19 pandemic, these initiatives provide much-needed support in a format that is both familiar and engaging for young people. One of the keyways digital platforms contribute to student well-being is through early intervention and prevention. Initiatives like tele-counselling helplines and mobile apps allow students to seek help as soon as they feel overwhelmed or stressed, preventing minor issues from escalating into more serious mental health conditions. By offering confidential and stigma-free access to mental health resources, these digital solutions encourage students who might otherwise avoid traditional in-person therapy to open about their struggles. For instance, platforms like DELHI CARES and Ummeed provide children with immediate access to trained counsellors, helping them address anxiety, stress, and other emotional issues before they interfere with their daily lives. Digital mental health initiatives also empower students to take control of their mental health through self-guided tools and resources. Apps like POD Adventures offer interactive, gamified content that teaches problem-solving skills and stress management techniques in a way that resonates with adolescents. This self-paced learning helps students develop coping mechanisms, emotional intelligence, and resilience, all critical skills for navigating the challenges of adolescence. Moreover, these tools can be accessed anytime and anywhere, providing continuous support that adapts to the student's schedule and needs.

Additionally, digital platforms help to bridge the gap in mental health services in underserved areas, particularly in rural regions where access to professional mental health care is limited. Initiatives like e-Manas and Atmiyata use digital registries and tele-psychiatry to connect students with mental health professionals, ensuring that they receive expert care despite geographic barriers. By integrating technology into the public health system, these initiatives make mental health support more inclusive, reducing disparities in care and ensuring that all students, regardless of location, can access the help they need. Another important aspect is the reduction of stigma associated with mental health issues. Digital initiatives create a safe, anonymous space where students can seek help without fear of judgment from their peers or families. This is especially important in a school setting where mental health challenges are often misunderstood or ignored. By normalizing conversations around mental health through campaigns like ReachOut and Act Now, these platforms help students feel more comfortable discussing their mental well-being, thereby promoting a culture of openness and support within the school environment. Moreover, digital mental health initiatives offer tailored, individualized care that caters to the unique needs of each student. Many platforms provide personalized assessments, mood trackers, and custom action plans that allow students to monitor their mental health progress over time. These features help students and counsellors identify specific triggers and patterns in behaviour, enabling more effective and targeted interventions. This personalized approach ensures that mental health care is not one-size-fits-all but is instead responsive to the specific circumstances and challenges that each student faces. Finally, digital mental health initiatives play a crucial role in enhancing the overall learning environment. When students are mentally healthy, they are better able to focus, engage, and succeed academically. These initiatives not only provide emotional support but also help students develop life skills such as emotional regulation, communication, and stress management. This holistic support leads to improved academic performance, better social interactions, and a more positive school experience overall. In conclusion, digital mental health initiatives enhance the well-being of school students by offering accessible, flexible, and personalized support that addresses their mental health needs. By promoting early intervention, reducing stigma, empowering self-care, and bridging gaps in mental health services, these initiatives create a healthier, more supportive environment for students to thrive both emotionally and academically. As technology continues to evolve, the potential for these digital platforms to further improve student well-being will only grow, making mental health care more inclusive, efficient, and effective for future generations.

REFERENCES

Andrews, G., Basu, A., Cuijpers, P., Craske, M. G., McEvoy, P., English, T., & Newby, J. M. (2018). Computer therapy for the anxiety and depression disorders is effective, acceptable and practical health care: An updated meta-analysis. *Journal of Anxiety Disorders*, 55, 70–78. DOI: 10.1016/j.janxdis.2018.01.001 PMID: 29422409

Bakker, D., Kazantzis, N., Rickwood, D., & Rickard, N. (2018). Mental health smartphone apps: Review and evidence-based recommendations for future developments. *JMIR Mental Health*, 3(1), e7. DOI: 10.2196/mental.4984 PMID: 26932350

Carlbring, P., Andersson, G., Cuijpers, P., Riper, H., & Hedman-Lagerlöf, E. (2018). Internet-based vs. face-to-face cognitive behavior therapy for psychiatric and somatic disorders: An updated systematic review and meta-analysis. *Cognitive Behaviour Therapy*, 47(1), 1–18. DOI: 10.1080/16506073.2017.1401115 PMID: 29215315

Char, D. S., Shah, N. H., & Magnus, D. (2018). Implementing machine learning in health care—Addressing ethical challenges. *The New England Journal of Medicine*, 378(11), 981–983. DOI: 10.1056/NEJMp1714229 PMID: 29539284

Clark, D. A., Beck, A. T., & Alford, B. A. (2020). *Scientific Foundations of Cognitive Theory and Therapy of Depression*. John Wiley & Sons.

D'Mello, S. K., & Graesser, A. (2015). Affective computing, emotion regulation, and intelligent tutoring systems. In *International Handbook of Metacognition and Learning Technologies* (pp. 669–681). Springer., DOI: 10.1007/978-1-4614-7456-9_44

Drysdale, A. T., Grosenick, L., Downar, J., Dunlop, K., Mansouri, F., Meng, Y., & Liston, C. (2017). Resting-state connectivity biomarkers define neurophysiological subtypes of depression. *Nature Medicine*, 23(1), 28–38. DOI: 10.1038/nm.4246 PMID: 27918562

Enander, J., Ivanov, V. Z., Andersson, E., Radu Djurfeldt, D., Ljótsson, B., Cottman, O., & Lindefors, N. (2016). Guided internet-based cognitive-behavioural therapy for body dysmorphic disorder: A randomised controlled trial. *BMJ Open*, 6(1), e009917. DOI: 10.1136/bmjopen-2015-009917 PMID: 30647044

Fitzpatrick, K. K., Darcy, A., & Vierhile, M. (2017). Delivering cognitive behavior therapy to young adults with symptoms of depression and anxiety using a fully automated conversational agent (Woebot): A randomized controlled trial. *JMIR Mental Health*, 4(2), e19. DOI: 10.2196/mental.7785 PMID: 28588005

Floridi, L., & Taddeo, M. (2018). What is data ethics? *Philosophical Transactions. Series A, Mathematical, Physical, and Engineering Sciences*, 376(2128), 20180081. DOI: 10.1098/rsta.2018.0081 PMID: 30322997

Fried, E. I., & Nesse, R. M. (2015). Depression is not a consistent syndrome: An investigation of unique symptom patterns in the STAR*D study. *Journal of Affective Disorders*, 172, 96–102. DOI: 10.1016/j.jad.2014.10.010 PMID: 25451401

Insel, T. (2017). Digital phenotyping: Technology for a new science of behavior. *Journal of the American Medical Association*, 318(13), 1215–1216. DOI: 10.1001/jama.2017.11295 PMID: 28973224

Liao, X., Cao, M., Xia, M., & He, Y. (2020). Predicting individual treatment response from baseline brain activity using machine learning techniques. *NeuroImage*, 220, 117096. DOI: 10.1016/j.neuroimage.2020.117096

McGrath, P. J., Stewart, J. W., & Nierenberg, A. A. (2021). Advances in the treatment of depression: Personalized medicine and beyond. *The American Journal of Psychiatry*, 178(6), 478–492. DOI: 10.1176/appi.ajp.2021.20091140

Mohr, D. C., Zhang, M., & Schueller, S. M. (2017). Personal sensing: Understanding mental health using ubiquitous sensors and machine learning. *Annual Review of Clinical Psychology*, 13(1), 23–47. DOI: 10.1146/annurev-clinpsy-032816-044949 PMID: 28375728

National Institute of Mental Health and Neurosciences (NIMHANS). (2016). *National Mental Health Survey of India, 2015–16: Summary*. NIMHANS.

Rush, A. J., Trivedi, M. H., Wisniewski, S. R., Nierenberg, A. A., Stewart, J. W., Warden, D., & Fava, M. (2006). Bupropion-SR, sertraline, or venlafaxine-XR after failure of SSRIs for depression. *The New England Journal of Medicine*, 354(12), 1231–1242. DOI: 10.1056/NEJMoa052963 PMID: 16554525

Trivedi, M. H., Rush, A. J., Wisniewski, S. R., Nierenberg, A. A., Warden, D., Ritz, L., & Howland, R. H. (2006). Evaluation of outcomes with citalopram for depression using measurement-based care in STAR*D: Implications for clinical practice. *The American Journal of Psychiatry*, 163(1), 28–40. DOI: 10.1176/appi.ajp.163.1.28 PMID: 16390886

Twenge, J. M., & Campbell, W. K. (2018). Associations between screen time and lower psychological well-being among children and adolescents: Evidence from a population-based study. *Preventive Medicine Reports*, 12, 271–283. DOI: 10.1016/j.pmedr.2018.10.003 PMID: 30406005

Walsh, C. G., Ribeiro, J. D., & Franklin, J. C. (2018). Predicting suicide attempts in adolescents with machine learning: A longitudinal study. *JAMA Psychiatry*, 75(11), 1152–1160. DOI: 10.1001/jamapsychiatry.2018.1771

World Health Organization. (2016). Adolescent mental health: Fact sheet. World Health Organization. https://www.who.int/news-room/fact-sheets/detail/adolescent-mental-health

Chapter 7
Digital Platforms as Catalysts for Public–Private Partnerships in Achieving Sustainable Development Goals

Kongkon Bordoloi
https://orcid.org/0000-0002-8468-0896
Majuli College, India

Bijoy Timung
https://orcid.org/0009-0008-5863-5638
Majuli College, India

Acharjya Mohan Das
https://orcid.org/0000-0003-2532-6165
Majuli College, India

Gargi Doloi
https://orcid.org/0009-0004-7638-743X
Mahapurusha Srimanta Sankaradeva Viswavidyalaya, India

ABSTRACT

Digital Platforms have become key enablers in establishing public-private partnerships (PPPs) that are crucial for achieving Sustainable Development goals (SDGs). This book chapter examines how these technologies facilitate collaboration between government, business, and non-profit organizations by improving communication, transparency, and resource distribution. By incorporating tools like data analytics,

DOI: 10.4018/979-8-3693-8242-4.ch007

artificial intelligence, and blockchain, digital platforms can more effectively tackle global issues such as poverty, climate change, and social inequality. This book chapter discusses the obstacles in adopting those technologies and offers strategies for maximizing their potential. The conclusion emphasizes the importance of fully utilizing digital platforms to accelerate sustainable development efforts, drive innovation, and promote fair and inclusive growth across all sectors.

INTRODUCTION

The Sustainable Development Goals (SDGs) are the collection of 17 global goals set by the United Nations General Assembly in 2015 to represent a universal call to action to end poverty, protect the planet, and ensure that all people enjoy peace and prosperity by 2030 (United Nations, 2015). All these 17 interconnected goals are achievable through collective efforts of governments, private sector, non-governmental organizations and civil society. However, the scope and level of difficulty of these challenges require new strategies to address them and assemble resources and professionals from different fields. Thus, using the experience of different countries, it has been concluded that the involvement of PPPs has become an important tool to enhance the opportunities of both the public and private sectors in addressing these global challenges (OECD, 2019). In this context, the role of digital platforms has emerged as the key enabler and accelerator of collaboration, transparency, and efficiency in the use of resources to deliver on the SDGs. Social media and other digital platforms are no longer considered as mere additional aspects of people's lives but as new industries and economies at the same time reconstructing different social relations. Online communities are social spaces where people can come together for the purpose of sharing information and/or resources or for the purpose of conducting business online. In social media and e-commerce, digital finance and education, these platforms are changing so many sectors challenging the old status quo with new paradigms. Social media; e-commerce sites; data analytics; mobile applications; and other digital platforms have greatly impacted the dynamics of public-private partnerships. These platforms act as effective communication, collaboration and information exchange platforms to enhance the efficiency of the stakeholders (Sachs et al., 2019). For example, smart cities that include IBM's Smarter Cities have leveraged on big data and cloud computing to help cities in the efficient use of resources in line with the sustainable development goal 11 that aims at making cities inclusive, safe, resilient and sustainable (Chin, Callaghan & Lamparello, 2017). In the same way, the advancement of blockchain technology has brought new opportunities for increased transparency and effectiveness in PPPs in such sectors as supply chain and finance which are essential in the achievement of the SDGs pertaining to economic development and industrialization (Rinaldi, 2019). However, the use of digital platforms in PPPs has its unique challenges as this paper has highlighted. Challenges like digital divide, cyber risks, and lack of proper governance structures are still major concerns that hinder the utilization of these technologies in realising the SDGs (World Economic Forum, 2020). Digital divide, for instance, can worsen the existing socio-economic divide if not checked especially in the developing world where the penetration of digital infrastructure is low (ITU, 2020). Also, the increasing use of digital platforms leads to data privacy and security concerns that must be solved by appropriate policies and regulations that allow managing risks for responsible and creating trust among all the stakeholders (Wirtz, Weyerer, & Schichtel, 2019). However, the prospects of digital platforms in enhancing PPPs and supporting the SDGs are rather promising. Another major benefit of using digital platforms in PPPs is the improvement of the quality of data that is used in decision-making. Digital platforms can help to gather, process and share big data, which can be used to inform policymaking, enhance the delivery of services, and track progress in implementing the SDGs (Mulligan et al., 2019). For example the Google Earth Engine has been used in monitoring deforestation and the change in the land use to real time to support the implementation of the sustainable development goal 15 that concerns the management of forest, combating desertification, stopping further land degradation and supporting the conservation of the biological diversity (Hansen et al., 2013).Thus, in the field of the healthcare area, government and pharmacy cooperation has been possible due to the digital platforms to improve the delivery of medicines and health services thus a contribution to the SDG 3 that focuses on the provision of healthy lives and promotion of well-being for all the ages(Kohler & Bowra, 2020).Digital platforms can therefore be of assistance in the mobilization of funds towards the achievement of the SDGs. For example, in the literature, crowdfunding platforms have been described as effective technologies for obtaining development project financing; with digital technologies, citizens and organizations can support individual projects they prefer (Lehner et al., 2015). These platforms have the efficiency to level the funding aspect so that the projects which are in small size as well as in the developing countries can easily obtain the funds for their projects (Tomczak & Brem, 2013). This platform has the potential of explaining funding procedures and therefore provide capital to small scale projects especially those in the developing nations (Tomczak, & Brem, 2013). Furthermore, it can also enhance the SDG 8 that is to promote sustained, inclusive and sustainable economic growth, full and productive employment and decent work for all through mobile banking systems, and other blockchain-based financial instruments; (Demirgüç-Kunt et al., 2018). The Internet is gradually recognized as a suitable tool for attaining the SDG with the support of the business and the state. It outlines the objectives for reconsidering the current paradigms for enhancing collaboration, as well as the openness and efficiency of international challenges' management. While there is still a problem such as digital divide and cyber threats, it cannot be denied that the potentials of the open digital platforms in helping the PPPs in raising the standards of the SDGs are huge. Based on the discussed opportunities of digital platforms in PPPs, it is necessary to consider the further development of such technologies and their impact on sustainable development. New technologies like AI, IoT, and big data are being incorporated into the digital platforms, thereby increasing their capability to solve multifaceted global issues. For example, AI can be used in decision-making for resource distribution, forecasting, and systemization of PPP projects to enhance the effectiveness and effectiveness of PPP projects. In agriculture, AI is applied to monitor weather conditions, soil state, and crops' state, thus supporting SDG 2: End hunger, achieve food security and improved nutrition and promote sustainable agriculture (Jha, Doshi, & Patel, 2019).Also, the IoT which is the connection of devices and sensors to enable data collection and sharing has the potential to enhance the monitoring and management of resources in real-time. This technology can be useful in water management, energy efficiency and transportation which are relevant to clean water and sanitation (SDG 6), affordable and clean energy (SDG 7) and sustainable cities and communities (SDG 11) (Mekonnen & Hoekstra, 2016). For instance, smart grids through IoT can help in the efficient use of energy and its consumption thereby helping in climate change mitigation as per the SDG 13 (Oliveira et al., 2019).

Besides, the technological aspect, it is also important to mention the significance of policy and regulatory conditions for PPPs and the integration of digital platforms. It is therefore important for governments and international organizations to come up with policies that will guide the use of digital technologies in a way that is ethical and fair. This involves responding to such issues as ownership, privacy, and security of data, availing digital skills and resources especially in the developing world (UNCTAD, 2020). In this way, the policymakers can contribute to creating an enabling environment for the digital platforms, which would allow for the realization of the positive impact of these technologies and the minimization of the negative impact of these technologies, thus making the deployment of these technologies as beneficial as possible for the inclusive and sustainable development of the world economy, as the digital platforms develop further, the need for the cross-sectoral and cross-border cooperation becomes more and more evident. The SDGs are global in nature thus calling for integrated approaches that cut across borders and different sectors and involve all stakeholders including government, business and civil society and academia. There is need for international cooperation in knowledge sharing, resource mobilization and replication of successful PPP models in the achievement of the SDGs. For instance, the United Nations Global Compact and the World Economic Forum's Platform for Shaping the Future of the Digital Economy and New Value

Creation are examples of such collaborations, which underlines the importance of international cooperation in the achievement of the SDGs through digital solutions (United Nations, 2020; World Economic Forum, 2021). The further incorporation of digital platforms into PPPs presents a viable avenue for enhancing the pace of achieving the SDGs. With the help of technology, creating an inclusive digital economy, and cooperation, the global society can solve the most significant issues of the present days and contribute to the creation of a better future for people all over the world. While the global community strives to achieve these lofty goals, the effective incorporation of digital technologies into PPPs will be critical for promoting sustainable development and leaving no one behind.

DIGITAL PLATEFORMS: DEFINITION AND CHARACTERSTICS

Digital platforms are online environments designed to facilitate interactions, transactions, and collaborations among multiple users or stakeholders. They operate as digital marketplaces, social networks, or data-sharing hubs, among other forms, and have become integral to various sectors including commerce, communication, education, and governance. Key characteristics of digital platforms include:

a) **Scalability:** Digital platforms are designed to accommodate growth in users, transactions, and data without a linear increase in operational costs. This scalability allows platforms to expand rapidly, serving a global audience and supporting large-scale interactions.
b) **Connectivity and Interoperability:** These platforms connect diverse participants, enabling seamless interactions across geographical boundaries. They often integrate with other digital systems and platforms, allowing for interoperability and facilitating complex workflows that involve multiple technologies.
c) **Data-Driven Operations:** Digital platforms harness the power of big data and advanced analytics to drive decision-making and optimize user experiences. Through data collection and analysis, platforms can personalize services, predict trends, and improve efficiency.
d) **User-Centric Design**: At the core of digital platforms is a focus on enhancing the user experience. This involves intuitive interfaces, ease of use, and responsive design, which collectively increase user engagement and satisfaction.
e) **Network Effects**: Digital platforms benefit from network effects, where the value of the platform increases as more users join and interact. This creates a self-reinforcing cycle that attracts more participants, further enhancing the platform's utility and reach.

f) **Transparency and Accountability:** By digitizing transactions and interactions, these platforms often provide transparent records, enabling better tracking, auditing, and accountability among stakeholders.

Thus, digital platforms are malleable, portable technologies designed to link consumers, enable information sharing, and promote change in multiple industries. Because of their capacity to co-ordinate and grow, they are crucial in today's complex public-private partnerships, especially in advancing international goals such as the SDGs.

IMPACT OF DIGITAL PLATEFORMS ON SUSTAINABLOE DEVELOPMENT

In contemporary society, technology has become the key enabler, changing the ways through which societies interact with these global goals. These are the e-commerce platforms, social media, digital finance, e-learning and many others, which present new opportunities that can help in attaining the SDGs. Sustainable development is influenced by digital platforms in a significant way since they bring about solutions that can enhance the achievement of the SDGs. These platforms are therefore instrumental in delivering improved economic growth, social inclusion and environmental stewardship in the future. However, to get the best out of it, there are some issues that need to be solved, for example, digital gap, environmental problems, and legal questions. In this way, it will be possible to use the potential of digital platforms and contribute to the achievement of the SDGs and the creation of a better future. Digital platforms have democratized access to global markets, enabling even small medium enterprises (SMEs) in remote areas to participate in international trade. This increased market access can drive economic growth by fostering entrepreneurship, creating jobs, and reducing poverty. The multifaceted impact of digital platforms on sustainable development, focusing on economic growth, social inclusion, and environmental sustainability are explained below:

1. E-commerce and Economic Growth

The e-commerce platforms such as Amazon, Alibaba and other similar platforms have brought about a new era of global trade because they allow small businesses and entrepreneurs to sell their products in foreign markets (Zhu et al., 2006). These platforms lower the hurdles of entry allowing MSMEs from rural and remote areas to engage in international trade. For instance, Alibaba's Taobao Villages has shown how e-commerce can impact rural economy in China positively, thus eradicating poverty and empowering the economy (Lin & Liu, 2018). This corresponds with the eighth SDG which is to ensure sustained, inclusive, and sustainable economic growth, full and productive employment, and decent work for all.

2. Job Creation and the Gig Economy

The emergence of platforms like Uber, Upwork, Fiverr and others has led to the creation of new jobs mainly in the urban areas (Sundararajan, 2016). These platforms have revolutionized conventional employment by providing flexible working arrangements hence enhancing economic development and decreasing unemployment incidences. However, the gig economy also has its drawbacks, including job insecurity and the absence of social protection that need to be resolved to achieve the goals of SDG 8.

3. Digital Financial Services

Mobile money apps such as PayPal, M-Pesa and use of blockchain has had a positive influence on the expansion of access to financial services especially in the developing world (Aker & Mbiti, 2010). For instance, M-Pesa has transformed the financial sector in Kenya by extending formal financial services to millions of people who previously could not access them, save or borrow money (Jack & Suri, 2014). This advancement contributes to the achievement of SDG 1 (No Poverty) and SDG 10 (Reduced Inequalities) since it offers financial services to the vulnerable groups.

4. Education and E-Learning Platforms

Technological advancement in the education sector has made learning easier, flexible and more accessible to everyone. Sites such as Coursera, Khan Academy, Google Classroom provide courses from renowned universities and colleges to learners across the globe and mostly at free of cost (Alalshaikh, 2015). This supports SDG 4 (Quality Education) as it offers education to all ages regardless of the location or financial status they are in. In the COVID-19 outbreak, e-learning platforms were very useful in maintaining continuity of learning especially in countries with limited physical learning infrastructure (Zhang et al., 2020). Nevertheless, the issue of digital divide persists, with poor students in different regions still unable to access the required technology and internet connection which only widens the inequalities in education.

5. Healthcare and Telemedicine

Companies such as Teladoc and Practo have made healthcare more accessible especially to the rural and remote areas (World Health Organization, 2016). These platforms allow patients to speak to healthcare practitioners without physically visiting them which makes the delivery of healthcare services more convenient and cheaper. This advancement is important in the achievement of SDG 3 (Good Health and Well-being) because it enhances the health of people by providing appropriate medical consultation and treatment especially in emergency situations such as the current COVID-19 pandemic. Digital platform has played a significant role in availing information to the people especially on ways to prevent diseases and improve on their health.

6. Social Inclusion and Equality

The use of social media such as Face book, Twitter and Instagram has been widely used to support social inclusion and equality (Sandoval-Almazan & Gil-Garcia, 2014). These platforms have empowered the minority groups to express their grievances, fight for their causes and even campaign for change. The hashtag revolutions such as #MeToo and #BlackLivesMatter have become worldwide trends thanks to the social media platforms. They help support SDG 10 – Reduced Inequality as they provide a voice to those who are marginalized and can result in bringing change to society. The use of social media also presents challenges, such as the spread of misinformation and online harassment, which need to be managed to ensure these platforms contribute positively to social inclusion.

7. Digital Platforms and Environmental Awareness

Social networks and other internet-based tools have been crucial in increasing people's awareness of environmental problems and encouraging environmentally friendly behavior. Some examples of these organizations include Ecosia, a search engine that plants trees using the money it gets from advertisements, and Earth911 which offers information regarding the recycling process (Gleick, 2014). These initiatives contribute towards the achievement of SDG 13 (Climate Action) since they promote collective action against climate change. Companies like Airbnb have brought in the sharing economy that when well managed has a lesser negative impact on the environment than conventional industries like hospitality and transport (Guttentag, 2015). Digital platforms enhance sustainable consumption and production thus meeting the goal of sustainable development goal 12 (Responsible Consumption and Production).

8. Smart Cities and IoT

Internet of Things (IoT) has made it possible to develop smart cities where the system of city's infrastructures are controlled through digital platforms (Caragliu, Del Bo, & Nijkamp, 2011). Smart cities use technology in utilizing energy, waste, and transport hence minimizing the impact on the environment. For instance, Barcelona City has incorporated IoT sensors to track the quantity of waste that is produced and the best routes for collecting the waste hence minimizing on emissions and cost of operations as explained by Cohen (2015). All these technologies are important in enhancing the realization of sustainable development goal number 11, Sustainable cities and Communities since they enhance the sustainability of cities as well as welfare of the inhabitants.

9. Sustainable Consumption and Production

Digital platforms have also helped in the promotion of circular economy through reuse and recycling of products. OLX and Freecycle are just examples of platforms that contribute to the buy and sell of used items and hence advocate for sustainable consumption (Stahel, 2016). Through increasing the useful life of products and decreasing the need for new resources, these platforms support the SDG 12 (Responsible Consumption and Production). The technology is being applied to increase accountability in supply chains so that the products are procured, manufactured, and delivered sustainably. This technology assists in the consumption patterns that are sustainable because consumers can make proper decisions on the products to buy.

PUBLIC-PRIVATE PARTNERSHIPS IN THE CONTEXT OF SDGS

PPPs are working relationships between the public and private sectors in which they agree to work together to achieve certain objectives that are usually related to the provision of public goods and services. As for the SDGs, PPPs are especially important because they allow merging the financial capabilities, ideas, and technologies of the private sector with the government's controlling and social orientation. These collaborations are especially important to solve multifaceted issues that the world faces today including poverty, inequity, environmental degradation, and lack of adequate basic human needs, for instance health and education.

PPPs work on different structures that can be contractual, or where the public sector is involved, a more strategic relationship with the private sector where risks and returns are shared. In the context of SDGs, PPPs are useful for mobilizing resources for large infrastructure projects, stimulating improvements in sustainability, and improving the quality of public services. For instance, the alliance with the private telecommunications companies has been very crucial in extending internet connectivity in the developing countries which contributes to the ninth industrial innovation and infrastructure and the seventeenth partnership objectives (World Bank, 2017). PPPs are not only a source of funds, but also a source of knowledge and experience exchange and capacity enhancement. While the private sector provides the new technologies, the better ways of managing, and the market solutions, the public sector offers the policies and the motivations to ensure that these practices respond to the public good. The effectiveness of PPPs in delivering the SDGs premised on the fact that these partnerships must be anchored on well-coordinated contractual relationships that set out the rights and obligations of the contracting parties in a manner that serves the intended sustainable development goals (Bovaird, 2004). Many PPPs over the years have been instrumental in the achievement of sustainable development. For instance, in the energy sector, the collaboration between governments and private entities has made it possible to establish projects that support SDG 7 on Affordable and Clean Energy, for instance through solar and wind power. The use of PPPs has helped to increase the availability of medical structures and services in areas where they are needed, thus contributing to the achievement of the third SDG (Good Health and Well-being). These historical examples demonstrate the potential of PPPs to address critical global challenges and advance the SDGs.

DIGITAL PLATFORMS AS ENABLERS OF PUBLIC-PRIVATE PARTNERSHIPS

Digital platforms are increasingly becoming vital tools for facilitating Public-Private Partnerships (PPPs) aimed at achieving the Sustainable Development Goals (SDGs). They act as marketplaces where the public sector organization can access private players for partnership in providing services and infrastructure, funding health care, education and environmental conservation. Through developing a virtual environment where the stakeholders can post the materials, information, and knowledge, the digital platforms contribute to the improvement of the PPPs' outcomes. For instance, blockchain technology can help in creating transparency and accountability in financial transactions between the partners that eventually can minimize the risks related to PPPs (Sarker, Ahuja, & Sahay, 2020). Digital platform application in PPPs also enhance the aspect of real time communication and information flow between the partners. Cloud systems and collaborative applications enable public and private individuals to cooperate effectively with one another irrespective of country borders. This level of connectivity also helps to fast forward project schedules and avail all stakeholders with project goals and objectives. Also, the results of the work that is done can be monitored using data analytics and performance tools which are crucial in decision-making and to show progress (Meijer, 2018). It has been pointed out there are a lot of cases where digital platforms have facilitated PPPs. For instance, in smart cities, IoT-based system has been employed to connect public service delivery with private sector developments including smart grids and ITS in the realization of SDG 11 (Sustainable Cities and Communities) (Amin, Khan, & Holz, 2019). Another example is the application of Digital health platforms in developing countries where the public health agencies partnered with private tech companies to provide the telemedicine facilities supporting SDG 3, which is good Health and Well-being (Gururaj, Saxena & Morsink, 2021). Such platforms not only bring efficiencies to the sectors but also help bring important services to the under-served population. These platforms also have a pivotal contribution in the achievement of the SDGs as they foster PPPs and present innovation and scalability for the global challenges.

CASE STUDIES OF DIGITAL PLATFORMS DRIVING PUBLIC-PRIVATE PERTNERSHIPS AND SUSTAINABLE DEVELOPMENT GOALS

Digital platforms have been found to be an effective tool in enhancing PPPs in the implementation of the SDGs. They rally round various players, allowing them to address set goals and objectives in an effective and efficient manner. Here are a few examples of how digital platforms have been used to support successful PPPs in different industries.

1. M-Pesa: Mobile Money and the Fight against Poverty (SDG 1: No poverty)

The use of an ICT-based platform to mobilize a PPP for sustainable development is perhaps best illustrated by M-Pesa, a mobile money service that was launched in Kenya with support from the Kenyan government and a private telecoms company, Safaricom. The innovation of M-Pesa has greatly enhanced the aspect of financial accessibility in Kenya especially for the persons who have not been able to get a physical account with a bank. SDG 1 (No Poverty) has greatly benefited from this platform by low-income earners, savers, and remittance beneficiaries who have gained better financial security through this platform (Jack & Suri, 2014). The experience of M-Pesa has resulted in such schemes in other countries as well; this demonstrates the role of digital platforms in PPPs for sustainable development. Drawing from the case of M-Pesa, it is crucial to understand that this digital platform has gone beyond the provision of financial services. M-Pesa has not only impacted on the achievement of SDG1– No Poverty but has also had a significant influence on several other Sustainable Development Goals.

For instance, it has ensured the provision of basic human needs such as health and education through mobile payments as provided by M-Pesa under the UN SDG 3 & 4. Services that are related to health such as paying for premiums for health insurance or receiving funds for medical purposes are now available to low-income people. Likewise, parents can use M-Pesa to pay for school fees directly, and guarantee that their children are able to attend school without uninterrupted. The experience of M-Pesa has been replicated in other parts of Africa and beyond and is evident that digital platforms can be scaled up to support PPPs for sustainable development. Tanzania, Ghana and India have copied this model, and adapted it to suit their environments to solve issues such as financial exclusion and other developmental issues. M-Pesa's impact also underscores the importance of supportive regulatory environments. The Kenyan government's collaboration with Safaricom, including the creation of enabling policies, was crucial to the platform's success. This highlights the role of effective governance and regulatory frameworks in fostering innovation and scaling digital platforms for development (Ndung'u, 2017).

2. Digital Green and Agricultural Development (SDG 2: Zero Hunger)

Partnering with the Indian government and private technology firms, a non-profit organization called Digital Green has created a digital tool for boosting agricultural yields and promoting sustainable practices. The platform incorporates videos in training farmers on proper ways of farming that would allow them to improve production and have less effect on the environment. This initiative helps to achieve SDG 2 on ending hunger, achieving food security and improved nutrition and sustainable agriculture as it seeks to address food security issues and enhance the wellbeing of smallholder farmers. This is evident with marked increase in the yields of crops and the use of appropriate farming methods by the farmers who have embraced the platform (Gandhi et al., 2016). The training that Digital Green offers using videos in the form of training modules is not only a novel approach to the sharing of agricultural knowledge but also an effective method of 'enabling' farmers by arming them with the knowledge and tools they need to make appropriate decisions. The use of local farmers in the videos makes the content familiar to the viewers and hence makes it more engaging thus making the message more effective. This method has enhanced better understanding and recall of knowledge and thus enhanced the uptake of improved methods of farming hence enhancing productivity in the agricultural sector (Gandhi, Veeraraghavan, Toyama, & Ramprasad, 2009). The platform has also used data and analytics to curate content and monitor the effectiveness of the programs it airs. Farmers report the adoption rates of various practices, and the results obtained to Digital Green. This feature makes it possible to update the training consistently and makes sure the training material is most effective. This feedback loop has helped the platform to make a lot of progress in the increase of the practice of sustainable practices as well as the productivity of agricultural yields (Toyama, 2011).

Digital Green also contributes to the achievement of the third sustainable development goal, that is, Climate Action through encouraging practices that have least effects on the environment and practices that build up the resilience of the climate. These are content on water conservation, soil health management and the use of organic inputs to enable farmers to cope with the prevailing climatic conditions and reduce the impacts of agriculture on the environment. This focus on sustainability ensures that the benefits of increased productivity do not come at the expense of long-term environmental health (Gandhi et al., 2016). The following are some of the lessons and best practices that can be deduced from these case studies on the use of digital platforms in PPPs for the SDGs: First, successful initiatives require a great deal of cooperation between the public and private sectors with both bringing their strengths to the partnership. Second, the question of scalability and flexibility is important when speaking about mass popularity of the digital platforms; the example of M-Pesa and similar platforms' internationalization proves it.

So, these case studies demonstrate that user-centered design plays a crucial role in the development of digital platforms, to satisfy the needs of the target audience. M-Pesa and Digital Green serve as examples of how these platforms can be used to solve some of the major global challenges and the findings in these case studies can be used to draw lessons for future applications.

DIGITAL PLATFORMS AND PUBLIC-PRIVATE PARTNERSHIPS IN INDIA

Digital platforms are one of the most important innovations in the realization of PPPs for SDG in India. These platforms are creating the linkages of government, private sectors, and civil society organizations in the effective and efficient use of resources, increased transparency, and innovation. The present digital environment in India is gradually developing with digital initiations such as M-Pesa, Digital Green, and others in focus, proving that technology can be used to solve developmental issues. Consequently, this essay analyses the different trends of PPPs in India facilitated by digital platforms, its effects on the achievement of SDGs, and the emerging prospects and constraints. Technology has made it easier for PPPs to run through the increase in use of digital technology in India, which has improved communication, coordination and cooperation among the stakeholders. These platforms are efficient means of communication between the government agencies, private companies, NGOs and the public, aimed at achieving a common goal. Mobile applications, cloud computing, big data analytics, and blockchain technology integration into PPPs has enhanced the effectiveness and efficiency of these partnerships. Perhaps, the most famous example of the use of such platforms is the Digital India initiative that was started by the Government of India in 2015. This initiative is with an intention to make India a digitally empowered society and a knowledge economy. It offers a strong support for PPPs since it delivers digital services such as e-governance, digital facilities, and digital literacy programs. Digital India has played a key role in development of right conditions in India for successful PPPs by building the right support structures and policies. Another is the Unified Payment Interface (UPI) which was initiated by National Payments Corporation of India (NPCI) in conjunction with the Reserve Bank of India (RBI) and some of the private commercial banks. Another example is the Unified Payments Interface (UPI), developed by the National Payments Corporation of India (NPCI) in collaboration with the Reserve Bank of India (RBI) and various private sector banks. UPI has revolutionized the financial landscape in India by facilitating seamless, real-time payments between individuals, businesses, and government entities. This digital platform has not only enhanced financial inclusion but also provided a secure and efficient payment mechanism for PPPs engaged in various sectors, such as healthcare, education, and infrastructure. Another notable initiative is the Jan Dhan Yojana, a financial inclusion program launched by the Government of India. This program leverages digital platforms to provide access to banking services, insurance, and credit to millions of unbanked individuals across the country. The program has successfully opened over 400 million bank accounts, significantly reducing financial exclusion and contributing to poverty reduction.

Digital platforms are also playing a part in environmental sustainability in India in the sense they are encouraging sustainable practices and minimizing the environmental footprint in various sectors. The National Agriculture Market (eNAM) for instance is an online portal where farmers can sell their produce to various buyers across the country without the intervention of middlemen. The service of eNAM helps in cutting down on emissions of greenhouse gases in that it saves on transport of physical commodities and food waste. In the energy sector, there are various organizations such as EESL (Energy Efficiency Services Limited) to promote the use of energy-efficient technologies and practices. EESL is a joint venture of public sector undertakings under the Ministry of Power that has used digital media in the promotion of energy efficiency programs like distribution of LED bulbs and smart meters. These activities have led to tremendous change in the energy conservation and emissions of carbon, which has supported the attainment of SDG 13. Even though digital platforms have been useful in PPPs and the attainment of SDGs in the country, there are some challenges that are still present. The first of the challenges is the digital divide, which is the difference between the people who are connected to the internet and the people who are not. In India, the digital divide is even more apparent than in other countries, especially in rural areas where the Internet connection and computer literacy are still a problem. Solving this problem requires collective actions to advance digital assets, educate people on the use of technology, and guarantee that technology environments are friendly to all.

CHALLENGES AND OPPORTUNITIES IN LEVERAGING DIGITAL PLATFORMS FOR PUBLIC-PRIVATE PARTNERSHIPS

Though digital platforms offer a great potential to support the PPPs to realize the SDGs, their use and deployment are not without challenges. Some of the difficulties include the following: The first one is the digital divide which is the differentiation between the individuals who have access to the digital technologies and those who do not. This divide is especially marked in the development regions where issues of infrastructural development including internet connection and digital literacy may hamper the efficient use of digital platforms in PPPs. If not for these disparities, digital platforms are likely to widen the gap rather than reduce inequalities (Hargittai & Shaw, 2019). One of the problems of PPPs is the ever-increasing development of digital technologies. This is especially so because new technologies may be developed, or existing ones change with time and PPPs may be caught flat-footed. This can result in a misfit between the technology implemented in a project and the current innovations which can make some of the digital solutions outdated or suboptimal. For PPPs to be able to remain innovative and alert to the changes in technology, there is need to continuously invest in innovation and flexibility to change strategies as adopted for digitization (Bughin et al., 2017). Also, the application of AI and automated decision-making in PPPs has raised some ethical questions in the recent past. AI systems are strong, but they are prejudiced and can only replicate the prejudices of the data set that was fed to them. There is therefore a need to ensure that AI is used in PPPs in a manner that is ethical and transparent so that the public can have faith in the use of digital platforms for their benefits to be realized equitably. This involves not only technical solutions but also governance frameworks that emphasize accountability and inclusivity (O'Neil, 2016). Another major issue is that of data protection and security. Data protection and security remains another major issue. Digital platforms entail the use of data and information that may be collected and shared in large amounts, and this raises issues of storage, use and protection of this data. To protect the privacy and security of the individual, both the public and private sectors face a vast number of regulatory issues. If these concerns are not met, public trust will be eroded and legal sanctions will ensue, which is detrimental to the PPP (Dijck et al., 2018). Once more, the development and maintenance of such platforms can be costly and may prove unattainable for many organizations and especially those in developing nations. The costs involved in the construction of sound, secure and sustainable digital architecture can be significant. However, if there is a lack of funding for these partnerships, it means that the PPPs are likely to fail in effectively implementing digital solutions that have a potential for helping to achieve the goals set for the SDGs. Thus, the challenge of securing sustainable sources of finance, maybe using future financial instruments or blend finance is important in dealing with this challenge (Schmidt-Traub, 2015). However, there are several opportunities that digital platforms afford for innovation and development in PPPs. And one of the key benefits is that this approach may be scaled. Social media for instance can cover a vast audience in the shortest time possible thus the possibility of expanding successful PPP projects across regions or even internationally. For instance, the application that enables e-learning can be further developed to reach millions of learners around the globe and therefore be in support of SDG 4 (Quality Education).

Promoting transparency and accountability in PPPs is one of the profound opportunities in digital platforms. These platforms can transmit information in real-time on matters concerning the project in terms of advancement and financial operations and results. Through constant output of information on the functioning of PPPs, digital platforms help stakeholders to assess the efficiency of such cooperation. This increased openness also results in improved decision making since the decision makers are equipped with current, relevant information regarding the resources and other factors necessary to make changes in the organizational strategies. Moreover, it enhances responsibility since the nature of the data present entails that all stakeholders including the public keep on checking the performance of the partnership as well as the way they utilize resources (Meijer, 2018). It is, therefore, crucial to eliminate the digital divide especially in the developing countries to harness the full benefits of the digital platforms in delivery of PPPs. Governments can commit to infrastructure build up, jointly with the private sector, including broadband Internet connection and low-cost digital equipment. Moreover, programs that aim at enhancing the use of the digital platforms are important so that people and groups can use the device and internet well. That is why, training programs in digital skills provided within the framework of public-private partnerships can help people to leverage PPP projects in the field of digitalization and contribute to the achievement of inclusive and sustainable development objectives (Van Dijk, 2020). In conclusion it could be said that there are major barriers to the use of digital platforms in PPPs, but at the same time these barriers are opportunities for development. In this way, the issues of the digital divide, data protection and security, and transparency can become a key to the success of digital PPPs and foster sustainable development.

POLICY AND REGULATORY CONSIDERATIONS

The application of digital platforms in PPPs for SDGs is possible only if there are sound legal frameworks to support it. These frameworks are important so that the digital platforms are established within legal frameworks that will allow for innovation while at the same time preventing the harm of the public. Another is the creation of data governance policies that define how data is acquired, processed, disseminated and utilized within and across sectors. The use of data governance can help to avoid the abuse of data and guarantee that all the partners of the public and private sectors act according to ethical and legal norms, including the protection of privacy and information security (Taylor & Floridi, 2019). Furthermore, the role of regulations is to consider the issue of integration between various online services. Interoperability is essential in ensuring that various digital systems applied in the partnership of the public and private sector work together as intended. There is a need to set norms and procedures that will enable these platforms to share information and data hence improving the efficiency and effectiveness of PPPs. This calls for collaboration at both the national and the international level to harmonize the standards and ensure that the digital platforms are interoperable across the borders and across the sectors (Gasser & Palfrey, 2020). Governments and international bodies have the responsibility of establishing environment that supports development of the digital platforms for PPPs. Leveraging policies of the government, the government can encourage the private sector through the provision of tax exemptions, subsidies, or other forms of financial support for PPPs that seek to achieve the SDGs. Also, governments can contribute to the development of digital platforms through funding of communication networks like broadband which is crucial for the diffusion of the platforms especially in the rural areas (Cave, 2017).

International organizations including the United Nations, and the World Bank also play a significant part in disseminating best practices and establishing international benchmarks as well as fostering international cooperation. These organizations can assist in technical and financial terms in the implementation of digital platforms in LMICs. In addition, they can assist in co-ordination of policies in different jurisdictions to facilitate global expansion of digital platforms and support their contribution to the SDGs (Kende-Robb, 2018). As the digital platforms are getting more and more involved in the PPPs, questions of ethics and data protection arise. One of them is the risk of deepening social injustices if the use of online environments is not controlled. For instance, the algorithms applied in digital platforms can be such that they perpetrate biases, hence denying some people services or opportunities. It is imperative to understand how to create and manage digital platforms in a fair manner for the purpose of attaining sustainable development (Eubanks, 2018). Another significant factor is data privacy since social media and other digital platforms tend to gather extensive amounts of personal information. This is why governments and their private sector partners must ensure that data protection laws are adhered to protect individual's rights to privacy. This includes Following the General Data Protection Regulation (GDPR) in Europe that sets high standards in data protection and has been a benchmark to other countries. It is critical to be open about the use of data and share information about how user data is processed in the digital platforms employed in PPPs to ensure that the public has trust in the platforms (Zuboff, 2019). Therefore, the integration of digital platforms into PPPs for the attainment of the SDGs needs policy and regulatory framework. The government and other international organizations require coming up with a set of rules that will govern the innovation without compromising the public interests. Ethical issues must be also addressed as well as data privacy that must be protected in these initiatives as well. In this way, stakeholders can make use of the full advantages of digital platforms for sustainable development that is as well safe and fair.

FUTURE DIRECTIONS AND EMERGING TRENDS

As the digital platforms grow, several trends are likely to emerge, and affect the PPPs and the achievement of the SDGs. One of the most impactful trends is the use of AI in digital platforms. Machine learning, data analytics, and other AI tools can be used to improve decision-making processes, the allocation of resources and the accuracy of future outcome predictions. This can enhance the quantity and quality of PPPs as they get to be more efficient, effective, and have methods and processes explained or even done for them (Brynjolfsson & McAfee, 2017). Another of the trends that is becoming noticeable is the application of blockchain technology. Blockchain is a solution for an effective and decentralized creation of the record-keeping system that can enhance the PPPs' transparency and accountability. Using blockchain technology, it is possible to make records of transactions and agreements such that all the involved parties are likely to view the only correct representation of the facts. This can be especially useful in supply chain and in financial operations where security and identity are paramount (Tapscott & Tapscott, 2016). Future of PPPs appears as more connected and intertwined with each other and with other digital ecosystems and actors. These systems will be more integrated, and this will give a boost in the realization of the goals set in the SDGs. Such integration can result in the creation of better solutions that would address several aspects of sustainable development simultaneously (Gasser & Palfrey, 2020). An increase in the use of data analysis in the management of PPPs is set to be the key driver in the future evolution of the concept. Most of the digital platforms that employ big data and analytics enable one to gauge productivity, stakeholder engagement, as well as the success of projects. This approach will enhance the quality of the decisions made and therefore the performance and efficiency of the PPP projects and hence enhance accountability (Mayer-Schönberger & Cukier, 2013).

Internet of Things (IoT) and 5G networks that are still in their development stages are also expected to disrupt PPPs. IoT devices can gather information from different sources in real-time and this can be useful for monitoring and managing projects. For example, application of smart sensors in infrastructure projects can provide information on usage and maintenance requirements making the project more efficient and sustainable (Atzori et al., 2010). On the other hand, 5G will improve the networks and data transfer rates thereby providing more interactive digital platforms (Chen et al., 2018). In the context of using digital platforms in PPPs, it is possible to identify that the future is characterized by very active development of new technologies and constant changes in trends that can be both beneficial and problematic. AI, blockchain, IoT and 5G technologies can improve the efficiency, credibility and expansiveness of PPPs and thus support the SDGs implementation. It is therefore important for stakeholders to be aware of these developments and be able to harness the full potential of these technologies in achieving sustainable development. In addition, the implementation of PPPs with the help of AI, blockchain, IoT, and 5G creates new opportunities for developing organizational and methodological approaches to creating new business models and value creation models. Since these technologies facilitate efficient processes and improved transparency, they reduce the threshold for the small-scaled business to partner with the large-scaled business, which could potentially demoralize PPPs and encourage the efficient economic growth (Schwab, 2017). In addition, the availability of big data enables the delivery of services that are most relevant to the communities, which would also make PPPs more consistent with the principles of sustainable development. These digital innovations can enhance risk management in PPPs since they offer insights into possible problems and alert the stakeholders to such problems. For instance, with AI analytics one can predict possible delays in infrastructural projects or areas of weakness in supply chain that may lead to over cost control and project failure (Agrawal, Gans, & Goldfarb, 2018). This proactive measure not only strengthens the PPPs but also increases the durability of the development process, which is helpful in the efficient use of resources to avoid wastage. The use of digital technologies in PPPs can be seen as a part of the processes that take place in the context of digitalization of the economy and business, which is considered as one of the main factors promoting economic growth and competitiveness.

When governments and private entities work together on digital platforms, they can complement each other's activities – for example, the public sector has extensive experience in regulation, while the private sector is full of technological solutions (Mazzucato, 2018). This integration is important for solving modern transnational problems, including climate change and social injustice, which cannot be solved by a particular sector or country alone.

Thus, as PPPs are still developing because of these technological trends, it is crucial for the stakeholders to address the ethical issues of the digital platforms. Concerns like data privacy, cybersecurity, and digital inclusion technological have to be solved to make sure that positive outcomes of the technological progress do not deepen social divides (Zuboff, 2019). When it comes to the design and utilization of digital platforms, PPPs can play a significant role in the enhancement of the ethical features by ensuring that the created platforms are ethical and fair for the users.

CONCLUSION

Digital platforms represent a transformative force in Public-Private Partnerships (PPPs) aimed at achieving the Sustainable Development Goals (SDGs). Such platforms bring remarkable opportunities for enhanced cooperation, productivity, and openness in different spheres, including finance, healthcare, education, and infrastructure. From the examples of M-Pesa, Digital Green, Alibaba etc it is clear that digital platforms can complement the PPPs' activities and respond to the most urgent global needs and support sustainable development. This integration of digital platforms into PPPs is however not without some challenges. Challenges like the availability of the internet, privacy, and the requirement of proper regulation to support the application of such technologies must be resolved to the utmost. Equal access to digital content, privacy, and proper polices are critical for reaping the opportunities offered by online solutions while minimizing the threats. Future opportunities for PPPs include artificial intelligence, blockchain, IoT, and 5G networks as the technology frontiers for PPPs. These innovations are said to help to improve data usage for decision making, increase transparency, and enable more integrated and scalable solutions. This is because the use of digital platforms is set to assume even more importance in the promotion of sustainable development as the various platforms develop further. Governments, private companies, and international organizations must work together to counteract the current issues and successfully implement new technologies. In this way, they can guarantee that the SDGs are achieved using the digital platforms in an inclusive, equitable and secure manner. It can therefore be concluded that PPPs in the digital age will pave the way towards the resolution of global problems and sustainable development if the opportunities will be seized wisely and cautiously.

REFERENCES

Agrawal, A., Gans, J., & Goldfarb, A. (2018). *Prediction machines: The simple economics of artificial intelligence*. Harvard Business Review Press.

Aker, J. C., & Mbiti, I. M. (2010). Mobile phones and economic development in Africa. *The Journal of Economic Perspectives*, 24(3), 207–232. DOI: 10.1257/jep.24.3.207

Alalshaikh, S. (2015). The role of e-learning in the implementation of the sustainable development goals. International Journal of Education and Development using ICT, 11(1), 92-103. DOI: DOI: 10.1080/09751122.2015.11669057

Amin, M., Khan, A., & Holz, H. (2019). Smart city initiatives: PPP approaches and digital platforms. *Journal of Urban Technology*, 26(4), 3–18. DOI: 10.1080/10630732.2019.1649484

Atzori, L., Iera, A., & Morabito, G. (2010). The Internet of Things: A survey. *Computer Networks*, 54(15), 2787–2805. DOI: 10.1016/j.comnet.2010.05.010

Bovaird, T. (2004). Public-private partnerships: From contested concepts to prevalent practice. *International Review of Administrative Sciences*, 70(2), 199–215. DOI: 10.1177/0020852304044250

Brynjolfsson, E., & McAfee, A. (2017). *Machine, platform, crowd: Harnessing our digital future*. W.W. Norton & Company.

Bughin, J., Hazan, E., Ramaswamy, S., Chui, M., Allas, T., Dahlström, P., & Trench, M. (2017). *Artificial Intelligence: The next digital frontier?* McKinsey Global Institute.

Caragliu, A., Del Bo, C., & Nijkamp, P. (2011). Smart cities in Europe. *Journal of Urban Technology*, 18(2), 65–82. DOI: 10.1080/10630732.2011.601117

Cave, J. (2017). *Digital government: Leveraging technology to improve public sector efficiency and responsiveness*. OECD Publishing.

Chen, M., Ma, Y., Li, S., Wu, D., Zhang, Y., & Wang, L. (2018). A survey on 5G: Architecture and design principles. *IEEE Transactions on Network and Service Management*, 15(3), 1085–1104. DOI: 10.1109/TNSM.2018.2847682

Chen, S., Sun, S., Peng, H., & Wang, H. (2018). Digital platform strategy: Effects of competition and collaboration. *Journal of Management Information Systems*, 35(4), 978–1001. DOI: 10.1080/07421222.2018.1524823

Chin, W., Callaghan, C., & Lamparello, N. (2017). Smarter Cities: Bridging the Knowledge Divide with Corporate-NGO Partnerships. *Sustainable Cities and Society*, 29, 329–339. DOI: 10.1016/j.scs.2017.01.001

Cohen, B. (2015). The smart city wheel: A visual model for understanding the relationship between technological, environmental, and social dimensions of urban sustainability. *Sustainable Cities and Society*, 10(1), 1–8. DOI: 10.1016/j.scs.2014.07.007

Crawford, J., & Shinn, D. (2021). Digital learning: The impact of digital platforms on quality education. *International Journal of Educational Technology in Higher Education*, 18(1), 1–14. DOI: 10.1186/s41239-021-00262-6

Demirgüç-Kunt, A., Klapper, L., Singer, D., Ansar, S., & Hess, J. (2018). *The Global Findex Database 2017: Measuring Financial Inclusion and the Fintech Revolution.* World Bank., DOI: 10.1596/978-1-4648-1259-0

Dijck, J. V., Poell, T., & de Waal, M. (2018). *The platform society: Public values in a connective world.* Oxford University Press., DOI: 10.1093/oso/9780190889760.001.0001

Eubanks, V. (2018). *Automating inequality: How high-tech tools profile, police, and punish the poor.* St. Martin's Press.

Gandhi, R., Veeraraghavan, R., Toyama, K., & Ramprasad, V. (2009). Digital Green: Participatory video and mediated instruction for agricultural extension. *Information Technologies and International Development*, 5(1), 1–15. DOI: 10.1162/itid.2009.0014

Gandhi, R., Veeraraghavan, R., Toyama, K., & Ramprasad, V. (2016). Digital Green: A large-scale model for agricultural extension. *Information Technologies and International Development*, 12(4), 47–61.

Gasser, U., & Palfrey, J. (2020). Interoperability in the digital age. Berkman Klein Center for Internet & Society. DOI: DOI: 10.2139/ssrn.3522971

Gasser, U., & Palfrey, J. (2020). *Born digital: How children grow up in a digital age* (2nd ed.). Basic Books.

Gururaj, K., Saxena, S., & Morsink, C. (2021). Telemedicine and digital health platforms in developing countries: A PPP approach. *Global Health Research and Policy*, 6(1), 45–55. DOI: 10.1186/s41256-021-00209-8 PMID: 34847956

Guttentag, D. A. (2015). Airbnb: Disruptive innovation and the rise of the sharing economy. *Current Issues in Tourism*, 18(12), 1192–1217. DOI: 10.1080/13683500.2013.827159

Hansen, M. C., Potapov, P. V., Moore, R., Hancher, M., Turubanova, S. A., Tyukavina, A., Thau, D., Stehman, S. V., Goetz, S. J., Loveland, T. R., Kommareddy, A., Egorov, A., Chini, L., Justice, C. O., & Townshend, J. R. (2013). High-Resolution Global Maps of 21st-Century Forest Cover Change. *Science*, 342(6160), 850–853. DOI: 10.1126/science.1244693 PMID: 24233722

Hargittai, E., & Shaw, A. (2019). Digital inequality: Differences in young adults' use of the internet. *Communication Research*, 46(2), 375–397. DOI: 10.1177/0093650217715225

Hargittai, E., & Shaw, A. (2019). Mind the skills gap: The role of Internet know-how and gender in differentiated contributions to Wikipedia. *Information Communication and Society*, 19(4), 424–442. DOI: 10.1080/1369118X.2014.957711

Jack, W., & Suri, T. (2014). Risk sharing and transactions costs: Evidence from Kenya's mobile money revolution. *The American Economic Review*, 104(1), 183–223. DOI: 10.1257/aer.104.1.183

Jack, W., & Suri, T. (2014). Risk sharing and transactions costs: Evidence from Kenya's mobile money revolution. *The American Economic Review*, 104(1), 183–223. DOI: 10.1257/aer.104.1.183

Jha, A., Doshi, A., & Patel, S. (2019). Artificial intelligence and its role in advancing agriculture: A review. *Journal of Cleaner Production*, 240, 118208. DOI: 10.1016/j.jclepro.2019.118208

Kende-Robb, C. (2018). The role of international organizations in facilitating digital transformation. *World Development*, 114, 1–6.

Kohler, J. C., & Bowra, A. (2020). The Role of Global Health Partnerships in Improving Access to Medicines in Low- and Middle-Income Countries. *Globalization and Health*, 16(1), 1–10. DOI: 10.1186/s12992-019-0535-0 PMID: 31898532

Lehner, O. M., Grabmann, R., & Ennsgraber, C. (2015). Entrepreneurial Impacts of Crowdfunding on Sustainability-Oriented Startups. *Journal of Business Research*, 68(4), 911–917. DOI: 10.1016/j.jbusres.2014.11.031

Lin, J., & Liu, W. (2018). E-commerce and Taobao Villages: A path to poverty alleviation in rural China. *Journal of Rural Studies*, 60, 123–134. DOI: 10.1016/j.jrurstud.2018.04.004

Martens, T. (2018). E-Estonia: The rise of digital governance. *Public Administration Review*, 78(1), 36–45. DOI: 10.1111/puar.12973

Mayer-Schönberger, V., & Cukier, K. (2013). *Big data: A revolution that will transform how we live, work, and think*. Houghton Mifflin Harcourt.

Mazzucato, M. (2018). *The entrepreneurial state: Debunking public vs. private sector myths* (Revised ed.). Penguin Books.

Meijer, A. (2018). Digital platforms and public governance: The enabling role of technology in public-private partnerships. *Government Information Quarterly*, 35(4), 637–644. DOI: 10.1016/j.giq.2018.09.002

Mekonnen, M. M., & Hoekstra, A. Y. (2016). Four billion people facing severe water scarcity. *Science Advances*, 2(2), e1500323. DOI: 10.1126/sciadv.1500323 PMID: 26933676

Mulligan, G., Andersen, R., & Kimbler, L. (2019). The Role of Digital Technologies in Enabling Sustainable Development. *Journal of Environmental Management*, 248, 109293. DOI: 10.1016/j.jenvman.2019.109293

Ndung'u, N. (2017). *A digital financial services revolution in Kenya: The M-Pesa case study*. Center for Global Development.

O'Neil, C. (2016). *Weapons of math destruction: How big data increases inequality and threatens democracy*. Crown.

Oliveira, J. A., Silva, L. A., & Lima, M. M. (2019). IoT-enabled smart grids: A comprehensive review. *Energy Reports*, 5, 169–183. DOI: 10.1016/j.egyr.2019.09.007

Rinaldi, D. (2019). Blockchain Technology as a Tool for Public-Private Partnerships. *Journal of Public Administration: Research and Theory*, 29(4), 501–511. DOI: 10.1093/jopart/muz011

Sachs, J., Schmidt-Traub, G., Kroll, C., Lafortune, G., & Fuller, G. (2019). *Sustainable Development Report 2019: Transformations to Achieve the SDGs*. Bertelsmann Stiftung and Sustainable Development Solutions Network., DOI: 10.1017/9781108472026

Sarker, S., Ahuja, M., & Sahay, S. (2020). Blockchain technology and public-private partnerships: A framework for sustainable development. *Information Systems Journal*, 30(6), 889–915. DOI: 10.1111/isj.12261

Schmidt-Traub, G. (2015). Investment needs to achieve the Sustainable Development Goals: Understanding the billions and trillions. SDSN Working Paper. Sustainable Development Solutions Network.

Schwab, K. (2017). *The Fourth Industrial Revolution*. Crown Business.

Sundararajan, A. (2016). *The sharing economy: The end of employment and the rise of crowd-based capitalism*. MIT Press.

Tapscott, D., & Tapscott, A. (2016). *Blockchain revolution: How the technology behind bitcoin is changing money, business, and the world*. Penguin Random House.

Taylor, L., & Floridi, L. (2019). Regulating in an algorithmic world: Policy and the public sector. *Philosophy & Technology*, 32(1), 1–14. DOI: 10.1007/s13347-018-0338-9

Tomczak, A., & Brem, A. (2013). A Conceptualized Investment Model of Crowdfunding. *Venture Capital*, 15(4), 335–359. DOI: 10.1080/13691066.2013.847614

Toyama, K. (2011). Technology as amplifier in international development. *Proceedings of the 2011 iConference*, 75-82. https://doi.org/DOI: 10.1145/1940761.1940772

Van Dijk, J. (2020). The digital divide: A research review of the digital gap in the information society. *Annual Review of Sociology*, 46(1), 113–133. DOI: 10.1146/annurev-soc-121919-054532

Wirtz, B. W., Weyerer, J. C., & Schichtel, F. T. (2019). An Integrated Approach to Open Government: An Analysis of the State of Open Government in Europe. *Public Administration Review*, 79(4), 488–502. DOI: 10.1111/puar.12921

Zhang, W., Wang, Y., Yang, L., & Wang, C. (2020). Suspending classes without stopping learning: China's education emergency management policy in the COVID-19 outbreak. *Journal of Risk and Financial Management*, 13(3), 55. DOI: 10.3390/jrfm13030055

Zhu, K., Dong, S., Xu, S. X., & Kraemer, K. L. (2006). Innovation diffusion in global contexts: Determinants of post-adoption digital transformation of European companies. *European Journal of Information Systems*, 15(6), 601–616. DOI: 10.1057/palgrave.ejis.3000650

Zuboff, S. (2019). *The age of surveillance capitalism: The fight for a human future at the new frontier of power*. Public Affairs.

ADDITIONAL READING

Cordella, A., & Bonina, C. M. (2012). A public value perspective for ICT enabled public sector reforms: A theoretical reflection. *Government Information Quarterly*, 29(4), 512–520. DOI: 10.1016/j.giq.2012.03.004

Hanna, N. K. (2011). *Transforming government and building the information society: Challenges and opportunities for the developing world.* Springer Science & Business Media. DOI: 10.1007/978-1-4419-1506-1

International Telecommunication Union (ITU). (2020). *Measuring Digital Development: Facts and Figures 2020.* ITU.

Margetts, H., & Dunleavy, P. (2013). The second wave of digital-era governance: A quasi-paradigm for government on the Web. Philosophical Transactions of the Royal Society A: Mathematical, Physical and Engineering Sciences, 371(1987), 20120382. https://doi.org/DOI: 10.1098/rsta.2012.0382

Meijer, A. (2018). Public accountability in the information age: Reframing the value and challenges of transparency. *International Review of Administrative Sciences*, 74(3), 229–237. DOI: 10.1177/0020852307086399

OECD. (2019). *Public-Private Partnerships: Infrastructure and Public Procurement.* OECD Publishing., DOI: 10.1787/9789264203453-

UNCTAD. (2020). Digital economy report 2020: Digitalization, trade, and development. United Nations Conference on Trade and Development. https://unctad.org/webflyer/digital-economy-report-2020

United Nations. (2015). Transforming Our World: The 2030 Agenda for Sustainable Development. United Nations. https://sdgs.un.org/2030agenda

United Nations. (2020). The UN Global Compact: Annual report 2020. United Nations. https://www.unglobalcompact.org/library/5670

World Economic Forum. (2020). The Global Risks Report 2020. World Economic Forum.

World Economic Forum. (2021). Platform for shaping the future of the digital economy and new value creation. World Economic Forum. https://www.weforum.org/platforms/shaping-the-future-of-the-digital-economy-and-new-value-creation

KEY TERMS AND DEFINITIONS

5G Technology: 5G is the latest wireless cellular network technology that provides higher speed, higher availability and higher capacity in comparison with the previous networks.\

Artificial intelligence: Artificial intelligence, or AI, is technology that enables computers and machines to simulate human intelligence and problem-solving capabilities.

Blockchain Technology: Blockchain technology is a decentralized and distributed digital ledger system that securely records transactions across multiple computers or nodes in a way that ensures the integrity, transparency, and immutability of the data.

Digital platform: A digital platform is the software and technology that is used to integrate business processes and functions.

ICT: It is a term meaning "Information and Communication Technology. In other words, ICT education refers to educational methods that incorporate information and communication technology.

IOT: The internet of things, or IoT, is a network of interrelated devices that connect and exchange data with other IoT devices and the cloud.

Public-private partnerships: Public private partnerships refer to a contractual agreement between a public sector organization and a private sector firm.

Sustainable Development Goal: The SDGs are a new set of goals, targets and indicators that have been adopted by the UN member states and which are expected to form the development agenda and political policies of the countries over the next 15 years.

World Economic Forum: It is an independent international organization committed to improving the state of the world. As stated in its mission, it, "engages business, political, academic and other leaders of society to shape global, regional and industry agendas."

Chapter 8
E-Learning as a Global Vessel Towards Inclusive and Quality Education

John Marvin D. Renacido
Aklan State University, Philippines

Ersyl T. Biray
https://orcid.org/0000-0002-5094-5841
Aklan State University, Philippines

ABSTRACT

E-learning is easily accessible on the Internet, which opens up countless opportunities for the learning population and academic institutions. As the technological world skyrockets, so does the educational system that serves us at the forefront of other advancements. This chapter will discuss how the new learning model has proven that growth does not only lean toward one area but knows no bounds—a digital classroom where flexibility and creativity are at its center.

E-LEARNING AS A MEANS TO COMPETENCE AND INCLUSIVITY

Accessibility of E-Learning

E-learning is currently available on the internet, allowing students and practitioners access to information and development with a swipe of their hands. This adaptive approach enables countless opportunities in a wide range of industries. As the technological world skyrockets, so does the educational system that serves

DOI: 10.4018/979-8-3693-8242-4.ch008

us at the forefront of other advancements. This new model of learning has proven that growth does not only lean toward one area but knows no bounds—a digital classroom where flexibility and creativity are at its center.

Enhanced Learning Experience

E-learning allows more avenues on how a student will develop academically. A classroom setup may be comfortable for the majority, however, the cyberspace has undeniably more opportunities to offer. Humans rely on traditional methods as it is more convenient, however, this will lead to stagnancy of progress. As technology thrives in the society, people shall accept the development and privileges of new advancements. Stifling students in penetrating these digital shift will disable them to cope effectively with the trends of technology and the world. The surge of online learning platforms can be exploited to augmenting the intellectual growth of learners, and limiting interaction between students and digital outlets will be a significant loss in their learning experience.

There is no doubt that AI is capable of re-envisioning almost every aspect of the world with education being no exception. However, this technology should be approached with sobriety considering its ethical and social consequences. By accepting the advantages of AI while anticipating possible negative outcomes, its full potential in education will be harnessed resulting to better and more engaging interactions with learners (Stracqualursi & Agati, 2024).

Disability Prevalence

In a learning environment, students' profile are random in the teaching field. Their differences in terms of learning pace, methods, and abilities are normal. However, we shall take note that there are some learners who require special attention and guidance. They are the disabled ones. Some of the prevalent issues faced are dyslexia, speech or language impairments, and chronic health problems. Although they lack the same qualities as usual learners do, they still need to indulge in the power of education. Equality must always be upheld in the classroom regardless of what the background of the students.

Learning Disabilities are a growing global problem as they affect 79.2 million people all over the world and are continuously on the rise (UNICEF, 2021). These disabilities would range from problems with listening, thinking, speaking, reasoning, reading, writing, spelling to even mathematics which brings about an enormous call for specialized educational services. In the case of the United States, out of the total population of school-age children, over 15% are enrolled in special programs because of learning disabilities which is roughly an estimated 2.3 million children exposing the magnitude of the issue. This demand is even greater in such countries that are still developing economically as their resources are very scarce (National Center for Education Statistics, 2022). Learners with learning disabilities struggle with reading, writing, and mathematical reasoning, and as a result, they are less likely to achieve academic success than their age counterpart. This is demonstrated through poor performance in standardized tests in areas like reading, science, math as well as other subjects (Asghar et al., 2017).

Challenges of the Marginalized

Apart from fostering an inclusive environment established by the facilitator, E-learning is one way to resolve students' disability problems. The challenges that arise in their lives can be accessibility concerns, technological know-how, social isolation, and lack of support. Disabled learners struggle to adapt in an online classroom setup or utilize digital platforms due to their respective inabilities. Their access is restricted by their own lapses and undeniably there is a possibility, that learning will be compromised. Furthermore, they can be left behind because of their illiteracy in technology navigation. Socialization is crucial for students in a classroom environment however due to mental disorders, they are immobilized. Such learners also encounter guidance and monitoring from educators who neglect their potential. This behavior should be taken into consideration as inclusivity in being infringed. The aforementioned problems can hinder the development of the marginalized community so it needs to be addressed immediately.

The eternal essence of learning cannot be associated with technology alone. It is the correct usage of technology that brings about the desired change. Provided the technology is used with a specific intent and a sound reason, it can benefit high academic achievement for both; disabled students and able students. Nevertheless, using educational technology in the classroom does not improve teaching and learning when used inappropriately or lightly (Zhai, 2021). Thus, it is important to investigate how exactly AI technologies support specific learning activities with the students with learning disabilities (SWLD) populations.

As for the latter case, the SAMR model, created by Puentedura (2006), seems to be an appropriate theory to consider when evaluating the levels of technology integration into learning. The Substitution, Augmentation, Modification, and Redefinition (SAMR) model was originally formulated to assess the impact of e-learning and has since adapted in a successful manner to examine the technology enhancement of different types of learning including mobile ones (Zhai et al., 2019). Its distinct features in defining different forms of technology integration make it possible to explain in what certain innovative teaching approaches differ from an outdated and traditional way of education which is just about using new equipment and materials (Terada, 2020).

Multimodal Learning

Diversity is an absolute aspect every cohort has, whether in their learning abilities, behaviors, or cultural identities. Through a digitalized system of education, tailored instruction becomes a vital component of attending to the varied needs of students. As being digital means being global, this barrier would easily be broken by forming a systematic process to ensure exact user treatment. Accessible data will be readily available to digital users searching for a particular learning environment aligned with their interests. In an e-learning setup, multimodal learning functions to engage students in a realistic sensory experience, primarily focusing on visual, auditory, and kinesthetic aspects. This escalates the engagement between the student and the resource material, stimulating more motivation for learning.

Each student has different learning styles and through multimodal approach in education, we can cope with this challenge. Using digital technology, various strategies can be developed in order to create a productive learning ground. For visual learners, images, videos, infographics, diagrams, and other supplementary aids will stimulate learner enthusiasm and growth while in terms of auditory learners, discussions, lectures, audiobooks, podcasts and other hearing-related materials can be presented. To those students who enjoy learning in reading or writing, textbooks, articles, notes, essays, etc. can be of help to them to make their learning experience high-achieving, on the other hand, to kinesthetic learners, experiments, simulations, role playing, and other hands-on activities can be injected.

Multimodal learning offers numerous benefits towards students and with its flexible matrix, a more inclusive, interactive, and effective educational experience will take place in the classroom. This method can be used for diverse learning preferences and enhanced engagement will arise when implemented. Students are more interested in listening to discussions if the teaching strategy suits their needs. Through the help of this type of learning, they can encounter their preferred way of instruction may it be in any aspect. On top of that, learners will also attain a more improved retention as their interest are also increased. It is vital especially in assessments and recitations that will be done in the learning process. This method also helps the effectivity and inclusivity of learning because of its access-friendly nature, catering all diverse abilities and disabilities of students. Moreover, creativity will be fostered among learners as they are engaged in different modes of learning. They will not be restricted in only one aspect but shall undergo holistic treatment. Multimodal learning also prepare students to real-world challenges that they may encounter outside the classroom. Information is portrayed in different forms in realistic contexts. With this approach, students are well-informed and well-familiarized by the diverse functions of data from the environment.

A teacher can implement multimodal learning by understanding first the learning abilities of the students. Every student has different learning styles so before you apply this method, you shall ensure that you already know it so you can anchor the appropriate needs of each learner. As teachers being the facilitator of the classroom, they can incorporate various modalities to equip students the versatility in embracing information. A teacher shall be aware of not overpowering one modality to another. A balanced approach must be implemented to achieve the needs of every student. Technology is one medium to share the diversity of cascading information. Teachers can leverage its strengths to provide the various learning modalities. Moreover, teachers may utilize active learning to stimulate students' authenticity in understanding the lessons.

Educational games can be injected in multimodal learning. A teacher can make their lessons interactive and at the same time, knowledgeable. Students may not be aware because of too much enjoyment but they are actually learning to grasp various modality concepts. Furthermore, a teacher can also implement group activities wherein multimodal learning is applied. In this way, learners may learn through their peers and collaborative skills is improved. Teachers can also put forth in the classroom the power of case-based learning. It is where contextualized projects and activities can be developed incorporating different modalities to enhance students' understanding with the external environment. A teacher can also integrate the use of personal journals of students to improve their visual skills as well as reading and writing skills. It also allows teachers to assess students' behavior and intellectual proficiency.

Contemporary advancements in the field of Artificial Intelligence (AI) especially generative AI have resulted in the emergence of Multimodal Large Language Models (MLLMs) as useful tools in satisfying certain critical needs. MLLMs are a type of artificial intelligence model that is used to create and comprehend text-like content in many different forms such as writing, images, motion pictures, and sound. This makes a wide range of applications possible – from making creative works to resolving issues (Bommasani et al. 2021).

Bewersdorff et. al (2024) infer that MLLMs can help learners by making them use all the available multimedia learning materials and presentations. With adaptive design options, either self-configured by ourselves or set up by our teachers, MLLMs can assist learners in the selection, arrangement and incorporation of textual as well as pictorial and other forms of information. This has the potential to improve learning processes quite considerably. For example, advanced learners with large amounts of background knowledge may prefer complex representations, while others with fewer competencies can modify the learning content to their preferences. Even so, this kind of versatility brings out the issues regarding the management of the use of MLLMs as concerns learner independence and the controlled application of AI in generative learning strategies. This is another rich area of opportunities for further research as well as for many applications.

Differentiated Instruction

In any type of classroom, students will always vary with each other, may it be in their learning styles, preferences, and behavior. Teachers themselves shall be the ones to adjust their teaching tactics to cope learners who are lacking in a certain aspect.

Differentiated Instruction is one method in order to address the diversity of students. A teacher shall tailor its instruction so students will be able to learn based on its desired learning experience. Through e-learning, students may indulge in self-paced learning. As students have various learning styles, they also differ in their learning pace. Some are slow-placed while others are fast-paced. Teachers may utilize this strategy to test students' learning abilities. Moreover, by differentiated instruction, learners may engage into different formats of learning, providing them more opportunities to absorb information.

Domorovskaya (2024) examined learning management system statistics to determine the extent of interaction in terms of task completion for students with and without differentiated content. The results indicated that students were more engaged and more successful working with differentiated content. This implies that offering alternatives in task performance, allowing students to select how they want to present their results and even time limits for course work improves performance.

Learners explore more depending on the depth and forms teachers present their discussions. Every teacher may tackle their lesson differently in one session, however through this method, teachers can utilize various techniques to discuss the content of their lessons. This allows students to be developed holistically and effectively. One key principle of this kind of learning strategy is the process. Differentiated instruction makes students engage in a variety of learning materials. This could pose a complex and rigorous type of process but a more meaningful and knowledgeable learning experience. In this type of tactical approach, teachers have to give students the chance to make a product, out of their prior discussions like portfolios, written assignments, multimedia projects, or authentic assessments. These affirm that they are competent or ready enough to continue with the following units. Moreover, teachers shall establish a learning environment where positivity and flexibility thrive, a key component in upholding differentiated instruction. Learners must feel that their contribution or participation to the class is valued and not discouraged. If their motivation is being tarnished, then definitely learning is non-progressive.

Adaptive Learning Platforms (ALP) is useful for students in an e-learning setting. Its algorithm makes sure that students will encounter appropriately-challenged tasks and receive personalized learning assessments and instruction. Similar to ALP, Learning Management Systems (LMS) offers tailored mechanisms to every student in order for them to develop according to their strengths and receive feedback depending on their personal performance. Differentiated Instruction becomes effective, like other strategies, if the teacher composes engaging contents. Digital games is one way to stimulate their attention and interests. To encourage collaboration and skill enhancement, flexible grouping can be actualized in diverse set of learners. Online forums, peer-based learning, and group projects are examples which deepens understanding and foster creativity among students. Personalized feedback can be given to students through e-learning sites according to their performance and progress. This feedback may help close individual learning gaps by suggesting improvements.

When students are given learning experiences aligned with their interests, learning styles and needs, they become more engaged in the learning process. This results in higher motivation levels, participation rates, and retention. Through differentiated instruction, students can learn at their pace and obtain appropriate assistance. This can result in better academic outcomes and a more profound comprehension of the content. When students are suitably challenged and given individualized responses, they acquire much self-assurance about what they can do. Thus, they become risk-takers and will venture into new concepts. E-learning platforms that provide personalized learning experiences can make students concentrate on areas where they need more assistance, advancing them at a quicker pace. Therefore, time and resources shall be used well by the two parties involved — students and teachers.

Collaboration and Peer Instruction

At the expanse of scope, collaboration among different groups or students will surface, leading to a more fun and thrilling way of interacting. Peer instruction allows the sharing of insights gathered by each student, igniting knowledge, communication, and creativity. An interactive design also brings more learning, deepening their sense of belonging and purpose. With numerous students connected to the program, response and resolution will no longer require much effort. Through e-learning, continuous assessment and feedback will be delivered to the students, evaluating individual progress in the enrolled training courses or other instructional activities.

A study by Malsakpak et al. (2024) found that merging of E-learning (EL) and Collaborative Learning (CL) models led to significant improvement in undergraduate nursing students' College Academic Self-Efficacy (CASE). This success, in turn, was ascribed to the increased levels of interaction, provision of adequate teaching facilities, and delivery of effective services.

Peer and teacher interactions foster curiosity, interest, creativity, stimulation, boosting engagement and motivation levels. Learner perspectives are varied., understanding is deepened and accountability is fostered among them which leads to better retention of information. In collaborative learning situations, one learns how to communicate, solve problems, show empathy and negotiate—skills required at work and in life. A collaborative learning environment fosters familyhood or support, thus, reducing loneliness associated with online studying.

The learning process is marked by active involvement of students, contrasting with mere consumption of information passively. Input from fellow students could be more relatable and actionable as compared to just the instructor alone. Learners tend to take time explaining the concepts to fellow students, deepening their knowledge in those areas making them spot where they still require clarification.

On the other hand, this method also poses some challenges if applied. Some learners may eventually experience isolation or lack of interest if there are no classmates or instructors beside them. Moreover, accommodating different learning styles and pace within an online collaborative atmosphere may be strenuous for teachers. Live sessions and group work among various time zones can present challenges in terms of logistics. Meanwhile, in a collaborative setting, asynchronism and absence of direct observation makes it hard to measure one's input.

Strategies for a collaboration and peer instruction can be implemented towards a successful e-learning environment. It is noteworthy that teachers shall leverage tools that have strong e-learning systems, resource-sharing settings, and adaptability to various internet speeds in order to optimize or ease communication. Multimedia tools, interactive simulations, as well as quizzes and games can enhance active involvement and retention of learners. Furthermore, ice-breaking tasks, casual chats, and small study sets shall be employed to create a sense of belongingness and assistance networks. Instructors can create or specify expectations whereby everything must have order so that virtual manners and useful responses are observed. They may also capture live streams, use asynchronous resources or offer flexi-timetable learning options to learners from divergent place on time or their ways of learning. It is necessary to supervise group efforts regularly, provide feedbacks and offer guidance on technical issues or disputes. In addition, active listening skills must be emphasized and probable misunderstanding in online forums shall be addressed. Teachers also need to monitor attendance levels, engagement rates, as well as learning areas where students may experience difficulties so as to offer personalized support and modify course materials correspondingly.

Interactive Design

Learners must be involved with information that they can actively use instead of just consuming them. This means that as learners manipulate content, they will give answers, get feedback and put into practice what they know under a vibrant and exciting atmosphere.

Using a combination of pictures, videos, sounds and words provides a vibrant and captivating method of learning, catering variety of learning styles. They help learners get instant feedbacks on their level of comprehension and what they need to work on. In authentic situations, students can practice their skills and knowledge in a secure setting, which connects theories with practice. Learning through game-based or immersive simulations is an enjoyable way to study because it stimulates participation while enhancing the retention of facts. Instructional platforms stimulate connections among students through web-based discussion boards, joint tasks, and collaborative endeavors. Active examination and participation in study materials are stimulated by digitized workbooks, interactive e-books, and similar resources.

This traditional learning has an element that it can be quite boring but introducing interactivity helps engage the students' mind, attention as well as make them feel part of their own study process. By receiving feedback soon after, things will stick in mind easily. The use of case studies and role plays helps learners develop skills in critical thinking as well as decision-making.

Sahraie et al. (2024) stress that even though e-learning strategies that involve media, such as PowerPoint presentations and videos, are helpful, they are not sufficient conditions for ensuring success or generating positive feelings. While multimedia facilitates visualization and provides backup, it is not enough since true engagement demands interactivity with content, the teacher, and other learners as well.

The use of interactivity helps the learner practice on real-life skills which creates self-assurance for their future professions. Furthermore, personalized e-learning tools can accommodate variances in styles and speeds of learning among users, offering individual feedback and customized courses.

Instructors may deduce their requisites, modes of receiving knowledge, and technical know-how to design the appropriate process of learning. They shall involve specific, measurable, achievable, relevant, and time-bound (SMART) objectives that will form a basis of guidance in design as well as ensure that they are in line with the learning goals. Not every course calls for a similar degree of interactivity. It may depend on the subject matter, course aims, and learner's interests. Hence, it is crucial to choose suitable forms of interaction, tools, and platforms that support the desired level of interactivity, provide seamless integration, and offer accessibility for diverse learners. They shall continuously test the course, gather feedback from learners, and refine the design based on insights to optimize engagement and effectiveness.

Moreover, teachers shall ensure that the design is accessible to all learners regardless of their technical skills, abilities, or devices and consider accessibility features and alternative formats for diverse learners. It may take a lot of effort to come up with interesting and useful interactive e-learning courses, including time commitment, knowledge and skills, and technology. The design shall also be planned carefully, considering the time frame and money available. Apart from engagement metrics, it is also important to consider how effective interactive e-learning is and in order for learning to be meaningful, it is necessary to evaluate the ability of learners to apply their knowledge in real-life situations.

Continuous Assessment and Feedback

E-learning has grown to be an essential instrument of imparting knowledge and skills in the ever-changing world of education. Continuous assessment and feedback, however, are the most important factors that determine the effectiveness of e-learning. It is from this standpoint that the modern approach departs from traditional ones which primarily rely on rare evaluations to provide students with ongoing chances to monitor their performance, find out areas needing improvement as well as have personalized support.

In a recent study, Rui (2024) developed an innovative intelligent audio-processing algorithm that specifically focuses on analyzing the students' singing sounds through different processing techniques. In this case, the algorithm is capable of detecting problems with the voice with regard to the tune, the tone, the rhythm, etc., and gives recommendations within the time frame provided. This means that the students can assess which aspects of their singing carry weaknesses and correct them straight away. It shows that e-learning powered by IoT devices is able to disrupt vocal music training to a great extent. As such, by replicating the settings of a physical classroom and providing feedback in real-time, students are likely to be more engrossed in the learning process and improve their vocal abilities.

Students' progress is best tracked by frequent assessments than by the usual traditional ones that are done only at long intervals. Instructors can identify their learners' areas of strengths and weaknesses through constant evaluations which enable them to improve on what needs to be improved upon. Therefore, this promotes an understanding of the subject as well as better outcomes for students. Continuous assessment and feedback can be a powerful motivator for learners. Recognizing how much progress they have made after getting constant assessment creates a sense of achievement, motivating them not to give up on learning activities. Such a strategy also promotes ownership over one's learning since individuals become partakers in determining aspects needing change and moving together toward realization of goals set.

There is an argument for case-based learning and self-examination among students, or personal accountability in their learning process. The process of assessing yourself continuously allows one to keep track of the progress against standards and objectives. In this way, they develop personal insights that allow them to identify the necessary changes for improvement, increasing their sense of ownership resulting into more independence and accountability towards one's own academic success.

Continuous assessment gives teachers valuable information about how well their students are learning. Therefore, through regular feedback, teachers have an opportunity to find out student weaknesses and after that modify their teaching styles according to the supposed problems. Such a personalized strategy enables more effective educational approaches because it addresses specific requirements of different students, leading to better academic performance outcomes than before. In e-learning, continuous evaluation forms a basis for adaptable learning. Using learner responses, e-learning platforms dynamically change the path of learning by analyzing them and considering performance data to include further support in areas where learners are having difficulties and speeding up in areas that they have mastered. This makes it such that the right level of challenge and support is provided to each learner maximally.

Various feedback mechanisms shall be integrated into e-learning platforms and used during the entire period of learning process. Through ongoing feedback for questions, tasks, and practice, students can rectify their problems and enhance their skills by understanding. Continually assessing student progress using tests, projects, and debates offer chances for comments and course modification. Overall evaluation of learning achievement is through assessment tools such as exams, projects or presentations that gauge the level of a student's completion hence including all aspects of learner competence.

Individualized feedback should be aligned to the specific needs of every learner person considering his/her style of learning. Teachers may apply AI-driven devices to give personalized feedback on drafts, coding activities and other evaluations. They may give personalized advice and assistance through comments on assignments, discussions, and projects. Furthermore, they can stimulate students' involvement with assessments by providing forums in which they can share their own perceptions, seek clarification or advice or share responses regarding earlier work from colleagues and tutors. They can also allow students to offer helpful remarks about one another's tasks to promote teamwork spirit while sharpening cognitive skills for analysis in argumentation. Learners may be given the freedom to access their assessments and feedback throughout the learning process as transparency helps in accountability giving them power over their learning.

Continuous assessment and feedback may be too demanding in terms of time for teachers, especially in large online courses. Meticulous planning coupled with technological use could help mitigate this challenge. It is vital that students become truly engaged with the comments they receive from tutors so as to improve on the subject matter being taught. Fostering a culture of feedback as well as giving explicit directions on how to use evaluate properly will boost learner interaction with educators' comments. Learners can access their assessment results and feedback during the whole learning process. Such transparency fosters accountability and enables learners to own their learning.

E-LEARNING METHODS

Learners look for a place where they can learn comfortably and considerably. E-learning websites and applications are recommended mediums for clear and smooth learning. One tool for students to engage despite the limitations of face-to-face interaction is audio and video-based learning. It allows for a sensory experience where its instruction or presentation reinforces understanding more than pure text. E-learning is activity-based, which denotes that it comprises experimentation, exploration, and expression concepts. It will test students' practical knowledge, creativity, and social literacy. Another effective way e-learning can help is through peer-to-peer learning. This type of instruction will bring students together, cascading their thoughts with the group. To further actualize the learning experience of students, AI voiceover and avatars act as real-time chat assistants and offer beneficial information for students.

Audio and Video-based Learning

Audio and video have numerous benefits. For instance, they make learning more interesting and interactive by capturing the attention of learners. Multimedia content stimulates auditory and visual processing, leading to greater understanding and recall of information. Audio and video can be adapted to accommodate diverse learning needs, including those with visual or auditory impairments. Flexibility in learning schedules is enhanced since students can access audio and video contents at any place at any time.

High-quality audio and video content creation can be expansive often including specialized devices, software, and know-how. Effective audio and video content delivery requires dependable web access, devices that are compatible, and suitable file types. Overusing audio and video can confuse learners especially when dealing with complex or dense information and may easily distract learners from their main focus thus inhibiting understanding.

Audio and video-based education materials are produced and distributed with the help of several technologies that are unique in their functions and benefits. Tools such as Audacity, GarageBand, Adobe Audition, and Logic Pro are used for recording, editing, and mixing audio. Online platforms provide an extensive collection of sound effects royalty-free, music and voice-overs that enhance audio content. Tools like Google Cloud Text-to-Speech and Amazon Polly can transform written words into computer generated voice for use as narration or as descriptions in audios.

Programs such as Adobe Premiere Pro, Final Cut Pro, and DaVinci Resolve facilitate high-end video editing inclusive of transitions, effects and color correction. Camtasia, Snagit and OBS Studio are some tools for capturing as well as editing screen activities to produce tutorials, demonstrations or presentations. Some services like Vimeo, YouTube and Kaltura may provide options for adding interactive elements, quizzes and branching scenarios in video content. New technologies like Synthesia, Elai and Colossyan Creator use AI avatars to generate lifelike videos with personalized characters and voice-overs.

Interactive e-learning courses that incorporate audio, video, and other multimedia elements are made convenient with platforms such as Articulate Storyline, Adobe Captivate and Ispring Suite while the delivery of online courses is simplified by platforms such as Moodle, Canvas and Blackboard which also monitor learner progress and manage assessments.

Setting definite learning outcomes and ensuring that they are in line with all audio/visual components is necessary. Teachers shall present captivating images and sound that draws in attention from viewers and keeps them interested respectively. Audio/video clips must be short to deal with certain ideas or abilities only. They can also purchase good microphones, cameras, lights as well as editing programs to make professional-looking and sounding materials. Moreover, they can provide subtitles, captions, and transcripts to enhance accessibility for all learners, incorporate quizzes, polls, and other interactive elements to encourage active learning and engagement, and monitor learner engagement, feedback, and performance to assess the effectiveness of audio and video content and make necessary adjustments.

Activity-Based Learning

Activity-based learning (ABL) is an essential component of e-learning that promotes active engagement with content as opposed to just sitting in front of a screen consuming it. When learners participate actively in the process of learning, they are more likely to remember what they learned than if they did not. In E-learning, the meaning of ABL goes beyond lectures and quizzes, it encourages students to put into practice their knowledge through simulation or hands-on activities or real-life contexts. This strategy enhances understanding, facilitates recall, fosters critical thinking abilities and improves problem-solving skills.

John and Alaaraj (2024) point out that engagement is an important factor that explains the relationship between activity-based learning and students' academic performance. When educators apply activity-based learning in their teaching practice, they create a more interesting and productive learning experience geared towards the academic performance of the students, thus readying them for their careers. This altitudinal submission makes it possible for students to appreciate the importance of independent inquiry and problem solving which will be useful in their work in the future.

Here, learners engage themselves directly using the knowledge and abilities they have acquired through diverse activities. Such activities should be carried out how they would have been done outside class because it makes learning more applicable and also interesting in life. Also, collaborative learning takes place since there are other people often involved in these activities, thus, enhancing communication as well as teamwork among learners. Then again, immediate feedback is given by providing comments on progress made. Learners can tell which aspects require improvement, thus, modifying their learning strategies. Finally, continuous learning involves the interactive trend associated with ABL that encourages exploration by learners, leading to constant skill updates.

ABL provides many advantages for students and teachers which helps improve the effectiveness of online learning while increasing engagement. Active participation combined with application of knowledge leads towards a better understanding of concepts. Hands-on activities together with problem-solving exercises enhance memory retention and long-term recall. ABL promotes critical thinking skills, communication, cooperation, and problem-solving that are vital for success in different areas. Engaging activities and instant feedback create a sense of achievement, motivating people towards learning.

ABL helps you tailor your own style or needs thus offering personal experiences in the center of learning. When students are engaged within the curriculum, they will not be distracted by any other issues and thus be able to concentrate. Through these activities, their understanding and progress can be tracked so that changes can be made in teaching methodologies if necessary. Educators use ABL which enables them to keep records on how their students perform consequently giving ways that help improve courses as well as personalization. This adaptable approach can be utilized in different subjects and learning levels.

ABL-based activities in e-learning are endless. They can include everything from simple interactive exercises to complex simulations or student collaboration. Interactive quizzes and gamified quizzes are used to check everything learned in a fun manner. Real-world case studies and situations challenge learners to apply their knowledge in practical instances. Interactive simulations as well as role-playing activities make it possible for learners to grasp diverse points of view and practice certain skills in a secure setting.

Group projects promote teamwork, communication, and problem-solving which allow students to offer ideas that will contribute to a common outcome. Interactivity within video presentations enables students to pause, wind back, or review particular concepts at their own pace. Giving students hands-on experience with coding exercises along with coding challenges are ways through which learning can be made easier for technical subjects.

Maximizing the effectiveness of ABL by e-learning is possible if some practices are taken into consideration. Teachers must define precise learning outcomes that directly connect activities with objectives. They shall provide dynamic activities based on the different learning styles of the students to keep them involved and ensure activities are hard enough for them to learn, but not too hard so as to demotivate them. In addition, they must give instant and understandable responses on how they perform and mention their strengths along with areas that need improvement. They may also involve suitable technological gadgets in these activities for better participation and immediate responses. Furthermore, they can utilize class tasks or forums or internet collaboration tools to inspire relationships between learners by collaborating with peers and examine whether students engage, provide comments, or respond in order to evaluate whether done activities have been effective and identify when modifications should be made.

According to Santhi and Malathi (2024), active learning is one of the methods that bring students into the learning process effectively. This approach utilizes practical, active, and real situations so that students may strive to learn and enhance their abilities. This strategy enables students to keep the information for a long time, enhances creativity, critical thinking, and even the ability to solve problems. The attainment of activity-oriented instruction is dependent on the capacity of the teacher to involve the learners in the specified activities that are in sync with the curriculum and the learning targets. Activity based learning, if properly planned, prepared, and executed, will be an effective and constructive way in promoting the interactive learning process in the classroom.

Peer-to-Peer Learning

The peer-to-peer learning (P2P) revolutionizes the e-learning world by destroying the conventional system of education and paving way for a more engaging and collaborative learning environment. Instead of depending on instructors or outside resources, P2P learning is about students who cooperate with each other to learn and share knowledge. By doing so, it encourages active involvement in the process and promotes taking control of one's own learning while enabling people to draw from different angles.

This teaching strategy encourages teamwork learning where ideas, experiences and knowledge are shared by those together seeking to learn something. It is a participatory method, involving all students in a certain place where students can make contributions during discussions or while solving problems. It gives students insights coming from different backgrounds thereby making it richer. It highlights the customization of learners as some prefer knowing things slowly compared to others.

P2P Learning has its advantages to all learners. One is a better comprehension as conceptual discussions and feedback from peers will aid in deeper understanding because they are more comprehensive. In this approach, students will be required to express their thoughts and evaluate different viewpoints, developing their critical thinking abilities. It also fosters greater enthusiasm in learning as discussions are more motivating and engaging when it involves active participation and ownership. Learners will attain higher levels of self-esteem when they converse with fellow students and receiving constructive remarks will boost their confidence and allow them to take on risks easily. Through P2P Learning, students will have better interpersonal skills. Group work develops communication abilities necessary for different professions such as law enforcement agencies.

While students indulge to this kind of learning, educators as well embrace various benefits from it. P2P learning is a means of having students participate fully in the learning process. It ensures that they pay attention while minimizing distractions, hence, teachers will have outstanding performance and results. By engaging students in group tasks, these common experiences can yield profound insights into their level of understanding and overall development which helps teachers customize instructions according to what their students need. Moreover, peer-assisted learning calls for collaboration among learners, thereby promoting active and vibrant learning contexts. Educators can facilitate debates or provide direction without concentrating on transmitting knowledge, only through P2P means of teaching. Various subjects and instructional stages can utilize P2P learning, making it an adaptable methodology in all areas of education. P2P learning can be done via various methods and each method has its own merits which are tailored towards distinct types of learners and purposes.

A teacher can apply the concept of P2P Learning by leveraging some of these bridges of learning. First, we have Internet Forums and Discussion Boards which are platforms that enable learners to hold asynchronous conversations, exchange ideas and inquiries. Also, Group Projects and Collaborative Activities which inspire collaboration, communication as well as problem identification among learners who contribute towards a common goal and Peer Tutoring and Mentoring where older students assist others with academic work through tutorial sessions causing people with rich experience pass their information across in a transformative sense. Through Peer Review and Feedback, learning aids in better understanding and quality improvement when learners give each other constructive criticism. Social learning software that support P2P learning are provided by dedicated platforms like Peer Square and EducateMe and are used for collaboration, assessment and exchange of knowledge.

Shalin Hai-Jew (2021) who authored, "Practical Peer-to-Peer Teaching and Learning on the Social Web," makes an exciting case for incorporating peer learning into new educational setups. The book demonstrates and elucidates the possibility of distributed online resources, frequently produced by a variety of experts, that can help support learning in addition to a classroom environment. In this essay, two actual practical lesson plans adapted from Hai-Jew will be laid down to show how peer learning may be realistically introduced into high schools and colleges.

The first of the lesson plans is "Curating the Social Web," aimed at high school students, preparing them with critical skills on how to negotiate through the vast and largely overwhelming landscape of online information. The students are divided into groups and assigned specific topics. Every group embarks on a quest to search the social web for relevant resources, including videos, blog posts, and articles. The material to be extracted here is just information judged critically. At every point, students are urged to identify the strengths and weaknesses, which may include factors regarding credibility of sources, possibilities of bias, and accuracy. These operations foster critical thinking and media literacy, allowing students to be mature consumers of online information. The lesson concludes with resource lists that have been well-thought out and then shared with the class members, thus making them an active participant in the process of knowledge sharing.

The other course is "Peer-to-Peer Learning in the Classroom." This course is for college-level students. The aim will be to expose them to the idea of peer learning and how it can be implemented in a classroom setting. Students are grouped together and given chosen topics relevant to the curriculum of the classroom. The collaborative task is to create a collaborative project such as a presentation video or blog post that explores their assigned topic from various perspectives. The project will challenge the student to use online resources, share his expertise, and learn from each other in the creation process of the final product, which will be presented to the class. This approach gives the student ownership and encourages participation, fostering deeper understanding and critical thinking.

Lesson plans on both sides underline the need to think critically, to use media wisely, and to collaborate. They allow active participation in learning by students themselves, going beyond passive intake of information. Peer-to-peer learning is embraced here, where educators can then create a more dynamic, engaging, and empowering space for active participants in knowledge sharing. According to Hai-Jew, social web resources can therefore be exploited to improve educational outcomes, including effective collaborative and interesting learning for all.

In order to ensure high effectiveness of P2P Learning in e-learning there are some general guidelines one should follow. Teachers shall outline specific guidelines and expectations for student participation so that all students know their roles as well as what is associated with them. They must also construct a protective and broad-minded ambiance where students feel at ease discussing their thoughts and accepting comments. Moreover, they shall give harmony and control to ensure that conversations remain focused and that every student has an opportunity to engage. Instructors must also implement technological instruments which promote joint effort, interaction, and appraisal thus heightening the P2P studying experience and observe student participation, criticism and achievement so as to determine how effective the P2P learning tasks are then adjust accordingly.

AI Voiceover and Avatars

These features use machine learning techniques to create the voice impressions which allows them to mimic human speech.

AI voiceovers have three main benefits including enhanced accessibility, reduced labor and time requirements, in addition to low production costs among others. It is essential for any organization that provides both formal and informal education services to become familiar with and use artificial intelligence tools in line with the current trends of distance education. The use of AI voiceovers is way cheaper than hiring professional voice talent. AI voiceover generation can be done quickly and quite easily, avoiding the need of scheduling and recording sessions. It allows for quick updates and changes to the course content because they can be edited or revised with ease. Moreover, this privilege makes it possible for students with visual impairment or reading difficulties to have access to educational materials through AI voiceovers and many AI voice generators feature real-time translation options which allow e-learning materials to cater for global audiences.

AI voiceovers are helpful in different classroom activities injected by the instructor. It provides a natural and captivating narration to form recorded lectures. It also allows for screencast videos where therein explains software applications and online tools with clear and concise audio. It can also produce animated explainer videos, bringing complex concepts to life with engaging and informative narration. Through, whiteboard videos, AI voiceovers can provide a clear and concise audio explanation for visual demonstrations. Teachers can add a professional and engaging voice to interviews with subject matter experts and make tutorial videos, guiding learners through hands-on tasks with clear and concise instructions. AI can also produce videos that provides audio narration for interactive elements and branching scenarios.

AI is used to generate digital images of people called avatars. They mimic human interactions, thus, making learning appealing and satisfying. Utilizing AI-based Avatars is a clever way to obtain increased engagement, animate lifelike characters, and produce realistic expressions which capture learners' attention more effectively. Also, custom avatar options allow for a tailored learning experience that caters to individual preferences and Al avatar generation is more affordable than traditional video creation methods. Users can easily update video content with new information by modifying the avatar's script or appearance. Through this application, text-to-speech and text-to-video features increase the accessibility of contents for diverse learners.

Al avatars have various applications in e-learning which definitely reinforce knowledge of diverse learners. It can simulate conversations in various languages which allow learners to practice effectively. Companies may deploy Al avatars to facilitate new employees' training by providing real time assistance and respond any question posed. Al avatars help students who are having trouble with complicated technical procedures comprehend better by reducing them into simple instructions that can be easily understood. Al powered simulations where users negotiate or deal with conflicts are essential for learning soft skills such as negotiation or customer service negotiation. Assessments and quizzes can be made easier by utilizing Al avatars which are capable of providing instant feedbacks. Children's education has also been made more interesting through the use of avatars which has turned lessons into fun tales or games. Moreover, compliance training is made easier through the use of Al avatars which clearly explain legal and industry-specific regulations to learners. Health and safety training in some areas like health care has made use of AI avatars to simulate an emergency situation where one can practice their response without any danger. For professionals looking for up-to-date materials, Ai can give tutorials and resources that reflect current trends in different fields of work. In addition, Al avatars can be utilized in explainer videos because they are usually brief and made in bulk. In any presentation software such as PowerPoint, you can also use Al avatars to underscore your point. It is simple to use and anybody can do it-just make use of avatars to produce interesting video clips.

E-LEARNING PLATFORMS

Sample platforms for e-learning are Coursera, LinkedIn Learning, Skillshare, edX, and Moodle. They offer courses with various options depending on the inclination of the learner. This is achieved through the partnerships they have linked into, where different instructors specializing in different fields share their expertise and collaborate to create an educational port on a global scale.

Coursera

Coursera is an online educational platform that is available on a global scale, and it provides a wide range of courses from top universities as well as companies from all over the world. The platform aims to provide education that is accessible to all and of high quality through the focus on affordability, accessibility, and diversity in learning formats.

There are many courses that may be audited without payment, thus allowing students to tap relevant information without paying anything. This course can be taken at any time of the day or night and the student sets their own pace regarding how fast they want to complete it. People from different language backgrounds can now learn together, thanks to the introduction of multi-lingual courses in Coursera. In recent years, Coursera has incorporated a number of accessibility features such as Closed Captioning and Transcription, which have been able to aid open educational resources (OER) initiatives often empowered by various universities around the globe.

Coursera emphasizes quality education through its partnerships with top-tier institutions and its commitment to evidence-based teaching and learning strategies. It collaborates with over 300 leading universities and companies, including Stanford, Duke, Google, IBM, and Microsoft, ensuring high-quality content and instruction. It prioritizes evidence-based online teaching and learning strategies to ensure effective and engaging learning experiences. The average rating across courses on Coursera is 4.7 out of 5 stars, reflecting the high quality of the learning experience. Report reveals that 73% of learners who complete courses indicate positive career-related outcomes, underscoring the pragmatic benefit and impact of Coursera's programs.

Coursera acknowledges the significance of diversity and inclusion in learning. Specifically designed courses on diversity as well as inclusion in education are offered by Coursera for the purpose of equipping learners with skills on how to enhance equity in their educational settings. In an effort to promote equal opportunities for all learners, Coursera aims at removing obstacles to access to education particularly for students from marginalized communities. United Nations High Commissioner for Refugees (UNHCR) partners with Coursera so that they can offer educational opportunities for displaced persons and refugees.

To enable varying modes of learning and objectives, Coursera has different available learning formats. Distinct subjects or skills are delivered in individual courses. There are specializations or course collections that aim at helping students to acquire knowledge on specific areas of study. These programs confer professional certificates which equip individuals with employable competencies for job placements. Coursera also offers educational degrees like bachelor's and master's programs offered by top-ranked universities.

Coursera has the potential of fully delivering comprehensive learning experiences due to its capability of developing engaging and accessible pathways of education. Let's consider, as an example, a possible lesson plan for an introductory course on Data Science that can endow participants with foundational knowledge and skills to enter the rapidly expanding field of data science. This course will run over the period of three weeks, one per subject of interest.

The first week would be foundational in nature and would be the base of understanding the field. Module 1, "What is Data Science?," defines data science and introduces the reader to its core, while illustrating it in its various applications through a mix of companies from different industries. The module then focuses on the increased need for a new breed of professionals: data scientists, in a modern data-driven world.

Module 2: "Data Types and Sources," will discuss the kinds of data: structured, unstructured, and semi-structured; it will further explain different kinds of data sources-to be addressed -databases, APIs, and sources on social media. Quality and integrity of data would be of utmost importance as a critical factor for analysis. Finally, Module 3, "Data Visualization," will delve into the role and significance of data visualization, including common tools such as Python's Matplotlib and Seaborn. The learner would then be led through the construction of simple visualizations with best practices for communicating data insights.

Week two would focus on building on this groundwork by focusing on data analysis and interpretation. Module 4, "Statistical Concepts," would cover some of the statistical concepts like mean, median, standard deviation, and hypothesis testing. The module would focus on understanding data distribution and how statistical analysis should be applied to develop meaningful conclusions. Module 5, "Exploratory Data Analysis (EDA)," would take the learner through the process of EDA and show how patterns, trends, and outliers in data can be identified. It would be highlighted that such EDA has implications both for decision-making and in discovering insights that may lie hidden in the data.

Module 6, "Machine Learning Fundamentals," would introduce learners to the concept of machine learning, including supervised and unsupervised learning algorithms, model evaluation, and model selection; it would enable the learner to develop and evaluate machine learning models. It would end with applying knowledge from previous weeks: Module 7, "Case Study 1: Customer Segmentation," applies data science techniques to segment customers based on purchasing behavior. The results are then analyzed, and actionable insights are drawn for marketing campaigns.

Module 8, "Case Study 2: Fraud Detection," would cover the application of machine learning models in fraudulent transaction detection. This module would go even deeper into the issues and ethical concerns involved in fraud detection. Module 9 "Project: Data Science in Action," finally, would end with a final project in which learners apply their acquired skills to a real-world dataset. They would be guided to pick a topic that matches their interests and their career goals, meaning there would be much hands-on learning.

Coursera's impact penetrates far beyond the structure of this course. This would be the transformative power of e-learning: accommodating varied requirements and dreams for lifelong learning. It offers extensive courseware, multiple experiences of learning, and access from anywhere in the world. It allows learners to achieve new proficiencies, move ahead with careers, and continue personal development. Coursera will surely evolve more with the evolution of technology to help make lifelong learning accessible to anyone, anywhere.

LinkedIn Learning

LinkedIn Learning, which was formerly known as Lynda.com has transformed over the years to become an exceptional online learning platform. It encompasses thousands of video modules covering different disciplines such as business management, computer science, creative arts and personal development among many others. The primary beneficiaries are individuals who want to advance their skills and organizations interested in improving employee expertise and training.

In total, Linkedin Learning has more than sixteen thousand well-designed courses and are translated into seven languages. Moreover, these courses are constantly reviewed and revised so that they remain relevant to prevailing industry dynamics as well as current best practices. There are several types of training material on offer at this platform such as short clips or long documents, giving students an opportunity to pick what fits their pace best.

LinkedIn Learning's one positive characteristic is its concentration on the most required skills. The platform gives priority to the courses that help learners attain the required knowledge and abilities for succeeding in today's competitive job market. LinkedIn Learning has many advantages that individuals can reap especially from those who want professional growth and progress in their careers. It has the availability of a wide range of courses, allowing students to learn fresh skills or improve their current ones and increase their employability once again.

It provides courses specifically designed to help individuals advance their careers with topics such as job searching, networking, and leadership. Also for personal growth, Linkedin Learning is offering courses on communication, productivity as well as mindfulness. After completion of courses, certificates are awarded to learners, adding recognition and credibility to their LinkedIn profile.

LinkedIn Learning's strength lies in its ability to deliver focused, skill-based learning experiences. A potential curriculum like, "Mastering Public Speaking" course, showcase how the platform can effectively equip learners with the confidence and techniques to deliver impactful presentations. The course is structured across three weeks, each building upon the previous one to create a comprehensive learning journey.

The initial week focuses on establishing a solid foundation in public speaking. Module 1, "Understanding the Power of Communication," emphasizes the critical role of effective communication in professional settings. It highlights how public speaking builds credibility, influences others, and contributes to achieving professional goals. This sets the stage for the practical skills development to follow. Module 2, "Overcoming Stage Fright," directly addresses the common fear associated with public speaking. It provides practical strategies for managing anxiety and building confidence, including techniques for relaxation, visualization, and positive self-talk. This module aims to empower learners to confront their anxieties proactively. Module 3, "Crafting Compelling Presentations," delves into the structure and content of effective presentations. Learners are introduced to various presentation formats, learn how to develop a clear narrative, and explore techniques for audience engagement. This module provides the framework for creating impactful presentations.

Week two shifts the focus to the delivery and engagement aspects of public speaking. Module 4, "Nonverbal Communication," explores the significance of nonverbal cues—body language, voice modulation, and eye contact—in enhancing presence and impact. Learners participate in exercises designed to refine their nonverbal communication skills. Module 5, "Storytelling and Visual Aids," highlights the power of storytelling in presentations. Learners learn how to craft compelling narratives and effectively utilize visual aids to enhance their message. This module emphasizes the importance of connecting with the audience on an emotional level. Module 6, "Handling Questions and Feedback," equips learners with strategies for managing audience questions and receiving constructive criticism. They learn to respond confidently and professionally, transforming feedback into opportunities for growth and improvement.

The final week focuses on practical application and assessment of the skills learned. Module 7, "Practice and Feedback," provides a safe and supportive environment for learners to practice their public speaking skills. They receive constructive feedback from peers and instructors, refining their techniques and building confidence. This module simulates real-world scenarios in a low-pressure setting. Module 8, "Real-World Applications," explores real-world scenarios where strong public speaking skills are essential, such as job interviews, client presentations, and team meetings. Learners gain insights into adapting their skills to various professional contexts. Finally, Module 9, "Project: Delivering a Presentation," concludes the course with a final project requiring learners to deliver a presentation on a chosen topic. This project allows them to demonstrate their mastery of the course content and receive feedback, further refining their skills and building a portfolio of work.

In conclusion, this "Mastering Public Speaking" course on LinkedIn Learning demonstrates the platform's capacity to deliver a comprehensive and practical learning experience. By combining theoretical knowledge with practical application and feedback, the course empowers learners to develop the confidence and skills needed to excel in the art of public speaking.

Skillshare

Skillshare is a well-known platform for learning online that provides a variety of creative and professional development courses from industry professionals. This platform is suitable for people who want to try new creative activities, improve their current skills, or boost their careers. The core of the platform's philosophy is the need for project-based knowledge acquisition as it gives an opportunity for learners to demonstrate the real-world application of what they have learned using real-life experiences or artistic exercises. Students are therefore able to develop their portfolios through this method of instruction.

Skillshare offers a lot of advantages, especially to those who are looking forward to adopting different skills or improving their imagination. It enables users to have contact with professionals and take lessons from their industry such as accomplished painters, designers, business persons, and intellectuals who talk about contemporary issues related to art and craft. Thousands of courses can be found in different fields of creativity and talent, allowing aspiring learners to choose according to their personal preference or individual expertise. Students may participate in practical projects where they utilize knowledge gained previously while acquiring essential skills useful in practice from its application in real-life situations, as well as, become part of a worldwide network of artists where one can submit their works online for critical assessment, and draw lessons from other people's mistakes and successes. Students can enter courses whenever they feel like it, from any place and at a pace of their choice so that it is possible for them to study alongside other programs or activities.

The secret to the success of Skillshare has been its focus on offering concisely engaging, project-based courses. Below provides more detail into the lesson plans offered, but more so elaborate upon the structure and pedagogical approach that makes these courses such an effective learning experience. The examples picked here show the flexibility of the model presented here: across what could be termed either the open fields of creative vistas in graphic and photography design, through to business world entrepreneurship.

The very best example of the Skillshare approach would be "Mastering Typography: From Beginner to Pro," where a structured curriculum takes students step by step through Lesson 1 (Introduction to Typography), teaching them the rudiments in the class and applying the learning directly by looking into the best combinations of fonts to pair together and even making some layouts. Lesson 2: Building a Logo: builds on this base by exploring the topic of brand identity and color theory, culminating in the creation of a personalized logo. Building a Website Final Lesson: introduces the basics of web design, culminating in the design of a simple website using a relatively intuitive platform. The project-based strategy extends practice and confidence.

Similarly, the photography class, "Mobile Photography: Capture Stunning Images with Your Smartphone," uses that everyone appears to have a smartphone and writes on that as a very accessible means of teaching photographic fundamentals. Lesson 1: Understanding Composition-what are the key compositional elements and how are they created? Immediately, exercises are provided in mobile photography so that learning becomes hands-on. Lesson 2: Mastering Light and Shadow-the role of lighting in making images, even more hands-on work. The course ends with Lesson 3 (Editing Your Photos), which shows fundamental techniques of photo editing on easily accessible mobile apps. This is with the view of enabling learners to progress from conceptual understanding to actual application and post-processing.

An example of this model is the, "Freelancing 101: Build a Successful Career as a Freelancer," course. As seen here, Skillshare is so easy to adapt for professional development. So, in Lesson 1, Defining Your Niche, the learner performs a self-assessment to discover their strengths and opportunities in the market. Then comes Lesson 2: Creating a Portfolio, where one is taught the need for effective self-representation. The course ends with Lesson 3: Marketing and Networking, which teaches marketers and networking ways essential to get into a freelance career. The portfolio building and marketing plan give the results of actual work, giving self-confidence.

In conclusion, the Skillshare model portrayed through these examples is characterized by having practical application and instant feedback in store. This short lesson format combined with project-based learning ensures that the learning process is full of engagement and a sense of accomplishment. This makes learning not just easy and fun but, more importantly, successful regardless of the material at hand. Divergent fields feature consistent structures, showing how the approach could be adapted and how effectively it works.

edX

edX is a leading global digital learning stage that provides an extensive list of classes and projects from famous academic institutions around the world which started from August 2020 onward. It has turned out as a hub for people attempting to upgrade their skills, move up their career ladder, or even widen their area of knowledge.

It has evolved as a prime platform for eLearning, providing a wide variety of courses and programs from around the globe by different universities and companies. Therefore, it has turned out to be most peoples' destination to better their skills; advance their careers or simply want more knowledge. Well, as edX continues growing and adding more things to it, it will play a greater role in the future of online education.

The platform has been quite influential in the development of e-learning, which has contributed to different aspects. edX MOOC of its kind provides education that is free of charge, furthering accessibility irrespective of geographical location or financial constraints. This platform has introduced avant-garde techniques such as gamification, customized pathways for individual students, and a focus on community participation. To ensure that its courses meet the demands of industries and supply learners with valuable competencies for today's job market, edX has established partnerships with top-level academic institutions and corporations. Furthermore, edX is the leading site in online education research; by collecting data about how students behave online and adapting their courses accordingly, the platform has enhanced course design and learning results.

edX courses are designed to make learning more engaging and interactive, with a blended range of learning modalities to suit different learning styles. A sample lesson plan from the, "Minecraft, Coding and Teaching," course offered by the University of California, San Diego (UCSD) reflects how edX enables an entirely popular video game to teach coding skills.

In week 1, students are introduced to the world of coding and to coding education in a manner that will provide a developing sense of community for the learners. Explore the value of teaching coding and introduce the possibilities of using Minecraft as a learning tool; introduce students to the "Learntomod" software, which makes it easy to code with Minecraft. It's a coding practice in week 2. The learners code up some using several self-paced micro-coding exercises made available by the course materials and the Learntomod software. It is trial and error, and remediation of problem solving, thus making it very deep towards the concepts.

During week 3, the skills of students are enhanced that are acquired from coding, equipping students with ideas on how to create their lesson plans for teaching coding through Minecraft. A few examples from the instructors would be used as a basis and encouraged to modify them according to one's teaching personality and their students' requirements. This week mainly deals with how practical the information on coding can be in an educational environment.

The fourth or final week fosters community development and sustained learning. The students share lesson plans, give feedback to one another, and create new lesson plans together. This leads to a supportive learning environment and sustains continued interest in the course content.

This exemplary lesson shows the edX ethos of structured learning in a participative setting. The course provides a balance of theoretical and applied learning, forcing real-time interaction among the learners.

Moodle

Moodle is a free and open source that has been a widely-embraced learning hive, capable of managing course work as well as tracking students' progress in educational institutions, businesses, and organizations around the world.

Moodle's beginnings date back to 1999 when Martin Dougiamas, an educator and computer scientist from Australia, started putting together software. To enable learners to engage and mutually work together in a constructivist and social constructionist way, he set out to establish a platform for education. The initial iteration of Moodle was launched in August 2002, and since then it has been continuously developed and improved.

Moodle HQ, an Australian organization, manages and coordinates the Moodle initiative, which is financially backed by a consortium of accredited associates from all over the globe. Moreover, there is a dynamic open-source society that stimulates development through user inputs on how to expand or enhance the software platform.

The open-source nature of Moodle, coupled with its rich functionality, offers several advantages for both educators and learners. Moodle is free to use, making it an attractive option for institutions and organizations with limited budgets. Its open-source nature allows for extensive customization that enables educators to tailor the platform according to their specific teaching styles and curriculum requirements. It has a large active user community comprising developers and teachers who offer help, share resources as well as contribute to the continual development of the platform. In addition, Moodle was designed with an emphasis in mind so that every learner can monitor their progress or engage in online courses. It can also handle diverse user loads, making it ideal for small classrooms, larger universities, or even global organizations.

Moodle has far-reaching tools and resources that cater to diverse learning styles and subject topics. The following examples demonstrate the implementation of Moodle in effective lesson planning. First, an interactive quiz for language acquisition can be used to test vocabulary and grammar. It comes with images and audio for effective learning. This includes using Moodle's quiz module to create a multiple-choice quiz. The quizzes of Moodle have also been made to be personalized by providing a feedback function, and time management is encouraged with the help of a timer. Quiz results provide areas of support. Key Moodle features used include the quiz module, image and audio embedding, feedback function, and timer.

A task for collaboration in history is working on a research project that teaches teamwork and critical thinking through researching and presenting a particular topic in history. Students are separated into groups and each group will research a historical topic. The forum of Moodle is meant for group discussions, and sharing of resources is possible with a wiki, which allows collaborative writing and editing. Role assignments encourage individual contributions, and final presentations made, whether video or otherwise, are uploaded to Moodle. Discussion participation and research quality as well as presentation skills are the subjects of evaluation. Moodle features utilized are the forum, wiki, assignment submission, and video upload.

Finally, the flipped classroom model in science focuses on the classroom time on active learning and solving problems. Lectures are recorded or video tutorials are put up on Moodle to be viewed before class. The classroom time is for active learning and problem-solving. Moodle's assignment module is then utilized to collect and review students' work, and the instructor gives instant feedback through the messaging system. Course evaluations are based on participation by class, problem-solving ability, and submission of assignments. The features of Moodle that are relevant in this scenario are video upload, assignment submission, and the messaging system.

Moodle being open-source and very versatile is a tool highly useful for educators, trainers, and learners. The introduction of Moodle into lesson plans as well as making good use of its features creates an engaging and effective learning experience among various subjects and contexts. With advancing technology so will the role of Moodle form in shaping up the future of education and learning.

FACTORS TO CONSIDER IN CHOOSING THE RIGHT PLATFORM

Although e-learning platforms offer a variety of educational resources, students need to take into account some factors to find themselves suited to a particular learning system. As a student, you will assess if the target audience of the platform is congruent with your personal status. Another one is identifying the course contents and seeing if they will satisfy your desired outcome. Next, observe the features of the system and contemplate whether it will offer sufficient engagement as you immerse yourself throughout the course. Most importantly, a learner has to know if a course will demand a price for a specific program and see whether it's worth or appropriate to subscribe.

Target Audience

When selecting an educational platform, it is imperative that you understand your audience well since this is a strategic decision. Criteria like learner needs, preferences, and modes of learning will assist you in identifying a suitable platform for students' learning paths which will help in attaining expected end results. Also bear in mind that apart from delivering content, the platform must be able to provide an engaging and accessible learning experience that is in tune with its intended audience.

It is important to know exactly who your target audience will be before selecting the platform you want to use. This includes understanding them by looking at their demographics such as age, sex, geographical region, level of education, profession, and economic status which are key aspects to consider. As the facilitator of the peer group, you also need to consider the learning styles of your students if they prefer visual, auditory, kinesthetic, or mixed instruction. Moreover, a teacher must know the level of technological literacy they have to suit their capacity in a certain platform, as well as, consider their motivations and goals to identify the reason behind their interest. Time constraints shall also be inquired to determine how much time can they allocate for learning and what are their mode of learning preferences.

After you have identified your target users, you can then assess educational platforms relative to how well they can address those needs. To start with, instructors shall consider the content and curriculum of the platform if it really appeals to their interests. They also need to discover if the platform provides an engaging and interactive learning experience that matches users' preferred styles of learning. In addition, usability must be known if it is indeed easy for learners with diverse technical skills to learn from what is available on the site. Teachers shall look up if there is enough backing and materials for instructors, online discussion spaces, as well as, technical support in place by that site. And lastly but an essential input, one must know whether such a pricing plan is able to meet with requirements of the targeted audience.

Knowing your target audience greatly helps your desired platform to be reached. For busy professionals who would like to get better or develop their careers, a good option would be a website that has flexible and self-paced programs that can be accessed via phones. When it comes to secondary school students, a site containing games involving interaction between players, multimedia materials, and gamified learning experiences would be more attractive to these types of learners. In the case of disabled individuals, there must be screen readers and subtitles for students facing these challenges.

Course Content

Important factors for choosing an education platform are its course type and quality. It is essential that the platform fits into your course content requirements, ensuring that your students have a smooth and captivating learning experience at all times.

A teacher shall know what types and formats of content you want to provide to your students as this is necessary for choosing the right platform for them. In case learning courses are mainly based on texts, they need a platform with efficient text editing tools, document uploading options, and formatting possibilities. If courses contain videos, sound recordings, images, interactive components, etc., then they need to have a pod where different media forms can be uploaded, embedded, or streamed. If quiz makers, simulators, and games among others offer such interactive tools, then it means playful types of learners will be more engaged in their studies and keep the information better. The instructor then has to examine the best platform suitable for them. If your learners want to support collaborative work, online discussions, or peer reviews, then the platform ought to have things like discussion forums, chat spaces, and tools for editing shared documents.

It is essential to ensure that your content is accessible to everyone who is learning. Find platforms that are built on access standards so that individuals with disabilities can use the information therein. The platform must work together with reading screens, voice-into-text programs, and other similar technologies used in assisting handicapped people. To allow learners with auditory impairments to have access to video and audio messages, it should be in tandem with captioning as well as transcription facilities.

Features

For the premier educational platform to be developed, it is important to consider learning experience components. If an educator aims for good teaching, he/she must not forget that choose discerningly a suitable and conducive learning area. The platform should facilitate the teaching process and develop a healthy interaction between the teacher and his or her learners. The online sections must be established to ensure that, apart from delivering their course materials, they also have everything that helps in learning, communication, assessment, and progress tracking.

An all-encompassing educational system should have a variety of traits that aid different facets of learning. The platform shall facilitate the organization of courses into modules, units, and lessons with a clear path and coherence in the delivery. Also, it is important to have support for uploading different types of files (text, images, videos, audio) as well as powerful editing features. Multimedia such as videos, sound files, and interactive simulations must be incorporated into the platform seamlessly.

Moreover, inclusivity requires captions on all videos, transcripts for podcasts, and websites that are designed specifically for screen readers. The platform must also include multiple testing methods like exams, homework, and projects. In addition, automated scoring saves time and gives immediate feedback to the students as well as, instructors must have a chance to give individual commentaries to their learners about their progress and grades.

It is vital to have communicative and cooperative qualities in a platform to foster the personal growth of learners. One example is discourse areas, a space for discussion where learners engage in debates and receipt of inquiries, and give peer reviews to each other as well as course coordinators. Ticking Tock is also a distinctive feature that makes private messages more direct between teacher and student.

It will be advantageous if a platform has features such as pronunciation practice tools, interactive exercises, and language-specific dictionaries for courses in languages and such platforms for professional development programs shall have features like gamification, badges, and certificates. K-12 Learners will also find it engaging if the platform has interactive games, virtual field trips, and personalized learning paths among others.

Pricing

Choosing an appropriate academic platform involves pricing as an important factor. Organizations must make strategic decisions that will help them understand diverse pricing models, think about the cost determinants, and choose a platform that provides high quality at reasonable price points. Do not forget that the right platform must comfortably fit into your budget while having features, capabilities, and assistance to help you accomplish your academic objectives.

Different learning platforms usually have different pricing models in place with pros and cons. The per user/learner model charges fixed prices for each user or learner using this platform. This type of model is ideal for organizations with a steady base of learners but can be very expensive when dealing with fluctuating numbers. On the other hand, the per course model involves charging an established fee per every created course hosted within the platform itself. It fits organizations providing few or standardized courses however it might not work well if there are changes frequently. In terms of flat rate charges, a unitary fee is needed regardless of how many users or courses exist on it at any given moment. This will benefit those companies whose learners demand high amounts sometimes while learning goes down at other times. Not to mention, a platform's basic version is free while the premium one has extra services, features, or upgrades that come at an extra charge. This enables institutions to test out the platform before going for a paid option.

As an aspiring learner or user of a certain platform, we should be informed of its cost determinants. Prices are likely to go up on platforms that have advanced features such as automated grading, analytics dashboards, or proper communication tools. In the case of infrastructure support, the cost will often be higher for platforms meant to host many users or more comprehensive training packages. For some types of platforms, there may be increased costs due to extensive customization, branding, or integration plans. Moreover, there are platforms that offer dedicated customer support, onboarding assistance, or training resources at a higher cost than others while platforms developed for certain groups, like businesses, schools or individuals do likewise have different price structures.

In choosing a platform with reference to price, there are strategies that can be a basis to make an informed decision. First, you may set up a well-defined budget for your educational platform by considering the financial constraints of your organization and the benefits you expect from the platform. You can also look at different pricing options and select one that best matches your needs and expected use and remember to not just settle for the lowest price only. Factor in all the characteristics, features, and support available on each slot to identify where is the best place for your money. If there are particular requirements that come from your organization or if you have a large number of users, think about getting custom prices or discounts from service providers. For organizations that don't have much money, it would make sense to think about free or open-source platforms such as Moodle as this could save them a lot of cost.

BENEFITS OF E-LEARNING

As students delve into e-learning, there are advantages that they gain from its usage. These are time efficiency, easy growth analysis, transparency of the learning process, structured teaching, rich engagement, a safe learning environment, self-paced learning, and the availability of tutorial videos. These benefits drive students to develop their skills, increase their knowledge and productivity, and boost their interest or motivation in learning. As we have diverse kinds of learners, this type of education fosters an equitable and meaningful atmosphere, spurring more learning opportunities.

Time-Efficiency

One important advantage of e-learning is its time efficiency for both students and professors. E-learning sites enable their users to utilize their most precious asset – time, making education a more productive and harmonized endeavor by offering flexibility in what one learns at his/her own speed along with simplified content. Such time management leads to greater productivity, improved learning results as well as an easier and more interesting learning path.

The development and delivery of digital content have proven to be more time-saving than traditional classroom preparations. Once created, online courses and resources can be easily reused and revised, minimizing the lasting time investment for instructors. For educators, automated grading techniques are able to free up lots of time than assessing students' answers manually as a result allowing them devote their attention towards teaching thereby giving personalized guidance when needed.

Easy Growth Analysis

Analyzing growth has just become easier for many reasons including e-learning which gives people the power to see how individuals develop in real time. Changes can be made to courses as they are running to improve students' experiences. Continuous development through evidence is possible because it delivers better results for all those involved in the educational system.

The automatic capture of learner's activity by the e-learning platforms guides the e-learning apps on various things like time taken on modules, completion rate, scores from quizzes done, and how active one has been in the forums. It thickens our understanding of the motivation and advancement of each specific learner. While working on the quizzes and assessments against learners' performance, teachers can discover particular fields in which students have difficulties and modify their teaching methods henceforth. In this manner, students deal with knowledge gaps better. In addition, the information collected from online learning platforms may be utilized by educators to provide personalized comments that reveal students' strong points and weak ones that need more management. Such directed critique keeps students encouraged as well as focused.

Transparency of Learning Process

E-learning is heavily based on the concept of learning process transparency to achieve effective learning. This includes stating clearly what one is learning, how they will be learning it, and how their progress will be graded. Such a method enables most learners to comprehend it better, therefore, making them own their education.

Students are prone to engage actively when they understand the reasons behind their learning activities. As a result, such learners would cultivate motivation and participation in education as they are able to appreciate how relevant the subject matter is to them personally or professionally, thus, increasing their urge to learn. Moreover, transparency helps students develop metacognitive skills - the ability to understand and regulate one's learning. Understanding the mechanics of the learning process enables students to recognize personal strengths and weaknesses, and create appropriate study plans that can lead them into achieving better results academically. Students who know what is expected from them and what makes them successful feel more confident about themselves. As a result, they are able to assess their own progress and pinpoint areas where improvements can be made, thereby feeling empowered while taking control of their own learning, succeeding in school, and gaining confidence. Transparency creates a bridge between instructors' expectations and students' comprehension of course content. This would be especially valuable for minority group members or individuals who recently joined distance studying due to online opportunities to reduce such barriers. Furthermore, a sense of transparency promotes a more cooperative learning atmosphere. When students catch the drift about the learning process as well as reasons behind it, they tend to collaborate more with their mates and tutors thus resulting in a feeling that they have one thing in common.

Transparency in e-learning can be utilized through different ways to ensure students' progress is uncompromised and tracked. First in line, instructors shall define clearly what is to be learned by every module, unit, or course. In this regard, students are in a position to know what they ought to achieve and how these goals fit into the entire course plan. They can also present methods and criteria for appraising student achievements. The content entails rubrics, model assignments, and clear grade assignment guidelines. Communication shall also remain unrestricted between instructors and learners. This can happen through forums, discussion boards, or regular office hours that allow students to ask inquiries with respect to coursework, thus, getting their answers as soon as possible. Not to mention, peer feedback and collaborative learning activities should be facilitated. As a result, the students will have an opportunity to learn from each other, gain different perspectives, and improve their critical thinking skills. Moreover, you might want to provide frequent comments on student assignments and monitor their advancement during the term. It helps learners remain focused on their tasks, pinpoint areas that require improvement as well as make them feel appreciated during the process of acquiring new knowledge.

Engaging

The success of e-learning depends on the motivation of the students. E-learning platforms can make use of such elements as multimedia content, interactive activities, individualized routes for learning, application of real-life situations, games and competition, and social interactions among others to develop engaging and stimulating studying processes that encourage motivation and increase knowledge retention and skills improvement. We will continue to see more creative online education methodologies emerge in the future as technological advancement occurs, leading to a change in how we learn and grow.

E-learning platforms can make use of videos, animations, interactive simulations, and gamification among other things. In this way, different learning styles can be addressed while making the process more dynamic compared to the traditional text-only materials. E-learning involves interactive elements such as quizzes, polls, class discussion forums, and group projects which foster student participation. This promotes a feeling of belongingness and motivates students to openly engage with the ideas, enabling them to retain discussions for a longer time.

Adaptability is a major characteristic of e-learning platforms which are capable of accommodating various learning styles as well as different individual paces. Such learners have the liberty to advance at their own pace, revisit difficult concepts, and concentrate more on areas of interest. This tailored methodology cultivates control and self-motivation among students, hence promoting happier and more effective learning experiences. The integration of real-world scenarios alongside e-learning can make it effective in ensuring the relevance and applicability of what is learned in everyday life. As such, students' understanding and motivation levels can be improved through linking theory with practice.

Through gaming elements such as points, badges, leaderboards, or rewards it is possible to create an exciting environment for learning. These incentives promote active student participation in the completion of assignments as well as improvements, enhancing the overall fun of the study process. In addition, through forums, chat rooms, or group projects geared towards discussion between learners, e-learning platforms facilitate social interactions among users enabling them to share ideas which leads to mutual learning and creating a more captivating and constructive atmosphere for education.

Engaged learning contributes to students' intrinsic motivation and real interest in the discipline area. Consequently, this elicits further participation, heightened concentration levels, as well as, increased thirst for unearthing new ideas. Active involvement in learning activities stimulates various parts of the brain, leading to deeper processing which promotes information remembering. In turn, it results in improved educational performance as well as utilizing the acquired content in true-life settings.

The provision of stimulating learning experiences to individuals offers them a chance to acquire new abilities in an environment that is free from fear and opens its arms to its people. This method raises their faith in themselves, making them good at skills development. Consequently, they may feel more accomplished with what they have done.

Structured Teaching

The structured way of teaching is the methodology that puts more emphasis on creating a systematic, clear, and anticipatable learning environment. This includes shrinking complicated information into smaller and easier ones, giving out directives and anticipations plainly, and making use of visuals and habitual routines to help students learn. Though normally contradicted with aiding learners who have disabilities in learning, structured teaching principles can be extremely advantageous in e-learning settings as they increase engagement, enhance understanding, and contribute to student achievement.

E-learning platforms often showcase a plethora of information that may confuse students. Structured teaching organizes content into its logical units, providing a clear path for learners to follow and progress through it. Such structure reduces confusion and anxiety, allowing the students to focus on specific learning objectives. Through dividing complex concepts into smaller units, structured teaching enhances understanding and retention. In this approach, learners are able to gradually process information thus building a solid base before advancing to higher levels. The predictors of structured teaching provide a comfort zone and control for students. In every aspect of life, you are aware of what will be next, decreasing worries and ambiguities which enhances confidence and motivation to deal with education materials.

E-learning platforms can leverage structured teaching principles to create personalized learning paths. By tailoring the content and pace to individual needs, learners can progress at their own speed, revisit challenging concepts, and focus on areas of particular interest. This results in a greater degree of involvement while at the same time creating ownership feelings about one's learning. For instance, structured teaching could help make e-learning more accessible for students of different backgrounds such as students with disabilities or freshmen in the field of online education. Structured learning bridges the gap between the teaching environment and the comprehension abilities of the student with its well-defined steps and visual materials.

For every module, unit, or course, precisely specifying the learning outcomes enables students to know what they are required to learn and how it relates to the main course objectives. Instructors shall organize content into coherent chunks with headings, subheadings, bullet points, and other visual cues that aid in reading and understanding, assisting learners in spotting important information easily while browsing the material. They must also make use of visual aids such as diagrams, charts, infographics, or videos to help explain difficult ideas so that they stimulate interest during study time. Such functionalities will be particularly useful for those who prefer visual methods of learning.

To improve learning and give instant feedback, there are interactive activities such as quizzes, polls, or simulations, learners start processing information on their own and evaluate their understanding. Regular checkpoints and feedback throughout the course help in tracking student progress by identifying weaknesses, and giving them a path to follow. Learners use this opportunity to stay on track in a supported environment of learning.

Safe Learning Environment

An essential condition for efficiency in e-learning is a secure learning setting. Prioritizing safety, respect, and inclusiveness enables educators and creators of platforms to create online learning experiences that enhance learner empowerment, stimulate engagement, and ensure academic success. With the continuous development of technology, safeguarding learners from online threats while creating a conducive positive atmosphere for everybody becomes imperative.

A secure learning atmosphere helps to reduce anxiety and stress hence allowing learners to pay more attention to their studies without any fear of discrimination, harassment, or judgement. This creates a feeling of being at ease and confident which leads to active engagement by learners hence better academic results When learners feel safe they are likely to partake in discussions actively, raise questions, as well as share their ideas openly. Consequently, it leads to an electric type of classroom where everyone becomes involved, thus, team spirit is cultivated alongside the sense of belonging.

This kind of environment creates trust and respect among all teaching personnel, encouraging students to take risks on various issues such as trying out new techniques or facing hard questions. Through this critical thinking skills are enhanced just like problem-solving abilities while creativity is nurtured so that eventually better marks are achieved.

All the students regardless of their differences in background and even special needs can feel welcomed within a safe learning environment. This enables inclusivity as well as accessibility, giving equal chances for success to all learners. Online hazards like cyberbullying, bad content, and data breaches may pose dangers to students learning on e-learning platforms. Therefore, e-learning platforms shall establish strong security measures to protect learners from these threats. In this regard, secure learning management systems must be used alongside robust passwords and the provision of clear guidelines for online behavior should be provided. Teachers shall make sure to define what online behavior is acceptable by making rules against harassment, discrimination, or the use of foul language. This will help all students understand the boundaries of right and wrong things and create a respectful atmosphere of learning.

By employing moderation tools, it will be possible to track what goes on in the message boards where students discuss their issues over the Internet so that only decent messages are allowed. Consequently, harassment plus bullying are prevented, providing a more secure interaction zone for students together with their teachers as well as peers. The protection and responsible handling of learner data is critical. This can be done by having reliable learning management systems, encrypting sensitive information, and complying with relevant privacy laws and regulations.

Encouraging instructors to communicate openly with their students enables them to ask questions, voice grievances, and receive assistance from their teachers which is important for a closer teacher-student relationship. To encourage respect in the learning community, there should be diversity of course material, and inclusive language used throughout all studies offered. Such institutional policies make all necessary information at once available to everyone regardless of background, thereby creating more awareness among those who may not know it from personal experience.

Self-Paced Learning

Self-paced learning is a very influential approach that contributes positively towards enhancing e-learning effectiveness and accessibility. It allows individuals to achieve their learning objectives at their own pace and in their own way through flexibility, personalization, and control over the learning process. Although there are challenges with it, educators can devise strategies aimed at reducing them while promoting the advantages associated with this innovative mode of education. It is worth noting that as technologies develop further, self-paced learning will become more important in determining the direction of education.

Learning at one's pace provides unprecedented ease, as individuals can access course materials for free at any time and finish them whenever they want. This benefits particularly those who are too busy with jobs, families, or other activities that make attending classes in a traditional classroom difficult. This type of self-driven study gives an opportunity for learners to customize their learning experiences in accordance with their preferences and needs. Since this personalization gives learners mastery over what they learn, it makes them feel more motivated as well as involved in the process.

With no pressure from strict deadlines, self-guided studies can help students learn more about subject content in depth and digest information at students' own speed. As a result, learners develop a comprehensive understanding of what they learn while improving knowledge retention due to the ample amount of time available for revisiting concepts or practicing skills until one is sure about them. Self-paced education makes schooling available to everyone, even those who have physical, timing, or geographic constraints. Anyone with an internet connection can take part in the program from anywhere and at any time. This makes it possible for educational institutions and organizations to cater to a wider student base without being confined by physical classrooms.

Self-paced learning has its challenges despite its numerous advantages. Students' indulgence in procrastination and the absence of definite deadlines can make procrastination inevitable among some students. Some ways through which teachers may try to solve this problem are setting their dates for completion of assigned works, decomposing big undertakings into smaller pieces, or even using time management devices in general. In addition, a lack of stimulation may be faced by some of these students because of the absence of structure in ordinary classrooms. It will enable them to study on their own as an alternative option within such settings. The educators know what to do about it by providing simple learning goals for them, performing constant estimation, and making use of vibrant audio-visual content and exciting exercises. Student interaction is needed to attract anybody's attention who does not fit well into regular types of studying or is not used to this kind of lifestyle at all.

Self-directed learning can result in a lonely experience, particularly for students who perform better in a communal setup. Educators can take care of this by initiating online dialogues, developing virtual groups for studies, and including joint assignments. Furthermore, technical hitches may interfere with the educational process. Hence, educators should ensure that e-learning is dependable, and offer help and alternative ways of learning to those facing technical problems.

Availability of Tutorial Videos

In e-learning, tutorial videos are now a must-have component of learning that combines visual teaching, step-by-step guidance, and practical demonstrations. Educators are using tutorial videos that are easily accessible, flexible, and engaging to improve the quality of learning for their students.

Tutorial videos serve visual learners by allowing them to observe and understand concepts through demonstrations and visual representations. This can be helpful, especially in complex procedures, technical skills, or abstract concepts that are fenced off by text alone. It also decomposes complex tasks into small manageable parts providing learners with clear instructions accompanied by demonstrations they can follow at their own speed. This organizes learning which enhances comprehension and reduces confusion making the whole process more efficient and effective. Most often, tutorial videos exhibit real-life examples of the taught concepts that assist students in getting to know how practical what they learn is. Such linking with practical contexts enhances motivation, promoting real-life adjustment practices.

Since tutorial videos are available online, they are open for any learner anytime and anywhere there is an internet connection. This flexibility allows individuals who require that information to access it whenever it suits them best without being restricted by conventional learning environments' schedules. Correction of verbal errors is a step towards perfection for most people but in learning, it is about repeating what has been said by the instructor over again. This indicates that repetition and stabilization apply here as learners can always play back the instructional video to better understand it, go through hard sections or even relax themselves with these visual demonstrations. As learners may find mastering these skills easier through constant review of them, knowledge retention becomes easier as well through the ease of access to materials.

COMPARISON BETWEEN CONVENTIONAL AND DIGITAL EDUCATION

While e-learning seems like a bright door opening astounding privileges to digital users, traditional learning has its own unique characteristics that benefit other kinds of learners. These are social interaction and collaboration, structured learning and discipline, and teacher-led guidance and support, while in e-learning, accessibility and flexibility, cost-effectiveness, and global collaboration were its principal assets. These two ways of learning can both be effective, depending on the preferences of an individual. As long as growth is taking place, it is still progress.

Accessibility and Flexibility

Accessibility and flexibility are not only technical features but are also the fundamental principles that ought to govern the design and development of all online learning environments. An educational system that is more inclusive and equitable can be built by giving priority to accessibility and flexibility making it possible for all types of learners to realize their maximum potential. Therefore, this is not merely about doing things right, it is a future-wise investment in which all people will have access to digital-age education's transformative power.

Digital interfaces need to be designed in a manner that makes them accessible to people with visual, audio, and motor impairments by incorporating features such as keyboard navigation, screen reader software, and alternative text for images. Content should be provided through multiple formats like text, audio, video, or even sign language so that different types of learners can get hold of it easily. Virtual platforms must also include elements like assistive technology such as screen readers, text-to-speech programs, and closed-captioning systems. All of which enable disabled students to engage themselves completely during online classes.

A right to quality education is supposed to be available for each student bracing all forms of differences, promoting equality and justice in education. When students with disabilities have equal access to qualified teaching content, they are likely to do well, thus enhancing learning results for all learners. Academic success is more likely among disabled students who can easily access and interact with instructional materials resulting in improved learning outcomes in totality. By allowing disabled students to participate in online discussions, group work, or other classes, it builds an inclusive atmosphere and teamwork spirit among learners alike.

Personalized Learning

With the advancement of technology, personalized learning has become a common theme in modern education. This method accepts that one person learns differently from others in terms of personal approach to studies hence this mode intends to be designed to suit each student in a specific manner; thus promoting better understanding, encouragement engagement, and success. Hence, individualization in teaching can change the face of digital education by making it more engaging and effective as well as equal compared to conventional systems of learning. By embracing personalized learning, educators are able, not only to let students learn what they want but also to help them reach their full academic potential in an age of increasing complexity and dynamism in terms of information technology.

Learners can advance at their individual speeds with personalized education, concentrating on the aspects they require assistance in and looking into other subjects that attract them. This makes the whole process more interesting and relevant hence increasing the level of motivation as well as understanding of the concept better. When students believe that their learning is customized, such a feeling creates increased involvement and drive within them. This approach to education supports personal accountability, hence making learning more enjoyable.

Personalized education enables learners to spend more time on difficult subjects, go back to ideas they find hard, or eliminate already mastered materials. This intense focus gives rise to deep comprehension of concepts leading to memory enhancement. Not to mention, through this method, students can consolidate their ideas and use them subsequently in real situations, making them meaningful.

Learning can be made more collaborative if the student-centered way is adopted as it gives room for each student to choose and work with their partners to meet their objectives of studying. Through this collaborative process, learners get an opportunity to share their knowledge and experiences, thereby improving their communication and teamwork abilities. Furthermore, many personalized learning platforms utilize analytics to monitor student progress, pinpoint areas that require improvement, and adjust learning trajectories accordingly. This data-driven approach enables educators to make educated decisions with regard to curriculum design, instructional strategies, and learner support services, guaranteeing effective instructional delivery.

Today's Learning Management Systems (LMSs) come equipped with features such as adaptive learning models and tailor-made paths for individuals that facilitate personalized education, meanwhile, Adaptive learning technologies utilize algorithms to customize the learning experience according to each student's needs, therefore, providing individualized content, pacing, and feedback. Based on their own strengths, weaknesses, and goals for learning, educators can design tailored educational roadmaps for every student. Regularly giving relevant feedback combined with support that is specific to students' requirements keeps them motivated as they tackle problems or move towards achieving their targets.

Cost-effectiveness

Digital schooling comprises unassailable arguments concerning affordable costs, leading to great savings for both students and institutions. The use of technology in this manner makes it possible for digital education to provide equal quality education at a cheap price and fast manner, thus guaranteeing fairness and an all-inclusive educational paradigm. Nevertheless, for us to harness the full potential that comes with this innovative teaching method, it is important to address issues related to the digital gap and quality assurance.

Digital education minimizes operational costs associated with traditional classrooms, such as utilities, maintenance, and administrative staff. Furthermore, the absence of physical classrooms reduces the need for travel and commuting, saving both time and money for students and faculty. [Affordable Access to Educational Resources

Digital education platforms provide access to a vast library of online resources, including textbooks, videos, simulations, and interactive exercises, often at a fraction of the cost of traditional print materials. This accessibility allows students to access the information they need without incurring the expense of purchasing physical books or attending expensive workshops. Also, Digital education platforms do away with the expensive physical infrastructure such as buildings, classrooms, and libraries. Thus, educational institutions incur low overhead costs which enable them to use resources more efficiently in developing their curricula, upgrading their technology, and paying staff salaries.

Digital education makes it easier for students to save money since they can attend any course in any part of the world provided there is an internet connection. This means that expensive traveling, accommodation, and on-campus living expenses are not necessary anymore. Consequently, this makes education open to individuals who come from different backgrounds as well as having different incomes.

Educational content is effectively delivered through digital platforms with little or no cost incurred. Online courses can be created and distributed by educational institutions to more students at once, thereby minimizing the number of teachers needed and classrooms.

To be fair digital learning, its many cost benefits has some possible challenges. Lack of access to reliable internet connections and gadgets among some pupils still remains an impediment hence demand to close the gap on digitization. Digital platforms may also need to be efficiently used in teaching by educators through training and support programs. For online courses to serve their purposes well, quality must be ensured through good design of syllabus content and methods of evaluation.

Global collaboration

Digital education has transformed our traditional learning. One significant benefit is that it allows for worldwide collaboration. This helps students and educators from different backgrounds to work together, share knowledge, and deal with global problems.

International collaborative projects allow students to understand various cultures and worldviews. Students who interact with their counterparts across the globe are better placed to appreciate different customs, indigenous practices, etc. Researchers suggest that such exposures help in developing compassion and tolerance while embracing the whole idea of oneness through global citizenship. In this case, they gain preparedness for statehood in a world where cultures are becoming increasingly fused.

Global collaboration projects promote student inquiry and exploration of topics that spark interest among them. Using this method of learning based on asking questions, gives a better background understanding of concepts as they provide real life situations and multiple perspectives on an issue. International teamwork projects frequently include many languages' communication to give learners the finest chances of practicing their language capabilities and studying about various modes of interaction. Their exposure leads to improved fluency, self-assurance, and an understanding of culture.

Global collaboration projects can be employed to touch on urgent global concerns like climate change, poverty, or inequality. When students from different parts of the world work together, they are able to exchange information, resources, and viewpoints with one another for the purposes of coming up with innovative answers that could result in a more sustainable and fairer planet Earth.

Social Interaction and Collaboration

Traditional learning, which emphasizes person-to-person interaction, has significant advantages in social engagement and student cooperation. The atmosphere makes it easier to learn pivotal skills, interact with fellow students and prepare for a collaborative and communicative space that's emerging in the world. Nevertheless, while online education has its merits, it lacks the social and collaborative dimensions of face-to-face learning that ensure rounded development.

Conventional classrooms provide a natural setting for students to develop social skills and emotional intelligence. Through daily interactions with peers and teachers, students learn to communicate effectively, resolve conflicts, build relationships, and navigate social dynamics. This experience is crucial for their personal and professional development, preparing them for successful interactions in diverse settings. It also offers a conducive environment for collaborative learning, where students work together on projects, assignments, and discussions. This collaborative approach encourages students to share ideas, perspectives, and expertise, leading to a deeper understanding of concepts and a more engaging learning experience

Conventional education fosters a sense of community among students. Shared experiences, classroom interactions, and extracurricular activities create a sense of belonging and connection, promoting a supportive and inclusive learning environment. This sense of community is invaluable for students' well-being and academic success.

To become successful in various professional and personal settings, students are taught how to articulate their ideas effectively, engage with an audience, and respond to feedback via classroom discussions, debates, presentations, and group projects. The conventional classroom thus provides an opportunity for the development of communication and presentation skills.

This platform allows students to cultivate networks as well as relationships which prove beneficial in life. The students can create a better support network when they sustain their friendships with other colleagues along with teachers/mentors (shared learning experiences). Such connections can lead one to great chances while providing guidance together with a sense of belongingness

Structured Learning and Discipline

Structured learning, an important feature of traditional education, is a valuable structure for building discipline and academic achievement; conventional education provides students with clear expectations, consistent routines, and a supportive environment that are essential to their academic success as well as some important life skills. Digital education may be flexible and accessible but to lay a strong learning foundation, and build self-discipline among other things, conventional learning brings up students who can work orderly, consistently, or concentratedly in this world.

Traditional education generally has well-defined schedules, routines, and expectations. A predictable environment makes it easy for students to know what they are supposed to do, reduces anxiety, and gives them a sense of security. Through this structure, students can engage more effectively in learning as they do not have to worry about uncertainty or ambiguity.

A conventional classroom's structure limits distractions, enabling the learners to concentrate on the tasks at hand. This focused setting allows deeper processing of information, thereby leading to better understanding or retention. Structured learning typically includes time management strategies as well as organization tools. In this way, students learn how to stick to timetable plans, meet due dates, and prioritize activities allowing them to acquire essential skills outside school. One encouraging factor for constant effort plus accountability is that the formal education system is structured. The participation of students is crucial since it drives their engagement; they submit assignments in good time while they show their comprehension through exams, ensuring consistency in performance standards and fostering a responsible culture in academics.

The development of self-discipline is usually nurtured through a structured learning environment in formal education. With consistent routines, clarity in expectations, and frequent assessments, students learn how to manage their time wisely, prioritize tasks, and take responsibility for their own learning. This self-discipline becomes a valuable tool that students rely on throughout their school days and beyond. Structured learning environments (SLE) can be especially helpful to students having behavioral challenges. These programs offer enough support by providing the much-needed structure within which they acquire important behavioral skills as well as escape from negative emotions which improves their academic performance levels With SLE programs, there are clear expectations on behavior, resulting in definite consequences that serve as guidelines for understanding boundaries that govern social interactions for every student. In many cases, SLE programs offer personalized support that is kind of tailored to the needs of every student. This makes it easy for them to learn how to cope with different situations, develop emotional control mechanisms, and cultivate good relationships.

Unlike many institutions that frown upon the idea of data-informed education programs (in regard to the success of (SLEs), they employ data-driven monitoring in SLE programs which is done through data-based methods for tracking student performance and modifying intervention when necessary, making sure that students get exactly what supportive assistance they require, leading them towards full realization of their potentials.

Teacher-led Guidance and Support

The direct involvement of teachers in the courses they teach provides personalized guidance and support to students in conventional education. Teacher-led instruction, as it is commonly referred to, helps teachers tailor their teaching to the individual needs of their learners while addressing any learning difficulties that may arise. Moreover, it promotes a better understanding of concepts.

With teacher-led instruction, educators can differentiate their instruction by varying their methods and materials to meet the distinctive learning styles and requirements of the different students in their classrooms. This personalized approach guarantees that all students will receive adequate support for success no matter how fast they learn or where they are coming from. It gives room for teachers to give students who are struggling extra encouragement. Hence, there is an opportunity for offering individualized feedback or challenging gifted students with more complex tasks.

Direct interaction with their students can enable teachers to identify and tackle learning challenges as well as gaps in understanding. This helps them observe students' progress, give immediate feedback, and also provide targeted interventions to assist students in overcoming the obstacles they may face. In this way, personalized support ensures that students are provided with timely assistance, thereby averting the widening of the learning gap besides fostering confidence and motivation.

Direct instruction by teachers allows for guiding students through complex concepts, giving clear explanations, and facilitating discussions that stimulate critical thinking. Such interaction enables learners to ask questions, and look at different perspectives involved in a phenomenon or subject matter, developing deeper comprehension thereof. In addition, active engagement is encouraged by teacher-led instruction; which also creates a collaborative learning atmosphere in which learners learn from one another and draw on the teacher's expertise.

Teacher-led instruction creates firm relationships between teachers and students. The close contact enables teachers to understand their students very well and know their strengths and weaknesses individually, providing assistance according to each one's requirements. These relationships result in trust, promote communication as well as create a conducive environment for learning, making it easy for students to ask questions or request help.

This type of instruction becomes significant, especially to children with disabilities or additional needs. Educators are able to personalize help; adjust their teaching strategies, and establish inviting settings that meet specific demands of all learners. Additionally, they are able to partner with professionals who specialize in education like clinical psychologists on how such teenagers' emotional-social growth could be nurtured through academic coursework development plans.

HYBRID AND BLENDED LEARNING

Hybrid and blended learning are the interlock of e-learning and conventional learning. These two, however, have a subtle difference. Hybrid learning exists synchronously or on a real-time basis, while blended learning merges first-hand and virtual learning. If you are a learner who learns with head-on guidance, then hybrid learning is advisable, while if you are a flexible kind of learner, blended learning works for you.

The primary aim of hybrid learning is to make sure that students have a consistent experience regardless of whether they are studying online or offline. Hence, educational materials such as curricula, assessments, and other learning activities need to be established in a way that shifts smoothly from one modality to another. For instance, a hybrid course may require students to meet for live classes virtually and do assignments offline. This method seeks to ensure that there is an integrated educational experience with both online and offline parts contributing to achieving learning objectives.

In contrast, blended learning puts more emphasis on flexibility in terms of how people learn. The incorporation of technology serves to enhance traditional teaching methods. Some examples include extra resources available online, units with varying degrees of interactivity, or sites that allow individual learners to go at their own pace while still providing some form of guidance by teachers who remain in charge of all interactions within the classroom environment during this particular time period.

The digital divide is one of the drawbacks of online learning. Not all students have equal opportunities with regard to technological devices, internet bandwidth, and digital literacy training. In this case, whether you are in the marginalized section or not, that is not a reason for a novice to adapt to a modernized society. Hybrid and blended learning is an avenue for them to cope with the ever-evolving nature of technology. One way or another, they have to learn the necessary digital skills, or they will be left out.

Hybrid Learning

Hybrid learning is an educational approach that is dynamic in nature and combines the best of both worlds, traditional face-to-face teaching and e-learning. This model provides an opportunity for all students to have a flexible and personalized learning process meeting their diversity needs as well as those of the instructors.

Hybrid learning refers to a systematically organized mix of on-campus classes with distance learning activities. Some days or sections may be done physically while other curriculum parts can be worked out online during different time frames. This way, it leads to a flexible mode of study that accepts various styles and schedules at once.

In applying the hybrid model in the classroom, it has some sub-models that can be used as a guiding frame framework for instruction. First, we have the Flipped Classroom Model. Before attending the face-to-face session, students have an option to listen to pre-recorded lectures or watch video clips where they then engage in discussions, and activities or solve problems. Another is the Rotation Model where students engage in a variety of learning activities including online modules, group work, instructional sessions, and assignments done individually. We also have the Flex Model where students have more power as they select their courses and ways of learning, depending on what they require the most. The teachers give the necessary help but online learning is the kingpin. Next is the A La Carte Model which provides an additional layer to traditional classes with a choice of online methods, boosting flexibility and diversity in terms of available courses. Lastly, we have the Project-Based Model. This approach involves engagement in real-world activities with the use of digital materials and teamwork among students.

The Hybrid Learning method helps achieve better participation among learners through a more interactive learning experience achieved through the combination of both in-person teachings with online platform utilization. Many people have different kinds of flexibility when it comes to education which is why hybrid learning offers even more flexible classrooms that allow students to study at their preferred pace or time. With hybrid learning which integrates various forms of instruction, learners may understand better what has been communicated by instructors and how will they retain it.

The implementation of hybrid learning reduces the demand for real classrooms and teaching facilities that will in return, lead to a decrease in the total costs incurred by both institutions and their students during education. It also helps students have better preparation for a future where technology will have more and more importance at workplaces and in everyday existence.

Apart from the benefits given by hybrid learning, it also poses drawbacks. All students should have equal access to technology as well as reliable internet connections and to effectively implement hybrid learning strategies, teachers require sufficient training and support. Moreover, maintaining student engagement can be difficult in both online and offline settings as students may sometimes lose out on face-to-face social interaction due to combined learning procedures.

Blended Learning

Blended learning is something that has turned education and training around, giving it a dynamic, interactive, and effective mode of learning. Through the integration of best practices associated with online learning and traditional learning, blended learning empowers students to take charge of their education, develop vital abilities as well as obtain improved results. In line with the ever-changing technologies in many industries today, blended learning could ever be on the rise aiding in making it more personal to any student irrespective of their age or ethnicity.

Blended learning caterers for various preferences and styles of learning, enabling learners to select what suits them best regarding mode of study and pace. They can use the internet at their holes to go through the materials in their own time plus additional support can be provided during face-to-face sessions. The combination of online and offline activities such as interactive exercises, small group discussions, and hands-on training keeps students engaged throughout, fueling their motivation. The blended model of instruction normally results in lower traveling expenses, lower instructor costs as well as affordable resources as compared with conventional classroom primary teaching systems.

There are various models of blended learning, each with its unique approach to integrating online and offline components; Face-to-Face Model: This model combines traditional instructor-led sessions with online resources and activities, allowing students to control their pace of learning; Rotation Model: Students rotate through different learning activities, both online and offline, in a structured manner, often guided by an instructor; Flex Model: This model, also known as personalized learning, allows students to choose their learning path and pace, with instructors providing guidance and support; Gamification Model: This model incorporates game-like elements, such as points, levels, and challenges, to motivate students and enhance engagement; Online Lab Model: This model focuses on entirely digital learning, with minimal instructor interaction, and takes place before, during or after in-person sessions; Self-Blend Model: This model involves supplemental online resources like webinars, white papers, or video tutorials that may assist self-motivated learners; and, Online Driver Model: This model is entirely self-directed; it permits students to access the internet for personal study while interacting with teachers through chat rooms or online forums.

PERSONALITIES IN E-LEARNING

In the modern landscape of education, we have our leading pioneers, experts, or personalities who have worked out and conceptualized life-changing ideas for e-learning. They believe that in the digital world, knowledge is not absent but overflowing. These are Cathy Moore, Clark Aldrich, Clark Quinn, Craig Weiss, and Patti Shank. All of them have testified to the significance of e-learning in the present period. They agreed that virtual engagement has global potential and will have a transformative impact in the realm of education.

Cathy Moore

Cathy Moore is an internationally recognized leader in the field of e-learning who is known for her passionate advocacy of action-oriented, participative education that goes beyond conventional, information-heavy courses. Her contributions have fundamentally changed the face of e-learning with a focus on practical application, performance improvement and learner-centeredness.

She developed action mapping, a powerful framework for designing learning experiences that promote real-world performance enhancement. Through this model, design shifts away from mere information dissemination toward identifying specific actions required by learners as well as creating instructional contexts that would facilitate such actions. She is also a staunch advocate for performance support. She emphasizes the importance of providing just-in-time assistance and resources that learners can directly access at their workplaces. This approach departs from traditional courses by equipping students with the tools they require to work properly in their functions.

Moore has expressed support for micro-learning, which is the idea that learning experiences should be short and to the point instead of long-standing traditional courses. She suggests breaking down learning into more manageable components that are easier for learners to understand and therefore are highly relevant to them. Moreover, she is a renowned challenger of commonly held beliefs in e-learning. She tells designers to always question their understanding, investigate performance issues, and avoid having a "transfer of knowledge" mentality. Hence, her work fosters a more analytical and critical mindset in the design of e-learning programs.

Among other roles, Moore acts as a trustee of Serious E-learning Manifesto which focuses on improving the quality of e-learning by advocating for learner-centered principles, performance sensitivity as well as evidence-based design. In addition to this, she published her own 'L&D Manifesto' in 2022 where she suggested that workplace learning ought to move away from e-learning into nurturing all types of learning and development.

Works by Moore have had a deep-rooted effect on the e-learning sector, inspiring new designers to give prominence to the use, engagement of the learners, and improvement of performance among others. Her thoughts have inspired organizations worldwide causing them to change from the traditional way of learning which was more passive and focusing on the instructors in order to make it a more learner-centered experience that focused on actions and finally deliverables.

Clark Aldrich

Clark Aldrich is a prominent figure in the e-learning landscape, recognized for his pioneering work in educational simulations and serious games. He has significantly contributed to the evolution of e-learning, advocating for more engaging and effective learning experiences that go beyond traditional methods.

Aldrich's primary contribution lies in his passionate advocacy for simulations and serious games as powerful tools for learning. He argues that these interactive experiences offer a more engaging and effective way to teach leadership, innovation, and strategic skills compared to traditional methods like lectures and textbooks. He believes that these immersive environments provide opportunities for learners to apply knowledge, make decisions, and experience the consequences of their actions in a safe and controlled setting.

The e-learning industry has been significantly influenced by Aldrich's work. He has questioned the conventional approach to learning thereby evoking an interest in more interactive and attractive experiences. The simulations and serious games that he advocates for have sparked a style of education that is more liberal and effective; especially in areas such as leadership development, problem-solving skills as well as critical thinking.

Clark Aldrich is one of the pioneers in education simulations and serious game areas, arguing for their usage as strong learning instruments. He created many simulations for both educational settings as well as corporate ones making his name known in this field. Aldrich is a distinguished author who shares his ideas through publications, articles, or public talks As a result of this kind of work there have been profound changes within the e-learning industry; with an emphasis on how to make students learn using attractive materials.

Clark Quinn

Clark Quinn regards himself as an eminent personage in e-learning who is acknowledged for his contribution towards designing and strategizing learning technologies. He possesses a mix of skills that entail cognitive science and technology with actionable implementations to help organizations use tech to enhance their performance and achieve desired learning results.

Quinn has a Ph.D in Cognitive Psychology on which he bases his e-learning design approach; it focuses on how people acquire knowledge as well as think before designing effective learning experiences. He promotes 'cognitive design' where human cognition knowledge meets technological capability to solve real-life problems. Quinn has always talked against 'information dump and knowledge test' approaches to e-learning because they don't bring about any significant change in behaviors according to him. In addition, he advocates for a paradigm shift from traditional instructional methods to more engaging and effective learning experiences that prioritize the learners, focus on performance, and use evidence-based design principles.

Quinn provides just-in-time assistance and resources to learners in their work environment. Thus, this approach helps learners to have the tools necessary to do their work effectively. He advocates for micro-learning arguing that shorter focused learning experiences are better than long time set courses. In other words, he understands that learning should be broken into small pieces which can be easily understood by the users at the same time being applicable to their everyday lives. He has worked in different notable positions within the e-learning industry including research and development at Knowledge Universe Interactive Studio; and two Australian internet-based multimedia educational enterprises namely Open Net and Access CMC, from which he drew valuable management experience.

Respected in the domain of learning technology, he has served in various positions such as at the University of New South Wales, University of Pittsburgh's Learning Research and Development Center, and San Diego State University's Center for Research in Mathematics and Science Education. He extensively delivers keynote speeches both locally and internationally and has co-authored many articles, chapters, and five books on e-learning including "Engaging Learning: Designing E-Learning Simulation Games."

Learning Science advocates are at the heart of Quinn's e-learning design strategy since he knows that there is no better way than building on learners' cognitive mechanisms. By enhancing technology applications aimed at performance development, he suggests us to pursue beyond mere courses into constructing favorable learning experiences design as an example slice out of practices such as making use of social media.

Actively participating in the eradication of misconceptions concerning technological aspects of learning and e-learning that are more evidence-based is what Quinn has been doing. Abolition of false beliefs surrounding e-learning has seen him spearhead efforts such as the "eLearning Manifesto" which focuses on enhancing e-learning through learner-centeredness, performance orientation, and evidence-based design.

Patti Shank

Patti Shank is a highly respected figure in the e-learning industry, known for her expertise in instructional design, research, and an earnest quest for deeper learning and performance improvement. She is the author of the "Deeper Learning" series of books that provide pragmatic strategies for ameliorating learning results based on studies of training and education. These books explore matters such as writing and organizing for deeper learning, practice, and feedback for deeper learning, and memory management for deeper learning.

Shank puts emphasis on moving from mere transmission of information to teaching towards application. She believes that learners should be able to utilize what they learn in real situations so that their performance can be enhanced while still retaining knowledge over time. According to her, feedback and practice have critical importance in nourishing deeper learning, whereby its absence leads to a shallow understanding of concepts. She further suggests that there is minimal consideration for practicing these aspects in e-learning systems thus resulting in immature results.

A few issues Shank outlines about feedback and practices in e-learning include a lack of practice opportunities, non-credible practicing scenarios, and inefficient feedback mechanisms. To enable learners to gain proficiency, she states some practical solutions on how these problems can be tackled. She underlines the significance of appreciating the limitations facing working memories due to their restricted capabilities. As such, learning activities should be crafted in a manner that reduces cognitive load while maximizing working memory so as to ensure easy processing and retention by learners.

Also central to her argument is utilizing already known knowledge as well as establishing appropriate organizing structures within long-term memories which would boost both comprehension and application skills. She claims in e-learning design, it is important to make effectiveness the main objective rather than efficiency. According to her, a learner may go through an excellent course but not acquire any meaningful skills. As a result, Shank points out that we need to be able to strike a balance between efficiency and effectiveness so that the learning experiences are both attractive as well as significant. This enables her to talk to various learning professionals through online courses, articles and conferences she presents at. For these reasons, he shares his knowledge with many others.

Shank has received several accolades for his contributions towards the e-learning sector including being an award-winning contributing editor for Online Learning Magazine and research director with eLearning Guild.

Craig Weiss

The person who has become known as Craig Weiss has become a notable name in e-learning, known for his skill in learning technology, which has also helped him become one of the most influential figures in this industry. He assisted this industry by presenting lectures and writing articles; he was an analyst. All these efforts were aimed at making use of technology in a strategic manner, leading to improved learning and better business outcomes.

Weiss founded The Craig Weiss Group, a renowned research and advisory firm focused on the learning technology market. This professional organization provides important insights and analyses for L&D as it navigates through the intricacies of educational technologies. He is considered to be the face of his yearly awards otherwise known as the Learning Technologies Awards which celebrate the best products and solutions in learning technology products available in the market today. Such awards assist L&D professionals in identifying new tools that could help them improve on their training methodologies.

Weiss regularly writes articles, reports, and conducts investigations on trends pertaining to educational technologies providing useful insights on these trends that can be used by L&D practitioners. His work serves as an update on new developments for many companies involved in this field while aiding their decisions regarding technology acquisition. He is a strong supporter of effectively using advanced learning technologies to increase the quality of education and facilitate successful business activity. He constantly investigates and presents current trends concerning them in order for L&D experts to keep pace with changes.

Weiss firmly believes that partaking in collaborations among L&D practitioners can enhance their productivity. He does this by creating opportunities for networking and dialogues among L&P professionals which helps promote creativity. He is a frequently invited presenter at various trade conventions where he shares his expertise in the field of learning technology innovations and benchmarks. In addition, he has authored several publications related to learning technologies dispersing further information on them.

Weiss is the best expert in learning technology research, market analysis, identification of trends, and new product assessment. His work offers essential knowledge regarding the transformations in learning technology. He assists organizations in formulating and executing sound strategies for learning technologies that are consonant with their corporate objectives. By doing so, the use of technology is focused on achieving a specific desired outcome related to learning.

Weiss is one of the most reputable sources for insights about how learning technologies will develop in the future thus providing valuable guidance to L&D specialists. This prospective view helps companies prepare themselves for future developments in education and make informed decisions concerning investments in these platforms. He helped the use of learning technology and fostered innovation in the L&D sector. The advocacy he had for technology has driven the acceptance of new tools and methodologies, making learning be more engaging and effective.

He raised awareness of technological importance in education and development which was a reason for implementing various olden methods. This also assists in knowing that, there is a lot we can do with it. Weiss aided in joining L&D professionals thereby creating a common sense knowledge base as well as collaborative efforts among them. Consequently, his contributions to this domain have allowed professional experts to trade fables on what they regard as best practices, while at the same time enhancing community feeling of professionalism within the L&D environment.

REFERENCES

A framework for responsible AI in education. (2023, June 7). Grammarly. https://www.grammarly.com/blog/responsible-ai-education/

Admin. (2023, February 24). *Virtual and augmented reality in E-learning*. Bytecasting. https://bytecasting.com/home/virtual-and-augmented-reality-in-e-learning/?amp=1&webview_progress_bar=1&show_loading=0

Admin. (2024, January 6). *The Psychology Behind Gamification*: Why It Engages us | Web1Media. Web1Media. https://web1media.com/the-psychology-behind-gamification-why-it-engages-us/?webview_progress_bar=1&show_loading=0

Admin. (2024b, July 28). *Leveraging AI for spreading awareness and education in psychology. Envision Your Evolution*. https://www.envisionyourevolution.com/ai/leveraging-ai-for-spreading-awareness-and-education-in-psychology/34867/?show_loading=0&webview_progress_bar=1

Agente. (2024, January 11). *LMS gamification in 2024: Benefits, Types, and Examples* | Agente. https://agentestudio.com/blog/gamification-changing-elearning?show_loading=0&webview_progress_bar=1

AI-Powered Gamification in the Classroom - Planit Teachers. (n.d.). https://www.planitteachers.ai/articles/ai-powered-gamification-in-the-classroom?show_loading=0&webview_progress_bar=1

Alaghbari, S., Mitschick, A., Blichmann, G., Voigt, M., & Dachselt, R. (2021). A User-Centered approach to gamify the manual creation of training data for machine learning. *I-Com*, 20(1), 33–48. DOI: 10.1515/icom-2020-0030

Ali, K., Zahra, A., & Mohammad, M. (2021). *National Library of Medicine*. https://www.ncbi.nlm.nih.gov/pmc/articles/PMC8170558/?webview_progress_bar=1&show_loading=0

Aravindan, A. (2023, October 10). *Unlocking User Engagement: The Psychology behind Gamification in Mobile Apps*. Medium. https://medium.muz.li/unlocking-user-engagement-the-psychology-behind-gamification-in-mobile-apps-dce9c2a901de

Asghar, A., Sladeczek, I. E., Mercier, J., & Beaudoin, E. (2017). Learning in science, technology, engineering, and mathematics: Supporting students with learning dis-abilities. *Canadian Psychology*, 58(3), 238–249.

Augmented Reality in Education: Examples, Benefits, & Use Cases (2023). https://arborxr.com/blog/augmented-reality-in-education-examples-benefits-use-cases/?webview_progress_bar=1&show_loading=0

Ayo, S. K. (2022, January 5). *THE AI HIERARCHY OF NEEDS - Analytics Vidhya - Medium.* Medium. https://medium.com/analytics-vidhya/the-ai-hierarchy-of-needs-6d76aa6c5555?show_loading=0&webview_progress_bar=1

Best Adaptive Learning Platforms 2024 | Reviews & Comparison. (2024, February 26). https://edtechimpact.com/categories/adaptive-learning/

Bewersdorff, A., Hartmann, C., Hornberger, M., Seßler, K., Bannert, M., Kasneci, E., Kasneci, G., Zhai, X., & Nerdel, C. (2024). Taking the Next Step with Generative Artificial Intelligence: The Transformative Role of Multimodal Large Language Models in Science Education. *ArXiv*, abs/2401.00832.

Bhanabhai, M. (2023, January 15*). Gamification symmetry with Maslows hierarchy of needs – a model to #Improve, #Engage and #Perform.* Thealphaswarmer. Gamification Symmetry With Max, B. (2022). Maslows Hierarchy of Needs – A Model To #Improve, #Engage and #Perform. thealphaswarmer. https://www.thealphaswarmer.com/2022/09/gamification-symmetry-with-maslows-hierarchy-of-needs-a-model-to-improve-engage-and-perform/?show_loading=0&webview_progress_bar=1

Breon, C. (2024, March 18). *Unveiling the unseen: the spellbinding impact of augmented reality (AR) and virtual reality (VR) in entertainment and education.* Medium. https://medium.com/@breoncayden/unveiling-the-unseen-the-spellbinding-impact-of-augmented-reality-ar-and-virtual-reality-vr-in-6d8d908ace42

Bullock, M. (2023, July 28). *AI Meets Gamification: Unleashing the potential of artificial intelligence in employee motivation.*

Bullock, M. (2023a, May 28). *AI in Gamification – The Future of Productivity and Engagement. Spinify.* https://spinify.com/blog/ai-in-gamification/

Campbell, R. (2024, January 10). *AI and Collaborative Learning - Richard Campbell.* Richard Campbell. https://richardccampbell.com/ai-and-collaborative-learning-an-innovative-way-to-improve-education/

Çelik, F., & Ersanlı, C. Y. (2022). The use of augmented reality in a gamified CLIL lesson and students' achievements and attitudes: A quasi-experimental study. *Smart Learning Environments*, 9(1), 30. Advance online publication. DOI: 10.1186/s40561-022-00211-z

ChatGPT: the AI chatbot for gaming customer support. (2023, July 16). Dasha.AI. https://dasha.ai/en-us/blog/chatgpt-gaming-companies-technical-support?webview_progress_bar=1&show_loading=0

Choudhary, P. (2023, August 12). *Cons and pros of AI game development.* https://www.linkedin.com/pulse/cons-pros-ai-game-development-payal-choudhary

Claire, A. (2012). *The Game of Motivation: Gamification and Augmented Reality in Education.* oeb insights. https://oeb.global/oeb-insights/the-game-of-motivation-gamification-and-augmented-reality-in-education

Cojocariu, R. T. A. G. (2023, March 3). *Five ways you can use AI for Gamification - Gabriela Cojocariu - Medium.* Medium. https://medium.com/@gabriela.cojocariu/five-ways-you-can-use-ai-for-gamification-43919727e5c9

Cooper, C. (2023, December 16). *The power of AI driven gamification in business - Colin Cooper - medium.* Medium. https://medium.com/@colin-cooper/the-power-of-ai-driven-gamification-in-business-8d5165bf6e8a

Distinguishedsite. (2023, January 27). *AI's benefits and drawbacks for the gaming industry.* Medium. https://medium.com/@distinguishedsite/ais-benefits-and-drawbacks-for-the-gaming-industry-8be875218dbf

Domorovskaya, O. (2024). Differentiating E-Learning Content in ESL Courses to Meet Special Needs of Students with Learning Difficulties. *Journal of Teaching English for Specific and Academic Purposes*, 15-24.

FHS Doe, J. (2023). *Responsible AI integration in e-learning: Focusing on human skills.* E-Learning Journal.

EducationTimes. (n.d.). *How AI-powered gamification in education increases student engagement - EducationTimes.com.* https://www.educationtimes.com/article/campus-beat-college-life/99734287/how-ai-powered-gamification-in-education-increases-student-engagement?webview_progress_bar=1&show_loading=0

ELearning videos: The complete guide | DLI blog. (n.d.). Digital Learning Institute. https://www.digitallearninginstitute.com/blog/vr-in-training-and-elearning-everything-you-need-to-know?show_loading=0&webview_progress_bar=1

Esteem: Maslow's Hierarchy of Needs. (2024, September 19). The Interaction Design Foundation. https://www.interaction-design.org/literature/article/esteem-maslow-s-hierarchy-of-needs?webview_progress_bar=1&show_loading=0

Francisco. (2023, September 18). *Level Up Your learning: How AI Supercharges engagement in gamified Education - Teachflow.AI*. Teachflow.AI. https://teachflow.ai/level-up-your-learning-how-ai-supercharges-engagement-in-gamified-education/

Game On: Level Up Your Life with AI-Powered Gamification. (2024, May 3). https://www.motivacraft.com/game-on-level-up-your-life-with-ai-powered-gamification/

Gamification AI – Everything you need to know - centrical. (2024, June 4). Centrical. https://centrical.com/resources/gamification-ai/

Gamification and Self-Determination Theory – MetaDevo. (2023, June 21). https://metadevo.com/gamification-and-self-determination-theory/?webview_progress_bar=1&show_loading=0

GeeksforGeeks. (2024, May 14). *10 AI chatbots for educational tutoring*. GeeksforGeeks. https://www.geeksforgeeks.org/ai-chatbots-for-educational-tutoring/

Guilbaud, P., Sanders, C., Hirsch, M. J., & Guilbaud, T. C. (2022). Social-Emotional Competence for the Greater Good: Exploring the use of serious game, virtual reality and artificial intelligence to elicit prosocial behaviors and strengthen cognitive abilities of youth, adolescents and educators – a systematic review. *Lecture Notes in Computer Science*, 13317, 423–442. DOI: 10.1007/978-3-031-05939-1_29

Gupta, D. (2024, July 22). *7 Best Adaptive Learning Platforms in 2024*. The Whatfix Blog|Drive Digital Adoption. https://whatfix.com/blog/adaptive-learning-platforms/?webview_progress_bar=1&show_loading=0

Hai-Jew, S. (2022). *Practical Peer-to-Peer Teaching and Learning on the Social Web*. .DOI: 10.4018/978-1-7998-6496-7

Hill, M. (2024, March 22). *How to use augmented reality to gamify learning - inspired ideas - medium*. Medium. https://medium.com/inspired-ideas-prek-12/how-to-use-augmented-reality-to-gamify-learning-c05f1f8f7751

How AI and Gamification are Changing the Workplace. (n.d.). https://gamificationlabs.com/resources/blogs/how-ai-and-gamification-are-changing-the-workplace?webview_progress_bar=1&show_loading=0

How AI-Powered Gamification Can Boost Online Learning Engagement - CO/AI. (2024, September 4). CO/AI. https://getcoai.com/news/how-ai-powered-gamification-can-boost-online-learning-engagement/

How AI-powered gamification in education increases student engagement. (2023). https://l.facebook.com/l.php?u=https%3A%2F%2Fwww.educationtimes.com%2Farticle%2Fcampus-beat-college-life%2F99734287%2Fhow-ai-powered-gamification-in-education-increases-student-engagement%3Fshow_loading%3D0%26webview_progress_bar%3D1%26fbclid%3DIwZXh0bgNhZW0CMTAAAR2JtrUzyqRV2rpeizeTnIGC3ESt3-X5LblWUMvnI4OgSB3mLp0VZpSBaL0_aem_5LmV3ImIMywODciDp81dlw&h=AT05yb4M043T5YLXyNSyB3N9-GsqjhJ79e1EC2d8vVpx7f3Hio-gG97GHMy5zuy02XTqac2gzaNTxj-rSk5nTjjNo7mYsiqu2P3kSFR2O2sxQDcyrBzAHm2qUx7ebjrsnYe83Q

Iheringguedes. (2024, June 11). *Application of virtual reality (VR) in education and the learning theories.* Medium. https://medium.com/@iheringguedes/application-of-virtual-reality-vr-in-education-and-the-learning-theories-c6f7a48cafb1

Ivan. (2021, February 17). *AI & Gamification – Risks and Rewards.* Etrellium. https://www.etrellium.com/ai/the-issues-prospects-of-ai-and-gamification/

Jain, A. (2024, March 25). *Is AI-Enhanced gamification the key to eLearning success?* https://blog.commlabindia.com/elearning-design/ai-enhanced-gamification-elearning

Jain, S., & Jain, S. (2023, September 25). *Interactive Learning with Augmented Reality: Applications, Benefits and Challenges. Jumpstart Magazine.* https://www.jumpstartmag.com/interactive-learning-with-augmented-reality-applications-benefits-and-challenges/

Jihoon, K., & Darla, C. (2021). *Effects of Gamification on Behavioral Change in Education: A Meta-Analysis.* https://www.ncbi.nlm.nih.gov/pmc/articles/PMC8037535/

John, J. A., & Alaaraj, H. K. (2024). Perspective of Students on the Indirect Effect of Activity Based Learning Towards Academic Achievement by Mediating Engagement. In *Business Development via AI and Digitalization* (Vol. 2, pp. 645–661). Springer Nature Switzerland.

Julia, B., & Juan, V. (2024). *What are the best practices for ensuring data privacy when using AI and ML solutions?* LinkedIn. https://l.facebook.com/l.php?u=https%3A%2F%2Fwww.linkedin.com%2Fadvice%2F3%2Fwhat-best-practices-ensuring-data-privacy%3Ffbclid%3DIwZXh0bgNhZW0CMTAAAR2zSrV5D9Whtu2AakxN7iLIJIaM_gv17bVnqpzUm2_PmUvGTF91IZxpxoI_aem_KF93iw8vKkoCpT1x13tGrw&h=AT0Y3wqwoZwR8xkc5ybBdPcGS_1f9Wdz_E9a7qrk56WtSZol1SSar2RdnBEbJgA2L_H8vUHhZR9ozlpIcpqq0jKXuYhvm8jTmEhq3NjNy-vBTZ2f726LEp23ThsBNeVWpHLL6g

Kenyon, S. (2023, June 23). *Gamification and Self-Determination Theory - Sam Kenyon - Medium*. Medium. https://medium.com/@samkenyon/gamification-and-self-determination-theory-45a28494b672?webview_progress_bar=1&show_loading=0

Khaleghi, A., Aghaei, Z., & Mahdavi, M. A. (2021). A Gamification Framework for Cognitive Assessment and Cognitive Training: Qualitative study. *JMIR Serious Games*, 9(2), e21900. DOI: 10.2196/21900 PMID: 33819164

Kiyer. (2023, June 22). *AI learning and gamification for education. Internet Public Library*. https://www.ipl.org/div/machine-learning-ai/ai-learning-and-gamification-for-education

Krasko, A. (2022, July 28). *Gamification and Augmented reality learning: Engage, excite, educate*. https://www.banuba.com/blog/gamification-and-augmented-reality-learning-engage-excite-educate

Kurni, M., Mohammed, M. S., & Srinivasa, K. G. (2023). *AI-Enabled gamification in education*. In Springer eBooks (pp. 105–114). DOI: 10.1007/978-3-031-32653-0_6

Landers, R. N. (2015, July 5). *Psychological theory and gamification of learning*. NeoAcademic. https://neoacademic.com/2015/01/15/psychological-theory-gamification-learning/?show_loading=0&webview_progress_bar=1

Leading the way: Embracing responsible AI in education. (2024, January 19). MindSpark Learning. https://www.mindspark.org/post/leading-the-way-embracing-responsible-ai-in-education

Li, L., Hew, K. F., & Du, J. (2024). Gamification enhances student intrinsic motivation, perceptions of autonomy and relatedness, but minimal impact on competency: A meta-analysis and systematic review. *Educational Technology Research and Development*, 72(2), 765–796. DOI: 10.1007/s11423-023-10337-7

Li, M., Ma, S., & Shi, Y. (2023). Examining the effectiveness of gamification as a tool promoting teaching and learning in educational settings: A meta-analysis. *Frontiers in Psychology*, 14, 1253549. Advance online publication. DOI: 10.3389/fpsyg.2023.1253549 PMID: 37876838

Lucy. (2023, January 26). *Virtual Reality in STEM Education - Crowdmark*. Crowdmark. https://crowdmark.com/blog/vr-in-stem/

Majgaard, G., Larsen, L. J., Lyk, P., & Lyk, M. (2017). Seeing the Unseen—Spatial Visualization of the Solar System with Physical Prototypes and Augmented Reality. *International Journal of Designs for Learning*, 8(2). Advance online publication. DOI: 10.14434/ijdl.v8i2.22368

Malsakpak, M. H., & Pourteimour, S. (2024). Comparison of the Effects of E-learning Blended with Collaborative Learning and Lecture-Based Teaching Approaches on Academic Self-Efficacy among Undergraduate Nursing Students: A Quasi-Experimental Study. *Journal of Advances in Medical Education & Professionalism*, 12(2), 102.

Manthena, R. (2023, June 26). *Transforming Education through the Power of Virtual Reality (VR) and Augmented Reality (AR)*. https://www.linkedin.com/pulse/transforming-education-through-power-virtual-reality-vr-manthena-

Mastering The Challenges Of AI: Privacy, Security And Compliance Strategies (2023). Forbes. https://www.forbes.com/councils/forbestechcouncil/2023/08/18/mastering-the-challenges-of-ai-privacy-security-and-compliance-strategies/

Mathias, S. (2024, July 3). *Responsible AI Integration: 4 steps for education leaders | ThoughtExchange*. ThoughtExchange. https://thoughtexchange.com/blog/responsible-ai-integration-4-steps-for-education-leaders/

Mathias, S. C. E. S. (2024, July 3). *Responsible AI Integration: 4 steps for education leaders | ThoughtExchange*. ThoughtExchange. https://thoughtexchange.com/blog/responsible-ai-integration-4-steps-for-education-leaders/

MindSpark Learning. https://www.mindspark.org/post/leading-the-way-embracing-responsible-ai-in-education

National Center for Education Statistics. (2022). *Students with disabilities. U.S. Department of Education, Institute of Education Sciences*. https://nces.ed.gov/programs/coe/indicator/cgg/students-with-disabilities

Neendoor, S. (2024, August 16). *AI and Gamification: Enhancing Student Motivation and Achievement. Digital Engineering & Technology | Elearning Solutions | Digital Content Solutions*. https://www.hurix.com/ai-and-gamification-enhancing-student-motivation-and-achievement/

Nextech3D.Ai. (2024, March 28). *10 Ways Augmented Reality Can Be used in Education*. https://www.nextechar.com/blog/10-applications-of-ar-in-education

Nguyen, Q. (2024, July 3). *Harness the power of virtual reality (VR) and augmented reality (AR) in education*. Atomi Systems, Inc. https://atomisystems.com/elearning/virtual-reality-vr-and-augmented-reality-ar-in-education/?show_loading=0&webview_progress_bar=1

Ningthoujam, R. (2022, October 3). *Merging AI and gamification in hiring: The Pros & Cons*. Leena AI Blog. https://leena.ai/blog/ai-and-gamification-in-hiring/

Notebook, D. V. (2023, August 4). *A new perspective on Maslow's hierarchy of needs: integrating AI and post-pandemic impacts*. Medium. https://davincisnotebook.medium.com/a-new-perspective-on-maslows-hierarchy-of-needs-integrating-ai-and-post-pandemic-impacts-2b0d7480d794

Panjwani-Charani, S., & Zhai, X. (in press). AI for Students with Learning Disabilities: A Systematic Review. In Zhai, X., & Krajcik, J. (Eds.), *Uses of Artificial Intelligence in STEM Education* (pp. xx–xx). Oxford University Press.

Parris, J. (2023, March 28). *The Psychology of Gamification: Understanding motivation and behavior*. Medium. https://medium.com/@jamesparris_63299/the-psychology-of-gamification-understanding-motivation-and-behavior-54a3921dc8da?webview_progress_bar=1&show_loading=0

Phillips, C. (2018, June 4*). Chatbots for Tech Support 101 - Support Automation Magazine - Medium*. Medium. https://medium.com/support-automation-magazine/chatbots-for-tech-support-101-cfc0d4973ae8?show_loading=0&webview_progress_bar=1

PlayTours. (2023, September 18). *How AI becomes important role in gamification to boost employee engagement and team-building activity*. Medium. https://medium.com/@playtours/how-ai-becomes-important-role-in-gamification-to-boost-employee-engagement-and-team-building-762c1b824a10

Pravendrapatel. (2023, May 24). *AR and VR Technology in Education - Pravendrapatel - Medium*. Medium. https://medium.com/@pravendrapatel0012/ar-and-vr-technology-in-education-69da7c3a9897?show_loading=0&webview_progress_bar=1

Private site. (2010, September 2). https://adavox.wordpress.com/2010/09/02/how-games-fulfill-maslows-hierarchy/

Puentedura, R. R. (2006). Transformation, technology, and education. http://hippasus.com/resources/tte/puentedurat te.pdf

Radulovski, A. (2024, March 11). *Visualization of abstract concepts*. Women in Tech Network. https://www.womentech.net/how-to/7-visualization-abstract-concepts?webview_progress_bar=1&show_loading=0

Rankstar. (2023, June 15). *Artificial intelligence in enhancing gamification. CRM Automation & Gamification Platform*. https://smartico.ai/artificial-intelligence-enhancing-gamification/

Rashani, N. (2022, December 5). *Gamification and Self determination theory - Nimasha Rashani - Medium*. Medium. https://nimasharashani.medium.com/gamification-and-self-determination-theory-8d68edad4583

Reality, P. (2024, September 1). *The use of AR and VR in E-learning: Applications and Benefits*. PROVEN Reality. https://provenreality.com/use-of-ar-and-vr-in-elearning/?webview_progress_bar=1&show_loading=0

Rivera, P. (2024, January 19). *Securing customer data: Developing a data privacy plan for AI integration*. IntelePeer. https://intelepeer.ai/blog/securing-customer-data-developing-a-data-privacy-plan-for-ai-integration

Romero, I. (2023, February 14). *AI, Gamification & Education*. https://www.linkedin.com/pulse/ai-gamification-education-iv%C3%A1n-romero?show_loading=0&webview_progress_bar=1

Cojocariu, R. T. A. G. (2023, March 3). Five ways you can use AI for Gamification - Gabriela Cojocariu - Medium. Medium. https://medium.com/@gabriela.cojocariu/five-ways-you-can-use-ai-for-gamification-43919727e5c9

Sahu, S. (2023, July 13). *Ethical Considerations for AI integration in corporate learning initiatives*. https://www.linkedin.com/pulse/ethical-considerations-ai-integration-corporate-sahu-he-him-his-

Samuel, A. K. (2021, September 9). *THE AI HIERARCHY OF NEEDS*. https://www.linkedin.com/pulse/ai-hierarchy-needs-ayo-kehinde-samuel

Santhi, M. V., & Malathi, R. (2024). Implementation of Activity-Based Learning in Classroom Teaching. Strength for Today and Bright Hope for Tomorrow Volume 24: 3 March 2024 ISSN 1930-2940, 23.

Sarvaiya, D. (2024, May 9). *Augmented Reality (AR) In Education: Enhancing Learning Experiences through AR Technology*. Intelivita. https://www.intelivita.com/blog/augmented-reality-in-education/

Mathias, S. C. E. S. (2024, July 3). Responsible AI Integration: 4 steps for education leaders | ThoughtExchange. ThoughtExchange. https://thoughtexchange.com/blog/responsible-ai-integration-4-steps-for-education-leaders/

School, O. G. (2024, January 22). *How gamification makes you love to learn*. graduate.me. https://graduate.me/en/blog/gamification?webview_progress_bar=1&show_loading=0

Self-Determination Theory in Gamification | Gamification in Business Class notes | Fiveable. (n.d.). https://library.fiveable.me/gamification-in-business/unit-3/self-determination-theory-gamification/study-guide/oCoyee6Xr1qyIj9Y?show_loading=0&webview_progress_bar=1

Sindhya, K. PhD. (2023, May 15). *Maximizing productivity and potential: Applying Maslow's hierarchy of needs to AI in business.* https://www.linkedin.com/pulse/maximizing-productivity-potential-applying-maslows-ai-sindhya-phd?webview_progress_bar=1&show_loading=0

Skidos. (2023, July 20). *The Future of Educational Gaming: How AI & Gamification Revolutionize learning.* Medium. https://medium.com/@skidos2021/the-future-of-educational-gaming-how-ai-gamification-revolutionize-learning-40b0d674d1ce

Smartico.Ai. (2022, July 18). *How to use gamification to increase motivation.* https://www.linkedin.com/pulse/how-use-gamification-increase-motivation-smartico-ai

Smith, J. (2022). *Leveraging AI in e-learning for a human-centric approach.* Educational Technology Magazine.

Stracqualursi, L., & Agati, P. (2024). Twitter users perceptions of AI-based e-learning technologies. *Scientific Reports*, 14, 5927. DOI: 10.1038/s41598-024-56284-y

Superstore, V. (2023, July 12). *Transforming Education with Virtual Reality (VR): Unlocking a New Era of Immersive Learning.* Medium. https://medium.com/@TheVRSuperstore/transforming-education-with-virtual-reality-vr-unlocking-a-new-era-of-immersive-learning-86a8c499a252

Systementcorp. (2023, July 3). *The Psychology of Gamification: Understanding Why it works - Eye of Unity Foundation.* Eye Of Unity Foundation. https://eyeofunity.com/the-psychology-of-gamification-understanding-why-it-works/?webview_progress_bar=1&show_loading=0

Team, W. (2024, January 4). *8 Best adaptive learning platforms in 2024.* The Change Management Blog. https://change.walkme.com/adaptive-learning-platforms/

Tec, B. (2021, January 21). *5 Practical ways of using AR and VR in eLearning.* https://www.linkedin.com/pulse/5-practical-ways-using-ar-vr-elearning-bse-tec

Terada, Y. (2020, May 4). A powerful model for understanding good tech integration. Edutopia. https://www.edutopia.org/article/powerful-model-understanding-good-tech-integration

The Impact of Gamification on Learning: Real-World Applications. (n.d.). https://www.idolcourses.com/blog/gamificationandelearning?show_loading=0&webview_progress_bar=1

Tondello, G. (2016, April 26). *Introduction to Gamification in Human-Computer Interaction*. Gameful Bits. https://www.gamefulbits.com/2016/04/26/an-introduction-to-gamification-in-human-computer-interaction/?show_loading=0&webview_progress_bar=1

TrainBeyond. (2024, June 20). *Enhancing Learning with Virtual Reality Simulation Training*. TrainBeyond. https://www.trainbeyond.com/enhancing-learning-with-virtual-reality-simulation-training/

Turnitin. (n.d.). *Turnitin affirms guiding principles for responsible AI integration into education technologies*. https://www.turnitin.com/press/launch-responsible-ai-in-education

United States Artificial Intelligence Institute. (USAII®). (n.d.). *Transforming Online Learning: Boost Learner Engagement with AI-Powered Gamification*. https://www.usaii.org/ai-insights/transforming-online-learning-boost-learner-engagement-with-ai-powered-gamification. https://www.usaii.org/ai-insights/transforming-online-learning-boost-learner-engagement-with-ai-powered-gamification

Use AI and gamification to craft captivating eLearning : Articles | The Learning Guild. (n.d.). Copyright 2024 the Learning Guild. Copyright 2024: Powered by Cyclone Enterprise: Content Management Solutions and Dynamic Publishing System Developed by Cyclone Interactive Multimedia Group, Inc. http://www.cycloneinteractive.com, Powered by Cyclone and Powered by Cyclone Enterprise. Portional ColdFusion Programming Provided by Finial Software, Inc. www.finial.com. https://www.learningguild.com/articles/use-ai-and-gamification-to-craft-captivating-elearning/

Virtual reality: could it be the next big tool for education? (2024, September 10). World Economic Forum. https://www.weforum.org/agenda/2021/05/virtual-reality-simulators-develop-students-skills-education-training?webview_progress_bar=1&show_loading=0

Virtual Reality for Education: Experiential Learning made Possible – Queppelin. (2023, May 4). https://www.queppelin.com/virtual-reality-for-education-experiential-learning-made-possible/

Virtual Reality in Training: The Power of Immersive Simulations (n.d.) https://www.virtusstudios.com/post/vr-in-training-the-power-of-immersive-simulations?webview_progress_bar=1&show_loading=0

VR and AR for eLearning: Interview with Volker Kunze. (2024, September 4). HQSoftware. https://hqsoftwarelab.com/blog/augmented-and-virtual-reality/ar-in-elearning-interview/?show_loading=0&webview_progress_bar=1

Wairura, F. (2023, January 5). *Creating Interactive and Immersive Learning with Augmented Reality: Case Studies and Examples.* Medium. https://medium.com/@wairuraf/creating-interactive-and-immersive-learning-with-augmented-reality-case-studies-and-examples-48dde1a754a9

Webmaster. (2018, August 16). *Training with Virtual Reality and Simulations.* VR-Sim. https://vrsim.com/simulation-virtual-reality-vr-training-infographic/?webview_progress_bar=1&show_loading=0%20https://vrsim.com/simulation-virtual-reality-vr-training-infographic/?webview_progress_bar=1&show_loading=0

What are some of the benefits and drawbacks of using AI to create adaptive game mechanics? (2024, July 2). www.linkedin.com. https://www.linkedin.com/advice/0/what-some-benefits-drawbacks-using-ai-create-adaptive

What are some tools or platforms that support adaptive learning in online learning? (2024, August 23). www.linkedin.com. https://www.linkedin.com/advice/1/what-some-tools-platforms-support-adaptive-learning?webview_progress_bar=1&show_loading=0

What are the benefits and drawbacks of using AI in gaming? | Artificial Intelligence Hub. (2024, March 17). https://aicitta.com/posts/what-are-the-benefits-and-drawbacks-of-using-ai-in-gaming/?webview_progress_bar=1&show_loading=0

Whitfield, P. (2024, March 20). *The Psychology of Gamification.* Beyond Thought International. https://beyondthoughtinternational.com/the-psychology-of-gamification/?webview_progress_bar=1&show_loading=0

Wong, C. (2024, July 17). *Chatbots for Learning: Ways to Gamify Chat-Based Learning Environments.* https://articles.noodlefactory.ai/chatbots-for-learning-ways-to-gamify-chat-based-learning-environments

2U. Wordpress. (2023, December 6). *Augmented Reality in Education: Interactive Classrooms* | Maryville Online. Maryville University Online. https://online.maryville.edu/blog/augmented-reality-in-education/

Yee, C. (2023b, November 15). *Gamification and operant conditioning.* Yu-kai Chou. https://yukaichou.com/gamification-study/gamification-and-operant-conditioning/?show_loading=0&webview_progress_bar=1

Yie, D. L., Sanmugam, M., Yahaya, W. J. W., & Khlaif, Z. N. (2024). *The impact of gamification depth on higher educational students' intrinsic motivation and performance levels.* Higher Education for the Future., DOI: 10.1177/23476311241248994

Zahid, R. (2023, November 2). *AI-Powered Chatbots in Technical Support*. Tanbits. https://tanbits.com/blog/ai-powered-chatbots-in-technical-support/?show_loading=0&webview_progress_bar=1

Zhai, X. (2021). Practices and theories: How can machine learning assist in innovative assessment practices in science education. *Journal of Science Education and Technology*, 30(2), 1–11.

Zhai, X., Zhang, M., Li, M., & Zhang, X. (2019). Understanding the relationship between levels of mobile technology use in high school physics classrooms and the learning outcome. *British Journal of Educational Technology*, 50(2), 750–766.

Chapter 9
Enhancing Peer Engagement and Student Motivation Through AI-Gamified Interactive Learning Tools

John Marvin D. Renacido
Aklan State University, Philippines

Ersyl T. Biray
https://orcid.org/0000-0002-5094-5841
Aklan State University, Philippines

ABSTRACT

Artificial Intelligence (AI) has become widely accepted in diverse fields and applications in the fast-paced development of technology. It has even penetrated the threshold of education. This chapter will tackle the potential benefits of utilizing AI-powered gamification and interactive learning tools and lay down approaches to attaining a responsible approach to AI Integration. It will also explore interactive learning tools teachers can employ in the classroom and determine the impact of AI-powered gamification on peer engagement. By this, some drawbacks of using AI in education will be revealed to avoid frustration in coping with its mechanisms. Further, it will also provide virtual and augmented reality applications for a clearer view of how these devices work. This chapter will uncover the psychology of gamification to realize the underlying mental implications of this pedagogy for students.

DOI: 10.4018/979-8-3693-8242-4.ch009

BENEFITS OF AI-POWERED GAMIFICATION

Artificial Intelligence (AI) has a wide range of perceived usefulness in education. Gamification is one of its well-known strengths, especially for young learners. They find delight in playing online games which even results in addiction. That's how it attracts their attention, making them prone to unconscious learning of concepts. Integrating AI Gaming elements as instructional materials in the classroom allows students to foster their enthusiasm for learning. It also provides a personalized learning experience since AI automatically recalibrates to meet the desired level of difficulty or needs of each student. Another is that it fosters interactive learning since gaming has been made to engage with other users. Students will be able to create an environment where learning, enjoyment, and socialization are intertwined. AI-powered gamification also hones the collaborative skills of students. Since gaming has multiplayer modes in their algorithms, students will develop their communication and interactive capabilities. Lastly, AI gamification helps track student progress in a real-time manner. Unlike manual or traditional methods of instruction which take longer in evaluating their performances, this pedagogical technique will provide not just instant feedback but efficiency in teaching.

Jose and Jose (2024) identified a wide range of opportunities offered by AI platforms in education, as highlighted by study participants who viewed these opportunities as outweighing their concerns and associated risks. The study categorized these opportunities into twenty subthemes, encompassing areas such as enhancing learner motivation, facilitating template creation, utilizing AI as an educational aid, promoting proper training and fostering positive AI usage, harnessing AI for teaching challenging subjects, enabling personalized learning experiences, offering an interactive tutoring experience, supporting remote learning, facilitating self-study, providing comprehensive educational content overviews, giving instantaneous feedback and evaluation, functioning as search engines and chatbots, enabling content validation, efficiency in terms of cost and time, streamlining material preparation, facilitating skill and language enhancement, promoting familiarity with topics and vocabulary, enabling text-to-speech and speech-to-text conversions, editing multimedia elements, and facilitating content generation. This comprehensive list demonstrates the potential of AI platforms to revolutionize various aspects of education, from streamlining teacher workload to enhancing student engagement.

Increased Motivation

This AI-oriented hocus-pocus came into being as a mighty implement for raising enthusiasm in different environments, from training to work. By applying gaming design principles and using artificial intelligence capabilities, it can create attractive and customized educational experiences that pull to the order of paid satisfaction, recognition received, and obtained achievement motive which is intrinsic to us all.

According to Bat et. al (2024), the SBL (Scenario-based Learning) practice was reinforced by the emergence of a versatile WCV (Write, Curate, Verify) three-step prompt engineering process for the high-quality Generative AI-assisted scenarios development. This denotes the development of prompts, the enhancement of the output created, and finally the assessment of the output. In the study, it emerged that the Work Creating Value model or WCV model when used together with ChatGPT, made scenario-building processes more effective, thus facilitating the development of quality SBL materials quickly. In addition, the students reported a significant improvement in intrinsic motivation, learning performance, and attitudes toward the use of scenarios with GenAI.

In conventional gamification, game aspects such as points, badges, leaderboards, and contests act as motives for learners. However, Artificial Intelligence advances this concept through user data analysis to offer a personalized approach that addresses unique needs and tastes. With this form of customization, challenges always remain exciting and rewarding to keep people motivated and involved.

In real-time, AI can evaluate learner performance, identifying important strengths as well as weaknesses. Consequently, personalized content will be provided along with challenges targeted at particular individuals' requirements, ensuring they remain constantly challenged.

AI-based gamification can change tasks and challenge difficulty according to individual advancement to ensure that students are not overwhelmed or bored. This adaptive strategy ensures that learners remain committed and encouraged to continue improving.

AI provides an opportunity for practical experience in a secure environment with realistic situations simulating actual professional activities including making important choices. This urges users to apply their education. By using team challenges, quests, or virtual environments, it is possible for learners to collaborate among themselves while sharing knowledge. Such an approach is important in soft skills development, including the teamwork ability of learners.

Ng et al. (2024) carried out a mixed deep case study of the incorporation of AI in maker education. In this research, 35 secondary school students participated in an AI maker program that had a Synectic approach as students designed and constructed AI-improved recycling bins. The goal of the program was to improve students' motivation, career, confidence, cooperation, and AI capabilities over different levels of cognition. The results of the case study indicated a growth in students' motivation, AI literacy, and collaborative skills, showing the effective outcomes of AI-based maker education in the learning process.

By examining student information, AI modifies the difficulty of challenges and content. In this way, they are personalized to suit individual needs, ensuring that students remain motivated and challenged at all times.

Points, badges, and leaderboards provide immediate feedback and a sense of fulfillment, encouraging desirable conduct on the part of the learner to maintain moving ahead. Language learning applications such as Duolingo or Kahoot! utilize points, badges, and leaderboards to make the study of a foreign language more enjoyable by adding an element of fun to it. As learners progress through different levels they obtain items of reward; this makes it interesting not only for them but also their companions. Gamified platforms like Bunchball and Achievers motivate employees and boost productivity through challenges, points, and recognition programs. These platforms encourage healthy competition, foster collaboration, and reward high performers, leading to a more engaged and motivated workforce.

Gökrslan et al. (2024) accomplished a systematic literature review of 37 educational SSCI articles, which concentrated on the application of AI chatbots in the educational sphere. The purpose of this analysis was to review this literature more from a research angle and evaluate the pros and cons of using AI chatbots for students and teachers. This literature review analyzed what types of chatbots, years of publications, keywords used, and research strategies were applied. The study indicated that enhancement of students' motivation to learn and improvement in their language skills were the main advantages for students, whereas it was economic efficiency and less workload for the teachers. Despite that, the review presented some possible negative aspects, such as a lack of interaction, unhelpful responses to learners, worries regarding originality, and academic dishonesty.

Personalized Learning

By enabling customized learning experiences based on individual needs and preferences, AI-powered gamification has transformed the way we acquire knowledge. In this regard, artificial intelligence plays a critical role in analyzing learner data, determining their strengths and weaknesses, and modifying the learning path accordingly. Conventionally, in gamification, there are elements such as point badges or leaderboards used to motivate learners. With AI going deeper into it, it is examining students' behavior patterns in terms of preference and performance so that it can tailor learning for them in real-time.

Castro et al. (2024) specify a number of factors relating to the effectiveness of personalized learning in the context of education in general and in e-learning in particular. Customizing education is based on the understanding and consideration of differences between students. Adjusting the delivery of the learning content and the teaching approaches makes sure that the teaching and learning resources are appropriate for the learners' interests and abilities. Endowing different strategies of evaluation and feedback allows instructors to offer assistance to students in a more efficient and relevant way. Customization of interfaces and educational spaces enhances the involvement and inclusiveness of all users due to their variance in preferences and requirements. Integrating AI technologies opens up a number of channels for improving personalized learning. Particularly, these solutions enable such functions as automatic learner profiles, recommendations of personalized content, assessment systems, and smart interfaces, all of which serve to enhance the learners experience and add to the personalization of learning.

AI algorithms evaluate student performance data for weaknesses and strengths identification. This intelligent software is capable of customizing content lessons, level of challenges as well as questions that need to be practiced, delivered to an individual person's need making them be challenged enough at all times while also enjoying what they are doing at a right pace.

Through personalized learning, every student gets properly adjusted respectively when encountering difficulties during class assignments or activities, keeping him/her neither overloaded nor bored since they do not want to lose interest in his/her studies completely. Consequently, learners remain motivated throughout the process.

AI gives timely responses that are specific to different actions by learners so that they may know their progress as well as the areas they need to work on. This feedback is personalized according to individual needs and styles of learning, making it more effective and interesting to learners. Furthermore, AI-powered systems can simulate one-on-one interactions with learners in addition to offering personalized guidance and predictive insights that proactively support them. This personalized support helps the learners in overcoming difficulties and also keeps them encouraged.

According to Roozafzai and Zaeri (2024), the ability of AI to personalize instruction and the use of captivating animations together applies great motivation to learners, facilitates retention of knowledge, and elevates academic achievement. Such an approach is inclusive and flexible for all types of students. It emphasizes the need for more collaboration across different fields of study because there are new ways of doing things in education, and the research shows how significant the changes can be by going beyond education to include AI, animation, and personalization in learning for the education of such people in the 21st century.

Personalized learning experiences promote active participation of learners in the process of learning by giving them customized challenges, rewards and feedbacks which are very specific for everyone. Such an approach makes students feel like they own their studies, providing a motivation for further development. On individualized learning pathways as well as adaptive difficulty levels, learners receive challenges appropriate for their understanding level which facilitate comprehensive knowledge acquisition and retention. Besides, personalized feedback plus intelligent tuition systems offer goal-directed assistance to boost even more educational achievement.

As AI can determine individual strengths and weaknesses, it can improve pathways of learning which enable learners to concentrate on aspects demanding maximum assistance. This way, much time is saved thus, making the whole process an efficient one. In addition, AI has the capability of modifying content as well as challenges depending on the abilities of various learners thus enabling more accessible and inclusive education systems. In this case, all students are given equal chances irrespective of their origin or the method by which they acquire information.

By using AI for analyzing learner data, Khan Academy and Duolingo platforms adjust their challenge difficulties, contents, and learning pathways with regard to individual needs. Overall, this personalized methodology makes sure that learners are kept involved in a continuous manner as well as being challenged appropriately. Also, through Kahoot! and Quizlet, for example, AI forms personalized quizzes as well as learning activities based on one's progress and mode of learning. This individualized approach boosts involvement and thereby enhances the overall effectiveness of the whole process of learning. These are computer programs driven by artificial intelligence that create tailor-made education plans based on individual targets, key competencies, or deficiencies. These plans consist of specially designed educational materials, practice questions, and tests aimed at directing a student toward his desired result.

Interactive Learning

Teaching with game effects is characterized by the kind of atmosphere that feels alive and entails playing instead of facts which are boring for learners of all ages. Counteracting passive methods of education, gamification powered by AI is reshaping the educational scene by creating interactive and engaging experiences that promote effective learning. The use of artificial intelligence aims at tailoring content based on learner data, adjusting teaching approaches according to personal requirements eventually making it more immersive as well as captivating.

Rahioui et al. (2024) stressed that technology should be adopted in a systematic way into the virtual classroom, in accordance with the educational aims and objectives as well as the characteristics of the students. For example, interactive simulation games in biology raise the level of immersion and retention for the students. Moreover, AI-based adaptive learning systems can help biology students in developing their knowledge by personalizing the learning experience which will help them in understanding the content better and taking interest in the beauty of nature. This study aims at utilizing AI technology for bettering the interactive simulations of cellular dynamics, which can be implemented in the teaching of anatomy and physiology and even ecology.

Traditional gamification used points, badges, or leaderboards among others to motivate learners. AI takes this one step further customizing the whole process since it tracks behavior patterns among learners including their interests over time then suggests materials accordingly while still analyzing what has been done so far. With AI realistic simulations that can imitate real-life situations, students can practice skills without risk being developed. By that, they are not only personalized and interactive but also secured.

Lee (2024) delves into how AI can be used to achieve the goal of personalized learning with positive effects on academic performance. The role of AI systems is positively viewed by students and teachers, the study states, particularly noting the engaging nature of tasks assigned and the interactivity offered in an AI system. It also underlined the necessity of both AI and teachers. While teachers are vital for moderating the curriculum and caring for the emotional and educational needs of all students, AI helps teachers by offering content that is appropriate to individual student needs. It also looks at issues in relation to the students performing below the standard, emphasizing the importance of a variety of approaches and identifying problems early on. In encapsulation, this dissertation relates the use of AI in education and gives suitable guidelines on how to improve personalized learning and equity in education.

Based on personal achievement, AI can alter challenges and assignments' difficulty to prevent learners from being overwrought or jaded. In doing so, they will be kept motivated to forge ahead cheerfully, creating an interactive and fulfilling way of acquiring knowledge. Moreover, feedback is personalized according to individual needs and learning styles making it more effective, interesting, and helpful. By creating adaptive learning paths according to the progress made by different students, one can provide either additional assistance when needed or just simply more demanding tasks.

AI-driven systems that are able to replicate one-on-one interactions can help learners with customized guidance as well as suggestions about future events. Consequently, this support makes the learning endeavor more engaging since it helps one bypass challenges. Based on your performance, AI can change the difficulty of tasks and challenges so as not to sink yourself or get jammed up with monotony. In this way, learners remain motivated and feel compelled to progress, making it a more interactive and pleasurable learning process.

With adaptive paths for learning, it implies real-time tailored advice that learners receive according to their actions, concerning how they are progressing. Therefore, this reveals their weaknesses. It is more engaging because it factors into account the individual personality profiles and specific needs associated with different learning styles. In other words, the use of AI includes the creation of personalized learning routes such as responsiveness in terms of activities performed by learners from supportive tasks to demanding ones.

When the interactive simulations and personalized challenges are put into place, then learners will find themselves applying the knowledge in real-life scenarios, enhancing understanding as well as retention of information. Moreover, adaptive learning paths along with timely feedback serve as extra support that leads to better results during learning.

In a gameplay context, this approach trains students' ability to solve issues with both critical thinking and creativity. Such an application guides them towards acquiring skills valuable in the future when dealing with problems at their workplaces.

AI can modify content and difficulty for learners so that it serves various populations enabling education access for everyone. By doing this none of the learners may lack chances for accomplishment due to social-economic background or mode of comprehension.

For instance, Khan Academy, New Zealand has personal learning pathways depending on what is suitable for them and may include assignments, lessons videos chat rooms, etc., from which they remain engaged throughout the entire use of these links.

AI gives opportunities for developing immersive VR and AR learning experiences that enable learners to interact much better with the available online platforms. The use of such technology can help live real-life situations, help equip the students with practical experience, as well as facilitate overall appreciation towards education.

According to Radif and Hameed (2024), the invention of AI tools for e-learning is likely to change the current outlook on educational environments. This is because the use of AI technologies in educational systems allows for more effective and individualized learning. They show how Artificial intelligence can increase students' involvement, provide varied learning possibilities, and provide teachers with means to better the learning process. Nevertheless, the authors note that there are issues such as protecting data, reducing algorithmic bias, and ensuring that there is still a touch of humanity in education that needs to be tackled.

Enhanced Collaboration Skills.

AI-powered gamification has evolved into a strong instrument for promoting co-operation and teamwork in different spheres ranging from education to workplaces. This approach uses elements of game design together with artificial intelligence capacities to create interesting and personalized educational experiences that inspire people to work together on shared objectives.

According to Kim and Kwon (2024), in recent study, data derived from the multivariate analysis of covariance (MANCOVA) has demonstrated that the participants improved significantly in AI-related knowledge, attitudes, and behavioral intentions narrowing existing gaps. It was also featured that the improvement was seen for all the participants, irrespective of their gender, or initial level of knowledge. This indicates that appropriate and team-based AI approaches are likely to improve AI knowledge equally and alter attitudes and intentions in a positive manner. It was also found that both female and non-binary students engaged more and felt less anxious about AI with improved comprehension and a preference for collaborative learning environments.

In traditional gamification, there are team-based challenges and leaderboards which are meant to spur cooperation among those involved in the process. AI does a lot more than that by giving individual and group performance data, personalized feedback, and changeable challenges that promote collaborative effort.

AI can analyze individuals' strengths, and weaknesses as well as the particular ways they learn then make sure no one plays alone while creating a team composed of different individuals who are complementary based on these identified skills. The choice of the teams is specific to the individual members, Thus, any member has a designated role to play contributing to the total success of the group.

Team-based challenges and quests can be designed by AI, which requires collaboration, knowledge-sharing among the members of a team, and making use of their common skills to achieve one goal. This method promotes communication, cooperation as well as feeling of common accomplishment.

The level of difficulty for team challenges can be adjusted by AI depending on how teams perform together so that they are not bored or overstressed. It has the capacity to provide real-time feedback about the teams' progress indicating where changes need to be made and motivating them towards assisting one another. For weaknesses, strengths, and opportunities for development, information about team functioning could be retrieved through AI analysis. Such information could support focused comments aimed at making the best use of team dynamics while improving general collaboration across teams.

Team members who use AI-powered gamification are encouraged to communicate well with one another, share ideas freely, and collaborate in solving problems. This results in an increased sense of friendship among team members as well as shared success which enhances their cooperative skills including teamwork and communication abilities.

From different views and strengths of team members on challenging tasks, they learn how to combine them to come up with more creative and effective solutions, enhancing their problem-solving abilities. A group approach in such scenarios helps in improving the skills to solve problems and innovation. Working as a team creates challenges and rewards which give a sense of belongingness that pushes team members into doing their best. By doing so, greater motivation is created among employees, promoting overall engagement through building goodwill at work among co-learners.

One way in which enhanced collaborative skills can be achieved is through the sharing of knowledge among individual contributors in their respective fields so that their understanding of different concepts can become more holistic by team members sharing anything learned through teamwork, resulting in high consistency in performance across all teams involved therein. This form helps foster an environment where everybody learns from each other's experience, thereby encouraging lifelong learning while also facilitating knowledge transfer between learners.

Zheng et al. (2024) seek to enhance online collaborative learning using an AI-based method of providing feedback and feedforward. Such a method not only provides the receipt of feedback but also offers suggestions on what to do next to facilitate collaborative knowledge building, coregulated behaviors, and group performance. The findings indicated that the AI-enabled approach was better suited to improving these elements of online collaboration.

Real-time Assessment

With AI-based products that track student performance in real-time educators can recognize strengths or weaknesses of certain domains for fast support. This feature in AI-infused gamification has deeply changed the face of learning forever. Instead of providing traditionally assessed students, this method creates a dynamic and adaptable experience that promotes involvement while fostering a supportive environment for enhanced outcomes.

Adair et al. (2023) developed and validated virtual labs in which mathematical modeling skills can be automatically assessed from student actions within the learning environment. This study utilized both machine learning and knowledge engineering to proactively provide scaffolds guided by a pedagogical agent acting on the student's specific difficulties while working. Results indicate that for students who were scaffolded with automated scaffolds for the first virtual lab experience, they improved on that same practice in a second virtual lab session on the same sort of science topic but different in scenario- a near-transfer task. These results suggest that real-time automated scaffolds based on fine-grained assessment can effectively foster the mathematical modeling competencies of students in accordance with Next Generation Science Standards (NGSS).

AI-powered gamification combines advanced algorithms with machine learning to evaluate student behavior and performance on a constant basis. The result is a rapidly changing way of studying due to immediate feedback through different learning approaches. Furthermore, AI can provide immediate feedback on learner actions, highlighting areas for improvement and reinforcing correct answers. This real-time feedback loop helps learners understand their progress and identify areas where they need more practice.

The level of task difficulty can be adjusted by AI on an individual basis based on the performance of learners, preventing them from being either frustrated or bored. Such an adaptive method allows students to feel motivated to move on with their studies and stay engaged since their abilities are matched with the level of challenge they face.

Adaptive learning paths that change in response to how a learner performs can also be created by AI which means it provides extra help or more complex jobs when required. This individualized strategy makes sure that learners face challenges appropriate for their skill levels at all times while receiving needed assistance for success in the learning process itself. In addition, AI-powered systems can imitate teacher-student interactions and offer customized directions along with prediction insights in order to proactively aid learners. Such personalized aid helps students overcome obstacles and remain interested, turning learning to be an interactive and dynamic form of education.

In an atmosphere where there is an immediate response, this educative scheme entails clearer learning outcomes and better retention rates owing to its targeted support measures. This personalized approach ensures that learners are always challenged at the right level and receive the appropriate support to succeed. Moreover, real-time rewards and individualized challenges are given, keeping students involved in the educational process right away. This personalized nature creates a greater sense of ownership and achievement and promotes moving forward.

RESPONSIBLE APPROACH TO AI INTEGRATION

Applying AI into teaching practice will necessitate proper implementation to ensure students will understand how will they benefit from it and what needs awareness. Teachers shall impart what the students need to expect upon integrating AI into the classroom. This will acquaint students with the core objectives of the lessons and what are the do's and don'ts in terms of usage. Skepticism and critical thinking will surface during discussions and will produce in-depth and preliminary knowledge about this digital trend. Human skills are now deteriorating due to the reliance of learners on today's technology. It is crucial to note that even if the classroom is mediated by technology, students' natural capabilities must not be hindered but increased. As AI-powered gamification is being utilized, some of it requires the personal data of students, thus, careful monitoring must be observed and protective measures should be ensured.

Setting Clear Expectations

The instructor must make expectations regarding the use of AI in education known to students even though some aspects of it are acceptable or not. Integrating artificial intelligence (AI) into online education has many encouraging prospects but also many serious challenges. It personalizes student learning experiences, helps in automating processes, and increases access to education, but its introduction calls for a carefully planned and responsible approach. The need for responsible use of AI implies the establishment of clear expectations that would help address both the intended purpose of utilization and possible dangers in this technology.

AI can analyze student data so as to personalize learning paths for them, give them tailored feedback as well as recommend relevant resources which would increase student engagement and improve their learning outcomes. Platforms powered by AI can also change content based on individual learners' responses that they provide after attempting puzzles or other questions. An educator's duties are eased by the automation of grading multiple-choice questions and feedback on compositions through artificial intelligence. This gives instructors more time for personalized interaction with students.

The use of AI technologies allows for the development of accessible learning materials such as audio descriptions for videos, while visually impaired students benefit from text-to-speech functions. It ensures that every learner is treated equally across the board, thereby promoting inclusivity. By providing data-driven insights into student performance, AI helps teachers identify areas needing improvement in their teaching methods as well as those requiring extra help. This makes it possible for teachers to personalize their instructions better.

AI systems must operate transparently regarding how they decide on things. The learners deserve to comprehend how the algorithms work, how they shape the process of learning, as well as other factors behind their suggestions. Also, AI systems can inherit biases from the data they are trained on. It is important to take steps in order to identify and reduce any possible biases, so all learners receive fair and equitable AI-powered learning experiences. AI systems gather enormous quantities of student data. To guard against sensitive information, it must comply with relevant regulations, and ensure responsible use of student data, strong data privacy, and security frameworks.

Rather than replacing human educators, AI must be used in collaboration with them. Teachers stand to gain valuable tools from this technology. However, the teacher's judgment is still important when guiding students' learning process among other things.

The constant assessment and improvement of AI systems is important based on feedback from students, educators, and other stakeholders. This will enable AI to adapt to meet new demands as well as address emerging issues. Moreover, instructors shall be trained on how to utilize AI tools effectively, understand its capabilities as well as limitations, and consider ethical dimensions to facilitate the responsible integration of AI into their theoretical frameworks.

Introducing learners to basic concepts about artificial intelligence (AI), how it is used in e-learning, and promoting critical thinking around possible merits and demerits of AI. This enables students to use that kind of technology responsibly and consciously.

Platforms shall be developed for open dialogue and cooperation among educators, students, researchers, and policymakers regarding ethics issues, best practices, and future direction for the use of artificial intelligence. It will build a common understanding that lays down the ground for the right path where responsible upholding of AI happens.

Promoting AI literacy

The performance, limitations, and ethical considerations behind AI should be taught to students locally so as to ensure they have an understanding. This will also require them to think critically about everything, including what is generated by machines like computers.

The integration of artificial intelligence (AI) into e-learning presents an exclusive opportunity to customize learning experiences, automate tasks, and enhance accessibility. Nevertheless, for responsible AI integration in e-learning, it is not only about adopting the latest technology. It calls for a proactive strategy that focuses on AI literacy – equipping students, teachers, and stakeholders with knowledge, skills, and critical thinking abilities to comprehend, engage with, and shape the development of AI in education.

AI literacy is more than knowing just the technical details involved in AI. It involves developing an all-encompassing appreciation of how artificial intelligence works, may it be the possible advantages or dangers associated with it, as well as, what implications it has for the future of education. Learners and educators need to grasp fundamental AI concepts like machine learning, deep learning, and natural language processing. This would enable them to analyze critically AI-powered tools and know what such tools are capable of doing.

AI is already being used in various e-learning applications such as personalized learning platforms and automated grading systems Critical thinking about the potential impact of artificial intelligence (AI) on education, which includes its influence on learning outcomes, equity, and privacy is fostered by AI literacy. This promotes an ethical approach to integrating AI that takes into account these issues while minimizing risks.

Engaging in AI discussions empowers individuals to engage meaningfully in these conversations regarding its role in education as well as contribute meaningfully to policy debates, and ethical framework development for responsible AI usage among others.

AI concepts, ethical considerations, and practical artificial intelligence skills shall be introduced into school curricula at all levels. For example, such activities may include hands-on activities, project-based learning, and collaborative projects designed to encourage critical thinking and problem-solving. Teachers must receive training that is inclusive of all areas related to AI applications. It includes teaching them how best they can include it within their own lessons or modules. Therefore, teachers are able to utilize it in an accountable manner.

Organizing community events including conducting workshops, hackathons, and other forums is beneficial as it allows for interactions between learners, instructors, and specialists in Artificial Intelligence (AI).

Focusing on Human Skills

Integrating artificial intelligence (AI) into e-learning is a double-edged sword. Although it can be used to personalize the learning experience, automate tasks, and provide useful insights, it is important to note that technology must augment rather than replace human capacities and interactions. Therefore, the responsible approach for AI integration in e-learning implies development of human skills which will help in enhancing the educational sector by making sure that AI is only a tool for learning and not a substitute for personal contact as well as critical thinking.

While AI can automate the grading of multiple-choice questions or offer generic feedback, it lacks the capacity to understand the context and show compassion like human teachers. Consequently, a responsible integration strategy for AI should emphasize nurturing those personal attributes that cannot be imitated by machines. Although information may be provided by AI, students cannot learn how to differentiate between facts and opinions or think outside the box when trying to solve intricate issues. In this regard, teachers are essential in guiding these processes since they make sure that learners analyze data from different perspectives before drawing any conclusions.

AI can help with communication but can't entirely take over the advantages of human cooperation and communication. Students should be encouraged by teachers to take part in discussions, debates, and group projects which will nurture communication as well as teamwork greatly. Although AI is able to create content or analyze patterns, it does not have the capacity to encourage creativity and innovation. Educators should motivate their students to think unconventionally an explore unchartered waters in order to come up with a personal outlook which is different from all others.

Effective teaching and learning require emotional intelligence (EQ) as well as sympathy, which is something that AI lacks. These skills should be developed by teachers for themselves & their students, this will enhance understanding, compassion, and the ability to relate with others through emotions on a personal level. A responsible strategy for integrating AI should prioritize human-centricity so that human abilities can be augmented rather than replaced by machines.

Teachers can benefit from this technology in various ways, including feedback based on data on how well scholars perform, personalized admission recommendations, and automated assessment tools. This enables instructors to devote more time to engaging their students personally through mentoring, motivating them while they learn, and giving them psychological support.

Making individualized instruction possible, demands that every resource is tailored to meet the specific needs of each student with regard to subject matter or pace of progress among others. However, training should always include instructors' guidance regarding the usage of different software implementations so as not to confuse learners about where it comes from, its limits, and ethics.

AI can create collaborative learning environments by providing platforms for online discussions, group projects, and peer-to-peer feedback. Nevertheless, it is vital to strike a balance between tools driven by AI and human contact. Teachers should motivate learners to participate in face-to-face discussions, develop relationships, and enhance their strong communication abilities. If handled appropriately, these humanistic qualities will never go out of fashion both in the present and future.

Prioritizing Data Privacy

The possibility of personalizing learning experiences, automating tasks, and improving accessibility through the use of artificial intelligence (AI) in e-learning is enormous. Nonetheless, as this potential grows, protecting learners' data privacy becomes imperative. A prudent way to integrate AI into e-learning emphasizes data privacy as a crucial value. It shall be ensured that AI technology is employed in an ethical manner that promotes learners' interests without endangering their sensitive information.

E-learning platforms that are powered by AI collect immense amounts of information about learners' activities such as their learning habits and styles, performance measurements, preferences, and sometimes personal details. Such data can be invaluable when aimed at customizing the learning experience to meet individual needs of students or improving academic achievement but it also poses considerable danger if not properly managed.

E-learning platforms, frequently accumulate sensitive information including but not limited to names of students, home addresses, performance report cards, and even health-related details. Such information shall never be accessed without permission or leaked out for any use. Just like other digital systems, e-learning platforms may fall victim to data breaches and cyberattacks. Protecting learner data from unauthorized access and averting possible harm calls for security measures with a high degree of robustness.

Even where there is no legal requirement, ethics will demand that data belonging to learners must be treated with respect and used responsibly. The right usage of such data shall be under their control, its usage understood by the learner as well as being secure. The integration of AI in e-learning is best done when data privacy is put into consideration at all times during the lifecycle of developing or deploying any kind of AI system. Data protection shall be built in from the beginning rather than added later on. This entails having privacy safeguards embedded within the AI systems like limited storage space for every user's information, encryption protocols, and access barriers among others.

Collect what is strictly necessary and process it for its intended purposes. Do not go beyond what is required, and every so often, wipe data off which has got no use anymore. Always encrypt your data both in transit and at rest so as to prevent unauthorized access to it by outsiders. On servers, there must be an effective way of safely storing data, firewalls shall be put up besides other robust security measures like intrusion detection systems with regular audits done, to assess if they are indeed secure enough.

Be upfront about how you collect your clients' details, be specific on how they will be used, ask for permission from students before collecting their personal information as well as using it in any endeavor. You should give students options like being able to view or edit their own files or even getting rid of them altogether. It is important that there are clear mechanisms in place for holding individuals responsible for data privacy issues such as appointing specific officers designated duty for ensuring protection of personal data or constituting committees on ethics relating to handling of information. Additionally, one should regularly review and audit practices regarding stored records so that compliance with privacy laws can be ascertained along with best practices in this field.

AI-GAMIFIED INTERACTIVE TOOLS

AI has a variety of interactive learning tools that can be used to empower peer collaboration and improve learning outcomes. These are some of the paramount causes as to why these advancements are being optimized in academia. Adjusting to students' academic capacities and learning styles is critical to achieving desired results in a certain curriculum. Through the use of adaptive learning platforms powered by AI, personalized instruction is maximized, prompting effective assimilation of skills and knowledge. Virtual Reality (VR) and Augmented Reality (AR) are immersive devices that allow students to experience sensuous learning by creating artificial visuals. These pique students' creativity and interest as it puts them in a realistic world beyond limits. AI also offers applications like chatbots which operate timelessly and forward instant feedback of any kind. It is due to the extensive web reach of AI, allowing students to accumulate a plethora of ideas and information. In an AI-facilitated classroom, students will indulge in the so-called Natural Language Processing (NLP). This system provides students with a convenient and efficient learning method as learners can directly communicate with the instructional material and progress with the lesson without interference as it is completely hand-free. Gamified Learning Management Systems are platforms students admire in AI learning. Aside from its advanced and pleasing features, it stimulates motivation and engagement for peers and fosters collaborative learning on both ends.

Adaptable Learning Platforms

The adoption of AI-oriented gamification in adjustable learning frameworks is increasingly becoming prevalent ostensibly with a mind of achieving better students' performance outcomes through possession of fun and gamified aspects. Artificial intelligence fosters personalization of learning approaches, modifications of subjects to be studied, instantaneous feedback all merged with game-like features that motivate and involve the learners.

Gamification refers to the application of game design elements and principles in non-game contexts like education to improve motivation, engagement, and results. AI-enabled gamification goes beyond as it makes use of artificial intelligence to design game components that are custom-made for each student's requirements and preferences.

Holman et al. (2024) reviewed the current functionalities of Artificial Intelligence-Powered Personalized Learning (AI-PPLs) to demonstrate their potential, or already, impacts on teaching practices and on the learning outcomes of students. It is based on various AI-PPL features that will reflect adaptive learning environments customized with feedback mechanisms and demonstrate their capabilities to tailor learning experiences. The authors stress accessibility and inclusiveness in AI-PPL so that the need for educational provision is beneficial among diverse learners. In addition, they call for professional development to upgrade educators' competency and skills in the effective use of AI-PPL. This research offers real-world examples and guiding questions for faculty in special education to provide practical insight to educators and faculty members across the process of embracing AI technologies into their teacher preparation programs.

To create personalized challenges and rewards that align with each individual's targets and advancement, AI algorithms scrutinize student data. The purpose is to keep learners motivated to learn more and improve.

Such platforms use game-like elements through engrossing narratives, virtual characters, as well as interactive components in order to build an absorbing and integrative environment for the purpose of education. These motivate the learners to take an active role in their studies, hence, give better understanding of what they are learning. Learning activities' complexity is adjusted by AI according to student performance. It helps avoid boredom or frustration experienced by students when faced with learning materials that are either too complex or simple for them.

For instance, leaderboards together with progress tracking systems found in gamified approaches give scholars a sense of rivalry as well as accomplishment which motivates them to do their utmost. Additionally, this makes it possible for learners to monitor their advancement in relation to time., Furthermore, AI gives quick responses concerning learner performance, showing where they need improvement or rewarding correct answers. It helps maintain the interest and motivation levels of the trainees, while it provides useful information for customized education.

Halkiopoulos and Gkintoni (2024) conducted a systematic review of 85 studies based on the PRISMA methodology towards analyzing the impact of AI on education. Based on a pool of 818 records sourced from the different databases, the review states that AI can influence improvement in performance, engagement, and motivation of the students. It, however, exposed certain challenges such as bias and discrimination toward smooth implementation. The authors emphasize the transformational capabilities of AI in developing personalized and adaptive learning (AL) environments, which inspires further development and research in AI as a tool to enrich educational outcomes.

Virtual Reality (VR) and Augmented Reality (AR)

Virtual Reality (VR) and Augmented Reality (AR) are not only changing how we learn but also how we experience gamification. By bringing together these immersive technologies with the power of artificial intelligence (AI), the opportunity for personalized and engaging learning experiences has come.

AI-powered gamification advances traditional gamification using data and algorithms to customize and change it based on each individual user's needs. When introduced to VR or AR, things become fully immersive and engaging. Also, AI can analyze a learner's progressions such as strengths/weaknesses enabling individual personalization through VR & AR platforms providing relevant feedback, leading to better comprehension levels together with motivation.

AI has the capacity to modify levels of challenges or tasks inside VR&AR games so that they do not overwhelm nor bore student users who need something engaging enough compared to what they have been through in other school years. Within virtual reality (VR) and augmented reality (AR), artificial intelligence can create personalized content, scenarios, and challenges that keep it fresh for players. This helps prevent learners from falling into monotonous routines while triggering a sense of exploration.

AI-based virtual characters may interact with students in VR and AR environments, offering tailored assistance, comments, and advice. Avatars can modify their actions or responses according to the progress or tastes of the individual learner which makes the entire session more interactive and compelling.

Chatbots Offering Instant Support

Chatbots are increasingly being used to provide technical support, offering a quick and efficient way to resolve user issues. However, their potential goes beyond simple problem-solving. Through AI-powered gamification, chatbots can turn technical support into an interactive and engaging learning experience.

Oleh et al. (2023) also assessed the impacts of the Smart Sender platform's chatbot-driven e-classes in learning the English language. The findings reached a conclusion that the chatbot-based e-classes have motivated students, improved proficiency in reading and usage of the English language, as well as the inclination towards online learning. Students praised it for being user-friendly and effective in the use of the chatbot tool for enhancing their proficiency in the use of the English language.

Conventional technical support often involves long wait times, frustrating interactions and a lack of personalization. Chatbots that are powered by artificial intelligence (AI), on the other hand, offer a more efficient and user-friendly alternative. Therefore, they can handle many inquiries at once within a short period of time and provide instant replies while using large knowledge bases in order to give precise solutions.

The incorporation of game-like elements in order to boost engagement and motivation takes chatbot experience beyond merely problem-solving. Users gain knowledge independently and solve problems on their own through this method which transforms traditional help desk services into a learning platform.

In the realm of assessment and evaluation, Williyan et. al (2024) further recommend the shift towards technology-driven approaches with AI chatbots such as ChatGPT, Twee, and Questionwell incorporated into the assessment process. This new trend holds a great promise for enriching the methods of evaluation that could consequently lead to better student learning experiences. In other words, the study presents worthwhile insights into the development landscape of AI-augmented content in Indonesian EFL education. Adaptation and ingenuity in this regard would prove the potential of AI as a tool in refreshing pedagogies and real-life practices of language acquisition for students. For that reason, findings could be part of the discourse towards more meaningful educational settings by introducing AI into education. Practical implications can be achieved by making AI a content co-creator, effectively uplifting the quality of the teaching of the English language in Indonesia overall.

Natural Language Processing (NLP)

Natural Language Processing is one of the applications of Artificial Intelligence that enables machines to understand, interpret, and produce human language. Such revolutions in communication between man and machine will transform the future educational system forever because it comprises all aspects of learning.

Shin, et al. (2023) analyzed teachers' language in online Algebra video lectures to identify how teachers communicate with their students. They considered 125 online Algebra video lectures accessible on Math Nation, which is a digital learning mathematics environment, with the help of NLP and computational linguistic tools. They established that the differences in teachers' language use would enable them to distinguish the various forms of pedagogical communication in such videos. It demonstrates the potential of NLP when applied to the analysis and understanding of online video lectures' communication patterns, making any improvement possible in online learning effectiveness.

NLP is an important element in building AI-based games since it allows software programs to comprehend natural language input from humans as well as output that sounds like real dialogue between real people. Consequently, players can control characters within game environments or talk to them using their own words. Players can interact with virtual characters through dynamic and personalized conversations. The game's AI engine will use an analysis of player's choices during gameplay so that special plots and dialogues are generated, making the experience more captivating.

Natural language processing (NLP) can be employed to generate interactive quests and challenges that make use of players' language abilities to deduce solutions, mine information or perform tasks. Traditionally, educational games have benefited from this most as they help in learning new concepts and terminologies via gameplay.

On the part of player performance and understanding, NLP is useful in altering game difficulty levels. Feedback and responses from users can be used by AI to gauge their comprehension level and adapt the game accordingly so that it remains an appropriate challenge while keeping them engaged. In addition, the development of genuine dialogue interfaces is possible through NLP which allows gaming participants to utilize auditory instructions or textual inputs while playing. Therefore, it makes these gaming experiences more user-friendly compared to conventional controls, especially for individuals lacking confidence in using standard devices for playing games.

Rayati (2021) shows that NLP can significantly improve how English language teachers interact with their students. The study highlights the potential of NLP to create a more positive and engaging learning environment, leading to better communication, stronger relationships, and increased student motivation. By using NLP techniques, teachers can better understand their students' needs and help them develop their language skills, confidence, and overall learning experience.

Gamified Learning Management Systems.

Gamified Learning Management Systems (LMS) are changing the way we learn and train by including game aspects in traditional educational frameworks. This approach, powered by artificial intelligence (AI), is creating more stimulating, interactive, and efficient ways of learning.

Unal and Unal (2024) have compared a traditional face-to-face case-based learning environment with a new gamified online platform. The results showed that the gamified platform proved more effective in enhancing learning outcomes compared to the traditional setting, and consistent with the MUSIC (empowerment, usefulness, success, interest, and caring) model of motivation. This gamified platform perfectly espoused all these aspects, a significant influence on promoting student choice and real-world application, achievement recognition, engagement through game mechanics, and finally, the support of a learning environment through peer interaction and feedback. The platform has enabled students to apply the learned knowledge in reality, retain information, increase peer interaction, have more control over their learning, and aware of external resources. Besides these aspects, the comfortable design and accessibility of the platform enhance its appeal and effectiveness.

In many cases, conventional LMS platforms experience challenges related to learner engagement as well as motivation. On the contrary, gamified LMS employs game design concepts to present an enhanced immersive, and rewarding experience. Integrating aspects like points badges challenges and leaderboards among others makes this type of education much more exciting, leading to active involvement from learners within it.

By using AI, we can make it automatic to change the complexity of challenges and quizzes in line with how an individual learner is doing as well as whether he or she is grasping anything. As such, learners are always motivated to develop their abilities by being confronted with more obstacles. It is possible for AI to make learning paths that are specific to every learner's requirements and style. Therefore, they can spend their time in areas having less support or learning at their own pace. Learning performance can be used by AI for suggestions and feedback that are more specific. This way learners can identify where they need improvement and manage their learning objectives more effectively.

IMPACTS OF AI-POWERED GAMIFICATION ON STUDENT ENGAGEMENT

As we have come across some possible ways AI can alter learning, let us dig deeper by tackling the impacts of AI-powered gamification on peer engagement. This tactic will generate active participation in a cohort which furthers memory retention and improved social and communication skills. Not to mention, it will also develop intrinsic motivation of students to explore new concepts and grow fond of learning even more. By incorporating gaming elements in an educational endeavor students will savor its continuous feedback every time an activity or session occurs, giving students the chance to track their progress. Inclusivity matters significantly in a classroom as it can affect academic performance if not practiced. AI-powered gamification offers tailored instruction to students whenever some need special attention or advanced discussion. This will help students enjoy learning based on their own pace and mental capability. Aside from being a flexible avenue for personal and intellectual growth, it will also foster lifelong learning in the digital age as it encourages critical thinking, problem-solving, and collaboration skills inside the learning environment.

Active Participation

Changing traditional learning environments into enjoyable and interactive experiences is the key mission of AI-powered gamification in the education revolution. Most students become more engaged and continue taking part actively as one of the greatest influences this method has made.

Conventional classrooms often incorporate a lot of passive approaches that involve students listening to lectures or reading texts without much involvement. Conversely, gamification motivates involvement through game elements. AI also enhances traditional forms of teaching into personal learning experiences that take into consideration individual students' needs. This is crucial for encouraging their engagement.

Tzeng et al. (2024) developed a personalized learning path for massive open online courses (MOOCs) using an LSTM (long short-term memory) model, aiming to better meet individual student needs. The system analyzes students' video-watching behavior and groups them based on similar learning patterns. This information is then used to create personalized learning paths for each group, improving student engagement and progress. The study found that students who received personalized recommendations moved from a slow-progress group to a medium or fast-progress group. The study also found that the personalized learning paths positively impacted students' attitudes towards learning, motivating them to continue learning and achieve higher learning capacity.

AI can utilize learner's data such as progress reports or areas of their strengths/weaknesses to create unique rewards/prizes which help them stay motivated to be involved actively. Moreover, AI uses individual student performance to adjust the difficulty level of tasks and quizzes in order to keep them engaged and appropriately challenged.

AI-fueled gamification makes learning environments engaging and interactive, therefore, it helps stimulate learners' participation through simulations, virtual practices, or problem-solving situations. Not to mention, AI gives instant feedback regarding student performance, assisting them to know how they are progressing as well as where they need improvement. Such feedback given enhances active approaches to learning through internalizing.

Intrinsic Motivation

AI-driven gamification is transforming the educational sector into one where intrinsic motivation is emphasized through tapping into human beings' wish to challenge themselves, achieve more than before, and attain mastery.

Chiu et al. (2024) explored how teacher support influences students' intrinsic motivation and engagement when using AI technologies in learning. Their study, involving 123 Grade 10 students using chatbots, found that both teacher support and student expertise (self-regulated learning and digital literacy) are crucial for students' intrinsic motivation and competence in using AI. The study also found that teacher support satisfied the need for belonging but sometimes hindered the need for independence. This research provides insights into how to effectively integrate AI into learning environments, considering both teacher support and student skills.

Most standard classroom settings use external motivators such as grades, prizes or punishments to make students get involved with learning. Nevertheless, these can be very temporal in nature and rarely lead to an enduring passion for gaining knowledge. On the contrary, intrinsic motivation arises from the core wish to learn regardless of external circumstances. AI-powered gamification taps into intrinsic motivation by offering exciting and individualized e-learning experiences aimed at appealing to natural curiosity among the pupils and their yearning to acquire something new. Depending on the performance of individual students, AI is able to modify the level of difficulty in tasks and quizzes so that they are neither under-challenged nor over-challenged. As a result, this gives rise to an atmosphere of mastery and drives them to greater heights of achievement which culminates in more thorough learning and higher levels of satisfaction.

Chen and Chang (2024) explored whether using AI-assisted game-based learning enhanced learning outcomes in science, intrinsic motivation, cognitive load, and learning behavior. Analytics of learning behavior and interviews found that AI support for game-based learning may raise intrinsic motivation and lower cognitive load while fostering appropriate learning behavior for students in science learning. This study carries a number of implications that impact the design and implementation of AI within game-based learning environments so as to enhance the learning outcome and motivation among students.

With AI-enabled gamification, students are immersed in interactive learning environments where they engage with real-life problems through simulations and virtual experiments among others. This hands-on approach helps them apply the knowledge acquired in class thereby making it more meaningful. In addition, AI instantly provides feedback about how well each student performs, helping them see how far they have come as well as what they need to improve on. Through this method, learners get an opportunity to learn from their mistakes while acquiring a more profound comprehension concerning course material as well as gaining independence over their academic voyage.

Continuous Feedback

By providing students with real-time feedback, a factor that greatly affects their engagement and learning outcomes, AI-based gamification is transforming education. Conventional education focuses on rare assessments such as tests and quizzes to measure what students know. This leaves students uncertain about where they stand in terms of progress since there isn't much information forthcoming. If feedback is continuous, it implies ongoing updates regarding students' performance. Hence, students are able to see areas that require improvement and modify their approach accordingly.

AI-powered tools increase user engagement through continuous feedback while making use of sophisticated algorithms and machine learning to offer tailored instant analysis, concerning one's academic output. AI can assess the academic records of students, such as the ways through which they learn, what they have achieved so far, and how they performed in their previous examinations to give tailored feedback.

Lee et al (2024) proposed a Video-based Automatic Assessment System on the basis of GPT-4V. This approach makes use of Gen AI to identify classroom dynamics in fine detail. It has been noticed that the VidAAS is able enough to measure learning skills of a student accurately in behavioral or psychomotor domains and gives rationale explanations for the pertinent assessment. The system, though promising in such areas, also holds the possibility for improvement with regard to processing speed as well as refinement of cognitive and affective domains. VidAAS provides the condition for reflection-in-action and reflection-on-action but underlines the balance between AI-driven insights and human judgment. Guided by the findings, future avenues for research in design, implementation, and integration into teacher analytics are presented for VidAAS, while GPT-4V's usefulness for real-time, scalable feedback and a better understanding of classrooms is underlined.

AI is capable of crafting adaptable learning tracks that modify itself as per the performance of learners. For example, if a student does not understand one particular idea, it can provide some extra materials or explain it simply again. On the contrary, if he/she is doing well in certain areas; more advanced materials may be given for him/her to remain motivated.

Personalized Learning Pathways

AI-driven gamification is revolutionizing the education sector by developing tailor-made learning tracks that aim at each student's preferences and individual requirements. This strategy greatly limits disengagement while enhancing motivation among learners, thus, making the whole process more exciting and enjoyable.

In most cases, traditional education relies on a single approach to teaching where all students go through similar syllabi and receive common instructions. Such a technique does not take into account differences in styles, paces, or areas of interest, leaving many learners demotivated and bored. Personalized learning pathways have come to solve this issue by making sure that every learner has what they want.

Student data such as performance, learning style, and preferences are regularly examined by AI algorithms to provide real-time updates about their progress and needs. AI-supported gamification systems can update the information and challenges for each student, depending on their data. If a student has difficulty grasping a certain idea, the AI may suggest more resources, hints, or simplified explanations to make it easier. On the other hand, if they are too good at it, AI brings in tougher materials to keep them busy.

The student's performance along with their way of studying can determine how best to give personalized recommendations and feedback through an artificial intelligence system. Such feedback shows the students where they are good enough and where they require additional assistance so that they can get individualized help with respect to what they need.

When implementing AI-based games, institutions have seen the advent of adjustable learning paths which develop according to the speed of learning from each student in real time. As a result, this allows students not only to get stimulated continuously at a rate suitable for them but also to have all the tools necessary for success.

Lifelong Learning Skills

When learners use AI-powered games and interactive tools they acquire thinking critically, solving problems, and teamwork abilities which are keys to succeeding in this digital world. As you are aware, one can always learn from life's experiences but sometimes it takes a teacher to make us understand that we need to continuously adapt since nothing is constant except change itself and this is where AI-powered gamification has come in.

According to the theory of engagement, people learn best in an interactive and dynamic environment which is created through active participation (Smith & Jones, 2020). When students' interests are incorporated into lessons, they feel more valued as contributors to their own learning (Brown & Larson, 2016). Consequently, they develop a sense of ownership towards their education process.

The engagement a lot of us at times refer to, is not simply all about fulfilling certain demands. This involves nurturing a passion for studying which ends up expanding beyond the schooling sphere and into a life-long learning quest. The interaction that ultimately leads to true comprehension could be enabled by every educational task designed by this program in accordance with student interests and values (Sharmaa et al., 2015). This implies that engagement must go beyond just performing exercises meant for answering questions; instead, it demands building on experiences we have encountered, in addition to other abilities such as flexibility or resourcefulness.

DRAWBACKS OF AI-POWERED GAMIFICATION

While AI gamification grants learners numerous advantages, it also has a few negative effects in certain ways. Such shortcomings are due to limitations that come with AI, difficulties experienced when integrating it into gamification systems, and possible unforeseen consequences.

Instability and Absence of Control

One major drawback is its unpredictability which makes it difficult for developers to regulate the gaming process. This means that, as much as they want to control the processes involved in the gaming process, developers will find it hard especially when machine mishaps come into place. For instance, it might end up making some wrong decisions or generate irrelevant content, thereby leaving users confused or frustrated.

Possible Insufficiency in Inventiveness

Although there is fast production of materials by way of artificial intelligence (AI), they tend to have lesser depth, subtlety, and human aspects associated with the products made by human designers. Prolonged dependence on AI for content production may also hinder inventiveness resulting in less unconventional and all-encompassing experiences, particularly in narrative development and storytelling aspects.

Technical Challenges and Integration Issues

Integrating AI into gamification systems can be technically complex and resource-intensive. The algorithms behind AI consume a lot of computational power and may end up introducing bugs, errors, or unforeseen interactions which can ruin the whole experience of gaming. Therefore, programming has to be dressed in rigorous tests of AI integration for it to work properly within the context of games. Hence, long hours are spent on debugging processes that also require more finances.

Bias and Fairness Concerns

AI reaches diverse software applications and this makes it susceptible to bias and inaccuracy. It is beyond our control as normal users, what information AI intends to make as reference. Appropriate assessment and fact-checking are vital when we are using AI to dissect if the given information is relevant or precise. In other words, users still must confirm the data AI has produced for us to ensure the neglect of unwanted or unreliable information. AI applications require ethical standards to be introduced by instructors. This will make them familiar with responsible use, data privacy, and the potential for AI to worsen existing inequalities.

The source of any bias presented by Gamification is the data supplied from which its algorithm was developed. Consequently, this may result in some discrimination or favoritism where certain groups may get punished due to their gender, ethnicity, or economic status among others. As such, developers should ensure that they deal with it very carefully while training algorithms but simultaneously must develop ways to promote impartiality and inclusiveness.

Data Privacy and Security Risks

In most cases when artificial intelligence is applied in gamification scenarios there is need to collect user data that would help personalize experience during playtime thus exposing individuals to privacy violations considering these activities involve tracking players' movements on screen plus other behavior related elements found such as games' scores spent. Another concern raised here involves use of third parties who acquire private data without consent from actual users.

Decreased Human Interaction and Incentive

Excessive AI-based gamification can decrease human interaction and incentives. Users will get bored if the whole experience gets too predictable, automated, or lacks real challenge. Therefore, it is essential to maintain the balance between human agency and AI-powered personalization so that the users have a sense of control over their own learning or gaming path.

FEASIBLE SOLUTIONS FOR PERCEIVED DRAWBACKS

In an article by Chen and Lin (2024), it was discussed that artificial intelligence is a double-edged sword in early childhood education by presenting some of its positive effects (personalized learning, personalized interactive support, and increased accessibility to broadened learning experiences) and negative effects (overuse and misuse). In the nearly AI-ubiquitous world, young children are going to grow within the surroundings where they will be exposed to the AI-powered tools most of the time; therefore, authors suggest applying POWER (purposeful, optimal, wise, ethical, responsible) principles by maximizing benefits and minimizing drawbacks of AI use. The authors have further recommended the inclusion of the POWER principles in AI literacy as a necessity for promoting the right use of AI-powered tools.

Bowen and Watson (2024) present groundbreaking and powerful research on the seismic shifts that AI is already causing in schools and at work, thereby delivering priceless insights into what AI can do in the classroom and outside the class. From learning to utilize novel AI tools and resources to their advantage, educators will be emboldened and empowered to navigate through the challenges and opportunities AI poses. This volume provides practical suggestions for how AI can be most effectively integrated into teaching and learning environments, from interactivity in learning techniques to advanced assignment and assessment strategies. Bowen and Watson confront key questions about academic integrity, cheating, and emerging issues in this age of AI. In an age of AI, critical thinking skills, information literacy, and a liberal arts education are more vital than ever. Educators will be in a perfect position to prepare students with the skills they need to thrive under such change as AI redefines the nature of work and human thinking. This book becomes a compass for educators as they navigate through unknown territories of AI-powered education and the future of teaching and learning.

Smith et. al (2024) points out how AI tools can prove to be helpful in extending support, further engagement of learners with disabilities, in the growing area of personalized learning. As building leaders and associated educators increasingly look for alternatives to address learning loss and similar demands facing today's classroom, students with disabilities are sharing how and when innovations via AI tools can improve learning. SE leaders and collaborative educators should think of means of involving the students with disabilities in more ways to determine improvement means for the personalized learning experiences, especially through AI-tool applications. Student opinions based on effective elements of personalized learning will probably lead to further identification of where to innovate via the applications of AI tools to further improve delivery of individualized instruction and learning opportunities for students with disabilities. The second consideration would be the advancement of research that includes the addition of specific AI tools and subsequent student use to determine their perspective and the impact of such tools on the five themes associated with their research. With the addition of AI tools, future research should measure the impact of these additions on student use, perspective on learning, and associated student outcomes. Third, the inclusion of AI tools related to the basic elements of personalized learning (e.g., self-pace, data-driven decisions) would be helpful in understanding.

Using Bakhtin's notion of heteroglossia, Tang et al. (2024) conceptualizes GenAI not as a source of autonomous and complete knowledge but rather as a dialogic agent to facilitate collaborative dialogue and co-construction of knowledge among students. Such an approach would encourage students to critically engage with AI-generated content, incorporating multiple viewpoints within the learning process, hence cultivating those key epistemic skills. Initial results show active student involvement in dialogue with GenAI. For instance, follow-up questions showing critical thinking and creativity are indicators of the integration of various sources and the development of epistemic skills among students. Findings in this case shed light on key elements involved in working with multiple perspectives to develop epistemic skills in understanding AI in a holistic and ethic manner. The call of the research pushes even further a more extensive exploration of GenAI's pedagogic potential and its broader implications for educational practices as a rather promising avenue for pedagogical innovation and, by the same token, the growth of critical thinking skills in the digital era.

Perkins et. al (2024) examines the capacity of teaching staff assisted by AI detection software in Turnitin to detect AI-generated content in higher education assignments. 22 samples were generated using the Open AI's ChatGPT tool, which employed prompting techniques to minimize the chances of AI detectors. These assignment samples were then separately graded by 15 teaching staff with actual student-produced assessment. The AI detection tool was correct to identify 91% of the experimental submissions as containing AI-generated content, but only detected AI generation in 54.8% of the content. That again speaks to the difficulties posed by advanced prompting techniques in detecting AI content. The recommendations make a case to shift overall strategies for judging the performance of university students, keeping in mind the emergence of new Generative AI tools. This could be about a reduction of general dependency on assessments that may have applied AI tools to simulate human writing, or alternatively through the adoption of AI-inclusive assessments. Essential training should therefore be given to academic personnel and learners, in efforts to preserve academic integrity.

VIRTUAL AND AUGMENTED REALITY APPLICATIONS

Virtual and Augmented Reality is an innovative way to implement gamified components in a classroom. This allows students to experience a more engaging, interactive, and dynamic learning environment as these offer high-resolution and close-to-authentic experiences. Sample applications of VR technology in education are historical simulations, medical training, science lab emanation, and visualization of abstract concepts like fields of anatomy and physics. On one hand, applications for AR Technology in education are interactive instructional resources (textbooks and worksheets, and field guides), gamified learning, and 3D imitation of rarefied visuals in domains like engineering and architecture.

VR IN EDUCATION: BEYOND TEXTBOOKS

Students are immersed in computer-generated environments through VR, allowing them to experience historical events, understand scientific concepts as well as practice their skills in a safe and controlled environment. The following are some of the main areas where VR can be applied in education:

Akpinar (2024) designed the Virtual Reality Solar System Model (VRSSM) for the unit of "Sun System and Eclipses" for 6th-grade students and to find out what students think about using virtual reality applications in science classes. It was revealed that students want VR to be applied not only in science lesson but in all other lessons, believing that the knowledge they have accumulated is not partial and that they feel that through this application, they can be able to raise their level of science achievement. Apart from that, the students report that the application of technology enhances their interest towards the science lesson and has an impact positively on their learning. Results of this study are expected to find their way in the development and creation of three-dimensional virtual reality learning environments on any number of topics or curriculum levels.

Experiential Learning

As compared to traditional field trips, VR can transport students to different historical landmarks, natural wonders, or even distant planets. Most traditional methods of teaching rely too much on lecture delivery, use of textbooks, and note-taking which eventually leads to passivity among some students such that they cannot concentrate or find interest in what they are being taught (Maes et al., 2010). On the contrary, experiential learning encourages both hands-on as well as active learner participation so that they can use this knowledge where necessary. It enhances understanding, improves retention rate, and promotes critical thinking abilities.

The implementation of experiential learning has been revolutionized through the utilization of VR technologies. The students are taken deeper into simulations thereby offering possibilities to interact with different ideas like never before. To provide a better understanding of the past, students should study firsthand how historical events like World War II's Berlin Blitz influenced people.

VR enables learners to engage in interactive simulations that mimic real-life situations. For instance, a history student can stroll through ancient Rome or relive the experiences of a pioneer on the Oregon Trail. A science student can dissect a virtual frog or carry out an experiment in the laboratory of his/her choice.

VR provides students with an opportunity to visualize abstract ideas within a three-dimensional environment. This is particularly important for mathematics, science, and engineering where understanding spatial relationships is very vital. In addition, VR gives students the ability to touch and manipulate objects in a virtual world. This helps them develop practical skills and comprehend better the inner workings of certain things.

Simulation and Training

Virtual reality (VR) is a reality in education rather than a futuristic concept, especially in simulation and training. VR allows students an engaging way to learn from their mistakes and practice their skills while at the same time making them understand complex concepts deeply and safely in a controlled environment.

Virtual experiments help learners carry out experimental work, observe physical phenomena, and get familiar with lab procedures without any risk. VR simulations allow medical students to perform intricate surgical operations, thereby honing their skills and mitigating possible dangers from actual-life situations.

VR training simulations serve as an engaging substitute for traditional learning which often depends on lectures, textbooks, and rote memorization. These allow learners to be part of real-life situations without facing any dangers that may come with such spaces. This makes it possible to enhance deep comprehension, increase retention levels, and promote the development of analytical abilities.

In the field of healthcare, medical professionals are trained in surgical procedures, patient care, and other medical skills using VR technology. It enables learners to carry out practices in an uncontaminated space, refining their capabilities and self-assurance. Moreover, the aviation sector uses VR flight simulators to train pilots, allowing them to undergo numerous kinds of experiences without having to get on real flights.

For engineering purposes, VR helps train engineers in designing, building, and performing additional engineering activities. Learners can apply traditional non-engineering methods to visualize as well as apply different kinds of intricate structures and systems. In addition, social sciences make use of VR designs for historical immersive simulations which offer students various experiences across cultures at different historical times. Consequently, it promotes a better grasp by students when it comes to the subject matter surrounding history.

Visualizing Abstract Concepts

Virtual reality (VR) education is being revolutionized by an innovative and powerful means of visualizing abstract concepts. It is often difficult for traditional learning modalities to present complex ideas appealingly and understandably. In contrast, VR facilitates an immersing as well as interactive environment which helps students comprehend and internalize abstract concepts in a way never experienced before.

Students can explore the human body in 3D via VR, visualizing complex anatomical structures and systems in a way that is impossible for traditional textbooks. They can also use VR to create interactive simulations of physical phenomena, enabling them to understand and visualize complex concepts like gravity, energy, or motion.

Abstract concepts like mathematical equations, scientific theories or philosophical ideas may pose a challenge for some learners. Conventional learning approaches like lectures and textbooks usually do not provide concrete and appealing representations of these concepts. As a result, difficulty understanding leads to boredom, anger, disinterest, or even failure to comprehend. VR technology provides three-dimensional interactive spaces where one can visualize abstract concepts, thus, it addresses this challenge. VR immersive environments can be produced which allow learners access to three dimensional illustrations of abstract concepts. For instance, a student studying mathematics could view complicated geometric figures or change equations within a virtual space. Physics students can investigate the details of atoms or see how gravity works through simulation.

Apandi et. al (2023) constructed a virtual reality science lab using the ADDIE Methodology, which is a well-defined model for designing instruction. Furthermore, this study attempts to assess how the virtual reality laboratory impacted the extent of immersion that 37 science students underwent during the learning process. In pursuing this exploratory experiment, the participants were split into two distinct groups. There were two groups under study: Group 1 consisted of twenty participants who were exposed to scientific films in two dimensions. The second was Group 2, which had seventeen participants who conducted their science education in a virtual reality laboratory. From these results, it can be deduced that there is a significant presence in both cohorts, but the performance in the VR cohort is higher compared to the rest of the group. The current study provides the much-needed information for teachers and educational software developers who are working to produce virtual reality resources for science education. It is recommended that for further studies concerning instructional technology implemented with virtual reality, cognitive load should be an examined variable. In general, this work contributes to a growing body of evidence showing the positive and holistic effects of immersive learning in education.

VR facilitates student interaction with virtual objects that they can manipulate as a means to understand better some abstract concepts at hand. For example, economics scholars can create simulated markets to learn supply and demand principles. Contexts in which psychology students could benefit more include exploring virtual representations of human brain models for better comprehension within this field.

The safe controlled environment provided by VR gives learners the chance of exploring different possibilities associated with an abstract concept whilst manipulating various parameters and looking at the result produced for each condition change made. This approach supports deeper comprehension and promotes critical thought processes among students.

VR is being employed in the development of virtual laboratories within which learners can conduct research, investigate the entangled details of atomic structures, or observe the impact of gravity in a safe and controlled setting.

AR IN EDUCATION: ENHANCING THE REAL WORLD

Augmented reality (AR) is a technology that uses digital elements as overlays over physical structures to aid learning.

Lampropoulos (2023) draws attention to the possible use of AI, AR, and Intelligent Tutoring Systems (ITS) in education, directing the focus to the individual and combined potential. Analysis of some recent researches by the author unfolds the integration benefits, especially focusing on the convergence of AI and AR; such a combination can develop an interactive, immersive, engaging, and personalized learning experience-applicable to all educational levels. It, therefore places greater emphasis on the capacity of these technologies to provide all sorts of appeals for various specific needs, from learner psychological and cognitive states to unique characteristic, knowledge, preferences, interests, and performance. These technologies should meet educational demands, positively influence teaching and learning activities, and consequently improve outcomes as well as motivation for learning.

The following are some of the most important educational applications of AR:

Interactive Learning Resources

In conjunction with AR, textbooks come alive through 3D models, animations and even interactive components embedded into real-world objects making it much more fascinating. Changing the game in education is augmented reality (AR). It offers a new dimension of interactive learning resources that are meant to increase comprehension, engagement and applicability in real life. Unlike virtual reality (VR) which immerses users in an entirely digital environment, AR creates a blended experience by overlaying digital information over the real world.

This technology enables educators to create learning resources that are more interactive than ordinary books or lectures. For instance, AR helps bring abstract concepts to life by means of 3D models, animations, and simulations. This helps students explore human anatomy through 3D interactive models or visualize complex mathematical equations using virtual spaces.

Urhan and Akpinar (2023) introduced a learning application referred to as Augmented Reality Integration (ARI) based on the Physics Independent Learning (MPIL) model of the marine physics concept. The application focused on testing the ARI effect on 21st-Century Skills (21-CS), which comprises Critical Thinking, Collaboration, Communication, and Creativity. The research design used a Quasi-Experimental Method with 88 students between 20-22 years old who were randomly assigned into the experimental and control groups. After the intervention for 3 weeks, it was observed that utilizing ARI technology in physics learning can significantly enhance their Creativity Thinking and Critical Thinking about concepts of Marine physics, lead students to further improve in Communication, and Collaboration in solving the problems included in the ARI application, and provoke the motivation to learn concepts in physics.

Using AR enables students to interact with virtual objects and environments so that they will have some insights into the subject matter. For instance, they may do scientific experiments based on computer simulations within a laboratory setting or visit ancient monuments using augmented tours. In addition to this, AR allows us to have a closer look at historical landmarks, natural environments, or cultural sites during our school trips by providing additional information.

Augmented reality shrinks the distance between theoretical knowledge and its implementation as it allows the student to engage with real-life situations within a safe and regulated setting. Medical procedures can be performed on patients who do not exist by students or they may design and run their engineering prototypes in an imaginary space.

AR has made it possible for learners to take virtual field trips without ever having to leave their classrooms. They can visit historical sites, natural habitats, or any other place through this technology. Students can learn about scientific processes through experiments, interact with virtual models of scientific principles or understand them better by using augmented reality science laboratories. Textbooks can be made more interactive through the provision of 3D models among other features. Not to mention, educational games underpinned by augmented reality provide an enjoyable way of learning.

Gamified Learning

AR, short for augmented reality, is not only a futuristic idea but it is enhancing education in terms of gamification by making the education process interesting and more interactive. It makes use of the digital information on the real world; speculating between the physical real-world environment and the computer-generated one thus providing a distinct venue for learning to take place in a game-like manner.

AR will create amazing games and challenges that enhance the ability to think critically, solve problems, and cooperate with other players. AR makes possible the creation of interactive scavenger hunts that promote learning through exploration thereby increasing its enjoyment.

Chen et. al (2020) designed an augmented reality app, Mobile Plant, which is designed for the primary school plant curriculum, that combines games with augmented reality to boost students' interests in learning. A questionnaire shows that the game can reach positive results in terms of its game difficulty and absorption of content.

The non-verbal use of game elements to enhance students' participation has worked magic where they are concerned. This unique mode of learning makes gamified interactive experiences available for learners who can be fully immersed in this process without getting bored easily. In this regard, teachers have a chance to come up with study places that really capture their students as well as promote greater understanding among them.

The AR apps are capable of recording students' progress and granting points as well when they finish their schoolwork or reach targets. These points can be displayed on leaderboards which encourage friendly competition amongst the learners, motivating them to want higher scores. Furthermore, badges or unlocked achievements can be awarded to a student who has grasped a particular concept or has completed certain challenges. It acts as an encouragement for further academic knowledge acquisition by exhibiting a sense of achievement.

Levels with amplitude in difficulty can be designed into AR games through which students have to go through them one after the other. This way the path of development is ordered for this purpose directing students towards self-inducing challenges. It is possible to make difficult fun-filled challenges through Augmented Reality enabling the application of knowledge and ability among their counterparts. Such may include hunts, puzzles, or even simulations in virtual reality. This gamified technology may also lead to the creation of detailed stories wherein learners perform different roles in solving issues related to narratives that involve plots. Thus, learning becomes much more involving compared to conventional methods.

In AR surroundings, students are able to do virtual trials as well as investigate scientific principles and exhibit with computer-generated models. Students can also experience famous battles, go back in time to ancient civilizations, or meet historical people who were part of different stories through augmented reality simulations. With Augmented Reality settings, students can also get new words, improve their accents, and even have conversations with imaginary characters.

Seeing the Unseen

Education is undergoing a major transformation thanks to augmented reality (AR) that blurs the boundary between digital and physical worlds, enabling learners to see beyond what is seen and experience learning in unprecedented dimensions. AR allows the overlaying of digital information on real-life objects creating interactive experiences that consequently enhance comprehension and engagement. The power of this technology is especially significant in education where it makes abstract ideas concrete, brings distant realities closer, and offers immersive forms of learning.

Rahmat et. al (2024) study the effect of mobile augmented reality on physics learning achievement and students' opinions regarding using this technology. They gathered pre- and post-test data for computation of the normalized gain score in evaluating students' learning achievement. The result showed that students who used mobile augmented reality had a higher criterion for learning achievement compared to students who used textbooks. Data are obtained through interviews conducted with students after using mobile augmented reality and are described and analyzed. Conclusion on the student's point of view states that augmented reality is a new learning environment, improving students' understanding of physics concepts with an enhancement in the learning achievements of students and concrete abstract concepts by visual 3D simulations. Findings revealed that the enhancement of students' understanding of physics concepts after the use of mobile augmented reality.

Augmented Reality allows students to see the human body's 3D representations over their own vision of a person's body making them have more in-depth knowledge concerning its internal structures and systems. Using Augmented Reality, learners can also visualize and grasp complicated concepts concerning engineering by projecting 3D models together with animations over physical objects they are dealing with.

AR has that unique ability to make things otherwise unseen clearer. It transforms vague notions into visible realities. For instance, through augmented reality (AR), students can visualize the solar system using a 3D planetary globe, hovering above their textbooks. Hence, they are able to understand planetary scale relationships in ways that static pictures or texts cannot explain. Likewise, AR can also be used to visualize complex anatomical structures whereby students can explore the human body in three-dimensional ways, thereby comprehending its intricate functions better.

With AR technology, learners are transported to different temporal and spatial contexts so that they get to know more about the environment around them. For example, one could imagine a history lesson where students examined artifacts closely, and were able to see actual places where such artifacts have been found like the pyramids of Giza. Moreover, students can perform virtual experiments within an AR environment where they interact with 3D models that simulate real-world situations. This way they are able to understand scientific principles through hands-on experience without the constraints of traditional laboratories.

Even when physical trips cannot happen AR can make field trips more vivid. Students can visit historical places or nature habitats, or even journey into outer space via this technology which gives them a better insight about their surroundings. Students can also practice their skills in a safe and controlled environment which prepares them for real-life situations.[5] This makes it possible to create realistic training simulations for various professions such as healthcare, engineering, and manufacturing among others.

THE PSYCHOLOGY OF GAMIFICATION

In the last part of this chapter, it will unlock the psychology of gamification. This will discuss theories on how gamification affects the mental or cognitive state of its users. Delving deeper into this topic will navigate the psychological aspect of a person or student who immerses or indulges in a gaming experience powered by AI. Gamification exploits the intrinsic motivation of the users, which refers to a passion for engaging in an activity for its own worth rather than for any external recompenses.

SDT PSYCHOLOGICAL REQUIREMENTS

Self-determination theory (SDT) is a concept that was brought forward by psychologists Edward Deci and Richard Ryan, and it postulates that human beings possess inherent psychological requirements for autonomy, competence, and relatedness. The satisfaction of these needs increases an individual's motivation, well-being, and general happiness. According to Self-Determination Theory (SDT), this intrinsic motivation is based on three fundamental psychological requirements:

Autonomy

Autonomy means being in command of and directing one's own actions. It refers to being able to act voluntarily without being coerced by the situations or other people. In the aspect of gamification; autonomy refers to the ability to make important choices for personalized experiences that are able to distinguish someone from another.

The ability to customize experiences based on individual preferences and needs makes AI gamification stand out as a unique opportunity, thus, promoting autonomy. AI algorithms analyze user data and preferences, suggesting personalized goals that resonate with their interests and skill levels. This gives learners the feeling of ownership of their progress and makes them pursue significant aspirations.

AI can dynamically adjust the difficulty of tasks and challenges based on user performance, ensuring that the experience remains engaging and rewarding. This prevents learners from becoming frustrated or bored, fostering a sense of competence and encouraging them to continue playing. Moreover, AI can personalize the content and interface of gamified systems to cater to individual user preferences. This might include customizing character appearances, choosing preferred gameplay styles, or selecting specific learning modules. Such customization empowers users to feel a sense of control over their experience and fosters a deeper connection with the gamified system.

AI can create dynamic narratives and gameplay experiences that adapt to user choices. This allows users to explore different pathways, make decisions that impact the story, and experience a sense of agency within the game world. When users feel a sense of control and ownership over their experience, they are more likely to be intrinsically motivated to engage with the gamified system. This leads to more sustained engagement, as users are driven by their enjoyment and desire to achieve their goals, rather than external rewards.

The autonomy enhances the general user experience because it makes the gamified system more fun, individualized, and pertinent to different preferences and needs. This results in higher levels of satisfaction among learners and a probability of enduring engagement. Students who perceive themselves as autonomous are more likely to internalize knowledge and competencies through a gamified experience. As a result, such changes could be more long-lasting in terms of behavior since they will be encouraged to use their knowledge in real-life situations.

Competence

The desire to feel competent and effective in what we do. Gamification offers feedback, challenges, and opportunities for skill development which enables users to assess their progress while still enjoying a sense of mastery.

Competence is all about that feeling of being effective and mastering one's skills and actions. It also indicates one's ability to learn, grow, and eventually reach desired outcomes. In this context of gaming, it means giving learners challenges that are not only well-calibrated to what they can do but also offering them feedback on their progress to help them feel accomplished.

By examining user data and performance, AI algorithms can provide customized challenges that are neither too hard nor too easy. This way users remain interested and motivated thereby avoiding boredom or demotivation due to too little challenge. In turn, they continue playing and feeling accomplished.

The system can dynamically alter the level of difficulty in tasks or challenges based on how well users do making sure that it stays engaging and rewarding at all times. This prevents users from getting frustrated or losing interest hence fostering a sense of competence and motivating them to play more. In addition, AI can respond to user performance as quickly as possible such that it points out regions in which a person needs to improve and encourages the actions that he/she has taken correctly. This way they follow up on their progression, detect areas they require concentration on, and derive satisfaction from their developing abilities.

Artificial intelligence can give users distinct representations of their advancement like progress bars, merit, and badges. Hence, students can recognize what they have achieved, monitoring their development which motivates them towards further advancement. With this technology, AI is capable of giving prompt and accurate reactions to user performance by pinpointing areas where one has made mistakes while praising the right decisions. As a result, individuals are able to keep tabs on how well they are doing with regard to education levels or any other form of skill acquisition.

Relatedness

The need to relate with other people around us. Gamification usually features social aspects like leaderboards, team competitions, or cooperation tasks that help create communities among its clientele. Relatedness is an emotion that entails belongingness or connection with others, and social support. It signifies the need to be part of a group, have interaction with other people, and feel appreciated and accepted. Thus, in gamification, relatedness means creating a community spirit among users and stimulating social contacts.

Capinding and Dumayas (2024) discusses the effects of AI on learning experience, academic performance, job counseling, motivation, self-confidence, social communication, and dependency on AI. Overall, findings reveal that students considered AI to be good in most aspects. In a social lens, students have agreed that AI fosters teamwork, peer learning, and networking.

AI-based gaming introduces a new avenue for social engagement where one will feel relatedness among other players. For instance, dynamic leaderboards created by AI enable users to see how their progress compares with other people. This creates friendly competition among them which promotes cooperation and gives users a sense of social status and belonging in the game-like community.

AI can facilitate teamwork challenges and collaborative play that will motivate user's cooperation towards achieving similar objectives. The above-mentioned promotes shared goals that help tighten ties among members within the game-powered society. AI is also capable of making online friendships and chat groups that facilitate user connections involving like-minded individuals in gamified systems. This builds an atmosphere of acceptance among its participants enabling them to share experiences and help each other.

AI can utilize user data as well as individual tastes. Hence, it recommends such associations with different individuals who may have comparable interests or objectives. This stimulates social activity passing through the process where people become acquainted with one another in these gaming environments leaving their social intermediaries out altogether.

MASLOW'S HIERARCHY OF NEEDS

A psychologist known as Abraham Maslow in 1943 suggested that humans have a hierarchy of needs with basic physiological and safety at the bottom while self-actualization sits at the top. As such, individuals are motivated towards satisfying these needs in an ascending order based on the priority, attached to meeting lower-level ones.

Esteem Needs

Esteem needs represent the 4th level in the hierarchy, above safety and belonging and below self-actualization. It includes aspects such as self-esteem, confidence, achievements, acceptance, and respect from others. When these needs are satisfied, individuals feel good about themselves and their lives.

Kurtić et. al (2024) examined the effects of using ChatGPT on learning and academic achievement in the subject of probability. Two independent surveys were utilized to collect data from the students about the perception of learning with ChatGPT. The two surveys would assess the self-confidence of the students, their understanding of probability, and how challenging the problems are. Significant gains in self-confidence and comprehension of the probability concepts were obtained among students subsequent to the introduction of ChatGPT assistance. Qualitative information gathered from the surveys also supported the findings, showing a positive shift among the perceptions regarding the abilities of the students, as well as that of understanding the subject matter. Of course, this notwithstanding, a student's perception of the difficulty experienced in problem solving showed little to no trend. This could be due to intrinsic complexity-of problems of probability that are intrinsically coupled with the amount of underlying mathematical know-how or do not depend exclusively on external support.

Recognition and accomplishment is a means by which AI gamification can meet users' esteem needs through personalization of experience that creates feelings of achievement. Through user data analysis, AI can create personalized achievements as well as badges allocated based on specific occurrences experienced within the gamified system. Such rewards may therefore be unique to an individual's interests or aspirations, providing them with recognition and accomplishments.

Dynamic Leaderboards and Rankings created by AI allow for comparison with other users on the progress made in a game. Therefore, it instills a competitive spirit among the players as well as a feeling of achievement. For this reason, people perceive themselves as having a form of social rank and being recognized in the context of the entire gamified community. AI also provides personalized feedback to users highlighting their strengths and weaknesses that may need improvement. Such acts can help improve user confidence, motivating them within a certain gamified system.

Using AI, social recognition can be achieved including sharing of achievements among users with friends or followers. In this case, users will get accepted within their networks based on what they have accomplished. Subsequently, AI can tailor content and challenges posed in gamified systems to unique skill levels and interests for every player who may be playing such games. Hence, it is important that every player feels challenged yet capable enough to accomplish set goals specifically aimed at increasing feelings of competency or accomplishment which eventually contribute towards having an optimistic self-esteem image.

Social Belonging

There are needs to be loved and belong, which is the third level of the hierarchy between esteem needs and safety needs. These needs include a craving for companionship, privacy, friendship, acceptance, and a sense of community. When they are met, people feel that they belong, have purpose in life, and achieve emotional well-being. AI-powered gaming platforms provide a lucrative opportunity to create social experiences that satisfy learners' requirements of belongingness, providing them with a sense of unity and connection.

Pani et. al (2024) discusses the potential of AI chatbots in social support interventions that help an individual feel a sense of belonging, social support, and loneliness reduction. They reviewed the major areas where AI chatbots are already being used and their findings and tries to contrast AI-based friendly chatbots with AI-based assistant chatbots such as ChatGPT and Bard. The arguments, put together, propose the use of AI chatbots as an assistive tool that can improve general wellbeing by better time management, advice, suggestion, and collaboration with the user indirectly in instilling a sense of belonging and alleviating feelings of loneliness.

AI creates dynamic leaderboards that enable users to compare their progress with others hence fostering friendly competition as it motivates teamwork. It enables members to gain social status hence feeling included in the game community. AI also enhances team-based challenges and collaborative gameplay, prompting users to work together towards common goals. This helps create a sense of common purpose and consolidates ties within the gamified community.

Chat features and forums can be incorporated into gamified systems with the use of AI, which allows users to communicate with one another, exchange tactics, and provide assistance. By doing so, it encourages social interaction between them while also instilling a sense of belongingness among them. Furthermore, gamified systems are capable of developing virtual communities and social groups through AI that enable users to associate with like-minded individuals who have corresponding interests and ambitions. This creates a feeling of belongingness for its members, allowing them to share their experiences within the platforms. Using user data as well as preferences, AI can recommend turning points in addition to other users' recommendations based on their individual likings or targets. Hence, this enhances interpersonal relationships among varied individuals, thus, making them feel part of such communities.

BEHAVIORAL ECONOMICS

Behavioral economics refers to economics that incorporates psychological aspects together with other disciplines, influencing them in making decisions about why people behave like these.

Loss Aversion

There is a more personal incentive for somebody who does not want to lose anything than he/she would have had if there was a prospect of gaining something else that relates closely to participation. Streaks, milestones, time limitations, and rewards are some examples of game-playing techniques, basically tapping on this principle therefore encouraging learners not only to continue but also stay away from potential loss situations.

Gillanders (2020) suggests a new evaluation method that seeks to address the challenges of low student engagement and cheating by incorporating loss aversion and peer assessment in one methodology. In the task students were to grade a peer's work correctly, and a small percentage of marks that they had already 'secured' for completing that task could get lost. A more comprehensive rubric, on which the student could grade the work, was developed to support students grading the work. Using survey data and interviews, we found that the students, although they did not like the assessment strategy, were better engaged in the assessment process and believed that their critical thinking ability was improved because of the assessment. Implications of this study include more explicit guidance for students through, for example, rubrics, lecturer accessibility and exemplars.

NATURALISTIC DECISION MAKING

Naturalistic Decision Making (NDM) endeavors to comprehend how individuals make their choices in a realistic environment, most times when they are faced with time pressure and uncertainty.

Liu and Wang (2024) measured pre-post intervention levels of critical thinking with a standardized assessment tool. In the experimentation group, students utilized AI tools such as ChatGPT-3.5, Bodoudou, SummarizBot, etc., for generating and answering text-related questions as well as interacting through interactive quizzes and AI-assisted debates during classes. In contrast, in the experiment, the control group continued to pursue regular methods unaided by any AI tools. The findings statistically showed improvement in the skills of critical thinking for the experimental group compared with the control group and studies the requirement by the pre and postintervention assessment. This leads to the fact that AI tools really enhance critical thinking skills in English literature classes. This study contributes to the discourse on AI in education and has practical implications for integrating AI technologies to support and enrich the learning experience of EFL students in literature classes.

AI is increasingly becoming the tool being leveraged for improvement in thinking and decision-making. AI-based tools can analyze huge amounts of data and identify patterns that many might miss. This can make enable better decision-making by individuals and organizations by providing more breadth as well as depth of understanding of complex situations. Another great advantage is the capability of AI to simulate various conditions of scenarios and to forecast possible outcomes as well, which will enable the decision makers to have a trial of alternative scenarios to test the risks and returns on them. Augmenting human intelligence through AI empowers people to think more critically, more effectively make decisions, and thus attain better learning results.

Real-Life Scenarios

Gamification training that is grounded on realistic simulations with less time available as an option can help the users develop their ability to cope with decision-making under pressure so that they can act efficiently in similar instances encountered outside these settings.

OPERANT CONDITIONING

B.F. Skinner was the first person who introduced Operant Conditioning which was a theory of learning that emphasized how behavior could be modified through reward and punishment (Cooper et al., 2018). This principle underlies many aspects of gamification intended to make sure that one learns fast and practices what is right.

Operant conditioning is a kind of learning that focuses primarily on behavior modification, which was first presented by B.F. Skinner. That means behaviors that are followed by rewards (positive outcome) tend to be repeated and those followed by punishment (negative outcome) usually tend not to happen at all.

AI can personalize rewards as well as punishments based on an individual student's needs, ensuring that reinforcements are relevant for each student, and maximizing their effects on behavior change. Moreover, AI changes task challenges according to how well a learner is performing to give appropriate reinforcement regardless of the mastery level achieved. Hence, students are always challenged yet involved in the learning process without experiencing frustration because of too simple assignments or feeling overwhelmed due to excessive task complexity.

Through AI technology, instant responses can be obtained from students regarding how they performed examinations, thereby informing them what needs to improve while providing praise which leads us to real-time advice, making it easy for learners to understand the consequences of actions undertaken and motivating them towards ongoing education activities and skill enhancement.

It is possible for students to engage in learning new skills through AI-generated challenges and rewards which they find very interesting. These individualized challenges are tailored according to their personal interests and ambitions making them stay engaged in their studies. In addition, AI enables intricate virtual environments as well as simulations whereby students can make mistakes without any risk since there are corrections given instantly after every move made. It creates a more real-world scenario that enhances the ability to expand for a low-pressure atmosphere.

Xiao et al (2024) have explored the interplay between EFL learners' self-esteem (S-E), cognitive-emotion regulation (CER), academic enjoyment (AE), and language success (LS) in AI-supported online language learning. For this intention, a copy of the Foreign Language Learning Self-Esteem Scale, the Cognitive Emotion Control Questionnaire, the Foreign Language Enjoyment Scale, and a researcher-made test were distributed to 389 EFL learners in China. Effects of S-E, CER, AE and LS were searched and estimated on the data via confirmatory factor analysis and structural equation modeling. Those results indicated that online courses based on AI can help develop the cognition of CER and AE among learners. This suggests that those learners who were well-implemented in a strong system of self-efficacy can effectively regulate their cognitive and emotional operations in the process of AI-supportive language learning.

DELIBERATE PRACTICE

Deliberate practice is not simply about repetition, it's about active engagement with the learning process, constant feedback, and strategic adaptation to improve performance.

According to Akinleye et.al,2024, AI-driven platforms can allow teachers to become efficient and proficient only if the same platforms instill a learning culture and meet the needs of the changing teachers. This ensures a dynamic and successful environment for educationists and learners alike. With the journey ahead, innovation and collaboration would surely emerge to break open the largest scopes of unleashing AI's full potential in education while turning it into a proper tool for lifelong learning in an ever more complicated world.

AI can analyze student data, including strengths, weaknesses, and learning styles, to create personalized learning paths that target specific areas for improvement. This ensures that students are consistently challenged and engaged in deliberate practice that is relevant to their individual needs. AI can adjust the difficulty of tasks and challenges in real time based on student performance. This allows students to practice at the optimal level for their current skill level, avoiding frustration from tasks that are too easy or overwhelming from those that are too difficult. This constant adaptation ensures that students are continually pushed beyond their comfort zones, fostering growth and improvement.

AI has the ability to give immediate feedback on how well students perform. It highlights areas where improvement might be required. This instant feedback helps the learners to quickly pinpoint their mistakes hence accelerating the learning process. Moreover, AI can also offer detailed statistics about progress such that they can observe their advancement over time and find what needs more attention when practicing.

This technology comes with engaging challenges and incentives that make students practice all the time. These trials are based on personal interests as well as individual objectives. They keep learners motivated plus engaged within their studying procedure. For students to feel like they are achieving something, game elements such as points or badges can serve as motivation.

AI can make interactive simulations or virtual environments where students can learn certain skills without exposing themselves to real-life consequences. The environments may present plausible situations with feedback, enabling students to develop or sharpen their abilities without facing any negative effects in real life.

EXPERTISE ACQUISITION

Expertise acquisition is a process where individuals develop expertise by extensively practicing and learning within one domain or field. The motivation structures and feedback provided by gamification motivate users to acquire new skills:

The education system can be completely transformed by AI gamification through the provision of expertise acquisition. Personalized learning pathways, adaptive challenges, immediate feedback and engaging motivation are some ways in which AI can enable students to master their areas of choice effectively.

Hidayat (2024) measured whether AI-based personalized reading platforms are effective in enhancing reading comprehension among senior high school students. The results showed that the students exposed to the AI-based platform scored much higher in reading comprehension than the other students, implying an improvement in reading comprehension brought about by the AI-based platform. Educators and administrators should thus consider exploring AI-based personalized reading platforms in their teaching strategies for the improvement of reading skills among learners.

By collecting data on student strengths and weaknesses as well as learning styles, AI is able to make personalized teaching schemes designed to help students improve their specific skills. Such tailored experiences challenge students consistently, ensuring they are always engaged in deliberate practice that suits them based on their aspirations and aspirations, and enhancing deeper understanding and development of new abilities.

AI adjusts the difficulty level of tasks and challenges in real time according to how well or poorly one performs a given assignment or task. This helps learners work at the most appropriate stage for them since they will not feel bored with easy things nor will they get lost amidst difficult things. It facilitates constant adjustment, keeping learners within their uncomfortable zones for growth purposes eventually resulting in high competency.

AI can provide real-time feedback to students on their performance, showing them what they need to work on and offering detailed analytics about their progress. Such feedback helps students to easily identify and rectify mistakes, speeding up the learning process and allowing for a better understanding of concepts. The analysis shows the students' progress, clearly making them want to keep practicing towards perfection.

Chauke et. al (2024) proved through thematic analysis that it is helpful for postgraduate students and some use this AI tool to modify their research topics before presenting to the supervisor at the final stages of submission. Furthermore, ChatGPT assists the postgraduate students in detecting grammatical mistakes and parading their academic writing, which goes a long way in enhancing their writing skills. Based on the above findings, the research is concluded by recommending that an emergent AI ethical use policy should be developed immediately within South Africa's historically disadvantaged universities. In this respect, the policy should be established as forming into developing guidelines on ethics of utilization by postgraduate students in using AI tools such as ChatGPT to integrate responsibly and effectively into academic success.

The use of AI enables the creation of motivating challenges and rewards that drive students towards regular practice as well as more challenging goals. Personalized challenges based on individual interests help maintain motivation, engagement in learning, and sense of achievement.

By virtue of its ability, AI is in the process of developing engaging simulations and virtual environments that are able to train learners. It creates interactive simulations as well as virtually simulated environments that enable students to practice their skills in a secure and controlled atmosphere while getting instant feedback on their actions. Such environments replicate real-world situations and challenges, enabling learners to hone their abilities without risking anything. Therefore, it exudes the understanding of how knowledge is practically applicable.

THE POTENCY OF GAMIFICATION

It is vital to create interesting and productive experiences by utilizing psychological theories that are based on gamification in order to motivate end users, influence their behaviors as well as to drive the desired results. The full potential of gamification can be realized through harnessing insights from motivation science, decision-making, and learning theory for these ends and leaving an indelible mark on users.

In order to accomplish goals, set by the UN that are related to quality education and gender equality, Koravuna et al. (2024) emphasize the significance of promoting digital literacy among females. AI is revolutionizing the face of learning as it provides an individually customized experience for individual learners. The integration of gamification in AI can further enhance the level of learning through increased involvement among students, continuous learning and an interactive competitive atmosphere. This means that the inclusion and promotion of digital literacy among these technologies are highly important so that everyone can have good use of these advancements.

As gamification progresses in sophistication, so will its influence on different industries such as education, healthcare, and business. By embracing the power of gamification and its underlying psychological principles, we can unlock new opportunities across various domains relating to engagement, motivation, and learning.

REFERENCES

5 Activity-based learning principles for the digital classroom. (2020, November 4). Fierce Network. https://www.fierce-network.com/accessibility/5-activity-based-learning-principles-for-digital-classroom?webview_progress_bar=1&show_loading=0

7 Advantages of Self-Paced Online courses. (2024, June 18). Sophia University. https://www.sophia.org/blog/higher-education/advantages-of-self-paced-courses/?show_loading=0&webview_progress_bar=1

Accessibility and flexibility can lead to student empowerment. (2022, December 6). Instructure. https://www.instructure.com/resources/blog/accessibility-and-flexibility-can-lead-student-empowerment?webview_progress_bar=1&show_loading=0

Adair, A., Segan, E., Gobert, J., & Sao Pedro, M. (2023). *Real-Time AI-Driven Assessment & Scaffolding That Improves Students' Mathematical Modeling during Science Inquiry.* Grantee Submission.

Admin. (2024, February 29). *Building a safe and productive online learning environment. Safe Search Kids.* https://www.safesearchkids.com/building-a-safe-and-productive-online-learning-environment/?webview_progress_bar=1&show_loading=0

Administrator, W. (2022, October 13). *Differentiated Instruction in Online Classroom.* High School of America. https://www.highschoolofamerica.com/differentiated-instruction-in-online-classroom/?webview_progress_bar=1&show_loading=0

Ahuja, R. (2020, March 20). *Benefits of social and collaborative learning.* Thrive Global. https://community.thriveglobal.com/benefits-of-social-and-collaborative-learning/?show_loading=0&webview_progress_bar=1

AI voice overs for e-learning for diverse learners. (n.d.). Speechify. https://speechify.com/blog/ai-voice-overs-for-e-learning/?show_loading=0&webview_progress_bar=1

Akhil, R. (2022). *Digital E-Learning Market Future, Size, Growth Rate, Major Players, Online and Corporate E-learning Market.* Ken Research. https://www.kenresearch.com/blog/e-learning-future-market

Aldrich, C. (n.d.). *Copyright 2024 the Learning Guild*. Copyright 2024: Powered by Cyclone Enterprise: Content Management Solutions and Dynamic Publishing System Developed by Cyclone Interactive Multimedia Group, Inc. http://www.cycloneinteractive.com, Powered by Cyclone and Powered by Cyclone Enterprise. Portional ColdFusion Programming Provided by Finial Software, Inc. www.finial.com. https://www.learningguild.com/contributors/612/clark-aldrich/?show_loading=0&webview_progress_bar=1

Amazon.com. (n.d.). https://www.amazon.com/Simulations-Future-Learning-Revolutionary-Learning/dp/0787969621?webview_progress_bar=1&show_loading=0

Apandi, N. E. F. Z., Mokmin, N. A. M., & Rassy, R. P. (2023). A Study on the Users' Experience in Learning Using a Virtual Reality Laboratory for Medical Sciences. In *Proceedings of International Conference on Research in Education and Science* (pp. 1-16).

Area9 Lyceum. (2021b, March 19). *Activity-Based Learning*. Area9 Lyceum. https://area9lyceum.com/adaptive-learning/activity-based-learning/?webview_progress_bar=1&show_loading=0

Audio & video tips for E-Learning | The Rapid E-Learning blog. (n.d.). *The Rapid E-Learning Blog*. https://blogs.articulate.com/rapid-elearning/audio-video-tips/?webview_progress_bar=1&show_loading=0

Bai, S., Gonda, D. E., & Hew, K. F. (2024). Write-Curate-Verify: A Case Study of Leveraging Generative AI for Scenario Writing in Scenario-Based Learning. *IEEE Transactions on Learning Technologies*.

Behance. (n.d.). https://www.behance.net/search/projects/?search=interactive%2BeLearning&show_loading=0&webview_progress_bar=1

5. *Benefits Of Self-Paced Learning*. (2024). Academy of Mine. https://www.academyofmine.com/self-paced-learning-benefits/?show_loading=0&webview_progress_bar=1

10. *Benefits of Using LMS for Collaborative Learning*. (n.d.). https://www.opigno.org/blog/10-benefits-using-lms-collaborative-learning?webview_progress_bar=1&show_loading=0

Bloggers, C. I., & Bloggers, C. I. (2017, November 16). *5 Fab tips to design Interactive E-Learning Modules*. https://blog.commlabindia.com/elearning-design/interactive-elearning-modules-design-tips?webview_progress_bar=1&show_loading=0

Bowen, J. A., & Watson, C. E. (2024). *Teaching with AI: A practical guide to a new era of human learning*. JHU Press.

BrightCarbon. (2023, October 23). *Insights from an eLearning strategist: Q&A with Clark Quinn*. https://www.brightcarbon.com/blog/insights-elearning-strategist-qa-clark-quinn/?webview_progress_bar=1&show_loading=0

By Craig Weiss. (2024, September 16). *Craig Weiss*. https://elearninfo247.com/author/diegoinstudiocity/?webview_progress_bar=1&show_loading=0

Can Studios Ltd. (2023b, April 4). *Self-Paced learning*. https://www.linkedin.com/pulse/self-paced-learning-can-studios-ltd?show_loading=0&webview_progress_bar=1

Capinding, A. T., & Dumayas, F. T. (2024). Transformative Pedagogy in the Digital Age: Unraveling the Impact of Artificial Intelligence on Higher Education Students. Problems of Education in the 21st Century, 82(5), 630-657.

Caroline. (2022, April 6). *Multimodal Learning: engaging your learner's senses*. LearnUpon. https://www.learnupon.com/blog/multimodal-learning/

Castro, G. P. B., Chiappe, A., Rodríguez, D. F. B., & Sepulveda, F. G. (2024). Harnessing AI for Education 4.0: Drivers of Personalized Learning. Electronic Journal of e-Learning, 22(5), 01-14.

Cathy Moore. (2012, November 20). e-Learning Centre. https://www.e-learningcentre.co.uk/resources/brilliant-blogs/news-and-lots-of-lively-views-from-the-pay-gap-for-women-in-e-learning-to-practical-tips-on-instructional-design-always-worth-a-read-follow-her-on-twitter-cammybean-share/?webview_progress_bar=1&show_loading=0

Cathy Moore's blog. (2023, October 16). https://www.td.org/magazines/td-magazine/cathy-moores-blog?webview_progress_bar=1&show_loading=0

Cecilia. (2023, October 10). *Harnessing the benefits of structured instruction - kognity*. Kognity. https://kognity.com/resources/harnessing-the-benefits-of-structured-instruction/?webview_progress_bar=1&show_loading=0

Charleybrown. (2021, September 22). *5 Advantages of collaborative E-Learning*. Online Class Helpers. https://www.onlineclasshelpers.com/blog/5-advantages-of-collaborative-e-learning/amp/?show_loading=0&webview_progress_bar=1

Chauke, T. A., Mkhize, T. R., Methi, L., & Dlamini, N. (2024). Postgraduate Students' Perceptions on the Benefits Associated with Artificial Intelligence Tools on Academic Success: In Case of ChatGPT AI tool. *Journal of Curriculum Studies Research*, 6(1), 44–59.

Chen, C. H., & Chang, C. L. (2024). Effectiveness of AI-assisted game-based learning on science learning outcomes, intrinsic motivation, cognitive load, and learning behavior. *Education and Information Technologies*, •••, 1–22.

Chen, J. J., & Lin, J. C. (2024). Artificial intelligence as a double-edged sword: Wielding the POWER principles to maximize its positive effects and minimize its negative effects. *Contemporary Issues in Early Childhood*, 25(1), 146–153.

Chen, M. B., Wang, S. G., Chen, Y. N., Chen, X. F., & Lin, Y. Z. (2020). A preliminary study of the influence of game types on the learning interests of primary school students in digital games. *Education Sciences*, 10(4), 96.

Chiu, T. K., Moorhouse, B. L., Chai, C. S., & Ismailov, M. (2023). Teacher support and student motivation to learn with Artificial Intelligence (AI) based chatbot. *Interactive Learning Environments*, •••, 1–17.

Christina. (2024b, July 30). *Essential audio, video, and authoring technologies for creating E-Learning courses*. Blue Carrot. https://bluecarrot.io/blog/exploring-audio-video-and-authoring-technologies-for-effective-e-learning-course-creation/?webview_progress_bar=1&show_loading=0

Clark, A. (2003). *Simulations and the Future of Learning: An Innovative (and Perhaps Revolutionary) Approach to e-Learning*. ACM Digital Library. https://dl.acm.org/doi/10.5555/861424?webview_progress_bar=1&show_loading=0

Colman, H. (2024, July 2). *Multimodal learning: a Transformative approach for success*. Explore the eLearning World With Us. https://www.ispringsolutions.com/blog/multimodal-learning?f_link_type=f_inlinenote&webview_progress_bar=1&show_loading=0

Continuous feedback model could reshape eLearning evaluation : Articles. (n.d.). Copyright 2024 the Learning Guild. Copyright 2024: Powered by Cyclone Enterprise: Content Management Solutions and Dynamic Publishing System Developed by Cyclone Interactive Multimedia Group, Inc. http://www.cycloneinteractive.com, Powered by Cyclone and Powered by Cyclone Enterprise. Portional ColdFusion Programming Provided by Finial Software, Inc. www.finial.com. https://www.learningguild.com/articles/continuous-feedback-model-could-reshape-elearning-evaluation/

Cooper, J. (2024, August 21). *How to use AI eLearning Avatars for online Courses 2024*. Vidnoz. https://www.vidnoz.com/ai-solutions/elearning-avatar.html?show_loading=0&webview_progress_bar=1

Cote, A., & Cote, A. (2024b, September 9). *What is Self-Paced Learning: benefits and ways to address its challenges*. LearnWorlds. https://www.learnworlds.com/self-paced-learning/?show_loading=0&webview_progress_bar=1

Craig Weiss: the e-learning industry's most prolific psychic. (2013, December 18). https://oeb.global/oeb-insights/craig-weiss-the-e-learning-industrys-most-prolific-psychic/?show_loading=0&webview_progress_bar=1

Cudy. (2023) *5 Tips for Applying Differentiated Instruction in eLearning*. Cudy technology. https://blog.cudy.co/5-tips-for-applying-differentiated-instruction-in-elearning/?webview_progress_bar=1&show_loading=0

Daffrin. (2023, June 6). *5 things to consider when choosing an E-Learning platform*. BrainCert Blog. https://blog.braincert.com/5-things-to-consider-when-choosing-an-e-learning-platform/?webview_progress_bar=1&show_loading=0

Dani, V. (2024, June 17). *The Cost-Effectiveness of Digital Textbooks in Schools*. Kitaboo. https://kitaboo.com/cost-effectiveness-of-digital-textbooks-in-schools/?webview_progress_bar=1&show_loading=0

DavidAnderson. (2020, July 9). *20 Beautiful Examples of Interactivity in E-Learning Design #288*. Articulate - Community. https://community.articulate.com/blog/challenge-recaps/20-beautiful-examples-of-interactivity-in-e-learning-design-288/1138574

Demir, H. (2022, August 23). *What is e-learning? 12 Key Advantages of E-learning - 2022*. Ant Media. https://antmedia.io/what-is-e-learning-12-advantages-of-e-learning/?webview_progress_bar=1&show_loading=0

Digital Learning Innovations. (n.d.). https://www.kennesaw.edu/digital-learning-innovations/?show_loading=0&webview_progress_bar=1

Diversity and inclusion in education. (2024, February 20). Coursera. https://www.coursera.org/learn/diversity-and-inclusion-education?webview_progress_bar=1&show_loading=0

DSmith. (2023, September 22). *Global Collaborative Learning: The Future of Cross-Cultural Education*. Medium. https://medium.com/@smithd4466/global-collaborative-learning-the-future-of-cross-cultural-education-f0beae080050?webview_progress_bar=1&show_loading=0

Durant, I. (2023, August 16). *What is target audience for e-learners*. Peep Strategy. https://peepstrategy.com/what-is-target-audience-for-e-learners/?webview_progress_bar=1&show_loading=0

E-learning accessibility - Research and Development Working Group WIKI. (n.d.). https://www.w3.org/WAI/RD/wiki/E-learning_Accessibility?f_link_type=f_inlinenote&webview_progress_bar=1&show_loading=0

E-Learning. (n.d.). LinkedIn. https://www.linkedin.com/showcase/skills-e-learning/?show_loading=0&webview_progress_bar=1

E-Learning vs Traditional Training: A Cost-Effectiveness Analysis. (2023, January 16). https://bookboonlearning.com/blog/ld-budget/e-learning-vs-traditional-training-a-cost-effectiveness-analysis/?show_loading=0&webview_progress_bar=1

Eclassopedia. (2023, July 24). *The importance of personalized learning in the digital age*. https://eclassopedia.com/the-importance-of-personalized-learning-in-the-digital-age/?show_loading=0&webview_progress_bar=1

Edgar, F. (2019, October 5). *Elearning Industry - How Well Do You Know About your Target Audience?* https://www.linkedin.com/pulse/elearning-industry-how-well-do-you-know-your-target-frank-edgar?show_loading=0&webview_progress_bar=1

elearn Magazine: The Rock Stars of eLearning: An interview with Clark Quinn. (n.d.). https://elearnmag.acm.org/archive.cfm?aid=2465423&webview_progress_bar=1&show_loading=0

ELearning videos: The complete guide. (n.d.). Digital Learning Institute. https://www.digitallearninginstitute.com/blog/elearning-videos-the-complete-guide?show_loading=0&webview_progress_bar=1

Elearning Voice over - Generate engaging voice overs for e-learning. (n.d.). https://murf.ai/voiceover/elearning

Erathi, N. (2014, April 5). *Differentiated instruction and e learning [Slide show]*. SlideShare. https://www.slideshare.net/slideshow/differentiated-instruction-and-e-learning/33167778

Ewa. (2024, September 8). *We make learning happen*. Snabbfoting. We Make Learning Happen. https://snabbfoting.se/en/

Fatima, B. (2023, November 7). *Navigating Peer-to-Peer Learning: Methods, perks and challenges [Infographic]*. https://blog.commlabindia.com/elearning-design/peer-to-peer-learning-ways-infographic?webview_progress_bar=1&show_loading=0

Ferriman, J. (2023, February 2). *7 Benefits of E-Learning Videos*. LearnDash. https://www.learndash.com/7-benefits-of-e-learning-videos/?webview_progress_bar=1&show_loading=0

Fleiss, A. (2023, March 31). *How do I choose a good learning platform? Rebellion Research.* https://www.rebellionresearch.com/how-do-i-choose-a-good-learning-platform?show_loading=0&webview_progress_bar=1

Four incredible benefits of global collaboration. (2024, January 31). https://edtechimpact.com/news/four-incredible-benefits-of-global-collaboration/?show_loading=0&webview_progress_bar=1

Giaro, M. (2023, August 19). *How to pick the right online course platform: The 6 crucial criteria you should look for*. Medium. https://medium.com/swlh/how-to-pick-the-right-online-course-platform-the-6-crucial-criteria-you-should-look-for-11f5523d5982?show_loading=0&webview_progress_bar=1

Gillanders, R., Karazi, S., & O'Riordan, F. (2020). Loss aversion as a motivator for engagement with peer assessment. *Innovations in Education and Teaching International*, 57(4), 424–433.

Global collaboration in the classroom: working together for a better world – Digital Education. (n.d.). https://iteach4future.org/blog/global-collaboration-in-the-classroom-working-together-for-a-better-world/?webview_progress_bar=1&show_loading=0

Gökçearslan, S., Tosun, C., & Erdemir, Z. G. (2024). Benefits, challenges, and methods of artificial intelligence (AI) chatbots in education: A systematic literature review. *International Journal of Technology in Education*, 7(1), 19–39.

Gordana, U. (2024, January 19). *23 Benefits of Personalized online learning: Master your education*. Alt Gov. https://altgov2.org/benefits-of-personalized-online-learning/?webview_progress_bar=1&show_loading=0

Halkiopoulos, C., & Gkintoni, E. (2024). Leveraging AI in e-learning: Personalized learning and adaptive assessment through cognitive neuropsychology—A systematic analysis. *Electronics (Basel)*, 13(18), 3762.

Harman, J. (2021, January 10). *Diving into Deeper Learning with Dr. Patti Shank. Leading Learning.* https://www.leadinglearning.com/episode-213-deeper-learning-patti-shank/?webview_progress_bar=1&show_loading=0

Harry, C. (2023, December 12). *E-learning Market Growth Statistics & Trends.* Storm6. https://storm6.io/resources/industry-insights/e-learning-market-growth-statistics-trends/?show_loading=0&webview_progress_bar=1

Hashemi-Pour, C., & Lutkevich, B. (2024, June 26). *What is e-learning? Importance, benefits and use cases*. WhatIs. https://www.techtarget.com/whatis/definition/Web-based-training-e-learning?show_loading=0&webview_progress_bar=1

Heal, J. (2023, January 5). *Balancing Teacher-Led instruction and Student-Centered learning*. Edutopia. https://www.edutopia.org/article/teacher-led-instruction-student-centered-learning?show_loading=0&webview_progress_bar=1

Hehir, D. (2024, February 28). *Collaborative learning and how you can use it in E-Learning*. Capytech. https://capytech.com/en/blog/collaborative-learning-and-how-you-can-use-it-in-e-learning/?webview_progress_bar=1&show_loading=0

Hill, A. (2024, March 18). *Effective feedback: How to gather and deliver feedback through eLearning*. ELM Learning. https://elmlearning.com/blog/feedback-elearning/?show_loading=0&webview_progress_bar=1

Holman, K., Marino, M. T., Vasquez, T., Taub, M., Hunt, J. H., & Tazi, Y. (2024). Navigating AI-Powered Personalized Learning in Special Education: A Guide for Preservice Teacher Faculty. *Journal of Special Education Preparation*, 4(2), 90–95.

Holmes, J. (n.d.). *Continuous Assessment and Feedback: Benefits of Learning with a Teacher*. foreign-language-teachers.com. https://www.foreign-language-teachers.com/personalized-learning-continuous-assessment-and-feedback?show_loading=0&webview_progress_bar=1

Home | Moodle.org. (n.d.). https://moodle.org/?auto_signin=true&webview_progress_bar=1&show_loading=0

Home page - Unity Environmental University. (2024, August 1). Unity Environmental University. https://unity.edu/

Hood, R. (2023, April 13). *Exploring the benefits and impacts of personalized learning in eLearning*. Medium. https://medium.com/@hussain2023/exploring-the-benefits-and-impacts-of-personalized-learning-in-elearning-9b6a87b2f01c

How do you evaluate and compare different LMS pricing models and plans? (2023, March 28). www.linkedin.com. https://www.linkedin.com/advice/1/how-do-you-evaluate-compare-different-lms-pricing?show_loading=0&webview_progress_bar=1

How do you integrate video and audio with other online learning tools and platforms? (2024, March 27). www.linkedin.com. https://www.linkedin.com/advice/0/how-do-you-integrate-video-audio-other-online?webview_progress_bar=1&show_loading=0

How to enhance and strengthen collaborative e-learning environments. (n.d.). https://kinescope.io/blog/how-to-enhance-and-strengthen-collaborative-e-learning-environments?webview_progress_bar=1&show_loading=0

How to identify your target audience for eLearning program? (n.d.). https://www.e-learningpartners.com/blog/how-to-identify-your-target-audience-for-elearning-program-or-online-course?show_loading=0&webview_progress_bar=1

Huntsberry, W. (2014, November 25). *Is Digital Learning more Cost-Effective? Maybe not.* NPR. https://www.npr.org/sections/ed/2014/11/25/366401940/is-digital-learning-more-cost-effective-maybe-not?webview_progress_bar=1&show_loading=0

Hurley, L. (2024, July 5). *Benefits of eLearning.* Learnopoly. https://learnopoly.com/benefits-of-elearning/?show_loading=0&webview_progress_bar=1

Hurley, L. (2024a, May 18). *What is Hybrid Learning?* Learnopoly. https://learnopoly.com/what-is-hybrid-learning/?webview_progress_bar=1&show_loading=0

Hurley, L. (2024b, July 5). *Benefits of eLearning.* Learnopoly. https://learnopoly.com/benefits-of-elearning/?webview_progress_bar=1&show_loading=0

Jose, J., & Jose, B. J. (2024). Educators' Academic Insights on Artificial Intelligence: Challenges and Opportunities. *Electronic Journal of e-Learning*, 22(2), 59–77.

Juan, M. (2016). *5 Features You Need to Consider When Choosing an Online Learning Platform.* PC Mag. https://www.pcmag.com/news/5-features-you-need-to-consider-when-choosing-an-online-learning-platform?webview_progress_bar=1&show_loading=0

Kapp, K. (2021, June 7). *A Conversation with Clark Aldrich -Part One.* Karl Kapp. https://karlkapp.com/a-conversation-with-clark-aldrich-part-one/?webview_progress_bar=1&show_loading=0

Kim, K., & Kwon, K. (2024). Designing an Inclusive Artificial Intelligence (AI) Curriculum for Elementary Students to Address Gender Differences With Collaborative and Tangible Approaches. *Journal of Educational Computing Research*, 62(7), 1837–1864.

Kiwi. (2024, July 29). *Self-Paced Learning: Meaning & Benefits.* Kiwi LMS. https://startkiwi.com/blog/self-paced-learning-meaning-benefits/?webview_progress_bar=1&show_loading=0

Knowledge Hub Media. (2023, September 11). *The Benefits of Structured instruction in Education.* Knowledge Hub Media | Demand Generation Marketing. https://knowledgehubmedia.com/the-benefits-of-structured-instruction-in-education/?webview_progress_bar=1&show_loading=0

Kondrat, B. S. (n.d.). *5 Best Peer to Peer learning Platforms in 2024.* https://www.educate-me.co/blog/best-peer-to-peer-learning-platforms?webview_progress_bar=1&show_loading=0

Koravuna, S., & Surepally, U. K. (2020, September). Educational gamification and artificial intelligence for promoting digital literacy. In *Proceedings of the 2nd International Conference on Intelligent and Innovative Computing Applications* (pp. 1-6).

Kulkarni, A. (2020, November 3). *Benefits of using Videos in eLearning.* https://www.linkedin.com/pulse/benefits-using-videos-elearning-ajinkya-kulkarni?webview_progress_bar=1&show_loading=0

Kurtić, V., Bikić, N., & Durmiš, E. K (2024). Enhancing Students'confidence and Understanding in Probability Through ChatGPT: An Analysis of Ai's Impact on Learning Experiences.

Lamar Online. (2017, October 3). What are the benefits of Teacher-Led Schools? Lamar. https://degree.lamar.edu/online-programs/education/med-teacher-leadership/general-concentration/benefits-of-teacher-led-schools/?show_loading=0&webview_progress_bar=1

Lampropoulos, G. (2023). Augmented reality and artificial intelligence in education: Toward immersive intelligent tutoring systems. In *Augmented reality and artificial intelligence: The fusion of advanced technologies* (pp. 137–146). Springer Nature Switzerland.

Laney, K. (2023) *What Is Multimodal Learning? 35 Strategies and Examples to Empower Your Teaching.* Prodigy https://www.prodigygame.com/main-en/blog/multimodal-learning/?f_link_type=f_inlinenote&show_loading=0&webview_progress_bar=1

Leading Learning Podcast. (n.d.). https://leadinglearning.libsyn.com/leading-learning-podcast-episode-213-patti-shank?webview_progress_bar=1&show_loading=0

Learning, E. L. M. (2024, August 5). How to create Well-Designed Interactive eLearning. https://elmlearning.com/blog/design-interactive-elearning/?webview_progress_bar=1&show_loading=0

Learning, E. L. M. (2024, August 5). *How to create Well-Designed Interactive eLearning*. https://elmlearning.com/blog/design-interactive-elearning/?webview_progress_bar=1&show_loading=0

Learnnovators, & Learnnovators. (2020, May 17). *CATHY MOORE – CRYSTAL BALLING WITH LEARNNOVATORS*. Learnnovators. https://learnnovators.com/blog/cathy-moore-crystal-balling-with-learnnovators/?webview_progress_bar=1&show_loading=0

Lee, H. (2024). Examining the Effectiveness of Personalized Learning Through Artificial Intelligence (Doctoral dissertation, Indiana University).

Lee, H. (2024). Examining the Effectiveness of Personalized Learning Through Artificial Intelligence (Doctoral dissertation, Indiana University).

Lee, U., Jeong, Y., Koh, J., Byun, G., Lee, Y., Lee, H., & Kim, H. (2024). I see you: Teacher analytics with GPT-4 vision-powered observational assessment. *Smart Learning Environments*, 11(1), 48.

Lee, U., Jeong, Y., Koh, J., Byun, G., Lee, Y., Lee, H., & Kim, H. (2024). I see you: Teacher analytics with GPT-4 vision-powered observational assessment. *Smart Learning Environments*, 11(1), 48.

Limited, C. G. (2021, June 30). *Benefits of personalisation in eLearning*. https://www.linkedin.com/pulse/benefits-personalisation-elearning-comeandsee-global-limited?webview_progress_bar=1&show_loading=0

LinkedIn Learning. (n.d.). *Online Learning Platform for Businesses*. LinkedIn Learning. https://learning.linkedin.com/?webview_progress_bar=1&show_loading=0

LinkedIn Learning: online training courses & skill building. (n.d.). https://www.linkedin.com/learning?webview_progress_bar=1&show_loading=0

Litmos. (n.d.). *Clark Quinn, Ph.D.* https://www.litmos.com/blog/author/clark-quinn?webview_progress_bar=1&show_loading=0

"Living, breathing" education: an interview with Craig Weiss. (2013, July 25). https://oeb.global/oeb-insights/living-breathing-education-an-interview-with-craig-weiss/?webview_progress_bar=1&show_loading=0

Long, P. B. L. (2022, March 8). *Transparency in learning and Teaching: Small changes, big impact*. https://blogs.iu.edu/citl/2022/03/08/transparency-in-learning-and-teaching-small-changes-big-impact/?webview_progress_bar=1&show_loading=0

M, D. (2022, June 27). *Advantages of personalized learning.* https://www.linkedin.com/pulse/advantages-personalized-learning-dhanush-m?show_loading=0&webview_progress_bar=1

Mansaray, S. (2024, August 30). *The best online learning platforms in 2024.* Explore the eLearning World With Us. https://www.ispringsolutions.com/blog/best-online-learning-platforms?webview_progress_bar=1&show_loading=0

Marco, Y. (2022, December 19). *The importance of identifying your target audience in online course creation.* Medium. https://medium.com/@yassinmarco/the-importance-of-identifying-your-target-audience-in-online-course-creation-b1c14907993e?webview_progress_bar=1&show_loading=0

Marco, Y. (2022b, December 23). *The key factors to consider when choosing an online course platform.* Medium. https://medium.com/@yassinmarco/the-key-factors-to-consider-when-choosing-an-online-course-platform-6794b3de1281?webview_progress_bar=1&show_loading=0

Mishra, D., Bakhronova, D., & Djalilova, U. (2023b). *Activity-Based Learning: an analysis to teach learners using online methodologies.* In Studies in computational intelligence (pp. 163–171). DOI: 10.1007/978-981-19-6450-3_17

Moodle. (2022, October 7). *E-learning Co., Ltd.* https://www.e-learning.asia/service/moodle/?webview_progress_bar=1&show_loading=0

Moodle. (n.d.). *eLearning Learning.* https://www.elearninglearning.com/moodle/?show_loading=0&webview_progress_bar=1

Moore, C. (2011, July 5). *Checklist for strong learning design. Training Design.* Cathy Moore. https://blog.cathy-moore.com/checklist-for-strong-elearning/?show_loading=0&webview_progress_bar=1

Mozafaripour, S. (2024, March 20). *Benefits of Online learning – 16 Advantages to Learning online.* University of St. Augustine for Health Sciences. https://www.usa.edu/blog/benefits-of-online-learning/?webview_progress_bar=1&show_loading=0

Okpoho, S. (2022, December 19). *5 Advantages of setting up a secure and friendly ELearning environment.* Gopius. https://gopius.com/friendly-elearning-environment/?webview_progress_bar=1&show_loading=0

Okpoho, S. (2023, April 6). *The Best of audio and video in E-Learning: A Must Know.* Gopius. https://gopius.com/audio-and-video-in-e-learning/?webview_progress_bar=1&show_loading=0

Online, L. (2017, October 3). *What are the benefits of Teacher-Led Schools? Lamar.* https://degree.lamar.edu/online-programs/education/med-teacher-leadership/general-concentration/benefits-of-teacher-led-schools/?show_loading=0&webview_progress_bar=1

Online classes for creatives. Skillshare. (n.d.). https://www.skillshare.com/en/?show_loading=0&webview_progress_bar=1

Online courses, training and tutorials on LinkedIn Learning. (n.d.). LinkedIn. https://www.linkedin.com/learning/search?show_loading=0&webview_progress_bar=1

Orlando, J. (2018, October 22). *Continuous assessments for better learning.* The Teaching Professor. https://www.teachingprofessor.com/topics/online-teaching-and-learning/grading-feedback-online-learning/continuous-assessments-for-better-learning/?show_loading=0&webview_progress_bar=1

Owen, R. (n.d.). *Teacher-Led Instruction: What it is and How to Implement it in Your Classroom.* eduwinnow.com. https://www.eduwinnow.com/classroom-resources-teacher-led-instruction?show_loading=0&webview_progress_bar=1

Paes, H. (2024, February 18). *The concrete benefits of social collaborative learning.* Medium. https://medium.com/@hemersonpaes/the-concrete-benefits-of-social-collaborative-learning-6935324cf186?show_loading=0&webview_progress_bar=1

Patti, S. (2007). *Online Learning Idea Book: 95 Proven Ways to Enhance Technology-Based and Blended Learning* (1st ed.). Barnes & Noble., https://www.barnesandnoble.com/w/online-learning-idea-book-patti-shank/1100321641?show_loading=0&webview_progress_bar=1

Pros and Cons of traditional classroom learning. (2024, July 8). EducationalWave - Pros and Cons Explained. https://www.educationalwave.com/pros-and-cons-of-traditional-classroom-learning/?show_loading=0&webview_progress_bar=1

Ramirez, M. (2022, July 30). *Webinar Replay: 5 Steps to Stellar AI Voiceover for eLearning. WellSaid Labs.* https://wellsaidlabs.com/blog/replay-ai-voice-for-elearning/?show_loading=0&webview_progress_bar=1

Raymer, R. (2013). *The Rock Stars of eLearning: An interview with Patti Shank.* eLearn, 2013(6). DOI: 10.1145/2491560.2499129

Richardson, P. (2023, June 16). *The benefits of online learning: flexibility and access to education.* Medium. https://medium.com/@philrichardsonmail/the-benefits-of-online-learning-flexibility-and-access-to-education-9531697f2df4?webview_progress_bar=1&show_loading=0

Robinson, A. (n.d.). *What is hybrid learning? blended learning? understanding the models.* https://blog.prepscholar.com/what-is-hybrid-learning-blended-learning-models?webview_progress_bar=1&show_loading=0

Sandeep, R. (2023). *K-12 Education Benefits from Digital Accessibility.* codemantra. https://codemantra.com/k-12-education-benefits-from-digital-accessibility/?webview_progress_bar=1&show_loading=0

Scalise, K. (2007). Differentiated e-learning: five approaches through instructional technology. IJLT., 3. 169-182. DOI: 10.1504/IJLT.2007.014843

Schoolbox. (2024, January 19). *Continuous Feedback and Reporting with Schoolbox eLearning Tools.* https://schoolbox.education/feedback-and-reporting-elearning/?webview_progress_bar=1&show_loading=0

Shaheen, A. (2023, February 22). *The Benefits of Online Learning: Exploring the flexibility and accessibility of E-Learning and distance education.* https://www.linkedin.com/pulse/benefits-online-learning-exploring-flexibility-distance-shaheen?show_loading=0&webview_progress_bar=1

Shende, P. (2023, August 17). *E-learning Market Size, share, Growth, Trends Analysis, growth Potential & Forecast, 2022–2030.* Medium. https://medium.com/@poonam.shende23/e-learning-market-size-share-growth-trends-analysis-growth-potential-forecast-2022-2030-d4d5c3ee11b7

Singapore, T. M. (2021, February 5). *The benefits of structured teaching. Therapy Masters.* https://www.therapy-masters.com/post/the-benefits-of-structured-teaching?show_loading=0&webview_progress_bar=1

9700. *SkillShare courses [2024] | Learn Online | Class Central.* (2024, August 26). Class Central. https://www.classcentral.com/provider/skillshare

SkillShare Online Classes | Start Learning Today. (n.d.). Skillshare. https://www.skillshare.com/en/join/premium?show_loading=0&webview_progress_bar=1

Staff, C. (2024, May 23). *What is Coursera? Coursera.* https://www.coursera.org/articles/what-is-coursera?webview_progress_bar=1&show_loading=0

Staff, K. (2024, September 10). *Teacher-led reforms have a big advantage — Teachers.* Kappan Online. https://kappanonline.org/stanulis-cooper-dear-teacher-led-reforms-big-advantage/?webview_progress_bar=1&show_loading=0

Staff, T. (2022, January 20). *A useful framework for transparency in education.* TeachThought. https://www.teachthought.com/education/transparency-in-education/?show_loading=0&webview_progress_bar=1

Swaby, G. (2018, January 23). *Openness and transparency in online Education - Gordon Swaby - Medium*. Medium. https://medium.com/@gordonswaby/openness-and-transparency-in-online-education-267fd1bba1b6?show_loading=0&webview_progress_bar=1

Sylvester, T. (2023, May 22). *Mastering Interactive eLearning Design: Step-by-Step Guide*. Inventio Learning Designs, LLC. https://inventiolearningdesigns.com/interactive-elearning-design/?show_loading=0&webview_progress_bar=1

Tamm, S. (2023, July 11). *10 Major Advantages of E-Learning*. E-Student. https://e-student.org/advantages-of-e-learning/?webview_progress_bar=1&show_loading=0

Teacher-Led approach. (n.d.). *Multiple Means of Instruction: All-inclusive Learning*. http://multiplemeansofinstruction.weebly.com/teacher-led-approach.html?webview_progress_bar=1&show_loading=0

Team, G. (n.d.). *What is hybrid learning?* GoGuardian. https://www.goguardian.com/blog/what-is-hybrid-learning?webview_progress_bar=1&show_loading=0

Technavio. (2024, September 12). *E-learning market Forecast & Growth Analysis*. Technavio, https://analysis.technavio.org, All Right Reserved 2024. https://analysis.technavio.org/e-learning-industry-analysis-research?webview_progress_bar=1&show_loading=0

Technologies, T. (n.d.). *Twenty benefits of Digital Learning*. https://www.trigyn.com/insights/20-benefits-digital-learning?webview_progress_bar=1&show_loading=0

The advantages of social and collaborative e-Learning. (n.d.). https://traineasy.net/blog/63/the-advantages-of-social-and-collaborative-e-learning?webview_progress_bar=1&show_loading=0

The Benefits of Structured Instruction in Education. (2023). https://resources.industrydive.com/the-benefits-of-structured-instruction-in-education?webview_progress_bar=1&show_loading=0

The story of Action Mapping and its creation by Cathy Moore. (n.d.). Training Design - Cathy Moore. https://blog.cathy-moore.com/action-mapping-creation-by-cathy-moore/?show_loading=0&webview_progress_bar=1

Tiwary, A. V. (2020, February 4). *5 Reasons Why Online Education is More Cost Effective*. https://www.linkedin.com/pulse/5-reasons-why-online-education-more-cost-effective-tiwary?webview_progress_bar=1&show_loading=0

Top 10 Benefits of E-Learning For Students and Educators. (n.d.). https://snatika.com/single-blog/top-10-benefits-of-e-learning-for-students-and-educators?webview_progress_bar=1&show_loading=0

Top e-learning courses - Learn e-learning online. (n.d.). Coursera. https://www.coursera.org/courses?query=e-learning&webview_progress_bar=1&show_loading=0

Top Five Factors to consider when choosing a learning platform. (2019) https://moodle.com/news/top-five-factors-to-consider-when-choosing-a-learning-platform/?show_loading=0&webview_progress_bar=1

Top Online+education Courses - Learn Online+education Online. (n.d.). Coursera. https://www.coursera.org/courses?query=online%2Beducation&show_loading=0&webview_progress_bar=1

Toxigon. (2024, September 8). *How to choose the best online learning platform in 2024.* Toxigon. https://toxigon.com/how-to-choose-online-learning-platform?webview_progress_bar=1&show_loading=0

Transparent Teaching. (2022, May 25). Teach Online | Miami University. https://sites.miamioh.edu/teach-online/what-is-transparent-teaching/?webview_progress_bar=1&show_loading=0

Velora Studios, L. L. C. https://velora.com. (n.d.). *Top 10 things to look for when choosing the perfect online course platform.* Heights Platform. https://www.heightsplatform.com/blog/top-10-things-to-look-for-when-choosing-the-perfect-online-course-platform?show_loading=0&webview_progress_bar=1

Verda, P. (2024, August 8). *Find your target audience for education: a quick 6-Step guide.* MedCerts. https://medcerts.com/blog/find-your-target-audience-for-education-a-quick-6-step-guide?webview_progress_bar=1&show_loading=0

5. *ways students benefit from global collaboration.* (2023, May 4). ISTE. https://iste.org/blog/5-ways-students-benefit-from-global-collaboration?webview_progress_bar=1&show_loading=0

What are the benefits and challenges of social and collaborative learning in e-learning? (2023, May 17). www.linkedin.com. https://www.linkedin.com/advice/0/what-benefits-challenges-social-collaborative?webview_progress_bar=1&show_loading=0

What are the key factors to consider when choosing a training platform or tool? (2023, March 15). www.linkedin.com. https://www.linkedin.com/advice/0/what-key-factors-consider-when-choosing-training?show_loading=0&webview_progress_bar=1

What is Hybrid Learning? (n.d.). Continu. https://www.continu.com/elearning-glossary/hybrid-learning?webview_progress_bar=1&show_loading=0

Willoughby-Petit, P. (2023, December 19). *Activity-based learning for software.* Learning Lab LMS LXP. https://www.thelearning-lab.com/blog-elearning-platform/activity-learning-software?webview_progress_bar=1&show_loading=0

Willoughby-Petit, P. (2023a, May 25). *Peer-To-Peer Learning — Learning Lab LMS LXP.* Learning Lab LMS LXP. https://www.thelearning-lab.com/blog-elearning-platform/peer-to-peer-learning?webview_progress_bar=1&show_loading=0

Writer, E. G. (2018, May 17). *How to enable online global collaboration in your learning environment.* Medium. https://medium.com/@edmodo_staff/how-to-enable-online-global-collaboration-in-your-learning-environment-8725e30581e7

Yogyata, & Yogyata. (2024, July 23). *How eLearning Saves More Time than ILT? [5 Proven Ways Explained].* https://blog.commlabindia.com/elearning-design/elearning-time-saving-against-ilt?show_loading=0&webview_progress_bar=1

Young, N. (2024, March 22). *Structured Learning: Transforming education for behavioral challenges.* Teachfloor. https://www.teachfloor.com/elearning-glossary/structured-learning?webview_progress_bar=1&show_loading=0

Chapter 10
Exploring Faculty Research Engagement:
A Cultural Perspective at Maritime Institutions for Achieving Sustainable Development Goals

Froilan Delute Mobo
https://orcid.org/0000-0002-4531-8106
Philippine Merchant Marine Academy, Philippines

Roldan C. Cabiles
Bicol University Open University, Philippines

ABSTRACT

The mission of the Commission for Higher Education (CHED) is to assist in the development of a quality community that can address the social, political, economic, cultural, and ethical problems that impede the nation's human growth and ability to compete internationally. Additionally, it adopts a vertical typology within each horizontal type as well as a horizontal typology based on the functional differentiation of HEIs about service to the nation. The study was conducted at the Central Luzon College of Science and Technology, Philippines during the 1st Semester of Academic Year, 2023-2024. The respondents of the study were 80 fulltime and part-time faculty. The researcher recommends that the faculty maintain high standards in terms of conducting research to comply with international standards.

DOI: 10.4018/979-8-3693-8242-4.ch010

INTRODUCTION

The mission of the Commission for Higher Education (CHED) is to assist in the development of a quality community that can address the social, political, economic, cultural, and ethical problems that impede the nation's human growth and ability to compete internationally. Additionally, it adopts a vertical typology within each horizontal type as well as a horizontal typology based on the functional differentiation of HEIs about service to the nation.

The Commission has been strongly advocating for a stronger focus on research among HEIs. The 1996 National Higher Education Research Agenda (NHERA) outlines the objectives of higher education research as well as the procedures and specific actions that must be taken to carry them out by actively participating in community outreach, research, and education. As a result, faculty personnel at higher education institutes (HEI) are also responsible for producing and sharing information through the publication of journals and community outreach initiatives.

It would be helpful to learn if faculty from higher education institutions (HEIs) will take the initiative to perceive the institution's efforts to increase research productivity as well as their capacity to take on the challenge. Higher education faculty members are expected to be the primary producers of research and community outreach involvement in their institutions. The importance of faculty engagement in research and community extension will lead to considerations of the structures and leadership necessary to change institutional policies and practices relating to integration and facilitate collaboration between local and international community participants. Another important aspect of faculty involvement in research, instruction, and community extension is CHED's institutional accreditation as a Center of Development or Center of Excellence.

Under CMO No. 46's 2012 Policy Standard to Enhance Quality Assurance (QA) in Philippine Higher Education Through an Outcomes-Based and Typology Approach, Article V, Section 23.3, requires faculty members with relevant degrees in their areas of specialization as required by CHED to participate in research and development activities in their respective disciplines as evidenced by refereed publications and other scholarly publications.

Scholarly outputs of faculty must be published in a highly reputable refereed journal that is indexed in major databases such as EBSCO, ASEAN CITATION INDEX (ACI), ISI Thompson Reuters, DOAJ, SINTA, Scopus, Web of Science, PASUC, and CHED-accredited journals, per reference in the Joint Circular Memorandum between the Commission on Higher Education and the Department of Budget and Management series of 2022.

The Civil Service Commission (CSC) also agreed to approve the Model Merit System for Faculty Members of State Universities and Colleges (SUC) and Local Colleges and Universities (LCUs) with Resolution Number 05-1404 dated October 6, 2005, that pertains to the involvement of faculty in research and community extension.

Faculty members are required to be involved in three different areas: instruction, research, and community extension.

Research is a crucial part of college accreditation. Sansone & Harackiewicz referenced Maslow and Herzberg's motivational theory as the study's theoretical foundation. According to this theory, people would look for alternatives to satisfy their perceived needs when such needs are not met. It could be important to meet some of their unique demands to motivate teachers to pursue research. They also emphasized that it is expected of most faculty members to succeed in their pursuits of research, teaching, and service.

Lack of funding, a lack of library resources, a lack of time, and poor organizational support were some of the challenges experienced by faculty members. Sometimes, internal urges and the desire for rewards from the outside world compel people to take action.

The primary goal of this study was to evaluate the level of faculty participation and motivational strategies for research at the Central Luzon College of Science and Technology. It attempted to respond to the following:

Statement of the Problem

1. What is the level of research preparedness faculty in terms of the identification of the problem, designing a method, analyzing and interpreting data, up to the recommendation for future studies
2. What is the level of research capabilities of faculty.
3. Is there a significant relationship between the research preparedness and capabilities of the participants.
4. how may the level of perceived preparedness and capabilities of the respondents in working with research ethics be describe

Conceptual/Theoretical Framework

The research study approach served as the foundation for the research project. This capability approach is typically thought of as a dynamic and multifunctional framework as opposed to a precise theory of well-being (Qizilbash 2008; Robeyns 2005, 94–96; Sen 1992; 2009). are both used to refer to the same idea in the literature, while the latter is frequently understood to refer more precisely to Nussbaum's incomplete theory of justice. 'Capabilitarianism' is a phrase that some philosophers have begun to use (Robeyns 2016; Nielsen and Axelsen 2017).

The conceptual framework showing the relationship of the study shown in Figure 1

Figure 1. The conceptual framework of the study

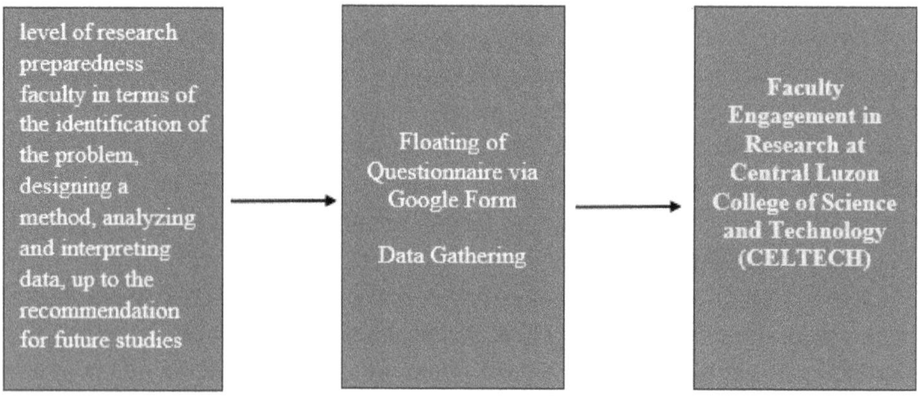

| level of research preparedness faculty in terms of the identification of the problem, designing a method, analyzing and interpreting data, up to the recommendation for future studies | → | Floating of Questionnaire via Google Form

Data Gathering | → | Faculty Engagement in Research at Central Luzon College of Science and Technology (CELTECH) |

Materials and Methods

The study was conducted at the Central Luzon College of Science and Technology, Philippines during the 1st Semester of Academic Year, 2023-2024. The respondents of the study were 80 fulltime and part-time faculty. Quantitative research design will be utilized achieving objectivity, control, and precise measurement, Leavy (2022). The study used a questionnaire consisting of four parts. It was an adopted questionnaire from the study of Manlapaz et al. (2020), titled "RESEARCH PREPAREDNESS AND CAPABILITIES OF ITED STUDENTS AND FACULTY Research Preparedness and Capabilities of ITEd Students and Faculty". For data collection, the researcher took the necessary consent and permits to transact with the groups and organizations concerned: the researcher coordinated with the Senior Vice President and Director for Academics, Training, Research, and Extension to request permission to conduct research through email.

Results and Discussion

This part presents and discusses the findings of the study. It includes the level of research preparedness faculty in terms of the identification of the problem, designing a method, analyzing and interpreting data, up to the recommendation for future studies.

Level of Research Preparedness

The level of research preparedness faculty in terms of the following: (1) identifying the background of the problem and an overview. (2) identifying the significance or importance of the study; (3) setting the objectives; (4) searching for and using related literature and the study

Figure 2. Identifying the Problem

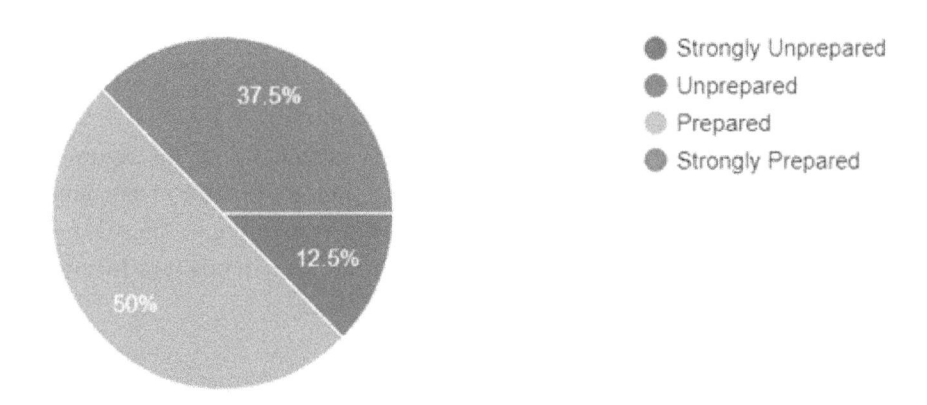

It can be gleaned from the table that the highest percentage of the figure is 50% and is described as "prepared." This result may indicate that the respondents are somehow prepared in terms of the following identifying the background of the problem and an overview. Moreover in the study of (Pangket et al., 2023), these difficulties, along with the challenges usually faced in the research reporting process, make it challenging to complete research successfully completed.

Figure 2: Designing a method

Figure 3. Designing a method

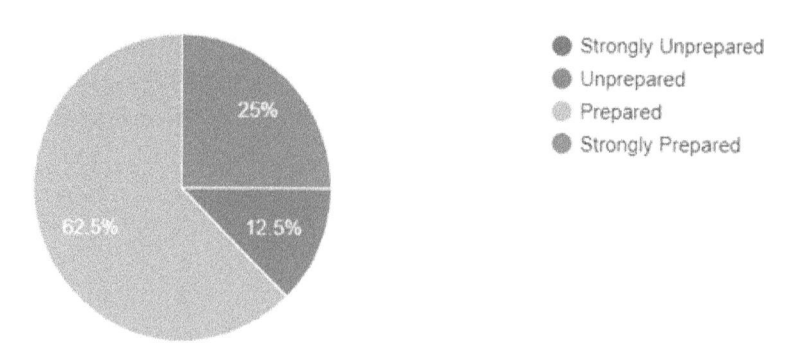

[Pie chart: 62.5% Prepared, 25% Unprepared, 12.5% Strongly Prepared; legend: Strongly Unprepared, Unprepared, Prepared, Strongly Prepared]

It can be gleaned from the table that the highest percentage of the figure is 62.5% and is described as "prepared." This result may indicate that the respondents are somehow prepared in terms of designing a method. According to the study of Sileyew (2020), the research approach also supports the researcher on how to come across the research result findings.

Figure 4. Analyzing data

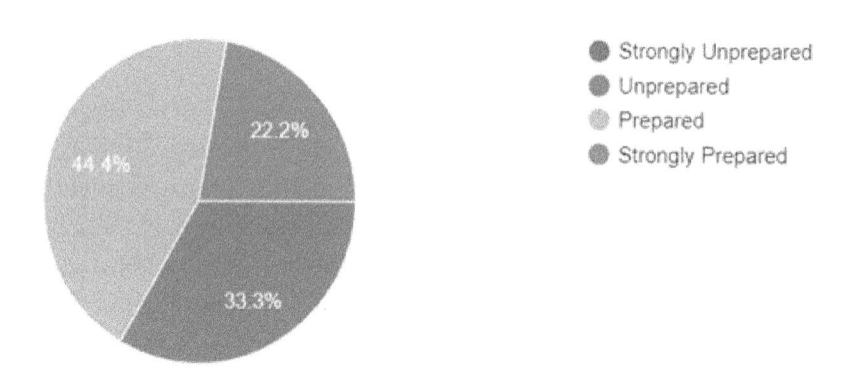

[Pie chart: 44.4%, 22.2%, 33.3%; legend: Strongly Unprepared, Unprepared, Prepared, Strongly Prepared]

It can be gleaned from the table that the highest percentage of the figure is 44.4% and is described as "prepared." This result may indicate that the respondents are somehow prepared in terms of analyzing the data. According to the study by Catzon (2023), how to analyze and extract true meaning from our business's digital insights is one of the primary drivers of success.

Figure 5. Interpreting data

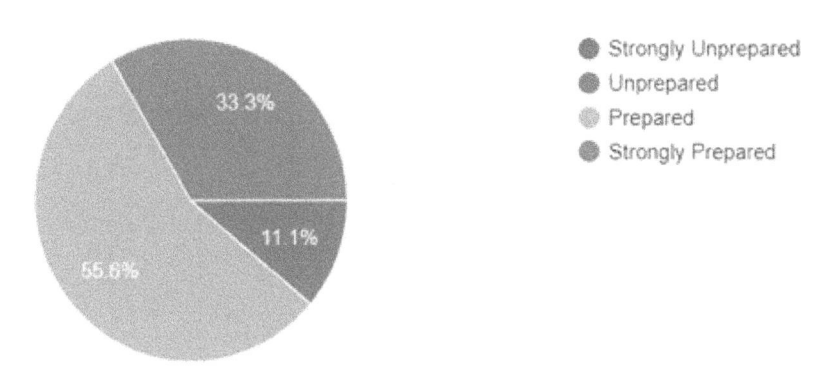

It can be gleaned from the table that the highest percentage of the figure is 55.6% and is described as "prepared." This result may indicate that the respondents are somehow prepared in terms of interpreting the data. According to the study by Kulkarni (2016), it is not only useful to understand the data behavior but also to choose the different statistical tests to be applied.

Figure 6. Formulating a conclusion and a recommendation

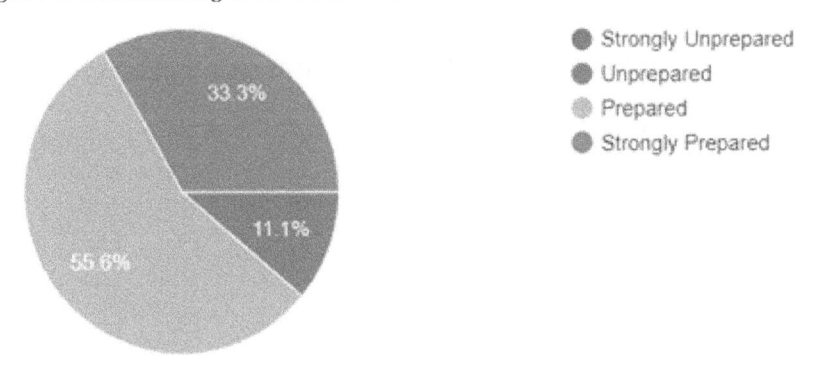

It can be gleaned from the table that the highest percentage of the figure is 55.6% and is described as "prepared." This result may indicate that the respondents are somehow prepared in terms of formulating a conclusion and a recommendation. According to the study by Nieto (2012), Based on our critical synthesis of the literature, in what follows, we briefly address what we see as positive future directions in four broad areas: teacher preparation for diversity.

Capabilities:

Figure 7. I have effective access to information and the skills therein.

It can be gleaned from the table that the highest percentage of the figure is 66.7% and is described as "agree." This result may indicate that the respondents somehow have effective access to information and skills. According to the study by Lefever et al. (2006), online surveys can access large and geographically distributed populations and achieve quick returns.

Figure 8. My training in conducting an interview with a resource person is sufficient.

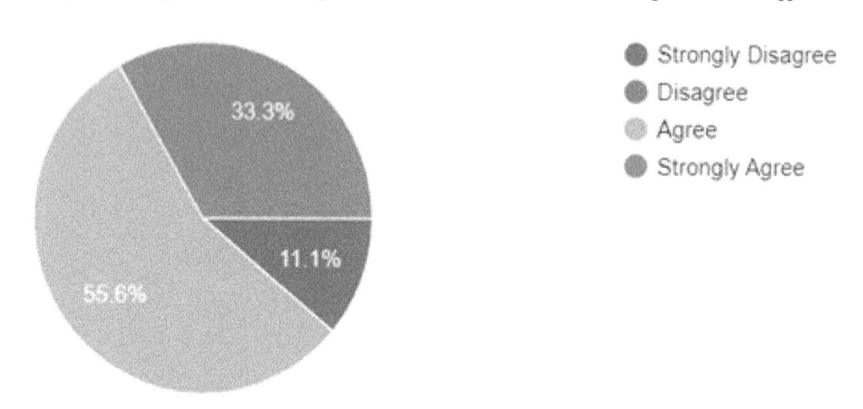

It can be gleaned from the table that the highest percentage of the figure is 55.6% and is described as "agree." This result may indicate that the respondents somehow have training in conducting an interview with a resource person, which is sufficient.

According to the study by Rowley (2012), in order to start to develop their skills in the craft of interviewing.

Figure 9. I am good at technical writing

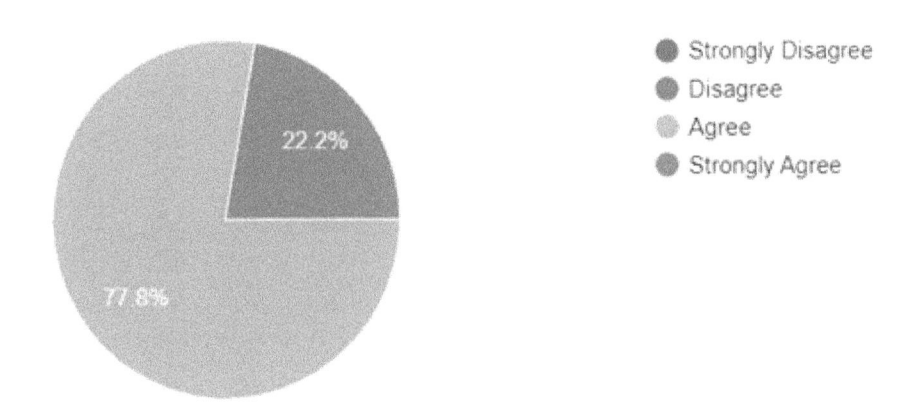

It can be gleaned from the table that the highest percentage of the figure is 77.8% and is described as "agree." This result may indicate that the respondents somehow believe that I am good at technical writing, which is sufficient. According to the study by Longo (1998), it can be constituted as an object of study according to five (of many possible) poststructural concepts.

Figure 10. I can perform statistical treatment of grouped and ungrouped data

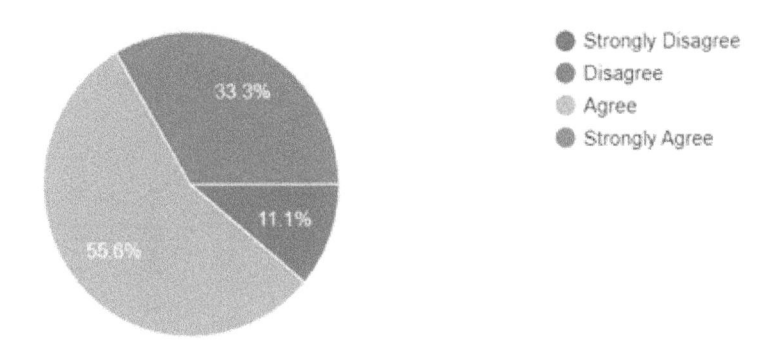

It can be gleaned from the table that the highest percentage of the figure is 55.6% and is described as "agree." This result may indicate that the respondents somehow believe that I can perform statistical treatment of grouped and ungrouped data.

According to the study by Bauer et al. (2008), this approach also permits one to formally determine the extent to which treatment effects vary over treatment groups and whether there is evidence that individuals within treatment groups become similar to one another.

Figure 11. I can decide on what kind of research design I am going to use

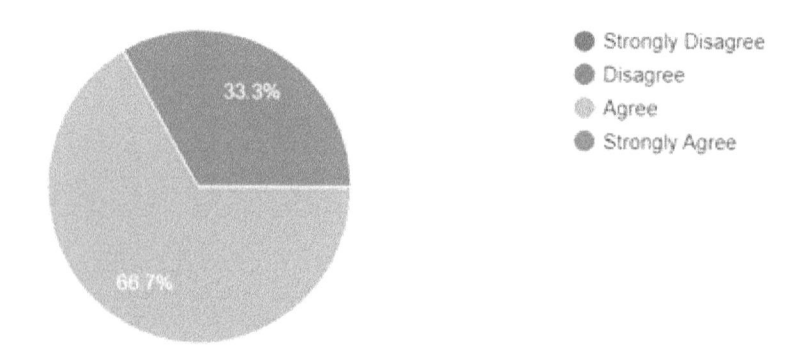

It can be gleaned from the table that the highest percentage of the figure is 66.7% and is described as "agree." This result may indicate that the respondents somehow believe that I can decide on what kind of research design I am going to use. According to the study by Bloomfield and Fisher (2019), how a researcher designs, structures, and implements a study can affect the research findings and is an important consideration regarding bias.

Figure 12. I know the difference between a conceptual and a theoretical framework by application

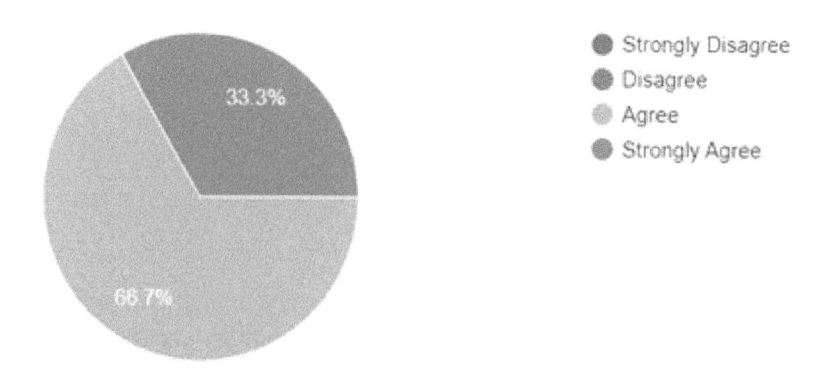

It can be gleaned from the table that the highest percentage of the figure is 66.7% and is described as "agree." This result may indicate that the respondents somehow believe that I know the difference between a conceptual and a theoretical framework by application. According to the study by Triandis (1995), a theoretical model that should prove helpful in keeping in mind, at one time, the major relationships among the key variables that define diversity and its consequences

Research Ethics

Figure 13. Truthfulness of mentioning the authors of a research paper are important as much as the findings.

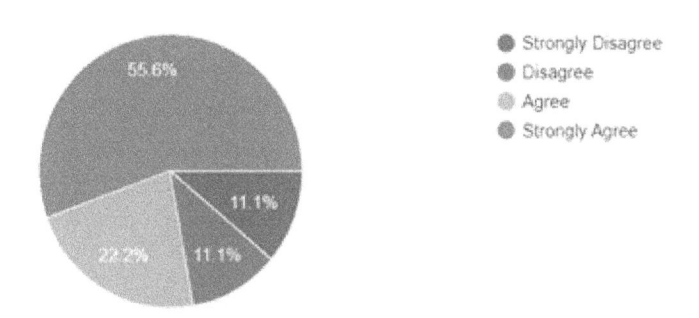

It can be gleaned from the table that the highest percentage of the figure is 55.6% and is described as "Strongly Agree." This result may indicate that the respondents somehow believe that the truthfulness of mentioning the authors of a research paper is as important as the findings. According to the study by Aksnes et al. (2019), citations reflect aspects related to scientific impact and relevance, although with important limitations..

Figure 14. The purpose of citations is to acknowledge the original authors

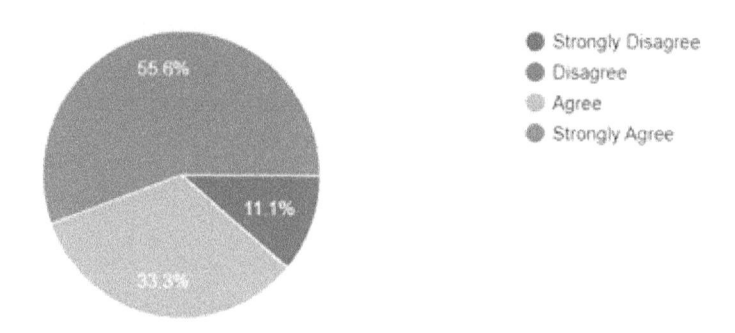

It can be gleaned from the table that the highest percentage of the figure is 55.6% and is described as "Strong Agree." This result may indicate that the respondents somehow believe that the purpose of citations is to acknowledge the original authors. According to the study by Aksnes et al. (2019), citations reflect aspects related to scientific impact and relevance, although with important limitations.

Figure 15. A researcher should not fabricate the findings of the study

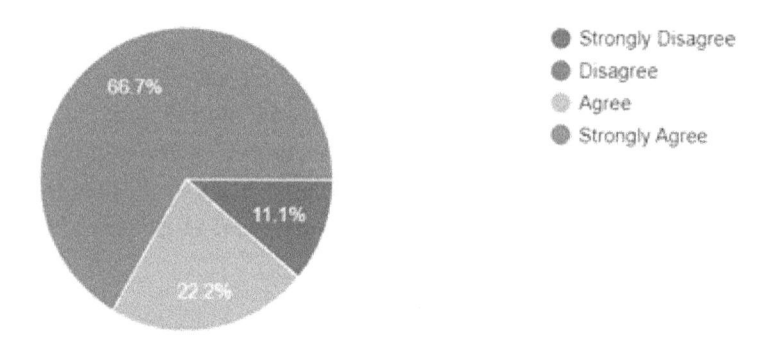

It can be gleaned from the table that the highest percentage of the figure is 66.7% and is described as "strong agree." This result may indicate that the respondents somehow believe that a researcher should not fabricate the findings of the study. According to the study by Lazer et al. (2018), fake news has a long history, but we focus on unanswered scientific questions raised by the proliferation of its most recent, politically oriented incarnation.

CONCLUSION

In conclusion, faculty that are highly involved in research are ready to conduct a research study. The results of faculty members in research preparation and capabilities are positively following international standards based on their institutional research mandates, indicating that their focus is on delivering quality research outputs that are publishable in a reputable journal indexed in Web of Science, Scopus, and ACI. The researchers concluded that faculty members are capable and ready to conduct research and are aware of the ethical standards of the research guidelines, which can be part of the research directions of the maritime institution towards achieving the sustainable development goal through education 5.0.

RECOMMENDATIONS

The researcher recommends that the faculty maintain high standards in terms of conducting research to comply with international standards, which are aligned with Education 5.0 and attain the goal of sustainable development.

REFERENCES:

Aksnes, D. W., Langfeldt, L., & Wouters, P. (2019). Citations, Citation Indicators, and Research Quality: An overview of basic concepts and theories. *SAGE Open*, 9(1), 215824401982957. DOI: 10.1177/2158244019829575

Bauer, D. J., Sterba, S. K., & Hallfors, D. D. (2008). Evaluating Group-Based interventions when control participants are ungrouped. *Multivariate Behavioral Research*, 43(2), 210–236. DOI: 10.1080/00273170802034810 PMID: 20396621

Bloomfield, J., & Fisher, M. J. (2019). Quantitative research design. *JARNA*, 22(2), 27–30. https://search.informit.org/doi/10.3316/informit.738299924514584. DOI: 10.33235/jarna.22.2.27-30

Calzon, B. (2023). *What is data analysis? Methods, techniques, types & how-to*. BI Blog | Data Visualization & Analytics Blog | Datapine. https://www.datapine.com/blog/data-analysis-methods-and-techniques/

Kulkarni, D. K. (2016). Interpretation and display of research results. *Indian Journal of Anaesthesia*, 60(9), 657. DOI: 10.4103/0019-5049.190622 PMID: 27729693

Lazer, D., Baum, M., Benkler, Y., Berinsky, A. J., Greenhill, K. M., Menczer, F., Metzger, M. J., Nyhan, B., Pennycook, G., Rothschild, D., Schudson, M., Sloman, S. A., Sunstein, C. R., Thorson, E., Watts, D. J., & Zittrain, J. (2018). The science of fake news. *Science*, 359(6380), 1094–1096. DOI: 10.1126/science.aao2998 PMID: 29590025

Leavy, P. (2022). *Research Design: Quantitative, Qualitative, Mixed Methods, Arts-Based, and Community-Based Participatory Research Approaches*. Guilford Publications.

Lefever, S., Dal, M., & Matthíasdóttir, Á. (2006). Online data collection in academic research: Advantages and limitations. *British Journal of Educational Technology*, 38(4), 574–582. DOI: 10.1111/j.1467-8535.2006.00638.x

Longo, B. (1998). An approach for applying cultural study theory to technical writing research. *Technical Communication Quarterly*, 7(1), 53–73. DOI: 10.1080/10572259809364617

Manlapaz, C. J., & Villanueva, M. M. (2020). RESEARCH PREPAREDNESS AND CAPABILITIES OF ITED STUDENTS AND FACULTY Research preparedness and Capabilities... ResearchGate. https://www.researchgate.net/publication/344328481_RESEARCH_PREPAREDNESS_AND_CAPABILITIES_OF_ITED_STUDENTS_AND_FACULTY_Research_Preparedness_and_Capabilities_of_ITEd_Students_and_Faculty?_tp=eyJjb250ZXh0Ijp7ImZpcnN0UGFnZSI6Il9kaXJlY3QiLCJwYWdlIjoicHJvZmlsZSIsInBvc2l0aW9uIjoicGFnZUNvbnRlbnQifX0

Nielsen, L., & Axelsen, D. (2017). Capabilitarian Sufficiency: Capabilities and Social Justice. *Journal of Human Development and Capabilities*, 18(1), 46–59. DOI: 10.1080/19452829.2016.1145632

Nieto, S. (2012). *Conclusion and recommendations.* https://bilingualreview.utsa.edu/index.php/AMAE/article/view/123

Pangket, W. F., Pangesfan, S. K. K., Cayabas, J. P., & Madjaco, G. L. (2023). Research writing readiness of graduate students in a Philippine state college. International Journal of Learning. *Teaching and Educational Research*, 22(4), 141–159. DOI: 10.26803/ijlter.22.4.9

Qizilbash, M. (2008), "Amartya Sen's capability view: insightful sketch or distorted picture?", in: Comim, Qizilbash and Alkire (eds.), pp. 53–81. DOI: 10.1017/CBO9780511492587.003

Robeyns, I. (2003). Sen's Capability Approach and Gender Inequality: Selecting Relevant Capabilities. *Feminist Economics*, 9(2/3), 61–92. DOI: 10.1080/1354570022000078024

Rowley, J. (2012). Conducting research interviews. *Management Research Review*, 35(3/4), 260–271. DOI: 10.1108/01409171211210154

Sen, A. (1974). Informational Bases of Alternative Welfare Approaches: Aggregation and Income Distribution. *Journal of Public Economics*, 3(4), 387–403. DOI: 10.1016/0047-2727(74)90006-1

Sileyew, K. J. (2020). Research design and methodology. In *IntechOpen eBooks*. https://doi.org/DOI: 10.5772/intechopen.85731

Triandis, H. C. (1995). A theoretical framework for the study of diversity. In *SAGE Publications, Inc. eBooks* (pp. 11–36). DOI: 10.4135/9781452243405.n2

Chapter 11
Facilitating Global Partnerships for Knowledge Sharing by Mediating Role of Digital Platforms in Achieving SDG 17 in Ethiopia

Shashi Kant
https://orcid.org/0000-0003-4722-5736
Bule Hora University, Ethiopia

Metasebia Adula
https://orcid.org/0000-0001-5732-2850
Bule Hora University, Ethiopia

Tamire Ashuro
https://orcid.org/0009-0001-0029-6863
Bule Hora University, Ethiopia

ABSTRACT

In the context of SDG 17, this study looks at how digital platforms might support international collaborations for knowledge exchange. Surveying a sample of 400 participants—this included international organization officials, development practitioners, and policymaker. The study employed both exploratory factor analysis (EFA) and confirmatory factor analysis (CFA) techniques to determine the principal aspects that underlie the utilization of digital platforms for international knowledge exchange.

DOI: 10.4018/979-8-3693-8242-4.ch011

The data's appropriateness for factor analysis was evaluated using Bartlett's test of sphericity and the Kaiser-Meyer-Olkin (KMO) measure of sampling adequacy. After that, SEM, was used to investigate the mediating function of digital platforms. The study's conclusions give development organizations, governments, and digital platform providers with insightful information on how to use digital technologies to promote international cooperation and knowledge sharing, which will eventually assist the larger objectives of sustainable development.

INTRODUCTION

In the framework of accomplishing the Sustainable Development Goals (SDGs), digital platforms play a critical role in fostering international partnerships for knowledge exchange in an increasingly linked world. SDG 17 is one of these objectives that highlights the value of partnerships for sustainable development and the necessity of cross-sector and cross-national cooperation. Ethiopia, a country endowed with abundant natural riches and a diverse culture, finds itself at a pivotal juncture. The incorporation of digital technology can act as a catalyst for international collaboration and information sharing, helping the country boost its socio-economic growth (Ibidunni, 2024). The idea of mediating relationships through digital platforms came forth as a result of the late 20th-century discussion on information technology and knowledge management. Academics are becoming more aware of how digital tools might help to overcome organizational and geographic barriers to enable real-time communication and teamwork. Research shows that nations that use digital platforms to exchange knowledge have seen increases in innovation, better governance, and more active communities. But there are several obstacles in Ethiopia's way of realizing these advantages, including as poor infrastructure, a lack of internet connectivity, and disparities in the country's population's degree of digital literacy (Dzhunushalieva & Teuber, 2024).

Although the future seems bright, Ethiopia has a number of real-world obstacles that prevent it from fully utilizing digital platforms for SDG 17. Inadequate legislative frameworks, socioeconomic inequality, and political instability are among the problems that impede productive knowledge exchange and cooperation. Furthermore, the nation's digital divide widens the gap among rich and poor, making it harder for marginalized people to access services and information. These difficulties highlight the necessity for a sophisticated comprehension of the best ways to incorporate digital platforms into Ethiopia's development plan (Schorr et al., 2021). By examining the relationship among digital platforms and international relationships in the Ethiopian context, this chapter seeks to close research gaps that currently exist. It will look at how these platforms may be used strategically to get over real-world obstacles and promote a more inclusive method of sharing information. This chapter will assist future scholars and legislators in developing policies that foster cooperation and promote sustainable development by summarizing the empirical research that has already been done, pointing out best practices, and offering doable suggestions. In the end, it aims to provide light on how Ethiopia may accomplish SDG 17 and become a role model for other countries pursuing comparable objectives in the digital era.

BACKGROUND OF THE STUDY

With a population of more than 120 million, Ethiopia is a country distinguished by its rich cultural heritage and significant historical legacy. Notwithstanding its potential, the nation confronts formidable obstacles to sustainable growth, which are made worse by complicated political issues and socioeconomic divides. In order to solve these issues, the Sustainable Development Goals (SDGs) of the United Nations, especially SDG 17, place a strong emphasis on partnerships and encourage cooperation among the public and private sectors. Given this, digital platforms play an ever-more-important role since they provide creative ways to encourage cooperation and information exchange amongst different parties (David et al., 2021). Digital platforms that facilitate knowledge sharing are emerging in tandem with the global trend towards the digital economy, wherein information technology is revolutionizing conventional means of communication and cooperation. By facilitating the interchange of knowledge, ideas, and resources, these platforms help stakeholders collaborate more successfully. Adoption of digital tools may promote inclusive development, empower local people, and improve information access in Ethiopia. Realizing the full potential of these platforms is hampered by the nation's still-developing digital environment, which is characterized by uneven infrastructure, low internet penetration, and disparate degrees of digital literacy (Kant & Adula, 2024).

Research shows that effective collaborations utilizing digital platforms have produced better results in a number of fields, such as agriculture, health, and education. Research suggests that nations with strong digital platforms for information exchange also have more innovative and robust governing systems. Nevertheless, there is still much to learn about using these discoveries in the Ethiopian setting. Previous studies frequently fail to take into account the distinct socio-cultural and economic elements that impact digital involvement within the nation. This disparity emphasizes the need for a targeted examination of Ethiopia's potential to leverage digital platforms to promote international collaboration and further its development objectives (Adula et al., 2023). The situation is further complicated by real-world issues including political unpredictability, financial limitations, and a dearth of appropriate policy frameworks. These elements make it more difficult to create long-lasting digital ecosystems that promote productive cooperation and information exchange. In order to create enduring relationships that support the SDGs, Ethiopia must address these issues. Through an analysis of the interactions among international collaborations and digital platforms, this research aims to provide light on the processes that might help Ethiopia get over these obstacles and use technology to further sustainable development (Jabo et al., 2024). In conclusion, the study's backdrop highlights the crucial role that internet platforms play in facilitating international collaborations for Ethiopian knowledge exchange. This research aims to contribute to the broader discourse on sustainable development by contextualizing the opportunities and challenges within Ethiopia's unique landscape. It will also provide insightful information for future researchers and policymakers navigating the complexities of digital engagement in Ethiopia.

STATEMENT OF THE PROBLEM

The aim of promoting partnerships for the goals, which is Sustainable Development aim 17 that Ethiopia aspires to fulfill, emphasizes the ideal state of a linked, cooperative approach to development. According to this perspective, digital platforms play a crucial role in facilitating information exchange, allowing a variety of stakeholders to work together productively across institutional and geographic borders. But there is a clear difference among this ideal and Ethiopia's actual situation today. Evidence suggests that despite the potential advantages of digital platforms, their use for establishing relationships is still patchy and uneven. Important inconsistencies arise in the literature when studies show that certain implementations have been effective in other settings but are unable to reproduce comparable outcomes in Ethiopia's distinct socio-cultural and economic environment (Guyo et al., 2023). Furthermore, there are a number of gaps in the study that prevent a thorough knowledge of the potential and problems related to digital platforms in Ethiopia. First, there are theoretical gaps since the unique socio-political dynamics of Ethiopian society are not sufficiently taken into account by many of the frameworks created for the analysis of digital partnerships. This gap makes it more difficult for these ideas to be applied in local situations, leading to conflicting findings about how well digital technologies promote partnerships. Moreover, there are still gaps in our understanding of the real-world experiences local stakeholders have while using digital platforms because most of the research is based on stories from around the world that might not accurately represent local circumstances (Dereso et al., 2023).

Contextual gaps exacerbate the situation by obscuring Ethiopia's particular struggles, which include socioeconomic inequality, a lack of digital literacy, and infrastructure deficiencies, in general talks about digital involvement. A lack of supporting legislative frameworks that can foster an inclusive digital environment and restricted access to technology for excluded communities are two practical issues resulting from these considerations. As a result, these obstacles hinder the formation of long-lasting collaborations that have the potential to propel the SDGs closer to reality (Durga et al., 2024). In order to close these gaps, this study offers a thorough investigation of the ways in which digital platforms might be used to support international collaborations for Ethiopian knowledge transfer. The research will enhance comprehension of the obstacles and possibilities by placing the results in the context of the nation's distinct socio-political and economic environment. Moreover, it will provide policymakers and practitioners with practical advice to help those craft policies that advance digital inclusion and strengthen cooperative endeavors (Panigrahi et al., 2023). By filling up these gaps in the literature, this study will also serve as a guide for future scholars, promoting more investigation into the complex interaction among digital platforms and sustainable development in Ethiopia. It seeks to stimulate innovative initiatives that may successfully harness the potential of digital tools for creating collaborations and accomplishing sustainable development goals by highlighting the need for customized solutions and localized methods.

THEORETICAL FOUNDATION

A number of theories offer a fundamental framework for comprehending the dynamics at work when examining the role that digital platforms play in promoting international partnerships for information exchange. The "Social Capital Theory," which holds that trust, norms, and social networks encourage cooperation among people and groups, is one relevant theory. Building social capital through digital platforms helps improve cooperation among different stakeholders in Ethiopia, such as local communities, NGOs, and government agencies. By utilizing these networks, digital technologies may promote partnerships—which are crucial for reaching Sustainable Development Goal 17—by fostering information exchange and helping to establish trust (Kant & Adula, 2024). "Diffusion of Innovations Theory" is another pertinent theoretical paradigm. This theory clarifies the ways in which new concepts and innovations move both inside and among communities. It is important to comprehend the elements that impact the adoption of digital platforms in Ethiopia. This entails investigating the ways in which technological preparedness, cultural attitudes, and the perceived advantages of digital tools influence their adoption. Using this idea, researchers may pinpoint adoption roadblocks and create plans that facilitate the efficient spread of digital technology to aid in the formation of partnerships (Nyoach et al., 2024).

"Constructivism" is another important concept in this discussion. Constructivist philosophy places emphasis on the social construction of knowledge through community interactions. This theory emphasizes the value of participatory approaches to knowledge exchange in the setting of digital platforms. Ethiopia can guarantee that digital projects are tailored to the unique requirements of varied groups and that they are culturally appropriate by including local stakeholders in their creation and execution. In order to foster a sense of ownership and promote active participation in partnerships, this participatory element is crucial (Asefa et al., 2023). Furthermore, "Collaborative Governance Theory" sheds light on the workings of multi-stakeholder participation methods. According to this notion, cooperation among different governmental sectors and levels is necessary for good governance. Leveraging digital platforms might help promote more inclusive decision-making processes in Ethiopia, where traditional governance institutions frequently meet difficulties. This idea emphasizes how crucial it is to set up official channels for cooperation in order to guarantee that all opinions are heard and that collaborations are just and long-lasting (Kant & Adula, 2024).

Last but not least, comprehending the differences in access to digital technology requires a comprehension of the "Digital Divide Theory." This idea tackles the disparity, which is frequently caused by socioeconomic considerations, among those who have easy access to digital technologies and those who do not. In order to guarantee that underprivileged groups in Ethiopia are included in the process of exchanging information, it is imperative that the digital gap be addressed. Researchers will better comprehend the obstacles preventing fair access to digital platforms and offer solutions that support inclusion by including this idea into their investigation (Ufua et al. (2021). When taken as a whole, these theories offer a thorough framework for examining the intricate interactions that exist in Ethiopia among global alliances and digital platforms. Through the use of these theoretical frameworks, the research will acquire a more profound understanding of the mechanisms that either support or impede efficient information exchange and cooperation. This knowledge will guide suggestions for policy and useful tactics meant to improve the contribution of digital platforms to the attainment of sustainable development objectives in the Ethiopian setting.

DEFINITION AND ORIGIN OF CONCEPTS

"Digital platforms" are online platforms that allow users to communicate with one other and exchange goods, services, and information. Social media networks, teamwork tools, online stores, and knowledge-sharing websites are a few examples of these platforms. The Latin word *plataforma*, which denotes a level surface or stage, is where the word "platform" first appeared. Within the digital realm, it developed in the latter half of the 20th century when technology started to facilitate intricate user interactions, progressing from basic webpages to intricate networks that foster cooperation and creativity. Digital platforms are now essential in many industries, acting as channels for information exchange and building alliances among international networks (Qureshi et al., 2021). The process by which people or organizations share knowledge, thoughts, and experience in order to promote cooperation and improve understanding is known as "knowledge sharing." It includes both formal and informal approaches, such as chats and organized training sessions. The idea of information sharing originated with knowledge management techniques in the 1990s, which highlighted the importance of learning and collective intelligence in businesses. The phrase has become more widely used in academic discourse throughout time, especially since globalization and technological developments have accelerated and facilitated the sharing of knowledge (Ufua et al., 2021)

The United Nations created the "Sustainable Development Goals (SDGs)" in 2015 as a collection of 17 interconnected global objectives with the purpose of addressing urgent social, economic, and environmental issues by 2030. Every objective has particular benchmarks and metrics to track development. The Millennium Development Goals (MDGs), which predominantly targeted underdeveloped nations, are where the SDGs got their start. With an emphasis on partnerships, inclusion, and environmental stewardship, the SDGs expanded this focus to encompass fairness and sustainability for all countries. The SDGs are now a global framework for development that influences tactics and policies all across the world (Nyoach et al., 2024). The networks, social norms, and social trust that promote collaboration and group action within a community are referred to as "social capital." It highlights how important social cohesiveness and relationships are to reaching both individual and group objectives. The work of sociologists like Pierre Bourdieu and Robert Putnam helped popularize the phrase in the late 20th century. The idea was first proposed by Bourdieu in the framework of social theory, and it gained popularity via Putnam's examination of civic participation and community development. Social capital is an important tool for cooperation and partnership in Ethiopia, especially in settings where mutual support and trust are critical for growth (Dereso et al., 2023).

Empirical Literature Review in Detail in Paragraph Forms

Global Partnerships and Knowledge Sharing

According to research, social cohesiveness, economic growth, and creativity all depend on efficient knowledge sharing. Ibidunni, (2024) conducted a well-known research that highlights the contribution that collaborative networks have to improving knowledge transfer within businesses. According to their results, partnerships—especially those that make use of digital tools—can result in better outcomes across a range of industries, including technology, health, and education. Moreno-Serna et al.'s systematic study from 2020 emphasizes the value of information sharing even more in accomplishing sustainable development goals. The authors contend that, especially in poor nations, collaborations cultivated through digital platforms can improve access to vital data and resources. Numerous case studies are summarized in this paper to show how digital cooperation has facilitated successful projects in fields including community development and disaster response. The research emphasizes how digital platforms may help varied stakeholders connect with one another and share knowledge and experience, which is essential for tackling complex global issues. Empirical research has started to examine the unique dynamics of information exchange via digital platforms in the Ethiopian environment. For example, Ufua et al.'s research paper from 2021 looks at how social media affects community involvement and information sharing in Ethiopia's rural areas. The results show that social media platforms have developed into essential resources for local communities to exchange knowledge on health, education, and agricultural methods. This study emphasizes how digital platforms have the capacity to empower underrepresented groups and promote inclusive engagement in knowledge exchange.

Even yet, there are still a lot of obstacles Ethiopia faces when trying to use international alliances for knowledge exchange. According to a research by Wang et al. (2024), socioeconomic inequality, poor internet infrastructure, and low levels of digital literacy are some of the obstacles that prevent people from effectively participating in knowledge-sharing projects. Their study highlights the need for focused initiatives to address these issues, such investments in infrastructure to increase internet access and training programs to improve digital skills. These results are consistent with the larger body of research on the digital divide, which emphasizes the significance of mitigating inequalities in order to provide fair access to opportunities for knowledge-sharing. Furthermore, research indicates a significant information vacuum about the contextual elements influencing international collaborations' capacity for knowledge exchange. Fewer research have looked at how local cultural, political, and economic settings affect the dynamics of partnership-building, despite the fact that many studies concentrate on the mechanics of cooperation. According to a meta-analysis by Ufua et al. (2021), successful partnerships must be customized to the particulars of each setting; a one-size-fits-all strategy to digital cooperation is insufficient. This finding necessitates more investigation into the unique sociocultural and economic contexts of nations such as Ethiopia in order to make sure that knowledge-sharing programs are applicable and effective.

Global Partnerships and Digital Platforms

Digital platforms have a tremendous influence on cross-border cooperation, as evidenced by an influential research by Moreno-Serna et al. (2020) that shows how these technologies improve communication and coordination among foreign partners. According to their results, digital platforms facilitate the formation of successful collaborations among firms by lowering transaction costs and streamlining procedures. Ufua et al. (2021) additional study delves into the particular methods by which digital platforms facilitate collaboration. Their study identifies key elements that contribute to the success of partnerships, including real-time communication technologies, data sharing capabilities, and collaborative project management systems. They draw the conclusion that digital platforms not only allow information exchange but also create trust and involvement among partners, eventually leading to effective collaborations in the sectors of health and education. Notwithstanding these encouraging results, the research also identifies important difficulties with digital platforms in partnership settings. Barriers include differences in digital literacy, technical inequities, and worries about data security and privacy, according to a thorough analysis by Ibidunni (2024). Despite the enormous potential of digital platforms, their study shows that these issues might erode confidence and participation, especially in developing nations. This emphasizes the necessity of focused initiatives to raise digital literacy and provide safe, fair access to digital resources.

Empirical research is starting to clarify the unique dynamics of digital collaborations in the Ethiopian environment. For instance, a research by Serna & Chaparro (2021) examines how digital platforms are used in agricultural partnerships and finds that farmer, cooperative, and agricultural organization collaboration has much improved thanks to these technologies. The study demonstrates how farmers may obtain market data, exchange optimal techniques, and synchronize their endeavors using digital networks, so augmenting their production and resilience. The report does point out that the full realization of these advantages is still hampered by issues with infrastructure and restricted internet access. Furthermore, scholarly works underscore the significance of contextual elements in molding the efficacy of digital collaborations. Successful digital partnerships, according to a meta-analysis by Li et al. (2023), must take local cultural, economic, and political factors into consideration. According to their results, collaborations that adjust to the particularities of their surroundings—like including local leaders and comprehending community needs—tend to be more powerful and long-lasting. This necessitates a thoughtful approach to digital platform design that puts inclusion and local participation first.

Digital Platforms and Knowledge Sharing

Zhang and Li's fundamental study from 2019 looks on how digital platforms help companies share knowledge, especially in the areas of research and education. According to their findings, social media, collaborative wikis, and online forums all greatly improve information availability, encourage group learning, and stimulate creativity. Digital platforms facilitate real-time engagement and resource sharing, allowing users to harness collective intelligence – an essential tool for problem-solving and decision-making. Moreno-Serna et al. (2020) are doing more study to examine the efficacy of particular digital platforms for knowledge exchange in enterprises. The study underscores the significance of platforms such as Microsoft Teams and Slack in dismantling organizational barriers and fostering cross-functional cooperation. The authors show via a number of case studies that these technologies help businesses make the most of their intellectual assets by supporting knowledge retention and distribution in addition to facilitating communication. According to the research, digital platforms' usability and design have a significant impact on how well they promote information exchange. On the other hand, a review by Serna & Chaparro (2021) points out important difficulties in using digital platforms for knowledge exchange. According to their investigation, there are a number of obstacles that might prevent successful interaction, including the digital gap, security concerns, and information overload. The authors contend that whereas digital platforms offer consumers never-before-seen access to information, they can also overload them, making it harder for them to separate useful information from noise. This research emphasizes how important it is to have efficient information management plans in addition to digital technologies so that users may successfully negotiate the challenges of knowledge sharing.

The literature also clarifies the contextual elements affecting how well digital platforms for knowledge exchange work. According to a research by Kumar et al. (2021), leadership and organizational culture have a significant impact on how digital tools are adopted and used. According to their findings, companies have a higher chance of using digital platforms for knowledge exchange successfully if they cultivate an environment of transparency and cooperation. This emphasizes how important it is to match corporate principles and practices with technology projects in order to optimize effect. New research has started looking into how digital platforms might improve knowledge exchange across different stakeholders in the Ethiopian environment. For instance, Kumar et al. research project from 2021 looks at the use of mobile applications in the spread of agricultural information. According to their results, farmers may now exchange best practices and market insights more easily because to digital platforms' substantial improvement in agricultural information availability. However, the study also draws attention to issues that might obstruct efficient information exchange, such as rural communities' low digital literacy and restricted internet access. Furthermore, study on the scalability and durability of digital platforms for knowledge exchange is needed, according to the literature. According to a meta-analysis by Li et al. (2023), knowledge of these platforms' long-term effects is crucial for guiding practice and policy. The authors support long-term research projects that evaluate the consequences of digital tool evolution for knowledge ecosystems as well as how they change over time.

Global Partnerships, Knowledge Sharing and Digital Platforms

In a seminal research, Kumar et al. (2021) investigate how digital platforms function as middlemen in international collaborations, facilitating more efficient knowledge and resource sharing among companies in various industries. According to their study, there are many examples of how NGOs, governments, and academic institutions have benefited from cross-border connections made possible by platforms such as Google Drive and Zoom, which have improved project outcomes and produced creative solutions for difficult problems. Serna & Chaparro (2021) conduct a thorough investigation of the ways in which digital platforms promote knowledge exchange in international collaborations. They name crucial elements that promote engagement as being user-friendly interfaces, teamwork tools, and feedback mechanisms. Their results imply that platforms are more effective at encouraging knowledge sharing when they offer open communication channels and encourage active involvement. This emphasizes how crucial platform functionality and design are to facilitating productive cooperation across partners with various specialties and backgrounds.

Furthermore, research indicates that trust is critical to digital collaborations. Liu and Zhang's (2022) study looks on the ways in which digital platforms might improve trust among international partners. According to their research, elements like peer reviews, user ratings, and secure communication methods help foster trust in digital contexts. According to the authors, building trust is essential to promoting information sharing since it increases the likelihood of collaboration among partners who have faith in the honesty and dependability of the platform and its users. Even with these encouraging results, there are still obstacles to overcome when using digital platforms to share information in international collaborations. Significant impediments include the digital divide, disparities in digital literacy, and worries about data protection, according to a review by Li et al. (2023). According to their study, involvement may be hampered by differences in access and capacity, especially in poor nations, even if digital platforms can promote the exchange of information. This emphasizes the necessity of focused initiatives to increase technology accessibility and boost digital literacy in order to enable all parties to participate fully in partnerships.

Particular studies conducted within the Ethiopian setting provide additional insight into the benefits and constraints associated with digital platforms for knowledge exchange. For instance, a study by Serna & Chaparro (2021) looks at the use of digital technologies in agricultural partnerships and discovers that farmers can now exchange vital resources and information thanks to apps like Facebook and WhatsApp. Nevertheless, they also point out that poor internet penetration and infrastructure constraints continue to be major obstacles to efficient information exchange. Their conclusions highlight how important it is to deal with these issues in order to properly utilize digital platforms for strengthening collaborations. The research also emphasizes how crucial contextual elements are in determining how well digital platforms for knowledge exchange work. According to a meta-analysis by Li et al. (2023), creating successful digital collaborations requires an awareness of local socio-cultural dynamics. In order to promote meaningful involvement and cooperation, the authors contend that platforms need to be flexible enough to accommodate local circumstances, taking into consideration things like cultural norms, language difficulties, and community needs.

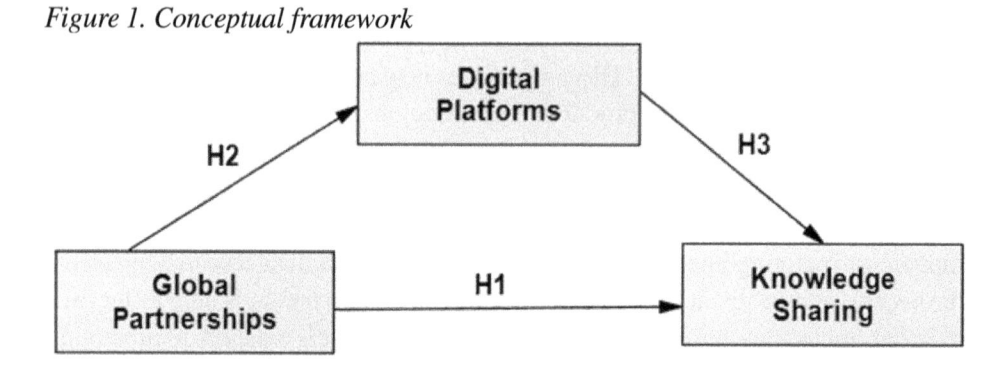

CONCEPTUAL FRAMEWORK

Figure 1. Conceptual framework

RESEARCH METHODOLOGY

The study utilized a quantitative methodology to investigate how digital platforms contribute to international collaborations for knowledge exchange. Using a stratified random selection approach, a sample size of 390 respondents was chosen to guarantee representation from a range of stakeholder groups, such as government officials, representatives of non-governmental organizations, and community people engaged in knowledge-sharing activities. This methodology facilitated a thorough comprehension of the dynamics operating across many industries and circumstances. The study used Bartlett's test of sphericity and the Kaiser-Meyer-Olkin (KMO) measure of sample adequacy to evaluate the validity and reliability of the measurement scales. Given that the KMO value was higher than the suggested cutoff point of 0.6, the sample was deemed sufficient for factor analysis. The next step was to improve the measuring scales and determine the underlying structure of the data using Exploratory Factor Analysis (EFA). The EFA validated the suitability of the survey instrument's items by revealing many unique aspects pertaining to the concepts of digital platforms, knowledge sharing, and partnership effectiveness.

The study then used AMOS software to do Structural Equation Modeling (SEM) in order to examine the proposed correlations among the components. SEM made it possible to analyze several links at once, giving researchers a thorough understanding of how digital platforms facilitate knowledge exchange in international collaborations. The root mean square error of approximation (RMSEA) and comparative fit index (CFI), among other model fit indices, showed values that satisfied the requirements for a good model fit. These metrics showed an acceptable fit. The scale was developed in accordance with accepted practices, starting with a careful analysis of the literature to determine pertinent dimensions and items for every construct. The first scale was then tested in a pilot study, and adjustments were made in response to comments and statistical analysis. In order to guarantee both content and construct validity, the final survey instrument had verified items that represented important constructs. To summarise, this study employed a rigorous sampling approach in conjunction with rigorous quantitative methodologies to explore the mediating function of digital platforms in promoting international collaborations for knowledge exchange. A strong analytical framework was made possible by the use of KMO, EFA, and SEM, which helped to clarify the links among important concepts and advance knowledge of how digital platforms can enhance collaborative efforts in various contexts.

DATA ANALYSIS

Table 1. KMO and Bartlett's Test

Kaiser-Meyer-Olkin Measure of Sampling Adequacy.		.904
Bartlett's Test of Sphericity	Approx. Chi-Square	1318.865
	df	88
	Sig.	.000

Source: Authors

The results of the Bartlett's test of sphericity and the Kaiser-Meyer-Olkin (KMO) measure of sample adequacy are shown in Table 1, which was done to determine whether the data was suitable for factor analysis. A high degree of sample adequacy was indicated by the KMO value, which was determined to be 0.904. This implies that the data were appropriate for this statistical method and that the sample size was adequate for carrying out factor analysis. Furthermore, an estimated chi-square value of 1318.865 with 88 degrees of freedom and a significance level of 0.000 was obtained using Bartlett's test of sphericity. This finding further supports the appropriateness of component analysis for the dataset by showing that the correlation matrix differs considerably from an identity matrix. When taken as a whole, these results confirm the data's robustness and provide credence to the study's later exploratory factor analysis.

Table 2: Total Variance Explained

Component	Initial Eigenvalues			Extraction Sums of Squared Loadings			Rotation Sums of Squared Loadings		
	Total	% of Variance	Cumulative %	Total	% of Variance	Cumulative %	Total	% of Variance	Cumulative %
1	4.1	32.35	32.35	4.1	32.35	32.35	3.0	21.51	21.51
2	1.7	9.87	42.22	1.7	9.87	42.87	2.6	16.57	36.42
3	1.7	9.87	52.10	1.7	9.87	52.10	1.8	14.68	52.10

Extraction Method: Principal Component Analysis.
Source: Authors

The overall variation explained by the variables derived from Principal Component Analysis (PCA) is summarized in Table 2. Three components were found, according to the initial eigenvalues, the first of which had an eigenvalue of 4.1 and explained 32.35% of the variance in total. This shows that a sizable amount of the dataset's information is captured by the first component. When paired with the first factor, the second component's eigenvalue of 1.7, or 9.87% of the variance, increased the total percentage to 42.22%. With an eigenvalue of 1.7, the third component continues to contribute 9.87% of the variance, keeping the cumulative variance at 52.10%. To improve the components' interpretability, the rotation sums of squared loadings were computed after extraction. The rotation totals of the second and third components were changed to 2.6 and 1.8, respectively, whereas the rotation total of the first component was decreased to 3.0, which accounted for 21.51% of the variance. With a better structure among the elements, the underlying constructs could be interpreted more meaningfully, which was the goal of this rotation procedure. Overall, the study shows that the three extracted components account for more than half of the variation in the dataset as a whole, demonstrating that the factor analysis was successful in capturing the key elements of the constructs that were being studied. These results offer credence to the reliability of the measuring scales employed in the investigation and lay the groundwork for more research.

Confirmatory Principle Component Examination

Using a kind of statistics called confirmatory principle component analysis, the principle component arrangement of a collection of directed proxies is confirmed. By using CFA, investigators can assess hypotheses based on the underlying frame job and correlatives among observable proxies. Table 3 of the inquiry used CFA to assess the premise that there is a relationship among the proxies being guided and the latent notions that support them.

Table 3: Covariances

Covariance			Approximation	S.E.	C.R.	P	Hy.
Digital Platforms	<-->	Global Partnerships	.251	.018	8.675	.00	H2
Digital Platforms	<-->	Knowledge Sharing	.317	.027	7.316	.00	H3
Global Partnerships	<-->	Knowledge Sharing	.266	.031	7.574	.00	H1

Source: Authors

The covariances among the three main components that the study looked at—digital platforms, global partnerships, and knowledge sharing—are shown in Table 3. Global Partnerships and Digital Platforms are said to have a covariance of 0.251 and a standard error (S.E.) of 0.018. The statistical significance of the link among the two constructs is supported by the critical ratio (C.R.) of 8.675 and the p-value of 0.00, which point to a positive association. This supports Hypothesis 2 (H2). Likewise, it is demonstrated that there is a 0.317 covariance among Digital Platforms and Knowledge Sharing, with a 0.027 standard error. This relationship's

C.R. is 7.316, and its p-value is once more 0.00, indicating its importance and bolstering Hypothesis 3 (H3). According to this research, efficient digital channels are essential for improving information exchange among Lastly, the covariance among Global Partnerships and Knowledge Sharing is recorded at 0.266, with an S.E. of 0.031. The C.R. of 7.574 and a p-value of 0.00 further validate this relationship, supporting Hypothesis 1 (H1). This indicates that stronger global partnerships are associated with increased knowledge sharing. In the context of the study, these covariance results emphasize the interdependence of digital platforms, international collaborations, and knowledge sharing, underscoring their combined significance in promoting productive cooperation and information exchange.

Table 4: Validity Concern

	CR	AVE	MSV	MaxR(H)	GP	DP	KS
GP	0.72	0.63	0.29	0.82	**0.63**		
DP	0.78	0.67	0.12	0.73	0.11	**0.69**	
KS	0.73	0.63	0.24	0.77	0.33	0.13	**0.62**

Note: GP= Global Partnerships; DP= Digital Platforms; KS= Knowledge Sharing
Source: Authors

The study's constructs, Composite Reliability (CR), Average Variance Extracted (AVE), Maximum Shared Variance (MSV), and Maximum Reliability (MaxR(H)) for Global Partnerships (GP), Digital Platforms (DP), and Knowledge Sharing (KS), are the main subjects of Table 4's validity concerns. With GP scoring 0.72, DP at 0.78, and KS at 0.73, the Composite Reliability ratings show adequate levels of internal consistency across the constructs. These numbers show that the measurement scales are dependable since they are higher than the generally recognized cutoff point of 0.70. Each construct's Average Variance Extracted (AVE) values—GP at 0.63, DP at 0.67, and KS at 0.63—are likewise encouraging. Every AVE number is higher than the suggested threshold of 0.50, suggesting that a significant amount of variance in the indicators is captured by the respective constructs. The constructs' discriminant validity is revealed by the Maximum Shared Variance (MSV) values. The MSV is 0.24 for KS, 0.12 for DP, and 0.29 for GP. These values show that the constructs are different from one another and support the discriminant validity further since they are less than the AVE values for each respective construct. Lastly, the Maximum Reliability (MaxR(H)) values—GP at 0.82, DP at 0.73, and KS at 0.77—corroborate the reliability findings. For the purposes of this study, the constructs of global partnerships, digital platforms, and knowledge sharing are both valid and reliable, as demonstrated by the validity metrics that collectively strongly support the measurement model's robustness.

Mediating role Examination

Figure 2. Structure Equation Model

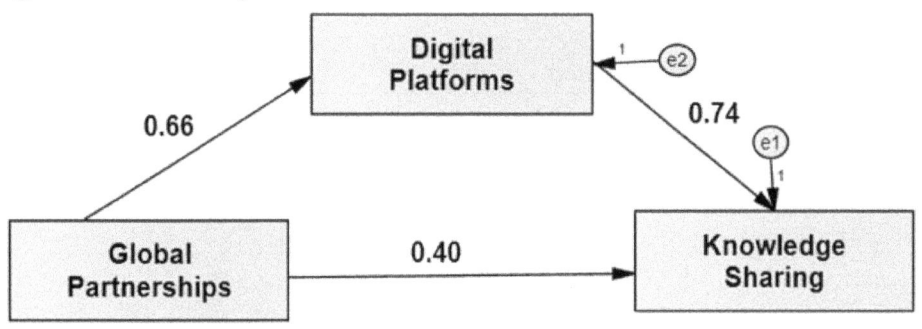

Model fit indices

Table 5: indices for Model Fit

Sig.	Chi-Sq	RMR	Fitness Goodness	Fitness Confirmatory	TLI	RMSEA
0.001	1.748	.029	0.911	0.910	0.905	.023

Source: Authors

The model fit indices are shown in Table 5, which offers a thorough evaluation of the suitability of the structural model. One frequent measure used to assess the model's goodness of fit is the chi-square value, which is statistically significant when the significance level (Sig.) is given at 0.001. The model appears to match the data well based on the chi-square value of 1.748. With a Root Mean Square Residual (RMR) of 0.029, the observed and projected values show a decent match, falling below the significance level of 0.05. Furthermore, the confirmatory fitness and overall model fitness goodness of fit indices are revealed to be 0.911 and 0.910, respectively. These results surpass the 0.90 acceptable standard, providing more evidence that the mode adequately represents the underlying data structure. When comparing the model's complexity to the number of estimated parameters, the Tucker-Lewis Index (TLI) is 0.905, which is likewise over the suggested threshold of 0.90, indicating that the model shows a strong match. Lastly, an outstanding match among the model and the data is shown by the Root Mean Square Error of Approximation (RMSEA), which is reported at 0.023, well below the threshold of 0.06. When taken as a whole, these fit indices confirm the structural model's suitability and robustness, offering compelling proof that the connections among the concepts of knowledge sharing, global partnerships, and digital platforms are well represented in the study.

Table 6: Regression Examination

Relative			Approx.	S.E.	C.R.	P	Ass.
Digital Platforms	<---	Global Partnerships	.843	.152	7.493	.00	H2
Knowledge Sharing	<---	Digital Platforms	.321	.148	2.791	.00	H3
Knowledge Sharing	<---	Global Partnerships	.935	.205	7.885	.00	H1

Source: Authors

A thorough analysis of the regression coefficients among the concepts of knowledge sharing, digital platforms, and global partnerships can be found in Table 6. Strong statistical measures back up the important links found in the investigation. With a standard error (S.E.) of 0.152, the regression coefficient showing the impact of global partnerships on digital platforms is stated to be 0.843. With a p-value of 0.00 and a critical ratio (C.R.) of 7.493, Hypothesis 2 (H2) is supported by a very significant association. This research emphasizes the critical role that cooperation plays in boosting digital engagement by indicating that more robust international collaborations are linked to higher efficacy in digital platforms. In addition, the evaluation of Digital Platforms' influence on Knowledge Sharing yields a regression coefficient of 0.321 and a S.E. of 0.148. This relationship's C.R. is 2.791, with a p-value of 0.00, indicating that this route is significant and verifying Hypothesis 3 (H3). The significance of digital platforms in promoting knowledge exchange among stakeholders is highlighted by this outcome. Finally, a strong correlation among knowledge sharing and global partnerships is demonstrated by the regression analysis, which has a coefficient of 0.935, a S.E. of 0.205, and a C.R. of 7.885. This relationship's p-value is also 0.00, which offers substantial support for Hypothesis 1 (H1). This suggests that successful international collaborations greatly improve information exchange, confirming the relationship among these concepts. Regression analysis, taken as a whole, emphasizes the crucial channels by which international collaborations impact digital platforms and information sharing, hence supporting the fundamental claims of the research and advancing our comprehension of cooperative dynamics in the context of knowledge transfer.

Table 7. Mediating role Effect

	Influence	worth	Path Influence
Global Partnerships → Knowledge Sharing	Direct Influence	.40	Direct influence stated
Global Partnerships → Digital Platforms → Knowledge Sharing	Indirect Influence	.66*.74=.49	Indirect Influence Ensued
	Whole influence	.89	Partial mediation

Source: Authors

Table 7 presents the link among Global Partnerships and Knowledge Sharing and the mediating function of Digital Platforms. The research provides a thorough understanding of the interactions among these dimensions by differentiating among direct and indirect impacts. The quantification of the direct influence of Global Partnerships on Knowledge Sharing is 0.40, suggesting a noteworthy impact that underscores the significance of cooperation in promoting knowledge exchange. The aforementioned direct link highlights the fundamental function that robust partnerships provide in facilitating efficient exchange of knowledge among involved parties. On the other hand, the indirect influence—that is, the effect of global partnerships on knowledge sharing through digital platforms—is computed as follows: 0.66 multiplied by 0.74 equals 0.49. This study highlights the crucial role that digital platforms play in improving information exchange and provides more evidence. When direct and indirect channels are included, the overall influence comes out to 0.89, indicating that global partnerships have a significant overall impact on knowledge sharing. The study comes to the conclusion that there is partial mediation, meaning that global partnerships still directly contribute to knowledge sharing even while digital platforms greatly improve the interaction. All things considered, these results draw attention to the intricate relationships that exist among digital platforms, knowledge sharing, and global partnerships. They also emphasize the critical role that digital tools play in promoting efficient communication and cooperation.

DISCUSSION

The study's conclusions offer important new perspectives on the complex interactions among knowledge sharing, digital platforms, and global partnerships. The findings demonstrate that global partnerships are essential for improving digital platforms, which help stakeholders share knowledge more effectively. This supports the idea that in order to fully utilize technology tools to optimize information flow, robust collaborative networks are necessary. The fundamental function of global partnerships is highlighted by their direct effect on knowledge sharing (0.40), which implies that successful partnerships naturally provide an atmosphere that is favorable to the exchange of information. Digital platforms' indirect influence (0.49) emphasizes how well they function as mediators in this interaction and shows how technology may improve the channels via which information is disseminated. This conclusion is especially pertinent to developing nations like Ethiopia, where the use of digital technologies may close information and communication gaps and strengthen local communities and organizations. Furthermore, a strong correlation among the constructs is shown by the overall influence of 0.89, indicating that bolstering relationships and improving digital capabilities would result in noteworthy advantages for knowledge exchange.

The report also highlights issues related to disparities in digital literacy and the digital divide, which may limit the usefulness of these platforms. As mentioned in the literature, removing these obstacles is necessary to guarantee that everyone has equal access to chances for knowledge-sharing. The analysis's partial mediation indicates that although Digital Platforms improve the link, Global Partnerships continue to have a direct influence on Knowledge Sharing. This highlights how crucial it is to build trust among couples and good human interactions in addition to not relying exclusively on technology. The study concludes by emphasizing the critical role that digital platforms play in moderating the impacts of international collaborations on knowledge sharing. Through the integration of technology inside collaborative frameworks, stakeholders can augment their ability to communicate and exchange information effectively. In order to guarantee that everyone can benefit from information sharing, future efforts should concentrate on developing digital infrastructure, enhancing digital literacy, and fostering partnerships that are flexible to local settings.

CONCLUSION

As a result, this study highlights the crucial interactions among digital platforms, knowledge sharing, and global partnerships. It also demonstrates the significant contribution that digital tools make to the advancement of cooperative endeavors. The results show that robust international alliances greatly improve the efficacy of digital platforms, which encourages more information exchange among interested parties. The study elucidates the impact of both direct and indirect factors, indicating that whilst collaborations establish the foundation for knowledge sharing, digital platforms serve as crucial intermediaries that enhance this procedure. The research does, however, also recognize that, especially in developing environments like Ethiopia, the digital gap and disparities in digital literacy might make it difficult to fully realize these advantages. It is imperative to remove these obstacles in order to guarantee that all parties involved may participate actively in knowledge-sharing initiatives. The knowledge gathered from this study not only advances our theoretical grasp of these concepts but also has applications for practitioners and policymakers who want to improve communication and cooperation. Maximizing the potential of information exchange in an increasingly linked world will ultimately depend on building strong international alliances and making investments in digital infrastructure. It is imperative that forthcoming studies persist in investigating these processes, especially within heterogeneous cultural and socioeconomic milieus, in order to devise approaches that guarantee just access to information and enable communities worldwide.

MANAGERIAL IMPLICATIONS

The study's conclusions have a number of significant management ramifications for companies looking to improve knowledge exchange through international alliances and digital channels. First and foremost, managers have to place a high priority on building robust networks of collaboration that encourage open communication and trust among stakeholders. Organizations may enhance the process of knowledge sharing by fostering ties with a variety of partners, including NGOs, government agencies, and academic institutions. This allows them to take use of the pooled expertise and resources available to them. Second, the importance of digital platforms as intermediaries emphasizes how important it is for businesses to make substantial investments in their IT infrastructure. It is imperative for managers to guarantee that the digital tools they utilize are easy to use and possess functionalities that enable instantaneous communication, exchange of data, and cooperative project administration. These investments strengthen partners' and workers' authority as well as the effectiveness of information sharing.

In addition, it is imperative to tackle the issues related to the digital divide. Managers have to put in place training initiatives to raise stakeholders' levels of digital literacy, especially in areas with restricted access to technology. Organizations may optimize participation in knowledge-sharing programs by providing personnel with the essential skills to efficiently utilize digital platforms. It is recommended that managers utilize a contextual approach in the development of their knowledge-sharing programs. With an understanding of the distinct cultural, economic, and social dynamics of the communities in question, companies will be able to customize their partnerships and digital platforms appropriately. This flexibility will encourage a sense of ownership and dedication among stakeholders in addition to improving the efficacy of information exchange.

PRACTICAL IMPLICATIONS

This study's practical implications emphasize measures that organizations may put into practice to improve knowledge exchange through international collaborations and digital platforms. First and foremost, institutions must to make a concerted effort to form and expand alliances with the public sector, the private sector, and civil society. Organizations may pool resources and expertise via the creation of collaborative networks, which fosters better information sharing and creative solutions to challenging problems. Secondly, it's imperative to invest in the infrastructure of digital platforms. It is recommended that organizations prioritize the selection and implementation of user-friendly technologies that enable smooth communication and cooperation. In order to promote widespread adoption and involvement, it is imperative that digital technologies are both accessible and compatible with the demands of all stakeholders.

Furthermore, it is important to give priority to training and capacity-building programs in order to raise the level of digital literacy among community members and partners. By offering courses and materials to improve digital platform usage abilities, people would be more equipped to participate to activities aimed at sharing information. This is especially crucial in places where access to technology may be restricted. Organizations should also take a flexible approach to knowledge-sharing tactics, modifying them to fit the unique socioeconomic and cultural settings of their partners. Organizations may handle particular difficulties and take advantage of opportunities by having a thorough understanding of local dynamics, which will encourage a sense of commitment and ownership among stakeholders. It is important to build methods for ongoing assessment and feedback in order to evaluate the efficacy of digital platforms and collaboration projects. Organizations may make educated modifications to ensure that their knowledge-sharing strategies stay powerful and relevant by routinely gathering user input.

THEORETICAL IMPLICATIONS

The study's theoretical ramifications advance our grasp of how international collaborations and internet platforms work together to promote knowledge sharing. Firstly, the results validate established ideas about knowledge management and collaboration, so bolstering the notion that robust collaborations augment the efficiency of digital platforms in fostering information sharing. This link highlights the need of social capital in cooperative environments, implying that efficient use of technology requires mutual trust and objectives amongst partners. Furthermore, the study expands the theoretical framework around information exchange by introducing the idea of digital platforms acting as mediators. The research highlights how important these platforms are in bridging the information distribution and collaboration gap, and it encourages more investigation into the particular characteristics and capabilities of digital tools that enhance collaboration. This aspect opens new avenues for research on the design and optimization of digital platforms tailored to different contexts and stakeholder needs.

The study also highlights how crucial context is to comprehending the dynamics of information exchange. Through an examination of the socio-cultural and economic determinants that impact the utilization of digital platforms in partnerships, the study adds to a more sophisticated theoretical framework that acknowledges the diversity of knowledge sharing in various settings. Scholars are encouraged by this viewpoint to explore the ways in which technology use and collaborative efforts are shaped by contextual variables. Lastly, the results demand a reevaluation of conventional knowledge-sharing approaches, which frequently ignore the mediating role of digital technologies. The research enhances the theoretical discourse on knowledge creation, sharing, and utilization in an increasingly digital and linked world by including the function of digital platforms into these models.

RECOMMENDATION

Several recommendations may be made to improve the efficacy of international collaborations and the use of digital platforms for knowledge exchange in light of the study's findings. Establishing strong collaborations with stakeholders from a variety of sectors, such as government agencies, non-profits, and academics, should be an organization's top priority. In addition to expanding the body of knowledge, this cooperative approach will promote a climate of trust and common goals, both of which are necessary for productive information sharing. Secondly, it is imperative that firms allocate resources towards the creation and execution of digital platforms that are easy to use. These platforms ought to be created with the end user in mind, including functions that make data sharing, collaborative work, and easy communication possible. It's important to regularly ask users for feedback to make sure the tools continue to relevant and accessible to all stakeholders involved.

Organizations can also concentrate on improving digital literacy among community members and partners. Putting in place training programs that provide people the know-how to utilize digital technologies efficiently may greatly increase involvement in knowledge-sharing projects. By increasing users' ability, such initiatives will enhance the influence of digital platforms on the diffusion of knowledge. Furthermore, while creating their knowledge-sharing plans, firms are urged to use a context-sensitive approach. Comprehending the distinct cultural, societal, and economic elements that impact stakeholder involvement can facilitate customized endeavors that strike a chord with regional populations, therefore boosting dedication and efficiency. In conclusion, the implementation of ongoing assessment and monitoring systems will be crucial in determining the effectiveness of digital platforms and collaborative efforts. Organizations may adjust their methods to suit changing requirements and problems and ensure continuous effectiveness in knowledge sharing by routinely assessing outcomes and collecting user insights.

FUTURE DIRECTIONS

Subsequent investigations about international collaborations and internet channels for information exchange ought to go into several auspicious avenues. Initially, longitudinal research may offer more profound understanding of the long-term effects of integrating digital platforms on knowledge exchange in collaborations. By tracking changes over time, these studies would enable researchers to spot trends and best practices that appear when businesses adjust to changing digital environments. Further in-depth assessments that look at the particular characteristics of digital platforms that best support information exchange are also required. Subsequent research endeavors may utilize comparative evaluations of diverse platforms to ascertain which features—like instantaneous collaboration instruments, data visualization functionalities, or user interaction attributes—optimizes knowledge sharing in diverse settings.

Further study is crucial in exploring the influence of cultural and socio-economic aspects on the efficacy of digital platforms. Comprehending the ways in which these contextual factors impact user engagement and information flow may assist firms in customizing their technology and strategies to more effectively address the demands of various stakeholders. Furthermore, it is still imperative to look at the problems caused by the digital divide. Subsequent investigations need to concentrate on pinpointing inventive approaches to close this disparity, guaranteeing that every prospective user has fair access to technology and instruction in digital literacy. Examining neighborhood-based projects that make use of available resources to improve online interaction is one way to do this. Lastly, there is a lot of room for investigation at the nexus among digital platforms for information exchange and artificial intelligence. Significant progress in the subject might result from examining the ways in which AI technologies can enhance knowledge management methods, such as by automating data analysis, customizing learning experiences, or enabling intelligent matchmaking among knowledge seekers and suppliers.

REFERENCES

Adula, M., Birbirsa, Z. A., & Kant, S. (2023). The effect of interpersonal, problem solving and technical training skills on performance of Ethiopia textile industry: Continuance, normative and affective commitment as mediators. *Cogent Business & Management*, 10(3), 2286672. Advance online publication. DOI: 10.1080/23311975.2023.2286672

Asefa, K., & Debela, K. L. (2023). Effect of Transformational Leadership on Organizational Performance: The Mediating Role of Employee Commitment and Expert Systems (AI) Inclusion in Ethiopia. *2023 International Conference on Communication, Security and Artificial Intelligence (ICCSAI)*, 305-310, DOI: 10.1109/ICCSAI59793.2023.10421269

David, K. G., Yang, W., Bianca, E. M., & Getele, G. K. (2021). Empirical research on the role of internal social capital upon the innovation performance of cooperative firms. *Human Systems Management*, 40(3), 407–420. DOI: 10.3233/HSM-190830

Dereso, C. W., Kant, S., Muthuraman, M., & Tufa, G. (2023). Effect of Point of Service on Health Department Student's Creativity in Comprehensive Universities of Ethiopia: Moderating Role of Public-Private Partnership and Mediating Role of Work Place Learning. In: Jain, S., Groppe, S., Mihindukulasooriya, N. (eds) Proceedings of the International Health Informatics Conference. Lecture Notes in Electrical Engineering, vol 990. Springer, Singapore. DOI: 10.1007/978-981-19-9090-8_13

Durga, P., Godavarthi, D., Kant, S., & Basa, S. S. (2024). Aspect-based drug review classification through a hybrid model with ant colony optimization using deep learning. *Discov Computing*, 27(1), 19. DOI: 10.1007/s10791-024-09441-w

Dzhunushalieva, G., & Teuber, R. (2024). Roles of innovation in achieving the Sustainable Development Goals: A bibliometric analysis. *Journal of Innovation & Knowledge*, 9(2), 100472. DOI: 10.1016/j.jik.2024.100472

Guyo, D. M., Kant, S., & Kero, C. A. (2023, November). Mediation of Marketing Intermediaries and AI Adoption Between Livestock Products Marketing and Economic Status of Pastoralist in Ethiopia. In *2023 International Conference on Communication, Security and Artificial Intelligence (ICCSAI)* (pp. 311-316). IEEE.

Ibidunni, A. S. (2024). Cross-border knowledge transfer and the innovation performance of developing economy small and medium enterprises: A moderated mediation effect of industry networks and localization of knowledge. *Technological Forecasting and Social Change*, 208, 123702. DOI: 10.1016/j.techfore.2024.123702

Jabo, B., & Kant, S. "Impact of Technical CRM on Ethiopia Bank Human-Computer Interface and Competitive Advantage as Mediators of Performance," *2024 IEEE International Conference on Computing, Power and Communication Technologies (IC2PCT)*, Greater Noida, India, 2024, pp. 679-682, https://doi.org/DOI: 10.1109/IC2PCT60090.2024.10486237

Kant, S., & Adula, M. (2024). AI Learning and Work Attitude Mediation Between Reward and Organizational Support in Ethiopia. In Gomathi Sankar, J., & David, A. (Eds.), *Generative AI for Transformational Management* (pp. 109–136). IGI Global., DOI: 10.4018/979-8-3693-5578-7.ch005

Kant, S., & Adula, M. (2024). Mediated by AI-Based Generative Re-Enforcement Learning and Work Attitude: Are Intrinsic Rewards Transforming Employee Perceived Organizational Support? In Gomathi Sankar, J., & David, A. (Eds.), *Generative AI for Transformational Management* (pp. 83–108). IGI Global., DOI: 10.4018/979-8-3693-5578-7.ch004

Kant, S., & Adula, M. (2024). Human-Machine Interaction in the Metaverse in the Context of Ethiopia. In *Impact and Potential of Machine Learning in the Metaverse* (pp. 196–212). IGI Global., DOI: 10.4018/979-8-3693-5762-0.ch008

Kumar, P., Ulseth, M., & Austin, S. (2021). Bridging the Gender Gap to Realize Capacity Building: The role of SDG 5 for SDG 17. In *Partnerships for the Goals* (pp. 78–87). Springer International Publishing. DOI: 10.1007/978-3-319-95963-4_122

Li, X., Wu, T., Zhang, H. J., & Yang, D. Y. (2023). National innovation systems and the achievement of sustainable development goals: Effect of knowledge-based dynamic capability. *Journal of Innovation & Knowledge*, 8(1), 100310. DOI: 10.1016/j.jik.2023.100310

Moreno-Serna, J., Sánchez-Chaparro, T., Mazorra, J., Arzamendi, A., Stott, L., & Mataix, C. (2020). Transformational collaboration for the SDGs: The Alianza Shire's work to provide energy access in refugee camps and host communities. *Sustainability (Basel)*, 12(2), 539. DOI: 10.3390/su12020539

Nyoach, T. D., Lemi, K., Debela, T., & Kant, S. (2024). Does Organizational Commitment Mediate the Relationship between Employee Relationship Management and Bank Performance? The Case of Banks in Ethiopia. *International Journal of Organizational Leadership*, 13(2), 355–376. DOI: 10.33844/ijol.2024.60419

Panigrahi, A., Pati, A., Sahu, B., Das, M. N., Nayak, D. S. K., Sahoo, G., & Kant, S. (2023). En-MinWhale: An ensemble approach based on MRMR and Whale optimization for Cancer diagnosis. *IEEE Access : Practical Innovations, Open Solutions*, 11, 113526–113542. DOI: 10.1109/ACCESS.2023.3318261

Qureshi, I., Pan, S. L., & Zheng, Y. (2021). Digital social innovation: An overview and research framework. *Information Systems Journal*, 31(5), 647–671. DOI: 10.1111/isj.12362

Schorr, B., Braig, M., Fritz, B., & Schütt, B. (2021). The global knowledge value chain on sustainability: Addressing fragmentations through international academic partnerships. *Sustainability (Basel)*, 13(17), 9930. DOI: 10.3390/su13179930

Serna, J. M., & Chaparro, T. S. (2021). Systemic Collaborative Platforms: Accelerating Sustainable Development Goals Transitions through Multi-Stakeholder Convening Arrangements (Doctoral dissertation, Universidad Politécnica de Madrid).

Ufua, D. E., Emielu, E. T., Olujobi, O. J., Lakhani, F., Borishade, T. T., Ibidunni, A. S., & Osabuohien, E. S. (2021). Digital transformation: A conceptual framing for attaining Sustainable Development Goals 4 and 9 in Nigeria. *Journal of Management & Organization*, 27(5), 836–849. DOI: 10.1017/jmo.2021.45

Wang, S., Li, Q., & Khaskheli, M. B. (2024). Management Economic Systems and Governance to Reduce Potential Risks in Digital Silk Road Investments: Legal Cooperation between Hainan Free Trade Port and Ethiopia. *Systems*, 12(8), 305. DOI: 10.3390/systems12080305

KEY TERMS AND DEFINITIONS

Composite Reliability (CR): A gauge of an indicator or item set's internal consistency with respect to measuring the same construct. Higher numbers denote stronger dependability. It shows how strongly the components correlate with one another.

Digital Literacy: The capacity to locate, assess, produce, and share information using digital tools. This covers abilities including using digital tools, accessing online platforms, and evaluating digital material critically.

Digital Platforms: Web-based instruments and technologies that help people communicate, work together, and exchange information. Social media, cloud storage, collaborative software, and niche apps made for certain sectors or jobs are a few examples of these platforms.

Discriminant Validity: An indicator of how unique a construct is within a certain research. It confirms that the concept represents a distinct component of the topic under study by making sure it is not overly similar to other constructs.

Global Partnerships: cooperative associations established among entities, institutions, and interested parties from many nations and industries with the objective of accomplishing common objectives, improving resource distribution, and tackling intricate worldwide issues.

Knowledge Sharing: The process by which people or groups share knowledge, skills, and perspectives in order to further practice and learning. Formal channels (like reports and presentations) or informal channels (like conversations and networking) can be used to accomplish this.

Mediation: The work done by an intermediary to improve or facilitate a connection among two or more entities, such as a digital platform. By bridging gaps among partners, digital technologies can facilitate information transfer, which is referred to in this context as mediation.

Chapter 12
Innovative Teaching Methods Using Technology in Accounting and Business Management

Michael B. Bongalonta
https://orcid.org/0009-0001-9989-626X
Sorsogon State University, Philippines

ABSTRACT

This chapter thus examines how technology can be embraced in teaching accounting and business management. The fast development of digital technologies impacted the traditional approaches and methodologies of teaching and learning and it provided educators the opportunity to incorporate innovative instructional techniques to engage and accommodate students and improve their understanding and memorizing capabilities. This chapter explores how accounting and business management curriculum integrates online simulations, VR, AR, AI, and big data analytics. By these technologies, learning activities are designed to be more engaging and challenging thus enabling students to be equipped with knowledge and skills for actual business settings. Furthermore, the challenges and future developments of using technology in teaching accounting and business management are presented highlighting the opportunity for educators in today's constantly developing educational environment

DOI: 10.4018/979-8-3693-8242-4.ch012

INTRODUCTION

Most often the information mentioned above shows how environmental education, particularly, accounting as well as business management needs has evolved in contemporary world society that is characterized by a constantly escalating pace of technological advancement. Technological interventions are evolving the conventional paradigms of learning delivery strategies and the incorporation of processes to cater to the needs of the new economy. The Fourth Industrial Revolution which is involved with the use of technology in teaching and learning processes requires adoption of the improved teaching strategies with the use of technology to ensure that the students are prepared to fit in the current labor markets (Schwab, 2016).

Both in accounting and business management critical thinking and analytical skills are fundamental and data and technology have played a very important role in delivering knowledge in these fields. Students are thus able to interact with realistic business conditions and problem-solving activities through online simulations, VR, AR, and AI as well as data analysis activity. The ensuing chapter affords a detailed examination of these tools and their implications in accounting and business management education. We also explore the difficulties of integrating technology into effective teaching practices and try to highlight the prospects that may define the educational landscape in these fields in the future.

1. The Role of Technology in Modern Education

The incorporation of technology has tremendously transformed the education sector to improve learning all over the faculties. As for the impact of IT in accounting and business management, the use of the concept helps to make the learning process more engaging and real-life-like, as it deals with tangible learning such as concepts (Gonzalez & Birch, 2020). In these areas, the technology is used to a larger extent not only for knowledge reproduction but also for learning important skills such as problem-solving, cooperation, and data evaluation.

Benefits of Technology Integration

Various advantages can be derived from the use of technology in education. For example, it is easier to engage a student when using digital resources since the content involved is interactive and easy to understand especially when graphics are involved in teaching complicated concepts. Many schools apply the case study approach and use online simulations and data visualization tools to help students learn such aspects of financial management as the decision-making of actual organizations. Such technology also promotes individual learning, mobility that adapts to the student's rate, and an immediate evaluation of the student's performance (Freeman et al., 2014).

In addition, the use of technology leads to social learning and interaction of students and tutors across geographic regions thus a global learning system. Social organizations are typical in almost all accounting and business management courses and activities that require teamwork and leadership; these collaborative sessions emulate actual organizational practices and expose learners to viable professional life situations.

2. Innovative Teaching Methods Using Technology

Principal of Virtual Reality and other computer-based simulations that are used to support learning in a virtual environment.

Multimedia presentations provide field experience and application of techniques in a safe environment since businessmen can try out various financial and managerial options. Other simulations such as marketing strategy simulation known as markstrat or systems of SAP's enterprise resource planning are common in the process of accounting and management learning (Lovelace et al., 2018). These platforms reflect actual decisions and give students valuable experience in the overall functionality of the financial and managerial control systems.

Virtual Reality (VR) to Augmented Reality (AR)

VR and AR are new revolutions in education. In teaching accounting and business management, VR can place learners in virtual scenarios within the business environment in which they deal with real but fictitious financial information for audits or managing budgets. AR benefits textbooks and other sources of knowledge because, for instance, students can look at balance sheets or financial forecasts in 3D Green (2020). These technologies help to make some abstract concepts tangible and allow the students to practice specific cases in a rather entertaining manner.

AI and ML – Artificial Intelligence and Machine Learning

AI and ML have become important in altering the delivery of personalized learning as they offer adaptive learning environments to students. In accounting education, AI-based tutoring like IBM's Watson Tutor, can detect students' learning behaviors and provide relevant learning resources so that students can enhance their understanding of difficult concepts in accounting (Kember et al., 2017). Furthermore, AI assists in the easy conduction of tests and evaluations and also frees teachers from the burden of grading through the usage of various techniques that are more engaging to the students.

Decision-making tools/Data analysis and data visualization

The knowledge of analyzing and interpreting data is one of the significant competencies in accounting and business management. The course content also includes data analysis applications such as Tableau and Power BI, for developing within the students the ability to make decisions based on data (Schneider et al., 2019). These tools enable students to draw trends, make projections about financial results, and analyze business indicators, which activities are critical to current management in today's world.

3. Benefits of Technology-Enhanced Learning in Accounting and Business Management

The use of technology in accounting and business management education offers numerous benefits that extend beyond the classroom:

1. Engagement and Motivation: Such approaches to learning create more interest in learning so that the student is fully involved in the learning process.
2. Critical Thinking and Problem-Solving: Using technology, students can employ abstract ideas and come up with realistic solutions used in actual business situations helping in decision making.
3. Flexibility and Accessibility: A flexible learning model has been made possible by the use of technology especially in online courses and other materials that can be accessed by students over the internet.
4. Skill Development: Digital tools have been identified as preparing the students in terms of technical competencies that are relevant in the market like data analytics and AI (Parsons & Taylor, 2019).

4. Challenges and Considerations

The incorporation of rich teachings in accounting and business management courses by incorporating technology poses a lot of potential in improving the results achieved. However, this integration brings out several factors that should be taken into consideration to enhance the effectiveness of the integration process.

1. 1. Infrastructure and Access The most crucial is the lack of favorable technical preconditions for developing and introducing the types of advanced educational technologies singled out above. An institution needs to make sure that it has the requisite technological tools such as hardware and networking to support the implementation of the technology-enhanced teaching approaches. This entails the availability of

computers with reliable internet connection, updated computers, and appropriate software applications in the system. Lack of infrastructure may result in technical problems which may greatly affect the viability of the technology-enhanced learning tools (Smith & Johnson, 2024).

1. 2. Integration and Compatibility The adoption of new technologies to enhance teaching and learning as well as other activities in education can at times be challenging due to issues of compatibility. There is a need to ensure that the various software applications and the learning technologies are compatible in a way as not complicate the learning process. Studies should be directed at the search for ideas on how to implement integration and various challenges that may occur when configuring one system in another (Lee & Davis, 2023). Further, it is recognized that the adoption may require reinvention or professional development training for the teachers whereby they can apply the new technologies efficiently as tools of instruction.

1. 3. Technical Support Technological support for students and other users while necessitating lecturers is also correspondingly required. One of the key factors that the institutions must have is the means to provide a solution in the event of a technical hitch. This entails having IT support staff and the user training can be done where problems can be solved easily. Incorporation of adequate technical support is essential to prevent the user from getting frustrated as a result of dealing with technical learning tools (Miller, 2023).

2. Pedagogical Considerations

2. 1. Teacher Practice Enhancement Although the use of teaching aids in classrooms assists in the delivery of content, it is not a total solution to teaching difficulties. Students exposed to technology-enhanced practices of teaching and learning indicated that such practices differed in their effectiveness based on how they blended into teaching practices. Teachers need to pick typified technology-enhanced learning activities in a way that is compatible with pedagogical goals and integrate appropriately within teachers' practice. More studies should be conducted to determine how technology integration into student learning can best be employed and effective pedagogy (Robinson 2022).

2. 2. Student engagement and motivation: One of the most important factors that have to be considered with the use of technology in education is the students' engagement and motivation. Interactive tools, the use of games, etc., are effective in motivating students, but not all students are the same as these tools. Technology must be used to meet multiculturalism perspectives of learning and implementation media tools are needed to meet the learning needs of clients. In future research,

the effect of different technologies should be compared and methods to solve the issues of different levels of motivation of students should be further investigated.

2.3. Concerning Tension between Technology-Enhanced Content Relevance and Quality it can thus be argued that it is of paramount importance that we enhance the quality of information. Textbooks and other instructional and educational tools and aids should therefore be well chosen and assessed in terms of educational quality and relevancy toward the course set goals and objectives. To address this, teachers should be able to review different online resources and applications in terms of their credibility, pertinence, as well as instructional usefulness. It could propose studies towards the identification of criteria for the assessment and the evaluation of high-quality education technology (Taylor, 2022).

3. Equity and Accessibility

3.1. Digital Divide The digital divide is another issue that is also prevalent in technology-infused learning. Students from disadvantaged backgrounds may not afford the devices or have access to high internet speed or other technological requirements. The existence of such a gap calls for concrete actions towards ensuring that technology is made accessible to all child learners to be able to benefit from technological support in learning. There is a need to continue strengthening institutional efforts alongside policymakers to come up with mechanisms needed to erase the digital divide and offer needed support to students in need (O'Connor, 2024).

3.2. Equal Skills for Every Learner To ensure that students with disabilities have a chance to use education technology, facilities have to be made accessible. This also entails ensuring that technology made available to the teaching-learning process is accessible to disabled students, be it visual, auditory, or motor disabled students. The studies should bring into light the provision of accessibility features in the learning technologies as well as assess the efficiency of the technologies in helping students with disabilities (Nelson & Davis, 2023).

3.3. Culture and Language Integration It is also important that the advancements in technology be integrated with culture and language pragmatics. Software and other teaching aids used in an educational setting should therefore be culture and language-sensitive to create equity in the learning institutions. It would be pertinent to focus on future research on how learning technology can incorporate various cultural and linguistic experiences and how to design the learning content for cultural sensitivity (Smith & Johnson, 2024).

4. Ethical and Privacy Concerns

4. 1. Data Privacy and Security With the increased utilization of technology in deliveries of education, there is handling of students' data which can be an issue of privacy and security. It is only significant to point out that institutions have to employ strong practices that will allow them to protect the data of learners and avoid privacy law violations. Further research should be centered on identifying strategies when it comes to data protection as a form of educational technology as well as the ethical dilemmas that surround the use of data (Davis & Thompson, 2024).

4. 2. Effectiveness of AI and Automation Concerns of AI and automation include: Decision-making Decisions made by intelligent systems need to be scrutinized to settle for the most vital decision rather than the quickest one. One of the major requirements is to guarantee that the use of AI and AI-supported tools and systems in the enterprise does not present and aggravate existing discrimination. It also emphasizes that research should investigate the positive and negative impact of implementing AI in learning contexts and offer rules regarding the proper and accountable use of the specified AI innovations (Lee & Davis, 2023).

4. 3. Effect on Teachers' Duties Change in roles and duties may occur in the teaching profession due to the incorporation of technology into teaching practice. Teachers may therefore be required to change their part from being the givers of knowledge and information but being the guide. Future work could look into the effects of technology on teaching positions and compare how educators can perform efficiently for development in digital contexts (Johnson & Adams, 2023).

5. Financial and Resource Constraints

5. 1. The market price of the hardware and software, as well as the additional expenditures on acquiring the latest technologies may pose a costly experience for academic institutions. Lack of funds may greatly affect the capacity to procure equipment and technology that are modern and innovative. Future research should address issues of where and how to find the greatest returns from continued investments in educational technology. Thus, white and Green (2024) also indicated that engaging in the search for funding and partnership might also play a role in the protracted financial difficulty.

5. 2. This means that the right distribution of resources is essential for the teaching practice to succeed through the use of technology. To incorporate technology in teaching and learning, institutions must follow appropriate strategies on how to organize resources such as cash, technologies, and human resources. It can also investigate how resources are known to be managed optimally to accomplish the

goals of a given organization that is known to have scarce resources (Williams & Brown, 2024).

5. Case Studies and Best Practices

Several institutions have successfully integrated technology into their accounting and business management programs: Several institutions have successfully integrated technology into their accounting and business management programs:

1. Harvard Business School: Simulation methods that Harvard applies to its business case studies have become a reference point for other organizations. In the same way, through the provision of simulated business environments for the students, Harvard has been able to boost the levels of student participation as well as aid learners to fully grasp the dynamics of various financial situations (Lovvorn & Chen, 2016).

2. Stanford Graduate School of Business: The incorporation of AI and ML into Stanford's curriculum has seen Stanford create algorithms to create learners' unique learning tools that change according to learners' progress thus enhancing learning success (Schneider et al., 2019).

Some of them are as follows: the first is admitting the use of a mixed approach, the second is using technology as an augmentor and not a replacer of conventional methods, and the last one is ongoing assessment of the use of technology in achieving the intended learning outcomes.

6. Future Trends and Directions

With enhanced learning technologies remaining an active area of discussion, it is important to uncover the subsequent research agendas that may improve the effectiveness and relevance of new approaches to teaching operation management, accounting, and business management disciplines.

1. Integration of Emerging Technologies

1. 1. Artificial Intelligence (AI) and Machine Learning The utilization of Artificial Intelligence and machine learning into the learning—enhancing tools seems to hold the sunrise prospects for developing personalized learning environments. Future studies could examine the possibilities of enhancing learning materials and assessment using AI in response to the student's performance and their learning preferences as well. For instance, AI can be applied to identifying tailor-made practice

questions or scenarios in accounting and business management that suit a student's learning level as noted from the performance history by Smith & Johnson (2024).

1. 2. Blockchain Technology is a sort of technology that can be effectively used in several fields including education to provide a guarantee for the honesty and reliability of academic credentials and certifications that are issued by academic institutions. Subsequent research may examine how blockchain may be leveraged to establish up-to-date and immutable records of academic credentials and personal achievements. Further, it may be engaging and useful to investigate how blockchain can be employed in protecting owners' rights of intellectual property for contents and assessments delivered in educational settings (Lee & Davis, 2023).

1. 3. Knowing well their potential to create an engaging learning environment, further research should be conducted to determine the effects of AR and VR on learning achievement. Researching how AR and/or VR can be used to model various intricate business situations as well as how the technologies can be incorporated into the current learning processes might reveal best and potential practices (Brown & Adams, 2022). Further, the analysis of the factors affecting cost-utility and practicality of AR/VR implementations in educational contexts may provide useful guidance for organizations who have contemplated the utilization of AR/VR for teaching.

2. AI and the Assessment and Evaluation of Technology Enhanced Learning

2. 1. Teacher Professional Development Concerns Research should involve finding out the concerns that teachers' professional development raises when implementing e-learning. Research in the comparative form could evaluate how effective certain categories of technology like, interactive simulations, online learning platforms, and the use of games in learning are to the learners' performance, interest, and satisfaction levels. Key Points: It is crucial to create more solid forms of evaluation and ways of assessing the effectiveness of students through the use of technology-enabled methods.

2. 2. Longitudinal Surveys that capture the impact of technology-enhanced education on the student's career and job progression may be useful. Stakeholders could examine how students who were early exposed to Ferris neo advanced technological tools on education prepare them for the workforce, flexibility, and promotion in accounting and business management of firms (Miller, 2023).

2. 3. Student and Instructor Perspectives It is important to understand both the students and the instructors' points of view concerning the use of technology in education. Research could assess the various technological tools from the perspective of efficiency, ease of use, and outcomes by different stakeholders. The use of questionnaires such as surveys, interviews, and focus groups could be used to estab-

lish qualitative data concerning experiences and tendencies which would result in proper decision-making consequently on integration of technologies (Clark, 2021).

3. Teaching Strategies and Teaching–Learning Resources

3. 1. The Other Instructional Models The use of online-based and face-to-face models of delivering instructions has become common. Further research has to be conducted on the use of varying degrees of blended learning and the effects that it has on students' achievement, participation, and satisfaction levels. Research could look at different combinations of face-to-face and online content and find out the most promising practices to apply such models in teaching accounting and business administration (Williams & Smith, 2024).

3. 2. Gamification Strategies Gamification for learning and improvement has the intention of raising the motivation level of students. Future studies could examine what particular approaches to gamification are more suitable specifically for varying categories of students as well as for various subjects. Exploring the impact of rewards like points, badges, and leaderboards for enhanced intrinsic motivation and learning outcomes or the accomplishment of learning outcomes could have been useful in contributing to knowledge on how to effectively adopt gamification approaches.

3. 3. Group Activity Support Technologies Technologies that enhance support group work/peer collaboration are essential in learning, environment institutions. It could be studied how these technologies affect group work, critical thinking abilities, and the lessons in general. The research on the viability of collaborative venues as applied in vehicle courses teaching teamwork and communication skills in accounting and business management could be insightful (Johnson, 2021).

4. What do Equity and Accessibility in Technology-Enhanced Education Mean

4. 1. Closing the Digital Divide This, means covering the gap in the availability of technologies in education is a vital issue. Subsequent studies should establish how integral technology may be implemented to narrow the gap of students who get left behind whilst providing every learner with an opportunity to reap the benefits of the integration of technology in education. Research could analyze the difficulties that students with various SES experience and identify ways to increase the use of educational technologies for such students (O'Connor, 2024).

4. 2. Types of research study that Accessibility for Students with Disabilities Research could cover include ways of making the technologies used in the teaching-learning process accessible to students with disabilities. The systematic investigation of accessibility design features for application in learning tools or platforms may

contribute to the promotion of teaching and learning affordances in approaches and technologies to embrace students' diverse learning needs (Nelson & Davis, 2023).

4. 3. International Views/Approaches: Interrogating the ways and means that technology-enhanced education is practiced and appreciated in different cultures and systems will give a broader point of view. Accompanying qualitative research could explore how and on what basis diverse countries and territories apply and incorporate educational technology into their teaching of accounting and business management, including the overall strengths and weaknesses seen in those systems (Smith & Johnson, 2024).

5. Ethical and Privacy Considerations

5. 1. Data Privacy and Security As CEM uses and shares a lot of data in delivering its educational technology, data privacy/ security becomes inevitable. The next studies should focus on how to avoid risks and violations of students' rights and how to enhance ethical issues of data use in technology-based learning. Exploring the measures that protect students' data but at the same time effective in providing students with sufficient learning experiences is crucial (Davis & Thompson, 2024).

5. 2. Future Changes with AI and Automation Education have been impacted by AI and automation by making important decisions based on data usage and biased assessment. Research could explore whether the integration of such AI-driven tools in education is ethical in the first place and then provide guidelines on how to make the development and use of such technologies ethical (Lee & Davis, 2023).

5. 3. Teaching/Learning Roles and Responsibilities Technological enhancement implies teaching learning roles and responsibilities in the following ways. Subsequent research studies should examine the impact of technology on teachers as well as its consequences on practice. It will be also useful to focus on the ratio between the use of technology resources in the process of learning and direct communication between students: Effective and supportive learning environments (Johnson & Adams, 2023).

CONCLUSION

Embracement of innovative teaching methods which include the use of technology is not just an added value to traditional teaching methods but rather the most appropriate way of preparing learners for the challenging business world. They enable the simulation of 'real-life scenarios, virtual reality, artificial intelligence, and data analysis in accounting and business management courses, ensuring that the students get to experience unique, and innovative methods of learning and problem-solving. However, the advantages of technology-driven education outweigh the obstacles, and the future of teaching in these fields will be defined by the usage of modern tools. To remain on the right side of irrelevance and relevant to our student's future employment in these continuously changing businesses, educators must come to terms with these improvements.

REFERENCES

Freeman, S., Eddy, S. L., McDonough, M., Smith, M. K., Okoroafor, N., Jordt, H., & Wenderoth, M. P. (2014). Active learning increases student performance in science, engineering, and mathematics. *Proceedings of the National Academy of Sciences of the United States of America*, 111(23), 8410–8415. DOI: 10.1073/pnas.1319030111 PMID: 24821756

Gonzalez, C., & Birch, P. (2020). Digital learning in higher education: Engaging students through technology. *Journal of Educational Technology*, 5(2), 45–53.

Green, D. (2020). Virtual reality and augmented reality: Transforming education in the 21st century. *International Journal of Educational Technology*, 8(1), 67–78.

Greene, S. (2018). Addressing the digital divide in education: Strategies for equitable technology access. *Education Policy Studies*, 12(3), 112–129.

Kember, D., McNaught, C., & Wong, F. (2017). Enhancing learning through technology in accounting education. *Journal of Learning and Technology*, 6(4), 99–112.

Lovelace, M., Ellingson, D. A., & Smith, D. (2018). Online simulations in accounting and business management education: Impact on student performance. *Journal of Business Education*, 12(3), 49–61.

Parsons, J., & Taylor, L. (2019). Preparing students for the workforce: The role of data analytics in accounting education. *Journal of Accounting Education*, 32(4), 312–325.

Schneider, A., Waldfogel, J., & McKinley, B. (2019). Data visualization tools for business decision-making. *Journal of Business Intelligence*, 11(3), 22–30.

Schwab, K. (2016). The Fourth Industrial Revolution. World Economic Forum.

Tapscott, D., & Tapscott, A. (2016). *Blockchain revolution: How the technology behind Bitcoin is changing money, business, and the world*. Penguin Books.

Chapter 13
Quality Education in Artificial Intelligence:
Promising Technologically Sustainable Transformation for Future Education

Miftachul Huda
https://orcid.org/0000-0001-6712-0056
Universiti Pendidikan Sultan Idris Malaysia, Malaysia

ABSTRACT

This chapter aims to examine the quality education in the age of Artificial Intelligence (AI) as an attempt to shape the future education through technologically sustainable transformation. The critical review from recently related literature will be employed in providing the perceptions concerning from both significant benefits and potential limitations of AI in the context of quality education. Utilizing the qualitative research design in focusing on the main objective, the findings revealed that the way to enhance quality education actualised into both teaching and learning practices amidst AI should do with enhancing the active involvement on questioning norms, analysing context, and evaluating evidence. The strategic potentials of AI adoption and development refers to enrich the utility of various facets of quality education including academic research and theory scrutiny. The study concludes that AI can be an asset in the development of quality education with caveats that require careful management.for quality education with AI applications effectively.

DOI: 10.4018/979-8-3693-8242-4.ch013

INTRODUCTION

In the recent years, the progress of advanced technology development has been widely emerged into the society in the various sectors such as business, social interaction and also education. The particular attention was given into the progress development encompassed into the societal worldwide mainly in the education sector (Abulibdeh, Zaidan & Abulibdeh, 2024). Moreover, the key point of such advanced technology development with its foundational scenario on bridging the progression of society requires the continued consistency in helping reform the innovation pathway. With this regard, the role of advanced technology progression on fostering the education reform should do with building the quality itself in ensuring the prominent acts to bring the reforming process throughout both progress and paves towards the innovation way (Goralski & Tan, 2020). Being significant to the quality education as the important scenario in underlying the learning instruction for instance, the technological skills integrated into the ability on building know-how on the way would help to perform and personalise the extensive means in approaching the appropriate method in the delivery process. It is true that the major needs to fulfil in resulting the quality of education for the human society should come up building the continued process, practices and pathways in exploring the ongoing trends mainly on the technological advancement. Since the massive expansion of technological innovation articulated into the Artificial Intelligence (AI), the current style of education practice has been gradually shifted from the physical form to the existential concept (Okunlaya, Syed Abdullah & Alias, 2022). In particular, its key potential of such existence concepts including the instructional design practices and process would bring the procedures in leading to the education scenario with being more attractive. Amidst the 21st learning century, the varied approaches at this point of view could be adopted particularly in helping to fulfil the quality education, in order to provide the related basic needs of education. With bringing the demands to fulfil through the strategic efforts in shaping the learning scenario, the continued support of emerging technologies requires the stable access of facilities together with material resources.

However, the emerging issues of AI-powered education scenario are locating at the collection process in which the source of information is questionable due to the lack of clarity about the rightful status. Moreover, the process of the way to achieve such information amidst the miles away from an educational institute for instance could lead the students in having the real time-online access to the initially related material (Huda et al., 2024). As a result, the attempts on taking the technology-supported learning process from both onsite and outside would need to obtain the benefits of continued access of the number of resources. It is especially the digitally material sources from an online platform in enabling the extensive value in giving the continued support of quality education. In particular, the key pillar in ensuring the quality education process and practices is strategized into teaching aspect, in which the educator should have the sufficient digital skills together with pedagogical abilities (Bahroun et al., 2023). Moreover, the consistent achievement in ensuring the teaching preparation for both adapting and adopting technology facility would benefit to the teachers' know-how on the way to obtain the effectiveness. With this regard, the continued support of such technology advancement could be achieved through the strategic pillars including the accessibility of learning materials, teacher expertise insurance assimilated into the quality learning achievement with the professional arrangement.

In addition, the number of study has been conducted along with the quality education in the digital age for instance (Cheng & Wang, 2023), while the scholarly attention has been lack of critically examining the AI-supported education with its essential transformation into the human entitlement. As a result, the need to expand further into looking at the crucial catalyst in achieving the sustainable progression in order to ensure the quality education should be taken into consideration. In particular, the continued exploration on dealing with the influential aspects, principles and factors leading to the quality education requires both substantial and instrumental aspect to help organise the gateway to impart the critical value, knowledge expert, skill ability. On this view, the constant feedback refers to give an insightful value in monitoring the progress in ensuring the fulfilment on expectation and targeted plan achievement. Thus, this chapter aims to examine the critical overview of quality education amidst the AI age by which the advancement of promising the technologically sustainable transformation for future education. The main value of this chapter points out that the strategic potentials of AI adoption and development refers to enrich the utility of various facets of quality education including academic research and theory scrutiny. The study concludes that AI can be an asset in the development of quality education with caveats that require careful management. A balanced approach that capitalizes on AI's strengths while being aware of its limitations is necessary for cultivating robust critical thinking abilities for quality education with AI applications effectively.

Quality Education and its Significance

Referring to the varied components of essential aspects to ensure the delivery scenario of information with relevant, effective and equitable pathway, the quality education remains key role of the entire process in the education setting. As the elements in ensuring the achievability of education pathway, the strategic attempts to determine the main indicator of how to access the quality places the know-how to make an education to be well prepared and obtained required the properly arranged assessment procedure (Hadi et al., 2024). With this regard, the objective point of building the yardstick to enhance the education quality should go through the multiple dimensions of planning, implementing and evaluating pathway. Considered as the principal indicator of education process and practices, the crucial point in looking at the gateway of solving initiative towards the emerging issues on the lack of learning achievement standard requires to have a sufficient transformation in directing the strategic approach properly in line with the targeted plan arrangement (Borham et al., 2024). As a result, the critical overview on addressing the varied literatures regarding the quality education should bring along with briefly analysing the wide range of key aspects in driving the standard of components to provide the high-quality education services. On this view, the extensive value of standardizing the instructional design such as curriculum arrangement has to do with getting prepared of teaching expertise quality together with the related material resources in order to result in the learners with a well-balanced norm.

In line with expanding the quality education, there is a need for reconstructing the goal plan arrangement and achievement through the real-field design of scenario in the sense that both teachers and students could have a suitable resource to have a sufficient comprehension about the lesson being taught. Moreover, the capability of managing the process and practices of learning instruction needs to come up with obtaining supporting system from both internal, namely learners and educators and external side, namely parents (Huda, 2024a). The particular point refers to contemplate the significance of advancing the continued support for learning instruction pathway to achieve the quality education. As a result, the monitoring direction of quality education would begin with continually upgrading the educational system in providing the learners with the related knowledge. With this regard, the part of necessary complement including skills, knowledge and values in leading to the continued growth in developing both individual and social advancement could stabilise in achieving the quality education as a catalyst for obtaining the economic success (Huda, 2024b). In terms of achieving such attainment, the criteria of producing the circumstance with the education trend and style require the active engagement to build the consistent pathway of having the learning experience in delivering the solving initiative towards the possible challenges. In particular, the strategic gateway of thinking skills and encouraging the belonging sense of own learning would play a key role in delivery system for quality education achievement. With this regard, the extensive value of wide range of aspects in the education process including curriculum arrangement, teaching strategy with assessment practice, school culture and community engagement should do with building the quality education enhancement. On this view, the curriculum arrangement requires the instructional design to gather the related information for the shake of national building agenda.

In addition, the standard assessment of qualifying the significance of quality education needs to gather the relevant information with its up-to-date pattern in ensuring the delivery process in a well-balanced pathway. On this view, the strategic gateway of providing the teaching strategy and practice requires the appropriate procedure in leading to the interactive learning circumstance so that the active engagement among the learners could be obtained properly in line with the plan arrangement (Huda, 2024c). With this regard, the active learning environment should do with the teaching practice in the sense that the evaluation process need to have a sufficient assessment in complementing the pathway in a well-fair arrangement within an accurate information transmission. As a result, the attempts to provide the continued support to the learning process needs to have an engagement in obtaining the feedback towards the learners' progress to lead to help improve the quality achievement (Huda et al., 2017). Moreover, the particular attention needs to be given to direct the improvement for the learning circumstance and culture in order to be with being supportive and inclusive. At this point of view, the strategic assessment to get a sufficient collaboration to promote the critical thinking as the result of quality education indicator has to come up the continued support from the community engagement involving the stakeholders, parents and local organizations. In terms of fostering the strategic assessment to shape the experiential expertise in education setting, way to maintain the quality education has to begin with having the required practices articulated into the commitment to achieve the progression together with the excellence in the instructional learning design (Mohamad Shokri & Salihan 2023). As such, the particular aspect of having the sufficient detail about the instructional process played a role in distributing the effective learning environment to result in the classroom instruction brought into the community outreach. The key priority of learners' active engagement in the teaching process could be also indicated into creating the positive circumstance in preparing the quality outcome to obtain the targeted destination in line with both inside and outside of the classroom.

Quality Education Assessment Criteria

Since the strategic role of quality education as the key indicator in looking at the process and practice amidst the society, an important part of the essence of quality education has been crucial mainly in developing the progression towards the learning instruction. With this regard, the assessment criteria of providing the quality education would result in creating the consistency of expanding both necessary knowledge expert and skill ability in helping succeed in life and contribute to the economy and society as a whole (Berlian & Huda, 2022). Attempts in fostering the social barriers are being the key point of education scenario with its features to provide the strategic chance with an inclusiveness to all regardless apart from the wide range of multi-background together with socioeconomic status. The significance of having the sufficient assessment on ensuring the quality education in society should do with building the relevant facilities and tools. As a result, such wide arrangement in giving an insightful value to play a strategic role in fostering to bring both knowledge and skills to shape the future generations could be empowered through the sufficient facility and equipment. With this regard, the need to drive the direction in targeting the destination of learning acquisition process should be taken into consideration on thriving in an ever-changing world scenario in the sense that the well-educated population could be essential to develop the innovation, economic growth, and social cohesion (Huda, 2022). In particular, the further orientation in promoting the quality education assessment requires both active and interactive engagement on building the teaching and learning practice. It is important to note that the continued supply and display for having the actively managed instructional design would lead to expand the learners with the critical thinking and responsible awareness in creating the citizenship with the patriotic sense. As the critical aspect of enhancing the quality education scenario to lead to the healthy society, the particular point should be transmitted into maintaining the important part of empowering the fundamental transition to achieve both success and prosperity in resulting the society with the civilised quality standard.

In addition, the assessment criteria to ensure the quality education has been a major concern in fostering the strategic direction to reach the learning destination. As the key to unlock the true potential of learners to grow their all aspect, assessment criteria would have the varied aspects in ensuring the targeted plan reached to the destination arrangement as the objective of education process (Omar, 2022). One of the significant contributions of having the quality education could result in helping to reduce the poverty together with producing the accessible and equitable chance to all the people from wide range of backgrounds. It is important to have a critical look at the strategic attempts to achieve the equitable access to the education facilities including digital technology support for learning process, learning material and resources, classroom management (Huda et al., 2022). With this regard, the wide range of monitoring process of assessment criteria to ensure the quality education achievement is progressively employed through the programs freely accessible in covering the learners with the multi backgrounds. As a result, the strategic gateway to sustain the quality education should do with running the relevant programs together with their several types in giving the chance to bring the individuals getting improved both knowledge and skills in their wide range of subject disciplines (Borham et al., 2024). In order to ensure the assessment criteria running smoothly, the proper arrangement to manage the way to enhance the improvement scenario could be obtained through the vocational training for instance. This program would have the strategic role in facilitating the monitoring scenario in providing the relevant information towards the targeted destination for quality education standard. On this view, both experiential and practical side as the major result to enhance the specific achievement is significant in helping ensure the quality education (Ali, 2023). As such, the continuing process in allowing the teaching and learning practice would be ready in giving such insightful value in refreshing both knowledge and skills related to the field of interest.

In line with equipping the assessment criteria to help achieve the quality education, the strategic enhancement to empower the area of field studies in following the learners' potential growth could be initiated in managing the learning programs related to the current trends and demand. On this view, the popular program for instance could be determined as the primary option among the learners in allowing them to gain the complete knowledge through the coursework at any basis (Jusoh et al., 2024). With this regard, the borderless space for gaining the learning practice through the instructional design could be employed through the online platform in enabling all learners from variety of places to have the equitable access to the learning acquisition process. On this view, the transitional expertise on managing the program relevant to the current trends of international learning system in offering the quality education scenario requires the strategic assessment programs in helping measure the process and practice of providing the experience and expertise in line with the education objective. In particular, the strategic gateway in looking at the whole process of assessment on helping measure the quality education requires the various criteria which could be potentially adopted in evaluating the quality of an education program including the learning outcome, relevance to the community and also the strategic approach of teaching practice (Rahim et al., 2024). Moreover, the key aspect of having the primary criteria to evaluate the educational program requires both knowledge and skill ability in producing the learners with all their potential growth as targeted plan arrangement. In terms of achieving the assessment criteria on ensuring the quality education, the targeted plan as noted in the instructional design could be delivered properly in line with the expected learning outcome (…). As a result, the potential value of having the assessment criteria in allowing the process and practices within the targeted measurement of quality education could play a significant role in ensuring the learning performance which is usually conducted through holding the exams and other similar assessments. It is important to take note that the strategic assessment in getting the learners' feedback would result in obtaining the relevant feedback in fostering the relevant criteria in assessing the learners' potential growth within the education practice. In terms of having the relevance to community, the quality education might have the potentiality of effective education program in highlighting the current needs of society, in enabling to obtain the relevant knowledge and skills (Hehsan et al., 2024). Preparing the learners with their relevant basic needs in terms of comprehension pathway and also strategic skills would result in helping to shape the continued practices of learning acquisition process in the attempts to solve the potential challenges.

Strategic Practice for Quality Education

Since the strategic attempts to enhance the quality education achievement, there are always containing both chances and challenges during the process. Such process and practices in maintaining the running process to go in line with the targeted plan should do with the potential chances and opportunities in ensuring the quality education (Muharom et al., 2024). One of which example is on bringing the job market of the graduation, social community contribution and also potential economic development. With this regard, the active engagement on monitoring the knowledge transition process and experience in contributing the society could be maintained in order to achieve the targeted plan as arranged in the objective standard quality. Both social and economic development are central as the outcome-based education process and practice so that the assessment could be placed in this particular result (Muhamad et al., 2024). The strategic transition of evaluating the critical look at the running progression to sustain the gateway to continue the curriculum design should be aligned with industry standards and trends. In particular, the continued support of promoting the critical thinking a result to initiate the problem-solving skills requires the early preparation of having the teaching approach together with the proper method of delivery process of knowledge being taught (Wahid et al., 2024a). Consisting of teaching approach enhanced to the employment pathway within the education program, it is crucial to sustain the strategic scenario in leading to the quality education achievement. At this point, the factor leading to determine the quality basis with an effective procedure refers to provide an innovative use in approaching the active engagement of learners in promoting the learning inquiry process. As such, the active employment in designing the appropriate technique to work together with the innovative initiative in creating the conducive classroom environment should build an attractive-based instructional design in line with the targeted plan arrangement.

In addition, the strategic appointment to generate the proper technique in enabling the learning instruction running within the targeted plan of objective achievement refers to have the sufficient preparation in leading to the balance of its aspect related to the quality education. At this point of view, the continued consistency of having the mutual work among the main actor and supporting system should be taken into consideration in ensuring the quality education to be with the destination journey as impacted into the objective scenario (Huda et al., 2024a). With this regard, the assessment criteria will begin with running the proper arrangement of project-related instructional design in which the quality education could come up with enabling the peer-to-peer learning process as the gateway for running the instruction practice. As a result, the additional gateway in helping create the positive classroom circumstance would result in the learning environment with an active collaboration, self-expression and also creativity. In particular, the strategic practice of dealing with the quality education agenda requires the sufficient supply for the education process together with its experiential attainment (Alwi & Ibrahim, 2022). As such, the point of the proper arrangement to result in the quality-based instructional design refers to the further elaboration of know-how in the way to drive the particular attention on ensuring the assessment criteria for quality education agenda. There should come up with the assurance of program and system in helping improve the strategic attempt on designing the section on criteria to have a sufficient evaluation for quality education program. Such arrangement would lead to the quality outcome with remaining to elevate the knowledge basis and practical skills amidst the society.

In line with having the sufficient composition of evaluation of quality education, the strategic attempts to assess the running program with its effectiveness requires to establish the scenario to achieve the learning outcome. All such arrangement should come up with the sufficient learning material and resources in enabling the quality delivery process and also absorbing process (Zamri et al., 2024). With this regard, the learning material resources with an adequate portion to the time of estimation are being the essential value to help deliver the quality education through the assessment criteria program. On this view, the further detail could be viewed into the following part of technology facility, textbook, laboratory, libraries, and other facilities necessary for effective learning enhancement (Huda et al., 2024b). Moreover, both schools and universities need to have a sufficient confidence on ensuring such resources would be freely accessible to all learners with their multi-background. It is important to note that having an equitable access apart from varied of ranges of socioeconomic status or geographic location would lead to advance the quality support services to the running program of education. As a result, the strategic practice of continuing the education program should provide the quality assurance of the support services in fostering the learners in having succeed for both intellectual, moral and social capacity (Yahya & Othman, 2022). It is especially in the academic aspect that the personally related manners including the essence of tutoring, counselling, mentorship, and other forms of assistance and guidance articulated into the advanced services would lead to enhance the learners with having the responsive awareness. As such, the essential element to help grow the learners' needs and preferences should come up with helping continually to those groups such as cultural differences, disability individuals and also language barriers. In overall pathway, the strategic gateway to evaluate the quality education requires an efficient transformation in adopting the current trends and demands throughout running the relevant education program.

Enhancing AI-Advanced Technology Development for Quality Education

Due to the massive technology development in the recent years, all the human society has been gradually shifted to the so-called norms with reconsidering the features of facilities. The advanced technology development has given a tremendous significance to the today's world, mainly in the education sector. It is in the education aspect that considering the multiple factors of which is through technology advancement would go beyond not only bringing the academic performance but also social transformation (Rahman, Jaafar & Huda, 2023). The in-depth assessment in driving the pathway to look into detail in strategic gateway in addressing the society's needs should do with generating the relevant employment throughout the effective pathway of instruction approach. With this regard, the strategic instruction throughout the process for quality education has been represented to the sufficient cohesion of teaching approach together with providing the adequately relevant resources (Cita Sari et al., 2023). The continued support of advanced technology development remarked the essential offer in giving the insightful value in managing the services delivery in the attempts to help improve the learning outcome. In line with the strategic effort in promoting the quality assurance on obtaining learning scenario, there should go through determining the assessment criteria in fulfilling the quality education programs. The significance of having the beneficial value in driving the quality education direction for both learners and community is required to prepare the related subject of learning materials (Huda et al., 2024c). Thus, the potentials of learner growth would contribute to the society in the sense that the whole process during the learning practice is signified into building the quality education as essential element in achieving the targeted plan.

In line with providing the varied significances to foster the individual in obtaining the full potentials of growth, the key contribution of positive learning environment has been set up throughout the advanced technology development. With this regard, the extensive value from both intellectual and social advancement could be the promising agenda to increase the learners' knowledge and skill (Zamri, Muhamad & Huda, 2023). At this point of view, the academic achievement should come up with elevating the intellectual and social growth in that the improvement could be achieved in enhancing the economic development progression. On this view, the strategic attainment in monitoring the better outcome including education, society and health sectors to help increase the quality education achievement. Furthermore, the increased monitoring system to sustain the social mobility in leading to the quality education requires the sufficient equipment of learning facility from the technology development (Masud et al., 2024). Such arranged scenario would enhance the essential value in providing the insightful value integrated into both necessary skills and practical knowledge. In particular, the requirement to follow such instruction needs to expand the potential contribution in bringing the workforce through accessing the high-quality education. As such, the learners with having the balance between knowledge and skills would lead to enhance their motivated essence through the technology-enhanced learning process (Huda et al., 2024d). Moreover, the insurance of having the security access during the learning process might become the essential agenda to lead as an outstanding point in bringing the future preparation with the prospect of economic development.

In terms of leading to help enhance the economic development by reducing the poverty rates, the strategic target of quality education is enhanced to improve in gathering the relevant information in building the quality outcome with the enhancing socioeconomic status. On this view, the community development as one of the major concerns for quality education is strategically to be promoted in building better outcome in the sense that could enhance the technology access to the process and practices (Huda, 2022). With this regard, the emerging points of bringing both services and support to help improve the learning scenario to have the sufficient prevention towards the challenging issues potentials are need to strategize the outcome of educated individuals with the sufficient knowledge comprehension. Moreover, the critical overview of engaging the technology-supported quality education would lead to expand the behaviour with the healthier sense as an attempt to maintain the balance scenario (Mohd Nawi, 2023). In particular, the strategic effort to build the quality education refers to have a sufficient link to increase the positive impact to help improve the learning instruction process and practices. As such, the continued improvement of having the quality education would result in raising the overall-based achievement including academic ability and social responsibility. At this point, the strategic attempts to increase the extent of quality education could provide the essential opportunity to develop the learners' quality achievement (Huda et al., 2024e). On this view, the strategic effort to enhance the education process and practices could be the leading point in obtaining the quality education.

Developing AI-Supported Practice Facility for Quality Education

The strategic effort to point out bringing the significant practice for the higher learning potentials should do with continuing to maintain the quality education, equitable and accessible. Moreover, the continued effort to ensure the equality access to all the individuals with diverse background is the main achievement goal within the scenario of mainly supported technology (Tan et al., 2024). In the attempts to promote the quality education, the wide range of beneficial access for both individual and social capacity might give a chance to improve the economic development. The key investment of quality education with the technology integration placed the continued benefits to help improve both individual and social learners in preparing to get involved into the society as a whole. The scenario of improving the economic opportunity to obtain the learning outcomes would increase the strategic opportunity in dealing with the investment to achieve the quality education (Wahid et al., 2024b). It is essential to have a critical look at maintaining the stronger and more prosperous future to help improve the social skills with the technology enhancement. However, the possible challenges during the practice requires the stability of having the risk arrangement scenario in enabling the act of what to do in line with facing it fluently. In the attempts to provide the quality education, the initial pathway should come up with building the accessible learning resources in giving the openness to the learning process (Musolin et al., 2024a). At this point of view, the strategic enhancement on managing the quality access should do with having an adequate technology and materials as required to achieve the effective instruction for teaching practice.

With regards to the strategic practice to have the sufficient knowledge and skills to lead to the ability in providing the quality education, the scenario of arranging the classroom portion needs to be taken in consideration in the sense that giving access achievable for teachers to provide the individual comprehension. At this point, the strategic attention might reach to give the learning inquiry process with the technology advancement in making the challenges as the opportunity for learning process (Musolin et al., 2024b). The particular attention needs to be given properly in identifying the areas in which the learners could have the access to the learning process and this might provide the support. Moreover, the additional value in having the continued support to help improve the quality education should do with building the professional development as the scenario of designing the equal and accessible learning. Since such arrangement is being the fundamental element to generate the opportunity in enabling the access for learning process, the gateway of technology enhancement needs to take into consideration in enhancing both knowledge and skills (Musolin et al., 2024c). In particular, the extent of obtaining the educational trends with the technology advancement would be the outstanding chance to support the struggle to obtain the mutual access to all learners in following the instruction process. Thus, the need to have a careful pathway in maintaining the techniques requires the strategic effort in ensuring the quality education at the achievement phase (Susilowati et al., 2018), At this point of view, the continued strategies adopted the know-how in the way to monitor the insurance of quality education assessment through implementing the wide range of effective teaching approaches.

In terms of having the sufficient access to the technology in supporting the quality learning, the scenario of designing the instructional process should bring along with providing the extensive value of personalized learning scenario. The particular attention needs to be given into building the learners' potential growth in enabling their knowledge comprehension and technology skills (Latif, Md Saad & Abd Hamid, 2023). As a result, the scenario of designing the effective teaching approach needs to cover the mutual involvement to incorporate the wide range of relevant practices in line with the raising pathway to the learners' active engagement. On this view, the engagement portion among the learners might have the following scenario including promoting the critical thinking skills to lead to the problem-solving initiative (Susilowati et al., 2018), The particular attention would also be given into sustaining the inquiry-based learning in order to build the project oriented instruction through the learning inquiry process. At this point, the role of advanced technology in the learning process might involve the integration procedure to the advanced technology tools into classroom arrangement. Moreover, the continued support to help improve the learning experiences could be obtained through the technology-supported learning platforms such as online resources, and educational apps (Abadi et al., 2018). As such, the extensive value of personalized learning scenario requires the attention to obtain the students' involvement in advancing the instructional approach in enhancing the learners' needs amidst their diversity background. Furthermore, the strategic ability accommodated with the continued efficiency of quality education practice needs to stabilise the approach in ensuring the learners' customized support (Aminudin et al., 2018a). The careful engagement as the guidance in the learning process is needed to have the sufficient facilitation from the technology advancement in achieving the potential growth of individual and social ability. On this view, the collaborative-oriented instruction would the learning scenario to lead to the environments in enabling to work together in shaping the appropriate practice to have the strategic ideas to improve the teaching strategy. Thus, the further enhancement could be portioned to enhance the quality of education as the main scenario to help produce the quality learning process and practices.

Sustaining AI-Empowered Practice Revolution for Quality Education

The strategic attempts on revolutionizing the advanced technology with its features have been widely adapted in adopting the particular facility to sustain the instruction process and practices. At this point, the gateway to provide the new opportunity in following the scenario in approaching the education practice requires the essential practice in delivering the process of knowledge acquisition (Zainuri & Huda, 2023). The role of AI in powering the instructional practice for teaching and learning played an essential role in helping improve the quality education through enhancing accessibility. Moreover, such initiative could also reach to increase the mutual engagement in advancing the personalized learning practices throughout the experiential-based performance. With following the positive support of advanced technology with AI-transformed instructional medium, the quality education is being the significant target of operation to achieve as the targeted plan arrangement (Maseleno et al., 2019). The ability in providing the mutual access to the instructional learning process and practice places the significant contribution of the material resources. It is especially in on online platform for instance that the access of quality educational materials would enable the learners to obtain the relevant information to support their learning process in that there could be the real time transaction in ensuring the delivery pathway of knowledge acquisition within the arranged plan. As a result, the beneficial value of AI-empowered technology facility in helping improvise the instructional design could reach out the particular arrangement to especially give the classroom management approach.

In line with benefiting the AI-based learning performance, the strategic initiative in monitoring the access and the procedures to go further determining the effectivity and consequence played a role to modernise the traditional-based learning management. Moreover, the classroom settings with the advanced technology adoption would help enhance the learning engagement at the leading features of both immersive and interactive pathway (Wulandari et al., 2018). In monitoring the progression to the learning experiences, the following features of AI-empowered instructional medium has given the platform to sustain the search engine pathway in helping improve the learning practice. The particular features of other similar platform such as virtual reality (VR), gamification and also relevant technology access are strategically being the medium of instructional practice with giving insightful value of being more fun and interesting for the learners (Aminudin et al., 2018b). It is especially for the learning platform where the AI-advanced instructional medium would enable the learners in interacting with their peers, members and teachers at the real-time-based scenario. In order to create the community sense in collaborating the advanced technology transition, the ability to form the access in performing the personalized learning together with its experiential pathway would result in designing the adaptive learning scenario (Huda, 2019). Such arranged systems throughout the algorithm use in helping manage the comprehension phase towards the related question for the learners to answer could be adopted in performing the individual learning ability. At this point of view, the detailed features in conducting such learning platform could reach to the decision system in enabling the learners to sustain their instructional performance. As such, the AI-empowered chat-gpt for instance has given the basic supply for early information description freely among the users prior to further clear identification and clarification from the primary sources.

In terms of helping monitor the basic principles of individual learning performance, the AI-empowered platform would allow the strategic gateway in the instructional process amidst their own personalised access. The additional part on managing AI-facilitated chatbots at this point could provide the database needed towards the given question so that the access to the learning inquiry process might have the feedback with an immediate basis (Yousefi and Tosarkani, 2023). Moreover, the strategic tool to enable to give the related information throughout the answering gateway might also become the significant features for the learning query pathway in having the give support by AI-empowered features. Moreover, the instructional process might go further in enhancing the constant response from each given question to provide a real time based response at the clearly descriptive point. The additional value in advancing the AI technology might transform the instructional design to sustain the learning performance as the gateway in approaching the quality education (Kembauw et al., 2019). The strategic approach to the education practice could provide the learning material sources to be more engaging, accessible and personalized within the achievement plan. Attempts to continue the further access to the learning material amidst the AI-instructed medium need to move forward leveraging the technology use in adopting the relevant information needed in enhancing the quality education. In ensuring the learning performance within the equal opportunity, the main destination in growing the development of learners' potentials would reach out quality education with its essential aspect of human development in acquiring the knowledge, skills, attitudes and values as demanded in achieving the growth potential (Huda, 2023; Syofiarti et al., 2021). The key emphasis in facilitating the quality education needs to have the access on managing the learning scenario mainly with the AI advanced technology development. As such, the significant contribution of such wide transaction of AI-supported instruction would reach in empowering the accessible pathway to achieve the quality education to all learners with the diverse background.

CONCLUSION

The emerging potentials given by the AI advanced technology in supporting the learning instruction could provide the substantial value in facilitating the access to the search engine –based platform. Such wide sophisticated features would enable in giving the prior information with the early brief description in that the accessible gateway to bring the users to have their personalised learning inquiry. The achievement to sustain the significant contribution of AI-supported instruction has been the strategic efforts to help achieve the quality education. This chapter did explore the essence of quality education in the age of Artificial Intelligence (AI) as an attempt to shape the future education through technologically sustainable transformation. The critical review from recently related literature will be employed in providing the perceptions concerning from both significant benefits and potential limitations of AI in the context of quality education. Utilizing the qualitative research design in focusing on the main objective, the findings revealed that the way to enhance quality education actualised into both teaching and learning practices amidst AI should do with enhancing the active involvement on questioning norms, analysing context, and evaluating evidence. The strategic potentials of AI adoption and development refers to enrich the utility of various facets of quality education including academic research and theory scrutiny. The study concludes that AI can be an asset in the development of quality education with caveats that require careful management. A balanced approach that capitalizes on AI's strengths while being aware of its limitations is necessary for cultivating robust critical thinking abilities for quality education with AI applications effectively.

REFERENCES

Abadi, S., Teh, K.S.M., Nasir, B.M., Huda, M., Ivanova, N.L., Sari, T.I., Maseleno, A., Satria, F., and Muslihudin, M. (2018). Application model of k-means clustering: insights into promotion strategy of vocational high school. International Journal of Engineering and Technology. 7 (2.27), 182-187.

Abulibdeh, A., Zaidan, E., & Abulibdeh, R. (2024). Navigating the confluence of artificial intelligence and education for sustainable development in the era of industry 4.0: Challenges, opportunities, and ethical dimensions. *Journal of Cleaner Production*, 437, 140527. DOI: 10.1016/j.jclepro.2023.140527

Ali, A. H. (2023). Pelajar Khalifah Profesional Tempaan Ulul Albab sorotan penerapannya berasaskan komponen QEI di UPSI. *Firdaus Journal*, 3(2), 51–63. DOI: 10.37134/firdaus.vol3.2.5.2023

Alwi, A. S. Q., & Ibrahim, R. (2022). Isu terhadap Penggunaan Teknologi Media Digital dalam kalangan guru pelatih jurusan Pendidikan Khas. *Firdaus Journal*, 2(2), 88–93. DOI: 10.37134/firdaus.vol2.2.9.2022

Aminudin, N., Huda, M., Ihwani, S.S., Noor, S.S.M., Basiron, B., Jasmi, K.A., Safar, J., Mohamed, A.K., Embong, W.H.W., Mohamad, A.M., Maseleno, A., Masrur, M., Trisnawati, and Rohmadi, D. (2018a). The family hope program using AHP method. International Journal of Engineering and Technology. 7(2.27), 188-193.

Aminudin, N., Huda, M., Mohamed, A.K., Embong, W.H.W., Mohamad, A.M., Basiron, B., Ihwani, S.S., Noor, S.S.M., Jasmi, K.A., Safar, J., Natalie, L., Ivanova, Maseleno, A., Triono, A., and Nungsiati. (2018b). Higher education selection using simple additive weighting. International Journal of Engineering and Technology. 7(2.27), 211-217.

Bahroun, Z., Anane, C., Ahmed, V., & Zacca, A. (2023). Transforming education: A comprehensive review of generative artificial intelligence in educational settings through bibliometric and content analysis. *Sustainability (Basel)*, 15(17), 12983. DOI: 10.3390/su151712983

Berlian, Z., & Huda, M. (2022). Reflecting culturally responsive and communicative teaching (CRCT) through partnership commitment. *Education Sciences*, 12(5), 295. DOI: 10.3390/educsci12050295

Borham, A. H., Huda, M., Rasid, M. S. A., Rahim, M. M. A., & Hamid, N. Z. A. (2024). Teaching approach for indigenous people: An empirical study from Pahang, Malaysia. [EduLearn]. *Journal of Education and Learning*, 18(3), 773–782.

Borham, A. H., Syahdiah, U., Mohsin, M. A., Huda, M., Rahim, M. A., Ilyas, D., & Sakni, A. S. (2024). Information and communication ethics in social media for indigenous people's religious understanding: a critical review. In *World Conference on Information Systems for Business Management* (pp. 287-302). Singapore: Springer Nature Singapore. DOI: 10.1007/978-981-99-8346-9_25

Cheng, E. C. K., & Wang, T. (2023). Leading digital transformation and eliminating barriers for teachers to incorporate artificial intelligence in basic education in Hong Kong. *Computers and Education: Artificial Intelligence*, 5, 100171. DOI: 10.1016/j.caeai.2023.100171

Goralski, M. A., & Tan, T. K. (2020). Artificial intelligence and sustainable development. *International Journal of Management Education*, 18(1), 100330. DOI: 10.1016/j.ijme.2019.100330

Hadi, A., Huda, M., Lyndon, N., & Nasir, B. M. (2024). Managing Professional-Ethical Negotiation for Cyber Conflict Prevention: Perspectives From Higher Institution Learners in the Pandemic Age. [IJCBPL]. *International Journal of Cyber Behavior, Psychology and Learning*, 14(1), 1–27. DOI: 10.4018/IJCBPL.344022

Hehsan, A., Huda, M., Mahsun, M., Asrori, A., Shafwan, M. H., Zakariya, D. M., . . . Layyinnati, I. (2024). Digital Muhadathah: framework model development for digital Arabic language learning. In *International Conference on Information and Communication Technology for Competitive Strategies* (pp. 13-29). Singapore: Springer Nature Singapore. DOI: 10.1007/978-981-97-0744-7_2

Huda, M. (2019). Empowering application strategy in the technology adoption: Insights from professional and ethical engagement. *Journal of Science and Technology Policy Management*, 10(1), 172–192. DOI: 10.1108/JSTPM-09-2017-0044

Huda, M. (2022). Towards an adaptive ethics on social networking sites (SNS): A critical reflection. Journal of Information. *Communication and Ethics in Society*, 20(2), 273–290.

Huda, M. (2023). Towards digital access during pandemic age: Better learning service or adaptation struggling? *Foresight*, 25(1), 82–107. DOI: 10.1108/FS-09-2021-0184

Huda, M. (2024a). *Empowering communication strategy for safe cyberspace: insights from trust-based quality information.* Global Knowledge, Memory and Communication.

Huda, M. (2024b). Trust as a key element for quality communication and information management: Insights into developing safe cyber-organisational sustainability. *The International Journal of Organizational Analysis*, 32(8), 1539–1558. DOI: 10.1108/IJOA-12-2022-3532

Huda, M. (2024c). Between accessibility and adaptability of digital platform: Investigating learners' perspectives on digital learning infrastructure. *Higher Education. Skills and Work-Based Learning*, 14(1), 1–21. DOI: 10.1108/HESWBL-03-2022-0069

Huda, M., Isa, N. K. M., Husain, H., Almunawar, M. N., Anshari, M., & Jailani, M. (2024). *Managing Organizational Stability in Digital Era: Emerging Trends of Trust in Cyberspace-Based Information. Customer Relationship Management: Methods, Opportunities and Challenges.* Nova Science Publisher.

Huda, M., Musolin, M. H., Ismail, M. H., Yauri, A. M., Bakar, A., Zuhri, M., & Hasanah, U. (2024c). From digital ethics to digital community: an Islamic principle on strengthening safety strategy on information. In *Proceedings of the Computational Methods in Systems and Software* (pp. 165-182). Cham: Springer International Publishing. DOI: 10.1007/978-3-031-53552-9_15

Huda, M., Musolin, M. H., Serour, R. O. H., Azman, M., Yauri, A. M., Bakar, A., Zuhri, M., Mujahidin, M., & Hasanah, U. (2024d). Digital record management in Islamic education institution: Current trends on enhancing process and effectiveness through learning technology. In *Software Engineering Methods in Systems and Network Systems - Proceedings of 7th Computational Methods in Systems and Software 2023.* Springer Nature Switzerland. DOI: 10.1007/978-3-031-53549-9_33

Huda, M., Rohim, M. A., Hehsan, A. B., Qodriah, S. L., Junaidi, J., Haron, Z., . . . Abas, H. (2024e). From Technology Adaptation to Technology Adoption: An Insight into Public Islamic School Administrative Management. In *International Congress on Information and Communication Technology* (pp. 57-68). Singapore: Springer Nature Singapore. DOI: 10.1007/978-981-97-3305-7_5

Huda, M., Serour, R. O. H., Musolin, M. H., Azman, M., Yauri, A. M., Bakar, A., & Hasanah, U. (2024b). Trust in electronic record management system: insights from Islamic-based professional and moral engagement-based digital archive. In *Proceedings of the Computational Methods in Systems and Software* (pp. 303-315). Cham: Springer International Publishing. DOI: 10.1007/978-3-031-53549-9_32

Huda, M., Shahrill, M., Maseleno, A., Jasmi, K. A., Mustari, I., & Basiron, B. (2017). Exploring Adaptive Teaching Competencies in Big Data Era. *International Journal of Emerging Technologies in Learning*, 12(3), 68–83. DOI: 10.3991/ijet.v12i03.6434

Huda, M., & Sutopo, L., Liberty, Febrianto, & Mustafa, M. C. (2022). Digital information transparency for cyber security: critical points in social media trends. In Advances in Information and Communication: Proceedings of the 2022 Future of Information and Communication Conference (FICC), Volume 2 (pp. 814-831). Cham: Springer International Publishing.

Huda, M., Taisin, J. N., Muhamad, M., Kiting, R., & Yusuf, R. A. (2024a). Digital technology adoption for instruction aids: insight into teaching material content. In *International Conference on Information and Communication Technology for Competitive Strategies* (pp. 59-68). Singapore: Springer Nature Singapore. DOI: 10.1007/978-981-97-1260-1_6

Jusoh, A., Huda, M., Abdullah, R., & Lee, N. (2024). Development of digital heritage for archaeovisit tourism resilience: evidences from E-Lenggong web portal. In *World Conference on Information Systems for Business Management* (pp. 53-74). Singapore: Springer Nature Singapore. DOI: 10.1007/978-981-99-8349-0_6

Kembauw, E., Soekiman, J. F. X. S. E., Lydia, L., Shankar, K., & Huda, M. (2019). Benefits of Corporate Mentoring for Business Organization. *Journal of Critical Reviews.*, 6(5), 101–106.

Latif, M. K., Md Saad, R., & Abd Hamid, S. (2023). Islamic Education Teachers' Competency in Teaching Qiraat Sab'ah for the Quranic Class. *Firdaus Journal*, 3(1), 19–27. DOI: 10.37134/firdaus.vol3.1.3.2023

Maseleno, A., Huda, M., Jasmi, K. A., Basiron, B., Mustari, I., Don, A. G., & Ahmad, R. (2019). Hau-Kashyap approach for student's level of expertise. *Egyptian Informatics Journal*, 20(1), 27–32. DOI: 10.1016/j.eij.2018.04.001

Masud, A., Borham, A. H., Huda, M., Rahim, M. M. A., & Husain, H. (2024). Managing information quality for learning instruction: Insights from public administration officers' experiences and practices. In *Software Engineering Methods in Systems and Network Systems - Proceedings of 7th Computational Methods in Systems and Software 2023*. Springer Nature Switzerland. DOI: 10.1007/978-3-031-54820-8_5

Mohamad Shokri, S. S., & Salihan, S. (2023). Modul pembangunan Program Huffaz Profesional Universiti Tenaga Nasional: Satu pemerhatian kepada konstruk pembangunan Al-Quran. *Firdaus Journal*, 3(2), 12–23. DOI: 10.37134/firdaus.vol3.2.2.2023

Mohd Nawi, M. Z. (2023). Media Variations in Education in Malaysia: A 21st Century Paradigm. *Firdaus Journal*, 3(1), 77–95. DOI: 10.37134/firdaus.vol3.1.8.2023

Muhamad, N., Huda, M., Hashim, A., Tabrani, Z. A., & Maárif, M. A. (2024). Managing technology integration for teaching strategy: public school educators' beliefs and practices. In *International Conference on Information and Communication Technology for Competitive Strategies* (pp. 385-400). Singapore: Springer Nature Singapore. DOI: 10.1007/978-981-97-0210-7_31

Muharom, F., Farhan, M., & Athoillah, S., Rozihan, Muflihin, A., & Huda, M. (2024). Digital technology skills for professional development: insights into quality instruction performance. In *International Conference on Information and Communication Technology for Competitive Strategies* (pp. 371-384). Singapore: Springer Nature Singapore. DOI: 10.1007/978-981-97-0210-7_30

Musolin, M. H., Ismail, M. H., Farhan, M., Rois, N., Huda, M., & Rohim, M. A. (2024c). Understanding of Artificial Intelligence for Islamic Education Support and Service: Insights from Empirical Literature Review. In Proceedings of Ninth International Congress on Information and Communication Technology. ICICT 2024. Lecture Notes in Networks and Systems. Springer, Singapore.

Musolin, M. H., Ismail, M. H., Huda, M., Hassan, T. R. R., & Ismail, A. (2024b). Towards an Islamic education administration system: a critical contribution from technology adoption. In Proceedings of Ninth International Congress on Information and Communication Technology. ICICT 2024. Lecture Notes in Networks and Systems. Springer, Singapore.

Musolin, M. H., Serour, R. O. H., Hamid, S. A., Ismail, A., Huda, M., & Rohim, M. A. (2024a). Developing Personalized Islamic Learning in Digital Age: Pedagogical and Technological Integration for Open Learning Resources (OLR). In Proceedings of Ninth International Congress on Information and Communication Technology. ICICT 2024. Lecture Notes in Networks and Systems. Springer, Singapore.

Okunlaya, R. O., Syed Abdullah, N., & Alias, R. A. (2022). Artificial intelligence (AI) library services innovative conceptual framework for the digital transformation of university education. *Library Hi Tech*, 40(6), 1869–1892. DOI: 10.1108/LHT-07-2021-0242

Omar, M. N. (2022). Inovasi pengajaran & pemudahcaraan menggunakan Aplikasi Ezi-Maq (MAHARAT AL-QURAN) untuk menarik minat pelajar menguasai Ilmu Tajwid. *Firdaus Journal*, 2(2), 79–87. DOI: 10.37134/firdaus.vol2.2.8.2022

Rahim, M. M. A., Huda, M., Borham, A. H., Kasim, A. Y., & Othman, M. S. (2024). Managing information leadership for learning performance: an empirical study among public school educators. In *World Conference on Information Systems for Business Management* (pp. 75-91). Singapore: Springer Nature Singapore. DOI: 10.1007/978-981-99-8349-0_7

Rahman, M. H. A., Jaafar, J., & Huda, M. (2023). Information and communication skills for higher learners competence model. In *Proceedings of the Computational Methods in Systems and Software* (pp. 357-375). Cham: Springer International Publishing.

Sari, Cita, D., Ali, A. H., Harun, M., Batre, N. M., Hanafi, M. S., Jaludin, Z. Y., Cittra Juniarni, Darodjat, Indria Nur, Ridha Harwan, & Iwan Kuswandi. (2023). Transformation of Artificial intelligence in Islamic Edu with Ulul Albab Value (Global Challenge Perespective). *Firdaus Journal*, 3(1), 1–9. DOI: 10.37134/firdaus.vol3.1.1.2023

Susilowati, T., Dacholfany, M.I., Aminin, S., Ikhwan, A., Nasir, B.M., Huda, M., Prasetyo, A., Maseleno, A., Satria, F., Hartati, S., and Wulandari. (2018). Getting parents involved in child's school: using attendance application system based on SMS gateway. International Journal of Engineering and Technology. 7(2.27), 167-174.

Susilowati, T., Teh, K.S.M., Nasir, B.M., Don, A.G., Huda, M., Hensafitri, T., Maseleno, A., Oktafianto, and Irawan, D. (2018). Learning application of Lampung language based on multimedia software. International Journal of Engineering and Technology. 7(2.27), 175-181.

Syofiarti, S., Saputra, R., Lahmi, A., & Rahmi, R. 2021). The Use of Audiovisual Media in Learning and Its Impact on Learning Outcomes of Islamic Cultural History at Madrasah Tsanawiyah Negeri 4 Pasaman. Firdaus Journal, 1(1), 36–44. (. https://doi.org/DOI: 10.37134/firdaus.vol1.1.4.2021

Tan, A. A., Huda, M., Rohim, M. A., Hassan, T. R. R., & Ismail, A. (2024). Chat GPT in Supporting Education Instruction Sector: An Empirical Literature Review. In Proceedings of Ninth International Congress on Information and Communication Technology. ICICT 2024. Lecture Notes in Networks and Systems. Springer, Singapore.

Wahid, A., Huda, M., Asrori, A., Abidin, R., Puspitasari, I., Hidayat, M. C., . . . Anwar, S. (2024). Digital technology for indigenous people's knowledge acquisition process: insights from empirical literature analysis. In *International Conference on Information and Communication Technology for Competitive Strategies* (pp. 41-57). Singapore: Springer Nature Singapore. DOI: 10.1007/978-981-97-1260-1_5

Wahid, A., Huda, M., Rohim, M. A., Ali, A. H., Kaspin, K. G., Fiqiyah, M., & Jima'ain, M. T. A. (2024b). Augmented Reality Model in Supporting Instruction Process: A Critical Review. In Proceedings of Ninth International Congress on Information and Communication Technology. ICICT 2024. Lecture Notes in Networks and Systems. Springer, Singapore. DOI: 10.1007/978-981-97-3305-7_6

Wulandari, Aminin, S., Dacholfany, M.I., Mujib, A., Huda, M., Nasir, B.M., Maseleno, A., Sundari, E., Fauzi, and Masrur, M. (2018). Design of library application system. International Journal of Engineering and Technology. 7(2.27), 199-204.

Yahya, S. F., & Othman, M. A. (2022). Penggunaan video dalam Pengajaran dan Pembelajaran Pendidikan Moral Tingkatan 2. *Firdaus Journal*, 2(2), 94–105. DOI: 10.37134/firdaus.vol2.2.10.2022

Yousefi, S., & Tosarkani, B. M. (2023). Exploring the role of blockchain technology in improving sustainable supply chain performance: A system-analysis-based approach. *IEEE Transactions on Engineering Management*.

Zainuri, A., & Huda, M. (2023). Empowering Cooperative Teamwork for Community Service Sustainability: Insights from Service Learning. *Sustainability (Basel)*, 15(5), 4551. DOI: 10.3390/su15054551

Zamri, F. A., Muhamad, N., & Huda, M. (2023). Information and communication technology skills for instruction performance: beliefs and experiences from public school educators. In *Proceedings of the Computational Methods in Systems and Software* (pp. 34-40). Cham: Springer Nature Switzerland.

Zamri, F. A., Muhamad, N., Huda, M., & Hashim, A. (2024). Social media adoption for digital learning innovation: insights into building learning support. In *International Conference on Information and Communication Technology for Competitive Strategies* (pp. 407-425). Singapore: Springer Nature Singapore. DOI: 10.1007/978-981-97-0744-7_34

Chapter 14
Shaping the Future of Education and the Futures of Learning Spaces in the Philippines Beyond 2050

Jimmy Maming
https://orcid.org/0000-0001-7601-7720
Nuevo School of Technology and Humanities Inc., Philippines

Eugene Escalona Toring
Indiana Aerospace University, Philippines

Kimberly Cui Nuevo-Toring
Indian Aerospace University, Philippines & University of the Visayas, Philippines

ABSTRACT

The foreseeable future educational environment in the Philippines is influenced by a complex interaction of elements such as technical improvements, shifts in population, economic expansion, and social changes. As we move beyond 2050, it is vital to conceive and investigate creative learning environments that promote innovation, analytical thinking, and lifelong education. This article investigates the Philippines' problems and prospects for building innovative learning spaces. It emphasizes the importance of fair opportunity for technological advances, training for educators, and suitable infrastructure. The report also looks at upcoming themes including individualized instruction, blended education, learning through experience, and lifelong learning.

DOI: 10.4018/979-8-3693-8242-4.ch014

INTRODUCTION

"There is no doubt whatever about the influence of architecture and structure upon human character and action. We make our buildings and afterward, they make us. They regulate the course of our lives" - Winston Churchill, 1924.

Imagine a Philippines where education is individualized, easily available, and smoothly incorporated into daily life, and where learning environments are not limited to conventional classrooms or institutions. In the future when education is a lifetime endeavor, people will be able to realize their full abilities and make valuable contributions to a flourishing community.

Over the years, the Philippines, a country having a rich cultural legacy and a fast-expanding population, has seen notable developments in education. However, the varied and changing demands of individuals in the twenty-first century might outgrow the conventional learning environments of the past. It is crucial to consider and investigate cutting-edge learning environments that might encourage innovation, analytical thinking, and lifelong learning as we go beyond 2050 (Castillo, Antiado, Reblando, 2019).

In the past, teacher-centered learning, standardized programs of study, and classroom-based instruction have been the mainstays of traditional learning environments in the Philippines. Even though these methods have been extremely important, it's possible that they won't fully equip pupils for the difficulties of the twenty-first century. A rising trend in creative learning environments that value customization, teamwork, and hands-on learning is meant to solve this. Technology is helping to drive this change, which attempts to create learning environments that are more effective and engaging (Morrisa and Imms, 2022).

Making the switch to cutting-edge learning environments offers both possibilities and problems. While spending on educator professional growth and infrastructure is necessary for successful implementation, ensuring fair availability of resources and technology is crucial to addressing the digital divide. Nonetheless, there are a lot of potential advantages to these creative strategies. They can promote entrepreneurship and innovation, raise educational attainment, and enhance educational results. The Philippines can develop a more inclusive and successful educational system that gives students the tools they need to succeed in the twenty-first century by embracing these new trends (Neill, S. and Etheridge, R., 2008).

Creative thinking and the development of entrepreneurial abilities can be fostered in students by innovative learning environments. Although there has been considerable discussion and research on the coming years of education, there aren't many in-depth studies that are especially concerned with what will happen to educational environments in the Philippines in and beyond 2050.

The Sustainable Development Goals, also known as the SDGs, cannot be achieved without innovative learning spaces. These places can support SDG 4 (Quality Education), SDG 5 (Gender Equality), SDG 8 (Decent Work and Economic Growth), SDG 9 (Industry, Innovation, and Infrastructure), and SDG 11 (Sustainable Cities and Communities) by offering inclusive, egalitarian, and individualized education. Collaborative learning environments, for instance, can promote innovation and entrepreneurship while tailored learning experiences can assist close disparities in education and improve learning outcomes.

By examining prospective outcomes, new trends, and difficulties that may influence the instructional settings of the future, this article seeks to close this gap and demonstrate how investment in educational facilities can also support equitable growth and economic success. It also offers an outlook on how learning environments may develop in the Philippines in the future. This study aims to educate lawmakers, educators, and stakeholders on the significance of investing in creative learning environments to satisfy the demands of future generations. It does this by examining various scenarios, emerging trends, and problems (Martínez-Ramos, et. Al, 2021).

Learning Spaces Defined

Learning spaces are physical or virtual places where instruction and learning take place. They cover an extensive variety of locations, including traditional classrooms, online platforms, libraries in general, and outdoor spaces. Learning environments are built to accommodate a variety of educational approaches, such as silent learning, collaborative instruction, hands-on education, and blended learning. To shed light on this phrase, consider the following definitions of learning environments from diverse authors.

Educause describes learning spaces as physical settings for many types of learning environments. They support a wide range of pedagogical approaches, including silent research, active or passive education, multisensory or physical instruction, industrial acquiring knowledge, and hands-on education, among others (EDUCAUSE, 2010).

Starr-Glass (2022) defines this term as an intentional location (real or virtual) intentionally created by the instructor in which participants could meet and participate in knowledge creation, whereas Davis (2010) proposed that educational spaces may promote new ways of instruction and learning while also fostering community. According to Simon Fraser University (2023), learning spaces are physical settings for many types of learning environments. They support a wide range of pedagogical approaches, such as silent learning, both passive and active education, multisensory or hands-on instruction, industrial learning, experiential education, and others. The University of Dayton (2023) supported this definition, which states that learning spaces are physical settings for various types of learning environments. They support a wide range of pedagogical approaches, such as silent study, either active or passive instruction, multisensory or physical learning, occupational education, hands-on training, and others.

Similarly, Iowa State University (2023) defines learning spaces as physical settings for various learning situations. They support a wide range of pedagogical approaches, such as silent study, either active or passive learning, multisensory or tactile education, industrial education, learning through experience, and others. According to the University of Michigan (2023), learning spaces are physical settings for a variety of learning contexts. They support a wide range of pedagogical approaches, such as silent research, active or passive schooling, visceral or hands-on instruction, practical studying, learning through experience, and others.

Stanford University (2023) emphasized the above criteria, stating that learning spaces are physical settings for many types of learning environments. They support a wide range of pedagogical approaches, such as silent investigation, both passive and active studying, multisensory or tactile instruction, industrial instruction, learning through experience, and others. subsequently, Harvard University (2023) concluded that educational environments are the material contexts for educational institutions of all types. They support a wide range of pedagogical approaches, such as silent study, actively or passively studying, tactile or physical instruction, industrial learning, learning through experience, and others.

One may argue that educative spaces are physical or virtual locations in which teaching and learning take place. They cover a wide range of locations, including traditional classrooms, online platforms, library resources, and outdoor spaces. Learning environments are built to accommodate a variety of educational approaches, such as silent research, learning together, hands-on study, and blended learning. Furthermore, according to several definitions, educational settings are designated areas where learners can gather and collaborate on knowledge generation. They might be virtual or real, and they accommodate a wide range of methods for instruction and instruction. Learning spaces are critical for developing effective and interesting learning environments that meet the different needs of learners.

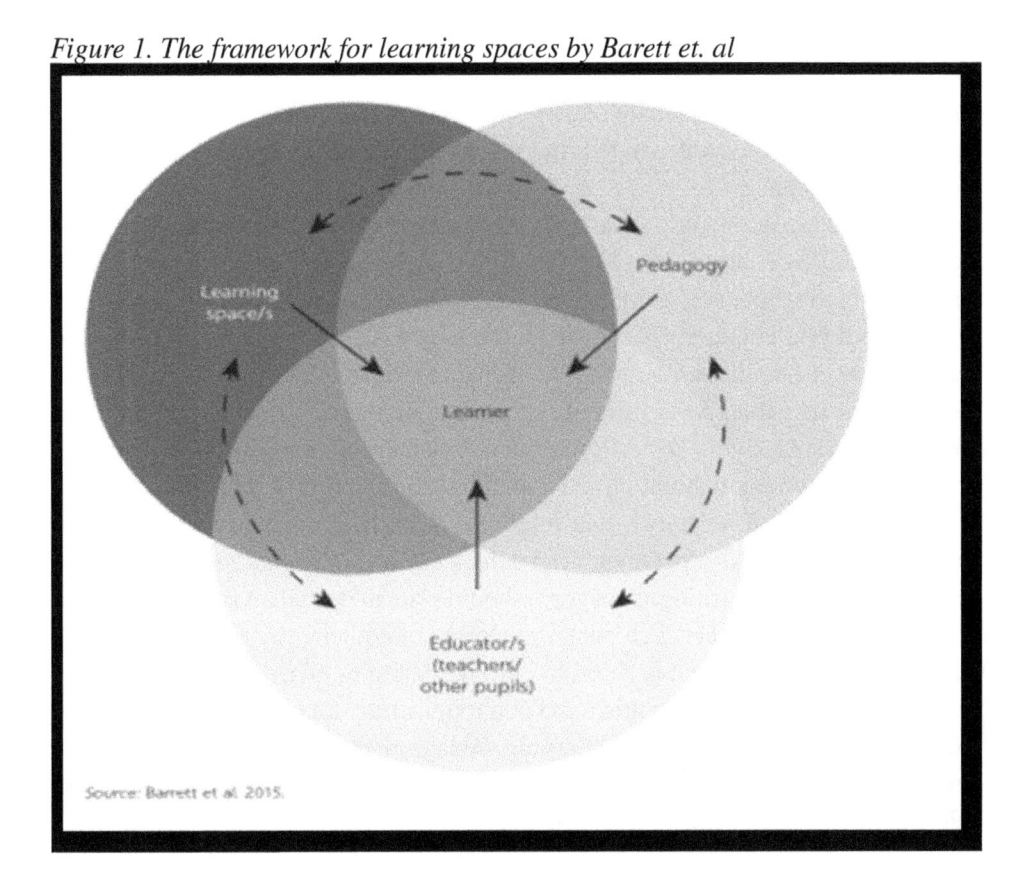

Figure 1. The framework for learning spaces by Barett et. al

Learning Interactions: Teachers, Spaces, and Pedagogy

Learning occurs within and across spaces. Whether in school classrooms or across tiny outside tables or peaceful library armchairs (Gonzalez, P.G., Noh, D., and Wilson, D., 2023). Learning interactions refer to the dynamic relationships between teachers, students, and the physical or virtual environments in which learning occurs. This framework highlights the interconnectedness of these three elements in shaping the overall learning experience.

According to Barret et al. (2015), teachers play a crucial role in creating and facilitating effective learning interactions. Their pedagogical approaches, teaching styles, and interactions with students significantly influence the learning process. Teachers can create engaging and supportive learning environments by employing a variety of teaching strategies: Teachers can use a mix of instructional methods, such as lectures, discussions, group work, and hands-on activities, to cater to different learning styles and promote active engagement. Another is to foster a positive classroom climate: Teachers can create a welcoming and inclusive classroom environment that encourages students to participate, ask questions, and take risks. Further, by providing personalized support, teachers can offer individualized attention and support to students, helping them to overcome challenges and achieve their learning goals.

Learning spaces also play a vital role in shaping learning interactions. The physical or virtual environment in which learning occurs can have a significant impact on student motivation, engagement, and academic performance. Effective learning spaces should be conducive to learning. This means that the physical design of learning spaces should be comfortable, well-lit, and equipped with the necessary resources. Further, it supports different learning styles, including visual, auditory, and kinesthetic learners, while fostering collaboration and communication. It should be designed to promote collaboration and communication among students and teachers.

In the context of Pedagogy, this refers to the methods and strategies used to teach and learn. Effective pedagogy can enhance learning interactions by focusing on student-centered learning: Pedagogy should prioritize student engagement and active participation, rather than passive learning. Another is by using technology effectively. Technology can be used to enhance learning experiences and provide new opportunities for collaboration and communication. Learning spaces also promote critical thinking and problem-solving. Pedagogy should encourage students to develop critical thinking and problem-solving skills. To illustrate this framework, below are examples of learning interactions:

1. A teacher using a flipped classroom approach where students watch lectures at home and then participate in group activities and discussions in class.
2. A teacher using a project-based learning approach where students work in teams to solve a real-world problem.
3. A teacher using a virtual reality simulation to provide students with immersive learning experiences.
4. A teacher creates a collaborative learning space where students can work together on projects and share ideas.

Learning interactions are complex and multifaceted. By understanding the interconnectedness of teachers, spaces, and pedagogy, educators can create more effective and engaging learning experiences for their students.

Emerging Trends in Learning Spaces

Personalized learning, enabled by technological improvements, is a promising method for meeting individual students' different requirements and learning styles. Customized learning platforms, for example, can use student performance data to change assignment difficulty and deliver focused feedback. This guarantees that learners are continually tested and supported, reducing boredom and dissatisfaction (OECD, 2019). Virtual reality simulations offer profound educational opportunities that can bring abstract ideas to life. For instance, pupils studying history can digitally visit past civilizations or investigate scientific phenomena firsthand. This can help with comprehension, participation, and ongoing retention of knowledge. Furthermore, artificially intelligent teaching systems can provide individualized support and guidance, adjusting to students' learning rates and responding to questions in real-time. This might be especially advantageous for students who struggle in typical school settings or need extra help.

Hybrid Learning

The convergence of online and in-person learning will increase, providing for greater adaptability and accessibility to education. Integrated learning models can offer the best of both worlds by allowing for collaboration, mentoring, and individualized support. (UNESCO; 2020). Hybrid learning is becoming more prevalent in the Philippines, providing a personalized and affordable approach to education. Here are some instances of how blended education is being used around the country.

K-12 Basic Education. Several educational institutions in the Philippines have implemented hybrid learning strategies, which combine online and in-person training. Particular topics or activities may need students to attend classes on campus, while others may be offered online. This provides more versatility and accommodates students with diverse learning styles and demands.

Higher Education. Educational institutions in the Philippines are also implementing hybrid education into their curriculum. Students, for example, can complement their on-campus coursework with online courses, or they may watch lectures online while also participating in group discussions and laboratories in person.

Vocational Training. Hybrid learning is especially useful in vocational training programs because it allows students to develop practical abilities through hands-on instruction while still acquiring theoretical concepts online. Culinary arts students, for example, may attend cooking sessions in person while also taking online nutrition and food safety courses.

Continuing Education. Hybrid learning is frequently employed in professional development initiatives, allowing professionals to upgrade or reskill without leaving their jobs. For example, instructors may take distance learning courses to strengthen their ability to teach, while managers may enroll in an online MBA program.

These are only a few instances of how blended education is being used in the Philippines. As technology advances, we ought to anticipate seeing numerous imaginative and successful hybrid approaches to education emerging in the future.

Experiential Learning

Experiential learning, in which students actively interact with the environment around them in their final days is becoming more common in modern education. This method understands that learning is more than just remembering facts and statistics; it also involves applying knowledge and honing critical thinking abilities. Experiential learning includes activities such as educational trips, internships, and project-based learning (Gardner, 2006).

Educational travels allow students to explore real-world locations and utilize their classroom skills in practical circumstances. Students studying biology, for example, may visit a nearby nature reserve to examine different ecosystems while recognizing species of plants and animals. Internships enable students to obtain direct involvement in their field of interest and apply their knowledge to real-world situations. A computer science student might volunteer at an IT firm to gain programming experience and learn industry best practices. Students participate in project-based learning activities, which encourage them to utilize their knowledge and skills to address real-world problems. Not to deny that students could collaborate on the project and then construct a powered-by solar energy water treatment system for a rural village.

Lifelong Learning

In today's fast-changing world around us, education is no longer a one-time experience limited to formal institutions. Individuals must engage in lifelong learning to get used to new technology, shifting employment markets, and societal changes. Learning environments will need to develop to enable this paradigm shift, including chances for lifelong learning (OECD, 2017). Illustrations of Lifelong Education Initiatives are shown below.

Online Courses and Platforms. Platforms such as Coursera, edX, and Udemy provide a wide range of online courses on a variety of topics, allowing students to learn at their speed and from any part of the world.

Community Colleges and Continuing Education Programs. These schools provide a wide range of workshops and classes for those looking to improve or reskill.

Corporate Training Programs. Many firms provide training programs for their staff to help them learn new skills and stay current with industry trends.

Mentorship Programs. Pairing seasoned experts with ambitious persons can provide invaluable advice and assistance for lifetime learning.

Libraries and Community Centers. These spaces can offer resources, workshops, and events to promote lifelong learning and engagement with the community.

Interestingly, Lifelong Learning can improve one's job prospects, development as an individual, interaction with others, adaptability, and ability to create supportive learning environments. To facilitate lifelong learning, learning environments must be adaptable, accessible, and inclusive. They should provide a wide range of educational designs, spanning through the internet, in-person, and hybrid alternatives. Furthermore, learning environments should be outfitted with the necessary technology and amenities to assist learning. In conclusion, lifelong learning is essential for individuals to thrive in the 21st century. By investing in innovative learning spaces and supporting continuous education, we can empower individuals to adapt to change, achieve their goals, and contribute to a better future.

Challenges and Opportunities

In any situation, challenges are always present as well as opportunities. The Philippines, a country with an extensive cultural past and a rapidly rising population, has seen substantial growth in education over time. However, traditional learning environments may be insufficient to address the diverse and changing necessities of learners in the twenty-first century. As we move beyond 2050, it is vital to conceive and investigate creative learning environments that promote innovation, analytical thinking, and lifelong education. The future development of educational environments in the Philippines is influenced by a complex interaction of elements such as technical improvements, population shifts, economic development, and social changes. These characteristics bring both obstacles and opportunities, necessitating meticulous investigation and strategic planning.

Digital Divide. The digital divide, the gap between those with access to technology and those without, remains a significant challenge in the Philippines. Ensuring equitable access to technology and digital literacy is crucial for creating inclusive learning spaces. (UNESCO, 2019).

Teacher Professional Development. Teachers will need to develop new skills and competencies to effectively facilitate learning in innovative environments. Investing in teacher professional development is essential for ensuring quality education. (OECD, 2018).

Infrastructure and Resources. Adequate infrastructure, including reliable internet connectivity and well-equipped learning spaces, is necessary to support innovative learning. Governments and private sector organizations need to invest in developing and maintaining quality infrastructure. (ADB, 2020).

Cultural Relevance: Learning spaces should be culturally relevant and inclusive, reflecting the diverse backgrounds and experiences of learners. This can involve incorporating local languages, customs, and traditions into the curriculum and learning environment. (UNESCO, 2018).

POTENTIAL SCENARIOS FOR THE FUTURES OF LEARNING SPACES

First Scenario. The Personalized Learning Hub

In this scenario, learning spaces become highly personalized and adaptive, catering to the unique needs and interests of each learner. Students have access to a variety of resources, including virtual tutors, personalized learning paths, and immersive simulations.

Second Scenario. The Collaborative Learning Commons

In this scenario, learning spaces are designed to foster collaboration, creativity, and critical thinking. Students work together on projects, engage in debates, and share ideas in open and inclusive environments.

Third Scenario. The Lifelong Learning Hub

In this scenario, learning spaces become centers for lifelong learning, offering a variety of programs and courses for individuals of all ages and backgrounds. These spaces provide opportunities for professional development, skill acquisition, and personal enrichment.

In a Nutshell, the futures of the academic environment in the Philippines is full of intriguing opportunities. By embracing new trends, tackling difficulties, and investing in creative learning settings, the Philippines can shape a future in which learning is open, welcoming, and empowering for everyone. This study has looked at prospective scenarios, analyzed new trends, and emphasized the need to tackle issues including the digital gaps, development for educators, facilities, and cultural relevance. By promoting innovative learning environments, the Philippines can make sure that its population has the abilities and knowledge required to flourish in a fast-changing world.

ACKNOWLEDGMENT

We express our deepest gratitude to all who have contributed to this endeavor's success. Your unwavering support and guidance have made this pursuit a reality.

Words could not express our special thanks to our son and inaanak, Eugene "Eugo" Nuevo Toring, Jr., for he is the source of our joy. We are eternally grateful to our parents, Dr. Jovenal Toring and Mrs. Cecilia E. Toring; Ret. Col. Jonathan O. Nuevo, Sr. and Mrs. Carissa Cui Nuevo; Mr. Clerio Candelario Maming and Mrs. Letecia Loquinto Bernabe, for their love, prayers, and sacrifices.

We also acknowledge the invaluable contributions of the administration, faculty, and staff of Indiana Aerospace University, the University of the Visayas, and Nuevo School of Technology and Humanities Inc. Their expertise and unwavering support have been essential to this project's success.

REFERENCES

Asian Development Bank (ADB). (2020). *Key Trends in Education in Asia and the Pacific*. ADB.

Castillo, Jr. F.G, Antiado, D.F. & Reblando, J.R.P (2019). Philippine Education System: Are We Moving Forward? *International Journal of Innovative Technology and Exploring Engineering (IJITEE)*, Vol. 8, Issue-12S.

Davis, J. A. (2010). *Learning Spaces: Designing for 21st Century Learning*. EDUCAUSE.

EDUCAUSE. (2010). *Learning Spaces: Designing for 21st Century Learning*. EDUCAUSE.

Gardner, H. (2006). *Multiple Intelligences: New Horizons in Theory and Practice*. Basic Books.

Gonzalez, P.G., Noh, D., and Wilson, D. (2023, Apr.). *Making the Space for Learning*. Project Zero. Harvard Graduate School of Business. Available from /sites/default/files/Making%20the%20Space%20for%20Learning.pdf

Harvard University. (2023). *Learning Spaces*. Retrieved from https://pz.harvard.edu/sites/default/files/Making%20the%20Space%20for%20Learning.pdf

Hughes, J., & Morrison, L. (2020). Innovative Learning Spaces in the Making. *Frontiers in Education*, 5, 89. Advance online publication. DOI: 10.3389/feduc.2020.00089

Iowa State University. (2023). *Learning Spaces*. Retrieved from https://www.lib.iastate.edu/visit-and-study/creation-and-learning-spaces

Johnson, D. W., & Johnson, R. T. (1999). *Active Learning: Cooperation, Competition, and Individualization in the Classroom*. Allyn & Bacon.

Martínez-Ramos, S. A., Rodríguez-Reséndiz, J., Gutiérrez, A. F., Sevilla-Camacho, P. Y., & Mendiola-Santíbañez, J. D. (2021). The Learning Space as Support to Sustainable Development: A Revision of Uses and Design Processes. *Sustainability (Basel)*, 13(21), 11609. DOI: 10.3390/su132111609

Morrisa, J. E., & Wesley Imms, W. (2022). Designing and using innovative learning spaces: What teachers have to say. *IUL Research.*, 3(6), 7–25. Advance online publication. DOI: 10.57568/iulres.v3i6.295

Neill, S., & Etheridge, R. (2008). *Flexible learning spaces: the integration of pedagogy, physical design, and instructional technology*. Semantic Scholar., DOI: 10.1080/10528008.2008.11489024

OECD. (Organisation for Economic Co-operation and Development). (2017). *Learning to Thrive: Skills for the Future*. OECD Publishing.

OECD. (Organisation for Economic Co-operation and Development). (2018). *Teaching and Learning International Survey (TALIS) 2018 Results*. OECD Publishing.

OECD. (Organisation for Economic Co-operation and Development). (2019). *Education 2030: A Global Education Transformation*. OECD Publishing.

Simon Fraser University. (2023). *Learning Spaces*. Retrieved from Retrieved from https://www.sfu.ca/students/myclassroom

Stanford University. (2023). *Learning Spaces*. Retrieved from https://news.stanford.edu/stories/2023/05/furniture-tech-upgrades-transforming-classrooms-learning

Starr-Glass, D. (2022). *Learning Spaces: Design and Pedagogy*. Routledge.

UNESCO. (United Nations Educational, Scientific and Cultural Organization). (2019). *Global Education Monitoring Report 2019: Learning to Change the World*. UNESCO.\

UNESCO. (United Nations Educational, Scientific and Cultural Organization). (2020). *Reimagining Education: A Global Dialogue*. UNESCO.

UNESCO. (United Nations Educational, Scientific and Cultural Organization). (2020). *Reimagining Education: A Global Dialogue*. UNESCO.

University of Dayton. (2023). *Learning Spaces*. Retrieved fromhttps://ecommons.udayton.edu/learnteach_forum/2023/

University of Michigan. (2023). *Learning Spaces*. Retrieved from https://lsa.umich.edu/technology-services/news-events/all-news/teaching-tip-of-the-week/learning-spaces-affect-student-engagement.html

ENDNOTES

[1] School Principal. Nuevo School of Technology and Humanities Inc. Tunga, Moalboal, Cebu, Philippines.

[2] Professor. University of the Visayas – Cebu City and Assistant Research Director & Professor. Indiana Aerospace University – Lapu-Lapu City

[3] Vice President for Operations and Director of Research and Innovations Offices. Indiana Aerospace University – Lapu-Lapu City

Chapter 15
The Effect of Experiment Videos Supported by Case Studies on High School Students' Environmental Awareness

Gamze Tunçay
https://orcid.org/0009-0003-3989-6457
Gazi University, Turkey

Zeynep Melike Güçlü
https://orcid.org/0009-0007-8888-147X
Gazi University, Turkey

Özge Özyalçin Oskay
https://orcid.org/0000-0002-9368-5381
Hacettepe University, Turkey

ABSTRACT

In 2015, the United Nations set the 2030 Sustainable Development Goals (SDGs) to address global challenges like poverty, inequality, health, education, and climate change. One key goal is quality education, aiming to provide free, equitable, and high-quality education for all. This study focused on improving environmental awareness and educational equality by using technology in schools without laboratories. A booklet with YouTube links and QR codes for experiments was developed, enabling 475 students across four cities to access experiment videos. Results showed a significant increase in students' environmental awareness and contributed to equal

DOI: 10.4018/979-8-3693-8242-4.ch015

learning opportunities.

In the 21st century, the rapid advancements in science, technology, and industry aim to provide people with a more comfortable and better living environment. However, the unconscious use of raw materials and the inadequate disposal of harmful waste from industrial facilities have significantly harmed the environment (Bozyiğit & Karaaslan, 1998). The only and most effective way to prevent environmental pollution and solve environmental problems is to educate individuals who make up society. Individuals should be raised with a sense of responsibility towards the environment, environmental awareness, and sustainable development goals (Çabuk & Karacaoğlu, 2003). When individuals are aware of the environment and potential problems, they act in a way that considers the environment in every action, in line with sustainable development goals (Gadenne, Kennedy, & McKeiver, 2009). One of the important concepts encountered in the process of creating environmental awareness and achieving sustainable development goals is environmental education. Environmental education is defined as "a continuous learning process that enables individuals to develop awareness towards their environment, recognize environmental values, attitudes, and concepts, and gain knowledge, skills, values, and experience to solve environmental problems in line with sustainable development goals" (Doğan, 1997; Vaughan, Gack, Solorazano, & Ray, 2003; Güven & Aydoğdu, 2012).

Environmental education is a multidimensional and long-term education that requires lifelong knowledge, values, understanding, and experience to achieve sustainable development goals. It is a significant area of work at every level of education, from preschool to higher education. Environmental awareness and environmental sensitivity should be developed from an early age, and this education should start in preschool and continue throughout life. Research on environmental education reveals that while there are numerous studies at the preschool, primary school, and undergraduate levels, there are insufficient studies at the high school level, specifically in the 9th, 10th, 11th, and 12th grades. The acquisition of environmental awareness and sustainable development goals should continue uninterrupted at every stage of education.

Since the environment is related to every aspect of life, it has become a common subject in many courses such as Turkish, Social Studies, Science and Technology, Physics, Chemistry, Biology, and Visual Arts. The acquisition of environmental awareness and sensitivity, the emphasis on practices in line with sustainable development goals, and the association of activities with daily life are essential (Polat, 2013). One of the most suitable teaching methods for this is the case study method.

The Case Study Method involves solving real-life problems in the classroom to facilitate learning. With this method, students understand the event, analyze the data, and evaluate the problem. It is possible to present scientific concepts to students using real-life examples through the Case Study Method, help them realize the relationship between real-life issues and science, and develop their scientific process skills (Çam & Köse, 2008).

Effective education on environmental awareness and sustainable development goals can only be achieved with teachers who have been trained in this area. If teachers know how to effectively teach environmental awareness, environmental sensitivity, and sustainable development goals using various methods and techniques, environmental education can be carried out more efficiently. Therefore, in the "Community Service Practices" course at a public university in Ankara, pre-service teachers have been asked to develop teaching materials that foster environmental awareness, environmental sensitivity, and sustainable development goals using new technologies and current teaching methods and techniques.

Sustainable Development Goals

In 2015, the United Nations Member States adopted the 2030 Agenda for Sustainable Development, drawing a shared roadmap for peace and prosperity for people and the planet. This framework includes 17 Sustainable Development Goals (SDGs), an urgent call to action for all countries—developed and developing—to address issues such as ending poverty and other deprivations, improving health and education, reducing inequality, and spurring economic growth. It also aims to combat climate change and preserve our oceans and forests (United Nations, 2024). The United Nations Turkey continues to support these goals to be achieved by 2030. The Sustainable Development Goals aim to end poverty, protect the environment, take measures against the climate crisis, ensure equitable prosperity, and promote peace (United Nations Turkey, 2024).

One of the 17 Sustainable Development Goals is quality education, which includes the objective "to ensure that all girls and boys complete free, equitable, and quality primary and secondary education leading to relevant and effective learning outcomes" by 2030.

Sustainable Development Goals and Education

Today, the world economy faces various social, environmental, and economic crises. While global changes have benefited society, problems such as inequality, terrorism, addiction, violence, gender discrimination, unhealthy living conditions, population growth, unplanned urbanization, low-quality education, unconscious consumption, climate change, environmental damage, income inequality, poverty, and unemployment affect the entire world. In this process, humanity has begun to understand nature. Communities known as knowledge societies today have contributed to the emergence of the concept of sustainability, which has gained importance due to the thoughts, discourse, and behaviors developed in response to these problems. It is now widely accepted that the world economy can remain stable and grow with the goals of sustainable development (Peşkircioğlu, 2016; Korkmaz, 2020).

Development in human-centered societies, which are strengthened by productivity-based growth, becomes sustainable when the gains from productivity increase are shared among parties, social justice is ensured, and resources for future generations are preserved. In this context, development is not based solely on the quantitative increase in goods and services produced individually but must also include the principles and outcomes of social development and environmental protection. This situation embodies the very essence of sustainable development in our era (Peşkircioğlu, 2016).

Sustainable development occurs without depleting our existing natural resources or disturbing the balance in the ecosystem (Aydede et al., 2019). The path leading to the concept of sustainable development began with the "Green Revolution" in the 1940s, seen as a significant innovation to meet the increasing food needs of the world's population. The Green Revolution started with agricultural developments in Mexico in the 1940s. Key points of the Green Revolution included the use of chemical fertilizers and pesticides, excessive water usage, and the destruction of wetlands, forest areas, and natural areas to open fields. It is a revolution with practices to solve today's global problems. Such developments have increased the importance of sustainable development and awareness (Teksöz, 2016; Şeker and Aydınlı, 2021).

Education for sustainable development aims to develop the knowledge, skills, perspectives, and values that will enable people to commit to creating a sustainable future (Zhang et al., 2020). The 2030 Agenda for Sustainable Development emphasizes the importance of incorporating sustainable development education principles at all educational levels. This education should encourage the development of sustainability competencies in preschool to higher education and informal education. Studies show that sustainable development education activities have become a significant focus in recent years and indicate the need for further research to operationalize and assess sustainability competencies (Cebrián et al., 2020).

Sustainable Development Goals and Chemistry Education

The aim of the study conducted by Loste et al. (2020) is to examine how sustainability tools such as green chemistry are perceived and considered beneficial in the fields of business and education. In the study, a survey was conducted with 565 participants who took an online course (MOOC) on sustainability tools. The sample group consisted of individuals from various professions in Spain and Latin America. The results of the study revealed that, although green chemistry is a successful tool in industry and chemistry, it is less known and considered less beneficial compared to other sustainability tools. However, after the training, there was an increase in the participants' perception of the benefits of green chemistry. In conclusion, it was emphasized that green chemistry should be promoted more in non-chemistry fields and that this awareness can be increased through education, regulation, and research.

The aim of the study conducted by Taha et al. (2019) is to compare the effects of traditional chemistry experiments and green chemistry experiments on students' environmental sustainability knowledge, awareness, and practices. The research was carried out within the framework of an experimental design, using a control group of 23 students and an experimental group of 23 students. The experimental group received training on the application of green chemistry experiments, while the control group performed traditional chemistry experiments. During the research process, a 48-item questionnaire was used to measure students' environmental sustainability knowledge, and a paper-and-pencil test was employed to assess their knowledge on reaction rates. The results showed that, although there was no significant difference in overall achievement between the two groups, the experimental group experienced a significant increase in green chemistry knowledge and environmental awareness. Furthermore, it was determined that green chemistry experiments were effective in enhancing students' environmental awareness.

The study conducted by Anastas et al. (2021) examines how the United Nations' Sustainable Development Goals (SDGs), announced in 2015, can be applied in the fields of chemistry and engineering, and their role in achieving these goals. The research emphasizes that the SDGs provide a universally applicable framework and highlights the importance of a sustainability-focused approach to the use of chemicals. Progress is evaluated through various examples and practices from different countries. Countries such as India, China, and Brazil are taken as case studies. The results underscore the importance of strategies such as using renewable resources, recycling waste, and sustainability education to reduce the environmental impact of the chemical industry. The study emphasizes that achieving the SDGs requires a systematic and holistic effort.

The study conducted by Michalopoulou et al. (2019) aims to evaluate the impact of the Sustainable Futures (SFOC) online course and the Sustainable Development Optional Unit (SDOU), developed by the University of Bristol, on the chemistry curriculum. The research examines how these educational materials contribute to chemistry education linked to the Sustainable Development Goals (SDGs) and what skills they help students acquire. The methods used include online and face-to-face interactions, student feedback, discussion points, video feedback, and portfolio-based assessments. The sample group is based on over 250 students from various faculties at the University of Bristol. The results indicate that these online courses and optional units provide students with in-depth knowledge and skills related to sustainable development, promote systems thinking and interdisciplinary collaboration, and make significant contributions to chemistry education.

The aim of the study conducted by Mitarlis, Azizah, and Yonata (2023) is to determine the feasibility of integrating green chemistry principles into laboratory practice and to evaluate how goals such as material savings, energy efficiency, and waste reduction can be achieved in this process. The research was conducted using practical laboratory experiments and student surveys related to the integration of green chemistry principles. The sample group consisted of students who participated in these practical laboratory experiments and surveys. The results of the study showed that the application of green chemistry principles provided material savings, reduced energy consumption, and prevented waste generation. It was observed that students' knowledge level of green chemistry increased from below 60% before the training to over 80% after the training. These findings revealed that the integration of green chemistry into education contributes to the SDGs (Sustainable Development Goals) and plays an important role in raising environmental awareness.

The aim of the study conducted by Petillion, Freeman, and McNeil (2019) is to increase student engagement and interest by integrating the UN Sustainable Development Goals (SDG) framework into introductory chemistry courses, as well as to support the learning of course concepts. To achieve this goal, a mixed-method approach, involving both quantitative and qualitative analyses, was used. Quantitative data were collected through surveys completed by 357 out of 649 students, while qualitative data were obtained through semi-structured interviews with 7 students. The results of the study showed that SDG-framed case studies helped students understand the societal relevance and applicability of chemistry concepts, positively impacted their learning processes, and increased student interest in the subject. However, some students expressed concerns about time constraints and a lack of conceptual support related to the case studies.

Quality Education

Educational content should reflect contemporary needs, such as crisis and disaster preparedness, and be suitable for the conditions children experience. Not only academic achievements but also 21st-century skills such as critical thinking and collaboration should be emphasized. Quality content increases inclusivity by addressing the needs of different children and helps them build a solid learning foundation (ERG, 2023).

Quality education is not only about increasing individuals' knowledge levels but also an essential social indicator of sustainable development. It integrates people into the constantly changing world, increases workforce productivity, and contributes to technological advancements. The positive relationship between quality education and sustainable development is a hallmark of developed societies (Cıvış, 2021). Quality education has a multidimensional structure, and its components vary according to the education policies of different countries. One of the aims of the Sustainable Development Goals is to achieve quality learning outcomes through free and equitable primary and secondary education (Kaynak et al., 2023).

Environmental Awareness

This section contains national and international studies related to environmental awareness and consciousness, along with the details of these studies. The research criteria for this topic include studies conducted with sample groups ranging from preschool to undergraduate levels. The focus is solely on environmental studies within the fields of chemistry, science, and extracurricular activities.

In the study conducted by Çabuk and Çabuk (2016), green chemistry is explained as methods that prevent the harmful effects of chemical products on the environment and human health. The aim of this project was to increase the environmental knowledge levels of 5-6-year-old children attending preschool through green chemistry applications. The project titled 'Protecting the Environment with Green Chemistry' was implemented for the first time in Isparta in 2016 and supported within the TÜBİTAK 4004-Nature and Science Schools project group. A total of 69 preschool children from Keçiborlu District in Isparta participated in the project, with 35 in the experimental group and 34 in the control group. During the project, children were provided with eight days of hands-on environmental education activities based on green chemistry. An experimental study was conducted in line with the impact of the project applications. Pre-post and follow-up tests were administered to the children who participated in the project. The results showed that the project 'Protecting the Environment with Green Chemistry' increased the environmental knowledge levels of preschool children.

The study conducted by Sancak (2019) aimed to examine whether the motivation of undergraduate students studying in science and mathematics fields towards learning science had a significant effect on their levels of environmental awareness. Additionally, it aimed to investigate whether students' motivation for learning science and their environmental awareness levels showed significant differences based on gender, type of high school graduated from, department, grade point average, mother's occupation, father's occupation, and monthly household income. The results revealed that students' levels of awareness of environmental issues did not show significant differences based on gender, type of high school graduated from, mother's occupation, or monthly household income, but did show significant differences based on department, grade point average, and father's occupation. Another finding was that there was a significant relationship between students' motivation levels for learning science and their awareness levels of environmental issues

The study conducted by Ercan and Sönmez (2015) aimed to determine how an original mobile learning application, based on the Android operating system, affected students' attitudes towards mobile learning, chemistry classes, and the environment, and how the education they received through the mobile learning method impacted their academic achievement, based on statistical data. The mobile application included sections on Water and Life, Chemistry at Home, Chemistry at School, Environmental Chemistry, and Industrial Chemistry.

The study was conducted with 64 tenth-grade students at a public school, consisting of 32 students in the experimental group and 32 in the control group. The data collected through tests were analyzed using a statistical program. Upon examining the analysis results, it was found that while there was no significant difference between the groups in the pre-test for academic achievement, environmental attitudes, and mobile learning attitude scales, a significant difference was observed in favor of the control group in the chemistry attitude scale. However, according to the post-test results, a significant difference was found in favor of the experimental group in the academic achievement test and the attitude scales for the environment and chemistry class. No significant difference was found between the groups in terms of attitudes toward mobile learning, although there was an increase in the average score of the experimental group.

The study conducted by Hithit (2021) aimed to determine the environmental attitudes of high school students using the New Environmental Paradigm Scale (NEP). The sample group consisted of 221 high school students. The data collection tools used in the study were the 'Personal Information Form' and the 'Revised New Environmental Paradigm Scale' (R-NEP) developed by Dunlap and Van Liere (2000). The obtained data were analyzed using the SPSS 24 software package. The research findings revealed that the environmental sensitivity levels of high school students were above average, and female participants reflected a more 'ecocentric' worldview compared to male participants. A low level of significance was observed in the relationship between students' environmental attitudes, worldviews, and the variables of gender, grade level, and age.

In the study conducted by Yiğit (2019), the aim was to examine the effect of recycling education practices in the 8th-grade Science course on students' environmental attitudes, environmental knowledge, and environmental behaviors. The study group consisted of 60 eighth-grade students studying in a public school. Two groups were formed, with 30 students in the control group and 30 in the experimental group. The experimental design of the study was a pre-test and post-test control group quasi-experimental design. While the experimental group received environmental education and activities focused on sustainable living and recycling, the control group followed the existing 2013 curriculum. The data collection tools used for both groups included the pre-test and post-test Environmental Attitude Scale (ÇTÖ), Environmental Behavior Scale (ÇDÖ), and Environmental Knowledge Scale (ÇBÖ). The data were analyzed using the SPSS 22 software package. At the end of the study, it was observed that the post-test averages from all scales showed significant differences in favor of the experimental group. The study concluded that recycling education practices aimed at sustainable living were effective in changing students' environmental attitudes, environmental knowledge, and environmental behaviors, thus serving the purpose of the research.

The study conducted by Kazaoğlu and Erkal (2022) aimed to examine the environmental awareness levels of university students and their behaviors towards environmental issues. The research included 392 undergraduate students from Hacettepe University, Beytepe Campus. To collect data, the "Environmental Awareness" scale and the "Behavior towards Environmental Issues" scale were used. The study found a positive relationship between students' environmental awareness and their behaviors towards environmental issues. Additionally, it was determined that views on environmental awareness were positively related to the sub-dimensions of the "Behavior towards Environmental Issues" scale, including establishment, creation, transformation into skills, perception, and adaptation to the situation. The levels of environmental awareness and behaviors towards environmental issues varied according to factors such as gender, family income level, class level, father's education level, sources of environmental information, environmental education status, number of people living in the family, preference for environmentally friendly products, membership in environmental organizations, and participation in environmental activities.

The study conducted by Doğan and Keleş (2020) aimed to determine the environmental awareness and behavior levels of middle and high school students and to investigate the variables affecting these characteristics. The study, conducted using a survey model, involved a total of 184 students—98 8th grade middle school students and 86 12th grade high school students—from the Silifke district of Mersin during the 2017-2018 academic year. The study explored whether the students' environmental behavior and awareness levels were influenced by their educational level (middle school-high school), school type (public-private), academic success, parental education level, number of siblings, and gender. The findings indicated that awareness scores were higher in middle schools compared to high schools, and higher in private schools compared to public schools, with female students scoring higher on behavior than male students. It was observed that academic success increased awareness but did not affect behavior. Students with higher awareness scores also had higher behavior scores. An increase in parental education level raised environmental awareness scores but did not affect environmental behavior scores. The findings suggest that while schools can create environmental awareness, they have not been successful in translating this into responsible environmental behavior.

The aim of this study conducted by Karagölge et al. (2019) was to determine the perceptions of final-year undergraduate students from different faculties at Atatürk University, who have received at least three years of chemistry education, regarding "Green Chemistry and Sustainable Development." This descriptive study used qualitative methods to collect data. A semi-structured interview form consisting of 19 open-ended questions, developed by the researchers, was used as the data collection tool. The sample of the study consisted of 43 fourth-year students at Atatürk University. Content analysis revealed that students had low perceptions of the concepts of "Green Chemistry and Sustainable Development." Factors such as the students' gender, the faculty they graduated from, and the department they are currently attending were considered, and it was found that students' views were similar and these variables did not affect their awareness of "Green Chemistry and Sustainable Development." To create awareness on topics closely related to the environment, such as "Green Chemistry and Sustainable Development," the first step is to raise awareness across all segments of society. Individuals raised with a lifestyle where the principles of green chemistry and sustainable development become behavioral norms are aware of their responsibilities and exhibit committed behaviors. In this context, chemistry course contents can be enriched with topics on "Green Chemistry Principles and Sustainable Development.

This study by Demir et al. (2023) was published as an international article in IJELS (International Journal of Education & Literacy Studies) in 2023. The research was conducted during the 2021-2022 academic year with 10 girls and 10 boys from 4th grade students at a primary school in Bartın. The study aimed to utilize school gardens, which play a significant role in environmental education, to help students develop environmental awareness and gain a sense of environmental responsibility. The data for the study were collected using a scale developed by Peker (2020) and a semi-structured interview form. The results indicated that environmental factors in education were effective in increasing students' environmental awareness. It was observed that the workshop activities conducted in the school garden enhanced the students' environmental awareness and had a positive impact on the 4th grade students. The recommendations of the study suggest organizing various activities in school gardens and reflecting them in the educational environment to develop a positive attitude towards the environment.

The study conducted by Ergin (2016) was published in the World Journal of Education (WJE) in 2019. The aim of the study was to determine the environmental awareness of teacher candidates. The sample group consisted of a total of 532 students randomly selected from all departments at Trakya University. The study was conducted during the fall semester of 2016-2017 with students from the Faculty of

Education and the Pedagogical Formation program. The data collection tool used was the "Environmental Awareness Scale" developed by the researcher. The scale was found to be reliable. Comprising three factors, the scale was found to be valid, reliable, and usable after statistical processing. High scores on all items and factors indicate a positive environmental awareness. A survey with 19 questions, prepared by the researcher to collect data on independent variables, was used. The study generally found that teacher candidates had very high environmental awareness.

The study conducted by Helvacı (2022) was published in the International Journal of Curriculum and Instruction (IJCI). The aim of the study was to reveal the effects of the E-STEM approach-based activity development processes on the environmental awareness levels and views of science teacher candidates. The sample group consisted of 11 teacher candidates from the Science Teaching Department, who were third-year students at a faculty of education at a state university in the Western Black Sea Region. It was observed that the environmental impacts of the E-STEM approach-based activity development process increased. The teacher candidates' levels of environmental awareness and their views on the process were positive.

The study conducted by Carangue et al. (2021) developed an understanding of integrating green chemistry into environmental education and managing its effects. However, the extent of green chemistry integration into the science curriculum is not widely known in the Philippines. The researchers identified the knowledge, perceptions, and challenges of chemistry teachers in the Philippines regarding Green Chemistry Education. Awareness of chemical hazards and their environmental impacts is demonstrated in lessons, but these issues are rarely discussed in detail during chemistry classes. This study provides an explanation of this issue. A moderate positive relationship was observed between teachers' knowledge and their perceptions of environmental awareness in green chemistry. However, no significant relationship was found between teachers' knowledge and perceptions when related to green chemistry integration.

The study conducted by Verep and Vural (2022) was published in the Journal of Anatolian Environmental and Animal Sciences (JAES). The research focuses on the reduction of natural resources due to technological advancements. Since this adverse situation affects the environment and the future of our children, who are our guarantee for the future, the study aims to increase their environmental awareness and consciousness. The study's objective is to gather data that can address this issue and send a message to correct the situation. To this end, many studies and research are conducted to raise awareness among primary and secondary school students about the environment. This study evaluates the success of various efforts to develop environmental sensitivity, awareness, or consciousness among primary school students by assessing the results of surveys conducted with criteria related to environmental awareness and consciousness.

The study conducted by Ridha, Hasan, and Sulastri (2020) aims to compare the environmental awareness levels of chemistry education students with those of non-chemistry education students. Using a quantitative research method with a survey, the study examined a sample group of 100 second-year students enrolled in the chemistry, physics, history, and geography education programs at FKIP Faculty in 2016. The results of the study revealed that while chemistry education students had high levels of environmental knowledge, their attitudes and behavior levels were lower than those of non-chemistry students. It was noted that environmental education is not sufficiently emphasized in chemistry courses, and therefore, there is a need to improve the environmental awareness of chemistry education students.

The aim of the study conducted by Hassan and Ismail (2011) is to examine the attitudes and practices of chemistry teachers regarding environmental education (EE) in Terengganu, Malaysia, and to determine the relationship between the integration of EE into the curriculum and students' environmental awareness and attitudes. The research was conducted using a quantitative method, with surveys administered to 127 chemistry teachers and 367 students. The data were analyzed using SPSS 7.0. The results show that teachers generally possess high knowledge about environmental concepts but have knowledge gaps in certain areas (e.g., sustainable development). While teachers exhibit a high attitude towards EE, they face obstacles such as exam-focused teaching and lack of materials. Additionally, a significant relationship was found between environmental awareness and attitudes. These findings suggest that EE needs to be implemented more effectively in the education system and that teachers require further support.

The aim of the study conducted by Ghazali and Yahaya (2022) is to examine university students' knowledge, awareness, and practices related to green chemistry in daily life. Designed as a quantitative study, the research used a survey method, with data collected from 392 students at public universities in Tanjung Malim and Kuala Lumpur. The sample consisted of students from both educational and non-educational fields, and the data were collected using a survey validated for expert validity and reliability. The results of the study revealed that students' levels of knowledge and application of green chemistry were "high," while their awareness level was "very high." No significant difference was found between educational and non-educational students.

The aim of the study conducted by Sulistina, Rahayu, and Yahmin (2020) is to examine the impact of guided inquiry learning strategies, which include socio-scientific topics related to the environment, on increasing the environmental awareness of chemistry teacher candidates. The research was conducted using both quantitative and qualitative methods, involving 30 chemistry teacher candidates. The results of the study found that guided inquiry learning strategies were effective in increasing students' environmental awareness.

The aim of the study conducted by Nurbait, Rahmawati, and Ridwan (2016) is to examine the effects of integrating Green Chemistry into education on students' environmental sustainability and their role in chemistry teaching. The research utilized a qualitative method, collecting data through tools such as students' reflection journals and interviews. The sample group consisted of teacher candidates, and educational programs were implemented to teach students the concepts and principles of Green Chemistry. The results showed that students understood the importance of Green Chemistry, developed awareness of environmental issues, and expressed a desire to integrate this knowledge into their future teaching roles. The study concluded that the integration of Green Chemistry into educational programs helps students develop environmental sustainability awareness and enables them to produce more sensitive and creative solutions to environmental problems.

Environmental Education

Environmental education is planned to contribute to individuals' understanding of the natural environment and positively influence their values and behaviors towards nature. Environmental education is significant in developing environmental awareness and sensitivity towards protecting and using the natural environment. Creating environmental awareness in society, protecting nature, and ensuring sustainability through environmental education have gained importance in recent years for Sustainable Development. Quality and extracurricular activities integrated with sustainable development-based environmental education can be an effective tool for Turkey to achieve the Sustainable Development Goals. Elementary school-aged children, who will be the adults of tomorrow, can act more consciously and sensitively about our common future (Yılmaz, 2019).

Globally, it is accepted that sustainable development fundamentally depends on education. Using effective environmental education strategies can enhance education's positive impact on managing natural resources. Students receiving environmental education acquire the knowledge, skills, and experiences necessary to manage their communities successfully and make informed decisions about managing natural resources. Education plays a crucial role in improving living standards and contributing to global development. Sustainable development means development that meets the needs of the present generation without compromising the ability of future generations to meet their own needs (Uralovich, 2023).

Within our research, an experiment booklet was designed through educational technology to provide equal education to students studying in schools without laboratories and to develop environmental awareness.

Case Study Method

This study conducted by Sümen and Şendur (2013) was carried out with 11th-grade students at an Anatolian High School in İzmir. The research compared experimental and control groups. The study aimed to determine the impact of case-based teaching methods on students' conceptual understanding and conceptual change in the topic of reaction rates in chemical reactions. In the experimental group, the topic of reaction rates was taught using case-based teaching, while in the control group, it was taught using the activities from the chemistry curriculum. The data collection tool used in the study was a concept test developed by Çakmakçı (2005). The data obtained from the concept test were analyzed both qualitatively and quantitatively. The results revealed a significant difference in favor of the experimental group. Additionally, it was found that case-based teaching was more effective in achieving conceptual change and ensuring students' conceptual understanding at the desired levels.

The study conducted by Şahin and Çakmak (2013) involved a research group of 24 prospective science teachers from the Faculty of Education at Giresun University. The research comparatively assessed the contribution of study sheets prepared according to case-based and Six Thinking Hats methods to the development of critical thinking skills in the context of heat and temperature. Data were collected using study sheets and journals prepared separately for each method, and were analyzed using document analysis techniques. According to the qualitative data obtained from these tools, while prospective teachers generally expressed views on analytical and truth-seeking aspects of critical thinking, they did not provide much feedback on self-confidence and curiosity aspects.

The study conducted by Ültay (2014) aimed to determine the conceptual knowledge of 12th-grade students regarding strong and weak interactions in chemical bonds and to examine the relationships between these concepts. The study was conducted using a descriptive approach and case study method. The sample group consisted of a total of 66 students from the 12th grade at a high school in Giresun. Data were collected using a concept map, a word association test, two drawings, and two two-tier questions. According to the obtained data, the majority of students drew the concept map hierarchically but failed to show the relationships between the concepts. In the word association test, most students were able to write 3 or 4 words related to the topic. In the question asking students to draw and show the weak interactions in an H_2O molecule, it was found that while most students recognized hydrogen bonds, they incorrectly labeled strong interactions as hydrogen bonds. The study concluded that students confused strong and weak interactions and did not fully establish the relationships between these concepts.

The study conducted by Demircioğlu et al. (2016) involved seventh-grade gifted students attending the Ordu Science and Art Center. The aim of this research was to propose an alternative method for finding the position of elements in the periodic table. The study utilized the case study method. Although the 2-8-8 rule is part of the curriculum for later grades, it was taught to these gifted students. Some students developed different rules for finding the position of elements.

The study conducted by Çam (2017) aimed to enhance Science Education pre-service teachers' conceptual understanding of acids and bases through case studies. This qualitative study involved presenting pre-service teachers with case studies related to acids and bases and asking them to provide their responses. The study was conducted with 72 first-year Science Education pre-service teachers. The results indicated that the responses of the pre-service teachers to the case studies improved scientifically over time and that they participated more actively in classes. When asked how they preferred the lesson to be taught, many indicated that they liked the case study method, citing the excitement of seeing the real-life applications of the concrete chemistry topics they learned. As a result, the case study method was observed to be effective in the conceptual understanding of acids and bases for pre-service teachers. The study suggests that this method could be applied in General Chemistry courses within Science Education programs.

In the study conducted by Gençoğlan (2017), an authentic case-based argumentation-based science learning approach was used. This approach was applied to investigate changes in 8th-grade primary school students' academic achievement in the topic of acids and bases, their attitudes towards science lessons, and their scientific process skills. The population of the research consisted of 8th-grade primary school students, with the sample including 69 students from Kahramanmaraş, divided into two classes. A quasi-experimental research design with pre-test and post-test control groups was used in this study. While the control group was taught using traditional methods (lecture, question-answer), the experimental group experienced the case-based argumentation-based science learning (CBABSL) approach. At the beginning and end of the application, both experimental and control groups were administered the Acids and Bases Achievement Test (ABAT), the Scientific Process Skills Test (SPST), and the Attitude Scale for Science Courses (ASSC). The results from the ABAT revealed that the authentic case-based argumentation approach significantly improved the students' achievement in the topic of acids and bases.

The study conducted by Çakmak and Akgün (2017) was published by the Canadian Center of Science and Education. The primary goal of this research is to ensure that students achieve the set objectives of the lessons at the desired level. The study highlights the importance of the case study method, including definitions and literature review related to this method. To achieve this goal, educators use various teaching strategies and methods. It is known that methods and materials that appeal to different sensory organs have an impact on students. The study indicates that using various teaching methods, techniques, and materials in education captures students' attention and alleviates the monotony of the lesson, thereby having a positive effect on teaching. Sometimes, students struggle to apply their theoretical knowledge in real life. In this context, various teaching methods are used to bridge theory and practice. The case study method is one of the effective methods for achieving this, as it is a teaching method that enables students to acquire knowledge and skills. It helps students develop the ability to handle problems they work on and to produce knowledge-based solutions in real life.

The study conducted by Sarı and Şengül (2018) examined changes in the academic achievement of science teacher candidates in general chemistry. General chemistry experiments were designed using the case study method combined with the Prediction-Observation-Explanation (POE) method. The sample of the study consisted of 42 science teacher candidates taking the General Chemistry Laboratory II course at a state university. The research employed a quasi-experimental design with pre-test and post-test control groups as a quantitative research method. Data were collected using the "Chemistry Achievement Test (CAT)" with established validity and reliability and worksheets based on the case study method combined with the POE method. Prior to the application, pre-tests were administered to the groups to ensure equivalence in academic achievement, and no statistically significant difference was found. After the application, post-tests on academic achievement were administered to both groups, revealing a statistically significant difference in favor of the experimental group.

The research conducted by Genel et al. (2018) developed a test through a pilot study to determine the level of understanding and misconceptions regarding chemical equilibrium concepts. The aim of this study is to identify the level of understanding of chemical equilibrium among high school students and to detect misconceptions. To achieve this, the study investigated the misconceptions related to this topic and ways to address them. The research utilized case study methodology. The sample consisted of 100 second-year high school students from a district center in Kağıthane, Istanbul. The test answers, results from interviews, and observational data revealed that students had misconceptions about chemical equilibrium. These misconceptions included issues related to changes until equilibrium is established, the rates of forward and reverse reactions at equilibrium, the effects of concentration, temperature, pressure, equilibrium constant, catalyst effects, the impact of solids on chemical equilibrium, the effect of noble gas addition on equilibrium, and the stoichiometry of chemical equilibrium. The study's recommendations suggest that curriculum developers should consider these misconceptions while developing their programs.

Kaya (2018) aimed to assess high school students' understanding of the atom concept using the case study method. Data for the study were obtained from administering a 12-item test to 271 final-year students from seven state high schools and conducting interviews with 10 students regarding the cases. Prior to the study, it was found that students did not understand the atom concept and had misconceptions about it. A common misconception was that "The atom is the smallest indivisible unit of matter." Other misconceptions about the structure of atoms included: "Atoms are spherical," "The atom's nucleus is spherical," "Electrons move in specific orbits around the atom," and "An atom consists of a nucleus, electrons, and orbits." Despite high overall levels of understanding of the atom concept, it was observed that many students only partially understood the structure of atoms and had some misconceptions in both areas. It was found that more than half of the students were unaware of subatomic particles such as quarks, leptons, gluons, and muons. The study concluded that nearly three-quarters of high school students understood the concept of atoms.

Mahdi et al. (2019) conducted a study published in the International Journal of Higher Education (IJHE). This study explored the use of the case study method to enhance students' critical thinking skills. Issues related to the content were explored, and the best scenarios were researched. The study discovered that the case study method encourages critical thinking and tends to develop students' critical thinking skills. The research employed mixed methods, and data analysis was conducted using the SPSS program. The sample group for this study consisted of 42 students enrolled in leadership and group dynamics courses within a business administration program.

Çoban et al. (2021) conducted a study published in the Journal of Educational and Social Research. The research was carried out before 2020. The aim of the study was to identify the teaching strategies of experienced chemistry teachers regarding solutions and the factors affecting the application of these strategies in the teaching environment. The case study method was used in the research. The study group consisted of four chemistry teachers. Data were obtained from scenarios, interviews, and classroom observations. According to the research results, teachers were aware of and able to use teaching strategies such as presentation, discovery, and research review, and they mentioned the use of visuals like videos/pictures/animations, models, experimental methods, or project preparation methods. However, classroom observations revealed that teachers predominantly used presentation methods, with only one teacher additionally employing the discovery method. The teachers attributed this discrepancy to factors such as deficiencies in content and pedagogical knowledge, limitations in laboratory facilities, high class sizes, lack of technical support for technological issues, a dense curriculum with short class periods, low student motivation, and the school and family's focus on exam-oriented studies.

In the article by Puri (2022), the case study method is described as a commonly used educational tool that brings students together. By implementing the case study method, which aims to enhance students' thinking skills, promote deeper understanding, and facilitate problem-solving, learning becomes more effective. The article explains that, as a result of discussions and analyses, students become more inclined to make critical decisions. In this method, the responsibility for learning rests with the students, while the teacher acts merely as a facilitator.

Experiment Videos

The study conducted by Howitz et al. (2020) examines how the face-to-face practical exams for General Chemistry Laboratory I (GCL-I) and Organic Chemistry Laboratory II (OCL-II) courses were adapted to remote education due to social movements in the summer of 2020. In GCL-I, traditional exams were replaced with Canvas exams and homework essays, while in OCL-II, some exam components were canceled, and alternative assessment options were offered. The sample group consisted of 1,403 students and 28 teaching assistants (TAs) for the GCL-I course and 104 students and 4 teaching assistants for the OCL-II course. The results show that while remote education provided some advantages, the lack of face-to-face laboratory experience hindered the thorough evaluation of fundamental laboratory techniques. Feedback from students and teaching assistants indicated that structured guidance and interaction strategies in remote education need to be improved in future courses.

In previous studies, research has also been conducted with undergraduate-level pre-service teachers and teachers. The views of teachers on topics supported by teaching methods and techniques used have been measured. However, the challenges that teachers sometimes face during lessons and throughout the term regarding specific learning objectives have not been addressed. In this study, there are learning objectives that will enable teachers to conduct their lessons more effectively and manage their time throughout the term. The learning objectives of each unit included have been prepared and made ready for teachers. In addition to student worksheets (study sheets) that will benefit students, teacher worksheets have also been prepared for teachers.

There is a study by Karaer (2014) in the previous literature, which corrects students' misconceptions about chemistry topics through observation and hands-on experience with chemistry experiments and provides long-term learning. In this study as well, content has been prepared to ensure active participation of students and provide hands-on, experiential learning. However, there has not been a study where chemistry topics are supported by experiments and case studies to raise environmental awareness. This study fills that gap.

When looking at studies conducted since 2013 up to the present day, there is no research aimed at increasing environmental awareness through case-study-supported chemistry topics at the high school level. Additionally, no contributions aimed at disadvantaged groups have been found in these studies. This study, aimed at increasing environmental awareness through case-study-supported chemistry experiments, is directed not only at advantaged groups but also at disadvantaged schools in regions without laboratories and students with hearing impairments, as the study includes experiment videos.

Chemistry Experiments in Chemistry Education

The study conducted by Karaer (2014) was published as a thesis in 2020. The study aimed to determine whether chemistry experiments conducted according to the 5E learning model, incorporating substances used in daily life, had an effect on student achievement and perceptions. The sample group consisted of 14 first-year students from the Chemistry Teaching Program at Ondokuz Mayıs University, who were enrolled in the General Chemistry Laboratory II course during the spring semester of the 2014-2015 academic year. Data were collected from the Reaction Rate Factors Achievement Test, a questionnaire, report papers, and semi-structured interviews with volunteer students. The findings indicated that experiments conducted according to the 5E learning model showed a significant difference between the pre-test and post-test average scores. The effect size calculation revealed that applying the 5E learning model had a very large effect. It was observed that while many students did not answer questions in the pre-test, they answered almost all questions in the post-test. Consequently, it can be said that experiments conducted according to the 5E learning model are effective in increasing teacher candidates' academic achievement levels, reducing misconceptions, providing meaningful and lasting learning, and developing positive attitudes and behaviors towards the laboratory, chemistry, and the teaching profession. The study suggests that the use of constructivist-based methods, techniques, and models is beneficial and should start from lower grades, and recommends determining students' existing prior knowledge before applying activities developed according to the 5E learning model, then implementing them and monitoring the process.

Purpose of the Research

The purpose of this research is to increase high school students' environmental awareness through technology and by enhancing the quality of education. In this context, an experiment booklet consisting of 5 experiments compatible with the achievements of the 9th and 10th grades in the 2018 Chemistry Curriculum of Turkey was designed. The selected achievements for the experiments are as follows:

Experiment 1: Bioplastic Production

Attainments:

1.1. Gives examples of the uses of common polymers.

a. Polymerization event is explained and the concepts of -mer, monomer and polymer are emphasized.

b. The positive and negative properties of polymers in different fields are emphasized

Experiment 2: Obtaining Adhesive from Milk

Attainments:

2.1. Gives examples of the uses of common polymers.

a. Polymerization event is explained and the concepts of -mer, monomer and polymer are emphasized.

ç. The harms of toys and textile products containing polymer materials are mentioned.

Experiment 3: Water Hardness Experiment

Attainments:

3.1. Explain the hardness and softness properties of water.

Experiment 4: Observing the Effect of Acid Rain!

Attainments:

4.1. Acids and Bases in Our Lives

4.2. Explains the benefits and harms of acids and bases.

a. Explain the formation of acid rain and its effects on the environment and historical artifacts.

Experiment 5: Effects of Lime and Caustic

Attainments:

5.1. Common Daily Life Chemicals

5.2. Explains the properties of cleaning agents.

a. Without going into structural details, explain how soap and detergent active ingredients clean dirt.

b. The benefits and harms of cleaning agents used in personal cleaning (shampoo, toothpaste, solid soap, liquid soap) are emphasized.

c. Cleaning agents used for hygiene purposes (bleach, lime source) are introduced.

These achievements have content that can be adapted internationally for students to increase environmental awareness. Teachers can use the experiment booklet anytime they see fit according to their students' cognitive levels. The experiment booklet includes safety precautions, case study texts, experiment sheets, chemistry questions related to the experiments, and information pages.

Initially, the case study method was used as the teaching method. Sample cases were written for the experiments, including scenarios from daily life. The purpose of using the case study method is to raise awareness of environmental problems we encounter in daily life in line with global goals. Experiments related to the relevant achievements and sample cases were selected. These experiments were conducted in the laboratory and recorded on camera. The experiment videos were uploaded to the YouTube platform, and the links to these experiment videos were converted into QR codes. QR codes were added to each page of the experiment booklet. These experiment booklets were sent to 475 students studying in schools without laboratories, and teachers were informed about the experiment booklet. The aim was to contribute to equal opportunities in education and enhance the quality of education for schools without laboratories by using one of the most accessible and convenient technological tools, YouTube and QR codes.

To examine the change in students' environmental awareness after the applications, the Environmental Awareness Scale was applied as a data collection tool before and after the experiments. Statistical analyses revealed a significant difference in students' environmental awareness levels after the applications.

CONCLUSIONS AND RECOMMENDATIONS

Efforts should be made to ensure equal opportunities for the purpose of each sustainable development goal, particularly for providing quality education as aimed in this study.

Environmental education should continue at all levels of education without interruption. The use of experiment videos that can be accessed independently of time and space is very important and effective in overcoming the negativities such as the lack of laboratory environment, lack of materials, and limited time to be allocated from the lesson time.

Case studies make it easier for students to make connections between chemistry topics and daily life.

In order for environmental education to be effective, there is a need for well-trained teachers who can use technology and have a good command of teaching methods and techniques. For this reason, it is very important for prospective teachers to gain experience in such applications, to develop their creativity, and to include these applications in teacher training programs.

Environmental education indirectly and directly serves many other sustainable development goals as well.

BOOKLET

Experiment videos supported by case studies and aligned with learning outcomes, along with teacher and student worksheets.

User Guide for the Booklet

This booklet is prepared for the study titled "The Effect of Experiment Videos Supported by Case Studies on High School Students' Environmental Awareness." The booklet includes 5 experiments. Each experiment has a teacher and student worksheet. It is recommended that photocopies of the student worksheets be distributed to students, followed by watching the corresponding experiment video. If your school has a laboratory, you can also perform the experiments, taking care to follow safety precautions. Answers to the questions in the student worksheets are provided in the teacher worksheets. You can contribute to the development of students' environmental awareness by conducting brainstorming sessions on the relevant experiments and topics in the classroom.

To Access Experiment Videos, Scan the QR Code.

Safety Precautions

Experiment 1: Use protective gloves and apron.
Experiment 2: Use protective gloves and apron.
- If acetic acid is used in this experiment, it should not be smelled or tasted.
Experiment 3: Use protective gloves and apron.
Experiment 4: Use protective gloves, goggles, and apron.
- To avoid any explosions, add acid to the water in the beaker gradually.
- Do not touch concentrated acids with bare hands, do not allow skin contact, do not smell or taste them.
Experiment 5: Use protective gloves and apron.
- Do not smell or taste the chemicals used.

TEACHER EXPERIMENT WORKSHEETS

Experiment 1: Bioplastic Preparation

Learning Outcome: It is recommended that this experiment and worksheet be related to the following learning outcomes.
10.4.1.2. Provides examples of the usage areas of common polymers.

a. The polymerization process is explained, focusing on -mer, monomer, and polymer concepts.

c. The positive and negative characteristics of polymers used in different areas are emphasized.

Experiment 2: Glue from Milk Preparation

Learning Outcome: It is recommended that this experiment and worksheet be related to the following learning outcomes.

10.4.1.2. Provides examples of the usage areas of common polymers.

a. The polymerization process is explained, focusing on -mer, monomer, and polymer concepts.

ç. The potential harms of toys and textile products containing polymer materials are discussed.

Experiment 3: Water Hardness Test

Learning Outcome: It is recommended that this experiment and worksheet be related to the following learning outcome.

9.5.1.3. Describes the hardness and softness characteristics of water.

Experiment 4: Observing the Effects of Acid Rain

Learning Outcome: It is recommended that this experiment and worksheet be related to the following learning outcome.

10.3.3. Acids and Bases in Our Lives

10.3.3.1. Explains the benefits and harms of acids and bases.

a. The formation of acid rain and its effects on the environment and historical artifacts are discussed.

Experiment 5: Effects of Lime and Caustic

Learning Outcome: It is recommended that this experiment and worksheet be related to the following learning outcome.

10.4.1. Common Chemicals in Daily Life

10.4.1.1. Explains the properties of cleaning agents.

a. Without going into structural details, it is explained how soap and detergent active substances clean dirt.

b. The benefits and harms of cleaning agents used for personal hygiene (shampoo, toothpaste, bar soap, liquid soap) are emphasized.

c. Cleaning agents used for hygiene purposes (bleach, lime water) are introduced.

Experiment 1: Bioplastic Preparation

Case Study

Nihal is a high school student. In her chemistry class, her teacher assigned a project task. She was asked to propose a solution to an environmental pollution problem. After researching, Nihal came across a news story that caught her interest. The news is as follows:

"The effects of microplastics on the body are still unknown. However, experts suggest that these particles may have long-term harmful effects and could negatively impact the developing immune system of a fetus in the womb. Plastic particles were found in the placenta of four healthy women who had normal pregnancies and births. These particles were detected on both the maternal and fetal sides of the placenta, as well as within the membrane where the fetus develops. The number of particles found was 12. The fact that the particles were blue, red, orange, or pink indicates that they might originate from packaging, dyes, cosmetics, or personal care products. The particles being 10 microns in size (0.01 mm) means they can enter the bloodstream and be carried through the blood. Researchers say that these particles might also have entered the bodies of babies. However, it was not possible to determine this since no such research has been conducted."

Should we come up with a solution to the problem that Nihal found?

Experiment Materials:

- 60 mL of distilled water
- 1.5 spatulas of vinegar
- 1.5 spatulas of glycerin
- 5 spatulas of cornstarch
- Beaker
- Stirring rod
- Graduated cylinder
- Food coloring

Procedure:

1. Fill the graduated cylinder with 60 mL of distilled water.
2. Transfer the water from the graduated cylinder to the beaker.
3. Add 5 spatulas of cornstarch to the beaker and stir.
4. Add 1.5 spatulas (approximately 5 mL) of vinegar and 1.5 spatulas of glycerin to the cornstarch-water mixture. Begin stirring.
5. Add 1 drop of food coloring to the mixture.
6. Stir until the mixture is homogeneous.

7. Heat the mixture on a stove or heater while stirring.
8. Once the mixture begins to boil, continue stirring for a short time and remove from heat once it turns into a gel.
9. Spread the mixture onto aluminum foil before it cools and shape it as desired.
10. Allow it to dry for a few days.

Student Worksheet Questions and Answers:

1. Investigate the environmental harm of plastics.
   o   Answer expected from students.
2. Plastic is composed of polymers. Is the bioplastic we obtained a polymer? Explain.
   o   Starch is made from cellulose. Cellulose is a monomer with a single-piece structure. When cellulose monomers combine, they form the polymer starch. Thus, we create a bioplastic (biodegradable plastic) from a plant-based polymer.
3. Compare the durability of the plastic we made with regular plastic.
   o   Answer expected from students.
4. Why has the use of bioplastics not become widespread?
   o   Despite being environmentally friendly, bioplastics have disadvantages such as high production costs and poor processability. The high production cost allows for the use of renewable resources, like agricultural waste, to produce bioplastics at lower costs.
5. What properties did vinegar and glycerin add to the bioplastic?
   o   Glycerin makes the bioplastic flexible and turns it into a gel. Vinegar helps the starch maintain a fluid consistency before drying by ensuring that the amylopectin in the starch remains aligned like amylose.

Experiment 2: Glue from Milk Preparation

Case Study
İpek is a biology teacher and wants her younger brother, who is in first grade, to be raised with high environmental awareness. She also wants to buy the least harmful stationery supplies for him. After researching stationery supplies, İpek found the following information about the harms of glues:

"Solvent-based adhesives are made with polymers. Unlike water-based adhesives, they contain a polymer solvent. Solvent-based adhesives are used in many industries including automotive, footwear manufacturing, furniture, and construction. Despite their versatility, a major issue with solvent-based adhesives is their environmental impact. The solvent they contain is harmful to air quality. Waste from solvent-based adhesives does not biodegrade easily. If not disposed of properly in waste collection bins, it can contaminate groundwater. It is a material that negatively affects the ecosystem and human health in many ways."

Let's help İpek make a less harmful adhesive. Let's create an eco-friendly glue together!

Experiment Materials:

- 250 mL beaker
- 250 mL Erlenmeyer flask
- Stirring rod
- Graduated cylinder
- Paper towel
- Skim milk
- Acetic acid (vinegar)
- Sodium bicarbonate (baking soda)
- Distilled water

Procedure:

1. Pour 125 mL of skim milk into the beaker.
2. Add 25 mL of vinegar or acetic acid to it.
3. Heat and stir until small curds form.
4. Remove the beaker from the heater and wait for the curds to settle at the bottom.
5. Using a funnel (place a paper towel inside the funnel), perform the filtration into an Erlenmeyer flask.
6. Transfer the solid remaining in the funnel to a beaker, and add 15 mL of water and half a spatula of baking soda.
7. Allow the glue in the beaker to dry for 30 minutes and then test it.

Student Worksheet Questions and Answers:

1. What is the purpose of using acetic acid or vinegar in this experiment?
    - The acid reacts with the casein protein in the milk. The casein protein coagulates, causing molecules to interact and form larger particles.
2. Why was baking soda added?
    - Baking soda neutralizes the excess acid (from the vinegar).
3. Write the equation for the reaction between acetic acid and baking soda (sodium bicarbonate).

    $CH_3COOH(aq) + NaHCO_3 \text{ (solid)} \longrightarrow CH_3COONa(aq) + H_2O(\text{liquid}) + CO_2 \text{ (gas)}$

4. What substance in the milk allowed us to obtain the glue?
    o   Casein protein

Experiment 3: Water Hardness Test

Case Study

Deniz, who visits her grandmother's house, notices that the dishes are not very clean after washing and need to be washed again before being placed in the cupboards. She thinks this is a waste of water and dish detergent. She investigates the reason behind the white spots on the supposedly clean plates and finds the following information:

"In hard water, when soap reacts with calcium, it forms 'soap scum', which leaves a significant amount of residue (scaling) when it evaporates. The lathering is minimal. Therefore, when using hard water, we need to use more soap or detergent to clean our hands, hair, and clothes, which increases the consumption of these products. Excessive detergent use has various negative effects on both the machine and the environment. Hard water also tastes unpleasant and leaves deposits in city water supply lines, hot water pipes, and boilers."

Burcu knows that reducing water waste is very important and is curious about which waters she uses in her life are hard. Let's check the hardness of the waters with Burcu!

Experiment Materials:

- Water from two different brands
- Distilled water
- Hard water
- 4 beakers
- German Hardness Measurement Device
- Stirring rod
- Liquid soap

Procedure:

Part 1

1. Pour the waters into the beakers in equal amounts.
2. Add one pump of liquid soap to each beaker.
3. Stir the beakers with the stirring rod.
4. Record the amount of foam produced.

Part 2

1. Put 5 mL of drinking water into the small tube of the German Hardness Measurement Device and add 3 drops of the indicator.
2. Add one drop of the titration solution to the tube and shake. Continue this process until a color change is observed. Record the number of drops added until the color change occurs.
3. Wash the tube and add 5 mL of distilled water. Add one drop of the titration solution and shake. Continue this process until a color change is observed. Record the number of drops added until the color change occurs.
4. Wash the tube and add 5 mL of hard water. Add one drop of the titration solution and shake. Continue this process until a color change is observed. Record the number of drops added until the color change occurs.
5. Refer to the table in the set and write down the hardness-softness status of the waters.

Student Worksheet Questions and Answers:

1. Is seawater hard water?
    o   Yes, it is hard water.
2. Does seawater show temporary hardness, permanent hardness, or both?
    o   Both.
3. Research the structures that cause hardness in water.
    o   Magnesium and calcium ions, which are present in large amounts dissolved in the water.
4. Can hard water be softened? How?
    o   Students are asked to research and share with their classmates.

Experiment 4: Observing the Effects of Acid Rain!

Case Study

Aslı has started researching the places she will visit with her family before their trip and has come across the following news:
"The photograph shows the Caryatids, statues built 2500 years ago on the Acropolis of Athens. The statues are made from a type of rock called marble, which contains calcium carbonate. Over time, it was discovered that acid rain caused darkening and erosion on the surface of the statues. As a result, it was decided in 1980 to replace the original statues with replicas and move them into the Acropolis Museum."
Aslı is very surprised by the strong effects of acid rain. Upon further research, she has found that acid rain also causes significant harm to nature. Now, shall we also observe the effects of acid rain together?

Experiment Materials:

- Concentrated sulfuric acid
- Concentrated nitric acid
- Beakers
- 3 marble cubes
- Measuring cylinder
- Distilled water
- Permanent marker

Experiment Procedure:

1. Add 400 mL of distilled water to each beaker.
2. Add 20 mL of each concentrated acid sample separately to the water. (You have prepared acid solutions.)
3. Label each beaker with the name of the acid solution to avoid mixing.
4. Carefully add the marble cubes, one by one, to the acid solutions in the beakers.
5. Record your observations.
6. To better understand the effect, you can leave the marble cubes in the solutions for 1 week.

Student Worksheet Questions and Answers:

1. How do acid rains form?
    o Acid rains form when fossil fuel (coal, oil) waste mixes with the natural water cycle. Combustion produces gases containing nitrogen and sulfur, which combine with water vapor in the air to create a chemical reaction. This reaction results in the formation of sulfuric and nitric acid droplets.
2. Where are acid rains most commonly observed in the world?
    o Acid rains are frequently observed in various regions of Europe, North America, and Asia.
3. What are the effects of acid rains on soil structure, vegetation, aquatic life, and human health? What preventive measures can be taken?
    o Students are expected to research and share their findings with their classmates.

Experiment 5: Effects of Lime and Caustic Soda

Case Study

Can is a high school student. He heard that Ayşe, the school janitor, did not come to school the previous day because she had been poisoned. When he asked why, the chemistry teacher explained: "Can, Ayşe tried to clean using a caustic chemical mixed with lime cleaner, and as a result, she got poisoned." After this conversation, Can starts researching the harmful effects of cleaning products on living beings and the environment, as well as the precautions that need to be taken. He finds an experiment related to the effects of caustic soda and wants to conduct it at school. The next day, he goes to his chemistry teacher and performs the experiment with him in class. Afterward, he shares the information he learned about the harms of cleaning products with his friends. Let's observe this experiment together!

Materials:

- 20 mL vegetable oil
- NaOH solution (20 g/100 mL water)
- Lime solution (slaked lime)
- 3 x 250 mL beakers
- Stirring rod
- Distilled water
- Digital balance
- Heater
- Wire mesh

Procedure:

1. Coat the inside of the three beakers with vegetable oil. Try washing these beakers with water.
2. Test by touching the beakers with your hand to see if the oil has been cleaned.
3. Add NaOH solution to one beaker, Ca(OH)2 solution to another, and a mixture of NaOH and Ca(OH)2 solutions to the third beaker, then heat for 15 minutes.
4. Pour out the solution, rinse the beakers with water, and test by touching the beakers with your hand to see if the oil has been cleaned.

Student Worksheet Questions and Answers:

1. What are the risks of acidic substances like vinegar and lemon coming into contact with metal kitchen utensils and marble kitchen counters?
   o Acidic substances react with metals and basic substances. Marble kitchen counters are basic due to the calcium carbonate in them. Therefore, acidic substances like lemon and vinegar can corrode these materials.
2. Why is it dangerous to mix cleaning substances?
   o Cleaning products are chemicals, and when mixed with another cleaning product, they can react chemically. This reaction might produce toxic gases or explosive substances.
3. What are the environmental harms of cleaning products? What precautions can be taken?
   o Students are asked to research this question.

Student Worksheets
Experiment 1: Bioplastic Production
Experiment 2: Making Glue from Milk
Experiment 3: Water Hardness Experiment
Experiment 4: Observing the Effects of Acid Rain
Experiment 5: Observing the Effects of Lime and Caustic Soda

Experiment 1: Bioplastic Production

Nihal is a high school student. Her chemistry teacher assigned a project to address an environmental problem. Nihal found an interesting news article: "Microplastics' effects on the body are not yet known. However, experts suggest that these particles could have long-term harmful effects, including negatively impacting the developing immune system of a fetus. Plastic particles were found in the placentas of four healthy women who had normal pregnancies and deliveries. The particles, which were blue, red, orange, or pink, could have come from packaging, paints, cosmetics, or personal care products. Each particle was 10 microns in size (0.01 mm), meaning they could enter the bloodstream and be transported. Researchers say that these particles might also have entered the babies' bodies, but this has not been studied yet."
Let's help Nihal find a solution to this problem!
Materials:

- 60 mL distilled water
- 1.5 spatulas of vinegar
- 1.5 spatulas of glycerin

- 5 spatulas of cornstarch
- Beaker
- Stirring rod
- Measuring cup
- Food coloring

Procedure:

1. Fill the measuring cup with 60 mL of distilled water.
2. Transfer the water to the beaker.
3. Add 5 spatulas of cornstarch to the beaker and stir.
4. Add 1.5 spatulas (about 5 mL) of vinegar and 1.5 spatulas of glycerin to the cornstarch-water mixture. Start stirring.
5. Add a drop of food coloring to the mixture.
6. Stir until the mixture is homogeneous.
7. Heat the mixture on a stove/heater while stirring.
8. Continue stirring until the mixture boils and turns into a gel, then remove it from the heat.
9. Spread the mixture on aluminum foil before it cools and shape it as desired.
10. Leave it to dry for a few days.

Questions:

1. Research the environmental harms of plastics.
2. Is the bioplastic we obtained a polymer? Explain.
3. Compare the durability of normal plastic and the bioplastic we made.
4. Why has the use of bioplastics not become widespread?
5. What properties did vinegar and glycerin impart to the bioplastic?

Questions: The term "polymer" comes from "poli-" meaning many and "mer-" meaning unit (part). Polymers are very large molecules formed by the reaction of many monomers. In other words, polymers are large molecules consisting of numerous atoms and molecules.

Experiment 2: Making Glue from Milk

Ipek is a biology teacher and wants her younger sibling, who is in first grade, to grow up with high environmental awareness. She also wants to buy the least harmful stationery products for her sibling. From her research on stationery products, Ipek found the following information about the harms of adhesives:

"Solvent-based adhesives are made from polymers. Unlike water-based adhesives, they contain a polymer solvent. Solvent-based adhesives are used in various industries, including automotive, footwear, furniture, and construction. Despite their versatility, one of the main problems with solvent-based adhesives is their environmental impact. The solvent contained in them is harmful to air quality. Waste from solvent adhesives is not easily biodegradable. If not properly disposed of in waste collection bins, it can contaminate groundwater and have various adverse effects on ecosystems and human health."

Let's help Ipek make a less harmful adhesive!

Materials:

- 250 mL beaker
- 250 mL Erlenmeyer flask
- Stirring rod
- Measuring cup
- Paper towel
- Non-fat milk
- Acetic acid (vinegar)
- Sodium bicarbonate (baking soda)
- Distilled water

Procedure:

1. Pour 125 mL of non-fat milk into a beaker.
2. Add 25 mL of vinegar or acetic acid.
3. Heat while stirring until small curds form.
4. Remove from heat and wait for the curds to settle at the bottom.
5. Use a funnel lined with paper towel to filter the mixture into an Erlenmeyer flask.
6. Transfer the solid part remaining in the funnel to a beaker and add 15 mL of water and half a spatula of baking soda.
7. Allow the glue to dry for 30 minutes before testing.

Questions:

1. What is the purpose of using acetic acid or vinegar in this experiment?
2. Why was baking soda added?
3. Write the reaction equation between acetic acid and baking soda.
4. Which component in milk helped us obtain the adhesive?

Experiment 3: Water Hardness Experiment

Burcu goes to stay with her grandmother and notices that dishes are washed again after drying because they are not very clean. She thinks this is a waste of detergent and water. She finds information about the causes of white stains on dishes: "In hard water, soap reacts with calcium to form 'soap scum,' which leaves a significant amount of residue (scaling) when evaporated. Lathering is minimal. Therefore, using hard water requires more soap or detergent to clean hands, hair, and clothes, increasing consumption. Excessive detergent use negatively affects both machines and the environment. Hard water also affects taste and leaves residue in city water supply lines, hot water pipes, and boilers."

Burcu knows reducing water waste is crucial and wants to test which of the waters she uses is hard. Let's find out the hardness of different waters with Burcu!

Materials:

- Water from two different brands
- Distilled water
- Lime water
- 4 beakers
- German Hardness Measurement Device
- Stirring rod
- Liquid soap

Procedure:
Part 1

1. Pour equal amounts of each water sample into separate beakers.
2. Add a pump of liquid soap to each beaker.
3. Stir the beakers with the stirring rod.
4. Record the amount of lather produced.

Part 2

1. Place 5 mL of drinking water into a small tube of the hardness measurement device and add 3 drops of indicator.

2. Add one drop of titration solution to the tube and shake until a color change is observed. Record the number of drops added until the color changes.
3. Wash the tube, place 5 mL of distilled water into it, and repeat the titration process. Record the number of drops added until a color change is observed.
4. Wash the tube, place 5 mL of lime water into it, and repeat the titration process. Record the number of drops added until a color change is observed.
5. Refer to the set table to determine the hardness of the waters.

Questions:

1. Is seawater hard?
2. Does seawater show temporary hardness, permanent hardness, or both?
3. Research the substances that cause hardness in water.
4. Can hard water be softened? If so, how?

Experiment 4: Observing the Effects of Acid Rain

Elif is a high school student. She found an interesting news article in her school library: "The environmental impact of acid rain is harmful to both plants and humans. Acid rain can decrease the pH of water in lakes, harming aquatic life. It can also damage buildings and monuments by reacting with calcium carbonate and corroding the structures. For example, the Parthenon in Athens has been significantly eroded by acid rain. Acid rain also damages crops, reduces soil fertility, and contributes to forest damage by weakening trees."

Elif wants to see how acid rain affects the environment and decides to conduct an experiment at school.

Materials:

- 100 mL beakers
- Distilled water
- Vinegar
- Three green bean plants
- Measuring cup
- Thermometer
- pH meter

Procedure:

1. Fill one beaker with 100 mL of distilled water. Label it as Control.

2. Fill another beaker with 100 mL of water and add vinegar until the pH drops to 4. Label it as Acidic.
3. Fill the last beaker with 100 mL of water and add vinegar until the pH drops to 3. Label it as Very Acidic.
4. Place a green bean plant in each beaker.
5. Monitor the growth of the plants over a period of two weeks, recording any visible changes.

Questions:

1. Compare the growth of plants in acidic and very acidic solutions.
2. Describe the visible effects of acid rain on the plants.
3. Research how acid rain affects different parts of the environment.
4. What measures can be taken to reduce the impact of acid rain?

Experiment 5: Effects of Lime and Caustic Soda

Case Study

Can is a high school student. He heard that Ayşe, the school janitor, did not come to school the previous day because she had been poisoned. When he asked why, the chemistry teacher explained: "Can, Ayşe tried to clean using a caustic chemical mixed with lime cleaner, and as a result, she got poisoned." After this conversation, Can starts researching the harmful effects of cleaning products on living beings and the environment, as well as the precautions that need to be taken. He finds an experiment related to the effects of caustic soda and wants to conduct it at school. The next day, he goes to his chemistry teacher and performs the experiment with him in class. Afterward, he shares the information he learned about the harms of cleaning products with his friends. Let's observe this experiment together!

Materials:

- 20 mL vegetable oil
- NaOH solution (20 g/100 mL water)
- Lime solution (slaked lime)
- 3 x 250 mL beakers
- Stirring rod
- Distilled water
- Digital balance
- Heater
- Wire mesh

Procedure:

1. Coat the inside of the three beakers with vegetable oil. Try washing these beakers with water.
2. Test by touching the beakers with your hand to see if the oil has been cleaned.
3. Add NaOH solution to one beaker, Ca(OH)2 solution to another, and a mixture of NaOH and Ca(OH)2 solutions to the third beaker. Heat for 15 minutes.
4. Pour out the solution, rinse the beakers with water, and test by touching the beakers with your hand to see if the oil has been cleaned.

Questions:

1. What are the risks of acidic substances like vinegar and lemon coming into contact with metal kitchen utensils and marble kitchen counters?
2. Why is it dangerous to mix cleaning substances?
3. What are the environmental harms of cleaning products? What precautions can be taken?

Information Page

2016 report by the U.S. Environmental Protection Agency (EPA) reveals that indoor air in homes and workplaces is two to five times more polluted than outdoor air. The main causes of this pollution include inadequate ventilation, burning toxic candles and air fresheners, and chemicals from cleaning detergents entering the air.

Cleaning detergents not only pollute the air inside your home. Their waste goes down the sink and drain, mixing with water and entering the ecosystem, causing harm to many species, especially marine life.

Chlorine, used as a bleach in detergents and laundry products, is one of the chemicals that pose serious environmental threats. Once used in World War I as a chemical weapon, it is now banned or restricted in many countries to protect the environment and human health. When used indoors, chlorine combines with moisture in the throat, larynx, and lungs, leading to acidic effects. Chlorine that ends up in water as waste interacts with other elements and minerals, creating dangerous toxic substances.

Phosphates, also used as nutrients in fertilizers, increase the nitrogen and phosphate levels in seawater when they mix. This leads to a rapid growth of plants like algae, decreasing the oxygen levels in the water and creating an environment where other marine life cannot survive.

Caustic soda, also known as sodium hydroxide, is widely used in food, cleaning, machinery, purification, and manufacturing industries.

ACKNOWLEDGMENT

This study was supported by TUBITAK.

REFERENCES

Anastas, P., Nolasco, M., Kerton, F., Kirchhoff, M., Licence, P., Pradeep, T., Subramaniam, B., & Moores, A. (2021). The power of the United Nations sustainable development goals in sustainable chemistry and engineering research. *ACS Sustainable Chemistry & Engineering*, 9(24), 8015–8017. DOI: 10.1021/acssuschemeng.1c03762

Aydede, M. N., Deveci, E. Ü., & Gönen, Ç. (2019). Environmental literacy and sustainability. In Hastürk, H. G. (Ed.), *Environmental Education* (pp. 249–276). Anı Publishing.

BBC News Turkish. (2020). *Microplastic particles found in babies' placentas: "Babies are contaminated before they are born"*. https://www.bbc.com/turkce/haberler-dunya-55412052

Bozyiğit, R., & Karaaslan, T. (1998). *Environmental knowledge* (1st ed.). Nobel Publishing.

Bulut, B., & Çakmak, Z. (2018). Reflections on sustainable development education and training programs. *International Journal of Turkish Literature Culture Education*, 7(4), 2680–2697. DOI: 10.7884/teke.4371

Çabuk, B., & Karacaoğlu, C. (2003). Examination of university students' environmental sensitivities. *Journal of Ankara University Faculty of Education*, 36(1-2), 1–2.

Çam, F., & Köse, Ö. E. (2011). The effects of life-based learning on student achievement in the nervous system. *Journal of Turkish Science Education*, 8(2), 91–106.

Cebrián, G., Junyent, M., & Mulà, I. (2020). Competencies in education for sustainable development: Emerging teaching and research developments. *Sustainability (Basel)*, 12(2), 579. DOI: 10.3390/su12020579

Cıvış, G. (2021). Quality education within the scope of sustainable development goals: Comparison of selected OECD countries and Türkiye [Master's thesis, Hasan Kalyoncu University].

Doğan, M. (1997). National Environmental Strategy and Action Plan Report on Education and Participation Group. Undersecretariat of the State Planning Organization (DPT) and Turkish Environmental Foundation.

Gadenne, D. L., Kennedy, J., & McKeiver, C. (2009). An empirical study of environmental awareness and practices in SMEs. *Journal of Business Ethics*, 84(1), 45–63. DOI: 10.1007/s10551-008-9672-9

Gencer, E. G., Korlu, Ö., Kesbiç, K., Akay, S. S., Kotan, H., & Arık, B. M. (2023). *Education monitoring report 2023*. Education Reform Initiative. https://www.egitimreformugirisimi.org/wp-content/uploads/2023/11/EgitimIzlemeRaporu2023.pdf

Ghazali, M. Z., & Yahaya, A. (2022). Analysis of green chemistry knowledge, awareness, and practice among university students. *Journal of Science and Mathematics Letters*, 10(1), 79–90. DOI: 10.37134/jsml.vol10.1.8.2022

Güntut, M., Güneş, P., & Çetin, S. (2019). *10 textbooks of secondary education chemistry*. Publications of the Ministry of National Education.

Güntut, M., Güneş, P., & Çetin, S. (2019). *9 textbooks of secondary education chemistry*. Publications of the Ministry of National Education.

Güven, E., & Aydoğdu, M. (2012). Development of an environmental awareness scale for environmental problems and determination of pre-service teachers' awareness levels. *Journal of Teacher Education and Educators*, 1(2), 185–202.

Hassan, A., & Ismail, M. Z. (2011). The infusion of environmental education (EE) in chemistry teaching and students' awareness and attitudes towards environment in Malaysia. *Procedia: Social and Behavioral Sciences*, 15, 3404–3409. DOI: 10.1016/j.sbspro.2011.04.309

Howitz, W. J., Thane, T. A., Frey, T. L., Wang, X. S., Gonzales, J. C., Tretbar, C. A., Seith, D. D., Saluga, S. J., Lam, S., Nguyen, M. M., Tieu, P., Link, R. D., & Edwards, K. D. (2020). Online in no time: Design and implementation of a remote learning first-quarter general chemistry laboratory and second-quarter organic chemistry laboratory. *Journal of Chemical Education*, 97(9), 2624–2634. DOI: 10.1021/acs.jchemed.0c00895

Kaynak, N. E., Altan, A. E., Abbak, Y., Alp, Z. A., Yavuz, E., & Toprak, E. (2023). A theoretical view of quality education in terms of sustainable development. *Iğdır University Journal of Social Sciences*, 34, 592–609.

Korkmaz, G. (2020). New teacher training degree programmes analysing education for sustainable development in the context of education for sustainable development. *Journal of Advanced Education Studies*, 2(2), 111–132. DOI: 10.48166/ejaes.742200

Loste, N., Chinarro, D., Gomez, M., Roldán, E., & Giner, B. (2020). Assessing awareness of green chemistry as a tool for advancing sustainability. *Journal of Cleaner Production*, 256, 120392. DOI: 10.1016/j.jclepro.2020.120392

Michalopoulou, E., Shallcross, D. E., Atkins, E., Tierney, A., Norman, N. C., Preist, C., O'Doherty, S., Saunders, R., Birkett, A., Willmore, C., & Ninos, I. (2019). The end of simple problems: Repositioning chemistry in higher education and society using a systems thinking approach and the United Nations' Sustainable Development Goals as a framework. *Journal of Chemical Education*, 96(12), 2825–2835. DOI: 10.1021/acs.jchemed.9b00270

Mitarlis, M., Azizah, U., & Yonata, B. (2023). The integration of green chemistry principles in basic chemistry learning to support achievement of sustainable development goals (SDGs) through education. *Journal of Technology and Science Education*, 13(1), 233. DOI: 10.3926/jotse.1892

Nurbaity, N., Rahmawati, Y., & Ridwan, A. (2016). Integration of green chemistry approach in teacher education program for developing awareness of environmental sustainability. In *Proceedings of the ASEAN Comparative Education Research Network Conference (ACERN), November 30th – December 01, 2016* (pp. 2148-2156). Universitas Negeri Jakarta. https://doi.org/DOI: 10.1234/5678

Özmen, H., & Karamustafaoğlu, O. (2019). *Research methods in education*. Pegem Academy.

Peşkircioğlu, N. (2016). 2030 sustainable development goals: Towards a global productivity movement. *Key to Development*, 28(335), 4–9.

Petillion, R. J., Freeman, T. K., & McNeil, W. S. (2019). United Nations Sustainable Development Goals as a thematic framework for an introductory chemistry curriculum. *Journal of Chemical Education*, 96(12), 2845–2851. DOI: 10.1021/acs.jchemed.9b00307

Polat, S., & Kırpık, C. (2013). Attitudes of pre-service teachers towards environmental problems. *Journal of Bartın University Faculty of Education*, 2(1), 205–227. DOI: 10.14686/201312026

Ridha, I., Hasan, M., & Sulastri, . (2020). Comparing environmental awareness between chemistry education students and non-chemistry education students. *Journal of Physics: Conference Series*, 1460(1), 012085. DOI: 10.1088/1742-6596/1460/1/012085

Şeker, F., & Aydınlı, B. (2021). Education and competencies for sustainable development from the perspective of science teachers. *E-Caucasian Journal of Educational Research*, 8(3), 460–479. DOI: 10.30900/kafkasegt.964116

Sulistina, O., Rahayu, S., & Dasna, I. W., & Yahmin. (2021). The influence of guided inquiry-based learning using socio-scientific issues on environmental awareness of pre-service chemistry teachers. In *7th International Conference on Research, Implementation, and Education of Mathematics and Sciences (ICRIEMS 2020)*, Yogyakarta, Indonesia. https://doi.org/DOI: 10.2991/assehr.k.210305.036

Taha, H., Suppiah, V., Khoo, Y. Y., Yahaya, A., Lee, T. T., & Muhamad Damanhuri, M. I. (2019). Impact of student-initiated green chemistry experiments on their knowledge, awareness and practices of environmental sustainability. *Journal of Physics: Conference Series*, 1156, 012022. DOI: 10.1088/1742-6596/1156/1/012022

Teksöz, G. (2016). Learning from the past: Education for sustainable development. *Boğaziçi University Education Journal*, 31(2), 73–97.

The Global Goals for Sustainable Development. (2024). *Quality education: Ensure inclusive and equitable quality education and promote lifelong learning opportunities for all.* https://www.kureselamaclar.org/en/global-goals/quality-education/

United Nations Department of Economic and Social Affairs. (2024). *Do you know all 17 sustainable development goals?* https://www.un.org/sustainabledevelopment/sustainable-development-goals/

United Nations Türkiye. (2024). *How does the UN support sustainable development goals in Turkiye?* https://turkiye.un.org/tr/sdgs

Uralovich, K. S., Toshmamatovich, T. U., Kubayevich, K. F., Sapaev, I. B., Saylaubaevna, S. S., Beknazarova, Z. F., & Khurramov, A. (2023). A primary factor in sustainable development and environmental sustainability is environmental education. *Caspian Journal of Environmental Sciences*, 21, 965–975.

Vaughan, C., Gack, J., Solorazano, H., & Ray, R. (2003). The effect of environmental education on school children, their parents, and community members: A study of intergenerational and intercommunity learning. *The Journal of Environmental Education*, 34(3), 12–21. DOI: 10.1080/00958960309603489

Yayla, Z., Çavaş, B., Çavaş, L., & Türkoğuz, S. (2011). Klasik kimya deneyleri. In Chemistry, R. S. (Ed.), *Classic Chemistry Experiments: RSC* (pp. 105–108, 189–191). Palme Yayıncılık.

Yılmaz, O. (2019). The necessity of environmental education at primary school level in Türkiye within the scope of sustainable development [Master's thesis, Ankara Hacı Bayram Veli University].

Zhang, T., Shaikh, Z. A., Yumashev, A. V., & Chłąd, M. (2020). Applied model of e-learning in the framework of education for sustainable development. *Sustainability (Basel)*, 12(16), 6420. DOI: 10.3390/su12166420

Compilation of References

Abadi, S., Teh, K.S.M., Nasir, B.M., Huda, M., Ivanova, N.L., Sari, T.I., Maseleno, A., Satria, F., and Muslihudin, M. (2018). Application model of k-means clustering: insights into promotion strategy of vocational high school. International Journal of Engineering and Technology. 7 (2.27), 182-187.

Abulibdeh, A., Zaidan, E., & Abulibdeh, R. (2024). Navigating the confluence of artificial intelligence and education for sustainable development in the era of industry 4.0: Challenges, opportunities, and ethical dimensions. *Journal of Cleaner Production*, 437, 140527. DOI: 10.1016/j.jclepro.2023.140527

Acampora, A., Preziosi, M., & Merli, R. (2020). Framing the tourism industry into circular economy practices. In *Proceedings of the 26th Annual Conference of the International Sustainable Development Research Society* (pp. 15-17).

Accessibility and flexibility can lead to student empowerment. (2022, December 6). Instructure. https://www.instructure.com/resources/blog/accessibility-and-flexibility-can-lead-student-empowerment?webview_progress_bar=1&show_loading=0

Adair, A., Segan, E., Gobert, J., & Sao Pedro, M. (2023). *Real-Time AI-Driven Assessment & Scaffolding That Improves Students' Mathematical Modeling during Science Inquiry.* Grantee Submission.

Admin. (2023, February 24). *Virtual and augmented reality in E-learning.* Bytecasting. https://bytecasting.com/home/virtual-and-augmented-reality-in-e-learning/?amp=1&webview_progress_bar=1&show_loading=0

Admin. (2024, February 29). *Building a safe and productive online learning environment. Safe Search Kids.* https://www.safesearchkids.com/building-a-safe-and-productive-online-learning-environment/?webview_progress_bar=1&show_loading=0

Admin. (2024, January 6). *The Psychology Behind Gamification*: Why It Engages us | Web1Media. Web1Media. https://web1media.com/the-psychology-behind-gamification-why-it-engages-us/?webview_progress_bar=1&show_loading=0

Admin. (2024b, July 28). *Leveraging AI for spreading awareness and education in psychology. Envision Your Evolution.* https://www.envisionyourevolution.com/ai/leveraging-ai-for-spreading-awareness-and-education-in-psychology/34867/?show_loading=0&webview_progress_bar=1

Administrator, W. (2022, October 13). *Differentiated Instruction in Online Classroom.* High School of America. https://www.highschoolofamerica.com/differentiated-instruction-in-online-classroom/?webview_progress_bar=1&show_loading=0

Adula, M., Birbirsa, Z. A., & Kant, S. (2023). The effect of interpersonal, problem solving and technical training skills on performance of Ethiopia textile industry: Continuance, normative and affective commitment as mediators. *Cogent Business & Management*, 10(3), 2286672. Advance online publication. DOI: 10.1080/23311975.2023.2286672

Agente. (2024, January 11). *LMS gamification in 2024: Benefits, Types, and Examples* | Agente. https://agentestudio.com/blog/gamification-changing-elearning?show_loading=0&webview_progress_bar=1

Agrawal, A., Gans, J., & Goldfarb, A. (2018). *Prediction machines: The simple economics of artificial intelligence.* Harvard Business Review Press.

Ahmadigol, J. (2016). New definition of educational technology. In 30th Annual Proceedings: Selected Research and Development Papers (Vol. 1). Presented at the Annual Convention of the Association for Educational Communications and Technology.

Ahuja, R. (2020, March 20). *Benefits of social and collaborative learning.* Thrive Global. https://community.thriveglobal.com/benefits-of-social-and-collaborative-learning/?show_loading=0&webview_progress_bar=1

AI voice overs for e-learning for diverse learners. (n.d.). Speechify. https://speechify.com/blog/ai-voice-overs-for-e-learning/?show_loading=0&webview_progress_bar=1

AI-Powered Gamification in the Classroom - Planit Teachers. (n.d.). https://www.planitteachers.ai/articles/ai-powered-gamification-in-the-classroom?show_loading=0&webview_progress_bar=1

Akar, E. (2015). *The Importance of Foreign Language Skills in the Hospitality Industry and Its Impact on Employee Performance: A Comparative Study*. Procedia - Social and Behavioral Sciences.

Aker, J. C., & Mbiti, I. M. (2010). Mobile phones and economic development in Africa. *The Journal of Economic Perspectives*, 24(3), 207–232. DOI: 10.1257/jep.24.3.207

Akhil, R. (2022). *Digital E-Learning Market Future, Size, Growth Rate, Major Players, Online and Corporate E-learning Market*. Ken Research. https://www.kenresearch.com/blog/e-learning-future-market

Aksnes, D. W., Langfeldt, L., & Wouters, P. (2019). Citations, Citation Indicators, and Research Quality: An overview of basic concepts and theories. *SAGE Open*, 9(1), 215824401982957. DOI: 10.1177/2158244019829575

Alaghbari, S., Mitschick, A., Blichmann, G., Voigt, M., & Dachselt, R. (2021). A User-Centered approach to gamify the manual creation of training data for machine learning. *I-Com*, 20(1), 33–48. DOI: 10.1515/icom-2020-0030

Alalshaikh, S. (2015). The role of e-learning in the implementation of the sustainable development goals. International Journal of Education and Development using ICT, 11(1), 92-103. DOI: DOI: 10.1080/09751122.2015.11669057

Al-Aomar, R., & Hussain, M. (2017). An assessment of green practices in a hotel supply chain: A study of UAE hotels. *Journal of Hospitality and Tourism Management*, 32, 71–81. DOI: 10.1016/j.jhtm.2017.04.002

Aldrich, C. (n.d.). *Copyright 2024 the Learning Guild*. Copyright 2024: Powered by Cyclone Enterprise: Content Management Solutions and Dynamic Publishing System Developed by Cyclone Interactive Multimedia Group, Inc. http://www.cycloneinteractive.com, Powered by Cyclone and Powered by Cyclone Enterprise. Portional ColdFusion Programming Provided by Finial Software, Inc. www.finial.com. https://www.learningguild.com/contributors/612/clark-aldrich/?show_loading=0&webview_progress_bar=1

Aldridge, D. (2023). Making learning engaging: Hands-on STEM education. LinkedIn. Retrieved September 15, 2024, from https://www.linkedin.com/pulse/making-learning-engaging-hands-on-stem-education-damien-aldridge-51bnc

Aleixo, A., Azeiteiro, U., & Leal, S. (2016). *Toward sustainability through higher education: Sustainable Development Incorporation in Portuguese Higher Education Institutions*. In Challenges in Higher Education for Sustainability (pp. 159-187). Springer. DOI: 10.1007/978-3-319-23705-3_7

Alfieri, L., Brooks, P. J., Aldrich, N. J., & Tenenbaum, H. R. (2011). Does discovery-based instruction enhance learning? *Journal of Educational Psychology*, 103(1), 1–18. https://doi.org/10.1037/a0021017

Ali, K., Zahra, A., & Mohammad, M. (2021). *National Library of Medicine*. https://www.ncbi.nlm.nih.gov/pmc/articles/PMC8170558/?webview_progress_bar=1&show_loading=0

Ali, A. H. (2023). Pelajar Khalifah Profesional Tempaan Ulul Albab sorotan penerapannya berasaskan komponen QEI di UPSI. *Firdaus Journal*, 3(2), 51–63. DOI: 10.37134/firdaus.vol3.2.5.2023

Alwi, A. S. Q., & Ibrahim, R. (2022). Isu terhadap Penggunaan Teknologi Media Digital dalam kalangan guru pelatih jurusan Pendidikan Khas. *Firdaus Journal*, 2(2), 88–93. DOI: 10.37134/firdaus.vol2.2.9.2022

Amazon.com. (n.d.). https://www.amazon.com/Simulations-Future-Learning-Revolutionary-Learning/dp/0787969621?webview_progress_bar=1&show_loading=0

Amin, M., Khan, A., & Holz, H. (2019). Smart city initiatives: PPP approaches and digital platforms. *Journal of Urban Technology*, 26(4), 3–18. DOI: 10.1080/10630732.2019.1649484

Aminudin, N., Huda, M., Ihwani, S.S., Noor, S.S.M., Basiron, B., Jasmi, K.A., Safar, J., Mohamed, A.K., Embong, W.H.W., Mohamad, A.M., Maseleno, A., Masrur, M., Trisnawati, and Rohmadi, D. (2018a). The family hope program using AHP method. International Journal of Engineering and Technology. 7(2.27), 188-193.

Aminudin, N., Huda, M., Mohamed, A.K., Embong, W.H.W., Mohamad, A.M., Basiron, B., Ihwani, S.S., Noor, S.S.M., Jasmi, K.A., Safar, J., Natalie, L., Ivanova, Maseleno, A., Triono, A., and Nungsiati. (2018b). Higher education selection using simple additive weighting. International Journal of Engineering and Technology. 7(2.27), 211-217.

Anastas, P., Nolasco, M., Kerton, F., Kirchhoff, M., Licence, P., Pradeep, T., Subramaniam, B., & Moores, A. (2021). The power of the United Nations sustainable development goals in sustainable chemistry and engineering research. *ACS Sustainable Chemistry & Engineering*, 9(24), 8015–8017. DOI: 10.1021/acssuschemeng.1c03762

Andersen, M. S. (2007). An introductory note on the environmental economics of the circular economy. *Sustainability Science*, 2(1), 133–140. DOI: 10.1007/s11625-006-0013-6

Anderson, K., Ryan, B., Sonntag, W., Kavvada, A., & Friedl, L. (2017). Earth observation in service of the 2030 Agenda for Sustainable Development. *Geo-Spatial Information Science*, 20(2), 77–96. DOI: 10.1080/10095020.2017.1333230

Andrews, G., Basu, A., Cuijpers, P., Craske, M. G., McEvoy, P., English, T., & Newby, J. M. (2018). Computer therapy for the anxiety and depression disorders is effective, acceptable and practical health care: An updated meta-analysis. *Journal of Anxiety Disorders*, 55, 70–78. DOI: 10.1016/j.janxdis.2018.01.001 PMID: 29422409

Ang, S. M. (2021). Awareness on sustainable development goals among university students in Malaysia. *Asian Journal of Research in Education and Social Sciences*, 3(1), 105–116.

Anud, E. (2022). Teaching performance of science teachers in the new normal and their technological pedagogical and content knowledge (TPACK) self-efficacy. International Journal of Applied Science and Research.https://doi.org/10.56293/ijasr.2022.5410

Apandi, N. E. F. Z., Mokmin, N. A. M., & Rassy, R. P. (2023). A Study on the Users' Experience in Learning Using a Virtual Reality Laboratory for Medical Sciences. In *Proceedings of International Conference on Research in Education and Science* (pp. 1-16).

Aravindan, A. (2023, October 10). *Unlocking User Engagement: The Psychology behind Gamification in Mobile Apps*. Medium. https://medium.muz.li/unlocking-user-engagement-the-psychology-behind-gamification-in-mobile-apps-dce9c2a901de

Area9 Lyceum. (2021b, March 19). *Activity-Based Learning*. Area9 Lyceum. https://area9lyceum.com/adaptive-learning/activity-based-learning/?webview_progress_bar=1&show_loading=0

Arizona State University. (2019). Social embeddedness initiative at ASU: Addressing community needs through deep engagement. https://www.asu.edu

Arockiasamy, S. (2018). Concept of educational technology. Viswa Bharathi College of Education for Women. Retrieved from https://drarockiasamy.wordpress.com/unit-i-concept-of-educational-technology/

Asefa, K., & Debela, K. L. (2023). Effect of Transformational Leadership on Organizational Performance: The Mediating Role of Employee Commitment and Expert Systems (AI) Inclusion in Ethiopia. *2023 International Conference on Communication, Security and Artificial Intelligence (ICCSAI)*, 305-310, DOI: 10.1109/ICCSAI59793.2023.10421269

Asghar, A., Sladeczek, I. E., Mercier, J., & Beaudoin, E. (2017). Learning in science, technology, engineering, and mathematics: Supporting students with learning dis-abilities. *Canadian Psychology*, 58(3), 238–249.

Ashesi University. (2019). Poverty Action Lab: Testing effective interventions in Ghana. https://www.ashesi.edu.gh

Asian Development Bank (ADB). (2020). *Key Trends in Education in Asia and the Pacific*. ADB.

Atanasova, N., Castellar, J. A., Pineda-Martos, R., Nika, C. E., Katsou, E., Istenic, D., Pucher, B., Andreucci, M. B., & Langergraber, G. (2021). Nature-based solutions and circularity in cities. *Circular Economy and Sustainability*, 1(1), 319–332. DOI: 10.1007/s43615-021-00024-1

Ateneo de Manila University. (2018). *Partnerships for sustainable development: Ateneo de Manila and Gawad Kalinga*. Ateneo Press.

Atmojo, I. R. W., Saputri, D. Y., & Fajri, A. K. (2022). Analysis of STEAM-based TPACK integrated activities in elementary school thematic books. *Mimbar Sekolah Dasar*, 9(2), 317–335. https://doi.org/10.53400/mimbar-sd.v9i2.49131

Attard, C., Berger, N., & Mackenzie, E. (2021). The positive influence of inquiry-based learning, teacher professional learning, and industry partnerships on student engagement with STEM. *Frontiers in Education*, 6. Advance online publication. https://doi.org/10.3389/feduc.2021.693221

Atzori, L., Iera, A., & Morabito, G. (2010). The Internet of Things: A survey. *Computer Networks*, 54(15), 2787–2805. DOI: 10.1016/j.comnet.2010.05.010

Audio & video tips for E-Learning | The Rapid E-Learning blog. (n.d.). *The Rapid E-Learning Blog*. https://blogs.articulate.com/rapid-elearning/audio-video-tips/?webview_progress_bar=1&show_loading=0

Augmentastic, P. V. T. LTD. (2023, April 12). How AR/VR is transforming STEM education: Unlocking new learning opportunities. Augmentastic PVT. LTD. Retrieved from https://www.augmentastic.com/how-arvr-is-transforming-stem-education

Augmented Reality in Education: Examples, Benefits, & Use Cases (2023). https://arborxr.com/blog/augmented-reality-in-education-examples-benefits-use-cases/?webview_progress_bar=1&show_loading=0

August, S. E. (2023, April 26). Integrating technology with best practices paves the way. American Association for the Advancement of Science. Retrieved September 15, 2024, from https://aaas-iuse.org/integrating-technology-with-best-practices-paves-the-way/

Aydede, M. N., Deveci, E. Ü., & Gönen, Ç. (2019). Environmental literacy and sustainability. In Hastürk, H. G. (Ed.), *Environmental Education* (pp. 249–276). Anı Publishing.

Ayo, S. K. (2022, January 5). *THE AI HIERARCHY OF NEEDS - Analytics Vidhya - Medium*. Medium. https://medium.com/analytics-vidhya/the-ai-hierarchy-of-needs-6d76aa6c5555?show_loading=0&webview_progress_bar=1

Bacova, M., Bohme, K., Guitton, M., Herwijnen, M. V., Kállay, T., Koutsomarkou, J., & Rok, A. (2016). *Pathways to a circular economy in cities and regions*. Interreg Europe Joint Secretariat.

Bahroun, Z., Anane, C., Ahmed, V., & Zacca, A. (2023). Transforming education: A comprehensive review of generative artificial intelligence in educational settings through bibliometric and content analysis. *Sustainability (Basel)*, 15(17), 12983. DOI: 10.3390/su151712983

Bai, S., Gonda, D. E., & Hew, K. F. (2024). Write-Curate-Verify: A Case Study of Leveraging Generative AI for Scenario Writing in Scenario-Based Learning. *IEEE Transactions on Learning Technologies*.

Baker, S., & Vandepeer, B. (2004). *Deployed force waste management report* (1st ed.). DSTO Systems Sciences Laboratory.

Bakker, D., Kazantzis, N., Rickwood, D., & Rickard, N. (2018). Mental health smartphone apps: Review and evidence-based recommendations for future developments. *JMIR Mental Health*, 3(1), e7. DOI: 10.2196/mental.4984 PMID: 26932350

Banchi, H., & Bell, R. (2008, October). The many levels of inquiry. *Science and Children*, 26–29.

Barron, B., & Darling-Hammond, L. (2008). Teaching for meaningful learning: A review of research on inquiry-based and cooperative learning. In Darling-Hammond, L., Barron, B., Pearson, P. D., Schoenfeld, A., Stage, E., Zimmerman, T., Cervetti, G., & Tilson, J. (Eds.), *Powerful learning: What we know about teaching for understanding* (pp. 11–70). Jossey-Bass.

Bauer, D. J., Sterba, S. K., & Hallfors, D. D. (2008). Evaluating Group-Based interventions when control participants are ungrouped. *Multivariate Behavioral Research*, 43(2), 210–236. DOI: 10.1080/00273170802034810 PMID: 20396621

BBC News Turkish. (2020). *Microplastic particles found in babies' placentas: "Babies are contaminated before they are born"*. https://www.bbc.com/turkce/haberler-dunya-55412052

Behance. (n.d.). https://www.behance.net/search/projects/?search=interactive%2BeLearning&show_loading=0&webview_progress_bar=1

Bell, P., Lewenstein, B., Shouse, A. W., & Feder, M. A. (2009). *Learning science in informal environments: People, places, and pursuits*. National Academies Press.

Bell, T., Urhahne, D., Schanze, S., & Ploetzner, R. (2010). Collaborative inquiry learning: Models, tools, and challenges. *International Journal of Science Education*, 32(1), 349–377. https://doi.org/10.1080/09500690802582241

Berlian, Z., & Huda, M. (2022). Reflecting culturally responsive and communicative teaching (CRCT) through partnership commitment. *Education Sciences*, 12(5), 295. DOI: 10.3390/educsci12050295

Best Adaptive Learning Platforms 2024 | Reviews & Comparison. (2024, February 26). https://edtechimpact.com/categories/adaptive-learning/

Bewersdorff, A., Hartmann, C., Hornberger, M., Seßler, K., Bannert, M., Kasneci, E., Kasneci, G., Zhai, X., & Nerdel, C. (2024). Taking the Next Step with Generative Artificial Intelligence: The Transformative Role of Multimodal Large Language Models in Science Education. *ArXiv*, abs/2401.00832.

Bhanabhai, M. (2023, January 15*). Gamification symmetry with Maslows hierarchy of needs – a model to #Improve, #Engage and #Perform*. Thealphaswarmer. Gamification Symmetry With Max, B. (2022). Maslows Hierarchy of Needs – A Model To #Improve, #Engage and #Perform. thealphaswarmer. https://www.thealphaswarmer.com/2022/09/gamification-symmetry-with-maslows-hierarchy-of-needs-a-model-to-improve-engage-and-perform/?show_loading=0&webview_progress_bar=1

Blasco, N., Brusca, I., & Labrador, M. (2020). Drivers for universities' contribution to the sustainable development goals: An analysis of Spanish public universities. *Sustainability (Basel)*, 13(1), 1–19. DOI: 10.3390/su13010089

Bloggers, C. I., & Bloggers, C. I. (2017, November 16). *5 Fab tips to design Interactive E-Learning Modules*. https://blog.commlabindia.com/elearning-design/interactive-elearning-modules-design-tips?webview_progress_bar=1&show_loading=0

Bloomfield, J., & Fisher, M. J. (2019). Quantitative research design. *JARNA*, 22(2), 27–30. https://search.informit.org/doi/10.3316/informit.738299924514584. DOI: 10.33235/jarna.22.2.27-30

Blumenfeld, P. C., & Krajcik, J. S. (2006). Project-based learning. In Sawyer, R. K. (Ed.), *The Cambridge handbook of learning sciences* (pp. 317–334). Cambridge University Press.

Borham, A. H., Syahdiah, U., Mohsin, M. A., Huda, M., Rahim, M. A., Ilyas, D., & Sakni, A. S. (2024). Information and communication ethics in social media for indigenous people's religious understanding: a critical review. In *World Conference on Information Systems for Business Management* (pp. 287-302). Singapore: Springer Nature Singapore. DOI: 10.1007/978-981-99-8346-9_25

Borham, A. H., Huda, M., Rasid, M. S. A., Rahim, M. M. A., & Hamid, N. Z. A. (2024). Teaching approach for indigenous people: An empirical study from Pahang, Malaysia. [EduLearn]. *Journal of Education and Learning*, 18(3), 773–782.

Bosone, M., & Nocca, F. (2022). Human Circular Tourism as the tourism of tomorrow: The role of travelers in achieving a more sustainable and circular tourism. *Sustainability (Basel)*, 14(19), 12218. DOI: 10.3390/su141912218

Boulding, K. E. (1966). The economics of the coming spaceship Earth. In Jarrett, H. (Ed.), *Environmental quality in a growing economy* (pp. 3–14). Johns Hopkins University Press.

Bovaird, T. (2004). Public-private partnerships: From contested concepts to prevalent practice. *International Review of Administrative Sciences*, 70(2), 199–215. DOI: 10.1177/0020852304044250

Bowen, J. A., & Watson, C. E. (2024). *Teaching with AI: A practical guide to a new era of human learning*. JHU Press.

Bozyiğit, R., & Karaaslan, T. (1998). *Environmental knowledge* (1st ed.). Nobel Publishing.

Brau, B. (n.d.). Constructivism. In Student guide to learning with technology. EdTech Books. Retrieved September 14, 2024, from https://edtechbooks.org/studentguide/constructivism

Breon, C. (2024, March 18). *Unveiling the unseen: the spellbinding impact of augmented reality (AR) and virtual reality (VR) in entertainment and education*. Medium. https://medium.com/@breoncayden/unveiling-the-unseen-the-spellbinding-impact-of-augmented-reality-ar-and-virtual-reality-vr-in-6d8d908ace42

BrightCarbon. (2023, October 23). *Insights from an eLearning strategist: Q&A with Clark Quinn*. https://www.brightcarbon.com/blog/insights-elearning-strategist-qa-clark-quinn/?webview_progress_bar=1&show_loading=0

Brinson, J. R. (2015). Learning outcome achievement in non-traditional (virtual and remote) versus traditional (hands-on) laboratories: A review of the empirical research. *Computers & Education*, 87, 218–237. https://doi.org/10.1016/j.compedu.2015.07.003

Bruder, R., & Prescott, A. (2013). Research evidence on the benefits of IBL. *ZDM Mathematics Education*, 45(6), 811–822. https://doi.org/10.1007/s11858-013-0542-2

Brynjolfsson, E., & McAfee, A. (2017). *Machine, platform, crowd: Harnessing our digital future*. W.W. Norton & Company.

Bughin, J., Hazan, E., Ramaswamy, S., Chui, M., Allas, T., Dahlström, P., & Trench, M. (2017). *Artificial Intelligence: The next digital frontier?* McKinsey Global Institute.

Bullock, M. (2023, July 28). *AI Meets Gamification: Unleashing the potential of artificial intelligence in employee motivation.*

Bullock, M. (2023a, May 28). *AI in Gamification – The Future of Productivity and Engagement. Spinify*. https://spinify.com/blog/ai-in-gamification/

Bulut, B., & Çakmak, Z. (2018). Reflections on sustainable development education and training programs. *International Journal of Turkish Literature Culture Education*, 7(4), 2680–2697. DOI: 10.7884/teke.4371

Burke, B. N., Reed, P. A., & Wells, J. G. (n.d.). Engineering byDesign™ – Maximizing design and inquiry through integrative STEM education: The setting. International Technology and Engineering Educators Association. Retrieved from https://assets-002.noviams.com/novi-file-uploads/iteea/resource_hub/ESP_EbD_v12.pdf

Butz, W. P., Kelly, T. K., Adamson, D. M., Bloom, G. A., Fossum, D., & Gross, M. E. (2004). *Will the scientific and technology workforce meet the requirements of the federal government?* RAND Corporation.

By Craig Weiss. (2024, September 16). *Craig Weiss*. https://elearninfo247.com/author/diegoinstudiocity/?webview_progress_bar=1&show_loading=0

Bybee, R. (2010). Advancing STEM education: A 2020 vision. *Technology and Engineering Teacher*, 70(1), 30–35.

Bybee, R. W. (2009). *The BSCS 5E instructional model and 21st century skills*. BSCS.

Bybee, R. W., & Landes, N. M. (1990). Science for life & living: An elementary school science program from Biological Sciences Curriculum Study. *The American Biology Teacher*, 52(2), 92–98.

Çabuk, B., & Karacaoğlu, C. (2003). Examination of university students' environmental sensitivities. *Journal of Ankara University Faculty of Education*, 36(1-2), 1–2.

Caeiro, S., & Azeiteiro, U. M. (2020). Sustainability Assessment in Higher Education Institutions. *Sustainability (Basel)*, 12(8), 10–13. DOI: 10.3390/su12083433

Calzon, B. (2023). *What is data analysis? Methods, techniques, types & how-to*. BI Blog | Data Visualization & Analytics Blog | Datapine. https://www.datapine.com/blog/data-analysis-methods-and-techniques/

Çam, F., & Köse, Ö. E. (2011). The effects of life-based learning on student achievement in the nervous system. *Journal of Turkish Science Education*, 8(2), 91–106.

Campbell, R. (2024, January 10). *AI and Collaborative Learning - Richard Campbell*. Richard Campbell. https://richardccampbell.com/ai-and-collaborative-learning-an-innovative-way-to-improve-education/

Campbell-Johnston, K., ten Cate, J., Elfering-Petrovic, M., & Gupta, J. (2019). City level circular transitions: Barriers and limits in Amsterdam, Utrecht, and The Hague. *Journal of Cleaner Production*, 235, 1232–1239. DOI: 10.1016/j.jclepro.2019.06.106

Can Studios Ltd. (2023b, April 4). *Self-Paced learning*. https://www.linkedin.com/pulse/self-paced-learning-can-studios-ltd?show_loading=0&webview_progress_bar=1

Capinding, A. T., & Dumayas, F. T. (2024). Transformative Pedagogy in the Digital Age: Unraveling the Impact of Artificial Intelligence on Higher Education Students. Problems of Education in the 21st Century, 82(5), 630-657.

Caragliu, A., Del Bo, C., & Nijkamp, P. (2011). Smart cities in Europe. *Journal of Urban Technology*, 18(2), 65–82. DOI: 10.1080/10630732.2011.601117

Carlbring, P., Andersson, G., Cuijpers, P., Riper, H., & Hedman-Lagerlöf, E. (2018). Internet-based vs. face-to-face cognitive behavior therapy for psychiatric and somatic disorders: An updated systematic review and meta-analysis. *Cognitive Behaviour Therapy*, 47(1), 1–18. DOI: 10.1080/16506073.2017.1401115 PMID: 29215315

Caroline. (2022, April 6). *Multimodal Learning: engaging your learner's senses*. LearnUpon. https://www.learnupon.com/blog/multimodal-learning/

Castillo, Jr. F.G, Antiado, D.F. & Reblando, J.R.P (2019). Philippine Education System: Are We Moving Forward? *International Journal of Innovative Technology and Exploring Engineering (IJITEE)*, Vol. 8, Issue-12S.

Castro, G. P. B., Chiappe, A., Rodríguez, D. F. B., & Sepulveda, F. G. (2024). Harnessing AI for Education 4.0: Drivers of Personalized Learning. Electronic Journal of e-Learning, 22(5), 01-14.

Cathy Moore. (2012, November 20). e-Learning Centre. https://www.e-learningcentre.co.uk/resources/brilliant-blogs/news-and-lots-of-lively-views-from-the-pay-gap-for-women-in-e-learning-to-practical-tips-on-instructional-design-always-worth-a-read-follow-her-on-twitter-cammybean-share/?webview_progress_bar=1&show_loading=0

Cathy Moore's blog. (2023, October 16). https://www.td.org/magazines/td-magazine/cathy-moores-blog?webview_progress_bar=1&show_loading=0

Cave, J. (2017). *Digital government: Leveraging technology to improve public sector efficiency and responsiveness*. OECD Publishing.

Cebrián, G., Junyent, M., & Mulà, I. (2020). Competencies in education for sustainable development: Emerging teaching and research developments. *Sustainability (Basel)*, 12(2), 579. DOI: 10.3390/su12020579

Cecilia. (2023, October 10). *Harnessing the benefits of structured instruction - kognity*. Kognity. https://kognity.com/resources/harnessing-the-benefits-of-structured-instruction/?webview_progress_bar=1&show_loading=0

Çelik, F., & Ersanlı, C. Y. (2022). The use of augmented reality in a gamified CLIL lesson and students' achievements and attitudes: A quasi-experimental study. *Smart Learning Environments*, 9(1), 30. Advance online publication. DOI: 10.1186/s40561-022-00211-z

Chacko, P., Appelbaum, S., Kim, H., Zhao, J., & Kim Montclare, J. (2013). Integrating technology in STEM education. *Journal of Technology and Science Education*, 5(1). Advance online publication. https://doi.org/10.3926/jotse.124

Chankseliani, M., & McCowan, T. (2021). Higher education and the sustainable development goals. *Higher Education*, 81(1), 1–8. DOI: 10.1007/s10734-020-00652-w PMID: 33173242

Char, D. S., Shah, N. H., & Magnus, D. (2018). Implementing machine learning in health care—Addressing ethical challenges. *The New England Journal of Medicine*, 378(11), 981–983. DOI: 10.1056/NEJMp1714229 PMID: 29539284

Charleybrown. (2021, September 22). *5 Advantages of collaborative E-Learning*. Online Class Helpers. https://www.onlineclasshelpers.com/blog/5-advantages-of-collaborative-e-learning/amp/?show_loading=0&webview_progress_bar=1

ChatGPT: the AI chatbot for gaming customer support. (2023, July 16). Dasha.AI. https://dasha.ai/en-us/blog/chatgpt-gaming-companies-technical-support?webview_progress_bar=1&show_loading=0

Chauke, T. A., Mkhize, T. R., Methi, L., & Dlamini, N. (2024). Postgraduate Students' Perceptions on the Benefits Associated with Artificial Intelligence Tools on Academic Success: In Case of ChatGPT AI tool. *Journal of Curriculum Studies Research*, 6(1), 44–59.

Chen, C. H., & Chang, C. L. (2024). Effectiveness of AI-assisted game-based learning on science learning outcomes, intrinsic motivation, cognitive load, and learning behavior. *Education and Information Technologies*, •••, 1–22.

Cheng, E. C. K., & Wang, T. (2023). Leading digital transformation and eliminating barriers for teachers to incorporate artificial intelligence in basic education in Hong Kong. *Computers and Education: Artificial Intelligence*, 5, 100171. DOI: 10.1016/j.caeai.2023.100171

Chen, J. J., & Lin, J. C. (2024). Artificial intelligence as a double-edged sword: Wielding the POWER principles to maximize its positive effects and minimize its negative effects. *Contemporary Issues in Early Childhood*, 25(1), 146–153.

Chen, M. B., Wang, S. G., Chen, Y. N., Chen, X. F., & Lin, Y. Z. (2020). A preliminary study of the influence of game types on the learning interests of primary school students in digital games. *Education Sciences*, 10(4), 96.

Chen, M., Ma, Y., Li, S., Wu, D., Zhang, Y., & Wang, L. (2018). A survey on 5G: Architecture and design principles. *IEEE Transactions on Network and Service Management*, 15(3), 1085–1104. DOI: 10.1109/TNSM.2018.2847682

Chen, S., Sun, S., Peng, H., & Wang, H. (2018). Digital platform strategy: Effects of competition and collaboration. *Journal of Management Information Systems*, 35(4), 978–1001. DOI: 10.1080/07421222.2018.1524823

Chen, Y. (2020). Designing learner-centered digital language learning experiences: A case study of a blended Mandarin Chinese course. *Computer Assisted Language Learning*, 33(5-6), 611–632.

Chiangpradit, L. (2024, July 10). 9 challenges of teaching STEM & how to overcome them. STEM Sports. Reviewed by S. Barton & H. MacLean. Retrieved from https://stemsports.com/8-challenges-of-teaching-stem/

Chin, W., Callaghan, C., & Lamparello, N. (2017). Smarter Cities: Bridging the Knowledge Divide with Corporate-NGO Partnerships. *Sustainable Cities and Society*, 29, 329–339. DOI: 10.1016/j.scs.2017.01.001

Chiu, J. L., Malcolm, P. T., Hecht, D., DeJaegher, C. J., Pan, E. A., Bradley, M., & Burghardt, M. D. (2013). WISEngineering: Supporting precollege engineering design and mathematical understanding. *Computers & Education*, 67, 142–155.

Chiu, T. K., Moorhouse, B. L., Chai, C. S., & Ismailov, M. (2023). Teacher support and student motivation to learn with Artificial Intelligence (AI) based chatbot. *Interactive Learning Environments*, •••, 1–17.

Choudhary, P. (2023, August 12). *Cons and pros of AI game development*. https://www.linkedin.com/pulse/cons-pros-ai-game-development-payal-choudhary

Christina. (2024b, July 30). *Essential audio, video, and authoring technologies for creating E-Learning courses*. Blue Carrot. https://bluecarrot.io/blog/exploring-audio-video-and-authoring-technologies-for-effective-e-learning-course-creation/?webview_progress_bar=1&show_loading=0

Ciobanu, A. (2013). *The role of student services in the improving of student experience in higher education*. Lumen Research Center in Social and Humanistic Sciences, Asociatia Lumen. DOI: 10.1016/j.sbspro.2013.08.654

Circular Economy in Tourism. (2019). Ellen MacArthur Foundation. https://ellenmacarthurfoundation.org/circular-economy

Cıvış, G. (2021). Quality education within the scope of sustainable development goals: Comparison of selected OECD countries and Türkiye [Master's thesis, Hasan Kalyoncu University].

Claire, A. (2012). *The Game of Motivation: Gamification and Augmented Reality in Education*. oeb insights. https://oeb.global/oeb-insights/the-game-of-motivation-gamification-and-augmented-reality-in-education

Clark, A. (2003). *Simulations and the Future of Learning: An Innovative (and Perhaps Revolutionary) Approach to e-Learning*. ACM Digital Library. https://dl.acm.org/doi/10.5555/861424?webview_progress_bar=1&show_loading=0

Clark, D. A., Beck, A. T., & Alford, B. A. (2020). *Scientific Foundations of Cognitive Theory and Therapy of Depression*. John Wiley & Sons.

Coder, Z. (n.d.). CoderZ: Engage students in STEM with coding and robotics. Retrieved September 14, 2024, from https://gocoderz.com/learn/

Cohen, B. (2015). The smart city wheel: A visual model for understanding the relationship between technological, environmental, and social dimensions of urban sustainability. *Sustainable Cities and Society*, 10(1), 1–8. DOI: 10.1016/j.scs.2014.07.007

Cojocariu, R. T. A. G. (2023, March 3). *Five ways you can use AI for Gamification - Gabriela Cojocariu - Medium*. Medium. https://medium.com/@gabriela.cojocariu/five-ways-you-can-use-ai-for-gamification-43919727e5c9

Colman, H. (2024, July 2). *Multimodal learning: a Transformative approach for success*. Explore the eLearning World With Us. https://www.ispringsolutions.com/blog/multimodal-learning?f_link_type=f_inlinenote&webview_progress_bar=1&show_loading=0

Commission on Higher Education. (2017). *Higher education reform agenda for poverty reduction in the Philippines*. CHED Publications.

Common Sense Education. (n.d.). Best robotics apps and websites for STEM classrooms. Common Sense Education. Retrieved September 14, 2024, from https://www.commonsense.org/education/lists/best-robotics-apps-and-websites-for-stem-classrooms

Conchas, D. M., Montilla, A. R. Y., Romblon, K. D. C., Torion, M. P., Reyes, J. J. R., & Tinapay, A. O. (2023). Assessing the experiential learning and scientific process skills of senior high school STEM students: A literature review. *International Journal of Multidisciplinary Research and Publications*, 6(2), 81–90.

Cong, T. T. (2016). *Factors attracting foreign tourists of Ho Chi Minh City* (Master's thesis). Ho Chi Minh City University.

Continuous feedback model could reshape eLearning evaluation : Articles. (n.d.). Copyright 2024 the Learning Guild. Copyright 2024: Powered by Cyclone Enterprise: Content Management Solutions and Dynamic Publishing System Developed by Cyclone Interactive Multimedia Group, Inc. http://www.cycloneinteractive.com, Powered by Cyclone and Powered by Cyclone Enterprise. Portional ColdFusion Programming Provided by Finial Software, Inc. www.finial.com. https://www.learningguild.com/articles/continuous-feedback-model-could-reshape-elearning-evaluation/

Cooper, C. (2023, December 16). *The power of AI driven gamification in business - Colin Cooper - medium*. Medium. https://medium.com/@colin-cooper/the-power-of-ai-driven-gamification-in-business-8d5165bf6e8a

Cooper, J. (2024, August 21). *How to use AI eLearning Avatars for online Courses 2024*. Vidnoz. https://www.vidnoz.com/ai-solutions/elearning-avatar.html?show_loading=0&webview_progress_bar=1

Cote, A., & Cote, A. (2024b, September 9). *What is Self-Paced Learning: benefits and ways to address its challenges*. LearnWorlds. https://www.learnworlds.com/self-paced-learning/?show_loading=0&webview_progress_bar=1

Craig Weiss: the e-learning industry's most prolific psychic. (2013, December 18). https://oeb.global/oeb-insights/craig-weiss-the-e-learning-industrys-most-prolific-psychic/?show_loading=0&webview_progress_bar=1

Craig, E., & Georgieva, M. (2017, August 4). AR and VR in STEM: The new frontiers in science. Retrieved from https://www.emorycraig.com/ar-and-vr-in-stem-the-new-frontiers-in-science

Crawford, J., & Shinn, D. (2021). Digital learning: The impact of digital platforms on quality education. *International Journal of Educational Technology in Higher Education*, 18(1), 1–14. DOI: 10.1186/s41239-021-00262-6

Cudy. (2023) *5 Tips for Applying Differentiated Instructionin eLearning*. Cudy technology. https://blog.cudy.co/5-tips-for-applying-differentiated-instruction-in-elearning/?webview_progress_bar=1&show_loading=0

D'Mello, S. K., & Graesser, A. (2015). Affective computing, emotion regulation, and intelligent tutoring systems. In *International Handbook of Metacognition and Learning Technologies* (pp. 669–681). Springer., DOI: 10.1007/978-1-4614-7456-9_44

D'Silva, I. (2010). Active learning. *Journal of Education Administration and Policy Studies*, 2(6), 77–82.

Daffrin. (2023, June 6). *5 things to consider when choosing an E-Learning platform*. BrainCert Blog. https://blog.braincert.com/5-things-to-consider-when-choosing-an-e-learning-platform/?webview_progress_bar=1&show_loading=0

Dagdag, J., Cuizon, H., & Bete, A. (2019). College students' problems and their link to academic performance: Basis for needs-driven student programs. *Journal of Research, Policy & Practice of Teachers &. Teaching Education*. Advance online publication. DOI: 10.37134/jrpptte.vol9.no2.5.201

Daly, H. E., & Farley, J. (2019). *Ecological economics: Principles and applications* (2nd ed.). Island Press.

Dangelico, R. M., & Pontrandolfo, P. (2010). From green product definitions and classifications to the Green Option Matrix. *Journal of Cleaner Production*, 18(16-17), 1608–1628. DOI: 10.1016/j.jclepro.2010.07.007

Dani, V. (2024, June 17). *The Cost-Effectiveness of Digital Textbooks in Schools*. Kitaboo. https://kitaboo.com/cost-effectiveness-of-digital-textbooks-in-schools/?webview_progress_bar=1&show_loading=0

Darling-Hammond, L., Flook, L., Cook-Harvey, C., Barron, B., & Osher, D. (2020). Implications for educational practice of the science of learning and development. *Applied Developmental Science*, 24(2), 97–140. https://doi.org/10.1080/10888691.2018.1537791

DavidAnderson. (2020, July 9). *20 Beautiful Examples of Interactivity in E-Learning Design #288*. Articulate - Community. https://community.articulate.com/blog/challenge-recaps/20-beautiful-examples-of-interactivity-in-e-learning-design-288/1138574

David, K. G., Yang, W., Bianca, E. M., & Getele, G. K. (2021). Empirical research on the role of internal social capital upon the innovation performance of cooperative firms. *Human Systems Management*, 40(3), 407–420. DOI: 10.3233/HSM-190830

Davis, J. A. (2010). *Learning Spaces: Designing for 21st Century Learning*. EDUCAUSE.

DC7. (n.d.). AR and VR STEM learning prototypes. Retrieved from https://www.dc7.co/research

Demir, H. (2022, August 23). *What is e-learning? 12 Key Advantages of E-learning - 2022*. Ant Media. https://antmedia.io/what-is-e-learning-12-advantages-of-e-learning/?webview_progress_bar=1&show_loading=0

Demirgüç-Kunt, A., Klapper, L., Singer, D., Ansar, S., & Hess, J. (2018). *The Global Findex Database 2017: Measuring Financial Inclusion and the Fintech Revolution*. World Bank., DOI: 10.1596/978-1-4648-1259-0

Dereso, C. W., Kant, S., Muthuraman, M., & Tufa, G. (2023). Effect of Point of Service on Health Department Student's Creativity in Comprehensive Universities of Ethiopia: Moderating Role of Public-Private Partnership and Mediating Role of Work Place Learning. In: Jain, S., Groppe, S., Mihindukulasooriya, N. (eds) Proceedings of the International Health Informatics Conference. Lecture Notes in Electrical Engineering, vol 990. Springer, Singapore. DOI: 10.1007/978-981-19-9090-8_13

Dewey, J. (1916). *Democracy and education: An introduction to the philosophy of education* (1966 ed.). Free Press.

Dewey, J. (1997). *How we think*.

Dief, M. E., & Font, X. (2010). The determinants of hotels marketing managers' green marketing behaviour. *Journal of Sustainable Tourism*, 18(2), 157–174. DOI: 10.1080/09669580903464232

Digital Learning Innovations. (n.d.). https://www.kennesaw.edu/digital-learning-innovations/?show_loading=0&webview_progress_bar=1

Dijck, J. V., Poell, T., & de Waal, M. (2018). *The platform society: Public values in a connective world.* Oxford University Press., DOI: 10.1093/oso/9780190889760.001.0001

Distinguishedsite. (2023, January 27). *AI's benefits and drawbacks for the gaming industry.* Medium. https://medium.com/@distinguishedsite/ais-benefits-and-drawbacks-for-the-gaming-industry-8be875218dbf

Diversity and inclusion in education. (2024, February 20). Coursera. https://www.coursera.org/learn/diversity-and-inclusion-education?webview_progress_bar=1&show_loading=0

Doğan, M. (1997). National Environmental Strategy and Action Plan Report on Education and Participation Group. Undersecretariat of the State Planning Organization (DPT) and Turkish Environmental Foundation.

Domorovskaya, O. (2024). Differentiating E-Learning Content in ESL Courses to Meet Special Needs of Students with Learning Difficulties. *Journal of Teaching English for Specific and Academic Purposes*, 15-24.

Dong, Y., Wang, J., & Yang, Y.. (2020). Understanding intrinsic challenges to STEM instructional practices for Chinese teachers based on their beliefs and knowledge base. *International Journal of STEM Education*, 7(1), 47. https://doi.org/10.1186/s40594-020-00245-0

Dostál, J. (2015). *Inquiry-based instruction: Concept, essence, importance and contribution.* Palacký University., https://doi.org/10.5507/pdf.15.24445076

Drysdale, A. T., Grosenick, L., Downar, J., Dunlop, K., Mansouri, F., Meng, Y., & Liston, C. (2017). Resting-state connectivity biomarkers define neurophysiological subtypes of depression. *Nature Medicine*, 23(1), 28–38. DOI: 10.1038/nm.4246 PMID: 27918562

DSmith. (2023, September 22). *Global Collaborative Learning: The Future of Cross-Cultural Education.* Medium. https://medium.com/@smithd4466/global-collaborative-learning-the-future-of-cross-cultural-education-f0beae080050?webview_progress_bar=1&show_loading=0

Durant, I. (2023, August 16). *What is target audience for e-learners*. Peep Strategy. https://peepstrategy.com/what-is-target-audience-for-e-learners/?webview_progress_bar=1&show_loading=0

Durga, P., Godavarthi, D., Kant, S., & Basa, S. S. (2024). Aspect-based drug review classification through a hybrid model with ant colony optimization using deep learning. *Discov Computing*, 27(1), 19. DOI: 10.1007/s10791-024-09441-w

Dzhunushalieva, G., & Teuber, R. (2024). Roles of innovation in achieving the Sustainable Development Goals: A bibliometric analysis. *Journal of Innovation & Knowledge*, 9(2), 100472. DOI: 10.1016/j.jik.2024.100472

Eclassopedia. (2023, July 24). *The importance of personalized learning in the digital age*. https://eclassopedia.com/the-importance-of-personalized-learning-in-the-digital-age/?show_loading=0&webview_progress_bar=1

Economy, C. (2021).. . *Circular Economy*, 39(7), 889–891.

Edgar, F. (2019, October 5). *Elearning Industry - How Well Do You Know About your Target Audience?* https://www.linkedin.com/pulse/elearning-industry-how-well-do-you-know-your-target-frank-edgar?show_loading=0&webview_progress_bar=1

EducationTimes. (n.d.). *How AI-powered gamification in education increases student engagement - EducationTimes.com*. https://www.educationtimes.com/article/campus-beat-college-life/99734287/how-ai-powered-gamification-in-education-increases-student-engagement?webview_progress_bar=1&show_loading=0

Edwards, D. B., Sustarsic, M., Chiba, M., McCormick, M., Goo, M., & Perriton, S. (2014). Achieving and Monitoring Education for Sustainable Development and Global Citizenship: A Systematic Review of the Literature. *Sustainability 2020, 12, 1383. S. Awareness of School Students about Sustainable Development in Education. PolySciTech*, 2014(1), 112–116.

Eizaguirre, A., García-Feijoo, M., & Laka, J. P. (2019). Defining Sustainability Core Competencies in Business and Management Studies Based on Multinational Stakeholders' Perceptions. *Sustainability (Switzerland), 11(8)*.

El Morabit, N. (2021). Educational technology: From a historical perspective to an empirical exploration of Moroccan learners' EFL speaking fluency. Global Journal of Human-Social Science: G Linguistics & Education, 21(11). https://doi.org/10.34257/GJHSSGV21N11

elearn Magazine: The Rock Stars of eLearning: An interview with Clark Quinn. (n.d.). https://elearnmag.acm.org/archive.cfm?aid=2465423&webview_progress_bar=1&show_loading=0

E-learning accessibility - Research and Development Working Group WIKI. (n.d.). https://www.w3.org/WAI/RD/wiki/E-learning_Accessibility?f_link_type= f_inlinenote&webview_progress_bar=1&show_loading=0

ELearning videos: The complete guide | DLI blog. (n.d.). Digital Learning Institute. https://www.digitallearninginstitute.com/blog/vr-in-training-and-elearning -everything-you-need-to-know?show_loading=0&webview_progress_bar=1

ELearning videos: The complete guide. (n.d.). Digital Learning Institute. https:// www.digitallearninginstitute.com/blog/elearning-videos-the-complete-guide?show _loading=0&webview_progress_bar=1

Elearning Voice over - Generate engaging voice overs for e-learning. (n.d.). https:// murf.ai/voiceover/elearning

E-Learning vs Traditional Training: A Cost-Effectiveness Analysis. (2023, January 16). https://bookboonlearning.com/blog/ld-budget/e-learning-vs-traditional-training -a-cost-effectiveness-analysis/?show_loading=0&webview_progress_bar=1

E-Learning. (n.d.). LinkedIn. https://www.linkedin.com/showcase/skills-e-learning/ ?show_loading=0&webview_progress_bar=1

Elkington, J. (1998). *Cannibals with forks: The triple bottom line of 21st-century business.* Capstone.

Ellen MacArthur Foundation. (2013). *Towards the circular economy: Economic and business rationale for an accelerated transition.* Ellen MacArthur Foundation.

Ellen MacArthur Foundation. (2019). *Circular economy in tourism.* Retrieved from https://ellenmacarthurfoundation.org/circular-economy

Ellis, J., Wieselmann, J., Sivaraj, R., Roehrig, G., Dare, E., & Ring-Whalen, E. (2020). Toward a productive definition of technology in science and STEM education. CITE Journal, 20(3). Retrieved from https://citejournal.org/volume-20/issue-3-20/science/ toward-a-productive-definition-of-technology-in-science-and-stem-education/

Enander, J., Ivanov, V. Z., Andersson, E., Radu Djurfeldt, D., Ljótsson, B., Cottman, O., & Lindefors, N. (2016). Guided internet-based cognitive-behavioural therapy for body dysmorphic disorder: A randomised controlled trial. *BMJ Open*, 6(1), e009917. DOI: 10.1136/bmjopen-2015-009917 PMID: 30647044

Erathi, N. (2014, April 5). *Differentiated instruction and e learning [Slide show].* SlideShare. https://www.slideshare.net/slideshow/differentiated-instruction-and-e -learning/33167778

Erickson, L. (2019, November 14). [STEM resources for robotics and coding. Mimio Educator. Retrieved from https://www.mimio.com/educator-blog/top-10-stem-resources-for-robotics-and-coding]. *Top (Madrid)*, 10, •••.

Eskrootchi, R., & Oskrochi, G. R. (2010). A study of the efficacy of project-based learning integrated with computer-based simulation – Stella. *Journal of Educational Technology & Society*, 13(1), 236–245.

Esposito, B., Sessa, M. R., Sica, D., & Malandrino, O. (2020). Towards circular economy in the agri-food sector. *Sustainability*, 12(17), 7406. DOI: 10.3390/su12177406

Estapa, A. T., & Tank, K. M. (2017). Supporting integrated STEM in the elementary classroom: A professional development approach centered on an engineering design challenge. *International Journal of STEM Education*, 4(1), 1–16.

Esteem: Maslow's Hierarchy of Needs. (2024, September 19). The Interaction Design Foundation. https://www.interaction-design.org/literature/article/esteem-maslow-s-hierarchy-of-needs?webview_progress_bar=1&show_loading=0

Eubanks, V. (2018). *Automating inequality: How high-tech tools profile, police, and punish the poor*. St. Martin's Press.

Ewa. (2024, September 8). *We make learning happen*. Snabbfoting. We Make Learning Happen. https://snabbfoting.se/en/

Fatima, B. (2023, November 7). *Navigating Peer-to-Peer Learning: Methods, perks and challenges [Infographic]*. https://blog.commlabindia.com/elearning-design/peer-to-peer-learning-ways-infographic?webview_progress_bar=1&show_loading=0

Fei, C., & Tse, A. W. C. (2024). Examining the Technological Pedagogical Content Knowledge (TPACK) of biology educators: A case study on pre-service and in-service teachers in preparation for applying STEM education. In Kubincová, Z. (Eds.), Lecture Notes in Computer Science: Vol. 14606. *Emerging technologies for education. SETE 2023* (pp. 108–119). Springer., https://doi.org/10.1007/978-981-97-4243-1_8

Ferriman, J. (2023, February 2). *7 Benefits of E-Learning Videos*. LearnDash. https://www.learndash.com/7-benefits-of-e-learning-videos/?webview_progress_bar=1&show_loading=0

FHS Doe, J. (2023). *Responsible AI integration in e-learning: Focusing on human skills*. E-Learning Journal.

Fichtman-Dana, N., Thomas, C., & Boynton, S. (2011). *Inquiry: A districtwide approach to staff and student learning*. Corwin Press.

Fiselier, E. S., Longhurst, J. W. S., & Gough, G. K. (2018). Exploring the current position of ESD in UK higher education institutions. *International Journal of Sustainability in Higher Education*, 19(2), 393–412. DOI: 10.1108/IJSHE-06-2017-0084

Fitzpatrick, K. K., Darcy, A., & Vierhile, M. (2017). Delivering cognitive behavior therapy to young adults with symptoms of depression and anxiety using a fully automated conversational agent (Woebot): A randomized controlled trial. *JMIR Mental Health*, 4(2), e19. DOI: 10.2196/mental.7785 PMID: 28588005

Fleiss, A. (2023, March 31). *How do I choose a good learning platform? Rebellion Research*. https://www.rebellionresearch.com/how-do-i-choose-a-good-learning-platform?show_loading=0&webview_progress_bar=1

Flick, L., & Bell, R. (2000). Preparing tomorrow's science teachers to use technology: Guidelines for science educators. *Contemporary Issues in Technology & Teacher Education*, 1(1), 39–60.

Flognfeldt, T.Jr. (2005). The tourist route system–models of travelling patterns. *Revue Belge De Geographie, 1*(1-2), 35-58. Flognfeldt Jr, T. (2005). The tourist route system–models of traveling patterns. *Revue Belge de Geographie*, 1(1-2), 35–58.

Floridi, L., & Taddeo, M. (2018). What is data ethics? *Philosophical Transactions. Series A, Mathematical, Physical, and Engineering Sciences*, 376(2128), 20180081. DOI: 10.1098/rsta.2018.0081 PMID: 30322997

Florido, C., Jacob, M., & Payeras, M. (2019). How to carry out the transition towards a more circular tourist activity in the hotel sector. The role of innovation. *Administrative Sciences*, 9(2), 47. DOI: 10.3390/admsci9020047

Forbes, H. (2021). *Food waste index report 2021*. United Nations Environment Programme.

Four incredible benefits of global collaboration. (2024, January 31). https://edtechimpact.com/news/four-incredible-benefits-of-global-collaboration/?show_loading=0&webview_progress_bar=1

Francisco. (2023, September 18). *Level Up Your learning: How AI Supercharges engagement in gamified Education - Teachflow.AI*. Teachflow.AI. https://teachflow.ai/level-up-your-learning-how-ai-supercharges-engagement-in-gamified-education/

Frandoloso, M. A., & Gasparetto Rebelatto, B. (2019). The participatory process of planning social and environmental responsibility at a Brazilian university. *International Journal of Sustainability in Higher Education*, 20(5), 917–931. DOI: 10.1108/IJSHE-01-2019-0017

Freeman, S., Eddy, S. L., McDonough, M., Smith, M. K., Okoroafor, N., Jordt, H., & Wenderoth, M. P. (2014). Active learning increases student performance in science, engineering, and mathematics. *Proceedings of the National Academy of Sciences of the United States of America*, 111(23), 8410–8415. DOI: 10.1073/pnas.1319030111 PMID: 24821756

Fried, E. I., & Nesse, R. M. (2015). Depression is not a consistent syndrome: An investigation of unique symptom patterns in the STAR*D study. *Journal of Affective Disorders*, 172, 96–102. DOI: 10.1016/j.jad.2014.10.010 PMID: 25451401

Gadenne, D. L., Kennedy, J., & McKeiver, C. (2009). An empirical study of environmental awareness and practices in SMEs. *Journal of Business Ethics*, 84(1), 45–63. DOI: 10.1007/s10551-008-9672-9

Game On: Level Up Your Life with AI-Powered Gamification. (2024, May 3). https://www.motivacraft.com/game-on-level-up-your-life-with-ai-powered-gamification/

Gamification AI – Everything you need to know - centrical. (2024, June 4). Centrical. https://centrical.com/resources/gamification-ai/

Gamification and Self-Determination Theory – MetaDevo. (2023, June 21). https://metadevo.com/gamification-and-self-determination-theory/?webview_progress_bar=1&show_loading=0

Gandhi, R., Veeraraghavan, R., Toyama, K., & Ramprasad, V. (2009). Digital Green: Participatory video and mediated instruction for agricultural extension. *Information Technologies and International Development*, 5(1), 1–15. DOI: 10.1162/itid.2009.0014

Gandhi, R., Veeraraghavan, R., Toyama, K., & Ramprasad, V. (2016). Digital Green: A large-scale model for agricultural extension. *Information Technologies and International Development*, 12(4), 47–61.

Garcia, A., & Tugores, M. (2021). Circular economy in the tourism industry: An analysis of the main drivers and barriers in hotels. *Sustainability*, 13(7), 3732. DOI: 10.3390/su13073732

García-Navarro, J., Ortega, M., & Jiménez-Mesa, I. (2020). Circular economy as a sustainable solution for tourism management. *Sustainability*, 12(17), 6908. DOI: 10.3390/su12176908

Gardner, H. (2006). *Multiple Intelligences: New Horizons in Theory and Practice.* Basic Books.

Gasser, U., & Palfrey, J. (2020). *Born digital: How children grow up in a digital age* (2nd ed.). Basic Books.

Gasser, U., & Palfrey, J. (2020). Interoperability in the digital age. Berkman Klein Center for Internet & Society. DOI: DOI: 10.2139/ssrn.3522971

Gawad Kalinga Foundation. (2020). Building sustainable communities: The Gawad Kalinga experience. https://gk1world.com

GeeksforGeeks. (2024, May 14). *10 AI chatbots for educational tutoring*. GeeksforGeeks. https://www.geeksforgeeks.org/ai-chatbots-for-educational-tutoring/

Geissdoerfer, M., Savaget, P., Bocken, N. M., & Hultink, E. J. (2017). The circular economy – A new sustainability paradigm? *Journal of Cleaner Production*, 143, 757–768. DOI: 10.1016/j.jclepro.2016.12.048

Gencer, E. G., Korlu, Ö., Kesbiç, K., Akay, S. S., Kotan, H., & Arık, B. M. (2023). *Education monitoring report 2023*. Education Reform Initiative. https://www.egitimreformugirisimi.org/wp-content/uploads/2023/11/EgitimIzlemeRaporu2023.pdf

Ghazali, M. Z., & Yahaya, A. (2022). Analysis of green chemistry knowledge, awareness, and practice among university students. *Journal of Science and Mathematics Letters*, 10(1), 79–90. DOI: 10.37134/jsml.vol10.1.8.2022

Giaro, M. (2023, August 19). *How to pick the right online course platform: The 6 crucial criteria you should look for*. Medium. https://medium.com/swlh/how-to-pick-the-right-online-course-platform-the-6-crucial-criteria-you-should-look-for-11f5523d5982?show_loading=0&webview_progress_bar=1

Gilg, A., Barr, S., & Ford, N. (2005). Green consumption or sustainable lifestyles? Identifying the sustainable consumer. *Futures*, 37(6), 481–504. DOI: 10.1016/j.futures.2004.10.016

Gillanders, R., Karazi, S., & O'Riordan, F. (2020). Loss aversion as a motivator for engagement with peer assessment. *Innovations in Education and Teaching International*, 57(4), 424–433.

Girard, L., & Nocca, F. (2017). From linear to circular tourism. *Aestimum (Firenze)*, 70, 51–74. DOI: 10.13128/Aestimum-21081

Global collaboration in the classroom: working together for a better world – Digital Education. (n.d.). https://iteach4future.org/blog/global-collaboration-in-the-classroom-working-together-for-a-better-world/?webview_progress_bar=1&show_loading=0

Gökçearslan, S., Tosun, C., & Erdemir, Z. G. (2024). Benefits, challenges, and methods of artificial intelligence (AI) chatbots in education: A systematic literature review. *International Journal of Technology in Education*, 7(1), 19–39.

Gonzalez, P.G., Noh, D., and Wilson, D. (2023, Apr.). *Making the Space for Learning*. Project Zero. Harvard Graduate School of Business. Available from /sites/default/files/Making%20the%20Space%20for%20Learning.pdf

Gonzalez, C., & Birch, P. (2020). Digital learning in higher education: Engaging students through technology. *Journal of Educational Technology*, 5(2), 45–53.

Goralski, M. A., & Tan, T. K. (2020). Artificial intelligence and sustainable development. *International Journal of Management Education*, 18(1), 100330. DOI: 10.1016/j.ijme.2019.100330

Gordana, U. (2024, January 19). *23 Benefits of Personalized online learning: Master your education*. Alt Gov. https://altgov2.org/benefits-of-personalized-online-learning/?webview_progress_bar=1&show_loading=0

Gore, C., & Figueiredo, J. B. (1997). *Social exclusion and anti-poverty policy: A debate*. International Institute for Labour Studies.

Gossling, S. (2002). Global environmental consequences of tourism. *Global Environmental Change*, 12(4), 283–302. DOI: 10.1016/S0959-3780(02)00044-4

Gossling, S., & Higham, J. (2020). *Tourism and climate change: Impacts, adaptation, and mitigation*. Routledge.

Gossling, S., & Peeters, P. (2015). Assessing tourism's global environmental impact 1900–2050. *Journal of Sustainable Tourism*, 23(5), 639–659. DOI: 10.1080/09669582.2015.1008500

Graham, C. R., Borup, J., & Smith, N. B. (2012). Using TPACK as a framework to understand teacher candidates' technology integration decisions. *Journal of Computer Assisted Learning*, 28(6), 530–546. https://doi.org/10.1111/j.1365-2729.2011.00472.x

Green, D. (2020). Virtual reality and augmented reality: Transforming education in the 21st century. *International Journal of Educational Technology*, 8(1), 67–78.

Greene, S. (2018). Addressing the digital divide in education: Strategies for equitable technology access. *Education Policy Studies*, 12(3), 112–129.

Greenhill, V. (2010). The 21st-century skills movement: A "quiet revolution" in education. *Education Canada*, 50(4), 6–10.

Guilbaud, P., Sanders, C., Hirsch, M. J., & Guilbaud, T. C. (2022). Social-Emotional Competence for the Greater Good: Exploring the use of serious game, virtual reality and artificial intelligence to elicit prosocial behaviors and strengthen cognitive abilities of youth, adolescents and educators – a systematic review. *Lecture Notes in Computer Science*, 13317, 423–442. DOI: 10.1007/978-3-031-05939-1_29

Güntut, M., Güneş, P., & Çetin, S. (2019). *10 textbooks of secondary education chemistry*. Publications of the Ministry of National Education.

Güntut, M., Güneş, P., & Çetin, S. (2019). *9 textbooks of secondary education chemistry*. Publications of the Ministry of National Education.

Gupta, D. (2024, July 22). *7 Best Adaptive Learning Platforms in 2024*. The Whatfix Blog | Drive Digital Adoption. https://whatfix.com/blog/adaptive-learning-platforms/?webview_progress_bar=1&show_loading=0

Gururaj, K., Saxena, S., & Morsink, C. (2021). Telemedicine and digital health platforms in developing countries: A PPP approach. *Global Health Research and Policy*, 6(1), 45–55. DOI: 10.1186/s41256-021-00209-8 PMID: 34847956

Guttentag, D. A. (2015). Airbnb: Disruptive innovation and the rise of the sharing economy. *Current Issues in Tourism*, 18(12), 1192–1217. DOI: 10.1080/13683500.2013.827159

Güven, E., & Aydoğdu, M. (2012). Development of an environmental awareness scale for environmental problems and determination of pre-service teachers' awareness levels. *Journal of Teacher Education and Educators*, 1(2), 185–202.

Guyo, D. M., Kant, S., & Kero, C. A. (2023, November). Mediation of Marketing Intermediaries and AI Adoption Between Livestock Products Marketing and Economic Status of Pastoralist in Ethiopia. In *2023 International Conference on Communication, Security and Artificial Intelligence (ICCSAI)* (pp. 311-316). IEEE.

Hadi, A., Huda, M., Lyndon, N., & Nasir, B. M. (2024). Managing Professional-Ethical Negotiation for Cyber Conflict Prevention: Perspectives From Higher Institution Learners in the Pandemic Age. [IJCBPL]. *International Journal of Cyber Behavior, Psychology and Learning*, 14(1), 1–27. DOI: 10.4018/IJCBPL.344022

Hai-Jew, S. (2022). *Practical Peer-to-Peer Teaching and Learning on the Social Web*. .DOI: 10.4018/978-1-7998-6496-7

Hajer, M., Nilsson, M., Raworth, K., Bakker, P., Berkhout, F., de Boer, Y., Rockström, J., Ludwig, K., & Kok, M. (2015). Beyond Cockpit-ism: Four Insights to Enhance the Transformative Potential of the Sustainable Development Goals. *Sustainability (Basel)*, 7(2), 1651–1660. DOI: 10.3390/su7021651

Halkiopoulos, C., & Gkintoni, E. (2024). Leveraging AI in e-learning: Personalized learning and adaptive assessment through cognitive neuropsychology—A systematic analysis. *Electronics (Basel)*, 13(18), 3762.

Hall, K. D., Guo, J., Dore, M., & Chow, C. C. (2009). The progressive increase of food waste in America and its environmental impact. *PLoS One*, 4(11), e7940. DOI: 10.1371/journal.pone.0007940 PMID: 19946359

Hannafin, M. J., & Hannafin, K. M. (2010). Cognition and student-centered, web-based learning: Issues and implications for research and theory. In M. Spector, D. Ifenthaler, & Kinshuk (Eds.), Learning and instruction in the digital age (pp. 11–23). Springer.

Han, Q. (2015). Education for sustainable development and climate change education in China: A status report. [The SPSSAU Project. SPSSA.]. *Journal of Education for Sustainable Development*, 2015(9), 62–77. DOI: 10.1177/0973408215569114

Hansen, M. C., Potapov, P. V., Moore, R., Hancher, M., Turubanova, S. A., Tyukavina, A., Thau, D., Stehman, S. V., Goetz, S. J., Loveland, T. R., Kommareddy, A., Egorov, A., Chini, L., Justice, C. O., & Townshend, J. R. (2013). High-Resolution Global Maps of 21st-Century Forest Cover Change. *Science*, 342(6160), 850–853. DOI: 10.1126/science.1244693 PMID: 24233722

Hargittai, E., & Shaw, A. (2019). Digital inequality: Differences in young adults' use of the internet. *Communication Research*, 46(2), 375–397. DOI: 10.1177/0093650217715225

Hargittai, E., & Shaw, A. (2019). Mind the skills gap: The role of Internet know-how and gender in differentiated contributions to Wikipedia. *Information Communication and Society*, 19(4), 424–442. DOI: 10.1080/1369118X.2014.957711

Harman, J. (2021, January 10). *Diving into Deeper Learning with Dr. Patti Shank*. Leading Learning. https://www.leadinglearning.com/episode-213-deeper-learning-patti-shank/?webview_progress_bar=1&show_loading=0

Harris, J., & Hofer, M. (2011). Technological pedagogical content knowledge (TPACK) in action: A descriptive study of secondary teachers' curriculum-based, technology-related instructional planning. *Journal of Research on Technology in Education*, 43(3), 211–229. https://doi.org/10.1080/15391523.2011.10782570

Harry, C. (2023, December 12). *E-learning Market Growth Statistics & Trends*. Storm6. https://storm6.io/resources/industry-insights/e-learning-market-growth-statistics-trends/?show_loading=0&webview_progress_bar=1

Harvard University. (2023). *Learning Spaces*. Retrieved from https://pz.harvard.edu/sites/default/files/Making%20the%20Space%20for%20Learning.pdf

Hasanah, U. (2020). Key definitions of STEM education: Literature review. *Interdisciplinary Journal of Environmental and Science Education*, 16(3), e2217. https://doi.org/10.29333/ijese/8336

Hashemi-Pour, C., & Lutkevich, B. (2024, June 26). *What is e-learning? Importance, benefits and use cases*. WhatIs. https://www.techtarget.com/whatis/definition/Web-based-training-e-learning?show_loading=0&webview_progress_bar=1

Hassan, A., & Ismail, M. Z. (2011). The infusion of environmental education (EE) in chemistry teaching and students' awareness and attitudes towards environment in Malaysia. *Procedia: Social and Behavioral Sciences*, 15, 3404–3409. DOI: 10.1016/j.sbspro.2011.04.309

Hattie, J. (2009). *Visible learning: A synthesis of over 800 meta-analyses relating to achievement*. Routledge.

Heal, J. (2023, January 5). *Balancing Teacher-Led instruction and Student-Centered learning*. Edutopia. https://www.edutopia.org/article/teacher-led-instruction-student-centered-learning?show_loading=0&webview_progress_bar=1

Hehir, D. (2024, February 28). *Collaborative learning and how you can use it in E-Learning*. Capytech. https://capytech.com/en/blog/collaborative-learning-and-how-you-can-use-it-in-e-learning/?webview_progress_bar=1&show_loading=0

Hehsan, A., Huda, M., Mahsun, M., Asrori, A., Shafwan, M. H., Zakariya, D. M., . . . Layyinnati, I. (2024). Digital Muhadathah: framework model development for digital Arabic language learning. In *International Conference on Information and Communication Technology for Competitive Strategies* (pp. 13-29). Singapore: Springer Nature Singapore. DOI: 10.1007/978-981-97-0744-7_2

Hıdıroğlu, Ç. N., & Karakaş, A. (2022). Transdisciplinary role of technology in STEM education. *Malaysian Online Journal of Educational Technology*, 10(4), 276–293. https://doi.org/10.52380/mojet.2022.10.4.411

Hill, A. (2024, March 18). *Effective feedback: How to gather and deliver feedback through eLearning*. ELM Learning. https://elmlearning.com/blog/feedback-elearning/?show_loading=0&webview_progress_bar=1

Hill, M. (2024, March 22). *How to use augmented reality to gamify learning - inspired ideas - medium*. Medium. https://medium.com/inspired-ideas-prek-12/how-to-use-augmented-reality-to-gamify-learning-c05f1f8f7751

Holman, K., Marino, M. T., Vasquez, T., Taub, M., Hunt, J. H., & Tazi, Y. (2024). Navigating AI-Powered Personalized Learning in Special Education: A Guide for Preservice Teacher Faculty. *Journal of Special Education Preparation*, 4(2), 90–95.

Holmes, J. (n.d.). *Continuous Assessment and Feedback: Benefits of Learning with a Teacher.* foreign-language-teachers.com. https://www.foreign-language-teachers.com/personalized-learning-continuous-assessment-and-feedback?show_loading=0&webview_progress_bar=1

Home | Moodle.org. (n.d.). https://moodle.org/?auto_signin=true&webview_progress_bar=1&show_loading=0

Home page - Unity Environmental University. (2024, August 1). Unity Environmental University. https://unity.edu/

Hood, R. (2023, April 13). *Exploring the benefits and impacts of personalized learning in eLearning.* Medium. https://medium.com/@hussain2023/exploring-the-benefits-and-impacts-of-personalized-learning-in-elearning-9b6a87b2f01c

How AI and Gamification are Changing the Workplace. (n.d.). https://gamificationlabs.com/resources/blogs/how-ai-and-gamification-are-changing-the-workplace?webview_progress_bar=1&show_loading=0

How AI-Powered Gamification Can Boost Online Learning Engagement - CO/AI. (2024, September 4). CO/AI. https://getcoai.com/news/how-ai-powered-gamification-can-boost-online-learning-engagement/

How AI-powered gamification in education increases student engagement. (2023). https://l.facebook.com/l.php?u=https%3A%2F%2Fwww.educationtimes.com%2Farticle%2Fcampus-beat-college-life%2F99734287%2Fhow-ai-powered-gamification-in-education-increases-student-engagement%3Fshow_loading%3D0%26webview_progress_bar%3D1%26fbclid%3DIwZXh0bgNhZW0CMTAAAR2JtrUzyqRV2rpeizeTnIGC3ESt3-X5LblWUMvnI4OgSB3mLp0VZpSBaL0_aem_5LmV3ImIMywODciDp81dlw&h=AT05yb4M043T5YLXyNSyB3N9-GsqjhJ79e1EC2d8vVpx7f3Hio-gG97GHMy5zuy02XTqac2gzaNTxj-rSk5nTjjNo7mYsiqu2P3kSFR2O2sxQDcyrBzAHm2qUx7ebjrsnYe83Q

How do you evaluate and compare different LMS pricing models and plans? (2023, March 28). www.linkedin.com. https://www.linkedin.com/advice/1/how-do-you-evaluate-compare-different-lms-pricing?show_loading=0&webview_progress_bar=1

How do you integrate video and audio with other online learning tools and platforms? (2024, March 27). www.linkedin.com. https://www.linkedin.com/advice/0/how-do-you-integrate-video-audio-other-online?webview_progress_bar=1&show_loading=0

How to enhance and strengthen collaborative e-learning environments. (n.d.). https://kinescope.io/blog/how-to-enhance-and-strengthen-collaborative-e-learning-environments?webview_progress_bar=1&show_loading=0

How to identify your target audience for eLearning program? (n.d.). https://www.e-learningpartners.com/blog/how-to-identify-your-target-audience-for-elearning-program-or-online-course?show_loading=0&webview_progress_bar=1

Howitz, W. J., Thane, T. A., Frey, T. L., Wang, X. S., Gonzales, J. C., Tretbar, C. A., Seith, D. D., Saluga, S. J., Lam, S., Nguyen, M. M., Tieu, P., Link, R. D., & Edwards, K. D. (2020). Online in no time: Design and implementation of a remote learning first-quarter general chemistry laboratory and second-quarter organic chemistry laboratory. *Journal of Chemical Education*, 97(9), 2624–2634. DOI: 10.1021/acs.jchemed.0c00895

Huang, B., Jong, M. S.-Y., Tu, Y.-F., Hwang, G.-J., Chai, C. S., & Jiang, M. Y.-C. (2022). Trends and exemplary practices of STEM teacher professional development programs in K-12 contexts: A systematic review of empirical studies. *Computers & Education*, 189, 104577. https://doi.org/10.1016/j.compedu.2022.104577

Huang, H. (2018). Integrating technology into Mandarin Chinese learning: A literature review. *Journal of Educational Technology & Society*, 21(1), 206–220.

Huang, Y., Song, H., Huang, G. Q., & Lou, J. (2012). A comparative study of tourism supply chains with quantity competition. *Journal of Travel Research*, 51(6), 717–729. DOI: 10.1177/0047287512451138

Huda, M., & Sutopo, L., Liberty, Febrianto, & Mustafa, M. C. (2022). Digital information transparency for cyber security: critical points in social media trends. In Advances in Information and Communication: Proceedings of the 2022 Future of Information and Communication Conference (FICC), Volume 2 (pp. 814-831). Cham: Springer International Publishing.

Huda, M., Rohim, M. A., Hehsan, A. B., Qodriah, S. L., Junaidi, J., Haron, Z., . . . Abas, H. (2024e). From Technology Adaptation to Technology Adoption: An Insight into Public Islamic School Administrative Management. In *International Congress on Information and Communication Technology* (pp. 57-68). Singapore: Springer Nature Singapore. DOI: 10.1007/978-981-97-3305-7_5

Huda, M., Taisin, J. N., Muhamad, M., Kiting, R., & Yusuf, R. A. (2024a). Digital technology adoption for instruction aids: insight into teaching material content. In *International Conference on Information and Communication Technology for Competitive Strategies* (pp. 59-68). Singapore: Springer Nature Singapore. DOI: 10.1007/978-981-97-1260-1_6

Huda, M. (2019). Empowering application strategy in the technology adoption: Insights from professional and ethical engagement. *Journal of Science and Technology Policy Management*, 10(1), 172–192. DOI: 10.1108/JSTPM-09-2017-0044

Huda, M. (2022). Towards an adaptive ethics on social networking sites (SNS): A critical reflection. Journal of Information. *Communication and Ethics in Society*, 20(2), 273–290.

Huda, M. (2023). Towards digital access during pandemic age: Better learning service or adaptation struggling? *Foresight*, 25(1), 82–107. DOI: 10.1108/FS-09-2021-0184

Huda, M. (2024a). *Empowering communication strategy for safe cyberspace: insights from trust-based quality information*. Global Knowledge, Memory and Communication.

Huda, M. (2024b). Trust as a key element for quality communication and information management: Insights into developing safe cyber-organisational sustainability. *The International Journal of Organizational Analysis*, 32(8), 1539–1558. DOI: 10.1108/IJOA-12-2022-3532

Huda, M. (2024c). Between accessibility and adaptability of digital platform: Investigating learners' perspectives on digital learning infrastructure. *Higher Education. Skills and Work-Based Learning*, 14(1), 1–21. DOI: 10.1108/HESWBL-03-2022-0069

Huda, M., Isa, N. K. M., Husain, H., Almunawar, M. N., Anshari, M., & Jailani, M. (2024). *Managing Organizational Stability in Digital Era: Emerging Trends of Trust in Cyberspace-Based Information. Customer Relationship Management: Methods, Opportunities and Challenges*. Nova Science Publisher.

Huda, M., Musolin, M. H., Ismail, M. H., Yauri, A. M., Bakar, A., Zuhri, M., & Hasanah, U. (2024c). From digital ethics to digital community: an Islamic principle on strengthening safety strategy on information. In *Proceedings of the Computational Methods in Systems and Software* (pp. 165-182). Cham: Springer International Publishing. DOI: 10.1007/978-3-031-53552-9_15

Huda, M., Musolin, M. H., Serour, R. O. H., Azman, M., Yauri, A. M., Bakar, A., Zuhri, M., Mujahidin, M., & Hasanah, U. (2024d). Digital record management in Islamic education institution: Current trends on enhancing process and effectiveness through learning technology. In *Software Engineering Methods in Systems and Network Systems - Proceedings of 7th Computational Methods in Systems and Software 2023*. Springer Nature Switzerland. DOI: 10.1007/978-3-031-53549-9_33

Huda, M., Serour, R. O. H., Musolin, M. H., Azman, M., Yauri, A. M., Bakar, A., & Hasanah, U. (2024b). Trust in electronic record management system: insights from Islamic-based professional and moral engagement-based digital archive. In *Proceedings of the Computational Methods in Systems and Software* (pp. 303-315). Cham: Springer International Publishing. DOI: 10.1007/978-3-031-53549-9_32

Huda, M., Shahrill, M., Maseleno, A., Jasmi, K. A., Mustari, I., & Basiron, B. (2017). Exploring Adaptive Teaching Competencies in Big Data Era. *International Journal of Emerging Technologies in Learning*, 12(3), 68–83. DOI: 10.3991/ijet.v12i03.6434

Hughes, J., & Morrison, L. (2020). Innovative Learning Spaces in the Making. *Frontiers in Education*, 5, 89. Advance online publication. DOI: 10.3389/feduc.2020.00089

Hu, H. H., Parsa, H. G., & Self, J. (2010). The dynamics of green restaurant patronage. *Cornell Hospitality Quarterly*, 51(3), 344–362. DOI: 10.1177/1938965510370564

HundrED. (2024). The impact of AR and VR on STEM education: A case study of Qatar Science and Technology Secondary School.

Huntsberry, W. (2014, November 25). *Is Digital Learning more Cost-Effective? Maybe not*. NPR. https://www.npr.org/sections/ed/2014/11/25/366401940/is-digital-learning-more-cost-effective-maybe-not?webview_progress_bar=1&show_loading=0

Hurley, L. (2024, July 5). *Benefits of eLearning*. Learnopoly. https://learnopoly.com/benefits-of-elearning/?show_loading=0&webview_progress_bar=1

Hurley, L. (2024a, May 18). *What is Hybrid Learning?* Learnopoly. https://learnopoly.com/what-is-hybrid-learning/?webview_progress_bar=1&show_loading=0

Hurley, L. (2024b, July 5). *Benefits of eLearning*. Learnopoly. https://learnopoly.com/benefits-of-elearning/?webview_progress_bar=1&show_loading=0

Ibarrientos, J. R. (2015). Implementation and Effectiveness of Student Affairs Services Program in One Polytechnic College. *Asia Pacific Journal of Multidisciplinary Research*, 3(5), 144–156.

Ibidunni, A. S. (2024). Cross-border knowledge transfer and the innovation performance of developing economy small and medium enterprises: A moderated mediation effect of industry networks and localization of knowledge. *Technological Forecasting and Social Change*, 208, 123702. DOI: 10.1016/j.techfore.2024.123702

Iheringguedes. (2024, June 11). *Application of virtual reality (VR) in education and the learning theories.* Medium. https://medium.com/@iheringguedes/application-of-virtual-reality-vr-in-education-and-the-learning-theories-c6f7a48cafb1

Insel, T. (2017). Digital phenotyping: Technology for a new science of behavior. *Journal of the American Medical Association*, 318(13), 1215–1216. DOI: 10.1001/jama.2017.11295 PMID: 28973224

International Labor Organization. (2018). *Decent work and poverty reduction in Southeast Asia*. International Labour Organization Publications.

Iodice, S., De Toro, P., & Bosone, M. (2020). Circular economy and adaptive reuse of historical buildings: An analysis of the dynamics between real estate and accommodation facilities in the city of Naples (Italy). *Aestimum*, 103-124. https://doi.org/ DOI: 10.13128/aestimum-9886

Iowa State University. (2023). *Learning Spaces*. Retrieved from https://www.lib.iastate.edu/visit-and-study/creation-and-learning-spaces

Ivan. (2021, February 17). *AI & Gamification – Risks and Rewards*. Etrellium. https://www.etrellium.com/ai/the-issues-prospects-of-ai-and-gamification/

Jabo, B., & Kant, S. "Impact of Technical CRM on Ethiopia Bank Human-Computer Interface and Competitive Advantage as Mediators of Performance," *2024 IEEE International Conference on Computing, Power and Communication Technologies (IC2PCT)*, Greater Noida, India, 2024, pp. 679-682, https://doi.org/DOI: 10.1109/IC2PCT60090.2024.10486237

Jack, W., & Suri, T. (2014). Risk sharing and transactions costs: Evidence from Kenya's mobile money revolution. *The American Economic Review*, 104(1), 183–223. DOI: 10.1257/aer.104.1.183

Jain, A. (2024, March 25). *Is AI-Enhanced gamification the key to eLearning success?* https://blog.commlabindia.com/elearning-design/ai-enhanced-gamification-elearning

Jain, S., & Jain, S. (2023, September 25). *Interactive Learning with Augmented Reality: Applications, Benefits and Challenges. Jumpstart Magazine*. https://www.jumpstartmag.com/interactive-learning-with-augmented-reality-applications-benefits-and-challenges/

Jha, A., Doshi, A., & Patel, S. (2019). Artificial intelligence and its role in advancing agriculture: A review. *Journal of Cleaner Production*, 240, 118208. DOI: 10.1016/j.jclepro.2019.118208

Jiang, H. (2018). The impact of language proficiency on service quality and customer satisfaction in the hospitality industry. *International Journal of Contemporary Hospitality Management*, 30(1), 426–445.

Jihoon, K., & Darla, C. (2021). *Effects of Gamification on Behavioral Change in Education: A Meta-Analysis.* https://www.ncbi.nlm.nih.gov/pmc/articles/PMC8037535/

John, J. A., & Alaaraj, H. K. (2024). Perspective of Students on the Indirect Effect of Activity Based Learning Towards Academic Achievement by Mediating Engagement. In *Business Development via AI and Digitalization* (Vol. 2, pp. 645–661). Springer Nature Switzerland.

Johnson, A. M., Jacovina, M. E., Russell, D. E., & Soto, C. M. (2016). Challenges and solutions when using technologies in the classroom. In Crossley, S. A., & McNamara, D. S. (Eds.), *Adaptive educational technologies for literacy instruction* (pp. 13–29). Taylor & Francis.

Johnson, D. W., & Johnson, R. T. (1999). *Active Learning: Cooperation, Competition, and Individualization in the Classroom*. Allyn & Bacon.

Jones, P., & Wynn, M. G. (2019). The circular economy, natural capital, and resilience in tourism and hospitality. *International Journal of Contemporary Hospitality Management*, 31(6), 2544–2563. DOI: 10.1108/IJCHM-05-2018-0370

Jose, J., & Jose, B. J. (2024). Educators' Academic Insights on Artificial Intelligence: Challenges and Opportunities. *Electronic Journal of e-Learning*, 22(2), 59–77.

Joshi, Y., & Rahman, Z. (2017). Investigating the Determinants of Consumers' Sustainable Purchase Behaviour. *Sustainable Production and Consumption*, 10, 110–120. DOI: 10.1016/j.spc.2017.02.002

Juan, M. (2016). *5 Features You Need to Consider When Choosing an Online Learning Platform*. PC Mag. https://www.pcmag.com/news/5-features-you-need-to-consider-when-choosing-an-online-learning-platform?webview_progress_bar=1&show_loading=0

Julia, B., & Juan, V. (2024). *What are the best practices for ensuring data privacy when using AI and ML solutions?* LinkedIn. https://l.facebook.com/l.php?u=https%3A%2F%2Fwww.linkedin.com%2Fadvice%2F3%2Fwhat-best-practices-ensuring-data-privacy%3Ffbclid%3DIwZXh0bgNhZW0CMTAAAR2zSrV5D9Whtu2AakxN7iLIJIaM_gv17bVnqpzUm2_PmUvGTF91IZxpxoI_aem_KF93iw8vKkoCpT1x13tGrw&h=AT0Y3wqwoZwR8xkc5ybBdPcGS_1f9Wdz_E9a7qrk56WtSZol1SSar2RdnBEbJgA2L_H8vUHhZR9ozlpIcpqq0jKXuYhvm8jTmEhq3NjNy-vBTZ2f726LEp23ThsBNeVWpHLL6g

Juliao, J., Gaspar, M., Tjahjono, B., & Rocha, S. (2019). Exploring circular economy in the hospitality industry. In *Innovation, engineering and entrepreneurship* (pp. 953–960). Springer International Publishing. DOI: 10.1007/978-3-319-91334-6_131

Jumaat, N. F., Tasir, Z., Abd Halim, N. D., & Mohamad Ashari, Z. (2017). Project-based learning from constructivism point of view. *Advanced Science Letters*, 23(8), 7904–7906.

Jusoh, A., Huda, M., Abdullah, R., & Lee, N. (2024). Development of digital heritage for archaeovisit tourism resilience: evidences from E-Lenggong web portal. In *World Conference on Information Systems for Business Management* (pp. 53-74). Singapore: Springer Nature Singapore. DOI: 10.1007/978-981-99-8349-0_6

Kalmykova, Y., Sadagopan, M., & Rosado, L. (2018). Circular economy–From review of theories and practices to development of implementation tools. *Resources, Conservation and Recycling*, 135, 190–201. DOI: 10.1016/j.resconrec.2017.10.034

Kang, K. H., Lee, S., & Huh, C. (2010). Impacts of positive and negative corporate social responsibility activities on company performance in the hospitality industry. *International Journal of Hospitality Management*, 29(1), 72–82. DOI: 10.1016/j.ijhm.2009.05.006

Kant, S., & Adula, M. (2024). AI Learning and Work Attitude Mediation Between Reward and Organizational Support in Ethiopia. In Gomathi Sankar, J., & David, A. (Eds.), *Generative AI for Transformational Management* (pp. 109–136). IGI Global., DOI: 10.4018/979-8-3693-5578-7.ch005

Kant, S., & Adula, M. (2024). Human-Machine Interaction in the Metaverse in the Context of Ethiopia. In *Impact and Potential of Machine Learning in the Metaverse* (pp. 196–212). IGI Global., DOI: 10.4018/979-8-3693-5762-0.ch008

Kapp, K. (2021, June 7). *A Conversation with Clark Aldrich -Part One*. Karl Kapp. https://karlkapp.com/a-conversation-with-clark-aldrich-part-one/?webview_progress_bar=1&show_loading=0

Kaynak, N. E., Altan, A. E., Abbak, Y., Alp, Z. A., Yavuz, E., & Toprak, E. (2023). A theoretical view of quality education in terms of sustainable development. *Iğdır University Journal of Social Sciences*, 34, 592–609.

Kembauw, E., Soekiman, J. F. X. S. E., Lydia, L., Shankar, K., & Huda, M. (2019). Benefits of Corporate Mentoring for Business Organization. *Journal of Critical Reviews.*, 6(5), 101–106.

Kember, D., McNaught, C., & Wong, F. (2017). Enhancing learning through technology in accounting education. *Journal of Learning and Technology*, 6(4), 99–112.

Kende-Robb, C. (2018). The role of international organizations in facilitating digital transformation. *World Development*, 114, 1–6.

Kenyon, S. (2023, June 23). *Gamification and Self-Determination Theory - Sam Kenyon - Medium.* Medium. https://medium.com/@samkenyon/gamification-and-self-determination-theory-45a28494b672?webview_progress_bar=1&show_loading=0

Kestin, T., den Belt, M., Denby, L., Ross, K., Thwaitea, J., & Hawkes, M. (2017). *Getting started with the SDGs in universities: A Guide for universities, higher education institutions, and the academic sector.* Sustainable Development Solutions Network.

Khaleghi, A., Aghaei, Z., & Mahdavi, M. A. (2021). A Gamification Framework for Cognitive Assessment and Cognitive Training: Qualitative study. *JMIR Serious Games*, 9(2), e21900. DOI: 10.2196/21900 PMID: 33819164

Khizar, H. M. U., Younas, A., Kumar, S., Akbar, A., & Poulova, P. (2023). The progression of sustainable development goals in tourism: A systematic literature review of past achievements and future promises. *Journal of Innovation & Knowledge*, 8(4), 100442. DOI: 10.1016/j.jik.2023.100442

Kim, K., & Kwon, K. (2024). Designing an Inclusive Artificial Intelligence (AI) Curriculum for Elementary Students to Address Gender Differences With Collaborative and Tangible Approaches. *Journal of Educational Computing Research*, 62(7), 1837–1864.

King, E. M., & Hill, M. A. (1993). *Women's education in developing countries: Barriers, benefits, and policies.* Johns Hopkins University Press. DOI: 10.1596/0-8018-4534-3

Kioupi, V., & Voulvoulis, N. (2019). *Education for Sustainable Development: A Systemic Framework for Connecting the SDGs to Educational Outcomes.* Sustainable Education and Approaches., DOI: 10.3390/su11216104

Kiwi. (2024, July 29). *Self-Paced Learning: Meaning & Benefits*. Kiwi LMS. https://startkiwi.com/blog/self-paced-learning-meaning-benefits/?webview_progress_bar=1&show_loading=0

Kiyer. (2023, June 22). *AI learning and gamification for education. Internet Public Library*. https://www.ipl.org/div/machine-learning-ai/ai-learning-and-gamification-for-education

Knowledge Hub Media. (2023, September 11). *The Benefits of Structured instruction in Education*. Knowledge Hub Media | Demand Generation Marketing. https://knowledgehubmedia.com/the-benefits-of-structured-instruction-in-education/?webview_progress_bar=1&show_loading=0

Koehler, M. J., Mishra, P., & Yahya, K. (2007). Tracing the development of teacher knowledge in a design seminar: Integrating content, pedagogy, & technology. *Computers & Education*, 49(3), 740–762.

Kohler, J. C., & Bowra, A. (2020). The Role of Global Health Partnerships in Improving Access to Medicines in Low- and Middle-Income Countries. *Globalization and Health*, 16(1), 1–10. DOI: 10.1186/s12992-019-0535-0 PMID: 31898532

Kondrat, B. S. (n.d.). *5 Best Peer to Peer learning Platforms in 2024*. https://www.educate-me.co/blog/best-peer-to-peer-learning-platforms?webview_progress_bar=1&show_loading=0

Koravuna, S., & Surepally, U. K. (2020, September). Educational gamification and artificial intelligence for promoting digital literacy. In *Proceedings of the 2nd International Conference on Intelligent and Innovative Computing Applications* (pp. 1-6).

Korkmaz, G. (2020). New teacher training degree programmes analysing education for sustainable development in the context of education for sustainable development. *Journal of Advanced Education Studies*, 2(2), 111–132. DOI: 10.48166/ejaes.742200

Kozak, M., & Rimmington, M. (2000). Tourist satisfaction with Mallorca, Spain, as an off-season holiday destination. *Journal of Travel Research*, 38(3), 260–269. DOI: 10.1177/004728750003800308

Krasko, A. (2022, July 28). *Gamification and Augmented reality learning: Engage, excite, educate*. https://www.banuba.com/blog/gamification-and-augmented-reality-learning-engage-excite-educate

Kräusche, K., & Pilz, S. (2018). Integrated sustainability reporting at HNE Eberswalde–a practice report. *International Journal of Sustainability in Higher Education*, 19(2), 291–312. DOI: 10.1108/IJSHE-07-2016-0145

K-Rockets. (2024, July 14). STEM education: Top ten best practices for teaching and learning. K-Rockets. https://k-rockets.com/stem-education-top-ten-best-practices-for-teaching-and-learning/

Kuhlthau, C., & Maniotes, L. K. (2015). *Guided inquiry: Learning in the 21st century* (2nd ed.). Libraries Unlimited.

Kulkarni, A. (2020, November 3). *Benefits of using Videos in eLearning*. https://www.linkedin.com/pulse/benefits-using-videos-elearning-ajinkya-kulkarni?webview_progress_bar=1&show_loading=0

Kulkarni, D. K. (2016). Interpretation and display of research results. *Indian Journal of Anaesthesia*, 60(9), 657. DOI: 10.4103/0019-5049.190622 PMID: 27729693

Kumar, P., Ulseth, M., & Austin, S. (2021). Bridging the Gender Gap to Realize Capacity Building: The role of SDG 5 for SDG 17. In *Partnerships for the Goals* (pp. 78–87). Springer International Publishing. DOI: 10.1007/978-3-319-95963-4_122

Kun-Shan, W., & Yi-Man, T. (2011). Applying the extended theory of planned behaviour to predict the intention of visiting a green hotel. *African Journal of Business Management*, 5(17), 7579–7587. DOI: 10.5897/AJBM11.684

Kurni, M., Mohammed, M. S., & Srinivasa, K. G. (2023). *AI-Enabled gamification in education*. In Springer eBooks (pp. 105–114). DOI: 10.1007/978-3-031-32653-0_6

Kurtić, V., Bikić, N., & Durmiš, E. K (2024). Enhancing Students' confidence and Understanding in Probability Through ChatGPT: An Analysis of Ai's Impact on Learning Experiences.

Lamar Online. (2017, October 3). What are the benefits of Teacher-Led Schools? Lamar. https://degree.lamar.edu/online-programs/education/med-teacher-leadership/general-concentration/benefits-of-teacher-led-schools/?show_loading=0&webview_progress_bar=1

Lampropoulos, G. (2023). Augmented reality and artificial intelligence in education: Toward immersive intelligent tutoring systems. In *Augmented reality and artificial intelligence: The fusion of advanced technologies* (pp. 137–146). Springer Nature Switzerland.

Landers, R. N. (2015, July 5). *Psychological theory and gamification of learning*. NeoAcademic. https://neoacademic.com/2015/01/15/psychological-theory-gamification-learning/?show_loading=0&webview_progress_bar=1

Laney, K. (2023) *What Is Multimodal Learning? 35 Strategies and Examples to Empower Your Teaching*. Prodigy https://www.prodigygame.com/main-en/blog/multimodal-learning/?f_link_type=f_inlinenote&show_loading=0&webview_progress_bar=1

Lasimbang, B., & Tayag, J. (2016). The role of state universities and colleges in poverty alleviation: An ASEAN perspective. *ASEAN Journal of Higher Education*, 10(3), 245–265.

Latif, M. K., Md Saad, R., & Abd Hamid, S. (2023). Islamic Education Teachers' Competency in Teaching Qiraat Sab'ah for the Quranic Class. *Firdaus Journal*, 3(1), 19–27. DOI: 10.37134/firdaus.vol3.1.3.2023

Lazer, D., Baum, M., Benkler, Y., Berinsky, A. J., Greenhill, K. M., Menczer, F., Metzger, M. J., Nyhan, B., Pennycook, G., Rothschild, D., Schudson, M., Sloman, S. A., Sunstein, C. R., Thorson, E., Watts, D. J., & Zittrain, J. (2018). The science of fake news. *Science*, 359(6380), 1094–1096. DOI: 10.1126/science.aao2998 PMID: 29590025

Leading Learning Podcast. (n.d.). https://leadinglearning.libsyn.com/leading-learning-podcast-episode-213-patti-shank?webview_progress_bar=1&show_loading=0

Leading the way: Embracing responsible AI in education. (2024, January 19). MindSpark Learning. https://www.mindspark.org/post/leading-the-way-embracing-responsible-ai-in-education

Learning, E. L. M. (2024, August 5). How to create Well-Designed Interactive eLearning. https://elmlearning.com/blog/design-interactive-elearning/?webview_progress_bar=1&show_loading=0

Learnnovators, & Learnnovators. (2020, May 17). *CATHY MOORE – CRYSTAL BALLING WITH LEARNNOVATORS*. Learnnovators. https://learnnovators.com/blog/cathy-moore-crystal-balling-with-learnnovators/?webview_progress_bar=1&show_loading=0

Leavy, P. (2022). *Research Design: Quantitative, Qualitative, Mixed Methods, Arts-Based, and Community-Based Participatory Research Approaches*. Guilford Publications.

Lee, C., & Li, S. (2021). Tourism and language: The role of Mandarin in enhancing tourist experience in Southeast Asia. International Journal of Hospitality Management, pp. 39, 47–58.

Lee, H. (2024). Examining the Effectiveness of Personalized Learning Through Artificial Intelligence (Doctoral dissertation, Indiana University).

Lee, U., Jeong, Y., Koh, J., Byun, G., Lee, Y., Lee, H., & Kim, H. (2024). I see you: Teacher analytics with GPT-4 vision-powered observational assessment. *Smart Learning Environments*, 11(1), 48.

Lefever, S., Dal, M., & Matthíasdóttir, Á. (2006). Online data collection in academic research: Advantages and limitations. *British Journal of Educational Technology*, 38(4), 574–582. DOI: 10.1111/j.1467-8535.2006.00638.x

Lehner, O. M., Grabmann, R., & Ennsgraber, C. (2015). Entrepreneurial Impacts of Crowdfunding on Sustainability-Oriented Startups. *Journal of Business Research*, 68(4), 911–917. DOI: 10.1016/j.jbusres.2014.11.031

Leicht, A., Heiss, J., & Byun, W. (Eds.). (2018). Issues and trends in education for sustainable development. *UNESCO Publishing*.https://unesdoc.unesco.org/ark:/48223/pf0000261445

Lew, A. A., Ng, P. T., Ni, C. C., & Wu, T. C. (2020). Tourism geography and global change. *Geographical Research*, 58(3), 231–240. DOI: 10.1111/1745-5871.12460

Li, X. (2021). Cross-cultural communication in the tourism and hospitality industry: A case study of Chinese tourists in Australia. Journal of Hospitality and Tourism Management, pp. 47, 148–156.

Liao, X., Cao, M., Xia, M., & He, Y. (2020). Predicting individual treatment response from baseline brain activity using machine learning techniques. *NeuroImage*, 220, 117096. DOI: 10.1016/j.neuroimage.2020.117096

Li, L., Hew, K. F., & Du, J. (2024). Gamification enhances student intrinsic motivation, perceptions of autonomy and relatedness, but minimal impact on competency: A meta-analysis and systematic review. *Educational Technology Research and Development*, 72(2), 765–796. DOI: 10.1007/s11423-023-10337-7

Li, M., Ma, S., & Shi, Y. (2023). Examining the effectiveness of gamification as a tool promoting teaching and learning in educational settings: A meta-analysis. *Frontiers in Psychology*, 14, 1253549. Advance online publication. DOI: 10.3389/fpsyg.2023.1253549 PMID: 37876838

Limited, C. G. (2021, June 30). *Benefits of personalisation in eLearning*. https://www.linkedin.com/pulse/benefits-personalisation-elearning-comeandsee-global-limited?webview_progress_bar=1&show_loading=0

Lin, J., & Liu, W. (2018). E-commerce and Taobao Villages: A path to poverty alleviation in rural China. *Journal of Rural Studies*, 60, 123–134. DOI: 10.1016/j.jrurstud.2018.04.004

LinkedIn Learning. (n.d.). *Online Learning Platform for Businesses.* LinkedIn Learning. https://learning.linkedin.com/?webview_progress_bar=1&show_loading=0

LinkedIn Learning: online training courses & skill building. (n.d.). https://www.linkedin.com/learning?webview_progress_bar=1&show_loading=0

Litmos. (n.d.). *Clark Quinn, Ph.D.* https://www.litmos.com/blog/author/clark-quinn?webview_progress_bar=1&show_loading=0

Li, X., Wu, T., Zhang, H. J., & Yang, D. Y. (2023). National innovation systems and the achievement of sustainable development goals: Effect of knowledge-based dynamic capability. *Journal of Innovation & Knowledge*, 8(1), 100310. DOI: 10.1016/j.jik.2023.100310

Li, Y., & Wang, L. (2023). Language proficiency and career advancement in the global tourism industry: The case of Mandarin-speaking professionals. *Journal of Global Tourism*, 56(4), 229–240.

Long, P. B. L. (2022, March 8). *Transparency in learning and Teaching: Small changes, big impact.* https://blogs.iu.edu/citl/2022/03/08/transparency-in-learning-and-teaching-small-changes-big-impact/?webview_progress_bar=1&show_loading=0

Longo, B. (1998). An approach for applying cultural study theory to technical writing research. *Technical Communication Quarterly*, 7(1), 53–73. DOI: 10.1080/10572259809364617

Loste, N., Chinarro, D., Gomez, M., Roldán, E., & Giner, B. (2020). Assessing awareness of green chemistry as a tool for advancing sustainability. *Journal of Cleaner Production*, 256, 120392. DOI: 10.1016/j.jclepro.2020.120392

Lovelace, M., Ellingson, D. A., & Smith, D. (2018). Online simulations in accounting and business management education: Impact on student performance. *Journal of Business Education*, 12(3), 49–61.

Lozano, R., Ceulemans, K., Alonso-Almeida, M., Huisingh, D., Lozano, F. J., Waas, T., Lambrechts, W., Lukman, R., & Hugé, J. (2015). A review of commitment and implementation of sustainable development in higher education: Results from a worldwide survey. *Journal of Cleaner Production*, 108, 1–18. DOI: 10.1016/j.jclepro.2014.09.048

Lucy. (2023, January 26). *Virtual Reality in STEM Education - Crowdmark.* Crowdmark. https://crowdmark.com/blog/vr-in-stem/

M, D. (2022, June 27). *Advantages of personalized learning.* https://www.linkedin.com/pulse/advantages-personalized-learning-dhanush-m?show_loading=0&webview_progress_bar=1

Majgaard, G., Larsen, L. J., Lyk, P., & Lyk, M. (2017). Seeing the Unseen—Spatial Visualization of the Solar System with Physical Prototypes and Augmented Reality. *International Journal of Designs for Learning*, 8(2). Advance online publication. DOI: 10.14434/ijdl.v8i2.22368

Mallow, S., Toman, I., & Van't Land, H. (2020). Higher Education and the 2030 Agenda: Moving into the 'Decade of Action and Delivery for the SDGs'. *IAU 2nd Global Survey Report on Higher Education and Research for Sustainable Development.*

Malsakpak, M. H., & Pourteimour, S. (2024). Comparison of the Effects of E-learning Blended with Collaborative Learning and Lecture-Based Teaching Approaches on Academic Self-Efficacy among Undergraduate Nursing Students: A Quasi-Experimental Study. *Journal of Advances in Medical Education & Professionalism*, 12(2), 102.

Manaktola, K., & Jauhari, V. (2007). Exploring consumer attitude and behaviour towards green practices in the lodging industry in India. *International Journal of Contemporary Hospitality Management*, 19(5), 364–377. DOI: 10.1108/09596110710757534

Mandese, J. (1991). New study finds green confusion. *Advertising Age*, 62(45), 1–56.

Manlapaz, C. J., & Villanueva, M. M. (2020). RESEARCH PREPAREDNESS AND CAPABILITIES OF ITED STUDENTS AND FACULTY Research preparedness and Capabilities... ResearchGate. https://www.researchgate.net/publication/344328481_RESEARCH_PREPAREDNESS_AND_CAPABILITIES_OF_ITED_STUDENTS_AND_FACULTY_Research_Preparedness_and_Capabilities_of_ITEd_Students_and_Faculty?_tp=eyJjb250ZXh0Ijp7ImZpcnN0UGFnZSI6Il9kaXJlY3QiLCJwYWdlIjoicHJvZmlsZSIsInBvc2l0aW9uIjoicGFnZUNvbnRlbnQifX0

Manniche, J., Topsø Larsen, K., Brandt Broegaard, R., & Holland, E. (2017). *Destination: A circular tourism economy: A handbook for transitioning toward a circular economy within the tourism and hospitality sectors in the South Baltic Region.*

Manolas, F. Alves, U. Azeiteiro, J. Rogers, C. Shiel, & A. Do Paco (Eds.), Universities as Living Labs for Sustainable Development: Supporting the Implementation of the Sustainable Development Goals (pp. 11–27). Springer International Publishing.

Manosuttirit, A. (2019). How to apply technology in STEM education lesson by project-based learning. *Journal of Physics: Conference Series*, 1340(1), 012044. https://doi.org/10.1088/1742-6596/1340/1/012044

Mansaray, S. (2024, August 30). *The best online learning platforms in 2024*. Explore the eLearning World With Us. https://www.ispringsolutions.com/blog/best-online-learning-platforms?webview_progress_bar=1&show_loading=0

Mansour, N., Said, Z., & Abu-Tineh, A. (2024). Factors impacting science and mathematics teachers' competencies and self-efficacy in TPACK for PBL and STEM. *Eurasia Journal of Mathematics, Science and Technology Education*, 20(5), em2442. Advance online publication. https://doi.org/10.29333/ejmste/14467

Manthena, R. (2023, June 26). *Transforming Education through the Power of Virtual Reality (VR) and Augmented Reality (AR)*. https://www.linkedin.com/pulse/transforming-education-through-power-virtual-reality-vr-manthena-

Marco, Y. (2022, December 19). *The importance of identifying your target audience in online course creation*. Medium. https://medium.com/@yassinmarco/the-importance-of-identifying-your-target-audience-in-online-course-creation-b1c14907993e?webview_progress_bar=1&show_loading=0

Marco, Y. (2022b, December 23). *The key factors to consider when choosing an online course platform*. Medium. https://medium.com/@yassinmarco/the-key-factors-to-consider-when-choosing-an-online-course-platform-6794b3de1281?webview_progress_bar=1&show_loading=0

Marr, B. (2021, July 23). 10 best examples of VR and AR in education. Forbes. https://www.forbes.com/sites/bernardmarr/2021/07/23/10-best-examples-of-vr-and-ar-in-education/

Martens, T. (2018). E-Estonia: The rise of digital governance. *Public Administration Review*, 78(1), 36–45. DOI: 10.1111/puar.12973

Martínez-Ramos, S. A., Rodríguez-Reséndiz, J., Gutiérrez, A. F., Sevilla-Camacho, P. Y., & Mendiola-Santíbañez, J. D. (2021). The Learning Space as Support to Sustainable Development: A Revision of Uses and Design Processes. *Sustainability (Basel)*, 13(21), 11609. DOI: 10.3390/su132111609

Maseleno, A., Huda, M., Jasmi, K. A., Basiron, B., Mustari, I., Don, A. G., & Ahmad, R. (2019). Hau-Kashyap approach for student's level of expertise. *Egyptian Informatics Journal*, 20(1), 27–32. DOI: 10.1016/j.eij.2018.04.001

Mastering The Challenges Of AI: Privacy, Security And Compliance Strategies (2023). Forbes. https://www.forbes.com/councils/forbestechcouncil/2023/08/18/mastering-the-challenges-of-ai-privacy-security-and-compliance-strategies/

Mathias, S. (2024, July 3). *Responsible AI Integration: 4 steps for education leaders | ThoughtExchange*. ThoughtExchange. https://thoughtexchange.com/blog/responsible-ai-integration-4-steps-for-education-leaders/

Mathias, S. C. E. S. (2024, July 3). *Responsible AI Integration: 4 steps for education leaders | ThoughtExchange*. ThoughtExchange. https://thoughtexchange.com/blog/responsible-ai-integration-4-steps-for-education-leaders/

Mayer-Schönberger, V., & Cukier, K. (2013). *Big data: A revolution that will transform how we live, work, and think.* Houghton Mifflin Harcourt.

Mazzucato, M. (2018). *The entrepreneurial state: Debunking public vs. private sector myths* (Revised ed.). Penguin Books.

McDonald, C. V. (2016). STEM education: A review of the contribution of the disciplines of science, technology, engineering and mathematics. *Science Education International*, 27(4), 530–569.

McGrath, P. J., Stewart, J. W., & Nierenberg, A. A. (2021). Advances in the treatment of depression: Personalized medicine and beyond. *The American Journal of Psychiatry*, 178(6), 478–492. DOI: 10.1176/appi.ajp.2021.20091140

Meadows, D. H. (2008). *Thinking in systems: A primer.* Chelsea Green Publishing.

Meijer, A. (2018). Digital platforms and public governance: The enabling role of technology in public-private partnerships. *Government Information Quarterly*, 35(4), 637–644. DOI: 10.1016/j.giq.2018.09.002

Mekonnen, M. M., & Hoekstra, A. Y. (2016). Four billion people facing severe water scarcity. *Science Advances*, 2(2), e1500323. DOI: 10.1126/sciadv.1500323 PMID: 26933676

Memorandum Order No, CHED. 09, s. 2013.

Michalopoulou, E., Shallcross, D. E., Atkins, E., Tierney, A., Norman, N. C., Preist, C., O'Doherty, S., Saunders, R., Birkett, A., Willmore, C., & Ninos, I. (2019). The end of simple problems: Repositioning chemistry in higher education and society using a systems thinking approach and the United Nations' Sustainable Development Goals as a framework. *Journal of Chemical Education*, 96(12), 2825–2835. DOI: 10.1021/acs.jchemed.9b00270

Mikhnenko, O., & Absaliamova, A. (2018). English for academic purposes and specific purposes: A literature review. *Journal of Language and Education*, 4(1), 4–14.

MindSpark Learning. https://www.mindspark.org/post/leading-the-way-embracing-responsible-ai-in-education

Mishra, D., Bakhronova, D., & Djalilova, U. (2023b). *Activity-Based Learning: an analysis to teach learners using online methodologies*. In Studies in computational intelligence (pp. 163–171). DOI: 10.1007/978-981-19-6450-3_17

Mitarlis, M., Azizah, U., & Yonata, B. (2023). The integration of green chemistry principles in basic chemistry learning to support achievement of sustainable development goals (SDGs) through education. *Journal of Technology and Science Education*, 13(1), 233. DOI: 10.3926/jotse.1892

Mohamad Shokri, S. S., & Salihan, S. (2023). Modul pembangunan Program Huffaz Profesional Universiti Tenaga Nasional: Satu pemerhatian kepada konstruk pembangunan Al-Quran. *Firdaus Journal*, 3(2), 12–23. DOI: 10.37134/firdaus.vol3.2.2.2023

Mohd Nawi, M. Z. (2023). Media Variations in Education in Malaysia: A 21st Century Paradigm. *Firdaus Journal*, 3(1), 77–95. DOI: 10.37134/firdaus.vol3.1.8.2023

Mohd Nizar, N., Ab Mutalib, N. H., & Taha, H. (2019). The Status of Knowledge, Attitude, And Behaviour of Postgraduate Students towards Education for Sustainable Development (ESD). *Jurnal Pendidikan Sains dan Matematik Malaysia, 9(2)*, 35–41. https://doi.org/DOI: 10.37134/jpsmm.vol9.2.5.2019

Mohr, D. C., Zhang, M., & Schueller, S. M. (2017). Personal sensing: Understanding mental health using ubiquitous sensors and machine learning. *Annual Review of Clinical Psychology*, 13(1), 23–47. DOI: 10.1146/annurev-clinpsy-032816-044949 PMID: 28375728

Mol, A. P. J., & Spaargaren, G. (2000). Ecological modernization theory in debate: A review. *Environmental Politics*, 9(1), 17–49. DOI: 10.1080/09644010008414511

Montalbo, M. T., & Salazar, J. P. (2019). Poverty in the Philippines: An analysis of urban and rural disparities. *Philippine Social Science Journal*, 14(2), 112–130.

Montenegro de Lima, C. R., Coelho Soares, T., Andrade de Lima, M., Oliveira Veras, M., & Andrade Guerra, J. B. S. O. D. A. (2020). Sustainability funding in higher education: A literature-based review. *International Journal of Sustainability in Higher Education*, 21(3), 441–464. DOI: 10.1108/IJSHE-07-2019-0229

Montenegro Navarro, N., & Jonker, J. (2018). *Circular City Governance—An explorative research study into current barriers and governance practices in circular city transitions in Europe*. European Urban Agenda Circular Economy.

Moodle. (2022, October 7). *E-learning Co., Ltd.* https://www.e-learning.asia/service/moodle/?webview_progress_bar=1&show_loading=0

Moodle. (n.d.). *eLearning Learning*. https://www.elearninglearning.com/moodle/?show_loading=0&webview_progress_bar=1

Moore, C. (2011, July 5). *Checklist for strong learning design. Training Design*. Cathy Moore. https://blog.cathy-moore.com/checklist-for-strong-elearning/?show_loading=0&webview_progress_bar=1

Moreno-Serna, J., Sánchez-Chaparro, T., Mazorra, J., Arzamendi, A., Stott, L., & Mataix, C. (2020). Transformational collaboration for the SDGs: The Alianza Shire's work to provide energy access in refugee camps and host communities. *Sustainability (Basel)*, 12(2), 539. DOI: 10.3390/su12020539

Morrisa, J. E., & Wesley Imms, W. (2022). Designing and using innovative learning spaces: What teachers have to say. *IUL Research.*, 3(6), 7–25. Advance online publication. DOI: 10.57568/iulres.v3i6.295

Mozafaripour, S. (2024, March 20). *Benefits of Online learning – 16 Advantages to Learning online*. University of St. Augustine for Health Sciences. https://www.usa.edu/blog/benefits-of-online-learning/?webview_progress_bar=1&show_loading=0

Muhamad, N., Huda, M., Hashim, A., Tabrani, Z. A., & Maárif, M. A. (2024). Managing technology integration for teaching strategy: public school educators' beliefs and practices. In *International Conference on Information and Communication Technology for Competitive Strategies* (pp. 385-400). Singapore: Springer Nature Singapore. DOI: 10.1007/978-981-97-0210-7_31

Muharom, F., Farhan, M., & Athoillah, S., Rozihan, Muflihin, A., & Huda, M. (2024). Digital technology skills for professional development: insights into quality instruction performance. In *International Conference on Information and Communication Technology for Competitive Strategies* (pp. 371-384). Singapore: Springer Nature Singapore. DOI: 10.1007/978-981-97-0210-7_30

Mulligan, G., Andersen, R., & Kimbler, L. (2019). The Role of Digital Technologies in Enabling Sustainable Development. *Journal of Environmental Management*, 248, 109293. DOI: 10.1016/j.jenvman.2019.109293

Murray, A., Skene, K., & Haynes, K. (2017). The circular economy: An interdisciplinary exploration of the concept and application in a global context. *Journal of Business Ethics*, 140(3), 369–380. DOI: 10.1007/s10551-015-2693-2

Musolin, M. H., Ismail, M. H., Farhan, M., Rois, N., Huda, M., & Rohim, M. A. (2024c). Understanding of Artificial Intelligence for Islamic Education Support and Service: Insights from Empirical Literature Review. In Proceedings of Ninth International Congress on Information and Communication Technology. ICICT 2024. Lecture Notes in Networks and Systems. Springer, Singapore.

Musolin, M. H., Ismail, M. H., Huda, M., Hassan, T. R. R., & Ismail, A. (2024b). Towards an Islamic education administration system: a critical contribution from technology adoption. In Proceedings of Ninth International Congress on Information and Communication Technology. ICICT 2024. Lecture Notes in Networks and Systems. Springer, Singapore.

Musolin, M. H., Serour, R. O. H., Hamid, S. A., Ismail, A., Huda, M., & Rohim, M. A. (2024a). Developing Personalized Islamic Learning in Digital Age: Pedagogical and Technological Integration for Open Learning Resources (OLR). In Proceedings of Ninth International Congress on Information and Communication Technology. ICICT 2024. Lecture Notes in Networks and Systems. Springer, Singapore.

Nadelson, L. S., & Seifert, A. L. (2017). Integrated STEM defined: Contexts, challenges, and the future. *The Journal of Educational Research*, 110(3), 221–223.

National Academies of Sciences, Engineering, and Medicine. (2011). Chapter 3: Practices that support effective STEM education. In Successful STEM education: A workshop summary (pp. 25–42). The National Academies Press. https://doi.org/10.17226/13230

National Center for Education Statistics. (2022). *Students with disabilities. U.S. Department of Education, Institute of Education Sciences.* https://nces.ed.gov/programs/coe/indicator/cgg/students-with-disabilities

National Institute of Mental Health and Neurosciences (NIMHANS). (2016). *National Mental Health Survey of India, 2015–16: Summary.* NIMHANS.

Ndung'u, N. (2017). *A digital financial services revolution in Kenya: The M-Pesa case study.* Center for Global Development.

Neendoor, S. (2024, August 16). *AI and Gamification: Enhancing Student Motivation and Achievement. Digital Engineering & Technology* | Elearning Solutions | Digital Content Solutions. https://www.hurix.com/ai-and-gamification-enhancing-student-motivation-and-achievement/

Neill, S., & Etheridge, R. (2008). *Flexible learning spaces: the integration of pedagogy, physical design, and instructional technology.* Semantic Scholar., DOI: 10.1080/10528008.2008.11489024

Nelson, C. E. (2022, January 30). STEM educational activities with virtual labs: Curriculum & skills. Connections Academy. https://www.connectionsacademy.com/support/resources/article/stem-educational-activities-with-virtual-labs/

Nextech3D.Ai. (2024, March 28). *10 Ways Augmented Reality Can Be used in Education.* https://www.nextechar.com/blog/10-applications-of-ar-in-education

Nguyen, Q. (2024, July 3). *Harness the power of virtual reality (VR) and augmented reality (AR) in education.* Atomi Systems, Inc. https://atomisystems.com/elearning/virtual-reality-vr-and-augmented-reality-ar-in-education/?show_loading=0&webview_progress_bar=1

Nguyen, T. C., Nguyen, T. C., & Nguyen, H. B. (2024). The role of information technology in STEM education. *Asian Journal of Education and Training*, 10(1), 18–26. https://doi.org/10.20448/edu.v10i1.532

Nielsen, L., & Axelsen, D. (2017). Capabilitarian Sufficiency: Capabilities and Social Justice. *Journal of Human Development and Capabilities*, 18(1), 46–59. DOI: 10.1080/19452829.2016.1145632

Nieto, S. (2012). *Conclusion and recommendations.* https://bilingualreview.utsa.edu/index.php/AMAE/article/view/123

Ningthoujam, R. (2022, October 3). *Merging AI and gamification in hiring: The Pros & Cons.* Leena AI Blog. https://leena.ai/blog/ai-and-gamification-in-hiring/

Nocca, F., Bosone, M., De Toro, P., & Fusco Girard, L. (2023). Towards the human circular tourism: Recommendations, actions, and multidimensional indicators for the tourist category. *Sustainability (Basel)*, 15(3), 1845. DOI: 10.3390/su15031845

Notebook, D. V. (2023, August 4). *A new perspective on Maslow's hierarchy of needs: integrating AI and post-pandemic impacts.* Medium. https://davincisnotebook.medium.com/a-new-perspective-on-maslows-hierarchy-of-needs-integrating-ai-and-post-pandemic-impacts-2b0d7480d794

Nurbaity, N., Rahmawati, Y., & Ridwan, A. (2016). Integration of green chemistry approach in teacher education program for developing awareness of environmental sustainability. In *Proceedings of the ASEAN Comparative Education Research Network Conference (ACERN), November 30th – December 01, 2016* (pp. 2148-2156). Universitas Negeri Jakarta. https://doi.org/DOI: 10.1234/5678

Nyoach, T. D., Lemi, K., Debela, T., & Kant, S. (2024). Does Organizational Commitment Mediate the Relationship between Employee Relationship Management and Bank Performance? The Case of Banks in Ethiopia. *International Journal of Organizational Leadership*, 13(2), 355–376. DOI: 10.33844/ijol.2024.60419

O'Neil, C. (2016). *Weapons of math destruction: How big data increases inequality and threatens democracy*. Crown.

OECD. (Organisation for Economic Co-operation and Development). (2017). *Learning to Thrive: Skills for the Future*. OECD Publishing.

OECD. (Organisation for Economic Co-operation and Development). (2018). *Teaching and Learning International Survey (TALIS) 2018 Results*. OECD Publishing.

OECD. (Organisation for Economic Co-operation and Development). (2019). *Education 2030: A Global Education Transformation*. OECD Publishing.

Okpoho, S. (2022, December 19). *5 Advantages of setting up a secure and friendly ELearning environment*. Gopius. https://gopius.com/friendly-elearning-environment/?webview_progress_bar=1&show_loading=0

Okpoho, S. (2023, April 6). *The Best of audio and video in E-Learning: A Must Know*. Gopius. https://gopius.com/audio-and-video-in-e-learning/?webview_progress_bar=1&show_loading=0

Okunlaya, R. O., Syed Abdullah, N., & Alias, R. A. (2022). Artificial intelligence (AI) library services innovative conceptual framework for the digital transformation of university education. *Library Hi Tech*, 40(6), 1869–1892. DOI: 10.1108/LHT-07-2021-0242

Olawumi, T. O., & Chan, D. W. (2018). A scientometric review of global research on sustainability and sustainable development. *Journal of Cleaner Production*, 183, 231–250. DOI: 10.1016/j.jclepro.2018.02.162

Oliveira, J. A., Silva, L. A., & Lima, M. M. (2019). IoT-enabled smart grids: A comprehensive review. *Energy Reports*, 5, 169–183. DOI: 10.1016/j.egyr.2019.09.007

Olsen, D. (1999). Constructivist principles of learning and teaching methods. *Education*, •••, 120.

Omar, M. N. (2022). Inovasi pengajaran & pemudahcaraan menggunakan Aplikasi Ezi-Maq (MAHARAT AL-QURAN) untuk menarik minat pelajar menguasai Ilmu Tajwid. *Firdaus Journal*, 2(2), 79–87. DOI: 10.37134/firdaus.vol2.2.8.2022

Online classes for creatives. Skillshare. (n.d.). https://www.skillshare.com/en/?show_loading=0&webview_progress_bar=1

Online courses, training and tutorials on LinkedIn Learning. (n.d.). LinkedIn. https://www.linkedin.com/learning/search?show_loading=0&webview_progress_bar=1

Online, L. (2017, October 3). *What are the benefits of Teacher-Led Schools? Lamar.* https://degree.lamar.edu/online-programs/education/med-teacher-leadership/general-concentration/benefits-of-teacher-led-schools/?show_loading=0&webview_progress_bar=1

Opara, E. C. (2023). *Educational technology for beginners: Basics of educational technology.* Printed in the United States of America.

Orlando, J. (2018, October 22). *Continuous assessments for better learning.* The Teaching Professor. https://www.teachingprofessor.com/topics/online-teaching-and-learning/grading-feedback-online-learning/continuous-assessments-for-better-learning/?show_loading=0&webview_progress_bar=1

Ortiz Rojas, M. E., Chiluiza, K., & Valcke, M. (2017). Gamification in computer programming: Effects on learning, engagement, self-efficacy, and intrinsic motivation. Retrieved from https://biblio.ugent.be/publication/8542410/file/8549234

Ouellette, A. M., & Wanger, S. P. (2022). Emerging International Issues in Student Affairs Research and Practice. *International Perspectives on Educational Policy, Research and Practice. Library of Congress Cataloging-in-Publication.* http://loc.gov

Owen, R. (n.d.). *Teacher-Led Instruction: What it is and How to Implement it in Your Classroom.* eduwinnow.com. https://www.eduwinnow.com/classroom-resources-teacher-led-instruction?show_loading=0&webview_progress_bar=1

Özmen, H., & Karamustafaoğlu, O. (2019). *Research methods in education.* Pegem Academy.

Paes, H. (2024, February 18). *The concrete benefits of social collaborative learning.* Medium. https://medium.com/@hemersonpaes/the-concrete-benefits-of-social-collaborative-learning-6935324cf186?show_loading=0&webview_progress_bar=1

Paletta, A., & Bonoli, A. (2019). Governing the university in the perspective of the United Nations 2030 Agenda: The case of the University of Bologna. *International Journal of Sustainability in Higher Education*, 20(3), 500–514. DOI: 10.1108/IJSHE-02-2019-0083

Pangket, W. F., Pangesfan, S. K. K., Cayabas, J. P., & Madjaco, G. L. (2023). Research writing readiness of graduate students in a Philippine state college. International Journal of Learning. *Teaching and Educational Research*, 22(4), 141–159. DOI: 10.26803/ijlter.22.4.9

Panigrahi, A., Pati, A., Sahu, B., Das, M. N., Nayak, D. S. K., Sahoo, G., & Kant, S. (2023). En-MinWhale: An ensemble approach based on MRMR and Whale optimization for Cancer diagnosis. *IEEE Access : Practical Innovations, Open Solutions*, 11, 113526–113542. DOI: 10.1109/ACCESS.2023.3318261

Panjwani-Charani, S., & Zhai, X. (in press). AI for Students with Learning Disabilities: A Systematic Review. In Zhai, X., & Krajcik, J. (Eds.), *Uses of Artificial Intelligence in STEM Education* (pp. xx–xx). Oxford University Press.

Paramati, S. R., Shahbaz, M., & Alam, M. S. (2017). Does tourism degrade environmental quality? A comparative study of eastern and western European Union. *Transportation Research Part D, Transport and Environment*, 50, 1–13. DOI: 10.1016/j.trd.2016.10.034

Parlier, M. (2024). The role of AR and VR in developing soft skills in STEM education.

Parr, A. (2022). *Knowledge-driven actions: transforming higher education for global sustainability*. UNESCO.

Parris, J. (2023, March 28). *The Psychology of Gamification: Understanding motivation and behavior*. Medium. https://medium.com/@jamesparris_63299/the-psychology-of-gamification-understanding-motivation-and-behavior-54a3921dc8da?webview_progress_bar=1&show_loading=0

Parsons, J., & Taylor, L. (2019). Preparing students for the workforce: The role of data analytics in accounting education. *Journal of Accounting Education*, 32(4), 312–325.

Patti, S. (2007). *Online Learning Idea Book: 95 Proven Ways to Enhance Technology-Based and Blended Learning* (1st ed.). Barnes & Noble., https://www.barnesandnoble.com/w/online-learning-idea-book-patti-shank/1100321641?show_loading=0&webview_progress_bar=1

Patton, L. D., Renn, K. A., Guido, F. M., & Quaye, S. J. (2016). *Student development in college: Theory, research, and practice* (3rd ed.). John Wiley & Sons., https://books.google.com.ph/books

Pedaste, M., Mäeotos, M., Siiman, L., de Jong, T., van Riesen, S., Kamp, E., Manoli, C., Zacharia, Z., & Tsourlidaki, E. (2015). Phases of inquiry-based learning: Definitions and the inquiry cycle. *Educational Research Review*, 14, 47–61.

Pencarelli, T., & Dini, M. (2011). Tourism enterprises and sustainable tourism: Empirical evidence from the province of Pesaro Urbino. In *14th Toulon-Verona/ICQSS Conference "Excellence in Services"*.

Perry, S. B. (n.d.). Project-based learning. The student's guide to learning design and research. EdTech Books. https://edtechbooks.org/studentguide/project-based_learning

Peşkircioğlu, N. (2016). 2030 sustainable development goals: Towards a global productivity movement. *Key to Development*, 28(335), 4–9.

Petillion, R. J., Freeman, T. K., & McNeil, W. S. (2019). United Nations Sustainable Development Goals as a thematic framework for an introductory chemistry curriculum. *Journal of Chemical Education*, 96(12), 2845–2851. DOI: 10.1021/acs.jchemed.9b00307

Philippine Statistics Authority. (2020). Poverty incidence among families: Annual report. https://psa.gov.ph

Phillips, C. (2018, June 4*). Chatbots for Tech Support 101 - Support Automation Magazine - Medium.* Medium. https://medium.com/support-automation-magazine/chatbots-for-tech-support-101-cfc0d4973ae8?show_loading=0&webview_progress_bar=1

Piaget, J. (1972). *The psychology of the child.* Basic Books.

PlayTours. (2023, September 18). *How AI becomes important role in gamification to boost employee engagement and team-building activity.* Medium. https://medium.com/@playtours/how-ai-becomes-important-role-in-gamification-to-boost-employee-engagement-and-team-building-762c1b824a10

Polat, S., & Kırpık, C. (2013). Attitudes of pre-service teachers towards environmental problems. *Journal of Bartın University Faculty of Education*, 2(1), 205–227. DOI: 10.14686/201312026

Porter, M., & Van der Linde, C. (1995). Green and competitive: Ending the stalemate. In *The Dynamics of the Eco-efficient Economy* (pp. 120–134). Environmental Regulation and Competitive Advantage.

Portz, S. (2015). The challenges of STEM education. The Space Congress® Proceedings, 3. https://commons.erau.edu/space-congress-proceedings/proceedings-2015-43rd/proceedings-2015-43rd/3

Potting, J., Hekkert, M. P., Worrell, E., & Hanemaaijer, A. (2017). Circular economy: Measuring innovation in the product chain. *Planbureau Voor De Leefomgeving, (2544).*

Powered Kids, S. T. E. A. M. (2023). The importance of incorporating hands-on learning in STEM education. Retrieved September 15, 2024, from https://www.steampoweredkids.com.au/post/the-importance-of-incorporating-hands-on-learning-in-stem-education

Pravendrapatel. (2023, May 24). *AR and VR Technology in Education - Pravendrapatel - Medium*. Medium. https://medium.com/@pravendrapatel0012/ar-and-vr-technology-in-education-69da7c3a9897?show_loading=0&webview_progress_bar=1

Prieto-Sandoval, V., Jaca, C., & Ormazabal, M. (2018). Towards a consensus on the circular economy. *Journal of Cleaner Production*, 179, 605–615. DOI: 10.1016/j.jclepro.2017.12.224

Prince, M. J., & Felder, R. M. (2006). Inductive teaching and learning methods: Definitions, comparisons, and research bases.

Private site. (2010, September 2). https://adavox.wordpress.com/2010/09/02/how-games-fulfill-maslows-hierarchy/

Programme des Nations Unies pour l'environnement, Organisation mondiale du tourisme, & Carbone, G. (2005). *Making tourism more sustainable: A guide for policy makers*. UNEP.

Pros and Cons of traditional classroom learning. (2024, July 8). EducationalWave - Pros and Cons Explained. https://www.educationalwave.com/pros-and-cons-of-traditional-classroom-learning/?show_loading=0&webview_progress_bar=1

Puentedura, R. R. (2006). Transformation, technology, and education. http://hippasus.com/resources/tte/puentedurat te.pdf

Purcell, W. M., Henriksen, H., & Spengler, J. D. (2019). Universities as the engine of transformational sustainability toward delivering the sustainable development goals: "Living labs" for sustainability. *International Journal of Sustainability in Higher Education*, 20(8), 1343–1357. DOI: 10.1108/IJSHE-02-2019-0103

Putri, A. R. A., Hidayat, T., & Purwianingsih, W. (2020). Analysis of technological pedagogical content knowledge (TPACK) of biology teachers in classification of living things learning. *Journal of Physics: Conference Series*, 1521, 042033. https://doi.org/10.1088/1742-6596/1521/4/042033

Qizilbash, M. (2008), "Amartya Sen's capability view: insightful sketch or distorted picture?", in: Comim, Qizilbash and Alkire (eds.), pp. 53–81. DOI: 10.1017/CBO9780511492587.003

Qureshi, I., Pan, S. L., & Zheng, Y. (2021). Digital social innovation: An overview and research framework. *Information Systems Journal*, 31(5), 647–671. DOI: 10.1111/isj.12362

Radulovski, A. (2024, March 11). *Visualization of abstract concepts. Women in TechNetwork.* https://www.womentech.net/how-to/7-visualization-abstract-concepts?webview_progress_bar=1&show_loading=0

Rahim, M. M. A., Huda, M., Borham, A. H., Kasim, A. Y., & Othman, M. S. (2024). Managing information leadership for learning performance: an empirical study among public school educators. In *World Conference on Information Systems for Business Management* (pp. 75-91). Singapore: Springer Nature Singapore. DOI: 10.1007/978-981-99-8349-0_7

Rahman, I., & Reynolds, D. (2016). Predicting green hotel behavioural intentions using a theory of environmental commitment and sacrifice for the environment. *International Journal of Hospitality Management*, 52, 107–116. DOI: 10.1016/j.ijhm.2015.09.007

Rahman, M. H. A., Jaafar, J., & Huda, M. (2023). Information and communication skills for higher learners competence model. In *Proceedings of the Computational Methods in Systems and Software* (pp. 357-375). Cham: Springer International Publishing.

Ramirez, M. (2022, July 30). *Webinar Replay: 5 Steps to Stellar AI Voiceover for eLearning. WellSaid Labs.* https://wellsaidlabs.com/blog/replay-ai-voice-for-elearning/?show_loading=0&webview_progress_bar=1

Rankstar. (2023, June 15). *Artificial intelligence in enhancing gamification. CRM Automation & Gamification Platform.* https://smartico.ai/artificial-intelligence-enhancing-gamification/

Rashani, N. (2022, December 5). *Gamification and Self determination theory - Nimasha Rashani - Medium. Medium.* https://nimasharashani.medium.com/gamification-and-self-determination-theory-8d68edad4583

Ravallion, M. (2016). *The economics of poverty: History, measurement, and policy.* Oxford University Press. DOI: 10.1093/acprof:oso/9780190212766.001.0001

Raymer, R. (2013). *The Rock Stars of eLearning: An interview with Patti Shank.* eLearn, 2013(6). DOI: 10.1145/2491560.2499129

Reality, P. (2024, September 1). *The use of AR and VR in E-learning: Applications and Benefits.* PROVEN Reality. https://provenreality.com/use-of-ar-and-vr-in-elearning/?webview_progress_bar=1&show_loading=0

Reeve, E. M. (2013). Implementing science, technology, mathematics, and engineering (STEM) education in Thailand and in ASEAN. *International Journal of Technology and Design Education*, 23(3).

Reeves, S. M., & Crippen, K. J. (2021). Virtual laboratories in undergraduate science and engineering courses: A systematic review, 2009–2019. *Journal of Science Education and Technology*, 30(1), 16–30. https://doi.org/10.1007/s10956-020-09866-0

Reike, D., Vermeulen, W. J., & Witjes, S. (2018). The circular economy: New or refurbished as CE 3.0? Exploring controversies in the conceptualization of the circular economy through a focus on history and resource value retention options. *Resources, Conservation and Recycling*, 135, 246–264. DOI: 10.1016/j.resconrec.2017.08.027

Reimagine Education. (n.d.). How virtual labs are revolutionizing science education. Retrieved September 14, 2024, from https://www.reimagineeducation.com/virtual-labs-science-education

Resnick, L. B. (1989). Introduction. In Resnick, L. B. (Ed.), *Knowing, learning, and instruction: Essays in honor of Robert Glaser* (pp. 1–4). Erlbaum.

Richardson, P. (2023, June 16). *The benefits of online learning: flexibility and access to education*. Medium. https://medium.com/@philrichardsonmail/the-benefits-of-online-learning-flexibility-and-access-to-education-9531697f2df4?webview_progress_bar=1&show_loading=0

Ridha, I., Hasan, M., & Sulastri, . (2020). Comparing environmental awareness between chemistry education students and non-chemistry education students. *Journal of Physics: Conference Series*, 1460(1), 012085. DOI: 10.1088/1742-6596/1460/1/012085

Rinaldi, D. (2019). Blockchain Technology as a Tool for Public-Private Partnerships. *Journal of Public Administration: Research and Theory*, 29(4), 501–511. DOI: 10.1093/jopart/muz011

Rivera, P. (2024, January 19). *Securing customer data: Developing a data privacy plan for AI integration*. IntelePeer. https://intelepeer.ai/blog/securing-customer-data-developing-a-data-privacy-plan-for-ai-integration

Robertson-Kraft, C., & Duckworth, A. (2020). *Positive psychology: character, grit and research methods*. University of Pennsylvania.

Robeyns, I. (2003). Sen's Capability Approach and Gender Inequality: Selecting Relevant Capabilities. *Feminist Economics*, 9(2/3), 61–92. DOI: 10.1080/1354570022000078024

Robinson, A. (n.d.). *What is hybrid learning? blended learning? understanding the models.* https://blog.prepscholar.com/what-is-hybrid-learning-blended-learning-models?webview_progress_bar=1&show_loading=0

Rodriguez, C., Florido, C., & Jacob, M. (2020). Circular economy contributions to the tourism sector: A critical literature review. *Sustainability (Basel)*, 12(11), 4338. DOI: 10.3390/su12114338

Romero, I. (2023, February 14). *AI, Gamification & Education.* https://www.linkedin.com/pulse/ai-gamification-education-iv%C3%A1n-romero?show_loading=0&webview_progress_bar=1

Rowley, J. (2012). Conducting research interviews. *Management Research Review*, 35(3/4), 260–271. DOI: 10.1108/01409171211210154

Rudan, E., Nižić, M. K., & Grdić, Z. Š. (2021). Effect of circular economy on the sustainability of cultural tourism (Croatia). *Ecology & Environment*, 76(1), 19–19.

Rush, A. J., Trivedi, M. H., Wisniewski, S. R., Nierenberg, A. A., Stewart, J. W., Warden, D., & Fava, M. (2006). Bupropion-SR, sertraline, or venlafaxine-XR after failure of SSRIs for depression. *The New England Journal of Medicine*, 354(12), 1231–1242. DOI: 10.1056/NEJMoa052963 PMID: 16554525

Sachs, J., Schmidt-Traub, G., Kroll, C., Lafortune, G., & Fuller, G. (2019). *Sustainable Development Report 2019: Transformations to Achieve the SDGs.* Bertelsmann Stiftung and Sustainable Development Solutions Network., DOI: 10.1017/9781108472026

Sahin, A. (2019). The role of interdisciplinary project-based learning in integrated STEM education. In STEM education 2.0 (pp. [page numbers]). https://doi.org/10.1163/9789004405400_006

Sahu, S. (2023, July 13). *Ethical Considerations for AI integration in corporate learning initiatives.* https://www.linkedin.com/pulse/ethical-considerations-ai-integration-corporate-sahu-he-him-his-

Samuel, A. K. (2021, September 9). *THE AI HIERARCHY OF NEEDS.* https://www.linkedin.com/pulse/ai-hierarchy-needs-ayo-kehinde-samuel

Sandeep, R. (2023). *K-12 Education Benefits from Digital Accessibility.* codemantra. https://codemantra.com/k-12-education-benefits-from-digital-accessibility/?webview_progress_bar=1&show_loading=0

Sanders, M. (2009). STEM, STEM education, STEMmania. *Technology Teacher*, 68(4), 20–26.

Santhi, M. V., & Malathi, R. (2024). Implementation of Activity-Based Learning in Classroom Teaching. Strength for Today and Bright Hope for Tomorrow Volume 24: 3 March 2024 ISSN 1930-2940, 23.

Saputra, J., & Prabowo, A. (2021). The Role of the School in Developing Student Development Tasks. *International Journal of Ethno Sciences and Education Research*, 1(4), 84–87. Advance online publication. DOI: 10.46336/ijeer.v1i4.244

Sari, Cita, D., Ali, A. H., Harun, M., Batre, N. M., Hanafi, M. S., Jaludin, Z. Y., Cittra Juniarni, Darodjat, Indria Nur, Ridha Harwan, & Iwan Kuswandi. (2023). Transformation of Artificial intelligence in Islamic Edu with Ulul Albab Value (Global Challenge Perespective). *Firdaus Journal*, 3(1), 1–9. DOI: 10.37134/firdaus.vol3.1.1.2023

Sarker, S., Ahuja, M., & Sahay, S. (2020). Blockchain technology and public-private partnerships: A framework for sustainable development. *Information Systems Journal*, 30(6), 889–915. DOI: 10.1111/isj.12261

Sarvaiya, D. (2024, May 9). *Augmented Reality (AR) In Education: Enhancing Learning Experiences through AR Technology*. Intelivita. https://www.intelivita.com/blog/augmented-reality-in-education/

Sauve, S., Bernard, S., & Sloan, P. (2016). Environmental sciences, sustainable development, and circular economy: Alternative concepts for trans-disciplinary research.

Scalise, K. (2007). Differentiated e-learning: five approaches through instructional technology. IJLT., 3. 169-182. DOI: 10.1504/IJLT.2007.014843

Scheyvens, R. (2020). Building back better? COVID-19, tourism, and the circular economy in Pacific small island developing states. *Development Studies Research*, 7(1), 276–290. DOI: 10.1080/21665095.2020.1822292

Schmidt-Traub, G. (2015). Investment needs to achieve the Sustainable Development Goals: Understanding the billions and trillions. SDSN Working Paper. Sustainable Development Solutions Network.

Schneider, A., Waldfogel, J., & McKinley, B. (2019). Data visualization tools for business decision-making. *Journal of Business Intelligence*, 11(3), 22–30.

School, O. G. (2024, January 22). *How gamification makes you love to learn*. graduate.me. https://graduate.me/en/blog/gamification?webview_progress_bar=1&show_loading=0

Schoolbox. (2024, January 19). *Continuous Feedback and Reporting with Schoolbox eLearning Tools.* https://schoolbox.education/feedback-and-reporting-elearning/?webview_progress_bar=1&show_loading=0

Schorr, B., Braig, M., Fritz, B., & Schütt, B. (2021). The global knowledge value chain on sustainability: Addressing fragmentations through international academic partnerships. *Sustainability (Basel)*, 13(17), 9930. DOI: 10.3390/su13179930

Schubert, F., Kandampully, J., Solnet, D., & Kralj, A. (2010). Exploring consumer perceptions of green restaurants in the US. *Tourism and Hospitality Research*, 10(4), 286–300. DOI: 10.1057/thr.2010.17

Schwab, K. (2016). The Fourth Industrial Revolution. World Economic Forum.

Schwab, K. (2017). *The Fourth Industrial Revolution.* Crown Business.

Scratch. (n.d.). Coding and robotics platforms for STEM. Retrieved September 14, 2024, from https://scratch.mit.edu

Şeker, F., & Aydınlı, B. (2021). Education and competencies for sustainable development from the perspective of science teachers. *E-Caucasian Journal of Educational Research*, 8(3), 460–479. DOI: 10.30900/kafkasegt.964116

Self-Determination Theory in Gamification | Gamification in Business Class notes | Fiveable. (n.d.). https://library.fiveable.me/gamification-in-business/unit-3/self-determination-theory-gamification/study-guide/oCoyee6Xr1qyIj9Y?show_loading=0&webview_progress_bar=1

Sellberg, C., Nazari, Z., & Solberg, M. (2024). Virtual laboratories in STEM higher education: A scoping review. *Nordic Journal of Systematic Reviews in Education*, 2, 58–75.

Sen, A. (1974). Informational Bases of Alternative Welfare Approaches: Aggregation and Income Distribution. *Journal of Public Economics*, 3(4), 387–403. DOI: 10.1016/0047-2727(74)90006-1

Serna, J. M., & Chaparro, T. S. (2021). Systemic Collaborative Platforms: Accelerating Sustainable Development Goals Transitions through Multi-Stakeholder Convening Arrangements (Doctoral dissertation, Universidad Politécnica de Madrid).

Shaheen, A. (2023, February 22). *The Benefits of Online Learning: Exploring the flexibility and accessibility of E-Learning and distance education.* https://www.linkedin.com/pulse/benefits-online-learning-exploring-flexibility-distance-shaheen?show_loading=0&webview_progress_bar=1

Shende, P. (2023, August 17). *E-learning Market Size, share, Growth, Trends Analysis, growth Potential & Forecast, 2022–2030*. Medium. https://medium.com/@poonam.shende23/e-learning-market-size-share-growth-trends-analysis-growth-potential-forecast-2022-2030-d4d5c3ee11b7

Shiel, C., Smith, N., & Cantarello, E. (2020). *Aligning campus strategy with the SDGs: An institutional case study*. In W. Leal Filho, A. L. Salvia, R. W. Pretorius, L. L. Brandli, E. DOI: 10.1007/978-3-030-15604-6_2

Sileyew, K. J. (2020). Research design and methodology. In *IntechOpen eBooks*. https://doi.org/DOI: 10.5772/intechopen.85731

Simon Fraser University. (2023). *Learning Spaces*. Retrieved from Retrieved from https://www.sfu.ca/students/myclassroom

Sindhya, K. PhD. (2023, May 15). *Maximizing productivity and potential: Applying Maslow's hierarchy of needs to AI in business*. https://www.linkedin.com/pulse/maximizing-productivity-potential-applying-maslows-ai-sindhya-phd?webview_progress_bar=1&show_loading=0

Singapore, T. M. (2021, February 5). *The benefits of structured teaching. Therapy Masters*. https://www.therapy-masters.com/post/the-benefits-of-structured-teaching?show_loading=0&webview_progress_bar=1

Sison, M. (2019). Evaluation of Student Affairs and Services Programs: A Tool for Quality Improvement. *International Journal of Education and Research.*

Skidos. (2023, July 20). *The Future of Educational Gaming: How AI & Gamification Revolutionize learning*. Medium. https://medium.com/@skidos2021/the-future-of-educational-gaming-how-ai-gamification-revolutionize-learning-40b0d674d1ce

SkillShare Online Classes | Start Learning Today. (n.d.). Skillshare. https://www.skillshare.com/en/join/premium?show_loading=0&webview_progress_bar=1

Smartico.Ai. (2022, July 18). *How to use gamification to increase motivation*. https://www.linkedin.com/pulse/how-use-gamification-increase-motivation-smartico-ai

Smith, J. (2022). *Leveraging AI in e-learning for a human-centric approach*. Educational Technology Magazine.

Soini, K., Jurgilevich, A., Pietikäinen, J., & Korhonen-Kurki, K. (2018). Universities responding to the call for sustainability: A typology of sustainability centres. *Journal of Cleaner Production*, 170, 1423–1432. DOI: 10.1016/j.jclepro.2017.08.228

Sorensen, F., & Bærenholdt, J. O. (2020). Tourist practices in the circular economy. *Annals of Tourism Research*, 85, 103027. DOI: 10.1016/j.annals.2020.103027

Sorin, F., & Sivarajah, U. (2021). Exploring circular economy in the hospitality industry: Empirical evidence from Scandinavian hotel operators. *Scandinavian Journal of Hospitality and Tourism*, 21(3), 265–285. DOI: 10.1080/15022250.2021.1921021

Srisawasdi, N. (2012). Fostering pre-service STEM teachers' technological pedagogical content knowledge: A lesson learned from case-based learning approach. *Journal of The Korean Association for Science Education*, 32(8), 1356–1370. https://doi.org/10.14697/jkase.2012.32.8.1356

Staff, C. (2024, May 23). *What is Coursera? Coursera.* https://www.coursera.org/articles/what-is-coursera?webview_progress_bar=1&show_loading=0

Staff, K. (2024, September 10). *Teacher-led reforms have a big advantage — Teachers.* Kappan Online. https://kappanonline.org/stanulis-cooper-dear-teacher-led-reforms-big-advantage/?webview_progress_bar=1&show_loading=0

Staff, T. (2022, January 20*). A useful framework for transparency in education.* TeachThought. https://www.teachthought.com/education/transparency-in-education/?show_loading=0&webview_progress_bar=1

Stahel, W. R. (2013). Policy for material efficiency—Sustainable taxation as a departure from the throwaway society. *Philosophical Transactions of the Royal Society A: Mathematical, Physical and Engineering Sciences, 371*(1986), 20110567.

Stanford University. (2023). *Learning Spaces*. Retrieved from https://news.stanford.edu/stories/2023/05/furniture-tech-upgrades-transforming-classrooms-learning

Stanney, K. M., & Cohn, J. V. (2009). Virtual environments. In Human-computer interaction (pp. 311–328).

Starr-Glass, D. (2022). *Learning Spaces: Design and Pedagogy*. Routledge.

STEMpedia. (n.d.). STEMpedia: Innovating STEM education through coding and robotics. Retrieved September 14, 2024, from https://thestempedia.com

Sterman, J. D. (2000). *Business dynamics: Systems thinking and modeling for a complex world*. McGraw-Hill.

Stracqualursi, L., & Agati, P. (2024). Twitter users perceptions of AI-based e-learning technologies. *Scientific Reports*, 14, 5927. DOI: 10.1038/s41598-024-56284-y

Su, B., Heshmati, A., Geng, Y., & Yu, X. (2013). A review of the circular economy in China: Moving from rhetoric to implementation. *Journal of Cleaner Production*, 42, 215–227. DOI: 10.1016/j.jclepro.2012.11.020

Sulistina, O., Rahayu, S., & Dasna, I. W., & Yahmin. (2021). The influence of guided inquiry-based learning using socio-scientific issues on environmental awareness of pre-service chemistry teachers. In *7th International Conference on Research, Implementation, and Education of Mathematics and Sciences (ICRIEMS 2020)*, Yogyakarta, Indonesia. https://doi.org/DOI: 10.2991/assehr.k.210305.036

Sultana, S. A., Rahman, M. T. M., Indhumathi, M., Keerthana, J., Kannadasan, & Nair, D. P. 2021. Student Welfare Services in Higher Educational Institution Hei in Puducherry:Study, A. (●●●).. . *Global Journal for Research Analysis*, 10(05). Advance online publication. DOI: 10.36106/gjra/0609142

Sundararajan, A. (2016). *The sharing economy: The end of employment and the rise of crowd-based capitalism*. MIT Press.

Superstore, V. (2023, July 12). *Transforming Education with Virtual Reality (VR): Unlocking a New Era of Immersive Learning*. Medium. https://medium.com/@TheVRSuperstore/transforming-education-with-virtual-reality-vr-unlocking-a-new-era-of-immersive-learning-86a8c499a252

Susilowati, T., Dacholfany, M.I., Aminin, S., Ikhwan, A., Nasir, B.M., Huda, M., Prasetyo, A., Maseleno, A., Satria, F., Hartati, S., and Wulandari. (2018). Getting parents involved in child's school: using attendance application system based on SMS gateway. International Journal of Engineering and Technology. 7(2.27), 167-174.

Susilowati, T., Teh, K.S.M., Nasir, B.M., Don, A.G., Huda, M., Hensafitri, T., Maseleno, A., Oktafianto, and Irawan, D. (2018). Learning application of Lampung language based on multimedia software. International Journal of Engineering and Technology. 7(2.27), 175-181.

Swaby, G. (2018, January 23). *Openness and transparency in online Education - Gordon Swaby - Medium*. Medium. https://medium.com/@gordonswaby/openness-and-transparency-in-online-education-267fd1bba1b6?show_loading=0&webview_progress_bar=1

Sylvester, T. (2023, May 22). *Mastering Interactive eLearning Design: Step-by-Step Guide*. Inventio Learning Designs, LLC. https://inventiolearningdesigns.com/interactive-elearning-design/?show_loading=0&webview_progress_bar=1

Syofiarti, S., Saputra, R., Lahmi, A., & Rahmi, R. 2021). The Use of Audiovisual Media in Learning and Its Impact on Learning Outcomes of Islamic Cultural History at Madrasah Tsanawiyah Negeri 4 Pasaman. Firdaus Journal, 1(1), 36–44. (. https://doi.org/DOI: 10.37134/firdaus.vol1.1.4.2021

Systementcorp. (2023, July 3). *The Psychology of Gamification: Understanding Why it works - Eye of Unity Foundation.* Eye Of Unity Foundation. https://eyeofunity.com/the-psychology-of-gamification-understanding-why-it-works/?webview_progress_bar=1&show_loading=0

Taha, H., Suppiah, V., Khoo, Y. Y., Yahaya, A., Lee, T. T., & Muhamad Damanhuri, M. I. (2019). Impact of student-initiated green chemistry experiments on their knowledge, awareness and practices of environmental sustainability. *Journal of Physics: Conference Series*, 1156, 012022. DOI: 10.1088/1742-6596/1156/1/012022

Tamm, S. (2023, July 11). *10 Major Advantages of E-Learning.* E-Student. https://e-student.org/advantages-of-e-learning/?webview_progress_bar=1&show_loading=0

Tan, A. A., Huda, M., Rohim, M. A., Hassan, T. R. R., & Ismail, A. (2024). Chat GPT in Supporting Education Instruction Sector: An Empirical Literature Review. In Proceedings of Ninth International Congress on Information and Communication Technology. ICICT 2024. Lecture Notes in Networks and Systems. Springer, Singapore.

Tapscott, D., & Tapscott, A. (2016). *Blockchain revolution: How the technology behind Bitcoin is changing money, business, and the world.* Penguin Books.

Tapscott, D., & Tapscott, A. (2016). *Blockchain revolution: How the technology behind bitcoin is changing money, business, and the world.* Penguin Random House.

Taylor, L., & Floridi, L. (2019). Regulating in an algorithmic world: Policy and the public sector. *Philosophy & Technology*, 32(1), 1–14. DOI: 10.1007/s13347-018-0338-9

Teacher-Led approach. (n.d.). *Multiple Means of Instruction: All-inclusive Learning.* http://multiplemeansofinstruction.weebly.com/teacher-led-approach.html?webview_progress_bar=1&show_loading=0

Team, G. (n.d.). *What is hybrid learning?* GoGuardian. https://www.goguardian.com/blog/what-is-hybrid-learning?webview_progress_bar=1&show_loading=0

Team, W. (2024, January 4). *8 Best adaptive learning platforms in 2024.* The Change Management Blog. https://change.walkme.com/adaptive-learning-platforms/

Tec, B. (2021, January 21). *5 Practical ways of using AR and VR in eLearning.* https://www.linkedin.com/pulse/5-practical-ways-using-ar-vr-elearning-bse-tec

Technavio. (2024, September 12). *E-learning market Forecast & Growth Analysis.* Technavio, https://analysis.technavio.org, All Right Reserved 2024. https://analysis.technavio.org/e-learning-industry-analysis-research?webview_progress_bar=1&show_loading=0

Technological Institute of the Philippines. (2020). *Innovating for change: The TIP innovation hub for micro-entrepreneurs.* TIP Manila.

Technologies, T. (n.d.). *Twenty benefits of Digital Learning.* https://www.trigyn.com/insights/20-benefits-digital-learning?webview_progress_bar=1&show_loading=0

Teksöz, G. (2016). Learning from the past: Education for sustainable development. *Boğaziçi University Education Journal*, 31(2), 73–97.

Terada, Y. (2020, May 4). A powerful model for understanding good tech integration. Edutopia. https://www.edutopia.org/article/powerful-model-understanding-good-tech-integration

The advantages of social and collaborative e-Learning. (n.d.). https://traineasy.net/blog/63/the-advantages-of-social-and-collaborative-e-learning?webview_progress_bar=1&show_loading=0

The Benefits of Structured Instruction in Education. (2023). https://resources.industrydive.com/the-benefits-of-structured-instruction-in-education?webview_progress_bar=1&show_loading=0

The Global Goals for Sustainable Development. (2024). *Quality education: Ensure inclusive and equitable quality education and promote lifelong learning opportunities for all.* https://www.kureselamaclar.org/en/global-goals/quality-education/

The Impact of Gamification on Learning: Real-World Applications. (n.d.). https://www.idolcourses.com/blog/gamificationandelearning?show_loading=0&webview_progress_bar=1

The story of Action Mapping and its creation by Cathy Moore. (n.d.). Training Design - Cathy Moore. https://blog.cathy-moore.com/action-mapping-creation-by-cathy-moore/?show_loading=0&webview_progress_bar=1

Thomas, J. W. (2000). *A review of research on project-based learning.* Autodesk Foundation.

Tiwary, A. V. (2020, February 4). *5 Reasons Why Online Education is More Cost Effective.* https://www.linkedin.com/pulse/5-reasons-why-online-education-more-cost-effective-tiwary?webview_progress_bar=1&show_loading=0

Tomczak, A., & Brem, A. (2013). A Conceptualized Investment Model of Crowdfunding. *Venture Capital*, 15(4), 335–359. DOI: 10.1080/13691066.2013.847614

Tondello, G. (2016, April 26). *Introduction to Gamification in Human-Computer Interaction*. Gameful Bits. https://www.gamefulbits.com/2016/04/26/an-introduction-to-gamification-in-human-computer-interaction/?show_loading=0&webview_progress_bar=1

Top 10 Benefits of E-Learning For Students and Educators. (n.d.). https://snatika.com/single-blog/top-10-benefits-of-e-learning-for-students-and-educators?webview_progress_bar=1&show_loading=0

Top e-learning courses - Learn e-learning online. (n.d.). Coursera. https://www.coursera.org/courses?query=e-learning&webview_progress_bar=1&show_loading=0

Top Five Factors to consider when choosing a learning platform. (2019) https://moodle.com/news/top-five-factors-to-consider-when-choosing-a-learning-platform/?show_loading=0&webview_progress_bar=1

Top Online+education Courses - Learn Online+education Online. (n.d.). Coursera. https://www.coursera.org/courses?query=online%2Beducation&show_loading=0&webview_progress_bar=1

Toxigon. (2024, September 8). *How to choose the best online learning platform in 2024*. Toxigon. https://toxigon.com/how-to-choose-online-learning-platform?webview_progress_bar=1&show_loading=0

Toyama, K. (2011). Technology as amplifier in international development. *Proceedings of the 2011 iConference*, 75-82. https://doi.org/DOI: 10.1145/1940761.1940772

TrainBeyond. (2024, June 20). *Enhancing Learning with Virtual Reality Simulation Training*. TrainBeyond. https://www.trainbeyond.com/enhancing-learning-with-virtual-reality-simulation-training/

Transparent Teaching. (2022, May 25). Teach Online | Miami University. https://sites.miamioh.edu/teach-online/what-is-transparent-teaching/?webview_progress_bar=1&show_loading=0

Triandis, H. C. (1995). A theoretical framework for the study of diversity. In *SAGE Publications, Inc. eBooks* (pp. 11–36). DOI: 10.4135/9781452243405.n2

Triplett, W. J. (2023). Impact of technology integration in STEM education. *Cybersecurity and Innovation Technology Journal*, 1(1), 16–22. https://doi.org/10.52889/citj.v1i1.295

Trivedi, M. H., Rush, A. J., Wisniewski, S. R., Nierenberg, A. A., Warden, D., Ritz, L., & Howland, R. H. (2006). Evaluation of outcomes with citalopram for depression using measurement-based care in STAR*D: Implications for clinical practice. *The American Journal of Psychiatry*, 163(1), 28–40. DOI: 10.1176/appi.ajp.163.1.28 PMID: 16390886

Tseng, K., Chang, C., Lou, S., & Chen, W. (2013). Attitudes towards science, technology, engineering and mathematics (STEM) in a project-based learning (PjBL) environment. *International Journal of Technology and Design Education*, 23(1), 87–102.

Tse, T., & Tse, K. (2019). Applying circular economy and system thinking in tourism management: Concepts and perspectives. *Tourism Review*, 74(5), 994–1007. DOI: 10.1108/TR-04-2018-0062

Turnitin. (n.d.). *Turnitin affirms guiding principles for responsible AI integration into education technologies*. https://www.turnitin.com/press/launch-responsible-ai-in-education

Twenge, J. M., & Campbell, W. K. (2018). Associations between screen time and lower psychological well-being among children and adolescents: Evidence from a population-based study. *Preventive Medicine Reports*, 12, 271–283. DOI: 10.1016/j.pmedr.2018.10.003 PMID: 30406005

Twum-Ampofo, E. &O sei-Owusu, B. Students' academic performance as mediated by students' academic ambition and effort in the public senior high schools in Ashanti Mampong Municipality of Ghana. *Selected Topics in Humanities and Social Sciences*. DOI: 10.9734/bpi/sthss/v7/13406D

Ufua, D. E., Emielu, E. T., Olujobi, O. J., Lakhani, F., Borishade, T. T., Ibidunni, A. S., & Osabuohien, E. S. (2021). Digital transformation: A conceptual framing for attaining Sustainable Development Goals 4 and 9 in Nigeria. *Journal of Management & Organization*, 27(5), 836–849. DOI: 10.1017/jmo.2021.45

UNESCO. (2019). *ICT in Education: A Critical Literature Review and Its Implications*. UNESCO.

UNESCO. (United Nations Educational, Scientific and Cultural Organization). (2019). *Global Education Monitoring Report 2019: Learning to Change the World*. UNESCO.\

UNESCO. (United Nations Educational, Scientific and Cultural Organization). (2020). *Reimagining Education: A Global Dialogue*. UNESCO.

United Nations Department of Economic and Social Affairs. (2024). *Do you know all 17 sustainable development goals?* https://www.un.org/sustainabledevelopment/sustainable-development-goals/

United Nations Development Programme. (2018). Sustainable development goals in the Philippines: A progress report. https://www.ph.undp.org

United Nations Türkiye. (2024). *How does the UN support sustainable development goals in Turkiye?* https://turkiye.un.org/tr/sdgs

United Nations World Tourism Organization (UNWTO). (2011). *Tourism toward 2030.* https://www.unwto.org/archive/global/press-release/2011-10-11/international-tourists-hit-18-billion2030

United Nations. (2015). *Transforming our world: The 2030 agenda for sustainable development (Report).* United Nations. https://undocs.org/A/RES/70/1

United Nations. (2015). Transforming our world: The 2030 Agenda for Sustainable Development. Retrieved from https://sdgs.un.org/2030agenda

United States Artificial Intelligence Institute. (USAII®). (n.d.). *Transforming Online Learning: Boost Learner Engagement with AI-Powered Gamification.* https://www.usaii.org/ai-insights/transforming-online-learning-boost-learner-engagement-with-ai-powered-gamification. https://www.usaii.org/ai-insights/transforming-online-learning-boost-learner-engagement-with-ai-powered-gamification

University of Cape Town's Bertha Centre for Social Innovation and Entrepreneurship. (2021). *Social innovation as a catalyst for poverty alleviation.* Bertha Centre Publications.

University of Dayton. (2023). *Learning Spaces.* Retrieved from https://ecommons.udayton.edu/learnteach_forum/2023/

University of Michigan. (2023). *Learning Spaces.* Retrieved from https://lsa.umich.edu/technology-services/news-events/all-news/teaching-tip-of-the-week/learning-spaces-affect-student-engagement.html

University of the Philippines Los Baños. (2021). *Empowering rural communities through sustainable agriculture: UPLB initiatives.* UPLB Extension Office Publications.

UNWTO. (2018). *European Union tourism trends.* UNWTO.

UNWTO. (2018). *Tourism for development – Volume II: Good practices.*

Uralovich, K. S., Toshmamatovich, T. U., Kubayevich, K. F., Sapaev, I. B., Saylaubaevna, S. S., Beknazarova, Z. F., & Khurramov, A. (2023). A primary factor in sustainable development and environmental sustainability is environmental education. *Caspian Journal of Environmental Sciences*, 21, 965–975.

Use AI and gamification to craft captivating eLearning : Articles | The Learning Guild. (n.d.). Copyright 2024 the Learning Guild. Copyright 2024: Powered by Cyclone Enterprise: Content Management Solutions and Dynamic Publishing System Developed by Cyclone Interactive Multimedia Group, Inc. http://www.cycloneinteractive.com, Powered by Cyclone and Powered by Cyclone Enterprise. Portional ColdFusion Programming Provided by Finial Software, Inc. www.finial.com. https://www.learningguild.com/articles/use-ai-and-gamification-to-craft-captivating-elearning/

Van Dijk, J. (2020). The digital divide: A research review of the digital gap in the information society. *Annual Review of Sociology*, 46(1), 113–133. DOI: 10.1146/annurev-soc-121919-054532

Vaughan, C., Gack, J., Solorazano, H., & Ray, R. (2003). The effect of environmental education on school children, their parents, and community members: A study of intergenerational and intercommunity learning. *The Journal of Environmental Education*, 34(3), 12–21. DOI: 10.1080/00958960309603489

Velora Studios, L. L. C. https://velora.com. (n.d.). *Top 10 things to look for when choosing the perfect online course platform*. Heights Platform. https://www.heightsplatform.com/blog/top-10-things-to-look-for-when-choosing-the-perfect-online-course-platform?show_loading=0&webview_progress_bar=1

Verda, P. (2024, August 8). *Find your target audience for education: a quick 6-Step guide*. MedCerts. https://medcerts.com/blog/find-your-target-audience-for-education-a-quick-6-step-guide?webview_progress_bar=1&show_loading=0

Vernier Science Education. (n.d.). Five research-based best practices for STEM education. Retrieved September 15, 2024, from https://www.vernier.com/blog/five-research-based-best-practices-for-stem-education/

Virtual Reality for Education: Experiential Learning made Possible – Queppelin. (2023, May 4). https://www.queppelin.com/virtual-reality-for-education-experiential-learning-made-possible/

Virtual Reality in Training: The Power of Immersive Simulations (n.d.) https://www.virtusstudios.com/post/vr-in-training-the-power-of-immersive-simulations?webview_progress_bar=1&show_loading=0

Virtual reality: could it be the next big tool for education? (2024, September 10). World Economic Forum. https://www.weforum.org/agenda/2021/05/virtual-reality-simulators-develop-students-skills-education-training?webview_progress_bar=1&show_loading=0

Voogt, J., & Roblin, N. P. (2010). 21st century skills discussion paper. Partnership for 21st Century Skills.

VR and AR for eLearning: Interview with Volker Kunze. (2024, September 4). HQSoftware. https://hqsoftwarelab.com/blog/augmented-and-virtual-reality/ar-in-elearning-interview/?show_loading=0&webview_progress_bar=1

Vygotsky, L. S. (1978). *Mind in society.* Harvard University Press.

Wahid, A., Huda, M., Asrori, A., Abidin, R., Puspitasari, I., Hidayat, M. C., . . . Anwar, S. (2024). Digital technology for indigenous people's knowledge acquisition process: insights from empirical literature analysis. In *International Conference on Information and Communication Technology for Competitive Strategies* (pp. 41-57). Singapore: Springer Nature Singapore. DOI: 10.1007/978-981-97-1260-1_5

Wahid, A., Huda, M., Rohim, M. A., Ali, A. H., Kaspin, K. G., Fiqiyah, M., & Jima'ain, M. T. A. (2024b). Augmented Reality Model in Supporting Instruction Process: A Critical Review. In Proceedings of Ninth International Congress on Information and Communication Technology. ICICT 2024. Lecture Notes in Networks and Systems. Springer, Singapore. DOI: 10.1007/978-981-97-3305-7_6

Wairura, F. (2023, January 5). *Creating Interactive and Immersive Learning with Augmented Reality: Case Studies and Examples.* Medium. https://medium.com/@wairuraf/creating-interactive-and-immersive-learning-with-augmented-reality-case-studies-and-examples-48dde1a754a9

Walsh, C. G., Ribeiro, J. D., & Franklin, J. C. (2018). Predicting suicide attempts in adolescents with machine learning: A longitudinal study. *JAMA Psychiatry*, 75(11), 1152–1160. DOI: 10.1001/jamapsychiatry.2018.1771

Wang, F., Kinzie, M. B., McGuire, P., & Pan, E. (2010). Applying technology to inquiry-based learning in early childhood education. *Early Childhood Education Journal*, 37(5), 381–389. https://doi.org/10.1007/s10643-009-0364-6

Wang, H. H., Charoenmuang, M., & Knobloch, N. A.. (2020). Defining interdisciplinary collaboration based on high school teachers' beliefs and practices of STEM integration using a complex designed system. *International Journal of STEM Education*, 7(1), 3. https://doi.org/10.1186/s40594-019-0201-4

Wang, M., Liu, R., Zhang, C., & Tang, Z. (2021). Daran robot: A reconfigurable, powerful, and affordable robotic platform for STEM education. *STEM Education*, 1(4), 299–308. https://doi.org/10.3934/steme.2021019

Wang, S., Li, Q., & Khaskheli, M. B. (2024). Management Economic Systems and Governance to Reduce Potential Risks in Digital Silk Road Investments: Legal Cooperation between Hainan Free Trade Port and Ethiopia. *Systems*, 12(8), 305. DOI: 10.3390/systems12080305

Webmaster. (2018, August 16). *Training with Virtual Reality and Simulations*. VR-Sim. https://vrsim.com/simulation-virtual-reality-vr-training-infographic/?webview_progress_bar=1&show_loading=0%20https://vrsim.com/simulation-virtual-reality-vr-training-infographic/?webview_progress_bar=1&show_loading=0

Webster, K. (2000). *Environmental management in the hospitality industry: A guide for students and managers.*

What are some of the benefits and drawbacks of using AI to create adaptive game mechanics? (2024, July 2). www.linkedin.com. https://www.linkedin.com/advice/0/what-some-benefits-drawbacks-using-ai-create-adaptive

What are some tools or platforms that support adaptive learning in online learning? (2024, August 23). www.linkedin.com. https://www.linkedin.com/advice/1/what-some-tools-platforms-support-adaptive-learning?webview_progress_bar=1&show_loading=0

What are the benefits and challenges of social and collaborative learning in e-learning? (2023, May 17). www.linkedin.com. https://www.linkedin.com/advice/0/what-benefits-challenges-social-collaborative?webview_progress_bar=1&show_loading=0

What are the benefits and drawbacks of using AI in gaming? | Artificial Intelligence Hub. (2024, March 17). https://aicitta.com/posts/what-are-the-benefits-and-drawbacks-of-using-ai-in-gaming/?webview_progress_bar=1&show_loading=0

What are the key factors to consider when choosing a training platform or tool? (2023, March 15). www.linkedin.com. https://www.linkedin.com/advice/0/what-key-factors-consider-when-choosing-training?show_loading=0&webview_progress_bar=1

What is Hybrid Learning? (n.d.). Continu. https://www.continu.com/elearning-glossary/hybrid-learning?webview_progress_bar=1&show_loading=0

Whitfield, P. (2024, March 20). *The Psychology of Gamification*. Beyond Thought International. https://beyondthoughtinternational.com/the-psychology-of-gamification/?webview_progress_bar=1&show_loading=0

Wilkinson, M. (2020). Best practices in STEM education. Retrieved from https://www.utc.edu/sites/default/files/2020-12/wilkinsonm2powerpoint.pdf

Willoughby-Petit, P. (2023, December 19). *Activity-based learning for software.* Learning Lab LMS LXP. https://www.thelearning-lab.com/blog-elearning-platform/activity-learning-software?webview_progress_bar=1&show_loading=0

Willoughby-Petit, P. (2023a, May 25). *Peer-To-Peer Learning — Learning Lab LMS LXP.* Learning Lab LMS LXP. https://www.thelearning-lab.com/blog-elearning-platform/peer-to-peer-learning?webview_progress_bar=1&show_loading=0

Wirtz, B. W., Weyerer, J. C., & Schichtel, F. T. (2019). An Integrated Approach to Open Government: An Analysis of the State of Open Government in Europe. *Public Administration Review*, 79(4), 488–502. DOI: 10.1111/puar.12921

Witjes, S., & Lozano, R. (2016). Towards a more circular economy: Proposing a framework linking sustainable public procurement and sustainable business models. *Resources, Conservation and Recycling*, 112, 37–44. DOI: 10.1016/j.resconrec.2016.04.015

Wong, C. (2024, July 17). *Chatbots for Learning: Ways to Gamify Chat-Based Learning Environments.* https://articles.noodlefactory.ai/chatbots-for-learning-ways-to-gamify-chat-based-learning-environments

Wong, C. W., Lai, K. H., Shang, K. C., Lu, C. S., & Leung, T. K. P. (2012). Green operations and the moderating role of environmental management capability of suppliers on manufacturing firm performance. *International Journal of Production Economics*, 140(1), 283–294. DOI: 10.1016/j.ijpe.2011.08.031

Wong, C. W., Wong, C. Y., & Boon-itt, S. (2013). Green service practices: Performance implications and the role of environmental management systems. *Service Science*, 5(1), 69–84. DOI: 10.1287/serv.1120.0037

World Bank. (2018). *Higher education and poverty reduction: Evidence from low-income countries.* World Bank.

World Health Organization. (2016). Adolescent mental health: Fact sheet. World Health Organization. https://www.who.int/news-room/fact-sheets/detail/adolescent-mental-health

World Health Organization. (2021). *The social determinants of health and poverty reduction in Asia: An overview.* World Health Organization Publications.

World Tourism Organization. (2018). *Tourism for development.* UNWTO.

World Travel and Tourism Council. (2023). Economic Impact Reports. Retrieved from https://wttc.org/Research/Economic-Impact

Writer, E. G. (2018, May 17). *How to enable online global collaboration in your learning environment*. Medium. https://medium.com/@edmodo_staff/how-to-enable-online-global-collaboration-in-your-learning-environment-8725e30581e7

Wu, H.-K. (2010). Modeling a complex system: Using novice-expert analysis for developing an effective technology-enhanced learning environment. *International Journal of Science Education*, 32(2), 195–219.

Wulandari, Aminin, S., Dacholfany, M.I., Mujib, A., Huda, M., Nasir, B.M., Maseleno, A., Sundari, E., Fauzi, and Masrur, M. (2018). Design of library application system. International Journal of Engineering and Technology. 7(2.27), 199-204.

Yahya, S. F., & Othman, M. A. (2022). Penggunaan video dalam Pengajaran dan Pembelajaran Pendidikan Moral Tingkatan 2. *Firdaus Journal*, 2(2), 94–105. DOI: 10.37134/firdaus.vol2.2.10.2022

Yang, D., & Baldwin, S. J. (2020). Using technology to support student learning in an integrated STEM learning environment. [IJTES]. *International Journal of Technology in Education and Science*, 4(1), 1–11.

Yap, J., & Ravago, M.-L. V. (2021). *Economics and poverty in the Philippines: Policy, research, and practice*. University of the Philippines Press.

Yayla, Z., Çavaş, B., Çavaş, L., & Türkoğuz, S. (2011). Klasik kimya deneyleri. In Chemistry, R. S. (Ed.), *Classic Chemistry Experiments: RSC* (pp. 105–108, 189–191). Palme Yayıncılık.

Yee, C. (2023b, November 15). *Gamification and operant conditioning*. Yu-kai Chou. https://yukaichou.com/gamification-study/gamification-and-operant-conditioning/?show_loading=0&webview_progress_bar=1

Yie, D. L., Sanmugam, M., Yahaya, W. J. W., & Khlaif, Z. N. (2024). *The impact of gamification depth on higher educational students' intrinsic motivation and performance levels*. Higher Education for the Future., DOI: 10.1177/23476311241248994

Yılmaz, O. (2019). The necessity of environmental education at primary school level in Türkiye within the scope of sustainable development [Master's thesis, Ankara Hacı Bayram Veli University].

Yogyata, & Yogyata. (2024, July 23). *How eLearning Saves More Time than ILT? [5 Proven Ways Explained]*. https://blog.commlabindia.com/elearning-design/elearning-time-saving-against-ilt?show_loading=0&webview_progress_bar=1

Young, N. (2024, March 22). *Structured Learning: Transforming education for behavioral challenges*. Teachfloor. https://www.teachfloor.com/elearning-glossary/structured-learning?webview_progress_bar=1&show_loading=0

Yousefi, S., & Tosarkani, B. M. (2023). Exploring the role of blockchain technology in improving sustainable supply chain performance: A system-analysis-based approach. *IEEE Transactions on Engineering Management*.

Yuan, X., Yu, L., Wu, H., (2021). Awareness of Sustainable Development Goals among Students from a Chinese Senior High School. Educ. Sci. 11, 458. *Special Issue Including Sustainable Development Goals (SDGs) Transversally in Education* DOI: 10.3390/educsci11090458

Zahid, R. (2023, November 2). *AI-Powered Chatbots in Technical Support*. Tanbits. https://tanbits.com/blog/ai-powered-chatbots-in-technical-support/?show_loading=0&webview_progress_bar=1

Zainuri, A., & Huda, M. (2023). Empowering Cooperative Teamwork for Community Service Sustainability: Insights from Service Learning. *Sustainability (Basel)*, 15(5), 4551. DOI: 10.3390/su15054551

Zamora-Polo, F., Sanchez-martin, J., Corrales-Serrano, M., & Espejo-Antunez, L. (2019). What Do University Students Now About Sustainable Development Goals? A Realistic Approach to the Reception of this UN Program amongst the Youth Population. *Sustainability (Basel)*, 11(13), 3533–3552. DOI: 10.3390/su11133533

Zamri, F. A., Muhamad, N., & Huda, M. (2023). Information and communication technology skills for instruction performance: beliefs and experiences from public school educators. In *Proceedings of the Computational Methods in Systems and Software* (pp. 34-40). Cham: Springer Nature Switzerland.

Zamri, F. A., Muhamad, N., Huda, M., & Hashim, A. (2024). Social media adoption for digital learning innovation: insights into building learning support. In *International Conference on Information and Communication Technology for Competitive Strategies* (pp. 407-425). Singapore: Springer Nature Singapore. DOI: 10.1007/978-981-97-0744-7_34

Zhai, X. (2021). Practices and theories: How can machine learning assist in innovative assessment practices in science education. *Journal of Science Education and Technology*, 30(2), 1–11.

Zhai, X., Zhang, M., Li, M., & Zhang, X. (2019). Understanding the relationship between levels of mobile technology use in high school physics classrooms and the learning outcome. *British Journal of Educational Technology*, 50(2), 750–766.

Zhang, T., Shaikh, Z. A., Yumashev, A. V., & Chłąd, M. (2020). Applied model of e-learning in the framework of education for sustainable development. *Sustainability (Basel)*, 12(16), 6420. DOI: 10.3390/su12166420

Zhang, W., Wang, Y., Yang, L., & Wang, C. (2020). Suspending classes without stopping learning: China's education emergency management policy in the COVID-19 outbreak. *Journal of Risk and Financial Management*, 13(3), 55. DOI: 10.3390/jrfm13030055

Zhu, K., Dong, S., Xu, S. X., & Kraemer, K. L. (2006). Innovation diffusion in global contexts: Determinants of post-adoption digital transformation of European companies. *European Journal of Information Systems*, 15(6), 601–616. DOI: 10.1057/palgrave.ejis.3000650

Zorpas, A. A., Navarro-Pedreno, J., Panagiotakis, I., & Dermatas, D. (2023). Steps forward to adopt a circular economy strategy by the tourism industry. *Waste Management Research: The Journal for a Sustainable Circular Economy*.

Zuboff, S. (2019). *The age of surveillance capitalism: The fight for a human future at the new frontier of power*. Public Affairs.

About the Contributors

Froilan Mobo is a Doctor of Public Administration graduate from the Urdaneta City University Class of 2016 and a graduate of the 2nd Doctorate Degree (Ph.D.) in Development Education program at the Central Luzon State University, Nueva Ecija, Philippines, Class of 2022. On March 11, 2024, Dr. Mobo was accredited and reclassified by the Commission on Higher Education (CHED) to the position of Professor II in the Philippine Merchant Marine Academy (PMMA), and this allowed him to work with different international research institutions, such as the Director and Research Consultant of the IKSAD Research Institute, Turkey. At present, he is in the process of finishing his 3rd master's degree, leading to social studies education at Bicol University. Recently, Dr. Mobo passed Batch 3—Certified Research Professional—and ranked in the top 5 in the National Examination and also passed the Certified Human Resource Associate (CHRA). He was appointed Editor-in-Chief of the International Journal of Multidisciplinary: Applied Business and Education Research, Malang, Indonesia, and appointed as a technical research evaluator by the Department of Science and Technology. He has published 107 research articles with 171 citations indexed in the Web of Science, Scopus, and ASEAN Citation Index.

***

Roldan Cabiles, a faculty member at Bicol University, Dr. Roldan C. Cabiles, holds the position of College Secretary and Planning Officer at the BU Graduate School. He likewise serves as the Program Adviser for the Master of Arts in English Education program offered via Open University. He earned his Doctor of Philosophy in Educational Foundations and MA in English Education from Bicol University Graduate School, Legazpi City, Philippines. He holds the academic rank of Assistant Professor II, having ascended from the rank of Instruction I at Bicol University.

Finally, he has provided guidance as an advisor for numerous research papers in undergraduate and advanced higher education.

Anjali Daisy is an assistant professor, Loyola Institute of Business Administration, Tamilnadu India. She holds a Ph.D. degree in the field of Emotional Intelligence. She assessed and developed an Emotional Competence Inventory for IT employees in Tamil Nadu as the outcome of her research work. She has done her MBA in PSG Institute of Management, Coimbatore. She secured University second position in B.Sc(Computer Science).She holds a Post Graduate Diploma in Labour Law and Administrative Law(PGDLL). She conducted EI training programs for diversified working professionals. She has published research papers in SCOPUS and SSCI indexed journals and wrote book chapters as well. She has presented papers at International conferences. She is also a reviewer in IGI Global. She has completed certification courses in the areas of Mind control, Competency Mapping, Strategic Performance Management, Psychology and Teaching in higher education offered by international premier institutes viz the University of Michigan, the University of Toronto, Yale University, and the University of Washington. She is able to incorporate global teaching-learning pedagogies in the courses she handles.

Zeynep Melike Güçlü is a chemistry teacher who is pursuing her master's degree in curriculum and instruction. Her areas of study are program development in education, argumentation and environmental education.

Jherwin P Hermosa, EdD, holds the academic rank of Assistant Professor 1 at the Laguna State Polytechnic University, San Pablo City Campus. He has also published books, poetry, and scientific articles in international circulations. He is currently pursuing a degree in Juris Doctor. His research interests are mostly social sciences, philosophy, and educational management.

Miftachul Huda is a researcher at Faculty of Human Sciences, Universiti Pendidikan Sultan Idris Malaysia. His research interest includes the field of educational studies: moral, Islamic and multicultural education, learning theory, adaptive teaching and learning technology. He has been experienced in working on research for more than five years. Contributing several works, he is currently the member of the advisory editorial board in some international journals. Traveling in some countries with scholarly intent makes him extensive experience on his research expertise in international trend and issues. Thus, he commits to contributing his knowledge to the benefit of society through professional and social activities.

Wes Harven Guillemer Maravilla has been an esteemed EFL/ESL language expert in Asia since 2019, bringing his expertise to diverse learners ranging from primary school students to adults. An advocate for the Communicative Language Approach and Project-Based Approach, Mr. Maravilla has dedicated his career to enhancing English language education. He holds a Master of Arts in Education, majoring in English Language Teaching from Chiang Kai Shek College in Manila, Philippines. Mr. Maravilla's research interests are vast and encompass technology and innovation, artificial intelligence, EFL/ESL methodologies, sustainable development goals, and specialized areas of English, including reading, oral expression, composition writing, and effective listening. His scholarly contributions include notable publications such as "Content-Based Learning," "Communicative Language Approach," "Assessment of Effectiveness of Zoom Platform on English Language Learning," and studies on "Thai and Taiwanese University Students' English Language Learning Experiences." Driven by a passion for improving language education, Mr. Maravilla constantly seeks new teaching methods and technologies to create effective and inclusive classrooms. He is also committed to using innovative strategies and technology to make everyday life easier for the community. By embracing modern educational tools, he strives to make learning more accessible and convenient, enhancing the well-being and growth of the society he serves.

Özge Özyalçın Oskay graduated from Hacettepe University Faculty of Education in 2001. She received her Msc.Degree in science education from the Hacettepe University in 2003, Ankara, Turkey. Then she received Ph.D degree at Hacettepe University, Faculty of Education, Department of Department of Mathematics and Science Education in 2007. She was appointed as Assistant Professor in Hacettepe University, Faculty of Education, Department of Chemistry Education in 2010. She received her Associate Professor title in 2013. She has been working at the same department as a Professor since 2018. Her main research interests are teaching and learning methods, educational technologies, flipped learning, technological pedagogical content knowledge.

Gamze Tunçay is a chemistry teacher who is pursuing a master's degree in chemistry education. The areas of study are virtual laboratories, technology integration in education and environmental education.

Index

Symbols

21st-century skills 1, 2, 3, 4, 5, 7, 8, 9, 14, 17, 18, 21, 22, 24, 25, 29, 30, 31, 32, 33, 81, 311, 444

A

Accounting Education 389, 399
Artificial Intelligence 145, 151, 154, 182, 200, 202, 204, 208, 213, 226, 265, 267, 271, 274, 275, 277, 278, 279, 280, 282, 284, 288, 289, 290, 291, 293, 294, 295, 296, 297, 302, 303, 304, 305, 316, 328, 329, 332, 334, 335, 336, 382, 383, 389, 394, 397, 401, 402, 415, 417, 418, 421, 422
Augmented Reality 5, 13, 34, 77, 88, 146, 264, 265, 266, 267, 268, 269, 270, 272, 275, 277, 293, 295, 307, 310, 311, 312, 313, 335, 389, 399, 423

B

Blockchain technology 182, 190, 194, 198, 205, 208, 395, 423
Business Management Education 388, 390, 399

C

case study method 440, 452, 453, 454, 455, 456, 459
chemistry education 442, 443, 444, 448, 449, 450, 457, 478
chemistry experiments 443, 454, 456, 457, 479
Circular Economy 117, 119, 120, 121, 122, 123, 124, 125, 126, 127, 128, 130, 131, 132, 133, 135, 136, 137, 138, 139, 140, 141, 142, 189
Classroom Management 66, 71, 77, 406, 414
Collaboration 3, 4, 5, 6, 7, 8, 14, 18, 19, 21, 29, 32, 35, 38, 41, 42, 43, 44, 45, 47, 50, 51, 55, 57, 60, 61, 62, 66, 69, 70, 72, 75, 76, 78, 80, 81, 82, 83, 86, 98, 100, 103, 120, 123, 124, 135, 146, 148, 163, 165, 167, 168, 172, 181, 182, 184, 190, 192, 194, 197, 202, 215, 216, 222, 223, 224, 225, 236, 248, 251, 252, 280, 281, 284, 285, 286, 289, 293, 298, 311, 319, 322, 332, 341, 342, 344, 360, 361, 365, 367, 369, 379, 380, 381, 382, 384, 396, 405, 409, 430, 431, 434, 444
Collaborative Learning 19, 85, 215, 216, 222, 223, 242, 252, 254, 265, 270, 285, 286, 291, 293, 326, 327, 330, 333, 338, 341, 427, 430, 434
Community Engagement 35, 40, 44, 53, 56, 57, 58, 60, 61, 102, 404, 405
Conventional Learning 248, 253, 255, 309, 426
Cultural Perspective 343

D

Differentiated Instruction 214, 215, 326, 331
digital Mandarin learning 1, 3, 4, 7, 8, 9, 14, 15, 17, 18, 21, 22, 23, 24, 25, 26, 27, 28, 29, 30, 32, 33, 34
Digital mental health education 143, 157, 158, 173
Digital Platform 168, 188, 190, 191, 194, 202, 208, 360, 368, 380, 386, 419
Digital platforms 2, 5, 6, 7, 13, 14, 16, 19, 20, 25, 27, 29, 144, 146, 150, 157, 161, 165, 171, 173, 174, 175, 176, 181, 182, 183, 184, 185, 186, 188, 189, 190, 191, 192, 193, 194, 195, 196, 197, 198, 199, 200, 202, 203, 205, 211, 251, 359, 360, 361, 362, 363, 364, 365, 366, 367, 368, 369, 370, 371, 373, 374, 376, 377, 378, 379, 380, 381, 382, 385
Diversity 13, 59, 183, 212, 213, 214, 228, 246, 255, 256, 330, 349, 353, 357, 381, 413

E

E-commerce 182, 186, 204
Educational Technology 31, 65, 66, 67, 68, 74, 86, 88, 89, 90, 93, 94, 96, 153, 154, 203, 211, 269, 273, 276, 356, 393, 397, 399, 451
E-Learning 62, 186, 187, 196, 202, 209, 210, 211, 212, 214, 215, 216, 217, 218, 219, 220, 221, 222, 223, 226, 227, 230, 234, 236, 240, 241, 242, 243, 244, 245, 246, 247, 248, 255, 258, 259, 260, 261, 262, 264, 266, 270, 272, 273, 280, 284, 289, 290, 291, 292, 300, 326, 327, 328, 329, 330, 331, 332, 333, 334, 337, 339, 340, 341, 395, 480
emotional well-being 144, 149, 151, 155, 156, 157, 169, 170, 172, 173, 319
employability 1, 4, 5, 6, 7, 8, 9, 21, 22, 24, 25, 29, 30, 32, 33, 34, 230
environmental awareness 188, 439, 440, 441, 443, 444, 445, 447, 448, 449, 450, 451, 456, 457, 458, 459, 460, 463, 471, 477, 478, 479
environmental education 388, 440, 441, 445, 446, 447, 448, 449, 450, 451, 459, 476, 477, 479, 480
Exploring 10, 24, 28, 108, 113, 127, 138, 139, 141, 155, 233, 267, 310, 324, 329, 333, 339, 343, 382, 396, 397, 402, 419, 423, 436

F

Faculty Engagement 344
Feedback and Assessment 23
future of education 147, 236, 289, 425

G

Gadgets 223, 251
Gamification 67, 96, 161, 163, 234, 239, 243, 257, 264, 265, 266, 267, 268, 269, 270, 271, 272, 273, 274, 275, 277, 278, 279, 280, 282, 283, 284, 285, 286, 287, 288, 293, 295, 298, 299, 300, 301, 302, 303, 304, 312, 314, 315, 316, 317, 318, 321, 323, 325, 335, 396, 414

I

Inclusivity 110, 145, 158, 195, 209, 211, 212, 239, 245, 288, 298, 444
innovation 3, 7, 49, 54, 55, 56, 57, 58, 59, 60, 61, 63, 64, 65, 66, 88, 98, 103, 112, 117, 120, 122, 135, 137, 138, 139, 140, 146, 154, 164, 168, 182, 190, 191, 192, 193, 195, 196, 197, 198, 203, 206, 259, 263, 286, 291, 306, 322, 360, 383, 384, 385, 402, 406, 423, 425, 426, 427, 433, 442
Innovative Teaching Methods 82, 387, 389, 397
Intelligence 145, 146, 151, 154, 156, 158, 171, 173, 175, 182, 200, 202, 204, 208, 213, 226, 252, 265, 267, 271, 274, 275, 277, 278, 279, 280, 282, 284, 288, 289, 290, 291, 293, 294, 295, 296, 297, 302, 303, 304, 305, 316, 321, 328, 329, 332, 334, 335, 336, 337, 365, 368, 382, 383, 389, 394, 397, 399, 401, 402, 415, 417, 418, 421, 422
Interactive Learning 27, 34, 67, 77, 83, 85, 155, 223, 237, 256, 268, 277, 278, 282, 293, 300, 311, 329, 405
Interdisciplinary Collaboration 35, 38, 41, 42, 43, 50, 51, 60, 61, 80, 98, 444

K

Knowledge Sharing 43, 184, 225, 359, 360, 361, 365, 366, 368, 369, 371, 373, 374, 376, 377, 378, 379, 380, 381, 382, 386

L

Leadership 26, 50, 53, 56, 102, 105, 109, 230, 259, 335, 338, 344, 368, 383, 384, 389, 422, 455
learning spaces 425, 427, 428, 430, 431,

433, 434, 436, 437, 438
Lifelong Learning 230, 286, 298, 302, 322, 425, 426, 432, 433, 434, 479

M

Mediation 127, 377, 378, 383, 384, 386
mental health awareness 168, 173
mindfulness apps 150, 151, 169, 171, 173
Multimodal Learning 212, 213, 328, 329, 335

N

Natural Language Processing 155, 161, 289, 293, 296, 297

O

Online Learning Platform 230, 334, 336, 341

P

Philippines 1, 3, 6, 7, 8, 11, 16, 26, 28, 30, 32, 35, 36, 37, 38, 40, 42, 43, 47, 48, 49, 52, 53, 55, 56, 57, 59, 60, 62, 63, 64, 65, 99, 100, 101, 102, 209, 277, 343, 346, 387, 425, 426, 427, 431, 432, 433, 434, 438, 449
Poverty Alleviation 35, 36, 37, 38, 39, 40, 41, 42, 43, 44, 45, 46, 47, 48, 49, 50, 51, 52, 54, 55, 56, 57, 58, 59, 60, 61, 62, 63, 64, 204
Poverty Reduction Programs 41, 48, 52, 60
Professional Development 26, 27, 65, 67, 68, 73, 81, 82, 85, 86, 87, 88, 93, 94, 232, 233, 239, 252, 294, 391, 395, 412, 421, 432, 433, 434
Public-Private Partnerships 44, 51, 61, 168, 181, 182, 186, 189, 190, 193, 195, 196, 200, 202, 205, 207, 208

Q

Quality education 39, 46, 102, 104, 107, 112, 187, 196, 203, 209, 228, 249, 250, 325, 392, 401, 402, 403, 404, 405, 406, 407, 408, 409, 410, 411, 412, 413, 414, 415, 416, 427, 433, 439, 441, 444, 445, 459, 476, 477, 479

R

Recycling 117, 119, 120, 122, 123, 129, 132, 133, 139, 141, 142, 188, 189, 279, 443, 446, 447
Reduce 60, 119, 121, 123, 128, 129, 131, 132, 134, 144, 145, 146, 152, 154, 156, 157, 159, 161, 168, 169, 171, 193, 195, 199, 242, 245, 288, 385, 406, 443, 474
Renewable Energy 119, 120, 123, 130
Research 4, 5, 6, 7, 8, 10, 26, 27, 28, 29, 30, 32, 35, 36, 37, 38, 40, 41, 44, 45, 48, 49, 51, 53, 54, 55, 56, 57, 58, 60, 61, 62, 64, 65, 66, 67, 68, 70, 71, 72, 73, 78, 79, 83, 86, 87, 90, 91, 92, 94, 95, 96, 98, 101, 102, 103, 104, 106, 108, 109, 110, 112, 113, 114, 115, 120, 121, 122, 125, 127, 128, 129, 130, 135, 136, 138, 139, 140, 141, 142, 144, 147, 150, 151, 154, 156, 157, 158, 159, 160, 161, 162, 163, 164, 169, 170, 171, 203, 204, 205, 206, 214, 234, 236, 260, 261, 262, 269, 279, 280, 281, 294, 300, 301, 305, 306, 310, 311, 324, 326, 327, 329, 331, 332, 334, 340, 343, 344, 345, 346, 347, 348, 352, 353, 355, 356, 357, 360, 361, 362, 363, 364, 366, 367, 368, 369, 370, 371, 373, 374, 376, 377, 378, 381, 382, 383, 385, 391, 392, 393, 394, 395, 396, 397, 401, 403, 416, 426, 427, 428, 437, 438, 440, 442, 443, 444, 445, 446, 447, 448, 449, 450, 451, 452, 453, 454, 455, 456, 457, 462, 466, 467, 469, 470, 471, 473, 474, 476, 478, 479

S

schools 76, 81, 88, 108, 115, 121, 143, 144, 145, 146, 148, 149, 150, 151,

153, 154, 155, 156, 157, 158, 161, 167, 169, 170, 171, 172, 173, 174, 225, 240, 305, 330, 335, 338, 388, 409, 433, 439, 445, 447, 448, 451, 455, 457, 459
SDG 8 1, 3, 4, 5, 7, 8, 9, 26, 29, 30, 183, 187, 427
SDG 17 359, 360, 361, 384
Simulations 5, 13, 15, 16, 72, 73, 74, 75, 77, 78, 79, 88, 146, 212, 216, 217, 222, 223, 227, 238, 243, 244, 250, 259, 274, 275, 282, 283, 284, 299, 300, 307, 308, 309, 311, 312, 313, 314, 321, 322, 323, 324, 327, 329, 387, 388, 389, 395, 399, 431, 434
Social Media 18, 156, 161, 168, 174, 182, 186, 188, 196, 198, 229, 260, 365, 366, 368, 385, 418, 420, 423
STEM Education 65, 66, 67, 68, 69, 70, 71, 72, 73, 74, 75, 76, 77, 78, 79, 81, 82, 84, 85, 86, 87, 88, 89, 90, 91, 92, 93, 94, 95, 96, 97, 98, 269, 271
stress management 150, 166, 173, 175
Student needs 34, 83, 85, 106, 283, 299
sustainability 11, 43, 48, 49, 53, 99, 101, 102, 103, 104, 107, 108, 109, 110, 111, 112, 113, 114, 115, 116, 118, 119, 120, 121, 122, 124, 128, 129, 133, 135, 136, 137, 138, 140, 141, 186, 189, 193, 194, 203, 204, 365, 384, 385, 417, 419, 423, 437, 441, 442, 443, 451, 476, 478, 479, 480
Sustainable Development 1, 2, 3, 5, 6, 8, 9, 10, 29, 30, 31, 35, 36, 43, 54, 63, 65, 99, 100, 101, 102, 103, 104, 106, 107, 108, 109, 110, 112, 113, 114, 115, 116, 117, 119, 136, 139, 141, 181, 182, 183, 184, 185, 186, 188, 189, 190, 191, 192, 193, 196, 197, 198, 199, 200, 201, 202, 205, 207, 208, 343, 355, 360, 361, 362, 363, 364, 365, 366, 383, 384, 385, 417, 418, 427, 437, 439, 440, 441, 442, 443, 444, 445, 448, 450, 451, 459, 476, 477, 478, 479, 480
Sustainable Development Goals 36, 63, 65, 99, 100, 101, 102, 103, 104, 106, 107, 108, 109, 110, 112, 113, 114, 115, 116, 119, 139, 181, 182, 190, 191, 192, 200, 202, 205, 343, 360, 361, 363, 365, 366, 383, 384, 385, 427, 439, 440, 441, 442, 443, 444, 445, 451, 459, 476, 478, 479
sustainable tourism development 3, 28, 29, 30, 123

T

technologically sustainable transformation 401, 403, 415
technology 2, 3, 6, 9, 16, 18, 23, 30, 31, 35, 37, 42, 43, 51, 62, 65, 66, 67, 68, 72, 73, 74, 75, 79, 80, 84, 85, 86, 87, 88, 89, 90, 91, 92, 93, 94, 95, 96, 97, 98, 144, 145, 146, 149, 153, 154, 156, 158, 159, 160, 162, 165, 168, 171, 173, 174, 175, 178, 182, 184, 185, 186, 187, 189, 190, 192, 193, 194, 195, 198, 200, 202, 203, 205, 206, 207, 208, 210, 211, 212, 213, 218, 230, 236, 245, 248, 249, 250, 255, 256, 259, 260, 262, 263, 264, 269, 270, 271, 272, 273, 276, 277, 282, 284, 288, 289, 290, 291, 296, 307, 308, 309, 310, 311, 313, 314, 316, 322, 323, 330, 332, 338, 339, 343, 345, 346, 356, 360, 361, 362, 363, 364, 365, 366, 368, 370, 377, 378, 379, 380, 381, 382, 387, 388, 389, 390, 391, 392, 393, 394, 395, 396, 397, 399, 402, 403, 406, 409, 410, 411, 412, 413, 414, 415, 417, 418, 419, 420, 421, 422, 423, 425, 426, 430, 432, 433, 436, 437, 438, 439, 440, 451, 457, 459, 478
Technology in Education 67, 73, 94, 98, 271, 307, 332, 388, 391, 395, 396
Tourism and Hospitality Management 1, 2, 3, 4, 7, 8, 16, 17, 19, 22, 25, 26, 29, 30
Tourism Sector 3, 11, 12, 14, 22, 23, 24, 26, 30, 33, 121, 122, 123, 124, 128, 135, 141

V

virtual counseling 143, 150, 169, 170
Virtual Reality 5, 13, 74, 77, 88, 153, 154, 161, 265, 267, 268, 269, 270, 273, 274, 275, 293, 295, 307, 308, 309, 310, 311, 312, 327, 389, 397, 399, 414, 430, 431

W

Waste Generation 119, 128, 444
Waste Management 109, 123, 135, 136, 142

www.ingramcontent.com/pod-product-compliance
Ingram Content Group UK Ltd.
Pitfield, Milton Keynes, MK11 3LW, UK
UKHW030621291224
453057UK00007B/58